National Identity
of Romanians in Transylvania

NATIONAL IDENTITY OF ROMANIANS IN TRANSYLVANIA

Sorin Mitu

Central European University Press

First published in Romanian as
Geneza identității naționale la românii ardeleni
by HUMANITAS, Bucharest, 1997

English edition published in 2001 by
Central European University Press

Nádor utca 15
H-1051 Budapest
Hungary

400 West 59th Street
New York, NY 10019
USA

An imprint of the
Central European University Share Company

Translated by Sorana Corneanu

Distributed in the United Kingdom and Western Europe by
Plymbridge Distributors Ltd., Estover Road, Plymouth, PL6 7PZ
United Kingdom

ISBN 963 9116 95 5 Cloth

Library of Congress Cataloging-in-Publication Data
A CIP catalog record for this book is available upon request

Printed in Hungary by Akadémiai Nyomda

Table of Contents

II. NEGATIVE DIMENSION OF THE SELF-IMAGE

III. IN BETWEEN THE GOOD AND THE BAD

IV. THE HISTORICAL DIMENSION OF THE POSITIVE
SELF-IMAGE

VII. BIBLIOGRAPHY

Acknowledgements

The present work, whatever value or interest there lies in it, is the result of contributions from a number of other persons besides the named author. My debt to those who offered their support in the making of this book and whom I do not even know how to begin to thank, is, therefore, immense.

My gratitude is first and foremost due to Professor Camil Mureșanu, who supervised my doctoral thesis. His observations and suggestions as well as the freedom he granted me in approaching a delicate subject matter were indispensable conditions for the completion of my project.

Professor Pompiliu Teodor encouraged me, as he has so many colleagues of mine, to be ever wise to new methodological developments and to attempt a complex-free tuning in to the concert of universal historiography.

To Professor Nicolae Bocșan I owe more than to anyone else my formation as a modernist historian, from the moment he handed me the first theme for research in my freshman year. Ever since, his unequalled warmth of heart, the totally disinterested support he never tired of offering in both scientific and human respects, have made me feel indebted to him in every single thing I have ever accomplished.

Dr. Ioan Chindriș offered substantial support in very concrete terms: I had access not only to his work as editor of the works of Bariț, Bărnuțiu and Pauleti, but also to the fresh materials he so generously provided. I am also grateful for the moral support he expressed both personally and publicly.

My colleagues and modernist fellows from both the Department of History and the History Institute have ceaselessly created the forum for a highly competent professional dialogue, by means of discussions or publications. For the same reasons I address my thanks to many of my students, whose questions and opinions often allowed me to find a way out of difficult problems.

As part of a project in support of Romanian higher education, the Soros Foundation for an Open Society helped me with considerable financial support with a view to completing this work. I assure the foundation of my warm consideration and I also wish to thank the co-ordinator of the programme of which my scholarship was part, my colleague Liviu Matei.

My friends and colleagues, many of them archaeologists, have also contributed to my project by their solidarity around the ideas and feelings that have created strong bonds among us.

I also wish to express my warm thanks to my parents, Corina and Marin Mitu, as well as to the Bozdoc family, to whom I owe so much for everything they have ever invested in me.

Finally, yet by no means lastly, pretentious though it may sound, I wish to thank Melinda, my wife, in a public manner as well, for her support and understanding, without which I doubt I could have brought the present research to an end. As it happened she has been my closest collaborator on this project, being confronted, maybe daily, with all my opinions, doubts and uncertainties concerning such a delicate subject.

I would like to thank the Humanitasl Publishing House, and especially its director Gabriel Liiceanu, and the co-ordinator of the Historical Series, Sorin Antohi, as well as my editor Vlad Russo to whom I am indebted for the publication of the Romanian version of this book.

As far as the English edition is concerned, many thanks and wholehearted appreciation should go to its translator, Sorana Corneanu. Her task has been especially difficult, as the book was initially destined to a Romanian public, familiar with both the archaic language of the quoted texts, and the rather specialised topic.

The initiative for the translation of this book into English belongs to Mona and Sorin Antohi, which is one more reason to express my warmest thanks. I would like to express the same gratitude and appreciation to my editors from CEU Press, especially, Richard Rados.

My hope is that I will not prove a total disappointment to all these people, and there are certainly others who generously offered their confidence and support.

Introduction: The Argument

MOTIVATIONS, CONCEPTUAL BACKGROUND

The starting point of the present study was, as should perhaps be the case with any scientific undertaking, a simple intellectual curiosity, a self-questioning as to a certain phenomenon of social reality. Yet by means of a process which I find extremely telling of what "scientific research" and "objectivity" mean in the area of the social and human sciences, this self-questioning gradually turned into a boundless "wonder", an experience of the order of surprise, bordering on sheer obsession.

I am referring to the interest I felt in one aspect of Romanian social reality: the impressive emphasis laid on the Nation, on the ideology surrounding it, and on the symbolic relationships individuals establish with this collective entity, that is, on their national identity. Within Romanian culture, the nation, as conceived during the early stages of the modern age by intellectuals searching for new forms of social cohesion, is a far cry from a mere ideological construct or an "imagined community": it is rather a fundamental frame to which the whole society is referred.

The elements of which it consists, the so-called national values, are decontextualised, divorced from the web of the other values with which they naturally belong in a "democratic" cohabitation, and become the top values of a rigid and artificial axiological hierarchy. Whether one is male or female, peasant or gentry, dull or smart, poor or wealthy, Catholic or Orthodox, matters less than what is seen as the major legitimising co-ordinate: one's belonging to the nation. Being a Romanian is, in the eyes of those intellectuals who are the leading voices of the national ideological discourse, the most wonderful and meaningful thing, even at the level of the individual's private life. Nor is this a matter of mere personal option or private affinity (that would be absolutely legitimate), but a statement of an overall social principle.

The majority of studies that have tackled the "national question" or the Romanian "spirit" so far, although undoubtedly remarkable in many cases for their analytical or speculative approach, have remained indebted to such an exclusive perspective, whereby the conceptual background against which they develop their arguments consists of the very system of values of the national discourse they endeavour to analyse. Thus, the angle from which these researchers view nationalist ideology is the same as that of the very subjects who engendered it in the first place, and such analyses are bound to speak the same language as the legend they pretend to scrutinise in a critical manner. Irretrievably under the spell of this fascinating modern mythology, the supposed spectators become characters in the play, actors and agents reproducing the discourse of national identity.

Such an approach may prove valid insofar as one takes it as a mere statement of ideological option, yet it can surely provide but an extremely poor method for an explanatory analysis. Bound to remain only a stereotypical reproduction of the discourse on identity, it does not succeed in deciphering and communicating any signification or motivation other than those it explicitly manifests as a self-justifying device.

The present study tries therefore to look at the question of the nation by taking a stance outside the self-legitimising discourse of the latter, by choosing a critical approach that is pluralist and relativising. Yet the relativisation of the presupposition that national values must be top priorities of human communities by no means entails the necessity of identifying another axiological hierarchy to replace the discarded one. The conceptual tenet underlying my analysis maintains that the system of values of national ideology is nothing but an alternative view, and a conventional one, too. Primarily, the nation itself and the values associated with it are but constructs of an ideological order, "realities" at the level of the social imaginary, whose "objective existence" is actually the outcome of their being circumscribed into historical contingency by groups of people who thereby endow them with substance and meaning.

I should make it clear from the very start that the "wonder" I felt (as mentioned above) at the way this "alternative view" took root and has persisted to this day as a hegemonic ideological principle at the level of Romanian culture and reality is an attitude for which I can hardly claim exclusiveness. On the contrary, the same stance has been lately assumed in truly valuable analyses of Romanian ideology and national identity, such as those by Sorin Antohi, Claude Karnoouh, or Katherine Verdery[1] (to mention only a few names whose association with my own honours me too much, perhaps).

Without claiming to break fresh ground, therefore, I have chosen to approach this subject from the perspective, and with the tools, of a historian, by means of an incursion into the roots of the issue. My analysis is applied to a concrete area and is circumscribed by a well-determined chronological, political and geographical context. It is also meant to throw light upon a coherent body of historical sources—a *sine qua non* of any research in the field. The assumption behind my work is that the study of national stereotypes, of the specific way in which Romanian society learns to describe and evaluate itself, can lead towards an understanding of the rise of national identity—an identity which is formed and finds expression at the level of cultural discourse, of public opinion and of the social imaginary.

I will proceed by giving a more detailed account of the elements that constitute the subject of my analysis.

WHY A SELF-IMAGE?

Earlier, as well as more recent, historical research has frequently (and perhaps excessively) insisted upon the fact that it was as a result of the projects of the Transylvanian School and, generally speaking, of the Romanian Enlightenment as a whole, that the bases were laid for the rise and affirmation of modern "national consciousness". Of course, the latter assimilated previous or coeval notions, such as the medieval humanists' sense of the existence of a "people", or the consciousness of ethnic identity of which much is made in folk mentality. Nevertheless, the new ideological and mental construction differed fundamentally from its predecessors due to the original way it became reflected in a modern national culture, to its vertically oriented accessibility at the level of the whole society, to its use of a systematic doctrine and sustained reflection on the national question, and, particularly, to its being "democratised" and "politicised", thus capitalising on the idea of "democratic politics seen as national ideology", as Fr. Furet[2] puts it.

Starting from, and on behalf of, the individual will, a social imaginary is reconstructed focused on the ultimate purpose of the individual's political action and animated by the "egalitarian passion", as in the theory of Tocqueville.[3] This new type of collective solidarity, which structures what we call, in a modern understanding of the term, a nation, represents in fact a society built by means of a language. Being of the nature of discourse, a construction, an over-invested projection of society, it is also, predictably, able to generate collective myths and images, to configure illusory realities and national mythologies that can legitimise, substitute or challenge everyday reality.

Coming back to Romanian historiography, we must observe that, due to its continuous interest in the subject we are dealing with and its eagerness to take notice of the *existence* of the "Romanian national consciousness", it neglected, in practical, conceptual, as well as methodological, terms, the *content* of that consciousness, the descriptive and functional elements of the national mythology. The mere observation that, at the beginning of the modern age, the Romanians started to ask themselves "Who are we?" and to become aware of their ethnic identity as extending over the whole national body and territory, and as being accompanied by several attributes such as language and historical destiny, is necessary but insufficient. Besides asking "Who are we?", the collective self-questioning and probing into the nature of identity also demands to know "What are we like?" and, even more importantly, "Why are we the way we are?", "Why are we different from, or similar to, others?" The answers the Romanian community gives to these questions configures its self-perception, and this image is in fact the element that makes national consciousness and identity consistent. From this perspective, the awakening of national consciousness will be considered only the first step towards the full shaping of a self-image and of a modern political and national mythology.

WHY THE TRANSYLVANIAN ROMANIANS?

Will the choice of a regional sample ensure the coherence of the subject in a satis-factory manner? Undoubtedly, during the first half of the nineteenth century the Transylvanian Romanians became unreservedly conscious of their ethnic-national belonging to the pan-Romanian community. This awareness, together with the special relationship established with the Danubian principalities, were to become important elements of Transylvanian self-perception. On the other hand, a simi-larly clear awareness began to take shape: that of a local, that is, Transylvanian, specificity, supported by marked regional stereotypes, even though this awareness is subsumed in the general Romanian identity and conceptualised as a provincial particularisation of the latter. As a rule, all seminal historiographical contribu-tions, from those of David Prodan, Pompiliu Teodor, Nicolae Bocșan and Ladis-lau Gyémánt to those by Zoltán I. Tóth, Keith Hitchins, Mathias Bernath or Emanuel Turczynski, have highlighted this *specific* character of the process whereby national solidarity arose in Transylvania during the eighteenth century and at the beginning of the nineteenth.[4]

What is important for the argument in the present study is the fact that the Transylvanian Romanians developed, at the beginning of the modern epoch, a certain view of the national community. When speaking about "We, the Romani-ans", they use the term to refer to the whole nation, yet their perspective is shaped by a certain bias and the examples they use to illustrate their opinions have to do, more often than not, with specifically Transylvanian issues. This specificity of the local reality leaves an unmistakable mark on the way they construct their self-image.

The issue of national identity and that of "discovering" the features that consti-tute it are raised here with an intensity unheard of in other areas of the Romanian space, due to the inferior political status of the Romanians in Transylvania, to in-ter-ethnic tensions, and to the fierce disputes with other competing nations. The self-image the Transylvanian Romanians come up with is shaped under the pres-sure of the constant threat they feel coming from "the other". The collective de-fence mechanism set off by this permanent fear and defiance favours the shaping of an original self-image that feverishly tends to make up compensating myths, imaginary spaces of mental security meant to provide symbolic protection to a threatened identity and injured national pride.

This is the source of one defining feature of their self-image, namely its mili-tant *nationalism*.[5] The Transylvanian Romanians' self-image emerges primarily as a reaction to the damaging images and hostile opinions thrown in their face by others: it is polemical and "militant". It is less concerned with itself, less focused on the Romanians' own reality, and more interested in the way others perceive and understand them.

These are aspects that can, I believe, validate the delineation of a distinct issue and of an autonomous field of research.

WHY THE BEGINNING OF THE MODERN ERA?

Firstly, it is important to note that the period covered by this work extends over a "long first half of the nineteenth century", which actually starts with the final three decades of the eighteenth century and ends with the period during which the 1848 Revolution struck solid roots in the collective memory of Transylvanian society, that is, the 1850s. From the point of view of traditional periodisation we seem to be dealing with two distinct epochs, namely the Enlightenment, as apparent in the work of the Transylvanian School, and the age of political and cultural Romanticism, whose climax was the revolution. Yet such a differentiation is hardly relevant to the question of the rise of national ideology, since both periods provided equally sustained contributions, through ceaseless and consistent efforts, to its fashioning and irreversible insertion into the matrix of the national culture of the Romanian discourse on identity. At the end of the eighteenth century and beginning of the nineteenth, the nation, its "traits" and "spirit" as well as the idea of the crucial role played by these aspects in the arena of social existence as a whole, settled for good in the minds of the people (starting with the intellectuals who claimed to have "discovered" them). So forcible was their insertion that it would become impossible to displace them, even when the challenger was a dogma with hegemonic and exclusive claims, such as the "internationalist" Marxism of the latter half of the twentieth century.

Therefore, precisely in order to preserve the coherence of the subject, I feel bound to consider in its entirety this long period of the genesis of the Romanian self-image, despite the specificity of certain modalities of ideological and cultural expression. All the more so, as in Transylvania the Enlightenment and Romanticism often interpenetrate to such a degree that they become almost impossible to distinguish.[6]

Should the above considerations seem unsatisfactory for a complete argumentation of my chronological choice, several other reasons of a different nature might well be added that will also open up additional areas of interest.

Taking into consideration what was referred to above as the structuring process of the modern nation, as in the theories of Fr. Furet in the case of the French Revolution[7], the coming into being and affirmation of the Romanian "national consciousness" would appear analogous to, and synchronous with, the evolutions in the Euro-Atlantic space. The 1791 *Supplex*, the revolutions of 1821 and 1848, and, generally speaking, the Romantic endeavour to build up a national mythology and a modern political imaginary, played, relative proportions considered, the same role in Romanian society as the American and French revolutions did for theirs, and functioned as ideological milestones on the road towards the emergence of a new national identity. Of course, this is not a question of analogies at the level of the respective structures, where differences remain striking perhaps even to this day. Revolution and Romanticism by no means sanction sudden changes in the social, economic and demographic spheres, and not even at the deep level of the political-institutional structures; their target area is consciousness. What does go through radical changes is the political and social *imaginary*, rather than the reality, at the level of which the main problems and troubles remain obviously the same.

The important shift is in the way individuals relate to this reality, in the way they view it and define themselves in relation to their own intrinsic nature, to the community to which they belong, and to the surrounding world. A new epoch is thus inaugurated, one that proves to favour consciousness, crises and momentous collective interrogations—an epoch, therefore, of the anxieties and problems faced by contemporary individuals, of the unavoidable challenges that place them in conflict with themselves and with the society to which they belong.

Hence the importance of the period that witnessed the birth of these "new times" and their insertion into the flow of human history as an era of a highly peculiar nature, whose universal signifier is the French Revolution and which triggered, in Romanian translation, the cultural, ideological and mentality-related transformations during the first half of the nineteenth century. The period under scrutiny functions as a matrix whose co-ordinates will come to define the whole contemporary sensibility and which accounts for the genesis of all the big ideas, myths and collective sentiments which still continue to animate us.

That is why the question of the self-image built by the Transylvanian Romanians at the beginning of the modern era sounds so familiar and relevant to the present-day reader that the whole story might well be regarded as a "roman à clef" that can be deciphered so as to give a picture of contemporary interests. The image Romania offers to foreign eyes; the achievement of a national consensus; the possibility of, and the steps towards, a way out of the crisis; attitudes towards the past and towards national values; cohabitation with others and European integration—all these are recurrent themes and motifs in my study. Yet their presence here is not the result of a previous selection and "cutting up", of a taking out of context (something hardly acceptable from an academic point of view) in order to respond to random questions and to the biased interests of the present. As a matter of fact, they are not as recent as we might be tempted to think and they are analysed here precisely because they were born during, and so can be traced back to, the epoch and the context under discussion. We will thus be able better to understand the way they have come down to us, by way of historical transmission, in the guise of obsessions and stereotypes actually formulated *illo tempore*. From this perspective the repeated allusions to, and mention of, such themes as are usually considered strictly "contemporaneous" will only draw the reader's attention to the remarkable longevity of the clichés of the discourse on identity and be indicative of a temporal route that can only make sense if one buys a return ticket.

SOURCES AND METHODS

In order to carry out an analysis of self-image and national identity we need to delineate those levels of social reality and collective consciousness against which the said phenomena can be highlighted. What instruments do we need to operate on them and what are the sources that will serve as their mouthpiece?

"National ideology" has already been the object of my research on several occasions.[8] I should make clear, however, for the sake of the conceptual and terminological desiderata of Romanian historiography, that the term "ideology" does not refer here to an ensemble of "clear ideas", to "systematic" scholarly reflection or to political or cultural doctrines. Certainly, "ideology" in its current usage and as I understand the term here, is large enough to include the above-mentioned ways of thinking, yet only as random components that are far from functioning as defining traits. From this point of view the present work has nothing to do with a study of the "history of ideas", even though frequent and profitable use is made throughout of the data offered by the latter. A piece of research dealing with the history of the social imaginary needs the history of ideas as a sort of auxiliary tool that is secondary in importance, yet indispensable. In the same way, the "positivist" history of the unfolding political phenomena plays a vital yet subordinate role in an attempt at an ampler reconstitution of the evolution and structures of a civilisation.

"Ideology", as we use the term here, stands for those social representations that are much more comprehensive and profound than any other and that ultimately perform the role of maintaining the internal coherence of a society. They grant meaning and legitimacy to the actions of a certain social group and satisfy its need to construct a self-image that will help it identify itself from the surrounding diversity. Thus, ideology provides a sort of ordering, a "rationalisation" of reality, by means of certain interpretative codes that make the world easier to grasp, intelligible and "user friendly". The materialisation of this system of beliefs in social action is yet another essential dimension of ideology.[9]

Finally we must add, this time for the sake of "foreign" historiography and social theory, that ideology cannot necessarily be equated with the notion of "false" representation, or the "distorted mirroring" of reality. One should be careful with the nuances of the term and evaluate it as a factor instrumental in legitimising and integrating human groups, as Ricoeur suggests, since these are functions as important as that of dissimulation and the "faked reflection of reality".[10]

In any event, I believe we can note the decisive role that this methodological perspective in the study of ideology and the social imaginary can have for both a comprehensive and sensitive understanding of historical reality. Social existence in its entirety seems to be symbolically constituted and to encompass a sense-making interpretation that surfaces in images and representations.[11] To the extent that this is the case, it is clear that all forms of actual manifestations, from ideas and mentalities to practical action or political life, are underlain by this deep stratum that needs to be dug out if we are to unveil their true face, rules and signification.

The present work takes as its basis this theoretical framework and the methodology of studies in the history of the social imaginary (which have known a sweeping development in recent Romanian historiography)[12]. As such, it is first and foremost aimed at providing a *descriptive analysis* of self-image in the chosen epoch and area. Some of the essential concerns of this research are the correct identification and description of the *themes, representations* and *clichés* contributing to this global image, and an analysis of the ways in which they express, and thus manifest, themselves.

Such an approach makes amends for the previous lack of this type of analysis, at least insofar as our topic is concerned. It also complies, on the other hand, with the habit of "palpable" demonstrations and the "staging" of sources that delight historians who like to hear their sources tell a tale full of "content" and "historical fact", which will presumably unfold by itself. At least up until the latest generations, Romanian historiography had a strong tendency to favour sources far more than concept, to start not from a question but from an archive or "discovery" that "calls for" display. In this respect, the precautions I took as to the scope and "degree of visibility" of the sources, as well as to the descriptive, fact-laden and exemplifying nature of the account, were absolutely necessary.

On the other hand, of course, I did not wish to remain at this level. Besides glossing the clichés, I was especially interested in unravelling the role they play in social action, that is, in the *functional analysis* of the images and stereotypes surfacing in the identity discourse.

In a nutshell, the method I use here can be divided into three main moments, which should be present in any investigation of a concrete case: a) the identification and delineation of the themes and clichés of self-image, followed by their description; b) an account of their genesis and of the evolution of their meaning, given that even the most (apparently) stable stereotypes have a history and a dynamics, changing with the political or cultural context; c) the deciphering of the functionality of the images and the ideological role they perform. Certainly, the three operations cannot visibly be carried out in this order for each and every step, for they will inevitably overlap in the actual presentation and analysis. What matters is for them all to be present, in one way or another, throughout the historical reconstitution.

The first moment consists of several operations: an enumeration of quotations that will give an idea of one particular cliché; the highlighting of the simplification the latter operates; and a demonstration of the significant nature of the respective theme, as compared with the context out of which it was derived and even with the entire body of sources.

The dynamics of the stereotype are considered from a viewpoint that is both synchronic, when we are interested in the internal coherence of the theme, and diachronic, when we are faced with an evolution. Sometimes the metamorphoses of a cliché can be highlighted by means of a chronological array of examples, selected from both the Enlightenment and Romantic eras. At other times the juxtaposition of two quotations that are absolutely identical in what they say yet separated by half a century in time (as will happen, for instance, in a comparison of Samuil Micu and Papiu Ilarian), will stand as proof of the endurance of a particular stereotype. It will also raise the question of the ideological functionality of a theme surfacing in cultural contexts so different in nature.

Undoubtedly, the third operation is of crucial importance for the analysis of self-image: it is never the case that representations are gratuitous or random, they always serve a purpose and have a well-defined social function. This is why they are not mere simplifications or distortions of reality, but ways in which the latter symbolically adjusts to the interests and ends of the group that constructs them. When Romanians say of themselves, at the beginning of the modern era (and not only then), that they are industrious and hospitable, tolerant and courageous, lyrical and intelligent, or, on the contrary, superficial and inconsistent, divided among themselves and lacking realism, sly and dishonest, these assertions are neither "false observations" nor, obviously, scientific or rationally provable truths. These are stereotypes made use of by the Romanians for purposes of a fairly specific symbolic nature: to distinguish themselves from others or to deny a denigrating image coming from outside, to build self-confidence and to stimulate national activism, to delude themselves and avoid responsibility when faced with an unpleasant situation, to legitimise a certain political action or behaviour, etc. The possible usage of the same cliché in support of quite diverse purposes and motivations and, in general, the tendency to instrumentalise social images, opens up an even wider scope for the manifestation of this unlimited functionality.

The sources of our historiographical research are located within the cultured, élitist level of Romanian society in Transylvania. The interest does not lie, as I mentioned before, in awareness of an ethnic identity as apparent in traditional peasant mentality, although a whole series of stereotypes that became effective in the new collective perceptions were nourished by that very segment. The new national identity, the emergent self-image was, on the contrary and *par excellence*, a construct of the intellectuals of the time and consolidated by means of political and cultural works. It functioned as part of a modern social imaginary, found expression at the level of public opinion, and thus gradually displaced older modalities of spiritual self-definition as used by the traditional community. Once fashioned at this level, the image would eventually radiate throughout the nineteenth century and well into the twentieth, as literacy, political culture and, generally, modern "national" culture made their way into the body of rural society.

It is for the above reasons that the rise of the modern self-image must be decoded from texts by the Transylvanian intellectuals of the Enlightenment, that is, of the pre-Romantic era around 1848. The sources will therefore be extracted from those intellectual domains that were of particular interest to the more or less enlightened minds of the time, such as historiography, philology, journalism, literature or travel accounts. We will also look at political texts, petitions, ideological discourses and programmes, as well as at instances of private writing, such as journals and private correspondence.[13]

I will therefore be interested, on the one hand, in works that had a wide circulation (by the standards of the time) and an effective impact on contemporary consciousness, such as Petru Maior's *History*, Bariț's periodicals, or popular calendars. On the other hand, and to an equal extent, I will also be interested in those writings that would be published at a much later date than their conception, such as Budai-Deleanu's *Gypsiad* or Cipariu's *Diary,* or those manuscripts that have been so far lying, unknown, in the silence of the archives. What I find fascinating is the recurrence of the same clichés in texts of the most varied extraction— the public debate, the private interrogation, or confessions made to a close and beloved friend. Similar images are to be found in the rostrum discourses of a pompous politician, in the academic considerations of a subtle and refined scholar, as well as in the less remarkable correspondence of a teacher or a country priest. What is at stake in the majority of the cases analysed here is not a transmission of sources, but a much deeper symbolic cohesion that coagulates society around several crucial obsessions and themes. This is so because self-image and discourse on identity are not primarily a question of the *spreading*, but one of the collective *assuming* of those ideological elements that make social consensus possible.

Due to this ubiquity, or ability to traverse the most diverse media, spaces and contexts, the discourse of national ideology seems to acquire (or, better put, could be seen as possessing) a somewhat autonomous substance, divorced from any other determination. At any rate, due to these qualities it lends itself beautifully to close literary reading in a thematic and structural analysis. The image is essentially a language, a discourse, and therefore it is only such a privileging of the *text*, of hermeneutics and of the belief in its capability of revealing the deep meaning of human existence, that can open the royal road towards the aim we have set for ourselves.

Text analysis is, obviously, the main technique used in this work. Yet, the risk was run of remaining too poorly equipped in face of a discourse thus divorced from the context of social action that generated it, alienated from the live presence of the people who contributed to its validation. I therefore tried to adopt other critical approaches as well. Certainly, on the face of it, the historian who approaches the realities of another epoch can by no means make use of the anthropologists' methods. By directly questioning their subjects, the latter bring life into the dumb message of the written texts, a life that is felt in the perspective and vivid presence of the informants, their gestures and intonation. The text is thus enriched by appendices that are often more eloquent than tens of pages of impersonal account. This is, in fact, what I have attempted here; I believe that the historian, too, can develop a sensitive relationship with the characters of his inquiry, unravel traces of their presence that are still alive, and thus establish a more direct dialogue with their value systems.

It often happens that the atmosphere familiar to the people of, say, 1800 infiltrates into our days. One can discover a street corner where the architecture has stayed the same; or a landscape that impressed our forefathers as it does us and made them exercise their literary abilities; or a certain dialectal nuance in the way our grandparents speak that preserves meanings to which people today can only turn a deaf ear. Such instances are the intuitions one can use, just like the anthropologist, in order to recreate a certain mental configuration or a state of mind of the times. The next step is to confront the result with the outcome of the patient and laborious rational analysis of the fragments of texts one is working with. I believe that the contact I had with the spaces where these people lived, and the familiarity I enjoyed with a specific cultural milieu and tradition enriched the body of methods and sources I developed. I often strolled the intricate small streets of Old Arad that had also been trodden by the frequently invoked heroes of my reconstitution, Moise Nicoară or Dimitrie Țichindeal, Diaconovici-Loga or Atanasie Șandor, the teachers of the 1812 prep school (preparandia) where I myself studied 170 years later. As a student, I used to live on the street where Avram Iancu lived when he was a student; I took and delivered courses in the same vaulted rooms of the Piarist Catholic College that have seen little change since they hosted Iancu and Sever, Hodoș and Papiu Ilarian. I tried, as often as I could, to look very carefully and decipher psychological traits in the faces of the "text authors" I was interested in as they appeared in paintings and engravings. I went through their correspondence and personal notes, through the love lines of their youth or their lists of daily errands. I tried thus to penetrate as deeply as I could the intimacy of several fragments of vivid and authentic existence.

It goes without saying that, for the sake of my analysis, I would not like these "anthropological" traits to be taken as sentimental outbursts and biased identification with the subject. All the more so as I made the claim at the beginning of this chapter for a necessary distance from the self-legitimating discourse and value system of national ideology, that is, from the subject of my research. Additionally, I do not agree with the "le folklore, c'est moi" type of perspective which has it that one must be born into, and thus be congenial with, a certain cultural reality in order to be able really to understand it. Researchers with radically different backgrounds have managed, perhaps, to seize the gist of the Transylvanian world better than I, in either its historical or contemporary dimensions.[14] Their accomplishment was indeed due to whole years of studying, of adjusting to, and living in the middle of, these realities, of engaging in a sensitive dialogue with the autochthonous value systems, with the people, their milieu and culture.

The examples I have mentioned prove that anyone has access to a subject such as the one with which we are concerned, provided that the sound, rational "text analyses" be accompanied by a good knowledge and *understanding* of the life behind them. For such an end the mere display of "neutrality" and "objectivity" is obviously not enough. Just as a biased positioning within the value system one claims to study is bound to mar one's ability to understand its hidden signification, so an inability to enter that world, however "closed" or "alien" it might be to one's nature, is equally likely to block access to signification. The only way may be, then, to be able successively to make your way into and out of the world to which you feel especially attached, to be able to look at it and grasp its meaning from both the inside and the outside.

Love and admiration for national values, which is absolutely acceptable as a personal option, is definitely an obstacle on the way to a true understanding of those values in their relationship with the ensemble of social realities. Hatred or contempt for them, usually projected from a different ideological stance, cannot favour such an approach either. Paradoxically, nor can "pure" indifference function as an appropriate intermediary for a sensitive and vivid cognitive encounter.

What is left, then, may be that critical and relativising "wonder", indiscriminately open to diverse experiences and flexible enough to be able to encompass both denial and acceptance in the attempt to come up with at least partially acceptable truth propositions, the sign of a cast of mind that intends both balance and a tinge of irony. What is left is that mere intellectual curiosity with which I started in the first place and beyond which, indeed, there is almost no arguing and proving.

*

However, since I mean this argument to be as loyal and complete as possible, I must add that alongside the basic motivations I have invoked so far, which, by their nature, should, I hope, be sufficient, there are also certain reasons of a purely personal nature, dependent on biography and chance. The vagaries of professional specialisation and evolution meant that I grew more familiar with this topic than with others, and that I explored it to the extent that my abilities allowed. The history of Transylvanian culture in the first half of the previous century and the method of comparative imagology have been, in fact, the subjects of my scientific concern for almost ten years. Last but not least, the fact that I am a Transylvanian myself, that I live in Cluj, as well as other biographical circumstances which I will not make explicit here but which might speak for themselves in the course of the book, made me particularly alive to problems of ethnic identity and nationalism.

To what extent this involvement with the subject helped me or, on the contrary, impeded my objectivity, is a matter I leave to the readers of the present study, be they Transylvanian or not, to decide upon.

*

The notes to this work contain bibliographical references abridged in forms such as, for instance, "3:Popescu 1985". The initial figure indicates the section of the bibliography in which I have placed the respective work; the author's name, or the title of the publication quoted follows in shortened form, and finally the year of publication. A list of these abridged references, which also represents the complete bibliography of the work, is placed at the end of the book. The quoted works are to be found there, grouped in sections (1.1: Manuscripts, 1.2: Papers and periodicals, 3: Specialised bibliography, etc.) Within each section the works are arranged in alphabetical order. The abbreviations used are standard (ms. = manuscript, ed. – edition/editor, B.A.R. – Biblioteca Academiei Române [The Library of the Romanian Academy]). The bibliography includes all works and sources actually used and quoted in the book.

NOTES

1 3:Antohi 1994, pp. 208–285, "Cioran and the Romanian Stigma. Mechanisms of Identity Formation and Radical Definitions of Ethnicity"; 3:Karnoouh 1990; 3:Verdery 1988; 3:Verdery 1991. For the manner in which my argument is organised I owe much to this latter work.

2 3:Furet 1978.

3 3:Tocqueville 1981, vol. II, part II; cf. Fr. Furet's preface to that edition.

4 See 3:Prodan 1971; 3:Teodor 1984, pp. 174–246; 3:Boçsan 1986, "The Enlightenment and the Nation"; 3:Gyémánt 1986; 3:Tóth 1946; 3:Tóth 1959; 3:Hitchins 1969; 3:Hitchins 1983; 3:Bernath 1972; 3:Turczynski 1976.

5 For a general discussion of the question of nationalism, several authors might be selected out of a large bibliography: 3:Anderson 1991; 3:Gellner 1983; 3:Hobsbawm 1990; 3:Smith 1986. In Romanian literature on the subject: 3:Mureșanu C. 1991; 3:Marga 1994, pp. 10–18; 3:Marga 1995, pp. 216–225 and pp. 226–238 "Romanian Ethnic Identification"; 3:Turliuc 1994 (accompanied by a useful bibliography); the excellent issue of *Polis* (no.2/1994) "Nationalism: Past, present and future" (including studies by B. Anderson, F. Fukuyama, E. Gellner, E. Hobsbawm, A. Marga, D. Pavel, A. Roth, K. Verdery, etc.).

6 See the discussion of the relationship between the Enlightenment and Romanticism in Transylvania in 3:Papadima 1975; 3:Marica 1976; 1.6:*GBC* 1973–1993, III, pp. 349–352 (the "Ioan Rusu" micro-monograph) and V, pp. 1–2 (the "Vasile Pop" micro-monograph).

7 3:Furet 1978.

8 This is the term also used, for instance, by Katherine Verdery in the title of her work "National Identity under Socialism. Identity and Cultural Politics in Ceaușescu's Romania" (3:Verdery 1991).

9 See, for an absolutely remarkable and comprehensive definition of ideology, 3:Ricoeur 1986, "In search of criteria for the ideological phenomenon". Also see 3:Verdery 1991, chp. I, "Ideology, legitimacy, hegemony".

10 Logically speaking, I cannot but ultimately agree with the current and highly fashionable opinion that ideology is not to be taken as (only) falsity, at least because there is no privileged position from which to utter the absolute truth. From this point of view, the present work does not mean to be a critique of national ideology but merely a presentation of it, since it holds that a biased critique can only illustrate the self-justifying discourse of another ideology. On the other hand, I feel compelled to remark that for an eastern European, who is still inscribed with the effects of "ideology", such a serene detachment from the latter is extremely difficult to assume. Convincing though it may sound, the theory that one cannot really step outside an ideology reproducing a certain problematic social order is challenged by a basic type of empiricism that says that one can certainly tell the difference between being part of communism or nationalism and being situated inside such paradigms as pragmatism or the scientific-technological ideology as it has been described by Habermas, even though the latter two will also remain, as they say, mere ideologies, justifying a certain power system, a certain manner of redistributing resources, or of manipulating things and people (in this respect, see 3:Marga 1992; 3:Habermas 1973; 3:Marga 1985). For a critique of such a "committed" type of ideology, in the attempt to contrast it with the "neutrality" of a positivist scientific cast of mind, see 3:Besançon 1978; 3:Besançon 1977.

11 3:Ricoeur 1986.

12 For the general topic of the political and social imaginary, see the classics 3:Baczko 1984; 3:Girardet 1986. Also see several Romanian studies: 3:Boia 1991 and the entire volume XL/1991 of the *Analele Universității București* Journal, the "Istorie" series; 3:Boia 1995a; 3:Boia 1995b; 3:Antohi 1991 and 3:Antohi 1994; the methodological syntheses (presented as synopses to doctoral theses) by Simona Nicoara (Cluj, the Modern History Department of the Babes-Bolyai University, 1996). From the viewpoint of techniques for the analysis of social psychology, see 3:Chelcea 1991; 3:Chelcea 1994a; 3:Chelcea 1994b; 3:Chelcea 1994c. For political mentalities after 1989, see 3:Mungiu 1995.

13 The source corpus used in this work, listed systematically according to the various categories of historical sources, is annexed at the end of the book (1: Period Sources).

14 I am thinking here, again, of Keith Hitchins, Claude Karnoouh, Gail Kligman and Katherine Verdery.

I. Self-image and Images Constructed by Others

REFLECTION ON ONE'S OWN CONDITION AS A REACTION TO IMAGES
CONSTRUCTED BY OTHERS

The most obvious feature of the self-image developed by the Romanian Transylvanians at the beginning of the modern era is its competitive tendency to exist as a vehement reply to the hostile images constructed by foreign observers.[1] Descriptions and analyses of the Romanian reality, either from a historical perspective or in its strict actuality, come in the first place, in fact, from these allogeneous observers, who thus fashion the first reference frame for a self-image still to be outlined.

A good illustration of this perspective, where the foundations are laid for stereotyped images, is the major book read by the generations of the first half of the nineteenth century, Petru Maior's *History of the Beginning of the Romanians in Dacia*. Over and above any other scientific or cultural motivations, the author argues for his stance in a preface that will eventually be much quoted, precisely for its mention of violently denigrating images invented by foreigners:

> Wondrous is the haste of those foreign authors who pour the vomit of their pens on the Romanian people [...] whenever it pleases them and never with due proof, they incriminate the Romanians with another forgery or downright lie and are persuaded that everybody has the duty to believe their fantasies. More, for sometime now, like donkeys scratching the back of their kin, they borrow slanders from one another, without bothering to search for the truth, and give all silly hearsay to print.[2]

It was awareness of such fierce adversity that would set in motion the intellectual effort to break the silence—a necessary step to take in order to stop the self-generating mechanism of hostility and calumny. For, as Maior puts it, "the more the Romanians hold their tongues and give no response to their wicked slanderers, the more obstinately these latter will endeavour to belittle the Romanians and ridicule them with all their might."[3]

Along the same lines, the well-known motto with which he prefaces his work ("The difficult thing is not to tell the truth"[4]) is not so much a self-critical urge to take into consideration the historian's own objectivity (as it has been abusively interpreted today), as a transparent allusion to the guilty *parti pris* of the other, of the lying foreigner who, in Maior's opinion, purposefully builds up a distorted image.

Doubtless in 1812, when the *History* was published, such a polemic spirit was no novelty. What the Buda censor accomplished was to make room for it in the social imaginary, by means of the expressiveness and virulence of his language, which both his contemporaries and posterity would come to admire. The final two decades of the preceding century had witnessed the vehement reaction of the Transylvanian School against such writings as Eder's critical annotations of the 1791 *Supplex*[5] or the historical works of Sulzer[6] or Engel.[7] A precedent was thus set for a whole tradition of polemical literature[8], illustrated by "Disputations", "Adversities", "Outraged Replies", "Critical Responses" and "Refutations"— which endlessly and obsessively reiterated a limited set of rather obscure and controversial historical and linguistic problems related to the Romanians' origin, language and continuity. Closely related to these themes, another series of images surfaced relating to the current situation of the nation, with political, social or ethnic-psychological connotations.

Thus, after Eder's notes had been argued against in *Widerlegung...* and *Responsum ad crisim...*[9], written, in all probability, by Micu and Şincai[10], the mode was taken over by Maior, between 1814 and 1816, in his series of *Animadversiones*[11] relative to Kopitar's criticism.[12] At the same time, a certain I. G.[13] signed a response to Martin Schwartner's allegations.[14]

The new pre-Romantic generation was self-consciously to continue this polemics. Theodor Aaron and Damaschin Bojincă took their cue from Maior's criticism, and in 1828 and 1834 translated, re-edited and enlarged the polemical writings of their master.[15] Meanwhile, the same Bojincă, together with Eftimie Murgu, started, in 1827, 1828 and 1830, a campaign[16] against the works of Sava Tököly.[17] The target of their attack was no random choice on the part of the two authors from the Banat, since the Serbian author, just like his predecessors who had specialised in "anti-Romanian" discourse, had managed to strike at the most sensitive area of Romanian national mythology and self-perception, one that would be constantly pursued by the Transylvanian School, that is, the theory of the Romanians' purity of origins and Latin essence.

Then, at the height of the Romantic period, at the time of the 1848 revolution, the same polemical motifs were taken over by a generation which, despite an ideological formation much more akin to modern trends, simply perpetuated the stereotype—the same competitive, "other-related" way of fashioning a self-image and reflection on the condition of the self. This was the period of the grand philological *querelles*, confronting, for instance, a Ioan Maiorescu with Schuller or Schnell.[18] Nor was Timotei Cipariu, although superior to his predecessors in the Transylvanian School, both in terms of his scientific status and his balanced and rational intellectual attitude, able to keep his distance from the personal and passionate confrontation with the opinions of "garrulous foreigners, who work their foul mouths and proffer falsities and bad lies in speaking of the Romanian language".[19] He thus inevitably referred, even when speaking of strictly current matters relating to the Romanian nation, to the same "Thunmann, Schlözer, Sulzer et al."[20]—an uneasy heritage for Romanian self-perception.

The difference from what had been going on before was that now the debate took place less and less frequently in the pages of scholarly papers and journals, previously published primarily in Latin or German, and was brought into the cultural pages of the periodicals of the time. Although the scholarly and sometimes pretentious tone was preserved in order to make it accessible only to a limited élite, it was by now obvious that the new medium would ensure that the polemics reached an ever wider spectrum of public consciousness and the social imaginary.

I will not devote more space here (since I will do so further on[21]) to George Bariț's articles, in which he argued against, proved false, refined or glossed the opinions of tens of foreign authors, in all scientific and cultural fields, and thus ultimately gave a genuine mirror variant of Romanian identity, essentially grown out of these external references. What I find extremely telling, though, is that, just as Bariț dealt with Engel[22], Andrei Mureșanu thought it fitting to write about the "old" Sulzer in 1846, more than fifty years after the death of the latter, thus reinforcing the progress of the valiant Swiss captain along the over-trodden paths of Romanian national mythology, which he had been, and would keep on, visiting for some while.

Like his fellow Eder, or the better-known Engel,[23] Sulzer would become truly popular, even though in a negative sense, within Romanian culture: he became one of the most effective elements shaping Romanian self-perception, one of those triggers of active reflection on the condition of the self. From then on, the stimulating presence of this enemy would become imperative for the galvanisation of the constitutive elements of self-image, for the conjuring and stirring of so many imaginary energies. As Mureșanu wrote:

> As many and differing opinions have emerged as foreigners have written about the Romanians; we should not wonder, then, that such writers, who care little about the good of the Romanians, have begun to form knowledge of them, either by pure chance or driven by some personal reasons, but at all events slanted by prejudice [...] yet, while we have ceased wondering about the straying of these foreign authors, the bigger is our pain as we find no other place to turn to when we want to learn about our past [...] but these very same pages written by foreign hands.[24]

The role played by foreign references and the polemical arguments against them in the shaping of the Romanian national identity receives a keen analysis in Alexandru Papiu Ilarian's *History of the Romanians of Higher Dacia*,[25] where it is clearly identified and delimited in a historical perspective: "The followers of Petru Maior", Papiu writes, "those Romanians who make the pride of their nation, who in his wake threw so much light on national history, were so victorious in confronting those foreigners who denied our glorious beginnings" that "they stirred the sleepy Romanians to a renewed awareness of the splendour of their nationality."[26] And, elsewhere: "In Banat and Hungary, scholars like Murgu and Bojincă, Teodor Aaron and others, followers of Petru Maior, were stern defenders of the golden origin of our people against foreign enemies, and thus awakened the national spirit and the love of culture among the Romanians."[27] The Transylvanian Romanians' consciousness and national culture were born, therefore, as Papiu has it, by an essentially polemical process of confrontation with the opinions advanced by foreigners who denied the elements of the Romanians' as yet amorphous identity.

The question may yet be raised as to how one is to explain this obsessive recurrence of attempts at demonstrating points that are taken as self-evident, this ceaseless reiteration of issues considered as long established and solved. If the Latin extraction of the language and the people, their continuity or pre-eminence, are irrefutable truths, already and undeniably certified by previous generations, why should every new generation be so keen on making the demonstration once again, on bringing "new arguments", as they put it, just as in a ritual, symbolic, yearly reconstitution of the mythical scenario of the genesis of the group identity? Is not such a perpetual re-visitation ultimately boring? Is it compatible with the requirements of science, which presupposes that facts and data once proven are taken for granted and acquire a certain degree of stability?

One obvious explanation is that the national "truths" are always in need of defence because they are always being contested by others. Yet in this case, an equally annoying obsession makes its way into the heart of the matter: if others are themselves so obstinate as to insist on denying self-evident and clearly established truths, such as those perpetually highlighted in Romanian discourse, then they must be, perpetually too, either incompetent or full of hatred, since their endeavour is to prove wrong what is undeniably right.

The dilemma we have thus formulated is, nevertheless, only a superficial one, because it uses rational, even "scientific" terms to explain aspects that are the exclusive prerequisite of the realms of ideology and national mythology. Despite the historiographical or philological tools they use when dealing with self-image, the Transylvanian intellectuals of either the Enlightenment or Romantic eras are scientifically minded only here and there, and as an option. The ultimate purpose of their discourse is the formation and consolidation of a national identity, therefore of an ideology, the internal logic of which cannot be posited in terms of a type of discourse that is rational and scientific. The "proofs" and "arguments" they bring to the fore to put down an equally ideological enemy are, indeed, simply the symbols of a ritual celebration of origins, a retrieval in the present of the mythical, primordial moments when the nation was born, moments that have been canonised in Romanian myth-history, the "ethnic-national Vulgate".[28]

Like any respectable myth of the primordial origins, the stereotypes of beginnings as they were constituted by the Transylvanian intellectuals point to a hazy origin that is projected back onto an obscure, controversial background. The original moment was that of a confrontation between a personification of the principle of Good, that is, us, and a hypostasis of the principle of Evil, that is, the indispensable foreigner. Although feared and denied, the foreigner is one element that self-consciousness cannot do without, since it provides the necessary contrast against which we can define our identity and which we will use in order to overemphasise our jeopardised condition in an unstable world.

SHOULD THE ROMANIANS REPLY TO CALUMNIES UTTERED BY OTHERS?

Becoming aware of, and finding the means to justify, both the practical and particularly the symbolic necessity to rebut calumnies uttered by others was a much more difficult process than we might think, especially if we consider the eventual progress of that practice. A significant component of Transylvanian self-perception, one that is closely related to the image of the ethnic-psychological profile of the nation, pictures the Romanians as an excessively patient, kind and quiet sort of people, who mind their own business and will never willingly react to the denigrating attacks thrown at them.

The "patience and quiet disposition of the Romanians", as Bojincă[29] calls it, was a familiar stereotype of the time, present at all levels of the social imaginary. Papiu Ilarian deplores that fact that "our history at that time [at the time of the Hungarians' appearance] is written by the Hungarians, for, as prince Cantemir says, 'it is much more to the liking of the Romanian soul to do a good deed than to put things down on paper'"[30] or, elsewhere, that "all we know about these movements of the Romanians [the peasant riots of the Middle Ages] has come down to us in notes made by the enemies of the Romanians; for the Romanians, who had to suffer God knows how many wrongs in those obscure times, who surely gave proof of their great virtue and love of freedom, would rather do good and noteworthy deeds than take written note of them, which they often could not or would not do, thus leaving this task to the enemy."[31]

Images that speak of the same attitude surface at the level of daily behaviour, too, as is apparent in a letter of 1815 telling of the trials undergone by the clergy in Arad in their confrontation with the Serbian ecclesiastic authorities: "God forbid, what calumny we Romanians hear from the Serbs", writes Gh. Popovici, vicar of Comlaus, "and what names they call us, and what raillery they throw in our faces. But what do I do? I remain silent."[32] A similar complaint forms the subject of a letter to Bariţ by several young Transylvanian intellectuals, in the summer of 1848, in reaction to the unfavourable comments made by the Hungarian papers with respect to the Romanian movements: "And thus much sadness has afflicted our young, and not without cause, since every man calls us foul names and throws dirt in our faces in the eyes of the whole world, and we say nothing in our defence, and nor could we without a publication in which we can show to the world all the lies and calumnies of our enemies."[33]

In an article written in the autumn of the same year, Bariţ himself admitted that "our custom, despite all we know, has been to put on a silent face in response to all those calumnies", while suggesting, however, that the time had come to "reply to the breeders of calumnies", since "there are among us weak-willed people who will lend their ears to any lie from a poisoned tongue, people who are so soft in the head that never will they be able to think for themselves."[34]

Indeed, the depiction of the Romanians as not good at replying as they should to their adversaries, either because of the lack of material and intellectual means or due to insufficient energy and will to do so, had another, quite predictable, side to it. As is most often the case, when self-perception brings to the fore a national characteristic taken as negative, the latter is over-incriminated in order to stimulate, by way of reaction, contrary attitudes and behaviour. The point is that this quietness, which is ultimately specific to the way Romanians are thought to behave in general, represents an extremely serious threat to the national cause.

The formula had been, as we have seen, forcefully launched by Petru Maior: "...the more the Romanians hold their tongues and give no response to their wicked slanderers, the more obstinately these latter will endeavour to belittle the Romanians and ridicule them with all their might."[35] Along similar lines, Damaschin Bojincă developed a quite elaborate meditation on the same subject when he addressed the issue of constructing an argument against Sava Tököly:

> Much forethought have I given: Should I reply to this *Disgrace from Halle* as to a worthless, pitiful, inarticulate and shapeless work, or not? My mind was set: It was not worth exercising my judgement in response to such aberrant deviation from the truth, it was not even worth considering it. Yet, when I saw that some people went so far as to kindle so much sanctimony, insolence and such ill-meaning hardened feelings in treating the Romanians, [people who] are not only dead to any shame (in seeing that the Romanians prove so humane and magnanimous as to make as if they don't even notice such hatred-breeding disgrace, and mouth no word against it), such people, then, are not only unmoved by the noble silence of the Romanians, but, persuaded that the Romanians are incapable of retort, are the more fierce in their calumny, and the more the Romanian men of letters keep to their silence, the more these haters of the Romanian people pursue their sullies [...] after seeing all this, I understood it was my duty, as one limb of our sweet Romanian nation, to defend my people, which never does anyone any wrong.[36]

Relying on this argumentation, and thinking of the "consequences ensuing from this patience and quiet disposition of the Romanians"[37], Bojincă mentions two reasons why he decided to reply to the *Disgrace from Halle*. Firstly, he published his book in Latin, that is, he meant it to be accessible to his foreign readers, "thinking that once we have acknowledgement or a word of remorse from outside, we will be more content unto ourselves as well"; secondly, he translated it into the mother tongue, so that the Romanians may "understand the way it is meet to answer any defamation of their nation, know what words of abuse such and such say, and what false figments are invented against Romanians, so that they see more clearly how these things go about and be less gullible and less easily fall prey to such delusions".[38]

Besides the consecrated theme of the external threat underlying the calumnies that too often reach Western ears, Bojincă introduces a much subtler idea here: the negative images invented by others may work on the Romanians' perception as well, undermining their confidence in the truth of their own image and condition, and thus making them lose heart in their efforts towards progress and enlightenment.

Yet the Romanians' polemical approach can hardly be said to be legitimate and justified in the absolute. It remains somewhat ambiguous. An extremely telling episode is that of the refutation of this very legitimacy, in the name of objectivity and scientific distance, by one of the participants in the dispute, the philologist Kopitar. He reproaches Maior precisely with having written in response to foreign criticism, with having replied to unjustified pieces of denigration and to biased attacks by giving them back the like, and moreover with making the preface of his

History a programmatic justification of his own polemical tendency and subjective passion, arguing for the necessity to give return to similar attacks by adversaries.

In an absolutely disconcerting manner, and somewhat against the evidence, Maior denies Kopitar's accusation: "…the words that the honourable reviewer puts into the mouth of (indeed glues onto) the author, saying that the foreigners' abuse and slander were the causes of the author's breaking the silence, are nowhere to be found in the short preface by the author."[39]

In fact, to the Transylvanian scholar, who wrote from within the national logic, things were as clear as they could be. His version, that is, the national myth-history, was coextensive with Truth and objectivity. It was an axiom, therefore it could not be accused of *parti pris* or subjectivity and could not be treated on a par with the foreign versions. As long as those other versions did not admit the validity of the Romanian variant, that is, the unique objective truth, they chose to exist in falsehood and uphold unprincipled opinions, thus one could not be wrong in attacking them by any means available.

THE REASONS FOR THE SLANDER

Why do foreigners slander the Romanians, spreading false versions of their origins and condition, when, as we have seen, the truth is undeniably on the Romanians' side?

The attitude of such foreigners is primarily explained by their political and national hostility, and only incidentally by ignorance, inaccuracy or sheer mistakenness. Foreigners have intentionally forged a tendentious image of the Romanians in order to perpetuate the Romanians' state of oppression and backwardness.

This is, for instance, the opinion expressed by Budai-Deleanu, who writes that "all views mentioned so far [detrimental to us] have been invented in the Hungarian and Transylvanian chancellor's offices by the enemies of the Romanian nation and then taken for granted by foreigners who know so little in this respect."[40] Şincai, in his turn, shows that "the enemies of our people […] have concealed whatever we might have written for the benefit of the nation, and it is from foreign hands that I have received what I have used for my writings so far and will from now on."[41] Şincai's assertion has, in fact, a fairly precise political implication: by keeping a check on Romanian history, foreigners actually limit their access to certain rights that they have inherited from time immemorial, which, once known, might help the Romanians bring about a radical change in the data regarding their current condition.

Yet besides this (would-be) "cool-blooded", pragmatic conspiracy designed in the laboratories of political analysis of the eighteenth century, foreign authors' attitudes are also interpreted by the Transylvanian intellectuals, especially as they advance into the era of Romantic nationalism, as meaning true national hatred of the fiercest and most irrational sort, only accountable for in terms of ethnic and confessional resentment and prejudice.

Such a tendency can already be decoded in the argumentation of the 1791 *Supplex*: even though it formally preserves the balanced and ceremonial tone of an en-

lightened chancellor's language, it actually gives free reign to a denunciatory exposure of national hostility. It contains the claim that the abusive introduction of those
paragraphs that establish the tolerated status of the Romanian nation into the text of
the *Approbatae* was done either "through inadvertence or by negligence" or with an
"intention to do wrong". Although the authors of the petition profess, with the same
formal elegance, not to be interested in discussing the validity of either of the two
variants, their interpretative preference is quite obviously implied in the subtext, especially when they state that there are in the *Approbatae* passages that tend to exhibit
"the editors' hatred rather than love for the Romanian nation".[42]

Certainly, Petru Maior would take this cast of mind to further extremes.
Anonymus, the *History* maintains, blackened the Romanians solely out of "the
intemperate love he had [...] for the Hungarian nation and the hatred for other
tongues [...] And maybe the Notary hated the Romanians the more for his being
a Catholic bishop [...] since hatred has long taken hold of the intemperate minds
of either party." What is more, Maior adds, "I am quite certain that, even to this
day, Paulus, the bishop of the Catholic Hungarians in Transylvania, would describe the Romanians to those who have no knowledge of them as the most backward people that ever existed."[43]

Yet another explanation for the critical tendency of foreign authors can be
added, one that goes beyond the idea of high politics as infused with national hatred and ulterior motives and that is thus slightly extraneous to the basic givens of
the self-image of the time while being more deeply rooted in the concrete social
and cultural circumstances of the day. Social politics under Emperor Joseph, as
influenced, for instance, by the 1781 tolerance edict, made it possible for Romanians to hold positions in the administration of the time, due to the process of political-social emancipation as well as to increased opportunities for education.
Generally speaking, the regime encouraged greater social mobility with a view to
making promotion in the administration or the army conditional on personal
merit rather than on ethnic or social origins.[44]

As can be expected, the effective embodiment of the idea remained to be desired. Yet even this purely theoretical chance offered to the previously excluded,
particularly in Transylvania, was enough to trigger the violent reaction of others,
who began to feel threatened. Bureaucrats of other nationalities, working for the
county, province, or even church administration, were all the more distressed by
the emergence of potential competitors for their jobs as they came as a completely
unexpected novelty, a breach into the unwritten law that had functioned until
then, one that did not even take Romanians into account in that area.

Competition for positions in the administration among bureaucrats of different nationalities explains a great deal of the virulence with which ethnicity was
attacked, since the same people were the leading figures of the intellectual élites
that were occupied with the creation of new national identities. By denigrating the
Romanians, Eder, Sulzer and Tököly actually meant to show that they, the Romanians, were not capable of holding positions within the system since they
lacked a cultured élite. Yet at the same time they denied the historical legitimacy
of the Romanians' national rising and insisted that the political-juridical status
quo, one that clearly discriminated against them, be respected.[45]

Without making too much of such an explanation, the Transylvanian intellectuals of the time were nevertheless alive to like motivations among the competition, particularly when they referred to certain personal reasons as to why their adversaries proved to be so keen on attacking them.

"There are", Maior writes, "people ready to swell their personal antipathy towards such and such a one into a general besmirching of the whole nation. I have known one man [he is referring to Sulzer] who went to the Romanian country as if expecting all people there to bow to him as to the Sun; yet not knowing the Romanian tongue, he received no respect. His grief and anger arisen therefrom found no better channel than to belittle and do violence to the Romanians"— visible in the theory Sulzer developed on the Romanians' migration from the south of the Danube. "I have known yet another [Eder] who, for the sole reason that one Romanian holding high office did not put in a word for a brother of his to enable him to get his own position", became an adept of Sulzer's theory and started to "work both his pen and his mouth to vomit the venom of his hatred upon all Romanians, to his very death".[46]

Șincai, noting that Emperor Leopold I himself "wanted to help the poor Romanians, who to this day are ignorant of their own good, and urged them to listen to good advice from the wise men of their own blood", believed that "the only reason why the foreign peoples [...] make a mockery of the teachings of the wise men of our nation is that they would have Romanians all as their slaves; for otherwise they will not have peace of mind and even if they did, that would make them poorer than the Romanians."[47]

At any rate, the idea that the Romanians are a favourite target of foreign slander and subject to others' efforts to perpetuate a negative image of them, one that would benefit others by keeping the Romanians in a subaltern position, was to become imprinted upon the Romanian collective imaginary. Here, for instance, is Timotei Cipariu:

> ...we speak the truth if we say that it was our neighbours who first blackened us, after they shamed us and began to see some good in sullying us; and the people of other lands, who knew us only from what our neighbours had to say, began to believe them, so that our neighbours, seeing their benefit and strengthened by the foreigners' blind confidence, did not shrink from besmirching not only what was bad in us, but also what was good and gracious and everything we held dear, our name and origin, our blood and language. And after they did us wrong in social life, they filled the world with books in which we were painted in such humiliating and disgraceful colours that they came to believe their own foul inventions.[48]

Therefore, as Cipariu would have it here, the defamatory attacks on the Romanians spring from stances adverse to them, and the hostile attitudes thus generated turn into negative stereotypes and images whose eventual persistence and wide circulation become incongruous with the actual facts.[49]

The Romanians, Object of Envy for Foreigners

Certainly, such a down-to-earth explanation for the attitudes of foreigners as that presented above, based on the idea of competition within the intellectual élites and the fight for self-affirmation, could not have met the needs of an ideology that was in search of general metaphysical foundations for the deep core of the nation. From this latter perspective, the idea that the Romanians are so fiercely denigrated because, in reality, foreigners envy them, was bound to be more persuasive; and so it was, to such an extent that it became a robust cliché in terms of self-image.

What could have made the dominant foreigners envy the poor and oppressed Romanians? Reasons for such envy were not, obviously, to be looked for in the wretched present condition of the latter but in the very elements that were being contested: their language, continuity, historical past, and, above all, noble Roman origins, which had always been the envy of those barbaric peoples whose descendants would give them no peace, be they Hungarian, Slavs or Germans. Within the hierarchy of values established by the Romanian national mythology, those origins held the central position: they could not have been expropriated in any way (they could, at most, be vainly contested), and so it was only natural that the hearts of the barbarians be gnawed by secret envy, since they did not enjoy the privilege of having been born Romans. That this perspective was very likely to be considered extremely relative, if not utterly preposterous, was an idea that did not excessively bother the self-consciousness of the epoch.

As usual, it is Petru Maior who gives expression to this stereotype, which he disseminates throughout his work. In his *History* he attacks those who, "envying the glorious descent of the Romanians from the most illustrious of kings and princes", deny the Latin purity of our blood.[50] Elsewhere he maintains that there are "certain Serbs and Greeks" who envy our Latin alphabet.[51] In *The History of the Church*, the envy-monger is Engel, who, "unhappy that the Romanians should have been among the first" to adopt the Christian faith (which they received directly from the apostles), doubts that the conversion happened at such an early date.[52]

The writings of Toma Costin (whoever this character really was) seem to display a more serene humour, different from the sanguinity of Maior's texts. Although the same cliché is made use of, Costin demonstrates superior critical awareness. If we place our inquiry into a rational paradigm, he states, origins cannot be taken as a reason for envy: "Do you really think, reader, that it is worthwhile for this nation to be envied for that small honour that chanced upon it when it was born of Roman fathers? Hardly could I have imagined that this honour might breed envy. It is certain that the virtues and glories of forefathers cannot be passed down by way of heredity, nor are they so specific of a people as to give anyone the right to pretend they were born with them."[53]

In turn, in Moise Nicoară's view, the name of the Romans, "so sweet a melody to our ears, so bright and mighty a sun to our eyes" is "that which other nations will (shall I say covet [pizmă]? No!) envy [invidie] us for."[54] The hesitant oscillation between synonyms of a language that had been little exercised in writing is an excellent indication of the author's search for a linguistic equivalent that could match the presupposed inner torment fuelling the foreigners' spite.

Language is equally expressive in Bojincă's writings: Sava Tököly's "straining" effort to deny our Latin origins is the "roar of the venom that had long been boiling in his bowels at seeing the Romanians' cultural ascent".[55] The organic, visceral metaphors fulfil the same function of revealing the inner struggle that secretly devours the foreigner faced with the glorious destiny of the Romanians. Even in the otherwise balanced opinion of Cipariu, the language—his favourite subject— is "a priceless treasure [...] envied by many other nations".[56]

So far we have surveyed the tendency of self-image to account for foreigners' envy in terms of their uneasiness with the Romanians' origins and historical past. Nevertheless, as the Romanians become more and more successful in claiming visibility in the arena of contemporary history, the explanation for foreigners' envy is itself displaced to bear on current topical issues. In 1847, for instance, the editors of *The Mouthpiece of Enlightenment* think that there lies in the heart of the Romanians "a nobleness akin to that of any other European people, which only hatred and envy could despise".[57]

However, the event that would give rise to a new imaginary target for allogenous envy within the progressively shaped space of a new myth-history was the revolution. In Blaj, writes Papiu Ilarian, "their enemies cannot but become envious of the Romanians' behaviour at this meeting", a behaviour that "will make the wicked defamers quake in their shoes".[58] After Bărnuţiu's speech, "the foreigners were filled with envy at the rebirth and glorious awakening and mighty future of the Romanians."[59] Yet, as compared with the other sort, this kind of envy is benign, speaking rather of foreigners' reluctant admiration, be they neutral or inimical, for the spectacular rising of the Romanians. Moreover, the praiseworthy feats of the revolution are such that the harmful potential of foreign envy, which is still gnawing, of course, at their hearts, is now reduced to silence and made inoperative. These feats, says Papiu, "seal the offensive lips of the envious enemies"[60] or at least promise to do so, as the delegation asking to see the emperor in July 1849 hoped they would, since they believed they had a right to wish that "the ill-meaning gossip and conjectures laid on these virtuous people solely by envy and jealousy will be reduced to silence in the face of what they have achieved for the sake of the monarchy".[61]

There is yet another side to this envy, one that is of the same visceral nature as that born out of the denial of Latin origins in Maior's or Bojincă's time. It has to do with the intense sense of frustration experienced by the pro-Habsburg Transylvanian Romanians at the end of the revolution, when they felt divested of their own victory. The revolution was "confiscated", its results misappropriated to benefit their "smooth-faced friends" (primarily the Saxons supported by the imperial bureaucracy and military officials), or, in some cases, even the former enemies, the Hungarians.

How can such an atrocious attitude on the part of one's own allies be explained? Obviously, only with reference to their spite in the face of the Romanians' exemplary behaviour, which might have placed them in a much more favourable light in Vienna. "The admirable victories of the highland Romanians", writes Papiu, were the reason why "hatred was begotten in the hearts of their enemies" so that the latter "started to concoct the shrewdest schemes [...] to confound the Romanians".[62] The enemies Papiu mentions are, precisely, imperial officials, jealous of the accomplishments of Iancu's or Axente Sever's guerrillas, or the Saxons, who tried to persuade the emperor of the Romanians' dishonourable behaviour during the revolution.[63] The same idea receives an even clearer formulation in a petition of April 1849: "The flawless zeal of the spirited Romanian people for the saintly cause of its much-honoured monarch has unfortunately stirred the jealousy and envy of those who never tire of finding ways to suppress their constitutional freedom and equality by law, granted by His Majesty to all peoples, for it seemed to them that the Romanians threatened to rise above the other nations in Transylvania."[64]

PERPETUALLY WRONGED, DESERTED, FORGOTTEN AND BETRAYED

The perception of such attitudes, taken as completely discriminatory against, and unjust to, the Romanians, meant that the revolutionary moment represented a turning point for the crystallisation of a theme that became essential to the national self-image: the Romanians as victims of others and of history, perpetually wronged, forgotten and deserted by everyone.[65]

The consolidation of that image mainly capitalised upon an old tradition of mediaeval history, which held that our great voivodes, Mircea the Old, Ştefan the Great and Mihai the Brave, were either deserted or too poorly assisted in their anti-Ottoman endeavours by their allies and neighbours, in general by a Christian Europe that proved dismayingly superficial and ungrateful.[66] Since the voivodes had been so brave, failure could only be attributed to the mistakes, unfair treatment and sometimes treason of their foreign allies. This cliché is explored, for instance, in Budai-Deleanu's *Gypsiad*, where Prince Vlad is prevented from reaping the fruits of his victory not by the boyars' opposition but because "No one soul of foreign kin / Will come strike a blow for him!"[67]

The revolution greatly intensified the idea, now sanctioned by examples and perceptions of extreme topicality. The isolated resistance of the highland Romanians [Moţi] in the spring of 1849, as well as the temporary withdrawal of the imperial troops in Wallachia[68], caused a keen sense of isolation among the Moţis, making them feel completely forsaken and with no way out of a terrible danger: "Not that at the beginning we received too much help, but now, with all our loyalty, we felt the spite, slander and injuries that have always been our lot and found ourselves alone, facing the fury of barbaric enemies", Avram Iancu reports retrospectively, commenting on the moment of the Austrians' withdrawal. He goes on: "The turmoil provoked by that incredible event in the highlanders' souls is beyond description and it took us a long while to bring peace and hope to their minds again."[69]

The letter of February 1849 delivered by the Prefecture of Auraria Gemina testifies to the same feeling, this time in the quick of events: "Stranded as we are here, in our mountains, we do not, yet cannot, know what the world is doing for us. We cannot, for we have been left to our own powers, deserted, and forced to defend ourselves from enemies who [...] rise like the stars on our lands and keep rushing in from all sides [...] What is worse, we do not know where the emperor's army lies, to where it has moved [...] for no one will let us know and no one cares to know where we are and what state we are in."[70]

The important thing for a discussion of self-image is the fact that such an intense collective feeling, experienced at a certain historical point by a relatively reduced section of the Romanian community, found room in the social imaginary that was passed on to posterity as part of the great explanatory tradition of the revolution, illustrated by the prefects' reports[71], revolutionary memoirs[72] or Papiu Ilarian's *History*.

The prefects' reports, for instance, are typical examples of explanatory narrative, meant to legitimate the Romanian choice of a course of action in terms both pragmatic, in Vienna's eyes, and symbolic, in the eyes of the Romanians. They weave a national "saga" inscribed with the image of a people "isolated and deserted by every single soul"[73]—the Romanians who, "cut off from the whole world [the phrase recurs many times], forgotten and deserted", spent "our time in the mountains...in complete ignorance of the state of things in the outer world."[74] The surrender of Sibiu by the imperials in the face of Bem's attack, as well as their re-grouping in Wallachia, are considered things "hard to explain"[75]. The suggestion is thus made, in defiance of the prudence reclaimed by the post-revolutionary political context and, as I have already intimated, for the special use of the Romanian readers of the reports, that, in abandoning the Romanians, Puchner's troops committed almost an act of treason, or at best proved to be guiltily incompetent. As if there were any gain for the Austrians in leaving the highlanders alone or in spiking their own guns by completely evacuating Transylvania. Yet the Romanians seemed to imply that if they themselves opposed resistance, the others should have done the same. The others' failure to meet these expectations, irrespective of the military circumstances or of any actual conditions, was bound to draw water to the "foreigners-unfair-to-the-Romanians" cliché.[76]

A version of the same stereotype was to function later, in 1848, as a powerful argument supporting a vindictive petitioner's sort of action. In the wake of an older tradition, the meeting of their demands has always been considered by the Transylvanian Romanians in relation to the situation of other, competing nations, and measured against the quantity of rights granted to others by imperial favour.

Of course, it has always been the fate of the Romanians never to be treated right, to receive less than their rivals, and, generally speaking, less than "everyone"—a confirmation of the eternal lowest position they occupy in any hierarchy. What makes things even less bearable is that, in fact, they deserve more than any other rival, since their conduct has been the best. They deserve more than anyone else and get less than everyone: this huge contradiction lends extraordinary intensity to their sense of injustice, leading to its continuing increase and to its impact on the Romanian self-image. There are other, secondary motifs also that make things worse: usually, those who receive more than the Romanians do are their enemies, and sometimes they are the very "rebels", the "bad guys" who wronged the empire and who are now all the better for it, while the Romanians, who only did right, get the worst of it.

The source of this image can be detected in the practice of petitioning, as carried out by Inochentie Micu, the *Supplex* and the memoirs of Vormärz.[77] The Romanians have inhabited the province from the earliest times, they outnumber all others in the province, they pay the highest amount of fiscal and military taxes, and yet they receive the worst treatment, both from a political-national point of view and in terms of the juridical status of the individual. The amends to be made in this case are conceived of in the same competitive terms, by comparison with the rights and status enjoyed by others: the Romanians should constitute themselves, just like the others, to form the fourth constitutional nation in Transylvania alongside the three already in existence.

In 1848 the arena of this inter-nation competition had acquired modern overtones: the medieval constitutional system of privileged nations was replaced by a system granting equal rights (*Gleichberechtigung*) to the nations of the empire, as stipulated in the Octroat constitutions of April 1848 and March 1849. However, the Romanians still felt mistreated, just as before, because of certain situations (such as the union of Transylvania with Hungary) that drove them once again into the corner of those who received nothing, while all the others (as the Romanians said) would be offered all that they themselves deserved, and maybe even more. "But now", states the petition handed to the emperor on 18 June 1848, "when laws have been given with the constitution of 25 April 1848 that certify the right of all the peoples in that province to their language and nationality, the Romanian nation of Transylvania loses both its language and nationality by this union with Hungary."[78]

"While other nations were fortunate enough to receive with triumphant joy the grace of Your Majesty's favours", the Romanians have nothing else to impart to the emperor but their "feelings of grief", claims a Lugoj memoir sent in November 1849.[79] The merchants of Braşov wrote to Bishop Şaguna in July 1848, assuring him that "the Romanians will not remain content with less than other peoples receive, as sacred justice requires."[80] The nation, another petition states, "believes it has the right to demand things [...] that have been granted to every other nation in the Austrian state".[81]

The injustice of not granting the Romanians their rights is all the greater as it is the Romanians who did the most for the cause of the dynasty, and "no other nation living in this great principality sacrificed more for the good of the throne", as is claimed in a letter of the Auraria Gemina Prefecture dated 24 February 1849.[82]

The same idea appears in the request for aid sent to General Jellačić on 28 April 1849: "Among the oppressed peoples in support of whom you have drawn your sword, the Romanians are the first who most urgently need the powerful shield of Your Excellency. They are the ones who in times of yore gave true support and have been to this day the ones who bleed the most."[83]. The emperor is informed, in a petition of January 1850, that "neither the Croats nor the Saxons nor the Serbs ever brought greater sacrifice for the sake of Your Majesty and of the sublime imperial house [...]; could such sacrifice and such faith and valour not be enough to persuade Your Grace to grant the loyal Romanian nation, as You have other peoples, the rights of free independence and national existence?"[84] On numerous other occasions similar mention is made of the long-expected realisation of the promise that the Romanians be granted the right to a "national existence, so that they can be the same with the Hungarians, the Croats, the Saxons and the Serbs".[85]

This enumeration of nations favoured by the emperor to the detriment of the Romanians will become an ever-present leitmotif of post-revolutionary petitioning, as it was taken to be a highly eloquent accusation of the injustice committed against the Romanians. A memorandum of 10 January 1850 denounces the fact that "the Romanians are expected to reveal higher qualities than the Saxons, Hungarians or Serbs" in order to be allowed to attain much-desired positions in the administration.[86] Bishop Erdélyi's petition of the same month argues for one of the main forms of vindication present in the Romanian political programme, that is, that they be allowed to have a national leader, by using the same strategy of invoking the situation of others: "Just as the Hungarians have their governor, the Saxons their *comes*, the Serbs their voivode and the Croats their ban, the Romanians demand that they have their own governor or prefect."[87] Everybody has one, only the Romanians do not; the injustice could not be clearer.

Another aspect appears in a document of July 1849. Whereas the peaceful and law-abiding Romanians were not allowed to "gather in their own national assembly", this right had been granted not only to "the Croats, the Czechs and the Poles" but "even the rebellious Hungarians".[88] Thus much-desired rights were conceded even to the rebels who had risen against the imperial authority, while the Romanians, even though they had sacrificed life and wealth for the cause of the emperor, were left out and had to put up with the mockery of those whom they had defeated on the battlefield but who had made it to the front ranks again and become masters after things had quietened down.

Frustration and the idea of the stolen revolution arrogated by others (no matter how relative such a perception might seem)[89], was opening a deep wound in Romanian public consciousness, as is apparent in the famous phrase used in a memorandum of January 1850: "The Szeklers were requited for their rebellion, and the Romanians were punished for their loyalty and support."[90] Such injustice, it is written elsewhere, might well have given rise to collective despair and extremism: "Could one expect then of a people so desperate and so deprived of its rights [...] anything short of extreme reactions?"[91]

It can be ultimately conjectured, however, that the theme of the injustice done to the Romanians in 1848, although solidly associated with the motif of the monarch's ingratitude and maltreatment, did not really shatter the myth of the good emperor, both at the level of popular sentiments and within the political-national imaginary as a whole.[92]

One proof of this is the Transylvanians' persistence in elaborating the ceremonious memoirs that they laid down at the feet of the throne, at least up until the time of the *Memorandum* (but in fact even after that), and their ever-renewed hope that news of a providential change for the better might come from the Hofburg or Belvedere palaces.[93] Despite dramatic protestations of defiance and disavowal by disappointed leaders such as Avram Iancu or Papiu Ilarian[94], or the tendency to move to the principalities since there was no more hope for Transylvania[95], the social imaginary would manage, once again, to have the emperor emerge from the "injustice-to-the-Romanians" affair with clean hands. The responsibility would be transferred onto other factors, such as Saxon schemes and calumnies, ill-meaning ministers or the secret police of the neo-absolutist regime, and the malefic capacity of the secular enemy (in particular the Hungarians) to grow back to its original size, like a reptile, even when it had apparently been decapitated. Collective resentment would thus be channelled to areas more agreeable to its own tendencies, that is, to more indefinite, crepuscular and mysterious zones, where the faceless agents of Evil are always at home. Even if the emperor kept face, one idea remained—namely, that the Romanians defined their condition as a function of a dangerous universal enemy, the ill-meaning foreigner who would forever do them wrong.

THE UNIVERSAL CONSPIRACY AGAINST THE ROMANIANS

The themes of the slander, envy and injustice inflicted upon the Romanians by others, together with the undeniable facts of their oppression and domination by all kinds of ethnic, political or social groups, was to lead to the emergence of another powerful stereotype, one that is often present in the social imaginary of any community facing similar situations: a belief in the existence of a generalised coalition of evil forces, conjuring to victimise and destroy.

This malign alliance had two main distinctive traits that made it a frightful force and that functioned as excellent arguments for the Romanians' incessant failures and, generally, for their state of submission and exploitation, which was perpetuated despite huge efforts towards emancipation.

The first trait had to do with the universal nature of the inimical alliance. There was a sense of the omnipresence of the enemy, encountered everywhere, at every frontier and among the Romanians themselves as well, leading to the feeling that any foreign group with which they came into contact would instantaneously fall on their necks. This topography of the big threat would give rise, on the one hand, to the widely embraced idea of *being surrounded* and, on the other, to that of the enemy lying in wait from within.

Indeed, the Romanians' relationship with any of the main neighbouring ethnic communities, be they Hungarians, Saxons or Serbs, was fraught at the level of perception not only with an irreducible conflict, but also with their domination by others, as well as with a sense of adversity and fear in the face of that threat. Even the vicinity of the Carpatho–Russians in the far north-west generated the same perception of discrimination and domination, as enforced by the bishopric of Mukacevo against the Greek–Catholic Romanians.[96]

In the wider picture of the principalities, the adverse coalition expanded to include, besides the Turks, primarily the Greeks and the Russians, whose threatening presence and unfavourable image fully reached Transylvania too, as perceived in particular instances of local contexts.[97] Even the small communities of the Slovaks in Banat or of the immigrant Macedo–Romanians in the western parts of the country or in Hungary[98], for instance, can be counted, as Moise Nicoară[99] counts them, among the elements of this truly universal coalition against the Romanians. A cliché is thus born of a people that is "surrounded and crushed by the barbarians, trampled by the whole world"[100], as Papiu Ilarian puts it, as well as the idea powerfully launched in 1848 that "everything had conspired against this nation".[101]

The second trait of the said alliance was its secrecy. The coalition of enemies was constituted as a conspiracy, which had its obscure ways, its mystifying intrigues and occult methods. On the one hand, the theme of the mystery veiling such political schemes had come down from the eighteenth century. This had been a time of such theories as that of the French Revolution as a plot in disguise[102], meant to overturn the monarchy, or of the practice of Freemasonry, with which Joseph's Vienna was quite familiar.

On the other hand, the nineteenth century had its own contribution of elements capable of reinforcing the idea of conspiracy: firstly, the activity of the secret opposition societies and the afferent plotting mentality[103]; secondly, the increased efficiency of the secret police of Restoration authoritarian regimes, trained to counteract subversive opposition by similar methods (Metternich's police apparatus was the vivid illustration of that principle).

As a result, the covert plans of the conspiracy against the Romanians could only be drawn up in such occult offices as the "Hungarian and Transylvanian chancellor's offices" mentioned by Budai-Deleanu.[104] There was more and more overlapping of that plot with the high and shadowy politics of the big ones (such as Vienna, in this case), who decided peoples' fates with total disregard for, and contempt of, their interests. The instruments meant to put those plans into practice were just as mysterious and impure: Jesuits, Freemasons, Jews, the secret police, whatever was ethnically and religiously alien, together with their acolytes recruited from among the Romanians—all specimens of the well-known stereotypical fauna of the lugubrious agents of Evil.[105]

Such an image of the universal anti-Romanian conspiracy, which seems so modern that it reminds one of the 1989 "agencies" and of the "war against the Romanian people"[106], is forcefully depicted in Moise Nicoară's writings between 1815 and 1819, which came out as part of a programme aimed at claiming a Romanian bishop for Arad.[107]

Certainly in Nicoară's case, the eloquence used to bring forth the motif of the universal plot is also due to his psychological profile, to his exalted imagination, often described (at least by his adversaries) as a pathological case. Yet an explanation can just as well ensue from the impact of a general mentality thoroughly imbued with a Romantic spirit. In such terms the case of the rebel from Arad is by no means exceptional: it has more to do with typicality than with individual peculiarity. The persecution complex, of which it is absolutely clear that Nicoară suffered, since he extrapolated many of his personal conflicts to the level of the entire nation, was an extremely popular disorder for the social imaginary of the Romantic era, as has been pointed out by pertinent research.[108]

The universal scope, obscure ways and devious practitioners of the conspiracy against the Romanians, that is, all the main elements of the cliché, are admirably outlined by Nicoară. His aim is also to unveil, expose and bring into dazzling light such a secret and hideous plot. A memoir to the emperor dated 15 August 1819 states:

> Much is whispered into Romanian ears and many and furtive are the ways they are roused, what with the police and its long hands reaching stealthily among all nations and rules and [all] kinds and classes of people, and with Macedonians here, or Serbs there, or Hungarians some other place, who wish for the good of the country, or others who work for uprising and mutiny, with Uniate Romanians here, or Lutherans there, or Calvinists or Papists, not to speak of the Jews, or with women who know their ways about all sorts of villainies, or county leaders [varmegii] or other high officers [diregători] and their orderlies [tisturi], who have business with the Romanians, and so on and so forth, that there is no end to it.[109]

Everybody has turned against the Romanians, from the Catholics to the Israelites; even though the juxtaposition of such elements makes no apparent sense, they are actually brought together by the underground conspiracy uniting them all behind the occult plot meant to destroy the Romanians.

What methods were used by these enemies who, although in great number, never acted but undercover? "First they rouse, by many cunning means, their [the Romanians'] envy, anger, violence, prejudice, fear of evil, hope for good or for some benefit of promotion by receiving honours, and other means which are not even spoken, to fit each man's mind, temper and state, and everybody is deceived by such promise of some good, high position or prosperity. So they start worrying and find no rest and finally, as if the seed of unrest had been born within, the spark rises at the slightest occasion of turmoil, rebellion and havoc."[110] Then, taking advantage of the atmosphere induced by such conflicts and turmoil among the Romanians and the Orthodox Serbs, in which they act as mere instruments, Vienna and the local and county administrations are able to see to their plans of spreading Catholicism and denationalising the Romanians.[111]

The scenario of the Serb and Hungarian agents disseminated mainly in Arad (and not in Timișoara, as in 1989!)—at any rate, in those western parts that are more prone to such destabilising actions, due to their cosmopolitan nature and their close contacts with the neighbouring countries—with a view to causing bogus turmoil as a cover for their machinations meant to undermine the Romanians' vital interests, is a constant of the Romanian political imaginary. The recurrence is surprising but can easily be explained, irrespective of certain coincidences, by those same imaginary mechanisms of the theory of the plot, which uses the new data of a certain historical epoch to reproduce the same general pattern of an age-old stereotype.

One quite significant fact with respect to the immense power the idea of the plot had in Nicoară's vision is that the emperor himself is accused of involvement, while, as we have seen, the latter would be broadly exculpated even after the great disappointment of the 1848 revolution. This is one of the few rare instances of Romanian anti-dynastic discourse at the time, which can only be ascribed to the huge dimensions the theory of the plot acquired in Nicoară's mind:

> ...that Your Majesty is the head and shadow organiser of that society and of that unknown rule, and that all that is done is done at your will and with your consent, so that you be able to ruin and destroy all laws and principles that keep the country and that you never tire to

do so [...] For the sake of those societies Your Majesty indulges in the direst tyranny and misrule, and allows every underling to do so too, and turns the laws so that he who will not join the league, or that lawless fellowship, is harmed and driven away.[112]

Another implicit tenet of the theory of universal conspiracy is that it must remain secret, undefined, hidden under the veil of a misty imprecision, which Nicoară himself, its fiercest enemy, tries not to, or dares not, tear apart completely. Although he, as we have shown, forcefully denounces the dangers of the plot before an ignorant audience, he is not willing to penetrate its core, as if afraid that the mere uttering of the malefic name, the *knowledge* of, and contact with, the absolute Evil, once unveiled in all its hideousness, might corrupt or be fatal to an honest spirit:

I do not know, yet nor do I wish to know, what is that misty rule hidden in the empire, or what its name is, what is that concealed and secreted society and what its aim and ends are. Those secretive or secret-keeping people are Freemasons, or masons of freedom; they are Catholics, they are the sort that wish to let loose the nation by revolution or mutiny and to secretly forge some new rule (or religion), and who thereby wish to raise a universal empire, or a rule for all; [...] I will not search into the aim of that hidden power or society.

These are the finishing touches of Nicoară's translation of his own 1819 appeal addressed to the emperor.[113]

This is yet another instance of the same juxtaposition of often incongruent elements: ultramontane Catholics[114] and freethinking Freemasons, Jacobins in favour of egalitarianism and the upholding of the universal empire, in a redo of Bonaparte's ideal. There was no need to be too clear about anything, it sufficed that there was no doubt about the existence of some organisations with obscure aims, which were, for additional suspense, usually conflated with the negative political clichés forged in Central Europe against the French Revolution and the Napoleonian Empire.

Another extremely interesting aspect of the motif of universal conspiracy as it appears in Moise Nicoară's vision is the feminine element of the plot, with its complexes and sexual alterity. In a letter sent to Theodor Popovici, rector of Chișineul de Criș, whom he accuses of having sold his soul to the anti-Romanian conspiracy, Nicoară thunders at the coalition members: "Now you're past being Macedonians and Uniates, now you can be Papists. You have fastened your devilish and whoring rule. There are enough of you now, and powerful enough to ensure that there will be no clean house left, no pure virgins and no immaculate homes."[115] The sexual connotations here go hand in hand with the dark face of the plot, which corrupts and soils whatever it touches, marring the purity and innocence of the party of Good.

One figure among the agents of Evil is, consequently, the *woman*—a throwback to the medieval mentality that feared and distrusted her, since she was the instrument of the devil and of the malefic spirits.[116] We have already seen that, besides ill-meaning foreigners, some of the agents of the universal conspiracy were those "women who know their ways so well about all sorts of villainies"[117], and who, elsewhere, appear as the dangerous instruments by means of which the conspiracy lures and corrupts weak spirits. Treason and enticement are caused by "the love of brass, gluttony, or the love of fame, praise and honours, or of gain and benefit, or fear and delusion, or pain, or the wish to live a better and easier life, or the love of the female kind"[118]—an illustration of the well-known motif of feminine seduction as a reason why men go to rack and ruin.

Moise Nicoară associates the theme of the "woman-as-agent-of-Evil-and-of-universal-conspiracy" with her status as privileged instrument of denationalisation. As we will see below[119], the inter-ethnic marriage, as a means of assimilating the Romanians in both ethnic and religious terms, has, in Nicoară's vision, mainly one face: the marriage between a Romanian man and a foreign woman who will inevitably seduce the former into turning against his own country.

It is not my aim to further explore such details here, yet it is worth mentioning that one persuasive approach to the correlation of misogyny, xenophobia and the obsession of the surrounded nation is the psychoanalytical one. We might take our cue here from the possibly authoritarian education of the child (as part of the usual family pedagogy of the age); as a consequence, the child was likely to develop an ethnocentric personality of the type described by Theodor Adorno.[120] After little Moise lost his mother at the age of eleven, his father would marry a Serbian woman.[121] The hard feelings harboured in his soul against the stepmother (as he confesses in his autobiographical notes)[122] would feed on her ethnic alterity, until he naturally came to project his resentment against foreigners at large and the insidious instrument they use to violate intimacy—woman. The complex would eventually surface in most unexpected ways, engendering a true persecution mania, as it did in the case of the violent accusations Nicoară brings forward even against his father when he felt alone and deserted by everyone in his lonely political-national attempt.[123]

Whether or not he was aware of it, Nicoară was re-living his childhood abandonment to the "stepmotherly" foreigners, as well as his father's treason both against his own son and against his people. This latter element is extremely apt to explain the thorough identification Nicoară would eventually elaborate between his personal destiny and the national cause.

However, such individual and subjective data left aside, it can be conjectured that Nicoară's cast of mind was largely representative of the public consciousness and political imaginary of the Transylvanian Romanian community. As is usually the case, a balanced usage of psychoanalysis in approaching a historical case will result rather in a metaphor, an analogon of a large-scale social reality[124]; for in order to try and explain the obsessions haunting a society subjected to deep complexes and collective psychoses, it is worth trying to analyse the *whole* community from a psychoanalytical perspective.[125]

THE ROMANIANS AS THE LAUGHING-STOCK OF OTHERS…

A quite unpleasant element of the Transylvanian Romanians' self-perception engendered by the critical images invented by foreigners is the painful feeling that they are (or could be at any moment) subject to the mockery of others.[126] Such an image is undoubtedly an extremely powerful blow to national pride and can therefore easily entail a perpetually alert bellicosity in the national identity discourse, the hypertrophy of a deeply wounded sensibility, always on its guard, awaiting, finger on the trigger, to be trampled down once again.

The examples illustrating this motif speak of a permanent fear in the face of the threat of foreign mockery. When, in 1804, the Greek Catholics of Reghin, driven by a powerful ethnic-religious community zeal, asked for a parish of their own, even though they had not yet managed to build their own church, Bishop Bob, temperate as always, urged them to give up their demand, lest "others should laugh in our face and say that we know nothing about canons".[127] Besides the violation of existing legal norms, the most persuasive argument for the abandoning of the initiative could not be other than the spiteful laughter of foreigners.[128]

George Crișan, superintendent of the Pogăceaua district, took a similar course of action in 1842. In a report to Bishop Lemeny, the rector speaks of the serious illegalities and abuses that Ion Pop, vicar of Budiul de Cîmpie[129], had indulged in, and expresses his belief that an official investigation committee should be sent to put an end to the abuses. On the other hand, he confesses his embarrassment at this new "occasion for shame" to be suffered in front of foreign people: "The need being felt, for the relief of these troubled people [he refers to priest Ioan's irritated flock], for a mixta commissio [a double committee, that is, one made up of both ecclesiastic representatives appointed by the Romanian bishopric and civilians from the county administration], so that the foreign people should not be again the spectators of our weaknesses."[130]

In other words, a good reason for cushioning the whole affair—a familiar practice in such cases—was found in this sad necessity of saving the face of a sensitive nation, always threatened by the infamous insults of foreigners.

The same applies to Dimitrie Iercovici's quite critical 1794 portrait of his fellow countrymen. The saddest thing to worry about in such situations was the shame to be endured in front of foreign people: "Pray, good and wise reader, ponder a while and consider what the other peoples will say […] of us […] Alas! We will be forever sorry to hear all these things from the mouths of other people."[131]

"We have become everybody's laughing-stock!", cries Nicolae Maniu in 1843, unnerved by the conflicts tearing to pieces the Blaj of Bărnuțiu and Lemeny, which will bring discredit on the Romanians and provide grist to the foreign enemies' mill once again.[132] In December 1848 the National Committee of Sibiu demanded that the vice-prefect Ștefan Moldovan take drastic measures for the protection of the Keménys' precious Grind library, which had been partially devastated by Romanian paramilitary formations. This time again it is not the seriousness of the act as such that is invoked but the same overwhelming argument of the shame and derision perpetually overshadowing the Romanians' deeds and, indeed, condition: "Such negligence, in the presence of prefects and other officials reputed for their knowledge and love of literature, may well belittle us in the eyes of foreigners, and have us pass for barbarians and vandals, to the perpetual shame of the Romanian people and its officials."[133]

The will to freedom from the burden of this stigma and its perpetual threat becomes apparent in the emphasis laid on this issue among other major political-national claims. The demand that "hideous and unbearably insulting names such as 'tolerated', 'allowed', or 'extra-nation'" be irremediably banned was the first issue addressed by the 1791 *Supplex*[134] and would continue to punctuate Transylvanian ideology up until Bărnuțiu's *Discourse*. The '48 leader would dwell a great deal on that idea by quoting several entire paragraphs rendered in the original, as if eager to perform the masochist ritual of exhibiting the stigma unjustly borne by the Romanians, of uttering again the hideous formulas used by medieval constitutions to decree that the Romanians belonged to the space of shame and derision.[135]

At a psychological level, the laughter of foreigners was a source of pain and sadness, all the more acute as the unjust mockery was often inflicted upon the Romanians' very efforts to make a complex-free case of their cultural identity. This is what happened, for instance, with respect to the pupils in the Arad Prep School who, on a Sunday of the year 1816, were mocked and admonished by Archimandrite Manuilovici for having dared to sing, "*Glory [mărire]* be to Thee, O Lord, for Thy Resurrection", in conformity with the canon of the Romanian Octoih [Orthodox book of religious songs], instead of "*Praise [slavă]* be to Thee, O Lord, for Thy Resurrection", as in the Slav-oriented tradition favoured by the Serbian ecclesiastic hierarchy. The pupils reacted to such injury in their *Demonstration*, designed to escalate the whole affair: "His holiness, of whom we spoke above, said unto us, before the whole flock in the church, *in total derision* [original emphases]: 'You, Socrates', twice and thrice, at which words we felt the darkest sadness, when instead of advice and good words we heard from such a holy man only calumny, at which everyone present fell laughing and mocking."[136]

Testimony to the same feeling of an injured collective and personal dignity, which threatened to shatter the young Romanians' enthusiasm in promoting their own national identity, came in 1845 in connection with the pupils of the Cluj Piarist high school, who had united around the manuscript journal *Diorile*. In the words of Papiu Ilarian: "We, brothers, are still sleeping the long dark sleep of ignorance, and if we raise our heads and start doing things, they said it would only make them laugh the harder!" But Papiu stands fast, like a natural born fighter. His generation is stirred by revolutionary passions and they are much more optimistic about the future of the nation than their timorous fathers from the beginning of the century. The sentence therefore continues in an attempt to reject the nasty mockery of the adversary: "Let them laugh, then! We'll see what comes of it and what their laughter is made of, other than weakness."[137]

Papiu operates on the symbolic level in order to try and find a way out of the trap of mockery by converting that obsession into the register of another theme successfully explored within the Romanian self-image: the ambition to prove to foreigners that Romanians are not what they think, and that the Romanians are as good as everyone else. The argument is meant to strike them dumb, to discourage their derisive and calumnious tendencies and should, in Papiu's optimistic opinion, be able to do away with any conflict and hostility whatsoever: "Let us show our detractors that we, too, are such sons of the land that admire the sciences, the arts and the crafts [...] And I would like to see who will then have the nerve to hold the Romanians in derision any more. You will see that they will try then to shake hands and ask for eternal peace with the Romanians."[138]

This was the result of the incredibly strong belief that Romanian suffering was due to the distorted image foreigners had of them and that the erasure of that image would immediately trigger a miraculous change for the better in terms of all data of reality.[139]

...BUT THEY WILL SHOW THE OTHERS (IN THE LONG RUN)

Although, on the face of it, the idea of denying the foreigners' calumny by factual proofs to the contrary looks like a more practical and realistic tendency, it was actually part of the same bellicose type of self-affirmation, one that relied on a polemical and destructive attempt to relate to an exterior point of reference rather than on a constructive consideration of the reality of the self. The Transylvanian scholars were persuaded that their intellectual creation and efforts for the betterment and enlightenment of the nation were much more conclusively legitimated if presented not as an end in themselves, but primarily as a means of raising the Romanians to the level of others, so that those others (as well as the Romanians themselves) should recognise Romanian equality.

The idea is given poetical shape by Dimitrie Țichindeal, on the occasion of such a propitious event as the opening of the Prep School in Arad:

> The time is nigh, Romanian, my brother,
> That you should try the treat of other,
> And have a feast of it like they
> Who raised to see the light of day.
> The grace of God be born in you,
> And prove to them God's gift is true.[140]

Budai-Deleanu, in his *Gypsiad*, has prince Vlad ask of the Gypsies (who function here, as elsewhere, as an *alter ego* of the Romanians[141]) to ensure that

> the day will dawn
> When chains will break,
> Your people will awake
> And no noisy laughter will they make.[142]

Another case in point are the reasons found by the intellectuals of the time for justifying their scientific or literary initiatives. Samuil Micu, in his *Short Information on the History of the Romanians*, states: "It is but a stain on the Romanians that they have no knowledge of the history of their people, for if we look around we see that all nations have put down on paper the deeds of their forefathers."[143] Similarly, Budai-Deleanu, in his preface to the *Romanian–German Lexicon*, upholds his undertaking in the same polemic terms: "Seeing that all peoples of Europe have long had their lexicons, while we are the only ones left who do not possess that which can be called the main wheel to the cart of culture, I felt the most urgent passion to the accomplishment of so high an aim."[144]

Petru Maior argues in the same way for the need for a history of the church: "It grieved me beyond words that all peoples who are in the least given to civility, have brought to light, by the tireless toil of the learned among them, and given to print, by the magnanimity of their rich, the rise, growth, changes and all matters of their churches; while the Romanian church, although our people are of a kin nobler than any other, and Christian from so early times that few others can claim primacy, is still devoid of such admirable work."[145]

Maior thus introduces the idea of reversing a hierarchy that shed a falsifying light on the true condition of the Romanians. Instead of accepting the laggard's position, since the Romanians alone had not yet managed to accomplish several cultural objectives, they should actually be numbered among the first on the list, thanks to their illustrious origins and venerable tradition. This way, the existing scarcity of Romanian cultural achievements would look like a mere insignificant accident rather than a serious shortcoming defining the real condition and image of the Romanians.

Moreover, Maior reinforces his polemical attitude, as he often does, with a finishing touch that rounds off his bellicose arguments on a striking note: "Parched and thirsty were all the Romanians, and I myself with them, for a history of their own, after all the sullying heaped on them from foreign mouths."[146]

This type of attitude displayed by an author towards his own intellectual creation, which was shaped by the Transylvanian School, was to receive the canonical status of a true stereotype, reigning as such in the forewords, introductions and dedications prefacing the whole book production of the decades prior to the revolution.[147] It even made its way into a book like the *Arabian Nights* in its 1836 Romanian translation by Ioan Barac, whose preface makes clear the motivation behind Rudolf Orghidan's financial support: "Seeing how all enlightened nations strive to write books and make them public, to the growth of their libraries, my heart and mind opened" and, we should add, so did the wallet of the rich Braşov-based Maecenas.[148] Barac, in his turn, gives theoretical formulation to similar ideas: "Our Romanian nation should learn from others and read the books that so many strive to bring to light, and have them printed and known in our national tongue as well, like all those nations who are busy gathering in their libraries all sorts of books."[149]

Thus every cultural achievement is cast in the role of an exclamation mark by which foreigners can see that the Romanians, too, are able to accomplish things as well as they do. The value of such achievements is actually weighed as a function of the quantity of respect it can provide the Romanians with, as well as of the symbolic equivalence it establishes, in terms of status, between "us and them". "We treasure that gazette of yours a good deal", is the comment in a letter sent to the editor, Bariț, in 1847, by the Romanian pupils of the Tîrgu-Mureş Calvinist college, "and we boast of it in front of the Hungarians. When they see us reading it aloud and ask, 'Mi az a Gazeta?' [What does "Gazeta" mean?], we proudly say that 'Gazeta' is exactly what they understand by 'Híradó'."[150]

In removing the emphasis from cultural onto political action, the revolution would strive to translate this tendency to equalise the Romanians' symbolic status with that of other nations, formerly placed in the area of intellectual creation, into the language of the civic and political conduct of the whole people. From this point of view, the decisive move for an invalidation of the slander aimed at them by others was to show that the Romanians were not only as gifted as their adversaries (as the Romanians of the time had it), but would leave their adversaries behind from that point on. And the Romanians had reason enough for such a claim, since the unleashing of energies brought about by the revolution shed light on their true capabilities, previously obscured by the distorting veil of adverse calumny. In his *History*, Papiu writes:

> The Hungarians say that you, Romanians, are but a mob of uncultivated, barbarian people, who gather only to raise havoc and kindle the flame of destruction all over the country. Let us come together, Romanians, young and old, from all sides of the Transylvanian land, let us hurry to Blaj and show our enemies and the whole world that the Romanians, although the most oppressed and defamed, are the most cultured people of the country [...]; let us show them that the seriousness of our assembly, the justness and maturity of our conclusions stand no reproof by any assembly and by any other conclusion the assemblies of the Hungarians and others have ever reached, from the fifteenth century to this day.[151]

The *National Paper* of 12 May 1848 (reproduced later in the same *History* authored by Papiu) cried enthusiastically: "Listen, peoples of Transylvania, listen and learn from this despised people, for it will show you what harmony, peace, good order and the respect of person and property are."[152] Papiu continues elsewhere to build the same superlative image of the assembly "that dispelled at once the old and deep-seated prejudice harboured by our neighbours as to the Romanians' character"[153]:

> The sobriety of the Romanians' conduct, whom the Hungarians and the Saxons were shameless enough to besmirch in every way, drew the foreigners' admiration. They foresaw then a great future for the Romanian nation, at which the Hungarians and the Saxons remained wordless [...], and then, out of moral constraint rather than by true love, the Hungarians and the Saxons declared publicly, on 15 May, that the Romanian people is indeed cultured, that the Romanian people deserves its freedom.[154]

The self-perception of the Transylvanian Romanians proved incredibly deft at using its imaginary retorts in order to transform the derisive scorn, thrown by the competing nations in the face of the most oppressed of the Transylvanian peoples, into an equally exaggerated admiration for "the most cultured people of the country" and of its exemplary destiny.

NOTIONS OF COMPARATIVE IMAGOLOGY AMONG THE TRANSYLVANIAN ROMANIANS OF A HUNDRED AND FIFTY YEARS AGO

The survey undertaken so far of the relationship between the Romanians' self-image and the images of them constructed by others has only revealed, all in all, a deeply ethnocentric perspective, one that is in fact only natural for the age and area under question, both of which witnessed the genesis and ascent of nationalisms. Even the attempts to break free from the terrifying space of the threat and hostility of others that have been sketched above, were nothing but imaginary compensations and returns of the old repressed obsessions, engendered by the same distorted, because ethnocentric, perception of the Romanians' relationship with those surrounding them.

There are nuances, however, to this general situation, elements that now and again relativise the said perception by means of a rational attempt on the part of the Romanians to consider themselves in the context of others. A question mark is thus raised against the uniqueness of the Romanians' doomed condition, on their being "the most" denigrated and "the most" envied of all, on the fact that everyone finds fault with them, and that they have to bear a stigma and face a hostility beyond any apparent explanation. The Transylvanian intellectuals' tentative considerations of comparative imagology in their day, usually unintended and far less demonstrative than the noisy disputes of violent polemics, tend to suggest that the Romanians are a people like all the others; that the way foreigners conceive of, and relate to, them is neither better nor worse than such perceptions and attitudes in general; that underlying any image, irrespective of any occult interests and hostility, there is a certain reality, which should be considered above anything else in a broad analysis of practical import or bearing on the question of identity. The lesson of alterity opens the Transylvanian Romanians to the idea that all nations are both relationally and reflexively defined by means of distorting ethnic images and stereotypes, which give the upper hand to imaginary differences and particularities, which can relativise one's conviction that one is as unique and different as one has been used to believing.[155]

This opening to others, the Romanians' insertion within a comparative series free from inferiority or superiority complexes, as well as the toning down of ethnically oriented images, are several elements capable of deflating the old mentality; they punctuate, now and again, the discourse of the Transylvanian intellectuals of the time.

Iosif Many, for instance, repeatedly offered "reports describing the Hungarians" in the pages of the Blaj and Braşov papers.[156] He also wrote about the Romanians in the Hungarian papers of Cluj[157], showing that "what we need is to learn about them, if not for any other reason, at least for the sake of good neighbourliness and cohabitation."[158] George Bariţ speaks of the same lack of true knowledge, which is a source of conflicts ("We are by now famous for our bad knowledge of one another, even though we live in the same country, we, the nations of Transylvania")[159], and suggests a drawing up of comparative studies free from prejudice, as well as a relativisation of the negative images and an opening to a world of differences and variety:

> Why then should we not look around and further away, so that, as Széchenyi says, we see that neither the devil is as black nor the angels as white as we believe them to be, but that the goblins (that is, or so it seems, us) are no more than brownish, while the angels only blond. Let us open wide our eyes and look well onto the peoples of Galicia, Italy [...], Portugal, Spain, or Ireland, and study them and see that the peoples of our country, besides their flaws that appear so from a moral and religious point of view, are in no way less developed than theirs.[160]

A first instance of such a shift in perspective is the work of Ion Codru Drăguşanu. His whole travelogue, a privileged locus for the knowledge-gathering and exploring of so many different realities, is written from the comparative point of view he professes at a certain point: "In my epistles I have described many countries and nations and tried to compare us, Romanians, for better or for worse, with other nations, some more cultured and some more barbaric than we are."[161] To reflect on one's own condition by contrast with others is, on the face of it, a strategy similar to the traditional polemical stance. But only on the face of it, since Codru Drăgușanu uses a much more serene and balanced type of comparison; and so does Bariț, too. They both offer relativising pictures by situating the Romanians in an indifferent, neutral position, at a "mid" level (whereas the characteristic self-evaluations of the Romanians placed them either on top or at the bottom of the list) within the hierarchy of a complex and differentiated world.

It is equally true that the enumeration of ethnic stereotypes he offers elsewhere, in almost exclusively negative terms and with direct import on the Romanian situation, was not able to change the ethnocentric perspective, the obsession with the surrounded people and the ill-meaning foreigner:

> This is how we stand, brothers, the Englishman only shows a loving face if we buy his products and give him all our precious savings; the Russian, now reborn under almighty tsarism, if we make room for him to set foot on Inferior Dacia on his way to old Constantinople, where he has a mind to raise a flock and be a shepherd; the German would wish us to give him room for colonies everywhere, with Geisaian and Andreian privileges; the Spaniard, although in misery now, will give us the high brow as he does everyone, for no one outnumbers his seventeen family names nor knows the language of pride as well as he does [...] Much aid cannot be hoped for from the Italian, unless he finds a helping hand himself. The Poles, a courteous people, will never rise, nor do they deserve to, for, just like our Hungarians, they are second to the Muslims in the whole world for their love of hegemony.[162]

The very judgement and valorisation of other nations is done here as a function of the attitude they manifest towards the Romanians. From this point of view, the only ones who enjoy a favourable perception are the French: "There is only one nation in the world that deserves our esteem and gratitude. That is the French nation, who for half a century now has been shedding its blood and opening its purse for humanity, and which, if need be, will not spare the same for us and for our redemption."[163]

In fact, Codru Drăgușanu is by and large a man of his time when he does not take these clichés as distorted images, as a simplifying glance thrown by our perception on much more complex realities, but genuinely believes in their truth and capacity to give pertinent descriptions of the respective nations.[164]

There are nevertheless texts of a remarkable scepticism as to the validity of ethnic stereotypes. Such are, for instance, some of the considerations published in the *Friend of the People* paper, issued in Pest in 1848, a publication which makes constant attempts to encourage an atmosphere of openness and tolerance.

Up until the suspension of censorship imposed by Metternich's regime, it is claimed here, the Romanians (together with the other peoples in Hungary) had been kept in darkness and had thus been deprived of any real or substantial knowledge of other nations or of "what other nations think of us [...] No knowledge have we had so far of other nations, other than that the Italian plays and walks the bear, that the Englishman builds railways, that the German always has something to hack, and that the Russian and the Turk are enemies of our kin; but we never knew why this should be so, neither knew our parents more than we do. For the tyrannical government has closed the door to knowledge and learning."[165] Some of the essential features of stereotype formation are admirably brought to light here: the simplifying nature of the cliché, pointed out by a selection of ridiculous images that illustrate the flimsiness of such categorisation; the emphasis on the decisive role lack of information plays in engendering the rigidity of prejudiced attitudes; the mechanism by which stereotypes are culturally transmitted within the family, from one generation to the next, given the absence of more consistent information regarding others. Even the animosities which the editorial staff, due to their political bent, considered most pernicious, that is, those towards the Russians, had to be explained in a rational way instead of being perpetuated by an insistence on certain images of the adversary, automatically reproduced along the lines of a tradition of prejudice.

It was obvious that such sensitivity to nuances in understanding the mechanisms by which images of others were produced was apt to give new dimensions to the issue of the relationship of the Romanian self-image with the more or less slanderous images constructed by foreigners and with a reality which could now be expected to fare better than when under the pressure of those same hypertrophied perceptions.

The same distrust of national stereotypes emerges, this time in a splendid, crystal-clear metaphorical formulation, from an anecdote translated from Hungarian by Iosif Many in *Journal for the Mind, Heart and Literature*, given the suggestive title "Defaming Tongue".[166] We should note here that criticism of ethnic clichés is often promoted by figures who are also remarkable for their openness and tolerance towards the Hungarians, such as Many or Sigismund Pop, the editor of the *Friend of the People*.[167] These intellectuals, whom the Romanians hold, at moments of crisis, to be traitors and renegades[168], believed that political and cultural dialogue, as well as a two-way circuit of information between the two nations, was the right way forward for the sake of their own people. Since their inclination was so powerfully hindered by the negative images and resentments projected by the Romanians onto the Hungarians (and the other way round), it was only natural that they favoured and tried to popularise those ideas that undermined the general theoretical bases of national stereotypes.

The anecdote in question tells how, when the devil was thrown out of heaven, his body broke into several parts which each fell in different countries of the world. His head fell in Spain, and that is why the Spaniards are "such a proud and haughty nation"; his heart fell in Italy, to the effect that "the Italian is sly and deceitful"; the stomach fell in Germany, "and ever since the German has had one nagging worry: to glut his insides"; the legs fell in France, which explains why "the Frenchman is so restless"; the sword fell in Poland, and so the Poles became a "heroic" nation, even though their heroism "comes to naught"; finally, his coat fell in Hungary and thus caused it to remain covered in darkness, from which "it has been striving to free itself to this day". But the devil's tongue, the anecdote goes, broke into smithereens which spread all over the face of the earth, "and that was the beginning of the reign of the devilish defaming tongue".[169]

The allegory has an exemplary meaning: all the "characteristics" and images the nations attribute to one another are but the expression of a generalised tendency to denigrate the other. This universal "defaming" is of a devilish nature, which means that the attempt to do away with it can only be a legitimate and desirable one.

A More Refined Attitude to the Images Constructed by Others

Taking these deviations from the dominant ethnocentric perspective as one pole of the scope of perception, one can delineate, even within that scope, a much larger and more diversified field of attitudes and options with respect to the perceptions conceived by foreigners, one capable of lending nuances to the polemical and univocal image we have sketched so far, even though the latter outweighs the others.

In 1796, in his *Short Information on the History of the Romanians*, Samuil Micu states that "the learned and wise writers, they all [...] cry out that the Romanians of Dacia [...] descend from the ancient Romans who came and settled in Dacia with Trajan the emperor. Nor can anyone claim that these writers tried to take sides with the Romanians, since they were neither kindred nor concerned with some benefit therefrom."[170]

Micu thus gives the blueprint of a theme that was to have a great future—the theme of the "impartial" foreigner, who, because objective, cannot write otherwise but in conformity with the Romanian version, and whose authority is invoked with satisfaction in support of Romanian arguments. The partiality and superficiality of the ill-meaning foreigner, always liable to be held as biased and subjective, are only referred to when he speaks ill of the Romanians; when, on the contrary, he speaks well of them, he suddenly becomes an objective and disinterested character whose statements are sought for and insistently underlined.[171] It is clear, however, that such a foreign character as could be entirely assimilated to the Romanian condition (even if he stood outside its physical space) was more of a fantasy, an imaginary *alter ego* and a necessary piece in the fabric of the Romanian self-image, one which, if not real, had to be invented.

This is not to say that there were not several real foreigners who wrote from within the Romanian vision and who made autochthonous perceptions their own—usually individuals who had settled or spent a longer time in the country, such as the German Thalson, chaplain in Alba-Iulia, or the Frenchman Vaillant.[172] Sometimes they even lent a helping hand to the strengthening of the self-image, or contrived new elements of the national mythology.

Vaillant played a quite important role in spreading the image of *La Roumanie*, ethnically and culturally unitary, inhabited by 8 million Romanians, which he was among the first to outline.[173] Thalson, in his turn, used, in 1842[174], a plethora of absolutely hyper-encomiastic terms, which could have been countersigned by any of the Romanian champions of Latinism—as Cipariu did in 1847 when he translated the German's reflections *in extenso*. Here is one example: the Romanians "are the saintly representatives of the true Romans; they are speaking monuments, gloriously passed down from father to son, from one century to another, to this day [...] I have spoken for you, Romanians! And I have tried to prove by argument that, as your tongue and customs show, you are descended from the great people of the Romans, so that you can proudly say today, as ever: we too are Romans! We are of Roman blood!"[175]

Thalson was simply carrying on the tradition of other enthusiastic "fans" of the Latin, who make of the Transylvanians "good savages"[176], to be found among the foreigners who lived for a longer or shorter while in Transylvania: Martin Opitz, Antonio Cosimelli or even Emperor Joseph II. All these forerunners are frequently invoked in the pages of Transylvanian papers, which thus help establish another stereotype—the foreigner amazed to discover the Romanians' Roman roots.

Just as Cipariu translated Thalson, Papiu Ilarian reproduces in his *History of the Romanians* whole pages from his favourite, the Frenchman Hippolyte Desprez.[177] "The Romanian peasant", writes Desprez (in Cipariu's translation), "is the living proof of the precious alliance of enthusiasm with irony, and he has preserved this amiable and simple gravity intact, which used to be the mark of the ancient peoples and is today to be found only in the savages"[178]—yet another illustration of the image of the "good savage", simple, authentic and uncorrupted by modern civilisation and at the same time an ideal instrument for the revolution, since he is the one able to start ingenuously from scratch and rebuild the whole political and social order.[179]

"This foreigner's penetration and insight into our domestic affairs", the young historian writes to Iacob Mureşanu, "his deep and impartial judgement is an occasion for wonder on our part, too, who should know ourselves better than anyone else."[180] More than an adept in terms of our perspective, the superficial foreigner featuring in other contexts has now managed to know the Romanians better than they know themselves! True, Papiu does not include all foreigners in this category, but he draws a demarcation line between the "German writers", who "are the most unfortunate judges of the Eastern peoples" and the French, who "are the most just and sharp. Famous among the Romanians today," the letter concludes, "are Gérando, Vaillant and, of late, Desprez".[181]

Our historian thus proves, at least on this particular occasion, that he entertains a more rational conception (as compared to the theory of the ill-meaning foreigner or to that of the universal conspiracy) by introducing the distinction between the good and the bad foreigner. Even if this Manichaean discrimination was, in fact, just another ideological simplification (Papiu insists, for instance, that French sympathy is due to a would-be solidarity among neo-Latin peoples), it undoubtedly lent a more refined and relativising approach to the foreign image.

Theodor Aaron, who had written a *Short Appendix to Petru Maior's History* along the lines of the polemical tradition, gave, as early as 1828, a clear outline of the paradigm of the good stranger/bad stranger dichotomy: "For some years now we have known the brave attempts towards a history of the Romanians' beginnings made not only by Romanian scholars, but by wise men of other countries too, many of whom, driven by a desire for the truth, have acknowledged the Roman blood flowing in Romanian veins, while others, full of anger and hatred (which it is plain they have sucked with their mothers' milk), fierce against the Romanians, brazenly proffer their slanders and villainies."[182]

Another distinction, besides that between the good and the bad, is that which tells apart those who have scarce or no knowledge of who the Romanians are but who are filled with good intentions, from the truly hostile who are deliberately turned against the Romanians.

Such differentiation is formulated as early as 1804, in the *Supplex*: "There are many who speak against the Romanians in Banat, some out of envy, and some out of ignorance."[183] The text seems to recommend lenience for the latter, rather than crushing polemics and violent back-biting.

Similar lenience and forbearance is to be found in another text of the Banat area, authored by chronicler Stoica de Hațeg—an instance of the exemplary cohabitation specific to that area.[184] There is evidence here of more openness and tolerance, due to the cosmopolitan nature of the region, to the absence of significant social differentiation (as opposed to the Transylvanian model), as well as to the policy of administrative, political and ideological levelling promoted by the Austrians in the eighteenth century. First and foremost, what distinguishes the rector of Mehadia from other contemporary historians is a refusal to base his intellectual approach on polemical intentions. His writing is not driven by the urge to combat foreigners who present the Romanian reality differently from how he sees it; he does not accuse them of being tendentious, even if he points out actual divergences in each party's opinions. If foreigners have overlooked certain aspects concerning the Romanian condition, this is due to a lack of information and especially to their not being greatly interested in such issues, which bear little importance from their point of view.

Stoica doubts neither their competence nor their rectitude and discovers something that comes as a surprising contradiction to the self-image of the time (and maybe even to today's perceptions)—namely, that Romanian concerns are actually less important to the foreigners than they are to the Romanians. Writing in 1829, the Banat rector claims:

> It is not my intention to blame the enlightened historians for having omitted and failed to mention in their writings some important and memorable events of the history of the world. Some they did not know, some they did not care to, and such events remained thus buried in eternal silence. No! It was only for the sake of my friends' requests and the authorities' charging that I took upon myself to reflect on and write about this country.[185]

In "Principles of Language and Writing", a work much more elevated than Stoica de Hațeg's modest chronicles, Timotei Cipariu holds to the idea of the foreigners' superficiality and lack of concern for Romanian problems: "...foreigners, who thought little of the attempt to probe deeper into the secrets of the Romanian language, as is their custom", approached the study of it only summarily and their careless analyses presented Romanian as a chaotic amalgam of foreign linguistic borrowings. "And it is no wonder", Cipariu goes on. "The language of a poor people, more accustomed to serving than to being master, does not look worthier of close attention than the people who spoke it."[186]

Despite the reproach implicit in his words, the noteworthy thing is that Cipariu does not take the unfavourable opinions of the Romanians usually held by foreigners as being the result of intentional calumnious tendencies, of national resentments or of obstinate biases. They are only seen as the outcome of a lack of real knowledge, due to the foreigners' ethnocentric perspective and to their tendency not to take notice of the Romanians.

At this point, Cipariu's position deviates radically from Stoica's, in that the philologist from Blaj proves very critical of that ethnocentric tendency. Although he has no trouble in seeing why this is the case, and shows that the real situation of the Romanians naturally makes them less worthy of interest and attention, Cipariu cannot help condemning that attitude, which he identifies as a species of narrow-minded and arrogant sufficiency.

All in all, however, it can be argued that Cipariu takes up a remarkably balanced and rational stance. Always careful to keep within the bounds of a strictly professional discussion, he reproaches the foreign authors not with sullying the Romanians or with wishing them ill; rather, he criticises them because he thinks they are in the wrong from a scientific point of view. Moreover, when he believes it is his fellow countrymen themselves who err in such or such a matter because of their very excess of polemical zeal, he does not hesitate to turn against them and to recognise the truth contained, possibly, in the foreigners' criticism.

Faced with foreign opinions denying the Latin origin of the Romanian language, Cipariu maintains, the Romanians fell into the other extreme and became the apostles of a ridiculous and overwrought sort of Latinism. "They became the true antipodes of the anti-Latinist foreigners" and their far-fetched etymologies "were an easy prey to the ridicule of poised foreigners, who said that the Romanians lack either enough philological training or a historical-moral sense".[187] The Romanians' attitude (just like, previously, that of the foreigners) could therefore be explained—as the result of such a dramatic reversal—either in terms of superficial information or of subjective involvement! True, Cipariu insisted on the idea that the denial of the Latinist bent was not entirely acceptable either, even if triggered by its inherent exaggerations.[188] However, what is ultimately worthy of note is that he tends to opt for a balanced and serene disposition in judging foreign opinions: "The time had come for the Romanians to be men of those dawning times of universal awakening and to open their minds and search carefully for what is right and what is false in the foreigners' judgements."[189] Just like his friend Bariț (whose attitude will be analysed towards the close of this chapter), Cipariu tries to strike a fair balance between reality, foreign criticism and self-image.[190]

Certainly, even if we were to leave Bariț or Cipariu aside, it would be inaccurate to maintain that the intellectual cast of mind of the time completely lacked the notion that foreign opinions and objections could be useful or true. Petru Maior himself admitted that "although it is meant to belittle the Romanians", Kopitar's allegation "is nevertheless praiseworthy, both because it comes from men of wisdom and because it may well serve as an occasion for further inquiries into, or a confirmation of, the truth".[191] That such criticism was a decisive occasion for national identity to gather momentum and assert itself was obvious even to contemporaries.

Budai-Deleanu even admits to the *necessity* of resorting to the   impartial judgement of foreigners when those who are too involved have divided opinions. When Mitru Perea confesses his confusion at the ambiguous image of Vlad-vodă as it emerges from various chronicles ("...some depict him as a fierce tyrant, others as a virtuous prince"), C. Adevărovici refers him to the objective examination of the external observer: "I think otherwise, namely that his friends wrote well of him, and his enemies badly; but let us see what foreigners wrote, for they took no part."[192]

Years later, Simion Bărnuţiu would raise the same issue. In response to Carlo Cattaneo's serious charge that the Romanians waste their time with sterile orthographic disputes instead of producing original works, Bărnuţiu agrees with the Italian scholar and believes that "an imputation coming from a foreigner, whom I take as a serious judge of these matters, is more precious than the observations of a Romanian journalist" (here he refers to himself!), who is at any time prone to a lack of objectivity because of his engagement with the issue at hand. "Here is how foreigners judge us", Bărnuţiu exclaims, "and rightly so."[193]

As noted above, one of the most discriminating attitudes towards foreign perceptions of Romanian realities is that of George Bariţ. The Braşov-based journalist also tends to start from a particular foreign reference when he approaches issues relating to Romanian society. Almost all his contributions on Romanian specificity, generously disseminated in the papers he edited prior to the 1848 revolution, are in fact annotated translations of accounts by foreign observers: Gérando, Vaillant, Bellanger, Paget, Chr. Witt, Benigni, Szentiváni, Willhelmi, to name only a few.[194]

Bariţ sets up a real programme in these terms: "Our concern, gentlemen, is to lend our ears to all foreign voices and listen carefully, whether they speak for, about, or against us."[195] It is apparent here that Bariţ gives evidence of much more discrimination than Maior or Bojincă in terms of the way foreigners write about the Romanians, which will obviously lead to a different way of relating the Romanians' own reality and image to foreign allegations.

On the one hand, Bariţ also makes room for the theme of the foreigners' generalised hostility towards the Romanians, of the universal conspiracy against them, which he formulates in extremely eloquent phrases: "I know it for a fact, as well as you do, that there is no other nation on which foreign people have poured out more abuse than they have on our heads", he writes, addressing an imaginary interlocutor, in an interesting article from 1838.[196] "Many found they had too slow a tongue and too poor a gift to give all the epithets and foul names they wished they could find [...] Let anyone have a look at statistical works [...] as well as at the stories of those travellers who saw the countries of the Romanians and he will find few who have not spoken of the evils we share with other nations as if they had only been our curse; they looked at our weakness through a microscope and they saw what is good in us through a veil [...]; and that is what meets the eyes of the whole Europe and appears in all cultivated tongues."[197]

On the other hand, in a note written two years later in which he shows that the Romanians had increasingly become a favourite subject of several foreign writers, be they Westerners, Saxons or Hungarians, the Transylvanian journalist is keen to underline the objectivity and sympathy displayed by these authors: "Note should be taken, however, of the fact that most of the voices now arising are not attuned to that alien passion we have met with in almost all writers from the past. It is plain, too, that they are somehow persuaded that there is some healthy seed of good life in us that may grow to last", writes Bariţ, and illustrates his words with a translation of an article from a Hungarian paper which eulogises the Romanians.[198]

It was not the first time Bariţ had given "crossover" samples of thought, as contemporaries remarked critically, when faced with such bewildering tail-turning. In fact, he was faithful to his own critical and meliorist rationalism; also, he willingly and deftly employed a journalistic tactic—that of voicing contradictory points of view in order to counterbalance the most diverse reactions and susceptibilities without offending any, with a view to gradually unravelling some poised and rational truths, which are always there in the midst of conflicting opinions.

Sensitivity to nuances when it comes to foreigners' opinions about the Romanians, even when critical, unfavourable images are at issue, is displayed by an 1844 commentary on a text harshly denouncing Romanian shortcomings: "I have always cherished the judgement or opinion that foreign people give of us when there is no sugaring the pill in their writing, for it is the best way we have to find out about others' full opinion of us, be they friends or enemies."[199] Importantly, Bariţ admits that foreign critiques may have a positive, useful function. They need be taken into account when fair, since they can help one discover drawbacks that one would never be willing to acknowledge by oneself but which one needs to be aware of and assume as such in order to be able to correct and eliminate them. Criticism can no longer be refused indiscriminately, by referring to the danger and tendentiousness it presumably contains, but should be analysed carefully and accepted as the case may be.

Similar assumptions are made in the 1838 article mentioned above[200], in which Bariţ argues quite subtly and cautiously for his stance, trying to examine it as thoroughly as possible. An imaginary friend reproaches him with "sullying habits, as some have come to complain, for you speak the truth too clearly and too early in your writings". Bariţ wonders how one can be accused of defamation for speaking the truth. Easily, the friend answers: truths can be upsetting and too harsh to be serenely accepted. One cannot be too careful with such susceptibility, all the more so as the Romanians' pride recoils in pain at foreigners' insults:

> This is the time, now, at the beginning, when you should handle people as you do glass and try to indulge them not drive them away, and lend your ear to their demands in all areas so that you learn what they like and what brings them harm. Many are those who believe you mean to laugh at the poor Romanians, which does them a lot of harm, when you say "Suffice the grievance they have from foreigners, why should their own kin sour the wounds?"[201]

Bariţ's dramatic set-up is all the more remarkable as the journalist brings persuasive arguments in support of either stance: the voice of truth and reason—insisting, in fact, that by opting for lucidity and a critical sense the nation will be on the winning side; and the voice of injured sensibility—which shows that a hasty unveiling of certain truths and the adoption of the same calumnious tone used by foreigners may well harm the national interest.

On the one hand, Bariţ exculpates himself: he never meant to insult anyone. On the other hand, however, "it is my heart's desire to learn the precious art of showing forth the wrongs and follies, and to purge the prejudices, first from my soul and then from the souls of others." He then sings to another tune, insisting on, and generally illustrating, the fact that the Romanians are denigrated and wronged. More than that, he argues decisively in favour of a combative reply to unfavourable external images and denounces the injuries that foreigners' distorted perceptions can bring to the Romanians at the level of international affairs.

> Yet we, with all the abuse others have been pouring out on us, have kept silent so far. Silent were the two provinces, although with their own constitution and rule no less than other peoples of Europe; they would not rise in their own defence and allowed those traits of character others purported to find in us to become fixed in the minds of every nation. No wonder, then, that no one stands up for them in parliaments and cabinets! If we are sure of being in the right, why do we remain silent and fear to speak up as men? Why don't we bend our force to erase such stains from our name?

By drawing up this long bill of indictment against the distorting images constructed by foreigners, Bariţ ensures that he is "covered" against potential replies and then inserts once again a plea for a careful observation of foreign perceptions, for they may prove true and just: "And if we find we deserve the blame, we should strive to undo our mistakes so that no one feels entitled to reprove and condemn us ever again."[202]

Here lies the deep significance of his argument, centred on the need for truth not on an attempt to avoid it or to hush it up. A sincere supporter of energetic combat against distorted and calumnious images, thus offering a safety valve and a target to injured nationalism, he also shows that unfavourable perceptions on the part of foreigners are not always based on hostile purposes but may well be founded on negative *realities* present within Romanian society. It is not the image that needs correction, therefore, but the reality underlying it; on the contrary, the image can help the Romanians to know the reality and to change it for the better.

This was probably the peak of objectivity that could be reached by Romanian reflection at that time on the relationship between self-image and images constructed by others, and one cannot but admit, considering the evolution of the idea to this day, that its lesson has remained an extremely valuable and lastingly valid one.

NOTES

1 For the role played by the discovery of the common "enemy" and the construction of "images of the adversary" in the process of fashioning national identities, see the whole discussion in 3:Anderson 1991, as well as applications to the Romanian case in 3:Shafir 1983 and 3:Volovici 1991.
2 "Foreword" to 1.4:Maior P. 1812; 1.9:Maior P. 1970, I, p. 91.

3 *Ibidem*.
4 *Ibidem*.
5 See "Prefatio editoris" (Editor's foreword) to 1.4:Eder 1791, pp. 2–7; 1.9:Fugariu 1983, I, pp. 142–144, 154–157.
6 1.4:Sulzer 1781–1782.
7 1.4: Engel 1794.
8 A detailed analysis of which, following all its international occurrences, is to be found in 3:Gyémánt 1986, pp. 61–119.
9 *Widerlegung der zu Klausenburg 1791 über die Vorstellung der Wallachischen Nation herausgekommenen Noten* and *Responsum ad Crisim Josephi Caroli Eder in Supplicum libellum Valachorum Transylvaniae iuxta numeros ab ipso positos*, edited respectively in 1.9:Pervain 1970, pp. 37–114 and 1.9:Pervain 1971, pp. 44–72 (fragments).
10 See the discussion on the paternity of these texts in 3:Gyémánt 1986, p. 72.
11 1.4:Maior P. 1814a; 1.4:Maior P. 1814b; 1.4:Maior P. 1815; 1.4:Maior 1816. See also 1.9:Maior P. 1976, II, pp. 199–248.
12 Barth. Kopitar, "Geschichte der Ursprungs der Römer von Peter Major", in 1.2:*Wiener Allgemeine*, no. 98, 7 Dec. 1813, pp. 1551–1565.
13 1.4:Costin 1812a; 1.4:Costin 1812b. As to the relationship Petru Maior/Toma Costin, see 3:Gyémánt 1986, p. 85.
14 1.4:Schwartner 1809.
15 1.4:Aaron Th. 1828; *Disputations on the History*..., translated and edited by Bojincă, in 1.5:Maior P. 1834, pp. 1–63.
16 1.4:Bojincă 1827; 1.4:Bojincă 1828; 1.4:Murgu 1830.
17 1.4:Tököly 1823; 1.4:Tököly 1827. For this polemics, see 3:Bocşan 1973.
18 Ioan Maiorescu, "A Refutation of M. I. K. Schuller's Opinion on the German Origin of the Romanian Language", in 1.2:*Journal for the Mind*, X, 1847, no. 15–22; also, in *ibidem*, VI, 1843, no. 11–13; X, 1847, no. 2–6; XI, 1848, no. 14–19.
19 Timotei Cipariu, "Principles of Language and Writing", in 1.2:*The Mouthpiece*, I, 1847, no. 35, p. 190.
20 Idem, "The Union", in *ibidem*, II, 1848, no. 67, p. 381.
21 See section 10, "A more refined attitude to the images constructed by others".
22 George Bariţ, "Ioan Hristian Engel", in 1.2:*Journal for the Mind*, VII, 1844, no. 1–3.
23 Or, later, Robert Roesler.
24 Andrei Mureşanu, "Sulzer on the Romanians", in 1.2:*Journal for the Mind*, IX, 1846, no. 30, pp. 236–240; 1.9:Mureşanu A. 1977, pp. 93–101.
25 Papiu's *History* may be considered the other work of reference for the period of our concern, alongside Maior's work. It thus rounds off the process of genesis that gave the Transylvanian Romanians a political and cultural imaginary in modern terms.
26 1.5:Papiu Ilarian 1852(II), pp. CIII sqq.
27 1.5:Papiu Ilarian 1852(I), pp. 208–209.
28 This phrase, which I find extremely suggestive, was coined by Sorin Antohi, see 3:Antohi 1994, p. 252 and *passim*.
29 1.4:Bojincă 1828, p. 7; 1.9:Fugariu 1983, II, p. 658.
30 1.5:Papiu Ilarian 1852(I), p. 7.
31 *Ibidem*, p. 20.
32 Gh. Popovici to Ioan Mihut, a letter of 15 November 1815, published in 1.9:Bodea 1943, p. 181.
33 Petru Suciu to George Bariţ, a letter of 3 July 1848, published in 1.9:Bodea 1982, I, p. 594.
34 George Bariţ, "The Romanians and the Despotic Reaction", article of October 1848, re-edited in 1.9:Bodea 1982, II, p. 937.
35 *Ibidem*.
36 1.4:Bojincă 1828, pp. 14–15; 1.9:Fugariu 1983, II, p. 660.
37 *Ibidem*, p. 7 and p. 658, respectively.
38 1.4:Bojincă 1828; 1.9:Bojincă 1978, pp. 8–9.
39 1.4:Maior P. 1814a; 1.9:Fugariu 1983, II, p. 223.
40 1.9:Budai-Deleanu 1991, p. 186.

41 1.9:Fugariu 1983, II, p. 128.
42 1.7:*Supplex 1791*, in 3:Prodan 1971, pp. 446, 458.
43 1.4:Maior P. 1812, pp. 93–94, 96–97; 1.9:Fugariu 1983, I, pp. 887–889.
44 See 3:Zieglauer 1881 and 3:Bernath 1972.
45 See a similarly constructed explanation, along sociological lines, of the rise of the various types of nationalism in Central Europe in 3:Karnoouh 1990: The Romanian or Carpatho–Russian Greek Catholic intellectual élite "exhibit the features of a stratum that mediates between the imperial and/or feudal power and the peasantry and thus represents a genuine embryo of an ethnic-national middle class in countries where the strata of craftsmen and bourgeoisie are either totally absent or reduced and allogenous. Where can such a social layer—a society of scholars—obtain its means of subsistence? Obviously, from state supplies. And what does it need in order to do that? Political existence!"
46 1.4:Maior P. 1812, pp. 47–48; 1.9:Fugariu 1983, I, pp. 881–882.
47 1.9:Fugariu 1983, II, p. 83.
48 1.1:Cipariu cca. 1846.
49 For the relationship between stereotypes and the factual realities from which they spring, see 3:Allport 1954; 3:Simpson, Yinger 1985, pp. 21–24, 71–90, 97 sqq.; as well as 3:Chelcea 1994a, pp. 67–69 or 3:Chelcea 1994b. It is also true that any hostile stereotype or prejudice also stems from a certain negative reality; yet it is equally true that stereotypes have an ulterior evolution that grows independent from the situations that generate them, as Cipariu states in the above-mentioned context.
50 1.4:Maior P. 1812, p. 15; 1.9:Fugariu 1983, I, p. 872.
51 *Ibidem*, pp. 334–335 ("Dissertation on the Romanians' Old Literature") and I, p. 923, respectively.
52 1.4:Maior P. 1813; 1.9:Maior P. 1976, p. 101.
53 1.4:Costin 1812a; 1.9:Fugariu 1983, I, pp. 856–858.
54 Moise Nicoară to Petru Maior, a letter of 5–8 December 1810, published in 1.9:Bodea 1943, p. 145.
55 1.4:Bojincă 1828, pp. 13–14; 1.9:Fugariu 1983, II, p. 660.
56 Timotei Cipariu, "The Union", in 1.2:*The Mouthpiece*, II, 1848, no. 67, p. 381.
57 "Bucharest", in *ibidem*, I, 1847, no. 16, p. 74.
58 1.5:Papiu Ilarian 1852(II), p. 207.
59 *Ibidem*, pp. 213–214.
60 1.9:Papiu Ilarian 1943, p. 99.
61 1.7:*Petition July 1849*, in 1.9:Păcăţian 1904, p. 601.
62 1.9:Papiu Ilarian 1943, p. 114.
63 *Ibidem*.
64 1.7:*Address April 1849*, in 1.9: Păcăţian 1904, p. 547.
65 An important study on the "self-victimisation" of Romanian identity is Sorin Antohi's "Cioran and the Romanian Stigma. Identity Mechanisms and Radical Definitions of Ethnicity", in 3:Antohi 1994, pp. 208–285. See also 3:Pippidi 1993, especially pp. 28–30.
66 Such images, which made their way into both cultured and folkloric tradition, never tire of laying ostentatious emphasis on the marked specificity of the Romanian stance as to the conflicts between the Turks and the West. Romanian reactions to Western initiatives evince distrust and a patronising tendency endorsed by the wisdom acquired through an experience of non-sharable particularity. Such perceptions were the basis of ulterior crucial elements of Romanian spiritual self-definition, all the way to Romantic historiography and Eminescu. See 3:Mitu S. 1992, p. 14.
67 1.8:Budai-Deleanu 1974–1975, I, p. 161.
68 Given that a serious monograph that should consider the 1848 Transylvanian revolution as a whole (including the period of the civil war) is still lacking, one can still refer to Bariţ's classic work, recently re-edited: 3:Bariţ 1994, pp. 101–582.
69 Avram Iancu's report concerning the battles of 1848-1849, drawn up in November 1849, re-edited in 1.9:Bodea 1982, II, p. 1035.
70 The Auraria Gemina Prefecture to the National Committee, a letter of 28 February 1849, published in 1.9:Dragomir 1944–1946, II, p. 77.

71 Published in German translation in 1.5:Laurian 1849.
72 See 1.9:Teodor 1972; 1.9:Bocșan, Leu 1988.
73 Avram Iancu's report, in 1.9:Bodea 1982, II, p. 1059.
74 *Ibidem*, p. 1053.
75 *Ibidem*, p. 1035.
76 It also foreshadowed what later came to be known as the "Yalta syndrome" and the "Americans-surrendering-us-to-the-Russians" cliché: Why didn't they start a Third World War in order to save us?
77 For a description and analysis of the historical sequence of Transylvanian petitions, although mainly undertaken from within the Romanian vision of the time, see 3:Prodan 1971; 3:Gyémánt 1986; 3:Maior L. 1992.
78 1.7:*Petition June 1848*, in 1.9:Păcățian 1904, p. 369.
79 1.7:*Petition December 1849*, in 1.9:Păcățian 1904, p. 636.
80 The merchants of Brașov to Bishop Șaguna, a letter of 20 July 1848, published in 1.9:Dragomir 1944-1946, II, p. 169.
81 1.7:*Petition February 1849*, in 1.9:Păcățian 1904, p. 521.
82 The Auraria Gemina Prefecture to the National Committee, a letter of 24 February 1849, in 1.9:Dragomir 1944–1946, II, p. 76; 1.6:Maior L. 1972, p. 73.
83 1.7:*Address April 1849*, in 1.9:Păcățian 1904, p. 546.
84 1.7:*Petition January 1850*, in *ibidem*, p. 645.
85 *Ibidem*, p. 646.
86 1.7:*Memorandum January 1850*, in 1.9:Păcățian 1904, p. 654.
87 1.7:*Petition January 1850*, in *ibidem*, p. 646.
88 1.7:*Reply July 1849*, in *ibidem*, p. 609.
89 The same feeling, only with different actors, was experienced by Romanian society after the events of 1989.
90 1.7:*Memorandum January 1850*, in 1.9:Păcățian 1904, p. 651.
91 1.7:*Petition January 1850*, in *ibidem*, p. 646.
92 A convincing illustration of the motif of loyalty to the emperor can be noticed, for instance, even after the end of the revolution, in a poem issued in the form of a leaflet by Timotei Cipariu, which exalts the idea of the Romanians' gratitude and loyalty to the Imperial House; see 1.1:Cipariu cca 1849.
93 See, for instance, 3:Maior L. 1992 and 2:Maior L. 1993.
94 See Iancu's refusal to meet the emperor on the occasion of the latter's visit to the Mountains (3:Dragomir 1965, pp. 273–282) or Papiu's reluctance when faced with the decoration offered to him (3:Albu C. 1977, pp. 93–95).
95 Bărnuțiu, Papiu, or those who came back: Maiorescu, Laurian (see 3:Urechia 1892–1901).
96 Talk of such discrimination lasted at least until the separation of the Romanian parishes, which eventually joined the bishopric of Oradea under the cure of Samuil Vulcan, and until the definitive extension of Romanian Greek Catholic jurisdiction throughout Maramureș (see the bibliography of the issue in 3:Ghitta 1994).
97 Such as the Romanians' conflict with the "Greeks" in Pest or Brașov.
98 Who, at another level of the Romanian self-image, are seen as an integral part of the Romanian national identity.
99 See 1.9:Bodea 1943, pp. 329, 341, 366, etc.
100 1.5:Papiu Ilarian 1852(II), pp. XCIX–C.
101 1.7:*Petition Januray 1850*, in 1.9:Păcățian 1904, p. 642. August Treboianu Laurian, too, wrote that "we are surrounded by people who would hate to see us better and have never meant us well"; see A.T.L., "Historical documents on the political and religious state of the Transylvanian Romanians", in 1.2:*Journal*, III, 1846, p. 95.
102 See, for instance, the famous work of Abbot Barruel (1.4:Barruel 1803) or the chapter dedicated to the theory of the plot (plus the bibliography) in 3:Godechot 1963.
103 See 3:Talmon 1968, chp. II, "La politique du complot et de l'émeute".
104 1.9:Budai-Deleanu 1991, p. 186.

105 Another imaginary actor of the anti-Romanian conspiracy, a telling presence in the Romanian political mythology of the epoch, is the famous "masked man", wearing a "short thick coat" or "black cloak", a specialist of red-herring policy and subversive actions. Such a character reportedly made his presence felt during Horea's mutiny (see 3:Prodan 1979, pp. 666–667, 703–706, etc.; Prodan's insistence on denying any possibility of an actual existence for Salis, the "man in the red shako", or the involvement of the Freemasons, etc., although undoubtedly slightly subjective, cannot but place more emphasis on the pregnant impact the theory of the plot had on the mutineers, at least as a "reality" of an imaginary nature). The same character in the same disguise was to feature as (would-be) assassin of Bărnuţiu and on the occasion of the Lemeny case in 1843. See 1.1:Pop 1843, as well as 3:Suciu 1938a; 3:Suciu 1938b; 1.1:Suciu 1938.

106 The phrase was launched at the beginning of the '90s by the widely read works of Dan Zamfirescu and Pavel Coruţ.

107 1.9:Bodea 1943, *passim.*

108 See Sorin Antohi's analysis of Ion Heliade Rădulescu's case in 3:Antohi 1994, p. 32.

109 1.7:*Appeal August 1819*, in 1.9:Bodea 1943, p. 329.

110 *Ibidem.*

111 *Ibidem*, pp. 329 sqq.

112 *Ibidem*, p. 348.

113 *Ibidem.*

114 Samuil Micu had also spoken, in his time, of the occult actions of the Jesuits; it was they who "urged the people of other nations" against Bishop Inochentie and the Romanian attempts at emancipation (1.9:Fugariu 1983, I, pp. 6–7), acting thus as true agents of the universal conspiracy. The same aversion to ultramontanism is to be found in Petru Maior (in the *Procanon*, for instance: see 1.9:Maior P. 1894) or, later, in Bărnuţiu, in the *Discourse* in Blaj, for instance (1.9:*Documents 1848 Transylvania 1977–1988*, IV, p. 11). All these attitudes were the outcome of rationalism under Joseph, itself adverse to the Jesuits and the "darkness" that went with this occult organisation. See also 3:Teodor 1984, pp. 83-98: "Jansenist and Gallican echoes in Romanian culture".

115 Moise Nicoară to Theodor Popovici, a letter of 1 Sept. 1819, published in 1.9:Bodea 1943, p. 352.

116 See 3:Delumeau 1978; 3:Duby 1988.

117 1.7:*Appeal August 1819*, in 1.9:Bodea 1943, p. 329.

118 1.9:Bodea 1943, p. 372.

119 See IV, 2 below: "Resistance to denationalisation".

120 3:Adorno 1950. For the individual reasons for ethnocentric behaviour, prejudice and discrimination, see 3:Simpson, Yinger 1985, pp. 71–90 and 3:Moscovici 1990, pp. 453–461.

121 1.9:Bodea 1943, pp. 16–18.

122 *Ibidem*, pp. 17–18; cf. 1.9:Bodea 1937.

123 1.9:Bodea 1943, p. 294.

124 For the issue of psycho-history, see 3:Szaluta 1987.

125 For a warning against the excessive "medicalisation" of explanations of social phenomena, see 3:Antohi 1994, pp. 234–236, 283–284.

126 See, for an extended discussion (plus bibliography) of the "theory of the stigma" as applied to the case of Romanian national identity, *ibidem*, pp. 224–239. From the viewpoint of this theory the self-image invoked in the present paragraph is but one of the typical behavioural features of the stigma-bearer, both individual and collective, be it "ethnic" or "tribal".

127 Bishop Ioan Bob to the faithful of Reghin, a letter of March 1804, published in 1.6:Maior P. 1968, p. 60.

128 The same idea is eloquently rendered in a 1803 circular letter in which Moldavian Metropolitan Bishop Veniamin Costache vituperates the alcoholic habits taken up by his priests. The habit "not only brings destruction and damnation to the soul and the body and leaves the house and the children in poverty and disgrace, but becomes the common talk of both Christian and other tongues, but first of the Jews, enemies of Christ and of the Christian name, who delight in the scandal and laugh and have a merry time." (See 1.9:Brătescu 1988, pp. 108–109). The danger of becoming the laughing-stock of the Jews, in a Moldavia where the subsequently popular anti-

Semitic logos were just being devised, was, in Costache's opinion, a propagandistic formula sure to terrify even the most insensitive priestly souls that had taken the high road to hell.

129 Ioan Pop, father of Alexandru Papiu Ilarian, was the future martyr of the national cause, executed by the Hungarian authorities during the revolution. Up until that point, however, he had proved to be, like so many of his fellow-priests of the time, an extremely rapacious and energetic character, who would beat his *jeleri* (peasants working on the nobles' estates, different from the serfs in terms of juridical status) and who built his private household with money abusively taken from the church (see the complaint sent to the Blaj bishopric by the Greek Catholic community of Budiul de Cîmpie on 1 June 1842: 1.1:*Complaint* 1842).

130 George Crișan to Bishop Ioan Lemeny, a letter of 15 June 1842, 1.1:Crișan 1842.

131 1.4:Iercovici 1794: "To the Reader"; 1.9:Fugariu 1983, I, p. 190.

132 Nicolae Maniu to George Bariț, a letter of August 1843, published in 1.6:*GBC* 1973–1993, III, p. 37. The "insult" brought to the "nation" and the "clergy" by these disputes also makes the object of complaints by representatives of the other party, Reverend Vasile Rațiu (see 1.1:Rațiu 1845) and Constantin Alpini, rector of Mediaș (see 1.1:Alpini 1845).

133 The National Committee to vice-prefect Ștefan Moldovan, official address of 16 December 1848, published in 1.9:Bodea 1982, II, pp. 1004–1005.

134 3:Prodan 1971, pp. 452, 464.

135 1.9:*Documents 1848 Transylvania* 1977–1988, IV, pp. 5–7.

136 1.9:Bodea 1943, p. 245.

137 Al. Papiu Ilarian, "Some preliminaries to *Diorile for the Mind and Heart*", in *Diorile for the Mind and Heart* (manuscript journal, Cluj), 1845, no. 1, *apud* 1.9:Papiu Ilarian 1981, p. 45.

138 *Ibidem*, p. 46.

139 Much more interesting considerations could undoubtedly be brought on the role this belief played in the conduct of the Romanian political class of the '90s.

140 1.9:Bodea 1943, p. 58.

141 See III, 3.1 below: "The Romanians like the Gypsies".

142 1.8:Budai-Deleanu 1974–1975, I, p. 37.

143 1.9:Fugariu 1983, I, p. 223.

144 *Ibidem*, II, p. 368.

145 *Ibidem*, II, p. 165.

146 *Ibidem*, II, p. 240.

147 A history of the phenomenon up to 1830 is readily accessible in the *BRV* (1.9:*BRV* 1903–1944, vol. II–IV).

148 Rudolf Oghidan, "To the readers", foreword to 1.5:Barac 1836; 1.9:Fugariu 1983, II, p. 742. In conformity with this national tradition, the tendency to support scientific creation for the sake of successful propaganda abroad is still present among official circles today, as is the willingness of some intellectuals to let themselves be inspired, since no other muse cares to assist them, by the reasons of a polemics extraneous to the cultural sphere as such.

149 1.5:Barac 1836, p. IV; 1.9:Fugariu 1983, II, p. 743.

150 The law students of the Tîrgu-Mureș Lutheran College to George Bariț, a letter of 19 January 1847, published in 1.9:Bodea 1982, I, p. 321; the foreign reference point invoked here was the Cluj paper *Erdélyi Híradó* ("The Transylvanian Herald").

151 1.5:Papiu Ilarian 1852(II), pp. 200–201.

152 Timotei Cipariu, "The National Assembly. Blaj, 15, 16, 17 May", in 1.2:*The Mouthpiece*, II, 1848, no. 1, p. 4; 1.5:Papiu Ilarian 1852(II), p. 256; 1.9:Bodea 1982, I, p. 492.

153 1.5:Papiu Ilarian 1852(II), p. 255.

154 *Ibidem*, p. 238.

155 The modern spirit of such suggestions, revealed by our analysis of the texts of the time, becomes even more apparent if we consider that they have not been substantially assimilated into Romanian culture to this day.

156 Iosif Many, "Pest and the Hungarians. (An excerpt from a journalist)", in 1.2:*The Gazette*, IX, no. 51, pp. 207–208. See Ioan Chindriș, the monographic study "Iosif Many", in 1.6:*GBC* 1973–1993, III, pp. 288–306.

157 3:Mitu M. 1992.

158 Iosif Many, *op. cit.*, (note 156), p. 208.

159 1.9:Bariţ 1962, p. 61.

160 *Ibidem*, pp. 98–99; 1.2:*The Gazette*, X, 1847, no. 96, pp. 381–382.

161 1.9:Codru Drăguşanu 1980, p. 225. I have chosen this edition here for the more fluent reading it allows, due to the orthographic and sometimes lexical modernisation.

162 *Ibidem*, pp. 232–233; pp. 260–261 in the Romul Munteanu edition (1.9:Codru Drăguşanu 1956). In the 1956 Munteanu edition, the censors eliminated the sentence referring to the Russians; the 1980 Albu edition kept it, but on the other hand cut off the passage referring to the Hungarians (which is quite surprising for the nationalist drive of the Ceauşescu epoch; it seems that the hypocrisy of the "solidarity of brotherly peoples" was still active, if selective and random). Today, the researcher has no other option but to reconstitute the text out of juxtaposed excerpts, or to collate at every step this edition with all the others: *princeps* (1865), Onciu (1910, 1923) or Cioculescu (1942).

163 *Ibidem* (the Albu ed.), p. 233.

164 See, for one of the most exhaustive collections of such national stereotypes, Hermann Keyserling, *Das Spektrum Europas* (2:Keyserling 1929).

165 1.2:*The Friend*, I, 1848, no. 11, col. 172.

166 A. Aur (= Iosif Many), "The Defaming Tongue", in 1.2:*Journal for the Mind*, III, 1840, no. 7, pp. 53–54.

167 As we have seen, Bariţ quotes Széchenyi, too, when he means to prove the relativity of ethnic images. See note 160 above.

168 A quite harsh remark on Sigismund Pop in 1.6:GBC 1973–1993, III, pp. 282–283.

169 A. Aur (= Iosif Many), *op. cit.* (note 166), p. 54.

170 1.9:Fugariu 1983, I, p. 238.

171 As has become apparent in such research as undertaken, for instance, by Catherine Durandin, the positive images foreigners formed of the Romanians, such as the much-invoked favourable image the French projected onto them in the first half of the nineteenth century, were themselves likely to be underlain by quite specific "interests" and reasons internal to the respective foreign societies (see 3:Durandin 1989, pp. 89–152 and 3:Antohi 1994, pp. 255–257). Equally, I might add, a negative image may well be an extremely objective and, ultimately, benevolent one. Yet, obviously, the nationalist nature of self-image was immune to logical arguments.

172 During the same period, the Hungarians, too, had such foreigners who had settled within their national vision, such as the Frenchman Auguste de Gérando or the Englishman John Paget, both married to descendants of the Transylvanian Hungarian aristocracy. For Gérando see 3:Iorga 1981, pp. 683–684; 3:Mitu M., Mitu S. 1996, pp. 226–227; 3:Adriaenssen 1991. For Paget see 3:Bodea 1960.

173 1.5:Vaillant 1844. On Vaillant: 3:Cudalbu-Slusanski 1937–1938; 3:Isar 1991, pp. 14–17 (with bibliography).

174 Dyonis Thalson, in 1.2:*Blätter*, VI, 1842, no. 45–47; also see idem, "Correspondenzen", in 1.2:*Satellit*, II, 1841, no. 15, p. 59.

175 *Idem*, "The Romans", in 1.2: *The Mouthpiece*, I, 1847, no. 47, p. 264.

176 Cf. 3:Pippidi 1980.

177 1.5:Desprez 1850. For Desprez' relationships with the Romanians, see 3:Maior L. 1968; 3:Isar 1991, pp. 18–19.

178 1.5:Papiu Ilarian 1852(II), pp. C–CII.

179 3:Durandin 1989, pp. 89–152; 3:Antohi 1994, pp. 255–257.

180 Al. Papiu Ilarian to Iacob Muresan, a letter of October 1852, published in 1.6:Pervain, Chindriş 1972, I, pp. 168–169.

181 *Ibidem*.

182 1.4:Aaron Th. 1828, pp. 11–12; 1.9:Fugariu 1983, II, p. 651.

183 1.7:*Supplex* 1804, in 3:Prodan 1970; also see 3:Prodan 1989, pp. 305–306.

184 A recent collection of self- and hetero-stereotypes characteristic of Banat in 2:Jurma 1994.

185 1.9:Stoica de Haţeg 1984, p. 9.

186 Timotei Cipariu, "Principles of Language and Writing", in 1.2:*The Mouthpiece*, II, 1848, no. 56, p. 314. The same lack of concern for Romanian problems on the part of foreigners is deplored

by Cipariu in a letter to Iacob Mureşanu of 27 December 1853, in which he is of the opinion that the Italians had better start studying hard the Romanian language if they want to shed light on the unsolved problems of Romanic philology (1.1:Cipariu 1853).

187 Idem, "Principles of Language…", in *loc. cit.*

188 *Ibidem.*

189 *Ibidem.*

190 A harsher attitude towards calumnies uttered by foreigners animates Cipariu in an unpublished 1846 manuscript. See 1.1:Cipariu 1846.

191 1.4:Maior P. 1814b, p. 4; 1.9:Maior P. 1976, II, p. 87.

192 1.8:Budai-Deleanu 1974–1975, I, p. 91.

193 Simion Bărnuţiu to Al. Papiu Ilarian, a letter of January 1853, published in 1.6:Pervain, Chindriş 1972, II, pp. 48–49.

194 See 1.9:Marica 1969, *passim.*

195 George Bariţ, "Foreign Literature for the Romanians", in 1.2:*Journal for the Mind*, VIII, 1845, no. 48, p. 383.

196 *Idem,* "Inquiry into the Nature of the Soul", in 1.2:*Literary Paper*, I, 1838, no. 5, p. 39 sqq.; no. 6, p. 46 sqq.

197 *Ibidem.*

198 *Idem,* "We, the Romanians", in 1.2:*Journal for the Mind*, III, 1840, no. 12, pp. 93–95 (translation of, and comments on, an article published in 1.2:*Századunk*, 1840, no. 6).

199 *Idem,* "On the Romanian Disease", in 1.2:*Journal for the Mind*, VII, 1844, no. 48, p. 375.

200 See note 196 above.

201 *Ibidem.*

202 *Ibidem* (pp. 39, 46–48).

II. The Negative Dimension of the Self-image

THE ROMANIANS AS SELF-DENIGRATORS: SHOULD THEY DENIGRATE THEMSELVES AS WELL OR NOT?

Undoubtedly, the way in which foreigners saw the Romanians and the images they wove around Romanian realities were traversed by unfavourable traits. Yet nor was the Romanians' self-image, despite its polemical reaction against such perceptions, devoid of negative descriptive elements, as we shall see. "Before others started to belittle and defame us", George Bariț wrote in 1839, "not long ago we used to have all kinds of sayings to belittle and insult ourselves. And this was so because we never thought nor trusted that something good might come out of us."[1]

Although the Brașov-based journalist believed that such a disheartening image had better be abandoned as soon as possible, the future would show that the self-denigrating passion is an essential component of the Romanian self-image, deeply rooted in the formative matrix of the national culture. We need only take one such instance in order to be persuaded that this is the case—a hundred years later, another Transylvanian, Emil Cioran would lavishly employ his stylistic gifts in theorising that tendency, in a book whose impact was as great then as it is now.

> Many peoples have poked fun at their own condition; self-irony is a given of any tormented and oppressed people. It is however rare that self-knowledge goes hand in hand with self-deprecation the way it has happened, to excess, with the Romanians. We would prove unfair to our own scourge if we were to contemplate only deficiency in that phenomenon, since it strikes an original note of bizarre significance. No other people is more apt to understand its own insufficiencies and to relish the rare delight of confessing them on any occasion. This is a collective self-denigration, a generalised "spitting in our own face", a bitter lucidity as to our own lot, which in some are born automatically and without conflicts while in others, the few, they cause lacerations. Could it be that "being Romanian" is not a pleasant evidence? What is sure is that the Romanian people is distanced from itself in a way that indicates a unique peculiarity in a people who lack historical consciousness.[2]

Certainly, if we leave the area of the ethnic-psychological obsessions or of the Romanians' stereotyped uniqueness, which Cioran has so remarkably formulated, and make for the space of rational analysis and comparative vision, we notice that such a negativist perception is by no means singular: its effects in numerous peoples and national identities has been well analysed and outlined in anthropological terms or from the perspective of social psychology. For instance, the "self-hatred" (*Selbsthass*) specific to the Jewish self-image[3], in terms of which Luca Piţu tried, in an original essay, to translate the Romanian self-perception[4], has long been known and analysed. Similarly, the seductive theory of the *stigma* allowed Sorin Antohi to decipher quite sagaciously the articulation of identity-making mechanisms in the case of Cioran himself.[5]

In fact, the theory of the stigma sheds significant light on the Romanian case as well, since both the way in which foreign images were configured and the impact they had on the Romanian Transylvanians' self-image can be convincingly explained with its aid.[6] Foreigners construct unfavourable images because their horizon of expectation (the "anticipated alterity") is belied by the striking differences exhibited by the Romanians' actual observed situation in relation to the external observers' pre-established schema. The Romanians' realisation that this was the case established a collective stigma at the level of their community identity. The stigma caused the stigmatised to display such attitudes and reactions as are absolutely typical of such a phenomenon: the obsessive fear that the stigma may be unveiled at any moment; the tendency to ape the "normal" foreigner even in terms of his disregard of the stigmatised; the shame, contempt and hatred for one's burdensome condition. Undoubtedly, such elements were quite capable of engendering the fabrication of a negative self-image.

The competitive manner in which self-perception is configured as a reply to images constructed by others, which we analysed in the previous chapter, created, in fact, paradoxical though it may seem, the propitious conditions for the emergence of negative self-stereotypes, if only by means of mere taking over from the other. That this could happen was due to the fact that, whereas sometimes the stigmatised tend to hide their stigma and behave as if it did not exist (even though they live with the obsession that the "deficiency" may be unveiled at any moment), at other times, particularly when the stigma becomes a matter of public knowledge, its bearers tend to indulge in the situation, to expose their handicap and thus to take over, often to overtax, the unfavourable image projected by the stigmatiser.

The texts mainly foreground the fear of those who promote the former behavioural variant in the face of the danger inherent in the generalisation of the latter, that is, when faced with the possibility that the foreigners' negative images influence and persuade the Romanians, too.

The Romanians, says Bojincă, must "learn well how to respond to those who defame the nation [...] and how to see through their lies and inventions about the Romanians, lest they be fooled into believing their concoctions".[7] Bariţ deplores the fact that foreigners who state that the Romanians are not part of Europe "come to inspire us with shame at ourselves by their descriptions", to the extent that his fellow countrymen tend to repeat the same things, even "indulging in such thoughts".[8] Similarly, Cipariu shows that the foreign scholars' irony with respect to the Romanians' Latinist exaggerations had become common currency among the Romanians as well: "That mockery, which the Romanians' philological inquiries have also embraced, is spreading like an epidemic among the Romanians themselves and cut short every soul's efforts, with no discrimination between men or opinions."[9] Generally speaking, all attitudes to the images constructed by foreigners that showed evidence of greater sensitivity to nuances (which we glossed in a preceding section) tended to take such criticism into consideration on account of the possibility that it might be right, and thus risked aligning themselves with the above-mentioned examples and additionally legitimating those fears.

Yet irrespective of what was said by foreigners or of the explanatory circumstances of the theory of the stigma, the dire Romanian realities of the time, whether political, economic or cultural, were enough to offer anyone, including Romanian intellectuals, plenty of arguments out of which pessimistic, unfavourable conclusions could be drawn and a gloomy image constructed.

Let us go on to survey several types of attitudes and reactions relative to the issue of the configuration of a negative self-image.

A somewhat surprising source of the Transylvanian Romanians' self-denigration, yet one that emerges in the fullest clarity, is the tradition of the Greek–Byzantine lamentation on the decay of the present as compared to the greatness of the past—a lamentation that usually makes direct reference to the motif of the conquest of Constantinople by the Turks.[10] This tradition had also been illustrated in the Moldavian–Wallachian literature of the sixteenth to eighteenth centuries, in the chroniclers' writings or in religious texts[11], from where it was taken over by the Transylvanians in the eighteenth century. We should also note that such a tradition, of a literary, expressive-formal nature, does not, in my opinion, constitute itself as a basic reason for the articulation of a negative image; however, it did provide that perception with certain ways of expression that would contribute to its configuration.

A true initiator in this respect was Gherontie Cotore, who provided Transylvanian culture, in a text of 1746, with a paradigmatic model of the lamentation on the present condition. Cotore draws a parallel between the Greeks and the Romanians and quotes from Patriarch Ghenadie's lament on the fall of Constantinople: "'Remember, brothers', says this Father, 'what our people was like and for how long; once it was wise, famous, brave, prudent, good, strong, and all the earth was at its feet [...] And now, alas, we have reason for shame, for all things are falling down and Constantinople has been taken.'"[12]

This picture of decay is eventually transferred to the Romanian situation, so that the Romanians are seen as even more capable of illustrating the huge contrast between the greatness of the past and the poverty of their current condition. Here, Cotore's lament becomes more eloquent than ever:

> Alas, alas! Fame and glory used once to be the fate of this Romanian people, until it fell back and now lingers under the desecration of others. Once it was brave and its sword mighty, now weaker are its arms than any other's. Wise it was in times past, now clouded in ignorance. Praised once, now scorned. Master once over Transylvania as well, now bereft of the rule of its own land. Obeyed once by other peoples, now their laughing-stock. Always ready with good deeds then, always up to villainies now. Rare and startling was then the sight of one impaled, now the stakes grow like trees. This is what the Romanian people has come to, and more lies in store for it [...], unless it consents to listen to the words of wisdom.[13]

In fact, Cotore's text is indebted to an age-old tradition[14], but he lays the foundations for the main themes of a negative self-image, as they will be developed during the Enlightenment and the Romantic age: the decay of the present as compared to the past; the insults of foreigners and the shame resulting from the Romanians' present condition, their cultural backwardness, their lagging behind other European peoples, their penchant for criminality and delinquency.

Samuil Micu follows in Cotore's wake: able to study his precursor's manuscripts in the Blaj library[15] he uses, as a comparison of the texts will show, similar sources. Thus, Micu makes definite room for the theme of lamentation within public consciousness by reproducing, in the introduction to his *History*, the words he claims Metropolitan Bishop Theodosie Veştemean of Wallachia (in fact a Transylvanian himself) uttered in 1680, when he deplored "the belittling and decay of this our Romanian people, which once was as powerful, learned and wise as the other great nations. And today it is so wretched and forlorn and so bereft of wisdom that neither learning nor science nor weapon nor law nor good order is left among this Romanian people [...] O, woe is me, that we should have come to this!"[16]

The tradition of the lament was to bear fruit particularly in the area of the epithets which defined, at every step, the Romanians' condition and which the Transylvanian intellectuals used self-referentially in texts meant for publication, in petitions and requests addressed to the authorities, as well as in their private correspondence. "Wretched", "needy" (the words used in the Romanian texts, *ticălos*, *nemernic*, *mişel*, are the equivalents of "miscreant", "infamous", and "rascal" in today's sense of the words; at that time, however, they meant precisely "wretched", and "needy"), "poor", "oppressed", "belittled", "decayed", and "ruined" are the omnipresent attributes accompanying any description of the Romanian state of things and outlining an image of the Romanian's "woe" as an inherent feature of his historical destiny.[17] Additionally, "tears" and "weeping" are always associated with reflection on these aspects, so that the image emerges of what Papiu Ilarian calls the "Plaining over Romania"[18], a suggestive phrase for this pessimistic vision, in contradiction with the self-confident term used by Bălescu—the optimistic "Song to Romania".[19]

Under certain conditions, however, the lament may be called on to perform a role in stark opposition to what it presupposes as a premise. The consternation produced by the contemplation of the Romanian disaster is sometimes deliberately emphasised and kindled precisely with a view to provoking the opposite reaction, that is, a national effort to find a way out of the deadlock.

Samuil Micu, for instance, believes that anyone who sets their eyes on the woeful situation depicted by Metropolitan Bishop Theodosie "will be filled with grief at the sight of such wretched times as we live in now and will look back to the worth and greatness of our fathers and will employ his mind and skill to learning and crafts and other praiseworthy deeds" in order to bring the nation back to the happy state of the old times.[20]

The same motif recurs four decades later with Ion Codru Drăguşanu, in a discourse delivered at a Ploieşti school, which employs the lamenting tone that is so specific to the Wallachian oratorical style[21] but also the optimistic urge to people to tear themselves out of this condition and build a better future for themselves:

The day of light and awakening has at last dawned for us, Romanians, as well. Woe betide us if we don't seize it and rise to the light, if we don't stand up and show a clean face to the world. Shame take us if we don't open our eyes and ears to see and hear what is being done and said around us. A plague on us if we remain forever blind, forever deaf, forever dumb [...] Romanians, brothers, what has become of the glory we once had among the peoples, what have we done with the memory of our ancestors' virtues? A mighty dark storm has ravished us, we have fallen low and to much grievance. The time is nigh for us to throw a veil over bygones and breathe in new inspiration, so that we may be born again to our antique selves.[22]

Another factor capable of encouraging the production of denigrating self-images came from the invitation to Romanians to a critical and unbiased reflection on their own condition, to a merciless regarding of the vanities and prejudices of a cloying self-perception.

Although keen on painting an image almost exclusively centred on positive aspects and on the denial of foreign opinions to the contrary, Damaschin Bojincă gives the impression, at a purely declarative level, that he is a fervent advocate of objectivity, no matter what sort of truth it might bring to the surface: "It is high time [...] we, the sons of the Romanian nation [...], started to keep brotherly council among ourselves and look honestly upon our sort, our good, upon the honour and fate of our nation."[23]

An equally lucid invitation is apparently launched by Papiu Ilarian when he quotes a significant paragraph from Széchenyi: "He alone is a truly wise patriot who looks for errors rather in himself than in others; for claims can be made on yourself, not on others."[24] The sole problem was that Papiu held the maxim valid for the Hungarians, not for the Romanians.

The difficulty of applying the desideratum of objectivity to an investigation of one's own condition is perfectly illustrated by the motif of the "damage" that a critical perspective can inflict on national pride. This immense collective susceptibility so frequently injured by foreigners could not be stirred without the risk of opening painful wounds, without the fear of provoking new and dangerous crises that might upset the fragile inner equilibrium of a vulnerable consciousness. Certainly, the pure and uncompromising champions of the critical spirit would continue to uphold their point of view, but the confrontation with the actual situation would force them to take it into account as well. Even though, generally, the critics' self-denigrating pathos condemned reluctance on the part of those "damaged" by the truth, it was seriously toned down by the aforementioned pressures.

As happens so often in his work, Budai-Deleanu tries to outdo the susceptibility of injured national pride by means of the relativisation inherent in the humour and burlesque spirit of the *Gypsiad*. Claiming that "a different sort of youth / Lived at the time of Vlaicu-vodă", he deplores the current state of things:

Gone is that valour,
And you, Wallachian soil, groan under fetters!(...)
You're prey to greedy foreign hands,
That sell you like wares in the market place!"[25]

Having reached the peak of his critique the poet mimics the violent reaction of the "damaged", and does so with the ulterior reason of placing their efforts between parentheses and neutralising them by means of irony.

> Slowly, now! Let the quarrel soothe to naught!
> I see eyebrows raised in spite
> And for my muse, fearful thought,
> I see designs vile and trite.(...)
> Of which God save us and forbid!
> And give them brain enough and wit
> To take the Gypsy prank we bid.
> Yet, for all that, the muse is known
> [the Gypsiad's author suggestively adds]
> To say no lie, but what is shown
> In its big mouth will make some groan.[26]

Mitru Perea, in his turn, writes a cogent explanatory footnote: "Swept by the heat of passion, the poet starts uttering things that nowadays might hurt and damage some". However, relativising irony is voiced again, with a view to dismantling the dense and obtuse vision of those who refuse criticism because they fear the truth it might unravel: "That is why he stops and, checking himself, blames it on the muse, as if she were an open mouth, as women are, who would sooner die than not say what they know of others."[27]

The same idea can be found in Simion Bărnuțiu. In a 1842 article, in which he attacks the internal administration and ultramontane tendencies of the Blaj bishopric, he also starts from the question of the "damage" his criticism may do to those who regard the Romanian church, despite its wrong-doings, as none other than the infallible pillar of the Romanian nationality.

> There are some who read in cold blood of the blood-shedding in Spain or the Caucasus[28] or in Afghanistan, but if it happens that they learn of some misdoing here at home, which cries to Heaven for undoing, they start changing colour and come over feverish and giddy. It is for such readers [...] that this tiny "galeate" prologue [*galeatus prologus* = "prologue for defence"] is meant, so that they be informed beforehand of the author's mind and know that he has no desire to harm anyone.

His sole purpose was to urge the Uniate clerics to read Petru Maior's writings (themselves critical of the hierarchy in Blaj)—a subtler way of winning them over to the Jansenist and Gallican ideas relating to the synodal administration of the church.[29]

In fact, Bărnuțiu is persuaded that things are in a much worse state than he had ventured to present them, and those prone to being "damaged" should be shaken into awareness much more powerfully than his amiable introduction achieves. He confesses quite explicitly to that concern in a letter accompanying the article sent to Bariț for publication: "Our downfalls are greater than I might have ventured to describe, so I only put my finger on some of them, but what I touched could no longer stay hidden from the public eye. Do not fear, sir, to give it to print if you find any value in it, all responsibility I take upon myself."[30] "True," the Blaj-based professor adds, "the article had better be published unsigned." A gesture equally telling of the hesitancy of the critical spirits of the time is that, when he actually publishes the article, Bariţ does so only in part.[31]

Although they did not lack the gift of denunciation of an Emil Cioran, it was clear that, under the quite different circumstances of the epoch in which they lived, the two Transylvanian opinion leaders could not afford to go that far on the road towards the goal about which they may well have been just as passionate: that of the radical transfiguration of their nation.

As we have seen in a previous chapter, with George Bariţ as with the others, the concern to protect those who might be "damaged" accompanies at every step, and, implicitly, blunts the sharp end of the critical spirit. Acutely aware of the tearing conflict between the need to speak the truth and uneasiness as to what might thus be revealed, Bariţ's journalistic work continually oscillates between the two hypostases. He knows only too well that a "clear and early" uttering of the truth hurts and "defames", therefore he listens to the voice advising him to "handle people as you do glass, and try to indulge them, not to drive them away, and lend your ear to their demands in all areas, so that you learn what they like and what brings them harm." That is the desirable course of action, even though the "desire to learn the precious art of showing forth the wrongs and follies, and purge the prejudice, first from my soul, and then from the souls of others"[32] remains the methodological and moral dictum that governs his analyses, despite the difficulties arising when a practical application of such a principle is attempted.

On the other hand, while the protection of national pride could be invoked for texts meant to become public, a critical and negative perspective on Romanian realities could be manifested unhindered in the prying-free pages of one's private correspondence and intimate notations, a privileged locus for uncensored confessions. "One single soul will not come to be here with me and for me!", Moise Nicoară notes the moment he finds himself abandoned by his fellow countrymen in his vindictive action. "Rottenness eats at the heart of our nation!!! Is this the blood of my kindred that grinds its gnashing teeth and pulls out a venomous tongue to put me to my death?"[33] Cipariu, in a letter to Bariţ, deplores the debility of his nation and argues for the abandonment of national hypocrisy in this respect: "There is no reason why we should fool ourselves. Our weakness is real, nothing fabricated about it, whatever we might like to think."[34]

A recurrent idea suggested by these records of self-distrust is that those negative aspects are so deeply rooted in the flesh of society that it will take decades and several generations for any hope of change to become legitimate.

That is what Ioan Buteanu thinks, for instance, as is apparent in a deeply dejected letter he writes at the beginning of 1849, in which he complains about the difficulties he has in mustering the people of his prefecture: "Vain has been my strife and toil, for the evil has struck roots in peoples' veins and guts, and only death can pluck it out. Growth and development—the basis of morality—find no place in their souls and our hope can only be with another generation."[35]

Ioan Maiorescu uses almost identical terms in a letter of 1838: "Little can we expect from the generation of our days, for little have they given so far."[36] Codru Drăguşanu, anticipating, or so it seems, the similar formula launched in 1990 by Silviu Brucan[37], sets decade-long terms for the perpetually delayed resolution of the Romanian crises: "I reckon I have counted enough, both good and bad, and I have more, but suffice it for now. There are healthy buds, there are also festering cankers from the deadly disease of our nation, and the next ten years, after which it is said things will be more stable, will not be enough for them to heal, and I would be glad to see them cured in fifty. God help us." [38]

Against the background of such pessimistic views on the fate of the nation, which are immediately correlated, from the competitive perspective, with the situation of foreigners, appears the motif of the "shame of being Romanian", as associated with the wish for assimilation to peoples that fare better. Although the texts testify to the spreading of this image (which will be analysed in a later chapter), it is usually criticised, particularly in public stance taking.

Bărnuțiu explains the reason why many people "have become uneasy and ashamed about being called Romanians", as invoked by the discontented themselves: "Well, they will say, what generous heart will cling to the Romanian people, which has come down so sorely and is so unlearned?" Bărnuțiu's reply to this is unequivocal: "To these people we answer that he who denies his nation because it has come down and is unlearned, and that not by its will, he is no more generous than he who denies his mother who gave birth to him because she is old and helpless." [39] Andrei Mureșanu uses similar terms ("Happy [...] is the man who is not ashamed of his nation, no matter how sickly it is" [40]), while Bariț attacks those boyars from the principalities who "deep down inside are still ashamed of being called Romanians". [41]

A more ambiguous position is evidenced in Codru Drăgușanu, who counterbalances the shame of being Romanian with the pride of being French, in a disconcerting premonition of a Ionesco or Cioran: "The sense of dignity has so deeply penetrated the French soul that each man is, so to speak, inebriated with his own self. The Frenchman's mouth fills with savour when he utters the name of his country and nation. And he has every right to feel so, and were I to be born again, I would implore Heaven that I see the light of day as a Frenchman." [42]

As we have seen so far, the search for an answer to the question, "Should we denigrate ourselves as well, or not?", will continually bring to the fore a large variety of nuances and intermediary attitudes. In his 1843 introductory lecture at Academia Mihăileană [the first Romanian high school in Moldavia], which was also published in Bariț's periodicals [43] and enjoyed great success among the Transylvanian Romanians, Kogălniceanu confesses to this oscillation, as well as his particular preference: "You will forgive this slight bent for my own nation, which does not mean I tend to falsify facts or try to excuse what is worthy of blame." [44]

Codru Drăgușanu speaks, too, of the problems and hesitations inevitably encountered by any rational and unbiased spirit. Even when willingly confronted only with the exigencies of his own consciousness, he does not find the choice between lenience and harsh, if equally superficial, criticism an easy task:

> Nothing easier than criticising; nothing harder than painting the truth or voicing the right judgement based on minute and just observations of all classes and all places one means to write about. My task is a portentous one. I intend to describe Romania as I have known it in the four years and a half since I've been here [...] The question remains, though, whether it so happened that my vision was slanted. [45]

At other times, however, the Transylvanian pilgrim makes an altogether differently motivated choice between the positive and the negative perspectives. When he speaks of his country to foreign ears he deliberately depicts a lighter image, even if he is convinced it does not reflect the truth. Why? Because "it is meet to do so", as Drăgușanu laconically justifies his deviation. It thus becomes clear that the truth has to be hidden from others—typical behaviour, from the perspective of the theory of the stigma, in one who fears that his handicap will be discovered to his shame. Consequently, writes the pilgrim, while in conversation with his French companions, "the occasion arose for me to give them only the good side of the story, which I did on principle, lest I should defile my country."[46] He is all the more careful, when he meets Hungarians, to deliver a "panegyric on Romania, although little deserved, which it is meet to do when you go over the borders of your country".[47] Although he admits that the praise he showers on his country is little deserved, Drăgușanu is convinced that dirty linen should be washed at home, and objectivity may well be tossed overboard once the frontier is passed.

Alexandru Papiu Ilarian also provides a good illustration for the same idea in an 1853 letter to Simion Balint. After describing Avram Iancu's serious psychic problems, Papiu recommends discretion. Significantly for the way in which the stigma and the complex of collective shame operate even in the case of a strong nature like Papiu's, the young militant explains that the shame brought on one individual automatically extends to the whole nation when it is made public. He thus opens the long career of the nation's prudery on the subject: "I would advise that in Vienna you do not write anything about him, for there are too many Romanians, both good and bad, and it's for the better if they are not privy to every single particular, either good or bad, of our nation, for they will judge us [...]; for we don't want to be spoken evil of, it would be a shame, anyhow, and the pain and suffering and honour and shame of one man is the pain or honour of all."[48]

Fostered within this retractile attitude in front of the unveiling of certain painful truths, and growing out of the necessity of cultivating national pride in order that the Romanians' awakening may be given moral support, self-image ends up by combating the tendency to self-denigration, even if it will never actually succeed in putting an end to it.

It was this tendency to which Budai-Deleanu gave expression when he wrote in the *Gypsiad*:

Poor though the country is,
The sweet thought one cherishes
Is to say, "We are from here!"

The footnote comment reads: "O, if only my people understood what a blessing it is to have one's own country, they would stop cursing themselves and defaming their own kin, thus humouring the foreigners who oppress them and who would laugh with joy to see our name wiped away forever from human memory."[49] Dimitrie Țichindeal reproaches Moise Nicoară with distrust of his fellow countrymen's abilities, and tries to dismantle the logical arguments of such a negative image. At the same time, he shows that the reality underlying it is not given once and for all, that it can and must be changed: "You're saying our people are cowardly and awkward. Why should you say that, and who are those people? When and how did you meet them? What folly did they commit to make you say they are cowardly? What they must do and learn in order to chase away cowardice you do not write."[50]

Papiu Ilarian, too, criticises his fellow countrymen's negative self-perception, their distrust of their own self-asserting capacities—attitudes that he believes are the more to blame as they disarm the nation at critical moments, throw doubt and confusion on the path the Romanians have to take, and thus play into the hands of the enemy. At the beginning of the revolution, he writes, no voice rose from among the Romanians against the union with Hungary. There were some who even militated in support of the idea, and "others believed Hungary to be the more potent nation and the Romanians, for centuries banished from the constitution, the more befallen, too unworthy of consideration to be listened to without scorn or to be able to give weight to their own words; they believed, then, that Romanian opposition could trigger nothing but ridicule."[51]

In his turn, Bărnuţiu sublimates criticism of this tendency (which for him equals the loss of national dignity) in words of rare violence, particularly meant to shed light on the use that adversaries may make of such conduct for their own legitimacy: "Who shall cherish the Romanian church, I ask, if the Romanians take shame in it? Who could respect the Romanians if they respect neither their own church nor themselves? Who can complain of being trampled down if he makes a worm of himself?"[52] Certainly, it might be argued that Bărnuţiu had forgotten the way he himself had condemned the Romanian church five years before[53], but such petty inconsistency was irrelevant by now, at the great hour of the revolution when "public will" and the discourse on power of the élite (whose prerogative it had become) merged beautifully in a unitary and self-sufficient fascicle.[54]

Abandoning the linguistic virulence of a Bărnuţiu, the criticism of the self-denigrating perspective finds much more rational ways of expression and more stable theoretical grounds under the pen of Alexandru Roman. Roman reproves Papiu Ilarian for judging too harshly in his *History* the priests and clerical circles—a steady pillar of the Romanian nationality (Roman refers primarily to the Greek Catholic hierarchy in Oradea, to whom he was fairly close)—and consequently for joining the ranks of those who were denigrating and blackening the Romanian nation.

Incidentally, this apparently surprising accusation—Papiu featuring as a detractor of the Romanians!—was but one of the paradoxes inherent in the Romanian self-image, since, as we have seen, almost all Transylvanian intellectuals opted for both attitudes in alternation. Few did it deliberately and in full awareness, however, as sometimes happened with Cipariu, Bariţ or Codru Drăguşanu, who in fact confess to doing it.

Coming back to the Oradea-based professor's observations, we should note first his subtlety in grasping the fact that the obsessive passion invested by the self-denigrator in constructing a negative image derives from a discrepancy between his excessive expectations as to his own nation, and its real situation, which is not actually as bad as when compared with his hypertrophied pretensions: "We must take the world and the course of things as the eternal laws of nature commend them and as they really are, not as they should be, and even less as we would like them to be.[55] Let us not allow [...] that the blaze of that sin[56] they ascribe to our men of letters (writers) be stuck on us. They had better cease their sarcasm, calumnies and vicious talk of how writing is unknown among us, and let experience speak, not some prefigured aims."[57]

Roman goes on to describe the way the passion of self-denigration has struck deep roots within the Romanians' conduct, in terms reminding one of a Cioran: "If two or three Romanians chance to gather together, they will before long start wailing and complaining [...]; it is as if this habit has grown together with our flesh and blood." Yet, Roman continues, he might think that is the truth "were I not too aware that all is due to the course of our unhappy fate that has been injuring us for so long; to innumerable worries, to our daily draught of woe [...] Here is my wish: that we slough off this wicked habit and hush down our wailing and start seeing to the bettering of our state [...] and break this black omen for good."[58]

At this point, Roman takes a definite departure from Cioran's ulterior path: the stigma of self-denigration is not so deeply rooted in some would-be inner datum of the Romanians that it cannot be wiped off; it is the natural consequence of some historical circumstances; it is a flaw, which should not be turned into a virtue but abandoned by means of an effort to better their actual situation and with the aid of a more rational process of relating a continually modified image to a reality that is itself dynamic and diverse. The stigma of Romanian backwardness, Roman might have said, in an *avant la lettre* paraphrase of Erving Goffman's theory, is not a reality to assume, but a mere perspective.

CULTURAL BACKWARDNESS

The most frequent negative theme accompanying almost any description of current realities is that of the Romanians' cultural backwardness. It governs the whole cultural discourse growing in the wake of the Transylvanian School, by means of the leitmotif of the "darkness" and ignorance in which Romanians struggle. It is, nevertheless, more than a mere particular, that is, Romanian, instance of some of the universal obsessions of the Enlightenment. The lack of modern culture is considered, in the Romanian case, to be a defining feature, a characteristic, which tells the Romanians apart from other peoples because they are not simply backward, they are the most backward of all, both among neighbouring nations and in the whole of Europe.

Such declarations, tough as they are, are clearly formulated by the very apostles of national awakening, which, as we shall see later, was no mere chance. "The Romanians", writes Andrei Mureșanu, "of all other peoples of Europe, tarry in their damnation under the impenetrable cloak of darkness."[59] Papiu Ilarian deplores the fact that "all peoples make progress in all the sciences and arts; it is only us, the Romanians, us, the unblemished descendants of the brave conquerors of the world, the Romans, who are still waiting."[60]

In 1855 Cipariu gave an eloquent illustration of this situation, pointing out all the defining elements of a modern civilisation that the Romanians lack almost entirely, a proof of their cultural backwardness:

> We are fast asleep! Hardly a word is uttered now and again worthy of today's civilisation, and no action taken whatsoever. Neither sciences nor arts flourish here, nor commerce or economy, and no state or military experts are to be found, nor schools or famous writers. In Romania one college, in Transylvania one academy (?) [the question mark is, obviously, Cipariu's], in the other Romanian lands some poor, wretched, God-forsaken gymnasium."[61]

For the priest of Blaj, as for any other inheritor of the Enlightenment, the general state of a society derives exclusively from its cultural advancement. If the Romanians do not have schools, they will not enjoy a better situation economically, politically, or socially either, nor will the moral and religious state of the nation—a sure indicator of the degree of culture and civilisation—fare any better.

Even for those such as Papiu Ilarian, interested to a greater extent in the political element, culture remains the motor of that realm, too, so that cultural drawbacks perfectly account for political failures: "For a nation that had declined in matters political, as the Romanians of Superior Dacia were then, there was no way left for renewal other than intellectual culture. But [before the union with the Church of Rome] the Romanians between the Carpathians and Tisza were in such a miserable state in this respect as well that rarely could a nation be found so bereft of all means of cultivating itself."[62]

Very rarely, of course, cultural poverty is valued positively, when it is shown as making it possible for the Romanians to remain immune to the attraction of other confessions, in particular the Protestant ones. Samuil Micu observes that the Romanian priests, "being fairly unlearned [...], rejected the new rites and teachings" of Lutheranism "and were adamant in preserving their own"[63], while Budai-Deleanu believes that the Romanian nation resisted Calvinist proselytism "either due to its strength and faithfulness or to the lack of culture for which it is blamed".[64]

The reiteration of the motif of cultural backwardness gives birth to verbal clichés to be found everywhere, in both Romanian and foreign texts. The Romanians are "culturally retarded"[65], "in the midst of spiritual decadence"[66], "raw and covered in ignorance"[67], "still on an inferior cultural level"[68], and among them "obscurantism reigns".[69]

In the wake of Enlightenment rhetoric, the metaphors used to express this state of things are based on the opposition between light and darkness, with all the possible intermediary nuances and possible illustrations of such elementary symbolism. Images are drawn from the vocabulary of the elements that refers to the displacement or disturbance of the light, which is the symbol of culture (e.g., the "foggy dark", the "mist" or the "clouds" of ignorance). There are references to phenomena that cause one to lose one's way (e.g., "traps", or the "labyrinth of darkness"[70]); and to the inability of either society as a whole or the individuals within it to reach out for the light—hence the clichés of "blinding" or "straying". Surely all these verbal illustrations, the rhetoric of an identity-wise ideology of collective self-victimisation *par excellence*, would gradually lose credit and become meaningless as a result of overuse?

What are the concrete elements starting from which the image of cultural backwardness was formed? Firstly, the scarcity of schools—which is over-insistently signalled in the contemporary texts, particularly in comparison with the situation in neighbouring nations. George Bariț published statistical data on the Transylvanian primary school, declaring: "We should learn by heart all these figures, for they are a lesson of deep as well as sad and shameful significance. The Romanians, of whom there are 1,120,000, have the least numerous and most contemptible schools", much less numerous, that is, than the Hungarians, the Saxons or the Szeklers. "This is the sure sign", Bariț adds from this comparative perspective, "by which we can judge the state of the religious, moral and intellectual culture in the nations of Transylvania. And here I have been given the chance I wanted to put together the numbers in the schools with the numbers in the prisons."[71]

For the Brașov-based journalist, the lack of primary-school education is serious not so much from a cultural and intellectual point of view as such, but from the perspective of what he calls the "moral and religious culture", the spreading of which is the main task of the popular schools. It is underdevelopment at this level that is chiefly responsible for the moral decay of the nation, since ignorance and lack of respect for Christian principles leads to immorality and delinquency and, generally, to neglect of the most basic norms of social cohabitation. The conditions are thus set for the existence of parishes where "no one in the congregation knows the Ten Commandments, and one wonders how they manage to keep them, how it is that the whole village is not yet in prison."[72]

Closely related to the deplorable state of primary education was the problem of illiteracy, which was an equally convincing illustration of cultural backwardness. The cultural efforts undertaken in other countries, claims the *Mouthpiece of Enlightenment*, "would be entirely lost on our people for the time being, since none of the commoners knows how to read".[73] Cipariu was to dwell on this idea on numerous occasions, as he does in a letter of 1848: "The Saxons and the Hungarians, *respectu numeri* [as far as their numbers are concerned], are 1 to every 3 Romanians, but as to knowledge of reading, the Romanians do not even number 1 to 3 of them [...] *Numerus sumus* [We are but number], nothing else."[74] Moreover, among the few literate Romanians, "the taste for reading is quite rare so far", as Bariț writes.[75] In an article with the significant title "Who among our audience reads our papers?", he shows that "the lack of a sufficient number of readers who might claim a right for themselves as representatives of public opinion" has a grievous influence on Romanian publications and, in general, on national political reflection and action.[76]

The poor cultural training of the priesthood was another component of the image under discussion. As early as 1791 the Transylvanian diet declared that the main cause of "the nation's lack of culture and education is its priests' ignorance: while they should be examples of good conduct for others and instruct them on the Christian duties [...], they are the first to break the rules and spur the believers into sinful deeds."[77]

It cannot be doubted that such affirmations also denoted the stereotypical way in which the Hungarians perceived the Romanians, but the image of an unlearned priesthood was just as widespread among the latter. Stoica de Haţeg pins it down to its historical dimension: "Our Romanians took to the natural law and a life in the wooded mountains, where they celebrate by the side of bears and wolves. If only they had monks or priests around them, but who can know? [...] But then, what makes a priest here, other than a mere sign written by hand saying 'I am a priest'!"[78]. The *Mouthpiece of Enlightenment*, referring to the contemporary period, declares that: "Among the Romanians [...], both priests and teachers, wherever they are, are all a piteous sight!"[79]

The 1814 petition by the Romanians from Arad underlines another idea, namely that of a close relationship between the poor cultural level of the clerics and the nation: "...and that is the plague whereof came the meanness and ignorance of our clerics and of this people. For they remained alone and banned from commerce with the most enlightened heads of the country, and all they had was story-telling and churchly books, which were not many either but mere sparks of Romanian nature and Christian law, by which they can at least be told apart from wordless bests."[80]

It was not only education at the lower levels of society that was viewed critically: higher culture, too, was embraced by the cliché of cultural backwardness. Although mass education was taking very timid steps, if at all, "higher" culture fared much better, which should have made room for a more optimistic vision. Nevertheless, the Transylvanian intellectuals seem just as discontent in this respect. When not simply denying the existence of any cultural progress they complain about its superficiality or irrelevance for society as a whole, thus initiating the tradition of the "forms-without-substance" line of criticism.[81]

The mentality of the time cultivated the belief that the Romanians lacked learned and valuable individuals capable of substantiating Romanian cultural institutions, forms and projects, even though the upholders of that idea were themselves learned and intelligent persons, whose very presence should have been enough to invalidate the cliché. Nevertheless, the idea held firm. Paul Iorgovici remarked, in 1799, that "no one of our Romanians from Banat took to such learning that might be capable of reforming Romanian schools"[82]. In 1796, Samuil Micu wrote: "The Romanian people cannot take pride in too many writers, for there has been little time for them to study hard and write profoundly, with all the uprising and fighting and worrying."[83] In around 1825 to 1829, Stoica de Haţeg, too, showed that "no good writers have been born in these parts, nor has there been any demand, nor favourable conditions."[84] At the time such complaints were voiced, they were somewhat understandable; the surprising thing is that they reoccur in an almost identical form towards the middle of the century when circumstances had already changed considerably.

"Few gifted men are there in Romanian culture", a petition from April 1850[85] claims. Ioan Maiorescu, in his turn, writes in 1843: "Once and for all, given the conditions of the principalities and of today's institutions, full contentment is never to be expected. The great lack of the men we need will not even allow us to do what can be done."[86] In almost identical terms, the idea reappears in Codru Drăguşanu: "We want mighty men in all realms and thus the nation will keep struggling in this vicious circle until God takes pity on us and saves us."[87] Elsewhere, the Transylvanian pilgrim adds: "In our society there are few learned men, fewer with breeding, and even fewer with good breeding. We do not have both extremities, for two extremities presuppose a middle to which they can both refer; we only have the worse side."[88] For Codru Drăguşanu, as for other enlightened spirits, or for Bariţ, this absence of "breeding", of education, automatically entails moral degradation; as a result of poor education, "in our society [...], instead of good breeding we see absolute corruption, instead of sound morality we see the reign of immorality and debauchery, instead of true religion we encounter coarse superstition."[89]

The motif of cultural backwardness was an expressive instantiation of one of the darkest spots of Romanian self-perception, since, besides the illiteracy of the masses and frailty of higher culture, it also connoted the moral and spiritual degradation of the nation.

THE ROMANIANS AS OCCUPYING THE LOWEST PLACE

As we have seen so far, any description of the poor cultural state of the Romanians necessarily relates to the situation of other peoples, be they directly connected to the Romanians or rather remote. In fact, the very concept of cultural backwardness makes no sense outside the terms of a comparison. Consequently, the worst part was not that the Romanians were simply backward, but that they appeared more backward then others, particularly as compared with their political and national adversaries who were thus entitled to justify their own domination. Here, as elsewhere, the image was not formed starting primarily from the Romanians' own reality but as a function of other images and realities of a superior standard that was altogether alien to their circumstances. This led to an extremely pessimistic self-evaluation, to the drawing of an imaginary hierarchy in which the Romanians could obviously do no better than the lowest position. "The thick mist of ignorance", writes Andrei Mureşanu, "has so disfigured the Romanian that, while all nations around rise to the awakening light, we alone have remained, from the Black Sea onwards, enslaved to the old barbarity".[90]

The ranking of the Romanians in the lowest position comes mainly from a comparison with the other Transylvanian nations—with the Hungarians and the Saxons, as, for instance, in Bariţ and Cipariu when they discuss Romanian education, and with the Serbs in the case of the western Romanians. In comparison with all of them the Romanians have to cope with the worst geographical location, the direst poverty, the poorest schooling, and the fiercest political and social oppression. All in all, the tight intertwining of these facets of backwardness ultimately makes them the slaves of all the others, as Samuil Micu believes: "The unlearned serve the learned, as is clear in the case of the Romanian people, who are, for the most part, unlearned and thus a slave to all other peoples."[91]

As the Romanians come to occupy more posts in the various countries of the Crown, the lowest position is invoked at the level of the whole Austrian monarchy as well, often with a view to gaining the emperor's compassion and persuading him that the Romanians deserve special imperial favour on account of the very status as victims that they have assumed.

The 1791 *Supplex* refers to "the supplicant nation [...] set at the furthest borders of the monarchy"[92], thus sketching the idea of a specific sort of disfavour, ultimately attributed to geographical reasons. From a strictly spatial point of view, the Romanians are located at the farthest remove from the "centre" of political life and of the civilised world, therefore they are at the bottom in all other respects. The 1814 petition of the citizens of Arad is much more explicit as to the position of the Romanians within the empire: "Why is it that the Romanian nation has only reached the lowest position in matters of education? Why is it that in the entire Austrian monarchy the worst wrongdoers are the Romanians? Why is it that this nation is always in danger of inner turmoil?"[93] The 1846 memoir of the Romanians from Răşinari finds it fitting to confirm, thirty years later, the consolidation of the same posture: "We feel like covering our faces with shame when we think that this bishopric, which numbers more than 600,000 souls, is the poorest in religious and scientific settlements throughout the monarchy over which the word of Your Majesty reigns."[94] Our "culture has remained wanting more than that of any of our fellow countrymen of other nations and confessions. Our pain and grief are thus, naturally, twice as great"[95], the petitioners from Răşinari add, in a reiteration of the drama of Romanian backwardness as compared with the condition of others.

Yet this obstinate clinging to the lowest position in every respect possible did not stop at the frontiers of the Habsburg Empire. Europe, a favourite frame of reference for an evaluation of the Romanian condition and achievements, would become, once again, the standard against which the Romanian vocation of always being at the bottom would be defined. As early as 1815 Moise Nicoară wrote to Piuariu Molnar about Romanian backwardness due to a lack of well-trained people to take care of administration and trade: "Quod nunc in tota Europa, quoad hac rem concernit, (Wallachians) ultimi locum teneant: in nulla quippe harum provinciarum quas incolunt, jure, quo deberent primum in administranda republica locum capiunt."[96]

During the first half of the eighteenth century the most propitious field for the manifestation of the "Romanians-at-the-bottom in Europe" stereotype was represented by the sphere of major cultural achievements, an area that provided enlightened Romanian intellectuals with the main understanding of the notion of "Europe" ("Enlightened Europe").[97] In relation to this model of progress, to the flowering of culture and civilisation, the Romanians were, if not in sheer opposition, at any rate at the bottom of it all. In 1855 Timotei Cipariu was still voicing this obsession: "Are not our ears buzzing with the tumultuous business of a Europe boiling with enthusiasm for higher and higher culture? And what do we do when the whole civilised world will not find its rest until it does more and more work? [...] We are sleeping!"[98]

Particularly at the beginning of the century, the cliché stating that the Romanians are the only ones left in Europe not having reached the level of the various cultural achievements of the time is to be found in all forewords or justifying accounts destined for the Transylvanian public. "All peoples in Europe have long had their own lexicons, we alone still lack them"[99], writes Budai-Deleanu in 1818, in his foreword to the *Romanian–German Lexicon*. "All nations joyfully took to" the study of geography, claims Nicola Nicolau in 1814, "...we, the Romanians, alone [...] lacked such inestimable and precious science."[100] "All the nations of awakened Europe" publish "periodicals and novels [...], it is only us, the Romanians [...] who are deprived of such precious gold" writes Alexie Lazăr, also in 1814.[101] "All enlightened peoples" write and read books, as Zaharia Carcalechi[102] puts it in a similar claim, "only we, Romanians, lack such precious treasure."[103]

It is true that the tedious recurrence of such statements may well have a bearing not only on the dramatic return of the obsession with occupying the lowest position, but also on another issue, pointing to much less profound concerns. Made meaningless from overuse, the formulas in question sometimes give the impression of being mere figures of style, meant to ornate the justifying discourse, to capture the benevolence of the reader by rhetorically overstating the ominous importance of the work they preface, one that will put an end, in the respective domain, to the enormous scarcity that used to place the Romanians at the bottom in Europe.

There are, however, some, very few, opinions that are at variance with this cliché. Such opposite opinions are articulated especially when the reference point for the Romanian position is no longer reduced to the generic formula "all the nations of Europe", but shrinks down to several concrete peoples, particularly among the Romanians' national enemies.

Carcalechi, for instance, in the foreword quoted, provides such a concrete identification of those in front of the Romanians: "Look how the Greeks, and even the Serbs, are so manly in their determination to print books, and the Greek nation, as well as the Serbs, are not only happy to have them, but eager to read them, too."[104] It is the Romanians alone who are still reluctant to take similar cultural initiatives. Up to this point, Carcalechi keeps within the limits of the cliché. The Greeks and the Serbs are not too high up the list themselves when compared to the West, the Germans or the Hungarians; on the other hand, they are the Romanians' main competitors in Hungary and, in general, in all trade centres of the empire where there are signs of a Romanian bourgeoisie. Moreover, the Romanians envy the Greeks' position beyond the Carpathians. For all these reasons, the Romanians should feel stimulated finally to rise from their present shameful position. According to Romanian perceptions the Greeks, for instance, who dominated them in the principalities, are a decayed nation, enslaved to the Ottoman Porte; therefore the Romanians have come to be the slaves of the Turks' slaves, which is unacceptable. The same goes, largely, for the Romanians' image of their relationship with the Serbs.

Under such circumstances Petru Maior will even end up fighting the cliché of the lowest position, that is, lower than the two peoples mentioned above. They do not fare better than the Romanians, Maior says, and what is more, it was the very oppression they perpetrated on the Romanians that has brought the Romanians to their low level: "After the Greeks and the Serbs themselves [...] plunged the Romanians into the deep mire of ignorance, they began spreading the word that the Romanians are unlearned and the dullest among all tongues, at which they laughed and scorned; and they are still laughing, even though both Greeks and Serbs (if we are exact about it) are equally, if not more, forlorn than we are."[105]

Constantin Diaconovici-Loga, too, believes that it is by no means compulsory for the Romanians to remain always at the bottom, even though for the time being "we are far behind" the other nations; but others, too, were at first where the Romanians are now and "today they shine all over the face of the earth", which logically entails that the Romanians may rise towards the light as well: "We are capable, indeed, like other nations, which, before they started to rise, were themselves covered in darkness."[106]

The Romanians should also note that their occupying the lowest position is conceived of in relation to their neighbours in Transylvania, either in the context of the Habsburg monarchy or of Europe as a whole, but not transcending, as a rule, the frontiers of the continent. Generally speaking, there is no such image as "the Romanians at the bottom of the world", which would also include the "savage" peoples, the Africans or the Asian nations.[107] This is due to the Transylvanian Romanians' Euro-centric vision, according to which the "world", circumscribing the modern model of civilisation, is reduced to the European continent and, possibly, to its extensions, such as the United States.[108] The Romanians occupy the lowest position only as part of the one comparison that can possibly hold water, that is, one relating them to the peoples belonging to European civilisation.

True, instances of derogation from this general rule do exist, as in the usage of terms like "barbarian" or "savage" to describe Romanian realities. Andrei Mureşanu, for instance, claims that if the Romanians persist in being satisfied with little and indulge in their backward state, "before long we will be reduced to a more wretched and decayed state than the slave in Africa".[109] The *Mouthpiece of Enlightenment* allows the justice of an article from *Erdélyi Híradó*, which holds that, given our cultural backwardness, it should come as no surprise that "in the lands from beyond the sea no one has any knowledge of this country, no one cares to keep a memory of it, or if they do, they think it is the land of savages."[110] Nevertheless, this "savageness" (in terms of degree of civilisation) is more of a metaphor, meant to emphasise that the Romanians lag behind the European standard.[111]

In terms of the continent, however, the Romanians are part of it, yet stand apart by not participating in its essential rhythms, by lacking more marked features that might individualise its position within the European framework. "The Russian has strong confidence in his almighty autocrat", writes Ion Codru Drăguşanu, "just like the Frenchman in his great and glorious nation, while the Englishman believes in money and excels in diplomatic dexterity, showing refinement in leading people by the nose. The Italian is slow in politics but superb in the arts, while the Spaniard is neither, but lives on the remainders of his past glory. What could we be proud of?"[112] No one is perfect, but everyone is on the up in some respect, except the Romanians.

The dullness of the Romanians' European condition is also seen as due to a lack of participation, to the fact that they lack the necessary will to take the way of progress, to make an effort and align themselves with others. The motif of the "sleep" in which the Romanians are enthralled while everybody else is waking up is one of the most widely circulated metaphors of the rise of national identity.[113] It reiterates the idea of Romanian uniqueness from this point of view, too: "We alone, brothers, are still sleeping the long sleep of inertia"[114], cries Papiu Ilarian in 1845; "We alone are still sleeping the sleep of torpor", cry his political adversaries too, the Romanian deputies to the Hungarian Parliament, in 1848.[115] "Careless of the regeneration of the world, we alone are dozing off", writes the moderate Cipariu as well in 1855.[116]

In fact, the grief and pain that go with the feeling of being the lowest are perhaps best illustrated in the writing of the priest from Blaj. Without being a consummate pessimist, or a sceptic at all costs, Cipariu simply looks at Romanian realities with a lucid and observant critical eye. But the results of this examination, which he undertakes from an absolutely rational stance, are as discouraging as can be. His correspondence before 1848 gives evidence, as we have seen[117], of deep distrust in the Romanians' aptitude for progress and ascent. The revolution, ultimately ending in another failure, would not make any difference. On the contrary. His memoirs, written in 1855, assume the task of passing on to posterity, through the introductory pages, an image of Romanian weakness and inability to leave catastrophe behind.[118] The 1838 journey he undertakes, following the steps of Dinicu Golescu, to Pest and Vienna, reveals once more the poor state of things at home as the distance separating the degree of civilisation in the two cities from our "slowness in everything"[119] becomes clearer. The same happens during his 1852 trip to Italy. When he discovers the cultural feats of the colony of Armenian Mechitharist monks in Venice, Cipariu contemplates with stupefaction the idea that even the Armenians are ahead of the Romanians: "Where do we stand, we, Romanians, who enjoy more political independence than the Armenians and who have perhaps more schools, wealthy monasteries, learned men, etc. than they do? Where do we stand in comparison with these monks? A handful of people could take the pains to do what they have done, alone, while we, who are so many, do nothing! It breaks your heart to see how even the Armenians are more advanced than us in literary matters."[120] To be worse than the Armenians was apparently the most eloquent proof of the shameful position occupied by the Romanians in the obsessively imagined hierarchy of nations!

THE ROMANIANS COMPARED TO THE GYPSIES

And yet the Romanians could do worse, as is demonstrated in texts comparing the Romanians' state with that of the Gypsies or of the Jews—ethnic groups that serve as ideal analogies for the position that the Transylvanian Romanians attributed to themselves, namely the lowest among peoples. Many have laughed at the Romanians, Timotei Cipariu writes bitterly, and adds, as an illustration of such distressing treatment, "as only the Jews and Gypsies have been laughed at".[121]

Sometimes the Romanians compare themselves with the Gypsies in terms of the discrimination and oppression to which the latter are subject. Bărnuțiu, for instance, shows that, according to the legislation that defined the status of the Romanians in Transylvania, "the Romanians are not true citizens but only suffered or tolerated, in the way of the Gypsies, who ramble here and there, carrying along their tents."[122] Generally speaking, and in many respects—their famous inability to opt for progress and give up a traditional way of life, their reputed quarrels and feuds that prevent them from concentrating on the essentials, as well as their status as oppressed people having to serve others—the Gypsies were an ideal receptacle for the incarnation of certain basic motifs of Romanian self-perception. The deep shame brought to Romanian vanity through such a comparison, or even identification, was a serious warning pointing to the Romanians' low position, and, as such, was meant to urge them to try and change things for the better.

It is not hard to guess that the most representative text in this respect is Budai-Deleanu's *Gypsiad*. There is no question that, at a certain level of interpretation and according to Ion Istrate's famous analysis[123], the *Gypsiad*'s "Rromas of Heaven" were but a burlesque antipode of heroic humanity, innocent actors in an upside-down world, as their non-adaptability to social conventions suggests.[124] Here, too, they feature as perfect analogons to Romanian identity as fostered during the Enlightenment. For, just like the Rromas, the Romanians of the time were themselves a degraded hypostasis of heroic humanity, of the golden age when the virtues inherited from their Latin ancestors were set off to advantage by the glorious feats of a Vlad the Impaler, while at present time they were no more than a reversed copy of their essential condition, crippled by the hardships of history.

In fact, the realm that the Romanians longed to inhabit was one of a flight from history, a mythical and ahistorical space/time continuum, sheltered from the ordeals that are bound to come up incessantly along the path of a terrestrial and historical condition that threatened to overwhelm them.[125] This is precisely the world of the Rromas of Heaven in the *Gypsiad*, which thus provides a perfect analogy to one of the basic themes of the Romanian self-image long before those created by Goga, Blaga or Cioran.

There is another level of interpretation, however, that reveals even more clearly the similarity between the Romanians and the Gypsies as portrayed in Budai-Deleanu's poem. From beginning to end the *Gypsiad* is underlain by an implicit meditation on the Romanians' condition. The poem is actually a mirror "Romaniad", either by faithfully projecting the Romanian image onto the Gypsy background, or, more often than not, by grotesquely deforming that image into exaggerated or parodic figures.

At the core of such an original way of reflecting one's own image lies an extraordinary ambiguity and tension in terms of signification, which may be one more proof of the baroque nature that has been attributed to the poem. On the one hand, replacing the Romanians with the Gypsies might look like an attempt to protect Romanian national vanity by avoiding calling a spade a spade and communicating unpleasant verities (a burlesque "Romaniad" with irony directed at negative aspects of the Romanians would certainly have been too hard to swallow). On the other hand, although the pill was sugared due to the relativising effect of humour and irony, the rather offensive comparison, and particularly the telescoping of the target sins inside the distorting mirror of Gypsy behaviour, seem deliberately to lead to one conclusion: complete blasphemy in the face of national identity, in a Voltairean manner allowing for rational criticism and a moralising spirit, but leading the way in the company of Sadean casualness and amused cynicism, in a staging where the rhythm is beaten out by an infinite roar of laughter.

Although the poem's commentators[126] have generally neglected the function of the *Gypsiad* world as an analogy for the existing condition of the Romanians, the fact is acknowledged by its very author in *Letter of Homage*, through a number of quite transparent allusions: "But you should pay close attention, for the story, it seems to me, is mostly an allegory in which the Gypsies stand for others as well, who used to do, and still do, the things Gypsies do at all times. The wise reader will know my meaning!"[127]

Indeed, allusions are often made to certain types of behaviour specific to the Romanians, such as that of the high Greek Catholic hierarchy, in particular Bishop Bob, with whom the enlightened leaders never managed to come to terms. In a reference to Petru Maior's writings that castigate the bishop, Budai-Deleanu writes, in the same letter to Mitru Perea:

> Your meaning came home to me when, writing fittingly of the Gypsies, you also, by the word of truth, duly touched the voivode, who ever since he has been here has never had his people at heart nor employed himself to any good, but only minded his own purse and the boyars' gorges. Lord, when will be the day when we can say we have a good voivode who loves the people? I thought I might hear soon that they had chosen you as their voivode, but, as I see, that bag of scum is still alive and a stench to the world.[128]

Obviously, the Gypsy community represents here the allegorical frame capable of indirectly evincing a contemporary situation: the "Gypsy gang" stands for the Romanian community and the "Gypsies' voivode" for their bishop.

As a matter of fact, the polemic atmosphere of the Old Regime favoured the allegorical pamphlet criticising contemporary realities under the guise of some exotic people, fantasy land or historical situation, a means to outwit the vigilance of the censors. It was an extremely frequent mode of expression, also present in Montesquieu, Voltaire and Benjamin Franklin, in the aftermath of Swift's negative utopia. With the Transylvanian Romanians, the most conspicuous representative of this tradition was George Bariţ, whose journalistic writings always refer to Transylvanian realities only by alluding to similar situations in other countries.[129]

Yet besides surface analogies or ruses necessary for the slipping in of the truth, the Gypsies are, in Budai-Deleanu's view, the carriers of much deeper symbolic equivalencies to Romanian specificity. When he writes, "I have become convinced, to my great grievance, that both our Gypsies and those of Egypt are of the same stock, and there as here they are a matter of ridicule and perpetual defamation, for they will not obey any law nor learn the manners of politeness, nor raise their minds with enlightened teachings"[130], it is plain that he envisages the essential themes of the Romanian self-image, not the features of fantasy Rromas: defamation and oppression by foreigners, reluctance to embrace progress and enlightenment, and cultural backwardness.

The Romanians' disunity, their splitting into factions—further clichés of national self-perception—are also and just as eloquently illustrated in the world of the *Gypsiad*. The interminable fights among the Gypsies, their useless, sterile disputes, such as that over the form of government to be adopted, were yet another mirror image shedding light on the Romanians' lack of national consensus: "I tremble, brothers, at the thought that, what with the Gypsies' endless quarrels, we might learn to love the brawling and the squabbling they are so fond of", notes one of the voices in the footnotes. Another adds: "Happy those who are too dull to understand! You might have seen, unless your brains are too fuddled, that only so far you have been spoken of a hundred times."[131]

In the process, Budai-Deleanu comes to reverse the data of the comparison between the Romanians and the Gypsies in a most offensive way for the former. It is not the Gypsies who are to remind them continually, by their own hapless state, of their predicament, but, on the contrary, the Romanians have hit the bottom so piteously that it is their turn to exist as a warning of the misery of decay, just like the Gypsies. Speculating on the motif of the fall of the great empires, yet directly alluding to the state of the Transylvanian Romanians, the poet declares:

> In days of yore to us still known,
> Many a people raised to a kingly throne,
> Mighty was their arm and wide their crown;
> Yet their sons today have sorely come down
> In our land; we'll be as much and soon, no doubt,
> If we should leave our men to flout.[132]

The cliché of the descendants of the Romans who are now the laughing-stock of the barbarians they once subjugated is one that definitely defines the Romanians. The six-line stanza above can fairly be decoded as follows: The Gypsies have fallen from the happy state they used to enjoy when they ruled over India; the same will happen to the Romanians if they persist in committing the sin that caused their disaster—the lack of national solidarity and of patriotism, which they display through such representatives as Bishop Bob or the Moldavian-Wallachian boyars, who neglect the welfare of the country and are only industrious when it comes to their own good. So the Romanians are as bad as the Gypsies, Budai-Deleanu seems to imply—that is, obviously, as bad as these imaginary Gypsies of a fictional world.

The real-life Gypsies, especially those bound by slavery in the principalities (significantly, nor can the Gypsies in the *Gypsiad* be located anywhere else), will always be a concern of the Transylvanians. In fact, almost all accounts by foreign observers travelling through the principalities dwell extensively on the subject.[133] Undoubtedly, the exoticism and unusualness of it also make for its fame[134], but so does the way the Danubian provinces as a whole come to be looked upon on account of it. The dire state of the Gypsies is considered, in a way, as a characteristic feature of the principalities as a whole, since they prove unable to better the juridical status and civilisation level—which, as it is, is a far cry from European standards—of a segment of their population, however "problematic" or numerically reduced it might be.

It is not only foreigners, however, who think that way: the Transylvanian Romanians do too, and relevantly so. The latter are incessantly critical of the institution of the Gypsies' slavery[135], often in the harshest terms, such as those used by

Cipariu to describe the situation in Wallachia, in a letter to Bariț: "They are the only ones left in Europe who still keep to the rules of slavery, if we can grant the name of European land to a country where men are treated like beasts."[136] The sad lot of the Gypsies therefore has a definite bearing on the Romanians, denying their very belonging to the European space of civilisation.

The issue of the Gypsies' slavery is looked upon rather differently by Codru Drăgușanu, who, like Budai-Deleanu, reverses the data of the comparison between the Rromas and the Romanians. The traditional occupations of the Gypsies (carefully analysed from the point of view of their specific contribution to the Wallachian economy) will disappear in the future, writes the Transylvanian pilgrim, "for poor Gypsies have already, and to a man, fallen in line or will do so soon; then farewell free industry! They too are trying to perform the claca, iobăgia and decima [three forms of statutory labour] just like the Romanians, who for now give no reason to be envied."[137] In other words, the Gypsies will end up in a worse state than before: they will come to be like the Romanians! Once again, meditation on the Romanians' own condition shows us in what is seen as the worst position: like the Gypsies, or worse than them...

THE ROMANIANS COMPARED TO THE JEWS

As we have seen, the Gypsies' slavery and their oppression were one of the basic reasons why the Romanians had chosen them as an element of reference for their own condition. The Jews could, nevertheless, just as appropriately illustrate the victim status: Romanian self-perception would therefore relate to them, too, on several occasions.

The general attitude manifested at that time by the Transylvanian Romanians towards the Jews (a relevant indicator of the degree of xenophobia of a society) was not devoid of certain anti-Semitic accents, due both to the inheritance of mediaeval mentality and to more recent cultural borrowings and reactions. Moise Nicoară, for instance, writes at the beginning of the century some quite offensive lines relating to the Jews, as associated with the anti-Christian spirit of the French Revolution and the spreading of it by the great enemy of the moment, Napoleon.[138] Iosif Many, in 1845 and 1847, translated from Hungarian[139] several moralistic sketches centring on the image of the Jew usurer or publican, the one who destroys the material well-being and corrupts the souls of the poor villagers who inevitably fall into his hands.

On the other hand, there existed a strong tradition of tolerance, too, as theorised by enlightened thinking and launched by the Josephine reforms.[140] That tradition, illustrated, for instance, by Timotei Cipariu[141] when he translated, in 1844 to 1854, fragments from Le Juif errant by Eugène Sue[142], is mainly the carrier of the motif of compassion for the Jew's unhappy lot, for the compulsory vagrancy of this character bereft of a land of his own. It is precisely this idea that the Transylvanian intellectuals would lay stress on when comparing the fate of the Jews with that of the Romanians.

Gherontie Cotore anticipates the theme as early as 1746 when he speaks of the Jews from the perspective of a biblical example, which he makes relevant for the present condition of the Romanians. If the Romanian people remain in the darkness they have chosen to live in by splitting from the Church of Rome, then "just like the Jews who, because of their unfaithfulness, were doomed to perish in the desert before they could reach the Promised Land, they [the Romanians] will not come to set eyes on the pledged land, namely the heavenly kingdom."[143]

For Cotore, the land that the Romanians are in danger of losing, just like the Jews, on account of their improper behaviour, is the very kingdom of the Lord. Those who come after Cotore, however, will take a much more secular line and speak of the earthly land of which the Jews were deprived, which should be a warning to the Romanians who are equally insecure about their owning and even inhabiting the land beneath their feet.

The example of the Jews who lost their fatherland is seen as relevant for the Romanians' case, since the sons of Israel did not end up that way only as a result of their own sins and errors. This, it is claimed, will also be the lot of the Romanians, and soon, too, if they persist in neglecting the national cause as they have done so far, and if they remain disunited and refuse to shake off the apathy that has brought them to the piteous state they are in. Unless the Romanians pluck up the courage to free themselves from their present state, Budai-Deleanu warns, "You'll be as you have been so far, / Accursed as the Jewish people are... / Like them astray and stripped of home."[144] In a footnote, Mitru Perea rounds off the warning: "Be as one and hold your hands [...] Behold [...] the Jews, who have no land and roam around the world like strangers, always on the road. No matter how small and poor one's land, I believe, the happier is the people that has a homeland and lives a life in it."[145]

Andrei Mureșanu was to voice exactly the same idea forty years later. If "today, when mankind steps ahead, urged by the spirit of the age", the Romanians continue in "the same listlessness and spite" with which they have looked upon the enlightenment of their people so far, then "we will be bound to wander around, stick in hand and children on our shoulders, like the Jews of beautiful Palestine used to; we will fall to true indigence, misery and humiliation and we will fill the prisons or die from hunger or its frightful effects".[146] The apocalyptic image painted by Mureșanu places the Romanians on the last frontier still separating them from the definitive loss of paradise, at the limit of universal damnation. Being chased away from a land they no longer deserve, the exodus and the condition of perpetual vagrancy are in store for them now, at the brink of chaos.

In fact, the theme of a people chased from its own land, pointlessly straying all over the world, grew into a true obsession with Mureșanu, as his journalistic work proves on many occasions. Behind it also lay contemporary projects for settling a German population onto Transylvanian land in order to achieve a better exploitation of the economic resources of the area—a project that was bound to bring about fears that the newcomers would simply take the place of the Romanians.[147] The Brașov-based poet would also give versified expression to the issue, again by means of an analogy with the situation of the Jews:

Give us a miracle, O Lord, like in the desert
When Your man, Moses, helped the Jewish folk!
And break the bondage and the dismal fate
Of this our crying nation appealing for Your aid.[148]

Today, however, no one lends their ears to Romanian prayers, and the menace of vagrancy looms up again as a fatality inscribed in the course of history:

It is the law of nature that nations once oppressed
Fall down, expire and vanish with no rest,
And in their hearth of old the families astray
Find once again a shelter, a place where to lay.[149]

Much less vent is given to another perspective on the Jews' unhappy lot, one to which the Romanian destiny is also related: the image that lays stress not so much on their mistakes as on their being oppressed and discriminated against by others. The Romanian deputies to the Hungarian Parliament wrote in 1848 that until that time the Romanians had been treated with "shameful tolerance, like that shown to the Jews"[150], and the bishop of Oradea, Vasile Erdélyi, considered in 1850 that "the age starting with the year 1659 has been for the Romanians what slavery in Babylon was for the Israelites, a state in which the Romanians still grapple, for those of them who live in Hungarian counties are under the rule of Hungary, those who dwell in Transylvania are subject to both Hungarian and Saxon laws, and those in Timişoara and Banat struggle under Serbian government."[151] Nevertheless, as we have seen, the Jews are regarded, as a rule, not so much as an oppressed people but as victims of their own sins.

In either case we are like them and, as with the Gypsies, the comparison swells up to the point where it becomes an identification labelling the Romanians as a pariah among nations, or as a people potentially deprived of its own land. Again as with the Gypsies, the Romanians' lot may well be even sadder than that of the Jews if they cultivate their irrepressible self-victimising tendency to ensure they are placed nowhere else but at the bottom. Europe, writes George Bariţ in 1842, has "a much poorer knowledge of us than they do of the Jews, who have their Moses".[152] We do not have even that, so we fare worse than the Jews, too.

MORAL AND BEHAVIOURAL "FLAWS" DUE TO THE NATION'S "SPECIFICITY"

An extremely severe and dark national self-image was created by features such as cultural backwardness, the low level of civilisation, social-economic misery, national oppression, and even alcoholism, robbery and criminality. These were nevertheless negative elements of a self-image that could generally be seen as the outcome of circumstances somewhat external to the Romanians' essential condition, the temporary results (even though covering a period of hundreds of years) of an unfavourable historical situation. They were not, therefore, definitively and inescapably imprinted onto the ethnic-psychological specificity of the nation, and their sources could be distinguished, explained, and possibly done away with by practical action, which would entail the erasure of those flaws as well.

Other negative features of self-perception were nevertheless considered intrinsic to Romanian nature and thus could explain by themselves, without the aid of further exterior historical circumstances, various unwelcome aspects of the mechanism of Romanian society. Within the Romanians' self-image, their inconsistency, superficiality, negligence and "Balkan" spirit, or lack of unity, were put forward as moral and behavioural features that defined Romanian conduct since they were vigorously inscribed into the patterns of the national specificity. In fact, they were little more than classic ethnic stereotypes and images, of a nature similar to those studied by imagology and social psychology—mental representations that human communities project both onto others and onto their own condition.[153] They are often present in the form of intimate confessions among the pages of private correspondence, which tend to generalise individual behaviour and to express exasperation triggered by particular situations. Certainly, they are also an indication of the heated replies of pugnacious personalities, as part of some personal disputes, but, as we will see, they almost always claim to be expressing some general value.

A basic cliché of the Romanians' self-image, active then as now, is inconsistency, an inability to go the distance once a thing is started. After settling in Wallachia, Ioan Maiorescu decides to blame it on the state of affairs in that area: "I have learned here never to trust anything until I see it with my very own eyes. There is a terrible fuss around everything at first, when they begin working, but then, God forbid such foolishness, hearts go stale and nothing will come of it. It has almost always been that way."[154] Atanasie Șandor notices the same tendency, in a commentary on the postponing of a national-cultural initiative by his fellow citizens in Arad: "They keep thinking on it, and reckoning what to do, and, in the Romanian fashion, whether to do it today or tomorrow, and thus they while away their time to no end."[155] This is also an echo of the regional stereotype related to the Transylvanian's slowness and his habit of taking his time to think things over before anything is said or done.

In addition to the above-mentioned flaw, there is the superficiality and indolence of the people, or the messy looseness of any Romanian undertaking. August Treboniu Laurian complains of the scarcity of readers among Romanians, due to their ignorance and poverty, and adds: "Consider, besides these, the laziness and listlessness inborn in the Romanian soul (do not take offence at these words!) and see for yourself why readers are so few among the Romanians."[156] Atanasie Șandor, upset about delays in payments of subscriptions to his papers, exclaims: "What can I do, since there is no teaching punctuality to the Romanians."[157] Vasile Pop, too, thinks that the "chief reason" for the low numbers of subscribers to Bariț's paper is "the indolence of our nation in these matters".[158]

In fact, their fellow countrymen's idleness and inability to ensure that their cultural-national initiatives are carried through is, as we will see in the next paragraph, a theme frequently tackled by the Romanian scholars of the time, confronted with so many material difficulties. They often complain that their papers remain undistributed, their books unsold, their appeals for subscriptions ineffective, and they are forever denouncing the lack of national zeal in the few potential readers within Romanian society.

Various other such flaws in the Romanians' character are constantly evoked. Ioan Maiorescu speaks of the "flightiness" that suits Wallachian Romanians "rather naturally"[159], while Cipariu tears a strip off a beneficiary of the Blaj foundations and blows the latter's greediness up to the size of a general monstrosity: "The Romanian has a short memory and no one is so ready to be ungrateful as he is [...] Our men are our greatest enemies, and they harm not only people but Romanian causes as well, for their own benefit, and only that. A monstrous Romanian said, in V(ienna): 'What got into this Ramonțai to raise foundations for the Romanians, he should have left them to his kin.' Hear him! Hear him! That's what the Romanian is like."[160] The superficiality, carelessness and negligence of the Romanians are also pointed out by Ion Codru Drăgușanu, who, in a comparative approach, shows that in Romania, just as in France yet in contrast with England, "one is always to expect faulty buildings, broken windows, blunt knives, damaged doors and many other things of the sort."[161]

The lack of a sense of realism and of a practical spirit is also one of the concerns of the Transylvanian intellectuals, all the more so as it was associated with other important themes within the political and social thought of the age, such as the attack on "forms without substance", the idea of gradual reforms or of the promotion of industry and trade. The Blaj-based professor Ioan Faur, for instance, alludes to the cliché in a letter to Papiu Ilarian: "The Romanians are used to feeding on hope; few wrack their brains to find ways towards the achievement of what lies in their power to do and what the times, reason and civilisation demand."[162]

Iosif Many's articles in the Hungarian periodicals issued in Cluj often insist on the same idea, as relevant to the particular degree of modernisation attained by the civilisational structures in Wallachia: "Indeed, Wallachia urgently needs material improvement, which not all are quick or willing to understand, so that many would rather waste time on political illusions than lend a helping hand to the government for the inception of such businesses as could be of undeniable help to the country."[163]

George Bariț's articles also include debate on the issue:

> One could be reduced to despair on seeing the foolishness of those people who, instead of immersing themselves completely in the study of the practical sciences that are of real help to humanity, all too often waste their time with shallow, sterile theories, with vain fantasies, with solving crosswords, enigmas, charades and other such trifles [...] But we are not yet ready to study the practical sciences, since we are not even done yet with our confessional disputes.[164]

Even if such flaws are manifest at the level of professional orientation or current politics, the two journalists put them down to what they call a cause/effect relationship between the characteristic lack of a practical spirit of which the Romanians are guilty, and such defects in their behaviour.

Taking these diffuse, non-systematic stereotypes and general statements on the Romanian "national specificity" as the background of our discussion, we will go on to analyse those self-attributed "deficiencies" that build up a coherently articulated theme at the level of the Romanian self-image. One of the most important of the deficiencies that we will cover in what follows is the would-be carelessness Romanians display when it comes to promoting national interests.

LACK OF ZEAL FOR THE NATIONAL CAUSE

To state that the Transylvanian intellectuals at the beginning of the modern age deplored the passivity of their fellow countrymen with respect to the nation's collective interests, and that, moreover, they took it as a defining feature of Romanian society, might seem at variance with the image constructed by militant Romanian historiography. According to the latter, the history of the Transylvanian Romanians is, after all, an uninterrupted chain of "battles" waged by the whole population, usually stirred into general "movements" and advancing steadily and undeterred towards the bright light at the end of the road: the forging of the united nation-state and union with the fatherland.[165]

In reality, however, the Romanian community in Transylvania was much more "pluralistic" than this unifying and simplistic vision might lead us to believe. Its members, like those of any normal society, were animated by the most varied of concerns and types of solidarity: from national interests, which could not be neglected (although here, too, options and solutions covered a dynamic and varied area), through political, confessional and social interests, to the usual personal or collective interests pursued with all the (merely human) individualistic "egotism" that the minimal space for freedom and the constraints and limitations of the age allowed.

Under such circumstances the militant intellectuals of the time, those who drew up the programme and schedule of national priorities and who called for the sacrificing of personal interests for the greater collective good of the nation, were the first to face the "resistance" and "passivity" of a multiform society that seemed to turn a deaf ear to the élite's appeals. Yet this apparent "passivity" was only a side effect of the exaggerated and impatient demands of the intellectuals, who believed that the nation did not come up to their expectations, that it did not conform to the plans and objectives they envisaged for it.

In fact, society was not deaf to the national programme, it was simply that it had many other deadlines to meet and priorities to see to. The countless particular interests and objectives of various groups or individuals would not easily melt away in the imaginary vessel in which the wizard-apprentices of the national cause meant to distil a unitary will and discover the universally applicable formula of collective emancipation and salvation. To them, society was "seriously disunited" and split, unable to focus its efforts and gather together around what was truly topical, that is, around what they considered to be topical and had established as such in the national programme. In reality, the society was naturally animated, in a Brownian motion, by its own dynamic rules, and the major hindrance came from the already existing legal, religious and moral constraints.

The militant intellectuals enlarged the spectrum of these constraints with the ideological exigencies of the national programme; they demanded that the new formula for social cohesion become so prominent as to subsume the other three, thereby welding it into a unique expression of the national will and action. The difference between the extent to which society, little prepared for such shift (with a bourgeois middle class too poorly cultivated), succeeded in adopting the national ideological programme and, on the other hand, the all-encompassing ambition of the authors of that programme, is able to explain the degree of disappointment felt by the Transylvanian militant élite, as well as the presence of such themes as a lack of national enthusiasm and solidarity at the heart of the identity they strove to build for that society.

The guilty, dispassionate look that Romanian society cast at the national cause manifested itself, in the first place, as a reluctance to support the cultural initiatives launched by the scholarly "intelligentsia". The public were always blameable for not reading and buying enough of the books, journals and papers written and published by the Romanian intellectuals.

Of course, the belief of these champions of the Enlightenment was that the dissemination of culture among the people by means of the spreading of books and literacy could almost entirely be equated with the complete emancipation of their nation. Bojincă, for instance, stated this idea quite plainly: "Should the Romanian nation be delivered from its darkness [...], we will get rid of any fault, trouble or oppression which spring from this very ignorance and darkness of the mind and burden each and every soul."[166] It follows that if the Romanians resist culture they will remain in the state of poverty and of political, social and national oppression that they are already in.

Otherwise, this strong belief in the power of culture to eradicate, by itself, all evils—a belief that might sound somewhat naive to modern ears—actually evinced an undeniable truth: without a solid nationalist ideological indoctrination, capable of offering new faith, establishing objectives and legitimising a new type of social solidarity, society did not seem willing to rise against an establishment that had its own ideological foundations, sanctioned by long tradition, and which, now with the dawning of the modern age (Josephine reformism and *Reformkor*) did not completely lack a certain capacity for inner reformation.[167]

Such considerations were indeed valid as far as the "national interest" was concerned, an interest the Transylvanian intellectuals undoubtedly stood up for, in all sincerity. Yet one cannot overlook the possible underlying influence and stimulation such efforts received from the intellectuals' pursuit of their own specific and limited interests, that is, from their dissatisfaction at not having their books bought or even published. On the one hand, there was the resentment caused by a lack of satisfactory financial rewards for their work, along with the sometimes extremely painful realisation that writing alone does not provide a living. This was especially the case with those who put a lot of work into their writing (see, for instance, the case of Bariț, who struggled endlessly with delayed subscription payments and was thus compelled to find other ways—private lessons, industrial business—of supporting his large family[168]).

An additional source of irritation was the difficulty of finding financial resources for the publication of books or papers, a problem then just as it is today.
Publishers could not risk the sums needed for the issuing of a scholarly work.
Certain printing houses specialising in Romanian publications, such as that run
by Barth of Sibiu[169], accepted only popular works, *Alexandriads*, almanacs or poetry
such as that written by Ioan Barac. The Romanian printing house of Blaj concen-
trated on religious writings and for the rest only allowed works by writers affili-
ated to the Capitulum or the bishopric (see the case of its manager, Reverend
Timotei Cipariu, who edited *The Mouthpiece of Enlightenment* and *Teacher of the
People*).[170]

Therefore, in order to publish a book, especially at the beginning of the century, one had to have a sponsor able to finance the printing costs. Such sponsors
were usually to be found among the Romanian merchants of Braşov or A-
Romanian ones from Pest, or among the prelates and boyars of the principalities.
As a rule, the foreword to such publications included elaborate praise of the Maecenas in question, as well as a complaint that there were not many of his kind in
Romanian culture. Another possibility was that of a "state order" carried out by
the printing press of the Buda University, which printed not only didactic and
moralising literature as ordered officially by the government but was also in favour
of similar private initiatives by Romanian intellectuals.[171]

Finally, a third possibility, and in fact the most frequent, was publicly to invite
potential buyers to subscribe in advance for the books and periodicals that were to
be published and that the subscribers would eventually receive by post. The
names of subscribers were usually mentioned at the end of the publication, since
they were not considered mere consumers of an indifferent merchandise (even if
the matter of the book could well be an indifferent one), but as patrons, to whom
the nation owed the greatest respect for their patriotic generosity. Both the problematic publication and sale and the overdone rhetoric of patriotism cast as a hook
to the few potential clients on whom the Transylvanian intellectuals could count
were an indication of the strained relationship they had with a readership almost
always accused of lacking in generosity.

On the other hand, however, the scant readership was a much more worrying
blemish on the public and social status of the intellectuals, on their prestige and
the acknowledgement of their value, to which they felt entitled and of which they
were in desperate need. Social prestige and the acknowledgement of their competence represent the very payment received by intellectuals in exchange for the
symbolic goods they produce.[172] Therefore, the lack of such acknowledgement is
what causes the greatest frustration, since without them, intellectuals will feel un-
paid, betrayed and bankrupt, no longer able to find a place for themselves in a
society that casts them out and seems to do easily without them.

How does one explain such a crisis at the level of transactions in symbolic
goods? Depending on one's perspective it could either be called an "over-
production" crisis or a crisis of "under-consumption". A disparity emerges, therefore, between the increased offer of cultural goods on the part of the Transylvanian intellectuals and the continuing reduced demand on the part of society. On
the one hand, improvements in education and in the individual juridical status of

the Romanians, initiated during the Josephine era and slowly consolidated thanks to the limited reformism of the Metternich age, had given them access to middle and upper level schools to a much greater extent than in the preceding age. The capacity for cultural performance was thus enhanced. On the other hand, the intellectual basis of the Romanian society remained fragile, due to widespread illiteracy and the weakness of the urban middle class.

Again, such a discrepancy is able to account for the resentments and frustrations of an intellectual minority that, although willing to become one with the people, was actually miles away from it.

We will go on to look at some illustrations of the theme of the lack of zeal for cultural initiatives—a flaw almost completely identified with attitudes towards the national cause.

I have already analysed the Romanian intellectuals' laments on the shortage of readers, rich patrons, and major achievements of any kind in Romanian culture.[173] All nations, they claimed, write and publish "in a manly way", becoming ever more civilised and refined and more aware of their rights. All have their books, journals, histories and geographies; the Romanians alone indulge in apathetic torpor and keep their distance from the universal effort towards enlightenment. The lack of "zeal" in Romanian readers even makes the Transylvanian scholars give up projects of a wider scope, as Dimitrie Iercovici confesses in his preface to the *Alexandriad* he printed in 1794: in addition to the popular book "I would also have some works of wise teaching in matters moral and of good conduct, but since I see that our people finds neither use nor interest in such books as are written and printed by wiser and greater men than me, I dare not give them to press."[174]

If this seems too early a date to start worrying about the scarcity of readers, we should note that fifty years later the Transylvanian intellectuals' views had not changed in the least. Asked in 1847 to give an account of the impression made by a book (of "moral writing" again) by Moise Sora Noac on Wallachian readers, August Treboniu Laurian answers Bariţ in terms similar to those used by Iercovici: "They will not be moved by things a thousand times wiser and greater."[175] In the same letter the idea appears again, as an echo of another editorial issue: "I resent having to repeat what I said above: our people are too coarse and crude to be moved so soon [...] Apathy, apathy and nothing else."[176]

Atanasie Şandor, too, writes of an absence of enthusiasm for reading in Romanian society, in a letter to Papiu Ilarian: "Books, Romanian books for the Romanians, that is what we need! The unhappy thing, though, is that there is such little desire in many of them, some not without learning, to buy Romanian books; such people are indeed not too literate, nor used to reading in the Romanian language, either using *slove* [Cyrillic spelling] or, even less, *litere* [Latin spelling]."[177]

Here, Şandor raises at least two questions of profound importance. For one thing, the lack of readers is not only due to illiteracy, but also to the reluctance of the literate, even the cultured among them, to devote too much time to reading. Secondly, and more worryingly, these cultured Romanians do not read Romanian books because they have grown used to reading foreign books, which, as can be seen in Şandor's allusion, could only horrify the poor intellectuals. Not only does that habit pave the way to denationalisation, by making its practitioners more and more familiar with the spiritual ambience of a foreign culture, it also makes the already scant group of Romanian book-buyers grow even thinner and weaker.

Faced, therefore, not only with a scarcity of books, schools and cultural achievements, but even with a lack of any willingness to put those in existence to good use, the Transylvanian intellectuals came to blame Romanian society as a whole for the fact that no good came out of it. It was not financial resources or favourable legislation that were lacking in the first place, but people who could bring to life the national programme of emancipation. "The great lack of capable men will not even allow us to do what could be done"[178], writes Ioan Maiorescu, and his colleague Laurian states sententiously: "We have but few true Romanians."[179]

Others, less easily given to desperation, hoped to shake their fellow country-men out of their lethargy and indifference towards the collective concerns of the nation by vehement urging and criticism. Bariț's wish is that those Romanian writers who are truly fighting for the good of the country should "make all sloth-ful and sluggish souls tremble at the sharpness of their pen".[180] To the same end, Iosif Many employs his poetic gifts in order to educate his idle contemporaries:

To our young I speak and say
Such pretty spring, such joyful day
Within your hearts can find no roof?
Lack you regard or love reproof,
Or have you no consideration
For our folk and for the nation?
Don't hold your brave heart in disdain,
We long for it to beat again.[181]

Contrasting the motif of the "torpor" and idleness of Romanian youth with the freshness of revivified nature, Many anticipates the theme of the chlorotic "vegetal people"[182], frozen in lethargic indifference to the dynamism and changes around them.

We have already seen how the incrimination of lack of zeal for cultural initia-tives extends into a general criticism of national inactivity. Whereas for the differ-ent generations of the Romanian Enlightenment the most grievous sin of Roma-nian society was its reluctance to support national culture, for the Romantic revolutionaries such as Papiu Ilarian the mortal sins were represented by too weak resistance to the Hungarian element, by lack of nationalist convictions, and by non-participation in active political militancy. Undoubtedly, just like the enlight-ened humanists before, the revolutionary minority of 1848 needed a public sup-porting it in the background, a public whose main task would have been to per-sonify the "will of the people", thus legitimating the actions of its leaders and re-sponding to the élite's "discourse on power". Since Romanian society was as pre-pared for a Jacobin revolution as it was for the elaborate discourse of high culture, the leaders of 1848 found themselves doomed to go on deploring the lack of na-tional zeal on the part of an indolent society.

Ioan Pușcariu, a young radical of Bărnuțiu's company in Sibiu, wrote on 26 March 1848 to Bariț:

I will only note that Romanians as spiritless as I found here I doubt might live anywhere else in the whole Transylvanian country. One says "Why should we ask the Saxons for this or that, for the Hungarians will give no matter what the Saxons will"; others say "Why should we make demands at all, for it might then serve the Saxons to boast they offered help in earnest and good will." Some under rule; some in bondage; others hoping for their own benefit, etc.; so much for a political nation.[183]

Pluralism of opinions or the pursuit of private interests were considered true heresies at the hour of the revolution when the national will and action had to merge in one focal nexus. Also, the core of the revolution had to be in the hands of a group of people able to claim the prerogative of producing the revolutionary discourse—a tendency that had just begun to take shape in the case of the Transylvanian Romanians' revolution, with the circulation of Bărnuțiu's *Provocation*.[184]

If, in March 1848, the hesitation Pușcariu speaks about could be put down to the confusion brought about by the outbreak of events, the discontent of the revolutionary leaders in the middle of the civil war is all the more significant. Petru Dobra and Ion Buteanu, for instance, complain repeatedly that the population in their area of authority, one extremely exposed to Hungarian attacks, offered unconvincing support to the resistance. In the long run the lack of enthusiasm of the population would extend to include the two prefects themselves. Consequently, seized by pessimism and tired of fighting both the enemy and what they called the indifference of their fellow countrymen, they agreed to negotiate with Dragoș. The bleak irony is that they would both meet their end as a result.[185]

At the beginning of 1849 Dobra complained that "our people of Zlatna move as the wind blows and many of them are so poor"[186], and Buteanu, in a touching premonitory letter ("What could be my private gain? Solely the Hungarian gallows awaiting me"[187]), gives voice to his deep dejection:

The people of Baia de Criș, who choose to favour the Hungarians rather than the national common cause and the interests of the dynasty, dared to say that they care little about the monarch's interests; that they are people of their land and have no complaints about Hungarian rule; that they will not come to the camps and fight; that they are sorry for having already risen against the Hungarians. See, brother, what sort of districts you govern, and what strong defenders of the sacred national cause you have![188]

What is left for the young militant intellectual to do under such conditions, when people will only look to their own affairs instead of taking an active part in the revolution?

In both positions [as military prefect and civilian administrator] I began first to employ the moral faculty and tried to show the right path to the people who had lost heart under the former rule, that of the Hungarians, by reporting acts of courage, which I thought might enliven and prompt them to heroic deeds. I used the power of the word, which I derived mainly from evangelical writ, as the only moral teaching the Romanians could have been prepared for. Vain has been my strife and toil, for the evil has struck roots in peoples' veins and guts, and only death can pluck it out. Growth and development—the basis of morality—find no place in their souls and our hope can only be with another generation. What is left for me to do? I can only use compulsion to bring them into line, and for their own sake, not out of delight in seeing my kinsmen punished, for it always grieves me to have to do it, [but] because there is no other way towards the general good of our Romanian nation.[189]

Some sources do speak of the Romanians' enthusiastic enlisting in the autumn of 1848, for instance in the troops of Colonel Urban or of the Romanian legions (largely prompted by the fear of the Szeklers' attacks, too[190]). Yet others reveal the hard time that both tribunes and prefects had in recruiting men for service in the camps [*loagăre*] of the paramilitary corps, or even in requisitioning the supplies necessary for the imperial troops or the Romanian guerrillas.[191] Under such circumstances they resorted to methods of recruitment and requisition used in the Austrian army and the former Hungarian administration, by alternating national propaganda with fines[192], with military executions of rebel villagers or with such measures as the demolition of a house owned by someone who would not serve in the paramilitary armed force.[193]

In practice, all the conflicting parties, the Austrians, Romanians and Hungarians (who also enlisted, in western areas, several thousands of Romanian volunteers in the army of General Bem[194]), used the same methods for recruiting cannon fodder. When the appeal of ideological principles (loyalty to the dynasty, the national cause or the war of liberation) did not bear fruit, a substitute was found in physical coercion, designed to "persuade" reluctant, non-revolutionary populations. Undoubtedly, all the above-mentioned factors need to be taken into account if one is to attempt an explanation for the population mobilisation during the civil war in Transylvania. Yet in all probability, for most of the Romanian or Szekler peasants involved, it was fear of the enemy and a desire to avenge the adversary's atrocities that drove them to take up arms, burn and kill. The intellectuals standing by their side, often terrified at the idea of massacre, tried to demonstrate for them the rightfulness of the cause for which they were fighting.

That being the case, the fact that indifference to the revolution and the inadequacy of the reasons for which people took part in it were primarily due to the traditional, rural structure of Romanian society, remained unnoticed. The Transylvanian intellectuals therefore often spread the image of the Romanians' neglect of the national cause, which came to be accepted as a defining trait of Romanian specificity.

One expression of that cliché, as banal as it was prominent in the Romanian social imaginary, was the idea of the Romanians as no longer fired by national enthusiasm as their ancestors had been. In 1842 Simion Bărnuţiu wrote: "Warmer was the blood filling the veins of our ancestors who fought for their rights, and stale is the heart of their grandchildren."[195] Papiu Ilarian takes up the idea, this time in tune with post-revolutionary despondency: "Are the Romanians of our day as ready and ardent when it comes to the raising of such an institution [a national university—the main objective of Romanian action in Papiu's opinion] as their blessed forefathers were when they struggled for the beginning of the schools in Blaj, which was an incomparably more difficult task for them than the establishing of a national university is today for their sons?"[196]

As a rule, Papiu explains all failings and defeats, at least partially, by the indolence and sloth of his fellow countrymen: national history is forgotten and remains unwritten "because of the Romanians' carelessness"[197]; the people of Banat have lost the autonomy of their province "because of overwhelming Hungarian intrigues" but also due to "our negligence and cowardice".[198] In general, the Romanians should manifest "more ardour for their holy rights".[199]

The harshness of the young historian's judgement, mainly targeted at the Romanians' lack of energy in opposing the tendencies of Hungarianisation, goes as far as even denying his nation the legitimacy of any effort at emancipation, since it seems so satisfied with its apathy and indifference to its own condition: "A nation that does not do what she can by herself, that will not help herself at all but hopes for aid from others, such a nation does not deserve anyone's succour!"[200]

Yet Papiu Ilarian's scepticism as to the Romanians' national zeal still leaves some room for an opposing attitude. The bunch of enthusiastic young men who took the revolution upon themselves were able to surpass the indifference of most Romanian intellectuals to the national cause, and, together with the people, showed themselves capable of remarkable energy and will to action—such is the conclusion of Papiu's *History*. As usual, the revolution is, in the eyes of its adepts, the providential means to expurgate all evils. It follows that the very lack of national zeal that the Transylvanian Romanians' self-perception projects onto itself could also disappear in the course of a whole series of revolutions. Yet, as the Romanian self-image has it, enthusiasm will only last as long as the revolution does; the paradoxical interpretation thus arises that the time of violent ruptures is a happier age than that of peaceful normality. What defines normality is that very absence of vital energy and of disinterested zeal that keeps the Romanians prisoners of the dire situation they are in.

KEEPING TO THE (BAD) OLD WAYS: ROMANIAN HOSTILITY TOWARDS PROGRESS

An accusation frequently levelled by foreigners at that time, yet one equally circulated as a constitutive element of the Romanian self-image, was that the Romanians could not advance on the path of civilisation because of their obstinate keeping to the old traditions and customs, to the routine of ancestral habits that had proved inefficient and incompatible with modern development but that they would not let go of for anything in the world. From this perspective, it was no longer a question of others preventing the Romanians from developing, but they themselves who *would not* take the step and give up their traditional behaviour, prejudices and lifestyle, that is, those elements that kept them divorced from the rhythms of contemporary civilisation.

In the opinion of the Transylvanian intellectuals, Romanian specificity was shaped by the "old way has got to be the way" type of philosophy, which was largely to blame for the existing state of things. True, the value of this ethnic-psychological trait was fraught with a certain ambiguity, since the capacity to preserve traditional ways unaltered, which presupposed resistance to denationalisation, was a positive feature, much cherished in the Transylvanian Romanians' social imaginary, particularly from the point of view of Romantic conceptions. Yet enlightened rationalism, more critical, as a rule, of traditions, prejudices and superstitions, was to remain an important element of Transylvanian ideology and sensibility for most of the first half of the nineteenth century. Therefore, the repudiation of the tendency to remain faithful to such customs as were incompatible with the exigencies of modern development would always benefit from a theoretical background capable of providing it with arguments and justifications. Naturally, the Romanians' keeping to the bad old ways and their hostility towards progress are, first and foremost, themes of the late eighteenth century and the first decades of the nineteenth, as elaborated by the Transylvanian School. Once settled in the collective imaginary, they would nevertheless reach out into Romanticism, especially since the contextual data that generated them underwent little change.

Closely related to many other elements of the self-image, the theme is primarily concerned with the Romanians' inactivity and their lack of enthusiasm for the cause of collective and individual emancipation, which appears as a typical attitude, a profoundly retrograde one, at once cause and effect of Romanian misfortunes. Along the co-ordinates of this vicious circle the core of the nation becomes inextricably evil; the Romanians wallow in the mire and love it, too.

In 1792 Sava Popovici of Răşinari wrote in his chronicle: "If man lends himself to ineptitude, ignorance, indolence and the reluctance to pursue true wisdom and learn good conduct, he will stray on vicious paths of deceit and perfidy, a pitiful villain subject to another."[201] The same incrimination of the Romanians' persistence in evil as a cause of their national subordination is to be encountered four years later in Samuil Micu: "Learning and science tell man apart from the beasts", he writes, and then deplores the absence of the desire to rise, specific, he thinks, to the Romanians, who "are still benumbed and, like the worm which looks for sweetness in horseradish, they think slavery and surrender will bring them happiness, alas, the woe of it!"[202]

The image of the vainly struggling worm that indulges in its own predicament (an image borrowed from folk paremiology), was, for all its extreme bitterness, a much cultivated one in the Transylvanian Romanians' discourse as a suggestive metaphor of their condition, defined by persistence in evil. It also occurs, for instance, in Dimitrie Iercovici, who wrote in 1796: "The Romanian nation is now free to enjoy all teaching and learning, that is, the Latin, Hungarian and German schools, and all kinds of other crafts are open now before the eyes of the Romanians", but the nation "still shrinks from drinking the water of wisdom", and "lies benumbed in its sloth, like the worm in its rot."[203] Several decades later Ion Codru Drăgușanu uses the phrase again with reference to the miserable *clăcaş* [serf] of Wallachia, who "agonises like the worm in its horseradish".[204]

Iercovici raises an issue that will become a leitmotif of the Romanian self-image: all conditions are now propitious for the Romanians to better themselves, yet they refuse to take the chance since they are so hostile to progress and tend to persevere in the way of evil.[205] They are now finally in a position to achieve cultural improvement, to have schools, books and enlightened intellectuals, but the population refuses to take advantage of such opportunities. All officials, the emperor, the governor, and all the heads of the nation, the bishops, the principals and the scholars, seek the good of the Romanians, only the Romanians could not care less about their own good. "I will tell you, gentle reader, for silence hereupon can no longer be kept, that the emperor, Joseph II [...], had a mind to help the ploughmen's hearts and hands [...] and showed enough grace to demand that some ways be found for granting the Romanian nation the blessing of learning, but vain was his struggle", writes Iercovici. Moreover, the governor, Bánffy, "carried out so well the enlightened emperor's will that now there are enough Romanian schools in the Principality of Transylvania, but to no end, for no fruit is borne." Bishop Adamovici and principals Eustatievici and Şincai, in their turn, made every effort to organise schools and print textbooks, yet so far "too little evidence have the Romanian people given of their learning before the enlightened heads of the province."[206]

While one might sense obedience to the authorities in Iercovici, official translator of the province, the same cannot possibly apply to the liberal spirit of Codru Drăguşanu who, fifty years later, uses similar ideas and formulations, so testifying to the endurance of the clichés devised during the age of Enlightenment. The following is a fragment of his speech, delivered in 1847 at a school in Wallachia:

> Now, all favourable means are here, ready at hand. Our high government, father to us all, has had schools built and has thus given as many occasions for enlightenment, for education, for improvement. The high government does not spare any effort to see us safely on the road to happiness, advancement and light. No cost is too great, he believes, for the flourishing of these institutions, the glory of our nation and country. How can we remain blind to his benevolent deed? How can we not see it is for our own sake? How can we love to wallow in ignorance and the dust of so many centuries?[207]

The Bucharest government (which the revolution was just about to wipe away), just like the government in Cluj, spared no effort to ensure the rise of the populations it administered, but the latter would rather lie in the darkness of their stupor. Also evident here is the Joseph II-type of exasperation felt by any form of enlightened politics based on centralism and authoritarian control when faced with the stubbornness of conservative societies, impervious to any project of planned collective happiness.

Returning to the age of the Transylvanian School, the same paradigm is well illustrated in the case of Gheorghe Şincai: "Mind you that Emperor Leopold [I] forced no one into union with the Roman Catholics, but he only meant to help the miserable Romanians, who to this day are blind to their own good."[208] Budai-Deleanu reduces the idea of the Romanians' persistence in "falling" into evil ways to the particular case of the population's civic and political behaviour:

> The crowd of evil-mongers
> Knows naught of sacred laws,
> No rule, no act, no flogging
> Will cleanse them of their flaws.

He explains in a footnote that "a nation given to villainy, unrest and decay cannot be put aright by laws and punishments, however saintly the law may be or fearful the compulsion."[209]

The motif of the Romanians keeping to the bad old ways also surfaces in the cultural discourse of the post-Enlightenment writers from Banat and Hungary, who benefited from the editorial facilities of the Buda University Press. It appears particularly in its expressive dimension, with insistence on eloquent, ornamental rhetoric. Accusatory vehemence always accompanies the favourite themes of cultural backwardness and lack of enthusiasm for supporting national initiatives.

Constantin Diaconovici-Loga, in his *Appeal for the Printing of Romanian books* issued in 1821, calls for a mobilisation of collective efforts with a view to cultural betterment, and challenges those backward mentalities that resist such actions and remain hostile to progress: "Fie those rusty minds that are not shamed to deal in such thoughts: my father too knew naught of these new conceptions, he was not a learned man, and who can say he did not live well? I reckon he never lacked either drink or food. This, I should think, is the manner of the beasts, but man has a duty to feed not only his body, but his mind too."[210] Here, it is the self-sufficiency of those who do not wish for more because they have managed with less that particularises the theme of the Romanians' persistence in evil.

The same question is given ample theoretical discussion in an 1829 work by Moise Bota.[211] At its earliest age (from a perspective contrary to Rousseau's, we might say), humankind was in a state of savagery and primitivism. Eventually, cultural, artistic and scientific progress, as well as the moral leap entailed by the aggregation of national collective solidarity (all of which were, in Bota's view, superior to the savage's egotistic individualism) led to the state of happiness now enjoyed by countries such as "Austria, England, France, etc."

Unfortunately, and herein lies the sorrow of the Transylvanian scholar, there are still to this day, in some areas, human communities that obstinately indulge in a state near to savagery, completely lacking any love of culture and remaining, like egoistic primitives, indifferent to collective progress. It is also worth noting Bota's nationalism (of Enlightened extraction), according to which national solidarity is an essential element of modern civilisation and a superior moral value that comes with it. Persistence in evil is manifest today in

> parties of people among whom some, although not really fallen all the way down to savageness, simple-mindedness, fright and terror, are nevertheless so given over to the bad that they will not rest until they break some law or rule handed down to us from times past [...], and are so at ease with their baseness and dark wickedness, and nor do they wish to part withal [...] Believe me, brother! This is a passion grown bitter with us Romanians. Every man knows in his heart that the growth of the nation is only thwarted when there is want of love for the land, for the sciences and for the enlightenment of the mind. Still, those who enjoy more riches than the rest are seized with so unabated a thirst for treasures that little do they care about the country or the thriving and advancement of its sons.[212]

Contrary to Micu, Șincai or Iercovici, who charged with adherence to evil the insensitive crowd, unmoved by the efforts of their leaders, Bota and Diaconovici-Loga are particularly critical of the hostility to progress to be observed in the rich. This is not necessarily a more democratic stance, which might differ consistently from the mere demophilia usually professed by enlightened minds. It is rather an integrationist view of society, in which society is seen as a complex organism where each actor, having his own well-established place within the hierarchy, must fulfil his social function, indispensable to the welfare of the whole. In addition, their criticism goes hand in hand with the motif of the Romanians' lack of national zeal in supporting cultural initiatives—it is in such terms that the merchants and well-to-do bourgeois could be, and frequently were, the favourite targets in the Transylvanian intellectuals' hunt for patrons.

The same motifs punctuate the justificatory rhetoric of Zaharia Carcalechi, in a moralising brochure printed in Buda in 1826.[213] Here, persistence in evil—which the Romanian self-image differentiates as a function of the various social levels—swells into a generalised national flaw, as is only "natural" for a globalising view of the nation:

> an insensitive people, one that willingly breaks our forefathers' laws, envies its kin, who is in want of the thriving love of enlightenment, good deeds and the bettering of its men, such a people cannot but fall into the darkness of misery and crashes by its own will [the supposed deliberateness of the Romanians' obstinate pursuit, "by their own will", of a backward state is a typical inference] down to the dire depths of idiocy, forever damned to suffer from its own wickedness! This has been (it grieves me to say) the travail of the Romanian nation to this day.[214]

In the wake of such enlightened considerations, Andrei Mureşanu developed, at the time of the 1848 revolution, an elaborate theory with respect to the Romanians' hostility to progress—a central motif in his journalistic work. To a certain extent he seems more sensitive to nuance, since he shows that the feature in question, which he attributes to the Romanians' social conduct, was acquired in the course of history and is due to certain conditions, being present in other peoples facing similar situations. All the same, the forceful and significant way in which it has settled as part of the Romanian lifestyle, something that is not to be encountered in other nations, has turned it into a defining feature of Romanian specificity. It is still possible for the Romanians to get rid of this characteristic, claims Mureşanu, yet he also insists that, given their present circumstances, the process is bound to be extremely difficult. In an article of 1843[215] he writes:

> One of the most pernicious traits of human nature is that it takes much more time and effort to unlearn bad old habits or customs than to learn new ways. Another one is that the longer darkness reigns over the mind and keeps light away, the harder it is to shovel the mind out of its numbness and stir it into wakefulness. But this has not only befallen the Romanian nation, others suffer from it as well, except that the burden of a sad fate is much harder on Romanian shoulders than on others, which these others know well how to turn to their own advantage.[216]

It is not the foreigners, however, who are primarily held responsible for the state of the Romanians, but the indifference to progress and awakening specific to Romanian society. Just like the intellectuals of the Enlightenment, Mureşanu shows that this is not a question of want of effort either on the part of the authorities or of a number of leaders devoted to national welfare, "yet the sad fact is that few have consented to make allowance for their efforts, and to this day there are some who believe that the generous idea of turning the Romanian people into a worthy bearer of the name of their forefathers, by enlightenment and advancement in the sciences, is unfit for the state of today's Romanians. Which is to say that in most hearts the seed of light sill lies buried under the gross matter of ignorance."[217]

The interesting formulation here is that "to this day" the Romanians will not change their attitude to modern progress, a phrase we have also met with in Carcalechi and elsewhere. In keeping with its own internal logic, the theme of the Romanians' persistence in evil tends to keep vindicating a venerable tradition: the Romanians have always been reluctant to embrace progress, therefore their present attitude is but an extension of that inclination.

As we have already mentioned, the motif in question also attempts to find self-justifying arguments in the self-image shaped by peasant mentality, at the level of folk paremiology and its tendency to cling to age-old, more or less pernicious, habits and customs—a defining feature of the Romanian ethnic-psychological profile. "The old way has got to be the way", "The old and the wise know better", "This is how our predecessors acted and the kind of life they chose, therefore it is only right for us to remain at their level". Such arguments readily lead to the perception of a horizon of self-satisfaction, a fatality attributed to that folk mentality which, according to Romantic conceptions, defines the Romanian national specificity.[218]

Since the Transylvanian intellectuals of 1848 obviously could not escape the influence of the Romantic vision, they grounded the Romanians' persistence in evil on such perceptions as are manifest at the folkloric level, even though their enlightened background urged them to criticise, discourage or ridicule the latter. Andrei Mureșanu writes in 1853 that, were the Romanians to get rid of their outworn customs which prevent them from developing industry, the sciences and the arts, "we could prove false the old saying, 'The Romanian's last-hour wits', which means to say that there is no hope of wisdom in the Romanian before he comes to little. The Romanian foresees nothing, he lets things slip and says, 'The way I lived is good enough for my son as well'."[219] Even such a radical Romantic and adamant supporter of the supremacy of rural values as Papiu Ilarian decries in 1848 the Romanians' settling into the unhappy orbit of a patriarchal existence inherited from their ancestors: "Romanians, the time has come! Do not tarry any longer, do not trust yourselves to the ways of your fathers and forefathers."[220]

Despite numerous such calls for a removal of Romanian resistance to change, the perception of the Romanians' ill-fated traditionalism would remain an important element of their self-image even at the promising hour of the revolution, as is apparent in the telling formulation used by the vice-prefect Ioachim Băcilă in January 1849 in his address to Avram Iancu: "The Romanian had rather listen to the evil than to the good word."[221]

"FORMS WITHOUT SUBSTANCE": THE MORAL CORRUPTION OF THE ROMANIANS BY MODERN CIVILISATION

The vogue of the "forms-without-substance" theory in Romanian culture[222] can undoubtedly be explained by certain "objective" particularities of Romanian evolution, having to do especially with the way Romanian society was rushed, sometimes even goaded, into its transition to modernity, and thus forced to cover over serious gaps. The tension that arose between appearance and essence, between, on the one hand, imported institutions and ideas and, on the other, Romanian realities, brought about a fundamental semiotic inadequacy, bound to short-circuit the very production of social meaning within the Romanian community. It therefore naturally triggered the birth of anti-modern criticism and its doctrinal coagulation around the Junimea group.[223]

Behind the aesthetic, political and cultural theories of Titu Maiorescu lies a whole tradition, long noted, particularly from the viewpoint of the history of ideas, by those specialists who have looked into Romanian reflections on the modernisation of Romanian society in the nineteenth century.[224] Apart from objective justifications legitimating it, the genesis of the theory of forms without substance cannot be properly understood, at least in its concrete manifestations if not in its very essence, unless its remarkable "predecessors" in the first half of the century are taken into account as well.

These numerous prefiguring instances, diverse and unequal as they are, should not be traced, however, only at the level of clear and systematic ideas, or of coherent doctrines such as the political traditionalism of the Restoration, or the German Romantic school of law philosophy. They should also be looked at from the wider perspective of the evolution of the social imaginary and of collective mentality, of self-image and of identity-shaping mechanisms.

In fact, identity and self-perception crises are merely an effect of modernisation, all the sharper as the latter quickens its pace. As a consequence, there is no escape from an inter-conditioning between critical reflection on modernity and an identity-centred problematic, as a fundamental and inextricable datum of one's existence.[225] Modernity, as mental space and general human condition, shelters the seed of a somewhat paradoxical attitude: the post-modern tendency to deny and ceaselessly reformulate not only tradition and the "oldness" against which it defines itself, but also its own bases and motivations—reason, individualism and "progress", individual and collective identity, which is a tendency that runs the risk of being (completely erroneously) taken for traditionalism and anti-modernity.[226]

Let us use these theoretical premises for a further survey of the "forms without substance" theme as applied to Romanian society by the Romanian Transylvanians' self-perception at the beginning of the modern era. From the viewpoint of doctrinal political ideology, the motif fitted well into the context of a reforming, liberal-moderate or even conservative thought, one that agreed to progress as based on evolving reforms, that had built upon historicist premises since the Enlightenment, that looked up to a tradition of Romanian society it considered organically grown, and that was legalist and abhorred ruptures, discontinuity and mob violence as exemplified by the fatal example of French ideology and the French Revolution.

For the most part, Romanian historiography has neglected or underestimated this important trend of Transylvanian political reflection in the first half of the nineteenth century. It nevertheless seems obvious to me that Bariţ's moderation and centrism, Cipariu's or Many's liberal Catholicism, or Bărnuţius' organicist nationalism, give the Transylvanian Romanians' political thought an orientation far removed from the model of individualist, voluntarist and radical liberalism of

French extraction. The confessed political creed of Bariț's generation is the ideal of the *juste milieu* and a "temperate advancement". The revolution itself (which they never call by that name[227]) was never associated ideologically, for all its violent democratic upheaval, with anything other than the same legalism of moderate liberalism, in addition to their solidarist nationalism and doubled by dynastic loyalism.

Under such circumstances the "forms without substance" motif can be considered firstly as an application of a general theme of conservative thought to the concrete case of Romanian society. The reasoning of the age ran as follows: the negative effects that attempts to put into practice the abstract, reality-free ideas of the French enlightened "ideologues" Voltaire and Rousseau can trigger in any society are to be noticed in the Romanian case as well, as they have left deep traces in the Romanians' very ways of living and thinking. This is how a political doctrine and a theory of evolution turn into self-image; this is how they are reflected in, and become grafted onto, the body of self-perception and collective identity.

As can be expected, such an ideological construct will only impose itself within a social representation if the interpretation of its data is in tune with the broad overview of the respective collective perception, and if it is indispensable for the process of shaping a national identity. The possibility of a "logical" correlation of the "forms without substance" motif with such themes of the self-image as the Romanians' superficiality and lack of a sense of reality, their fear of foreigners and of contamination with elements of foreign civilisation[228], that is, generally speaking, with the negative and self-victimising nature of that perception, offered exceptionally fertile ground for the reception of that doctrine and its assimilation into the very body of the social imaginary.

What, then, were the "forms without substance" capable of altering Romanian tradition, of cutting off the on-winding thread of organic continuity, since it could not really be claimed that modernity in general, and much less the political proposals of the French Revolution, had in any way invaded the Mioritic lands or struck deep roots in the core of Transylvanian Romanian society?[229] As is frequently the case, reality mattered less than the internal logic of self-perception, which could very easily build and assume completely distorted images of the so-called dangers presented by a modernity as yet little invested with actual existence. On the other hand, the dissolution of some traditional mentalities and life forms and the rather hastened pace of the transition to modernity in some domains, such as the area of culture or of the language, too abruptly subjected to renewals, were definitely disturbing and "threatening" signs of novelty. A mere pair of trousers, or the attempt to replace with an innocent top hat the patriarchal fur cap on the head of some merchant from Brașov, were often able to give rise to serious interrogations and identity crises.[230]

The Transylvanians often derided the "forms without substance" that prevailed among their fellow countrymen from the principalities, particularly from Wallachia. Here as elsewhere, however, the "visibility" of such forms was not so much due to a more modern or "democratic" political system than existed in Transylvania (apart from its being a "national" one), as to more openness in welcoming French ideology, culture and civilisation. It was the latter that managed to reduce to nothing what had still remained intact of the originality of the place, already compromised by Greek influence. Undoubtedly, among the sources of the theory of forms without substance lie the Transylvanian and Moldavian intellectuals' cutting judgements passed on the more mobile and dynamic "Wallachian spirit", that is, in fact, certain local stereotypes specific to the self-image of the Transylvanian or Moldavian Romanians. In this respect the make-up of the "Junimea" group, predecessors included (from Kogălniceanu to Ioan Maiorescu), is of undeniable significance.

Nevertheless, in terms of Transylvanian self-perception the forms without substance were not an issue confined to Wallachian territory but a feature of Romanian society in its entirety: the theme bears, as usual, on national specificity and identity and its occurrences refer as often to Transylvanian realities. As early as the end of the eighteenth century[231] the motif becomes apparent by means of clichés such as the demise of religious values as a result of an evolving, morally wanting lay culture; the corruption of mores and the debauchery engendered by a civilisation that gives the upper hand to material concerns over spiritual-moral ones; the shallow formation of the young generation, in both manners and knowledge, and its imperviousness to solid moral-Christian values; the opposition between authentic "culture" (which read, to the minds of the time, as a pre-eminently moral one) and "civilisation" as exclusively based on the values of material progress; the conflict between the traditional community's sense of solidarity and the selfish individualism of modern society; the jeopardy in which the specificity and originality of national culture and even language are placed by the tendency to borrow cultural and linguistic forms at odds with the autochthonous basic vocabulary.

The general formulas used to flaunt the "forms without substance" bear primarily on the sphere of the national culture, considered, in Enlightenment terms, as the main motor of development. Florian Aaron, for instance, believed that George Bariț gave proof of unjustifiable optimism as to Wallachian realities, and in 1838 wrote in response:

> Believe me, the echo resounds more sound itself. I am not saying we are not doing anything, but what we do is not in the way of which word has spread, nor to the purpose expected by all well-reasoning Romanians. The rust of the Greek fashion has not yet been wiped away; the craze for Gallic ways still reigns unabated; the Romanian literature is only in favour with the youth now in school; therefore, all literary production is either shut off or disdained, and anyway held in low esteem.

It is also true, he claims, that, "despite all that, here and there, some things do come out."[232]

Some of the basic motifs of the theory are already present in these quotations: the contradiction between essence and appearance, rendered here in the guise of the metaphoric disjunction between the sound proper and its fake echo; the condemnation of the pernicious French influence; the lack of substance of the cultural forms, to be noticed, for instance, in the existence of a literature without a readership. While for the sociological vision of political Junimism the expressions deprived of actual content were represented especially by the hollow institutions of the public and ideological model of development (e.g., a parliamentary system that was too representative for an as yet insubstantial civil society), for the Transylvanians of the first half of the century the main form without substance was culture itself, emptied of its moral core.

Similar critical considerations on the situation in Wallachia are to be encountered in a 1838 letter of Ioan Maiorescu. In his attack on the "luxury" and "flabbiness" reigning over his adoptive province—vices that, in his opinion, other peoples only take to in the high or even decadent phases of their development—the Transylvanian scholar proves unremitting:

> With us everything is upside down. The weaknesses other peoples fall into at the end of the road and with full gorges are with us from the first steps and on an empty stomach [...] I don't know what is to be expected from this our generation. But I fear no good is to come out of what we have now. Let them boast with what they will in our civilisation and praise advancements in literature, I for one, who like to search well into things and have a mind for the future, will never be mislead by outward forms.[233]

A healthy moral lesson, based on the principles of Christian morals, is, in the opinion of the Transylvanian intellectuals influenced by the tradition of German Enlightenment, the only content able to reinvest with authentic meaning the hollow cultural forms that gnaw at the heart of society. The absence of that moral-spiritual foundation, the disavowal of "materialism", "scepticism" and "Pyrrhonism", that is, the lack of moral principles that might inspire human action, is a basic theme illustrating the "forms without substance" theory in its Transylvanian variant at the beginning of the nineteenth century. "What will come of a society", asks George Bariţ, "where neither in church, nor in school, nor in the family nor outside it, is there any strong voice bespeaking a stoic, severe and truly manful nature that might face and fight, once and for all, this loathsome epicurism [..., which] reigns and rules, written on the face of most of what we call the élite of our society and which presents us with the sharpest of contrasts with the misery and woe of the majority of our people?"[234] In 1846 Gavril Munteanu puts his finger on a specific cultural form that is capable of murdering any moral fundament—the well-known, harmful influence of French culture and its love of vice: "We, the Wallachian Romanians, are endowed with everything except morals. Now, it is plain that we will never acquire that from the Pyrrhonism of French Romanticism."[235]

Ion Codru Drăguşanu, another Transylvanian who moved to the principalities during the same period, makes similar remarks in a discourse à la Maiorescu. Sometimes the "form without substance" is revealed by a comparison: in Paris, for instance, "most of the so-called cultivated Frenchmen have only a smattering of knowledge, just like our people here". At other times the theory grows out of an analysis of the Romanians' own reality: "In our society", writes the Transylvanian pilgrim, "some mere vain smattering passes for sound learning; instead of good breeding we have complete corruption, instead of morality reigns despondency and dissolution, instead of true religion we encounter deep superstition".[236] The village schools in Wallachia[237] look rather chic, with their small neo-classical gables, "yet it only looks good from the outside, while inside, God forbid, there is no real teacher, for some are only now being trained to become such, and painful is the process".[238]

There are two main "forms without substance" that Ion Codru Drăgușanu attributes to Romanian society, both reminders of a tradition that can be traced back to the most authentic Transylvanian Enlightenment.

One of them is based on the distinction between "learning", that is, the mere accumulation of information, of secondary importance, and "growth", that is, moral development. "Learning" is the form, "growth" the substance; needless to say, the former predominates with the Romanians when it is not entirely absent, which means that sometimes the Romanians are deprived of both the form and the educational content of a modern type of development. Here is how Codru Drăgușanu defines the two notions: "The growth of man is the development of the noblest sentiments ever, it should have as fundament religion, which shows man the principle and aim of his life, and as basis the eternal morals and the happiness of humanity. Growth is man's primary concern, learning only comes second; the one works within the heart, and the heart makes us men-lovers; the other works within the mind, and the mind is prone to stray."[239]

Obviously, the phenomena that are closely linked to the process of modernisation, such as the secularisation of education or the growing withdrawal of the church from public life[240], already noticeable during the Enlightenment, were liable to nourish (by way of reaction) resentments to such morally wanting "learning"—a true obsession of the *Aufklärung* in general and of Transylvanian pedagogical thinking in particular[241], from Bojincă[242] to Iosif Many[243]. It would eventually come to stand theoretical trial as one of the "forms without substance" that arose under the impact of a hasty modernisation that tried to make up the ground of the Romanians' painful belatedness.

Closely related to what has been said above, the second form without substance tackled by Codru Drăgușanu has to do with religion and the church—which he criticises in extremely severe terms. The church in Wallachia, he writes, is "so decayed that no one finds it in his heart to respect it".[244] Like the faith of the inhabitants (who, instead of "true religion" practice but "deep superstition"[245]), the church itself is nothing but a form without substance, an institution that no longer serves its true ends: "Behold the Pharisees who only clean the outside of the glass, while within lies materialism and dirty, deep-seated hypocrisy."[246]

This criticism of the church is not a new theme, and it is quite surprising to see how texts so widely separated both chronologically and from the point of view of intellectual formation, anticipate Drăgușanu's conclusions. Stoica de Hațeg writes in 1830: "We build churches yet we do not attend masses, we put up crosses yet we do not pray, we paint the face of tombs and offer our names and the memory of our dead to the altar yet set no *coliva* [funeral wheat porridge] before it."[247] The motif of the Romanians' superficial religiosity, alive solely to formal superstitions, and rigorously so, while deprived of any deep moral-Christian basis, was not only a peak of self-denigrating virulence (we are not even true Christians!) but also a frequent idea of the Enlightenment, yet another source nourishing the tradition of a form without substance.[248]

Another theme illustrating the theory in question is that of the "corrupted youth", of the improper moral and intellectual formation of the young generation who only embrace modernity for its vices, debauchery and moral corruption. The "flabbiness", apathy and lack of energy of the young prematurely grown old (images to be later given synthetic and most eloquent expression in Eminescu's poetry) round off the picture of this decadent youth, marred by modern education.

In his *Gypsiad*, Budai-Deleanu clearly anticipates the idea, along the very lines of the later satires of Eminescu, Junimea's favourite poet. Contrary to the young men of the times of the Wallachian voivode, who cultivated military virtues and prowess, today's *coconași* [sons of boyars] are but emasculated puppets:

> A flabby heart is all our young men's treasure,
> Who of their learning won't employ a word
> But only mind their daily search for pleasure,
> While in great terror they behold the sword.
> On pillows they would rather lie all day,
> Or in distractions and indulgence stray!(...)
> In ornaments and fair attires
> Brighter than any woman's garbs
> They pleasure take and all might tires,
> Or in the wasteful play of cards.
> These all are sapping our graceful young,
> The sons of this our most dear land![249]

One noteworthy detail in these lines is the effeminate, almost hermaphrodite nature of the young men described: it is known that imaginary bisexuality, the confusion of the sexes and, generally speaking, the crisis of masculine identity are familiar effects of the shock of modernity.[250]

The motif of "corrupted youth" is analysed at length and in detail by Ion Codru Drăgușanu:

> The wealthy boyars have lately taken to sending their young to academies in France, thence they come back in two or three years, dressed up in the latest fashion, with no more than a twisted idea of what their traditional customs are and morally corrupted by the most degrading of societies, Paris. With all this, they then fill the best of the Bucharest salons. It is not that in Paris or in France everyone is given to wantonness, but our youth will not care about the sound society of the family, they only look for lecherous distractions, wherever they may be found.[251]

The really significant concept here is that holding that evil comes from France. Corruption, debauchery, superficial education associated with atheism or the devastating revolution—in fact modernity as a whole, with all the traps it might keep in reserve—spring from the malefic source of this capital of modern civilisation and Slough of Despond called Paris. In fact, the vicinity of France and of Frenchman with the principle of Evil, often spiced with the immorality and vice they connote, such as, for instance, the "French disease" (syphilis) or "French love", is a well-articulated image of traditional Romanian mentality, also present at the level of peasant society.[252] The critical attack on France launched as a criticism of (superficial) modernity is thus able to incorporate clichés pertaining to a much older ethnic image.

The corruption of Romanian young by means of a Paris-based education is, in the case of Codru Drăgușanu, all the more relevant a motif as the pilgrim was known to be a close friend and admirer of France[253], which makes his critical appreciation strike a different note from that of a Florian Aaron or Ioan Maiorescu. Drăgușanu's attitude is apparent in the way (at variance, one might say, with the common perception of France from a Transylvanian perspective) in which he explains the moral degradation of the young students who had direct experience of the Hexagon: France does not carry the seed of corruption at its very core; what is more, its society is no more degraded than others; it is simply that Romanian youths tend to take over only the bad aspects of the French model.

In fact, we are led to understand, at stake is merely one of the negative aspects deriving from the ambiguous nature of modern civilisation, which for the Romanian imaginary was so significantly epitomised by the French model. Modernity brings with it the triumph of positive values, yet at the same time has in store numerous dangers and anti-values, hence the permanent need to keep an alert and critical eye on its developments. Superficial modernisation, devoid of adequate content (content that should have been the moral basis for the education of the Romanian young), is a "form without substance" that receives, as the Transylvanian intellectuals have it, perfectly relevant illustration in the model of the completely inadequate assimilation of certain elements of French civilisation into Romanian culture. The further step to be taken was the conceptual systematisation that would propose the "healthy" organic model of German culture, of which Titu Maiorescu was so fond, or to give theoretical ground, as Blaga would, to the differences between the superficiality of the "modelling" French influence and the fecund "catalytic" German one.[254]

The much-debated issue of a mimetic taking over of foreign surface forms that can only falsify the original foundations of autochthonous culture posits the question of the rapport between specificity, tradition and originality on the one hand, and, on the other, modernisation, innovation and opening towards the values of others. Given the obvious fragility of the traditions of a national culture that was then just about to acquire a taste of modernity, criticism of the borrowed modernising elements often had a bearing on another area, where tradition could not be debated: language. True, here too the adepts of accelerated modernisation could well maintain that neither was the Romanian idiom entitled to claim a longer and more solid tradition as language supporting a major culture. Up until that moment it had been used mainly as a mere tool of day-to-day communication by the lower classes, which made its enrichment and radical transformation absolutely necessary so that it could become the proper vehicle for science and high culture or for refined and cultured conversation to be used by the national élites.[255]

Nevertheless, the Transylvanian intellectuals declared themselves determined champions of the preservation of language specificity, on account of the fact that it was the carrier of a specific "genius". On the other hand, however, most of them did find it in themselves to re-create an altogether artificial language, one over-saturated with Latinate terms and expressions, while being strongly persuaded that the result could not but be the long sought for linguistic originality of some pristine times. "When it comes to language, everyone would be a tailor", writes Ion Maiorescu in a 1838 article. "They smooth it and they comb it, until the skin is peeled off it; then they give it another skin to try on. As with the language, so with the poor Romanian. Him, too, they would like to make thinner and fitter for new clothes, following the fashion of European civilisation, until he becomes a funny patchwork in which there is no trace left of his originality."[256] Timotei Cipariu uses similar terms in a letter to Bariţ of the same year: "Whatever they might think, a language such as ours is much too original and profound for any pompous tailor to come and dress it as he will... Until we stop looking up to other, foreign languages and taking them as models without searching well into our own language, we'll remain prisoners of this noisy clatter."[257]

Despite his remarkable opening towards, and high appreciation of, the values of universal culture, the reverend from Blaj was insistently in favour of a severe critical filtering of foreign models. He finds it proper and fit that the Romanians take over and imitate valuable elements of foreign cultures, yet only on condition that selective vigilance never be abandoned. Obviously, however, as an adept of the theory of the "forms without substance", he too believes that the Romanians manifest a unique, quite damaging one-sided tendency towards an indiscriminate imitation of the useless trifles they observe in others rather than towards the assimilation of true, substantial values.

In 1846, when praising a Hungarian theatre company, Cipariu wonders: "Why won't the Romanians imitate other nations in this respect? They, who imitate everybody in trifles and with so much obsequiousness."[258] Nine years later he raises similar questions, in a diary that represents his noetic testament:

> Is it not time we shook darkness off the eyes of this mind of ours, which cannot bring itself to see clearly the light of culture bestowed on us today, not by itself? When it comes naturally to man to imitate, how can it be that [we] alone will not rise at least in imitation? I mean imitation of good, noble, heart-strengthening, mind-raising, manly things, not of vain inanities, for these latter neither cultivate nor enlighten, but lead men to despondency, weakness of mind and dissolution.[259]

In 1848 Iosif Many, a colleague of Cipariu's on the editorial staff at the *Teacher of the People*, wrote much to the same effect in addressing his peasant readership: "Do not feel ashamed to learn from another if the occasion so arises. If you know how to read, take now and again a good book and read it, but beware of those damned vain books, wherein lies no good teaching for the bettering of the heart. Do not welcome into your bosom the disorder, folly and frailty of others."[260]

The reasonable compromise between opening towards the values of others and sifting away what was rotten in foreign cultures was the sole solution that these Transylvanian *Aufklärers* of such a balanced and rational cast of mind could possibly imagine. The problem arose when it came to the question of the criteria to be used for a selection of what was acceptable and what was not. Who was to be the infallible judge able to tell right from wrong? As the Transylvanian intellectual generations left the Enlightenment behind and headed towards the Romantic era, the area in which those criteria would be more and more sought for was that of the "specificity" and unmistakable genius of the Romanians' own originality, that is, the realm of imponderables that could never be weighed on the universal and cosmopolitan scales of Reason.[261]

Naturally, orientation within the realm of culture thus became much more difficult. In order to be able to keep faith in values and establish certain reference points, which became harder and harder to find, the Transylvanian scholars tended more and more evidently to embrace the particular: "Let us keep to our own, lest we lose direction." Not even German wisdom was of any use, wrote Codru Drăguşanu, not to mention that they had their shortcomings, too: "We should strive for our own acquisitions, since major science and culture, if foreign, even when coming from the classical well of the German land, is of no use for the Romanians; they should be grown on native soil, for only thus will they bear fruit and be of good consequence for us."[262]

Another theme illustrating the presence of the forms without substance in the social imaginary of the Transylvanian Romanians at the beginning of the modern era is that of the opposition between "culture" and "civilisation", if we are to use the terminology consecrated in the analysis of the Junimist doctrine.[263] Undoubtedly, at the time there were other terms, too, which covered just as well the meanings of the two notions whose references vary and which are sometimes even interchangeable.[264] The term "culture" in particular can also be invested with the negative connotation that makes it equivalent to "civilisation"; equally, "civilisation" can itself be "positive", just like culture. Kogălniceau, for instance, in his well-known introductory course on national history of 1843, also published in Transylvanian periodicals[265], speaks of a civilisation that is "healthy, not superficial like the one we have".[266]

Such lexical imprecision aside, what we agree to call "culture" in a "positive", "healthy" sense, had to contain, in the Transylvanian Romanians' opinion, a moral substance capable of endowing it with value. It could not be extraneous to the religious values and perspective, and was close to such notions as originality, specificity and tradition.

"Civilisation", on the other hand, in its "unhealthy" understanding, was especially identified with the material side of progress and with a superficial modernisation, as was the case, for instance, with sartorial fashion or with certain social conventions. One could speak, in this sense, of the futile, pompous "luxury" that went hand in hand with moral decadence or spiritual shallowness.

"Civilisation" is often associated with the urban lifestyle or with the ways of the élites, that is, with their comfort and lack of authenticity and profundity, while "true" culture was expected to take it upon itself to conquer the mob of commoners not yet exposed to the damages of "civilisation". Obviously, for these belated supporters of the Enlightenment, "culture" had not yet reached the rural area (folk culture remained, in their view, at best a picturesque manifestation yet evidently inferior to major culture). Therefore it was not actually very clear where culture might hide its illustrious face, other than in the golden age of Greek and Roman antiquity—a privileged regressive utopia wherein the Transylvanian intellectuals stored their stock of nostalgia for that true healthy culture of which they dreamt, one too little suited to the circumstances of a mundane and, moreover, modern, world.

The social imaginary of other nations also puzzled at the time over the same questions, as is apparent, for instance, in the fragments from Mickiewicz translated by Iosif Many in Bariţ's *Gazette*.[267] The French, who were the first to enjoy the writings and lectures of the Polish refugee from the Collège de France, were actually on the lookout for such ideal models of the "good savage", untouched by civilisation and civic-minded—imaginary actors who might have paved the way to the democratic and social revolution as the radicals wanted it, or fulfilled the Christian socialist dream of moral revitalisation. The Poles or the Romanians were best for the job, which explains the French interest in their cause.[268]

What the French did not know, however, was that their favourites found themselves, for more or less good reasons, in the same predicament of being subject to civilisation and its corrupting force that stifles true culture, patriotism and the civic virtues. They too were looking for their own substitutes, havens and imaginary models. The fragments translated by Many were meant to offer his fellow countrymen, "grown flabby" with modern commodities and "luxury", a piece of warning that was as valid for them as for the readership along the banks of the Seine.

> I often speak to you that you live among civilised peoples, and thereby you yourselves can acquire a taste of civilisation. Know, however, that those who speak to you about civilisation are themselves unlearned in these matters. The word civilisation means citizenship, from the word *civis*, citizen. And the name of citizen was given to those who sacrificed themselves for the country, like Scaevola, Curtius and Decius, and such sacrifice was called citizenry [...]
> Later, in the vulgar confusion into which the languages had fallen, the word civilisation was used to mean fashionable dress, tasty victuals, comfortable public houses, wide roads and handsome theatre halls. Should now not only the Christian but the Roman pagan too rise from the dead and see what sort of people goes today by the name of civilised folk, they would ask, shaking with rage: What right do these people have to bear the name which comes from the word *civis* (citizen)?[269]

George Bariţ is of the same mind as Mickiewicz on the question of the superficial civilisation of material values as cultivated by intellectuals, élites and townsfolk, which he opposes to true culture, which should infiltrate among the "people". What Mickiewicz had called "civilisation" appears in Bariţ as "culture", but the meaning of the terms stays the same: "If you take culture to mean merely fashionable dress for the laity, red girdles for the priests, copious meals and a slothful life, the cultivation of foreign languages and sheer disdain for the national language [...], then you are only right in saying we are running away from the people so that they will never be able to catch up with us, but God save them if they never do."[270]

A telling similarity between the two texts is not only the recurrence of elements meant to illustrate the superficial nature of the "civilisation" or "culture" under attack (modern dress and excessive nourishment), but also the direct address ("you", "I speak to you"), the almost prophetic tone, meant to challenge and show the light to a crowd that has lost its way and is groping about, dazzled by the sham wonders of modern civilisation that can only lead it to destruction.

Ioan Maiorescu and Timotei Cipariu are even more trenchant in this respect. Paradoxically, they argue, the Romanians have taken over what is bad in modern civilisation, that is, the lack of moral foundation, without even enjoying the material advantages that usually trigger such corruption and decay. Maiorescu writes: "The weaknesses other peoples fell into at the end of the road and with full gorges, are with us from the first steps and on an empty stomach ."[271] Cipariu, in his turn, situates his discourse in the space of the regressive utopia of republican Rome: "Rome, before lapsing into barbarity, was a noble spirit and master over the whole world; both culture and ill feelings came to it with the Greek feuds. We are still barbarians, O how desperately so!", but we have managed to combine what had been worst in "the Romans' barbarity and the Greeks' vices". Faced with such a catastrophe, Cipariu's conclusion, although expressed in anger (as is evident in the modal form of his phrase), rejects not only civilisation, which contradicts culture, but culture itself, because it contradicts a natural state that may be the happier choice, since the human being is not yet unnaturally spoiled: "Therefore, we could say, together with Rousseau, that all culture can do is spoil humankind."[272]

On the other hand, the idea that the Romanians had had their moral core corrupted by the superficial glamour of modern civilisation, for all its (anyway doubtful) applicability in the case of some élites such as the Moldavian–Wallachian boyars, found its own adversaries who could bring evidence to the contrary.

The author of a moralising brochure called *Theological Teachings*, published in Sibiu in 1820, claims that there is nothing to worry about in this respect: "This booklet is a conversation I mean to engage in with my Romanians, so I will have no business arguing, alongside other moralists, against the fashions, the luxury and pomp in dress, for that fastidiousness never concerned the Romanians as it did the townsfolk of other nationalities."[273]

In 1848 the vice-prefect Prodan Probul wrote an appeal to the Hungarian citizens of Aiud in which he presents the revolution as a dispute between the Hungarian townsfolk and the Romanian peasants. He shows that, in case of a conflict, the latter, by virtue of their traditional lifestyle, can very easily do without any contact with the urban civilisation of the former, and can thus deprive them of a number of facilities:

> If the citizens of the towns so hate the new citizens that they chase them away and know nothing of them, then the representatives of the people are themselves forced to reject the townsfolk, which means they will not carry any merchandise to the town, nor materials, wood for tools, or fire wood, nor will they lend their cattle for carting, or put their grains on the market, etc. [...] The Romanian nation has no use of such imaginary needs as the pomp, luxury and fastidious tricks of the town, and so they can well stay at home.[274]

In exchange, were understanding and harmony to be achieved by means of a civic and political integration of the Romanians, with equal rights within the constitutional organism, they would align themselves to the co-ordinates of modern civilisation and enjoy its material facilities, for the common good of the whole Transylvania:

> If she is granted the civic rights prescribed by the union, which, I must confess, she [the Romanian nation] will buy whatever the price, there will be no more poverty and weakness; you cannot imagine how fond the Romanian people is of what is good and beautiful; were they rich and rid of the rags they're wearing now, could they not bring, given their number, more profit than what a mere bunch of the former nobles made? And then, Transylvania would be able to show the world a handsome trading route along the Mureș river.[275]

That Aiud would eventually be set on fire and pillaged by Prodan's peasant guerrillas in the tragic circumstances of the civil war is nevertheless one evidence of the difficulties that had to be surpassed in the attempt to place the Transylvanians on modern tracks, of the discrepancies between intentions and actual possibilities, not only at the level of imaginary projections, but of silent and impersonal relationships as well.

All the same, as compared with the above-mentioned exceptions that arise to contradict the idea of the Romanians being corrupted by urban luxury and civilisation, the more prominent tendency, which had more advocates and a larger audience, was the one in tune with the general tenets of the "forms without substance" theory.

In 1853 the national poet of the moment made the very future of the Romanians and the possibilities for progress of their country look as if they depended, in symbolic terms, on the abandonment of the futile luxury of shallow appearances, on the discovery of that miraculous filter—happy, if intangible, illusion—that might allow the Romanians to sift out of the plethora of elements and models of modern civilisation only what was good and valuable:

> Like shaky leaves will shrewd treason fall,
> With all its vainglory and gaudy apparel,
> Then, dear Romania, the bell will toll,
> With good taste and wit to stop your quarrel![276]

Mureşanu's lines are a suggestive illustration of that obsessive and chimerical search for the Essential Criteria that might do away with the "forms without substance"—a central illusion to the self-image of the Transylvanian Romanians at the beginning of the modern age that was passed on to the generations after them. In fact, obsessions aside, it might have become apparent that, in comparison with the deplorable state of the nation, a worse variant was not even possible, all the more so as that alternative for development was represented by the Western type of civilisation. Irrespective of any model, formula or method, the essential concern should have been direct confrontation with reality and a concerted will to surpass the present situation in order to reach the aim as soon as possible. The Transylvanian intellectuals did not lack that will. But the accelerated modernisation (or the mere "threat" of it), reshuffling the structures of a rural, patriarchal and conservative society, was prone to shock the body of ideological constructions and imaginary projections into powerful cultural reactions, among the expressions of which the "forms without substance" theory was only one instance.[277]

Such theoretical reactions, such permanent hair-splitting, the sick fear that the Romanians might lose their specificity by coming into contact with the modern civilisation that corrupts "minor" cultures, their "wavering", the sophistries and projects of the "original democracies" would keep on adding, as they do to this day, a poisonous touch to the Romanians' tedious and interminable transitions to modernity.

The Unhappy Lot of the Romanians

In the absence of a deep-running process of self-definition, or of substitution myths able to provide a good, even if illusory, balance to the affective stratum, the insistence laid on the negative dimension of the self-image, in conjunction with a burdening history and reality, ran the risk of engendering a tragic, unhappy self-consciousness, as well as the painful assuming of that condition.[278]

Many texts provide a convincing illustration of that idea: the Romanian's lot is to suffer and be miserable. Papiu Ilarian, for instance, places the whole of Romanian history, once again a worthy continuation of its Roman ancestors, under the sign of the famous Latin dictum: *et facere et pati fortia romanum est*. While the original meaning of Mucius Scaevola's adage laid special emphasis on the stoic virtues of patience and manly forbearance—a way, ultimately, to serenity—the Transylvanian Romanians' understanding of it mainly focuses on unmotivated suffering, stamped onto the Romanians as a curse of their existential condition. "One of our historians likened our history to a tragedy", wrote Papiu.[279] "Painful as it might have been to him, he was only right in saying that. Indeed, from the beginning to this day, it is, truly, a history of our passions."[280]

Naturally, for the young and militant historian, whose father had just been executed during the civil war by a Hungarian extraordinary court[281] (that being only one instance in a long series of tragedies and horrors), the formula of the unhappy lot of the Romanians was reinforced by the recent impact of the disasters of the revolution. The image, with its strong emotional overtones, was bound to impress his mind.

Ioan Buteanu, who was to end up on Hatvani's gallows as well, expresses the same idea in February 1849: "I believed that the lot of the Romanian was to suffer and, as a man, I decided to take it all with endurance."[282] Similarly, in December 1848, Bishop Şaguna painted the frightening picture of the civil war and its atrocities with the intention of capturing in its violent brushstrokes, just as in the drawings of Goya[283], the unhappy fate of Transylvania and particularly of the Romanian people:

> In my loneliness, my heart was bleeding and my eyes were shedding bitter tears over the dire situation of our country and of the peoples living in it [...] My mind went out to my nation, so persecuted by our enemies, to its pillaged and burnt villages, to the ravished churches and their blemished chalices, and to those many brothers of mine, both lay and holy faces, who were sentenced to a cruel death and now lie forgotten in fields and on roadsides.[284]

Identical tableaux are sketched in Andrei Mureşanu's poetry—certainly a reminder of cruel realities, but also an indication of some recurrent mental clichés, settled in the contemporary consciousness:

> Its lovely villages now levelled to the ground
> Are fallen prey to ugly croaking ravens,
> Come from wild deserts and searching every mound
> To feed on crushed corpses, eyes staring at the heavens.[285]

One telling connection is that between the misery-ridden individual fate of the Romanian and the collective destiny of the nation. Papiu, Iancu and Buteanu in 1848, and Moise Nicoară before them, all had individually unhappy lives, but at the same time their fate stands for, and is completely identified with, similar tribulations faced by the national community: "The Romanians' fate, I believe", writes Cipariu in 1838, in a note on the troubles that Eftimie Murgu had to suffer at the hands of his colleagues and the authorities in Bucharest, "is to be forever unhappy, each and every one."[286] Obviously, Murgu's fate was an ideal symbol for Cipariu's partial, if highly expressive, conclusion on the Romanian self-image. Expelled from Wallachia, at odds with the people in Iași, imprisoned by the county authorities before the revolution, "severed" from his fellows in the Pest and Debrecen parliaments during the revolution, imprisoned again by the Austrians afterwards—what else could be more expressive of the Romanians' cruel fate, a people chased all over the world by blind fatality![287]

Although, as we have seen, the revolution was greatly effective in establishing a privileged place for the motif of the Romanians' unhappy lot within the social imaginary, it was not the first to know such imaginary elaboration: the theme had been present before, as part of a self-image embracing the Romanians' age-long oppression as an essential ingredient. The 1791 *Supplex* mentions the "grievances of an afflicted nation" (*afflictae Nationis gravamina*), and the inhabitants of Hodac and Ibănești wrote in 1805 to Bishop Bob that "we live in hapless times and are more forlorn than ever."[288] Greek Catholic priestly administrator Simion Crainic uses similar terms in a letter addressed to the rectors of the Blaj diocese, in which he complains that "we have come, brothers, to live in such hapless times that we behold, through the mist of our tears, how our rights, our privileges and our old dear customs are torn down by wicked hands, reaching out from all sides."[289]

The real issue at stake in such formulations is not a context-bound misfortune suffered in such or such an age, therefore more or less easy to explain, but a consummate fate, a black omen, which operates irrespective of any human will or ability to turn the conditions of existence to some account or other.

Sometimes, such an explanation is able to elucidate everything and absolve the Romanians of any responsibility. According to an 1816 brochure, the darkness in which the Romanians have been dallying so far is not due to "any fault on the part of the Romanians, but to our bad fate who has been ever so zealous to grieve the Romanians and drive them away from the wisdom and glorious deeds of their fathers and make them of a kind with the beasts rather than with human beings".[290]

Timotei Cipariu also speaks of "the relentless fate of the times and circumstances that blew this nation from all sides"[291], and Petre Cermena shows that "the unfair times made it so that our nation [...] has ever been doomed to remain unseen and scorned".[292] Bariț, in his turn, exclaimed in 1842: "Heavenly Father! Do not lead us into temptation, that we believe there is a curse upon our heads."[293] From this perspective, the Romanians' enemies themselves no longer appear as personalised and subjectively turned against them as elsewhere, but as mere instruments of a superior force that impinges upon them in the form of awesome fatality.

It cannot be doubted that the theme in question, with both its meaning and expressions, fulfils a rather symbolic, sometimes even decorative, function, meant as a general explanation and unifying label of the wealth of adversities and catastrophes traversing the Romanians' existence. Since it lends itself so easily to expressive synthesis it was frequently used in poetry as a literary motif holding together numerous poems, lyrical meditations on the theme of the Romanians' unhappy lot. A parallel might seem possible with the *fortuna labilis* theme, specific to baroque poetry, yet such vicinity looks to me rather superficial and hardly valid, although, on the face of it, the latter could also be related to a pessimistic tendency in the perception of the cast of one's age.

There is an obvious relation, however, to the pre-Romantic type of sensibility, one lyrically bent towards elegiac meditations on the theme of oppressive fate—the proper means of expression for the tribulations of a sensitive yet hypertrophied ego, keen on freeing itself from the burden of the contingent and giving itself to the relief of confession.[294]

On the other hand, besides the literary import and conditioning of the motif, it can be much more convincingly explained as a transposition into poetical terms of certain obsessions that functioned at the level of the social imaginary and that undoubtedly tuned in to the poetic canon of the time. Moise Nicoară, for instance, struggles and strives with a literary language completely untrained for that sort of poetry, yet gives evidence, in 1811, of a typical pre-Romantic sensibility[295], of which Romanian literary historiography has made no mention. He gives voice to the theme in his *Cry and Complaint for the Lost Glory of the Romans*:

Dire and boundless, unrelenting fate,
Will you keep chasing me away,
Fearsome doom, before it be too late,
Will you not give us pause and point an open way?[296]

The fate that made the Romanians fall from the greatness of the past is a real "scourge"—yet another instantiation of their stigmatic unhappiness.

Nicoară also illustrates the typical conjunction of individual and national fates, in terms of the collective Romanian predicament:

You! Pitiless fate, companion of mine since my first day,
Are you not yet content with this my plight,
This awful ire that has been my sway
From cradle until now, a vicious bite?[297]

The misfortune that has encroached upon the poet since his earliest infancy has its source in the misfortune and sad lot of his people—a motif that was to know a long career in Romanian lyrical poetry, particularly in its Transylvanian variant, along the Coşbuc–Goga–Cotruş line.

Another pre-Romantic poet, Iosif Many, gives, in 1838, a sketch of a rather uncouth Luciferian revolt[298] against the "god" who allotted the Romanians such an adverse fate ("You, who poured your spite on the Romanians"[299]). It was an anticipation of the much more adroit attempt of Andrei Mureşanu, who, in 1847, wrote the poem *To My Muse*, entirely built on the theme of the Romanians' in-auspicious fate.

In an elaborate staging Mureşanu "reverses" the motif of national misery by asking his muse, with typically Romantic rebellious discontent and painful irony, to imagine another fate for the Romanians, different from the unfair share that had been allotted to them:

> Turn, muse, the odds for just one single day,
> And say there was and is for us a time of joy.
> Shuffle our people's future and redo their sad lot,
> If they bemoan and wail, you tell them they should not!(…)
> Why burden them with woe and poverty and strife,
> Why make them raise their face and ask for their right,
> Can you not see that nature itself will not vouchsafe
> Of its bright gold a share for sons of the same race?(…)
> It smiles on some and they are now of mind sublime,
> It frowns on others and they will fall to darkness cruel,
> Virtue in plenty for the few, but for the rest just brutal crime,
> Who are forever meant to suffer and with the passions fight their duel.[300]

The unrelenting fate giving birth to merciless realities makes any attempt at easing off look ridiculous and utterly impossible. Like the fairy-tale Fates she unfairly, yet unpredictably, shares out virtues and vices to the nations, or, rather, the conditions that might lead to a growth of those features, either negative or positive. For instance, the violence issuing from the lack of moral-Christian education may well throw the Romanians for eternity into the moral "misery" of criminal souls, battered by passions and vices. At stake here is also the Romantic Manichaeism that divides the world into the good and the wicked, the fortunate, endowed with genius and virtue, on the one hand, and the stigma-bearers, the "wretched", gnawed by foul passions, on the other.

Was there no possibility of escaping such steadfast inevitability? At the end of his poem, Mureşanu only makes room for the tiniest spark of hope, a quite doubtful one too, which looks more like a sombre piece of warning on the even darker surprises, in tune with the Romanians' unhappy lot, that the future may have in store for them:

> Hold, muse, your tongue and lie in wait
> For the last minute, whatever it may be,
> For he who is insensitive deserves his fate,
> The sombre death to come, the fatal fee.[301]

This idea is central to the thinking of the Braşov-based poet and journalist and is often present in his articles as well: there certainly is a possibility of bending the adverse fate, of achieving "another fate" for the Romanians, a better one, since human will at its strongest is nevertheless able to shape its own destiny. It is only that the clock is ticking away, that the preordained "fatal minute" of final collapse is drawing menacingly near while the Romanians' efforts and determination to change their fate are too anaemic and unconvincing, a far cry from what they should be. And "he who is insensitive" to the necessity of a collective mustering of forces in order to find the way out of their predicament deserves his lot and should perish.

As usual, Mureşanu's argument seeks to shock his fellow countrymen into shaking off their lethargy and "deadly sleep", which his, as well as his contemporaries', perception attribute to the Romanians' conduct and fate.

The implacable way in which merciless fate strikes the Romanians triggers the idea of an original sin, of a curse they have to expiate. Their lot in the present is therefore a ransom to be paid for the faults of their forefathers. Such a theory is nevertheless fraught with too high a level of ambiguity. On the one hand, it could provide a persuasive explanation for the misfortunes of the Romanians' lives, at least if taken as a metaphor meant to signify the vicissitudes of the past. On the other hand, however, relocating the burden of responsibility for their situation onto the heads of their ancestors could be considered too facile a solution, one which is at variance with the insistent urges based on the idea that it is the Romanians of the present who hold the key to the door out of crisis and their duty to make the necessary effort to find it.

Nevertheless, the expressive motif of the original guilt that accounts for the unhappy lot of the Romanians is clearly noticeable, even though nobody is really specific as to what that guilt might have been. Obviously, the Romantic signature is present here as well, with its sensibilities and typical way of thinking. The children are doomed to suffer for the sins of their fathers—a conception coming in the wake of both the Old Testament and the archaic peasant type of morality.

In the poem *The Voice of a Romanian*, Andrei Mureşanu depicts once again a Luciferian revolt against the destined grievance of that burdening original sin: "Heavenly Father, I humbly raise my eyes to You, / Yet vain my prayer is and a sad waste my sighs", the poet complains; the lament gradually turns into violent reproach:

> Maybe our fathers buried themselves in crime;
> But how can old evils resound, through time, in us?
> If that be true, the sons of a serf's line
> Should be born blind, their lives not worth a fuss.
> You say that sins at last shall be forgiven,
> Not weighed and searched, and not unjustly given
> From man to son; but now behold the hurt and pain
> Slipped down through ages, in erring preordained.[302]

There is an undertone reference here to an older tradition that identifies the source of the original sin in a way that leaves little occasion for Romanian self-esteem. Consequently, the covered reference to that tradition detectable in Mureşanu's poem looks somewhat disconcerting. The line mentioning the ancestors who "maybe" "buried themselves in crime" evokes the reason why (according to the view of the nobility) the peasants (i.e., in subsequent interpretations, the Romanians) were initially forced into the perpetual bondage of serfdom. As both Werbőczy's legislation[303] and a whole justificatory tradition associated with it maintain, the eternal bondage of the "infidel rustics" was but a punishment for the crimes they had committed during Dózsa's time and, before that, at Bobilna, and then periodically re-enacted, as, for instance, at the time of Mihai the Brave's coming to Transylvania or during Horea's mutiny. "Think that the serfdom you are now rid of", writes Bishop Lemeny in 1848 in a circular letter, urging his flock to obey the law, the authorities and the recruitment rules, "followed from your fathers' deeds, when they refused to protect the country and rose against the rulers of the land. And now our concern is that you do not rise again and resist, for then they might silence you by force of guns, which would be a greater damage than the first."[304]

According to this image, therefore, medieval serfdom was justified not only economically, but also morally, both as a punishment for an original sin and as a warning and practical measure, meant to prevent the eventual repetition of such blood-shedding conflicts. As the peasants would come to be identified, essentially, with the Romanians, not only from the point of view of the Hungarians but also of the Romanians who shared the Romantic conception of the nation, the imaginary elaboration of the theme would associate that typically medieval social pact with the national condition, with the might of a curse grafted onto the defining structures of Romanian fate.[305]

Of course, Romanian Romantics condemned the anachronism of serfdom from the point of view of the exigencies of their time; radicals like Papiu impugn it vehemently, in all its instances throughout history, starting from Werbőczy (while in Wallachia, Bălcescu will never forgive Mihai the Brave himself for binding the "Rumanians" in serfdom; the identification Romanian = serf is operative here as well).[306] Those more indebted to the heritage of Transylvanian *Aufklärung*, like Mureşanu, were nevertheless more moderate and sensitive to social distance: although they could not approve of serfdom either, they recognised the historical bases of the phenomenon and accepted it somehow (exclusively as far as the medieval period went) as a fatality pointing out the ways of a less fortunate world and time. Now, the same intellectuals thought, given the altogether different conditions, it was indeed absolutely necessary that serfdom be abolished, even if the pessimism inherent in motifs such as the Romanians' unhappy lot or their original sin, as illustrated by Mureşanu, were indicative of the hard time they had in finding a way out of this plight, largely due to their own reluctance, too.[307]

Irrespective of the concrete sphere in which it could be placed, which was usually overlooked (except for identifications such as that suggested by Mureşanu), the original sin operated somewhat destructively by discouraging any effort to better the Romanians' present fate. In 1855 Simion Balint wrote to Iosif Hodoş, who had previously confessed his inner turmoil as to the unfortunate destiny of the nation: "To no end are you troubling yourself with the fate of the nation; leave it, don't wrack your brains with it, for no help is possible *de praesenti*; the time will surely come for you to help them as you can, but for now maybe they still have ancient sins to expiate."[308] The inevitable stigma of the ancestral sin could thus function as glib justification of the easy way out: the inactive contemplation of the national catastrophe, which was not yet to see the day of its final expiation. Obviously, from a different point of view, the position of the priest from Roşia Montana could be interpreted as a mere proof of realism.

An eloquent expression of the motif of an original sin is to be met with in Ion Codru Drăgușanu. Like Andrei Mureșanu, the pilgrim from Făgăraș calls upon divine justice—the actual authority with the power to expiate the Romanians' collective guilt and bring about the ultimate ending of a destiny which it is not clear whether or not they deserve:

> When is it [Lord,] that we will see the day of final expiation for our ancient sins? How many generations will still endure Your wrath? Your word was, Lord, "I will punish wickedness up to the fourth generation, and bless piety up to the thousandth!" Have mercy, Heavenly Father, have mercy for we have had seventeen centuries of pain and woe! Have mercy at last, give us Your blessing up to the fourth generation and no more, and then, if we do not deserve Your grace, punish us again up to the thousandth, and humbly will we proclaim Your justice, to the end of time.[309]

Although more confident than Mureșanu as to a possible improvement in the Romanians' lives, Drăgușanu is equally careful to give the same warning: If the Romanians do not fully meet the exigencies conducive to the ending of the crisis, they will get what they deserve—misery now and forever!

The source of the original curse may be identified, in some cases, in a somewhat neutral historical circumstance, that is, the Romanians having deserted their original land of ancient Italy and Rome. Abandonment in the midst of barbarian peoples, severance of bonds with the primitive hearth of the autochthonous civilisation equalling a desertion of the divine protectors of house and family who ensured the tradition of the Romanians' forefathers—all these functioned as both cause and form of manifestation of the Romanians' unhappy lot and original sin. Contrary to their Italian brothers, for instance, who were to enjoy a happier fate, the Romanians were punished by having to remain separated from the cradle of their origins and be exiled like Ovid to the Black Sea, thrown into a northern, cold and hostile world.

The motif is present in accounts by numerous Transylvanian travellers to Italy (from the master-minds of the Transylvanian School to Cipariu, Papiu, Bărnuțiu, Hodoș, Laurian or Codru Drăgușanu)[310], as well as in the pre-Romantic verse of Nicolae Pauleti[311] or Iosif Many, who bitterly lament over the inauspicious fate that abandoned the Romanians on these cold shores, trodden by barbarians. It is no surprise, then, that frequent translations were made at the time from Ovid[312]— an ideal symbol, the man whose personal drama appeared as a perfect embodiment of the unhappy lot reserved for a whole branch of the Latin race. Pauleti tackles the theme in diatribes ("You, Romanian people, you leaf blown away by the wind of cruel fate"[313]), while Simion Balint addresses an emotional request to Papiu Ilarian, who was then completing his studies in Italy, that he "make known to those people this branch of their kin, broken and carried away on the world's waves".[314]

Papiu would even attempt, in his *History*, a "scientific" explanation (as far as "scientific" goes in the Romantic conception, certainly) of the "Romanians' sinister fate", to be blamed on the curse that made of Trajan's Dacia, beginning in 274, "a prey to the barbarians' fury". "Hereupon", he writes, "began the Romanians' fatalities in all things [...] which have never ceased, not to this day."[315]

Like any other element of the self-image, the motif of the Romanians' un-happy lot can be instrumentalised with a view to justifying, in symbolic terms, any political or cultural tendency. In 1848, for instance, it is invoked both by the ad-epts of the anti-unionist and pro-imperial attitude, who summon the Romanians to come to Blaj or else "you will remain as unhappy as you have ever been"[316], and by the adepts of the Hungarian cause, such as Bishop Lemeny, who, on the con-trary, urges his fellow countrymen to stay at home and submit to the authorities, for identical reasons: "Lest you should bring to your people, instead of joy, the last wreckage"[317]—an allusion to the "first wreckage", that is, the original sin that threw them into the bondage of serfdom, due to similar conduct of violence and law-breaking.

Bărnuţiu, in his turn, wrote a manifesto in November 1848, which he signed as head of the National Pro-Habsburg Committee, in which he urges the Romani-ans to avoid the useless violence and excess of which they are held guilty, since such behaviour can only bring them "a still greater sorrow than what you've been facing so far".[318] The telling thing in such stance taking is the form in which a warning is addressed to those who will not abide by the rule of conduct suggested by their leaders: should they keep to their improper ways they will fall lower than before, they will fare much worse than they have already become accustomed to. The burdening threat of this destiny must have been a pregnant element of the self-image of the nation, particularly at such troubled times, if its mere invocation could function as an argument able both to ensure symbolic legitimacy and inflict pressure on collective conduct.

However, as we have seen, a change for the better in the Romanians' fate re-mained an open possibility, if certain circumstances were fulfilled. "Now or never, set your fate aright"[319] was an explicit urge in that direction, even though it also, and just as clearly, pointed out, warningly, that defeat was possible and disastrous: should the Romanians fail to act now, they would never be able to. In spite of re-peated failings, deferrals and fresh beginnings in their attempt to set things aright, national culture would never tire of recalling Mureşanu's poem as one of its fa-vourite symbols, probably due to the spark of hope to be detected in the cadenced flashing of its lines—a promise which the inner balance of a consciousness ani-mated rather by torments and obsessions than by rational analyses and projections needed so badly.

Much confidence was placed in around 1840 in the possibility of abandoning the fatalistic and discouraging belief in bad omens and a hostile fate, now, in the new age of reason, progress and modernity. Here is Nicolae Pauleti: "Be no more fearful of omens, their song is long a bygone."[320] The motif of the dawning of a new era, emerging from the sign of fatefulness and heading towards a "rebirth" and an "awakening", offers an encouraging counterpoint to the depressing theme of implacable fate. The idea of a bright new day is also present in Mureşanu's po-ems:

> There is no final bell for such a race of glory,
> A mother of great heroes for times and times on end.
> If so far ills and wrongs are woven in her story,
> The time will come for Heaven to smile on her again.[321]

Divine grace may wipe out the original sin, on condition that the sinful repent and find the right path, which gives the poet occasion to soothe his Luciferian revolt:

When You behold, good Father, a people so forsaken
Kneeling in humble prayer, You won't abandon him!
You're just and seeing in the repentant a candid faith awaken,
In Your kind gracious mercy, You will forgive the sin.[322]

In another poem, of 1848, Mureşanu writes that despite all the misfortunes that have befallen the Romanians and that are still working their spell, the Romanians will not lose faith in the ultimate justice of divine providence:

Nor is our people fallen
A prey to black despair,
From Heaven and a truthful heart
He still hopes for repair.[323]

The poet's admonitions, elaborated in the thick of the disasters of the civil war, are now meant to stimulate faith in a promising future:

We did not perish when there was no hope for light,
When raging was our thirst for dear freedom bright,
Now, tyranny defeated and struggling in sharp pain,
Your day has dawned, brave brother, to rise and shine again.[324]

Leaving aside such oscillation, meant to counterbalance a burdensome confrontation with the tragic conditions of an unfortunate fate, one can assert, by way of conclusion, that within their self-image the theme of the Romanians' unpropitious fortune, either by itself or in conjunction with its reverse, plays a mock-compensating and self-deluding role, at variance with any sort of rational analysis in the face of painful realities. The failed attempts they have made so far to come out of the mire are thus "explained" away, absolved and put between parentheses, while responsibility is laid on that force that exceeds human will, that implacable fate they could not possibly counteract and that has thrown them into their present location, state and position. To the extent that they are willing to avoid such fatalism as is inevitable once that theory is embraced, the Transylvanian intellectuals try to inculcate the belief that the tables can be turned. At the same time, they warn that to achieve this demands an extraordinary effort and will on the part of the whole nation, a human intervention in the course of history that is deliberate and rationally planned, and more determination than has ever been shown in any previous attempt.

NOTES

1 1.2:*Journal for the Mind*, II, 1839, p. 69.

2 2:Cioran 1993, pp. 71–72; other editions, *princeps*: Bucharest, Vremea, 1936; Bucharest, Vremea, 1941; Bucharest, Humanitas, 1990.

3 Theorised in 3:Lessing 1930.

4 3:Pițu 1991, pp. 17–23.

5 3:Antohi 1994, pp. 208–285. I feel bound to salute Sorin Antohi's effort in founding the study of Romanian identity on the basis of a first-rate bibliography, offering thus both a theoretical horizon that Romanian research in the field has lacked almost entirely, and a series of impressively intelligent practical applications. I owe a lot to the suggestions and references offered with generosity in his studies.

6 I will reproduce here some of the elements of the theory of the stigma, as they are synthesised in 3:Antohi 1994, pp. 224–238, starting from Erving Goffman's ground-breaking study (3:Goffman 1963): "The patterns of social interaction within consecrated frames make it so that our behaviour in front of persons of our acquaintance does not require special concentration. Acquaintance produces an anticipated alterity, so that the stranger/foreigner is welcomed into a 'structure of expectation' that has pre-established the categories within which he can be perceived. These anticipated co-ordinates of the Other usually turn into normative expectations, which unconsciously build up a virtual social identity. Real social contacts may bring to light certain attributes of the Other that differentiate him from the profile/category we used in order to have a representation of him. If this attribute is a negative one, if it has a (potentially) negative effect on the social relationship, if it diverges from the anticipatory/normative stereotype, then we can speak of stigma. Therefore, the stigma is 'a special sort of discrepancy between the virtual and the actual social identities' [...] Manipulation of the stigma is a current phenomenon of any society, a process that occurs wherever there are identity-formation norms. Both 'normal people' and the stigmatised (ultimately, these are interchangeable roles) take part in the definition and upholding of the social constructs associated with identity, and we might say that theirs is a somewhat accomplice-like sort of participation [...]: the most spectacular common element is precisely the individual's art of taking strategic control over self-images and their products, which the others are likely to use [...] We are not talking of two opposed series of actual individuals, the stigmatised and the 'normal', but of a complex and ubiquitous social process in which any individual plays both roles, at least for a short while, under given circumstances: 'the normal and the stigmatised are not persons, but perspectives'."

7 1.4:Bojincă 1828, p. VI; 1.9:Bojincă 1978, p. 9.

8 George Bariț, "Foreign Literature for the Romanians", in 1.2:*Journal for the Mind*, VIII, 1845, no. 48, p. 383.

9 Timotei Cipariu, "Principles of language and writing", in 1.2:*The Mouthpiece*, II, 1848, no. 56, p. 314.

10 Certainly, the motif of the lamentation may be connected to much more widespread themes, such as the lost Paradise, the Ecclesiastes' lament, or the baroque motifs of the *fortuna labilis* type, all well represented in old Romanian literature, especially in the seventeenth century. Cioran goes as far as relating what he thinks is the Romanians' fatalistic spirit to the tradition of the lament (of the chorus) in Greek tragedy as it was known in the Balkan space (2:Cioran 1956; 3:Antohi 1994, p. 272). Obviously, such considerations are too general for an applied study, which, from the point of view of methodological exigency, cannot afford to reconstitute a tradition except by following a line of literary motifs and afferent mental attitudes that is at least probable, if not provable, at every step.

11 3:Mazilu 1984; 3:Mazilu 1976. For the uncertainty—and lamentation-ridden mental climate—see something of 3:Georgescu 1972, pp. 31–33, but especially 3:Nicoară T. 1990.

12 Gherontie Cotore, *On Those Petty Articles Which Have Caused So Much Grudge*, in 1.9:Comșa 1944, p. 97. For Cotore, see 3:Tóth 1944; 3:*Dictionary 1900, sub voce* (with bibliography).

13 *Ibidem*.

14 There have even been suggestions of echoes from the work of High Steward Constantin Cantacuzino (cf. 3:*Dictionary 1900*, p. 233).

15 Micu actually met Cotore in his youth.

16 Samuil Micu, "The History, Customs and Events of the Romanians", in 1.3:*Calendar Buda I*, 1806, in the annex; 1.9:Fugariu 1983, I, pp. 223–224.

17 See section 8 below, "The unhappy lot of the Romanians".

18 1.5:Papiu Ilarian 1852(II), pp. CII–CIII.

19 See 1.5:Bălcescu/Russo 1850.

20 Samuil Micu, *loc. cit.* (see note 16 above).

21 See 3:Mazilu 1986–1987.

22 1.9:Codru Drăguşanu 1956, p. 272.

23 1.9:Bojincă 1978. p. 105.

24 1.5:Papiu Ilarian 1852(II), p. XXXVIII.

25 1.8:Budai-Deleanu 1974–1975, I, p. 174.

26 *Ibidem.*

27 *Ibidem.*

28 He refers to the fights between the Russians and the Chechens—topical then as it is now.

29 Simion Bărnuţiu, "The Great Synod of the Bishopric of Făgăraş. *Prologus galeatus*", in 1.2:*Journal for the Mind*, VI, 1843, no. 4, pp. 26–29; no. 5, pp. 33–37; also see 1.9:Bogdan-Duică 1924, p. 212.

30 Simion Bărnuţiu to George Bariţ, a letter of 22 December 1842, published in 1.9:Bogdan-Duică 1924, *loc. cit.*

31 Romanian historiography mainly insists on the restrictions imposed on Bariţ or Cipariu by official censorship. However, it should be made clear that equally significant omissions and elisions were due to the self-censorship practised by the journalists of the time, always careful not to step on the toes of the authorities or to upset personal or collective vanities and sensibilities within Romanian society. Bariţ's position as to the political attitude of Bishop Lemeny, whom he will spare even decades after his death (see 3:Bariţ 1994) is one quite telling instance in this sense. As far as the much-debated bishop is concerned, another question of a similar nature would torment the minds of the epoch: to what extent was the charge of homosexuality brought against him (Bărnuţiu was even to take it to the Court) capable of "damaging" the prestige of a nation led by such a pastor? Was it not preferable that the hypocritical veil of discretion be used to save national modesty, as Constantin Alpini, rector of Mediaş, suggests, extremely distressed and ashamed, in a letter? ("Whether the B.(ishop) is a s-t (= sodomite) or not has not been made public so far, it could only have been presupposed by some. I, for one, was not let into this sooner than 1843, by Papp Iosi (= the Blaj-based professor Iosif Pop), whom I did not believe then. So, even if it were true, the thing should not have been brought out into the open, not to mention unveiled in front of the Throne, for much more ill was done and a much greater fuss raised by that indiscreet publication than would have been by keeping silent." See 1.1:Alpini 1845).

32 George Bariţ, "Inquiry into the nature of the soul", in 1.2:*Literary Paper*, I, 1838, no. 5–6.

33 1.9:Bodea 1943, p. 295.

34 Timotei Cipariu to George Bariţ, a letter of July 1838, published in 1.6:*GBC* 1973–1993, IV, p. 137.

35 Ioan Buteanu to Dimitrie Moldovan, a letter of 19 February 1849, published in 1.9:Dragomir 1944–1946, II, p. 73.

36 Ioan Maiorescu to George Bariţ, a letter of August–September 1838, published in 1.6:*GBC* 1973-1993, I, p. 218.

37 In the hyper-optimistic context of the moment, the post-December leader ventured the opinion that it would take at least twenty years for Romania to recover from its disaster; obviously, his allegation stirred a huge wave of indignation. Cf. 3:Mungiu 1995, p. 205.

38 1.9:Codru Drăguşanu 1956, p. 108.

39 Simion Bărnuţiu, "The Great Synod of the Bishopric of Făgăraş" (1842), in 1.9:Bogdan-Duică 1924, p. 214.

40 Andrei Mureşanu, "Introductory. Property (wealth, estate)", in 1.2:*The Gazette*, VIII, 1845, no. 80, p. 318; 1.9:Mureşanu A. 1977, p. 92; 1.9:Mureşanu A. 1988, p. 136.

41 George Bariţ, "A Note from the Letter-dealer", in 1.2:*The Gazette*, XI, 1848, no. 64, p. 268; 1.9:Bodea 1982, II, p. 710.

42 1.9:Codru Drăguşanu 1956, p. 254.

43 Mihail Kogălniceanu, "Speech at the opening of the national history course at the Academia Mihăileană", in 1.2:*Journal for the Mind*, VII, 1844, no. 11–13.

44 *Ibidem, apud* 1.9:Bodea 1982, I, p. 219.

45 1.9:Codru Drăguşanu 1956, pp. 92–93.

46 *Ibidem*, p. 168.

47 *Ibidem*, p. 90.

48 Alexandru Papiu Ilarian to Simion Balint, a letter of April 1853, published in 1.6:Pervain, Chindriş 1972, I, p. 132.

49 1.8:Budai-Deleanu 1974–1975, I, p. 21.

50 Dimitrie Ţichindeal to Moise Nicoară, a letter of 14 August 1816, published in 1.9:Bodea 1943, p. 243.

51 1.5:Papiu Ilarian 1852(II), pp. 96-97.

52 *The Discourse* delivered by Simion Bărnuţiu on 2/14 May 1848 in Blaj Cathedral, published in 1.5:Papiu Ilarian 1852(II) under the title *The Relationships between the Romanians and the Hungarians and the Principles of National Freedom*. See 1.9:*Documents 1848 Transylvania* 1977–1988, IV, p. 12.

53 See note 39 above.

54 Evidently, despite the methodological belatedness of Romanian historiography, it could be said that the terminology and concepts proposed by François Furet (3:Furet 1978), which we have used here, fit exactly the case of the Romanian 1848 revolution as well, whose real signification is thus revealed.

55 If we were to be faithful to our protochronism, we should also note the way in which Alexandru Roman anticipates Erving Goffman's theory of the stigma (see note 6 above), as he discovers, in the terms of the American sociologist, that the stigma is born out of the contrast between the virtual and the actual social realities. Certainly, this would be pushing things too far, since Roman's affirmations are but the result of common-sensical observations, which does not degrade them in any way. On the contrary.

56 The terms Roman uses are absolutely explicit of the stigmatic nature he attributes to the said practice.

57 Alexandru Roman to Alexandru Papiu Ilarian, a letter of August 1851, published in 1.6:Pervain, Chindriş 1972, II, pp. 305–306.

58 *Ibidem*.

59 A.N. (Andrei Mureşanu), "Why we are so late", in 1.2:*Journal for the Mind*, VI, 1843, no. 42, p. 329.

60 Al. Papiu Ilarian, "Preliminaries to *Diorile for the Mind and the Heart*", in *Diorile for the Mind and the Heart* (manuscript journal, Cluj), 1845, no. 1, *apud* 1.9:Papiu Ilarian 1981, p. 44.

61 1.9:Cipariu 1972, pp. 32–33.

62 1.5:Papiu Ilarian 1852(I), p. 195.

63 Samuil Micu, *Historia Daco-Romanorum sive Valachorum* (1778), *apud* 1.9:Fugariu 1983, I, p. 9.

64 1.9:Budai-Deleanu 1991, I, p. 312.

65 1.7:*Memoir August 1848*, in 1.9:Dragomir 1944–1946, II, p. 179.

66 1.2:*The Mouthpiece*, II, 1848, no. 70, pp. 393–394 (transl. from 1.2:*Zeitung*, 1848, no. 116); 1.9:Bodea 1982, I, p. 428.

67 1.5:Papiu Ilarian 1852(I), p. 75.

68 Prince Metternich to Count Sedlnitzky, head of the police, official note of 15 February 1835, published in 1.9:Bodea 1982, I, p. 96.

69 Ioan Faur to Al. Papiu Ilarian, a letter of March 1852, published in 1.6:Pervain, Chindriş 1972, II, p. 127.

70 1.4:Bojincă 1830, p. V; 1.9:Fugariu 1983, II, p. 719.

71 George Bariţ, "From Transylvania. An old worry", in 1.2:*The Gazette*, VI, 1843, no. 40, pp. 157–158; 1.9:Bariţ 1962, pp. 78–80.

72 *Ibidem*.

73 "German Literature", in 1.2:*The Mouthpiece*, I, 1847, no. 3, pp. 11-12.

74 Timotei Cipariu to George Bariț, a letter of March 1848, published in 1.6:*GBC* 1973–1993, IV, p. 299.

75 George Bariț, "From the editors", in 1.2:*The Gazette*, I, 1838, no. 1, pp. 3–4; 1.9:Bariț 1962, p. 47.

76 *Idem*, "Who of our audience reads our papers?", in 1.2:*The Gazette*, XIV, 1851, no. 61, pp. 253–254; 1.9:Bariț 1962, p. 141.

77 The 1791 reply of the Transylvanian Diet to the memoir *Supplex Libellus Valachorum*, published in 1.9:Păcățian 1904, p. 137.

78 1.9:Stoica de Hațeg 1981, p. 60.

79 "Primary Education in France", in 1.2:*The Mouthpiece*, I, 1847, no. 35, p. 189.

80 1.7:*Petition July 1814*, in 1.9:Păcățian 1904, p. 144. See, for the issue of the memoir, 3:Gyémánt 1986, pp. 152–153.

81 See section 7 above, "Forms without substance".

82 1.4:Iorgovici 1799, p. 27; 1.9:Iorgovici 1979, p. 139.

83 1.9:Fugariu 1983, I, p. 234.

84 1.9:Stoica de Hațeg 1981, p. 311.

85 1.7:*Appeal April 1850*, in 1.9:Dragomir 1944–1946, I, p. 195.

86 Ioan Maiorescu to George Bariț, a letter of August 1843, published in 1.6:*GBC* 1973–1993, I, p. 267.

87 1.9:Codru Drăgușanu 1956, p. 101.

88 *Ibidem*, p. 271.

89 *Ibidem*.

90 A.N. (Andrei Mureșanu), "Why we are so late", in 1.2:*Journal for the Mind*, VI, no. 42, p. 330.

91 1.9:Fugariu 1983, I, p. 234.

92 1.7:*Supplex 1791*, in 3:Prodan 1971, pp. 454, 466.

93 1.7:*Petition July 1814*, in 1.9:Păcățian 1904, p. 141.

94 1.7: *Memoire 1846 Rășinari*, in 1.9:Păcățian 1904, p. 167.

95 *Ibidem*, p.166.

96 Moise Nicoară to Ioan Piuariu Molnar, a letter of 1815, published in 1.9:Bodea 1943, p. 33.

97 See 3:Marino 1995, esp. pp. 157–190: "The Romanian 'Lights' and the discovery of Europe"; 3:Bocșan, Duma, Bona 1994, pp. 14–17; 3:Antohi 1994, pp. 254–259.

98 1.9:Cipariu 1972, pp. 32–34.

99 1.9:Fugariu 1983, II, p. 368.

100 1.4:Nicolau 1814–1815, I: "To the Reader!"; 1.9:Fugariu 1983, II, p. 204.

101 1.9:Fugariu 1983, II, p. 218.

102 Obviously, Carcalechi is not a Transylvanian, but the *Romanian Library* was issued in Buda and mainly targeted at the Romanian readership from the Austrian monarchy.

103 Zaharia Carcalechi, "To the Readers", in 1.2:*The Library*, I, 1829; 1.9:Fugariu 1983, II, p. 680. The same ideas could be found in 1.3:*Calendar Buda II* (Carcalechi), 1825: "Review of the *Romanian Library*".

104 1.9:Fugariu 1983, II, p. 680.

105 *Ibidem*, I, pp. 919–920.

106 1.4:Diaconovici-Loga 1821, p. 10.

107 For the image of the Orient and of Africa, see 3:Anghelescu 1975; 3:Radosav 1985. For the theory of *Orientalism*, see 3:Said 1978; 3:Antohi 1994, pp. 216–218, 268–269.

108 For the Transylvanian Romanians' image of America, see 3:Mureșan C. 1982; 3:Mitu S. 1993a (with bibliography); 3:Nicoară S. 1993; 3:Vári 1993.

109 1.9:Mureșanu A. 1977, p. 67.

110 1.2:*The Mouthpiece*, II, 1848, no. 58, p. 323.

111 The last decades of the century will witness a powerful amplification of the Romanians' tendency to relate to extra-European realities, usually "African" ones, both from the point of view of foreign images and of their self-image. See, for instance, the phrase "Romania—Europe's Ethiopia", circulated mainly during the latter part of the Ceaușescu regime, or Ioan Gyuri

Pascu's recent hits (e.g. "Africa—Such a burning dream"), 2:Pascu I.G. 1995. For the identity-wise relationship between Romania and Europe/Africa also see 3:Verdery 1991, chp. I.

112 1.9:Codru Drăgușanu 1956, p. 121.

113 It has also been recently revived by Dan Pavel, see 3:Pavel 1994.

114 Al. Papiu Ilarian, "Preliminaries to *Diorile for the Mind and Heart*", in *Diorile for the Mind and Heart* (manuscript journal, Cluj), 1845, no. 1, *apud* 1.9:Papiu Ilarian 1981, p. 45.

115 An appeal signed by five Romanian deputies to the Hungarian Parliament, addressed to their fellow countrymen, on 24 September 1848, published in 1.9:Dragomir 1944–1946, II, p. 31.

116 1.9:Cipariu 1972, p. 32.

117 See 1.6:*GBC* 1973–1993, IV, pp. 71–308.

118 1.9:Cipariu 1972, p. 29 sqq.

119 Timotei Cipariu to George Bariț, a letter of December 1838, published in 1.6:*GBC* 1973–1993, IV, p. 141.

120 1.9:Cipariu 1972, p. 140.

121 1.1:Cipariu cca. 1846. Cioran conceived of his identity in similar terms when he confessed to being attracted to Hungarian and Gypsy music and to the various virtues attributed to the Hungarians (2:Cioran 1993b, p. 19). The intention to shock is obvious: while, at the time he wrote (1977), the peoples Romanians most despised were the Hungarians and the Gypsies, he professes to liking these two in particular. Similarly, in Cipariu's age, the most scorned ethnic groups were the Gypsies and the Jews. Cioran illustrates yet another fundamental idea for the Romanians' identity relationship with the Gypsies: if it were not for them, the Romanians would really be at the bottom and, in fact, this may happen at any moment (2:Cioran 1993a, p. 74). After 1989, the same identity-defining relationship, with all its labyrinthine intricacies, was beautifully illustrated by the anecdote of the Romanians/Gypsies who ate the swans from the public gardens in Vienna. Even a complete nationalist like Adrian Păunescu cultivates the same paradox in poems like "From station to station" or "Nomad Romania" (2:Păunescu 1993–1994).

122 1.9:Bogdan-Duică 1924, p. 203.

123 See 3:Istrate 1982, pp. 318–351.

124 The motif of "Gypsydom-Heaven" has been beautifully refined into the jewel of "The Small Gypsiad", co-authored by Șerban Foarță and the "Phoenix" band (see 2:*Phoenix*).

125 The idea of the Romanians' off-history existence, for a thousand years by some estimations, has been amply theorised in Blaga's philosophy or Cioran's essays; it has also been turned into re-markable poetry by Blaga. It might not be a mere coincidence that the two are both Transylva-nians and thus the carriers of the "song of our passions", an extension of the self-victimising reading grill the Transylvanians use to read their history and assume an unhappy fate. Also see 3:Pippidi 1993, p. 29; 3:Antohi 1994, p. 213. The relativity of such a perception is demonstrated by its surfacing in other peoples as well. Claudio Magris quotes a witticism attributed to Chan-cellor Kreisky: "'Austria made its exit from history and she is all the happier for it.' Every true inheritor or imitator of the Habsburgs", Magris goes on, "is ill at ease in the great theatre of the world, on the stage of world history, where he was commissioned to play the generalist actor." (3:Magris 1986, chp. IX.)

126 Some observations in 3:Pițu 1991, p. 21; 3:Antohi 1994, p. 54.

127 1.8:Budai-Deleanu 1974–1975, I, p. 7.

128 *Ibidem*, pp. 6–7.

129 See 3:Mitu S. 1991.

130 1.8:Budai-Deleanu 1974–1975, I, p. 5.

131 *Ibidem*, p. 323.

132 *Ibidem*, p. 30.

133 Similarly, today's foreign perception of Romania includes compulsory references to the Roma-nian Gypsies' situation, to the despair of those inhibited by this image.

134 See an account of the state of the Gypsies in the Principalities at the time in 3:Djuvara 1989.

135 Iosif Many, for instance, writes about it for the use of the Hungarian readership as well; see "Moldavia", in 1.2:*Híradó*, 1844, no. 26, pp. 152–153; "A rabszolgák emancipatiója Oláhország-ban" ("The Emancipation of the Gypsy Slaves in Wallachia"), in *ibidem*, 1844, no. 95, pp. 567–568.

136 Timotei Cipariu to George Bariț, a letter of January 1845, published in 1.6:*GBC* 1973–1993, IV, p. 205.

137 1.9:Codru Drăgușanu 1956, p. 104.

138 1.9:Bodea 1943, p. 143.

139 "The Money Lender (A Caricature)", in 1.2:*Journal for the Mind*, VIII, 1845, no. 28–29 (transl. from Nagy Ignác, "Az uzsorás"); "The Melancholy of a Hungarian villager", in 1.2:*The Mouthpiece*, I, 1847, no. 30–33.

140 That, despite the fact that, from a practical point of view, Joseph II had not abolished all restrictions discriminating against the Mosaics, such as, for instance, the interdiction on cross-weddings between Jews and Christians—one of Moise Nicoară's concerns as well. See 3:Carmilly-Weinberger 1994, pp. 81–87; 1.4:*Decree 1786*.

141 Cipariu seems to be ignorant even of the clichés that would have a future—those of the venal Jew merchants and publicans. While in Bucovina, although he finds it rather bothering that the Romanians are being numerically overpowered by the Jews, he thinks that even though "the Jews have taken over all trade and manufacture", at all events, "the truth is that the Jews are lovers of labour, wherever they are, and one can trust them to solve things well and swiftly" (1.1:Cipariu 1850).

142 Eugène Sue, "The sleepless Jew", in 1.2:*Journal for the Mind*, VII, 1844, no. 36; VIII, 1845, no. 2–7.

143 1.9:Comșa 1944, pp. 97–98.

144 1.9:Budai-Deleanu 1974–1975, I, p. 21.

145 *Ibidem*.

146 1.9:Mureșanu A. 1977, p. 91.

147 See "From the statistics drawn up in Transylvania", in 1.2:*The Gazette*, VII, 1844, no. 21, pp. 161–163; "Introductory. Colonisation", in *ibidem*, VIII, 1845, no. 7, pp. 25–26; "Introductory. A new plan for improvement in several branches of the economy of our country", in *ibidem*, VIII, 1845, no. 52, pp. 205–206. Cf. 3:*Ideology of Generation* 1968, pp. 245, 266, 272.

148 Andrei Mureșanu, "A Sigh" (1845), in 1.8:Mureșanu A. 1963, p. 33.

149 *Ibidem*.

150 "A national reply given to Baron Nic. Iojica by the Romanian deputies in the Hungarian Diet", in 1.2:*Journal for the Mind*, XI, 1848, no. 32, pp. 249 sqq.; 1:9.Bodea 1992, II, p. 895.

151 1.7:*Petition January 1850*, in 1.9:Păcățian 1904, p. 642.

152 George Bariț, "The Romanians and Hungarianism", in 1.2:*Journal for the Mind*, V, 1842, no. 9, p. 65 sq.

153 For the inconsistency of theories on "national specificity", as well as for the idea that peoples' "defining features" are, generally speaking, but false clichés and representations of the self and of others, not sociological realities, see 3:Dyserinck 1981; 3:Mitu S. 1993b, p. 95; 3:Heitmann 1985, pp. 13–16. See the same for the persistence of the theory of the "national specificity" in Romanian culture.

154 Ioan Maiorescu to George Bariț, a letter of May 1840, published in 1.6:*GBC* 1973–1993, I, p. 234.

155 Atanasie Șandor to George Bariț, a letter of May 1845, published in *ibidem*, II, p. 300.

156 August Treboniu Laurian to George Bariț, a letter of March 1847, published in *ibidem*, I, p. 127.

157 Atanasie Șandor to George Bariț, a letter of August 1848, published in *ibidem*, II, p. 360.

158 Vasile Pop to George Bariț, a letter of January 1840, published in *ibidem*, V, p. 44.

159 Ioan Maiorescu to George Bariț, a letter of 26 August 1838, published in *ibidem*, I, p. 214.

160 Timotei Cipariu to George Bariț, a letter of 25 June 1847, published in *ibidem*, IV, pp. 292–293.

161 1.9:Codru Drăgușanu 1956, p. 143.

162 Ioan Faur to Al. Papiu Ilarian, a letter of March 1852, published in 1.6:Pervain, Chindriș 1972, II, p. 127.

163 "Oláhország" ("Wallachia"), in 1.2:*Híradó*, 1844, no. 42, pp. 248–249. Also see "Moldavia", in *ibidem*, no. 26, pp. 152–153; "Oláhország", in *ibidem*, no. 59, p. 352.

164 George Bariț, "Souvenirs from my travels. 21 October 1852", in 1.2:*The Gazette*, XV, 1852, no. 85–86, 88, 99; 1.9:Bariț 1962, pp. 153–154.

165 Despite the fact that, at the time (i.e. up until 1859), the said land did not yet even exist on the political map of Europe.

166 1.4:Bojincă 1830, p. 15; 1.9:Bojincă 1978, p. 105.

167 A partial analogy can be suggested with the communist regime under Ceaușescu, undermined from within by the form of nationalism he himself had been encouraging, a form that gave birth to another legitimising ideological reference point that would discard the communist one (see the thesis of Katherine Verdery's book, 3:Verdery 1991).

168 See 3:Netea 1966.

169 See 3:Popa L. 1994.

170 All the same, Cipariu himself was always complaining about the scarcity of funds for the editing of his books; see, for instance, the argument of a letter of 1853, addressed to Iacob Mureșanu (1.1:Cipariu 1853).

171 For the activity of the above-mentioned press, see 3:Veress 1982.

172 See 3:Verdery 1991, chp. I; 3:Bourdieu 1971.

173 See section 2 above, "Cultural backwardness".

174 1.4:Iercovici 1794, "To the reader"; 1.9:Fugariu 1983, I, p. 191.

175 August Treboniu Laurian to George Bariț, a letter of November 1847, published in 1.9:Bodea 1967, pp. 310–311.

176 *Ibidem.*

177 Atanasie Șandor to Al. Papiu Ilarian, a letter of July 1851, published in 1.6:Pervain, Chindriș 1972, II, p. 317.

178 Ioan Maiorescu to George Bariț, a letter of August 1843, published in 1.6:*GBC* 1973–1993, I, p. 267.

179 August Treboniu Laurian to Pavel Vasici, a letter of November 1846, published in 1.9:Bodea 1967, p. 293.

180 George Bariț, "Inquiry into the nature of the soul", in 1.2:*Literary Paper*, I, 1838, no. 6, p. 48.

181 Ardelean Aurelie (= Iosif Many), "Spring song", in 1.2:*Journal for the Mind*, III, 1840, no. 21, p. 168. The song was also "published", with slight differences, in 1.1:*Aurora* 1838–1840, no. 22/1840 (B.A.R., Rom. ms. 460–461, f. 168r–169r). The same "resuscitation" from the lethargic sleep of national idleness is the subject of one of Cipariu's poems, untitled, of 1833–1835 ("The printing house", in 1.8:Cipariu 1976, pp. 87–88).

182 See the poem "I believe", in 1.2:Blandiana 1991, p. 75 ("I believe we are a vegetal people, / What else is there in our placid expectation / For the shedding of leaves?").

183 Ioan Pușcariu to George Bariț, a letter of 26 March 1848, published in 1.9:Bodea 1967, pp. 316–317.

184 For the text of the *Provocation*, see 1.9:*Documents 1848 Transylvania* 1977–1988, I, pp. 90–92; but rather in 1.9:Bărnuțiu 1990, pp. 33–35, 73–76, with a discussion of all variants and a thorough bibliography.

185 For a presentation of the events (yet, obviously, without any highlight on the two leaders' pessimism) see 3:Dragomir 1965, pp. 126–178; 3:Dragomir 1989, pp. 53–96, "Ioan Buteanu, prefect of Zarand between 1848 and 1849".

186 Prefect Petru Dobra to the vice-tribune George Musescu, a letter of 30 March 1849, published in 1.9:Bodea 1982, II, p. 1017.

187 Prefect Ioan Buteanu to Dimitrie Moldovan, a letter of February 1849, published in 1.9:Dragomir 1944–1946, II, p. 74.

188 *Ibidem*, pp. 73–74.

189 *Ibidem*, p. 73.

190 1.9:Bocșan, Leu 1988, pp. 61–62 and *passim*; 3:Neamțu 1988; 3:Bolovan I. 1994, pp. 166–167.

191 Using such terms as "paramilitary corps" or "guerrillas" for the Romanian fighters in 1848 might seem far-fetched in the context of Romanian historiography, although the absolute appropriateness of those terms to the situation in question cannot be doubted. In the language of the time, the term used is *Landsturm*, with the Romanian equivalents "lancers" or "crowds" (organised in legions and their sub-echelons). The term denotes the territorial irregular troops, the "militias" set up by the Austrians starting with the autumn of 1848, formed of Transylvanian Romanians and Saxons. (Obviously, there were plenty of Romanians fighting among the

regular troops, the already existent frontier guard and line regiments, in which there was massive enlisting at the epoch.) Also, paramilitary corps were formed spontaneously, too, for reasons of self-defence, by urban and rural communities, taking as a model the institution of the "national guards" established by the Hungarian revolution. In fact, the setting up of pro-Habsburg irregular troops by the imperial authorities was meant to counteract the similar corps already functioning on the Hungarian side—primarily the national guards in the Transylvanian towns, as well as other irregular troops (*szabad-csapat* = "sniper corps", *önkéntes* = "volunteer" troops, etc.). The term "guerrillas" is particularly appropriate in the case of the corps fighting in the Apuseni mountains, since the tactics used were based on ambush fighting, intercepting communication lines, and swift incursions into areas controlled by the enemy. The Romanian historiography prefers romantic terms, such as "the groups of Moţis (Highlanders)" or "the army of the Romanians". It thus cultivates the idyllic image derived from *Iancu's March* and Bălcescu's accounts, of highlanders sitting around the fire, reading fragments from Lamennais and roasting sheep before cheerfully setting off for the battle camp. In fact, the combatants in question were people who fought in the woods, attacked and looted mountain towns—certainly, as a reply to, to score points in comparison with, the similar operations of the Hungarian paramilitary corps. The notion of "guerrilla" is also accountable for in historical-etymological and comparative terms, since, just like their anti-Napoleonic Spanish homologues, who consecrated the term, these *guerrilleros* of the Apuseni, too, are peasants fighting with rudimentary weapons, sometimes fearsome ones, against a better organised and better equipped foreign occupant, who treats them just as ferociously, with no respect for the usual rules of warfare. Unfortunately, although there are acknowledged studies dedicated to "Iancu's army", authored by generals and superior officers (see 3:Topliceanu, Ucrain 1989), they have not even managed to elucidate these elementary questions of military terminology.

192 See, for instance, a formal letter addressed by Axente Sever to his centurions, dated 20 December 1848, published in 1.9:Dragomir 1944–1946, II, pp. 48–49. We find there that those who "flee from the camp" will be "amerced...twelve zloties" each; those who do not present themselves "lance in hand before their captain" when the bell board is struck "will take twenty-five" (it is not clear whether "twenty-five" refers to zloties too, or to strokes of the rod; in any case, it seems to be an effective solution, since the conclusion is that "this way our poor captain will no longer have to yell all day long before people turn up"); "those who defy all that" will be "marked" so that "they be within reach and ready for military punishment".

193 *Ibidem*, p. 391. The collection of documents published by Silviu Dragomir actually contains hundreds of such confessions telling of like difficulties encountered by the military and civilian "administration" established by the revolution. These are texts that both Dragomir and the other exegetes of the issue have nevertheless almost entirely overlooked. For the Romanian revolutionary administration in Transylvania, see 3:Dragomir 1989, pp. 186–213, "The legions and the prefects" (in apologetic terms). For the same, as considered from the point of view of formal details of a purely administrative nature, see 3:Maior L. 1967 and 3:Maior L. 1972.

194 3:Bariţ 1994, p. 403; 3:*Of Trans. Hist. (II)* 1963, pp. 100. 103.

195 Simion Bărnuţiu, "The Great Synod of the Bishopric of Făgăraş (...)", in 1.9:Bogdan-Duică 1924, p. 214.

196 1.5:Papiu Ilarian 1852(I), p. 224.

197 *Ibidem*, p. 74.

198 1.5:Papiu Ilarian 1852(II), pp. CXV–CXVIII.

199 *Ibidem*, p. CXXXVI.

200 1.5:Papiu Ilarian 1852(I), p. 224.

201 *Apud* 3:Prodan 1971, p. 276.

202 1.9:Fugariu 1983, I, p. 234.

203 *Ibidem*, p. 190.

204 1.9:Codru Drăguşanu 1956, p. 103.

205 A similar theme arising after 1989 is that of the "change of mentality"—the change in the worn-out ways of individuals who keep to their preference for authoritarian control and centralism, despite legislative and institutional liberalisation.

206 1.9:Fugariu 1983, I, p. 190.

207 1.9:Codru Drăgușanu 1956, p. 272.

208 1.9:Fugariu 1983, II, p. 83.

209 1.8:Budai-Deleanu 1974–1975, I, p. 302. Here too, Budai-Deleanu rounds off the debate around the forms of government with a memorable phrase, a familiar dictum of eighteenth-century political reflection, coming down from Montesquieu, and one that is still highly applicable to similar debates of our day: "Where the nation is good, both monarchy and democracy will be good, but when the nation is bad, either one will be as bad." Certainly, the phrase would lose all relevance in the event that the self-stigmatising view on the Romanian condition were abandoned and the ethnocentric and exclusionist self-image altered.

210 1.4:Diaconovici-Loga 1821, pp. 11–12; 1.9:Fugariu 1983, II, p. 565.

211 1.4:Bota 1829, "Foreword".

212 Ibidem, 1.9:Fugariu 1983, II, p. 693.

213 1.4:Carcalechi 1826.

214 Ibidem, pp. 13–14; 1.9:Fugariu 1983, II, pp. 635–636.

215 Andrei Mureșanu, "Why we are so late", in 1.2:Journal for the Mind, VI, 1843, no. 42, pp. 329–331.

216 1.9:Mureșanu A. 1977, p. 34.

217 Ibidem; Andrei Mureșanu, op. cit. (in 1.2:Journal for the Mind), p. 330. In the 1977 edition of Mureșanu's journalistic work, edited by Livia Grămadă, the last sentence is re-tailored in accordance with the exigencies of a censorship that proved extremely touchy as to the image of the Romanian national specificity.

218 In the case of this so-called folk vision, it is actually a question of the image of an image, since the "folklorism" of Romantic extraction distorts from the very beginning, due to its own inherent ideological assumptions, the authenticity of archaic, traditional perspectives. For the role of "folklorism" in the construction of Eastern European national identities, see Claude Karnoouh's remarkable work 3:Karnoouh 1990.

219 Andrei Mureșanu, "The Romanian and music", in 1.2:The Telegraph, I, 1853, no. 61–63; 1.9:Mureșanu A. 1977, p. 151.

220 1.5:Papiu Ilarian 1852(II), p. 105.

221 Vice-Prefect Ioachim Băcilă` to Avram Iancu, a letter of 31 January 1849, published in 1.9:Dragomir 1944–1946, II, p. 220.

222 For the "pre-history" of the theory see 3:Ornea 1975, pp. 166–168, and especially 3:Marino 1995, pp. 191–198, "The History of the 'forms without substance' theory". For the presence of Junimism in Transylvania see 3:Iercoșan 1983 (pp. 26–52, "Pre-Junimist elements").

223 3:Antohi 1994, pp. 24 25; 3:Alexandrescu 1983.

224 See, for instance, 3:Ibrăileanu 1970, pp. 31–61; 3:Lovinescu 1972, pp. 196–197.

225 See 3:Le Rider 1990, chps. I–IV.

226 Ibidem; 3:Lyotard 1979.

227 See 3:Bocșan 1990; 3:Bocșan 1994; 3:Bocșan 1995.

228 See 3:Mitu S. 1992, pp. 11, 20.

229 It has become a general, if paradoxical, rule that modernisation encounters the strongest resistance precisely where it is most inconsistently and incompletely adopted; traditional societies prove the more frightened at the perspective of its approach as, once vigorously settled, everyone will be persuaded that, "bad" though it might be, it is still preferable to the Old Regime.

230 For the role of the "hat" in defining alterity see 3:Mitu S. 1992, p. 10.

231 For the presence of enlightened criticism in the principalities see 3:Georgescu 1971, chps. II, V. The critical forms in question here were nevertheless somewhat at variance with the spirit of the "forms without substance", as they attacked traditional values and championed new, "progressive" ideas, while conservative criticism generally acts to the contrary.

232 Florian Aaron to George Bariț, a letter of 7 February 1838, published in 1.6:GBC 1973–1993, I, pp. 9–10; 1.9:Bodea 1982, I, pp. 102–103.

233 Ioan Maiorescu to George Bariț, a letter of August–September 1838, published in 1.6:GBC 1973–1993, I, p. 218.

234 G. Pop (= George Bariț), "From the Romanian Buzau", in 1.2:The Gazette, XV, 1852, no. 28–29; 1.9:Bariț 1962, p. 148.

235 Gavril Munteanu to George Bariț, a letter of July 1846, published in 1.6:*GBC* 1973–1993, VI, p. 211.

236 1.9:Codru Drăgușanu 1956, p. 271.

237 For primary education in Wallachia during the constitutional epoch see 3:Iscru 1975.

238 1.9:Codru Drăgușanu 1956, p. 100.

239 *Ibidem*, p. 271.

240 See 3:Besançon 1978.

241 See 3:*The History of Pedagogy* (II) 1966; 3:Manolache, Dumitrașcu, Pîrnuță 1968; 3:Protopopescu 1966, pp. 154–162; 3:Țîrcovnicu 1970, pp. 76–109; 3:Țîrcovnicu 1978, pp. 213–235; 3:Mîrza 1987.

242 For Bojincă's pedagogical conception see 3:Țîrcovnicu 1964; Nicolae Bocșan, "Morals and pedagogy", in 1.9:Bojincă 1978, pp. XXXIII–XXXVIII.

243 His pedagogical ideas are expounded in: y (= Iosif Many), "Népiskoláink statisztikája" ("A Statistics of our popular schools"), in 1.2:*Híradó*, 1843, no. 41, pp. 241–242; *idem*, "Ideas on the advancement of the people", in 1.2:*The Gazette*, IX, 1846, no. 57, p. 226; *idem*, "Ideas on the balanced union of the cultivation of moral and soul faculties with the transmission of knowledge", in 1.2:*The Mouthpiece*, I, 1847, no. 27, pp. 143–144; no. 28, pp. 149–150.

244 1.9:Codru Drăgușanu 1956, p. 99.

245 *Ibidem*, p. 271.

246 *Ibidem*, p. 99.

247 1.9:Stoica de Hațeg 1984, p. 86.

248 The cliché of the Romanians' superficial religiosity, as part of the negative side of the self-image, was to know a long career in texts such as 2:Rădulescu-Motru 1984, pp. 56–67 (1904), which dwells on the excess of "formalism" in Orthodoxy; 2:Drăghicescu 1995, pp. 276 292 (1907); 2:Ralea 1977, p. 598 ("National atheism"); 2:Cioran 1993a, pp. 78–84. For the same issues also see 3:Ornea 1995, pp. 103–105; 3:Marga 1995, pp. 230–231.

249 1.8:Budai-Deleanu 1974–1975, I, p. 173.

250 3:Le Rider 1990, chps. V–VIII.

251 1.9:Ion Codru Drăgușanu 1956, p. 97.

252 See 3:Mitu S. 1992.

253 See 3:Condeescu 1946.

254 2:Blaga 1994, pp. 192–214, "Modelling and catalytic influences".

255 For the same issues, also see section VI, 3 below, "Language and the alphabet".

256 Ioan Maiorescu, in 1.2:*Literary Paper*, I, 1838, no. 16, p. 122.

257 Timotei Cipariu to George Bariț, a letter of January 1838, published in 1.6:*GBC* 1973–1993, IV, p. 109.

258 Timotei Cipariu to George Bariț, a letter of 27 July 1946, published in *ibidem*, p. 267.

259 1.9:Cipariu 1972, pp. 29–30.

260 Iosif Many, "A Word welcoming the times", in 1.2:*The Teacher*, I, 1848, no. 19–20.

261 See, for an analogy, the passage from the concept of "universal literature" to that of "national literature" (3:Marino 1992, pp. 31–38.)

262 1.6:Codru Drăgușanu 1956, p. 206.

263 3:Ornea 1975, pp. 140–145. A classic approach to the subject in 3:Spengler 1923 (*princeps* ed. 1918), I, pp. 142–145.

264 See 3:Febvre 1930; 3:Tonnelat 1930; 3:Bochmann 1977; 3:Duțu 1982, pp. 99–101.

265 1.2:*Journal for the Mind*, VII, 1844, no. 11–13.

266 1.9:Bodea 1982, I, p. 220.

267 Iosif Many (trans.), "Fragments from the books of Mickiewicz's travels", in 1.2:*Journal for the Mind*, VI, 1843, no. 15, pp. 117–119.

268 See 3:Durandin 1989.

269 Iosif Many, *op. cit.*, pp. 117–118.

270 George Bariț, "Who among our readership reads the papers?", in 1.2:*The Gazette*, XIV, 1851, no. 61, pp. 253–254; 1.9:Bariț 1962, p. 141.

271 Ioan Maiorescu to George Bariț, a letter of August–September 1838, published in 1.6:*GBC* 1973–1993, I, p. 218.

272 Timotei Cipariu to George Bariț, a letter of February 1845, published in *ibidem*, IV, p. 216.
273 1.4:*Teachings* 1820, p. 150; 1.9:Brătescu 1988, p. 337.
274 Appeal by Vice-Prefect Simion Prodan Probul to the inhabitants of Aiud, dated 19 October 1848, published in 1.9:Bodea 1982, II, p. 990.
275 *Ibidem.*
276 Andrei Mureșanu, "One morning on the Surul" (1853), in 1.8:Mureșanu A. 1963, p. 62.
277 For an explanation of the anti-liberal trends as reactions to the phenomenon of modernisation, see 3:Zeletin 1991, pp. 245–287, "The reaction against the Romanian bourgeoisie. Towards a social psychology of the Romanian culture of the latter half of the nineteenth century."
278 The Romanians' "unhappiness" as an element of their self-image was the more troubling and hard to bear as the theme of "happiness" as indefeasible right and ultimate end of the earthly existence of the human being was central to the Enlightenment and easily noticeable in the Romanian case as well (see 3:Mauzi 1969; 3:Muscă 1980; 3:Bocșan 1986, pp. 211, 215, 227–230.)
279 The work Papiu has in mind, without giving exact reference, is August Treboniu Laurian's dissertation, "Historical documents on the political and religious state of the Transylvanian Romanians", published under the signature A.T.L. in 1.2:*Journal*, III, 1846, pp. 95–330. The first sentence of that study is: "The Romanians' history is in itself a tragedy." The passage is also quoted and extensively commented upon by Timotei Cipariu, in a *Literary note*, unpublished (1.1:Cipariu cca 1846).
280 1.5:Papiu Ilarian 1852(I), p. 1.
281 3:Albu 1977, p. 73; 3:Totu, Florea, Abrudan 1984, p. 207.
282 Ioan Buteanu to Dimitrie Moldovan, a letter of 19 February 1849, published in 1.9:Dragomir 1944–1946, II, p. 74.
283 See 2:Harris 1964. Here too, the analogy offered by the *Disasters of War* triggers a comparison between the Spanish *guerrilleros* and the peasant highlanders from the Apuseni—both fighters in atrocious wars, using similar weapons, against foreign armed invasions.
284 The speech delivered by Bishop Șaguna at the political meeting in Sibiu, 28 December 1848, published in 1.9:Păcățian 1904, p. 502.
285 Andrei Mureșanu, "In Memoriam. To the Hurmuzachis", in 1.8:Mureșanu A. 1963, p. 45.
286 Timotei Cipariu to George Bariț, a letter of July 1838, published in 1.6:*GBC* 1973–1993, IV, p. 134. The personal "sorrows" and "despairs" as correlated with the general problems of the nation are also the subject matter of an 1845 letter addressed to Ștefan Moldvai (1.1:Dragomir 1845).
287 See, for Murgu's fate, I.D. Suciu's introductory study to 1.9:Murgu 1969, pp. 12–90; 3:Dragomir 1946, V, "Murgu's straying".
288 The founders of the Runcu monastery and the inhabitants of the Hodac and Ibănești villages to Bishop Bob, a letter of the summer of 1805, published in 1.6:Maior P. 1968, p. 81 (also see pp. 78–111). The inhabitants of the two villages, who were to make their presence felt in history once again, and violently so, in March 1990, down the streets of Tîrgu Mureș, enacted, not surprisingly perhaps, a preview of the theme of "the Romanian children and teachers chased away from schools by the Hungarians"—a theme that played such an important role in initiating and upholding the wave of nationalism in 1990. In 1805, the owner of the place, Baron Bornemisza, seized the estate of a monastery that had made it possible for the regional school to exist and thus forced the children to interrupt their studies. The inhabitants reported the abuse and the civil and ecclesiastic authorities (the latter represented by Petru Maior, rector of Gurghiu) made investigations. Opinions differed: the civil authorities claimed that the school, being in bad condition and hidden in the forest, was improper anyway, and had to be got rid of; the rector and the Romanians argued that it had nevertheless served many generations. Finally, the Uniate bishopric came to terms, using the mediation of the civil authorities, with the baron. The latter was to keep the monastery estate but give up another and take it upon himself to build a school for the Greek Catholic Romanians in Gurghiu and to rebuild the church of the monastery in Ibănești. The fact is that the baron kept on shirking his duty, yet the building he constructed to look like a Swiss villa would go on as a Romanian school up until 1912, when it was replaced by new premises made of stone... To their shame, the Romanian and Hungarian Transylvanians of 1990 proved even less willing to come to an agreement in sharing out their

schools than their forefathers two hundred years before. On the other hand, neither was president Iliescu's administration any more deft in clearing up the disputes than the baron Bornemisza. On the contrary.

289 1.1:Crainic 1845.

290 1.4:*Teachings* 1816, p. 127, "Honest reader!"; 1.9:Fugariu 1983, II, pp. 312–313.

291 Timotei Cipariu, "Principles of language and writing", in 1.2:*The Mouthpiece*, II, 1848, no. 60, p. 338.

292 Petre Cermena to Pavel Vasici, a letter of 23 January 1849, published in 1.9:Bodea 1982, II, p. 957.

293 George Bariţ, "Zlatna, 7 March" (obituary for Vasile Pop), in 1.2:*The Gazette*, V, 1842, no. 10, p. 37. See similar phrasings, in 1843, in Vasile Moldvai (1.1:Moldvai 1843).

294 See 3:Van Tieghem 1924–1948; 3:Monglond 1930; 3:Anghelescu 1971, esp. pp. 177–205; 3:Cornea 1972, pp. 24–34.

295 It is likely he acquired such sensibility through Hungarian influence: Kazinczy, Kisfaludy (see 3:Sőtér, Pándi 1965).

296 Moise Nicoară, "Cry and complaint for the lost glory of the Romans", a 1811 poem published in 1.9:Bodea 1943, p. 154.

297 *Ibidem*.

298 For that hypostasis of Romantic mythology see 3:Tacciu 1973, pp. 13–52, "The myth of the fallen angel"; also see 3:Tacciu 1982–1987.

299 1.1:Many 1838a, f. 34v.

300 Andrei Mureşanu, "To my muse" (1847), in 1.8:Mureşanu A. 1963, p. 35.

301 *Ibidem*, p. 37.

302 *Idem*, "The voice of a Romanian" (1843), in *ibidem*, p. 28.

303 See 3:Prodan 1967–1968.

304 A circular letter from Bishop Ioan Lemeny, dated 21 October 1848, published in 1.9:Păcăţian 1904, p. 464.

305 For "peasantness" and "ruralness" as distinctive traits and elements of Romanian self- and hetero-identification, see 3:Heitmann 1985, chp. I; also 3:Karnoouh 1990.

306 See, for Papiu, 3:Chindriş 1983, pp. 97–107, "Serfdom"; for Bălcescu: 3:Giurescu C.C. 1977, pp. 32–33.

307 Contrary to this view, Papiu, and with him the majority of Romanian culture and historiography until, say, David Prodan, condemns serfdom also in its historical, medieval dimension, in terms similar to those used to criticise its manifestations in 1848 or in the twentieth century, ignoring thus the specific (mainly economic) motivations that might have legitimated it in a much anterior age. Such a perspective was reinforced by Marxist conceptions, due to their relentless concern with social conflicts that might fuel class struggle, the motor of the evolution of society towards progress and communism. The nationalists, in their turn, have been more than willing to identify at this level a justification *avant la lettre* of their doctrine by overtaxing conflicts and underestimating the specific determinations of the respective medieval tensions of a social-economic, often religious or ethnic nature, which differs substantially from its understanding in terms of modern nationalism.

308 Simion Balint to Iosif Hodoş, a letter of March 1855, published in 1.6:Hodoş 1944, p. 54.

309 1.9:Codru Drăguşanu 1956, p. 79.

310 See August Treboniu Laurian, in 1.2:*Journal for the Mind*, XVIII, 1855, no. 38–39, 42; XIX, 1856, no. 12–13, 18, 22; 1.9:Codru Drăguşanu 1956; 1.9:Cipariu 1972 (his "Italy" letters); 1.6:Pervain, Chindriş 1972 (correspondence from Italy); 3:Isopescu 1930; 3:Marcu 1935; 3:Lascu V. 1981; 3:Mitu S. 1987-1988; and 3:Mitu S. 1988a, respectively.

311 See 1.8:Pauleti 1980, esp. pp. 153–165, 301–381.

312 See 3:Lascu N. 1957; 3:Lascu N. 1974.

313 Nicolae Pauleti, "To those who love the Romanians", in 1.8:Pauleti 1980, p. 82.

314 Simion Balint to Papiu Ilarian, a letter of December 1852, published in 1.6:Pervain, Chindriş 1972, II, p. 10.

315 1.5:Papiu Ilarian 1852(I), p. 2.

316 Appeal for the convocation of the second assembly in Blaj, April 1848, published in 1.9:Bodea 1982, I, p. 445.

317 A circular letter from Bishop Ioan Lemeny, dated 21 October 1848, published in 1.9:Păcăţian 1904, p. 464.

318 Manifesto of the "Committee for the Romanian Nation", dated 25 November 1848, published in 1.9:Bărnuţiu 1990, pp. 68–69.

319 Andrei Mureşanu, "A resounding echo" (1848), in 1.8:Mureşanu A. 1963, p. 38.

320 Nicolae Pauleti, "A souvenir for bracing hearts", in 1.8:Pauleti 1980, p. 155.

321 Andrei Mureşanu, "The voice of a Romanian" (1843), in 1.8:Mureşanu A. 1963, p. 30.

322 *Ibidem.*

323 *Idem*, "In Memoriam. To the Hurmuzachis", in *ibidem*, p. 45.

324 *Ibidem.*

III. In between the Good and the Bad

IDLE OR DILIGENT?

Were we to discuss the issue of the attitude to labour in the most general of terms, without referring to the Transylvanian Romanians' self-image or to any other social representations to the point, we would have to admit that idleness and diligence are extremely relative notions, which can be approached from widely varying viewpoints.[1] As can be expected, ethnic stereotypes do not hesitate to share these qualities out to certain nations and social groups. The Germans are almost always considered "industrious" (true, here as elsewhere, the cliché only obtains as to the modern Germans, not to Tacitus' indolent barbarians[2]), while the southern Italians, for instance, the Gypsies, or the Black Africans are labelled as "idle". An important role is played here by the idea of the climatic conditioning of human behaviour[3], since it often happens that the excessive "heat" of the southern regions explains, in the logic of those images, their inhabitants' slothfulness. Codru Drăgușanu, for instance, has left an absolutely illuminating writing on the subject, in which he describes the Lazzaronians who idle away their days in unimaginable torpor under the scorching sun of Naples. It is also true that he finds they are of the same stock as the craftsmen [trocari] from Brașov, without troubling himself with the fact that the latter lived in a much harsher climate.[4]

Certainly, if we leave such clichés aside and admit that human biological data are identical in individuals belonging to any race or ethnic group, clichés such as the Germans' "industriousness" or the Gypsies' "laziness" become relative to the extreme, and indeed meaningless. The Transylvanian intellectuals feeding on the cosmopolitan and universalist tradition of the Enlightenment were of the same opinion (at least when it came to denying the accusations brought by foreign people against the Romanian character). Toma Costin and Eftimie Murgu, for example, were determinedly against those generalisations whereby a moral trait or a certain type of behaviour was ascribed to a whole nation: "That a Romanian might differ, in his being, from other mortals", writes Murgu, is an absurdity that could only surface in the mind of an ill-meaning character like Sava Tököly[5]. Toma Costin, too, in referring to the same problem of the Romanians' supposed indolence, writes that "all the generic vices that are imputed to a people or to an individual are unfair, for there is no such thing as generic vice, and we are equally in the wrong when we take advantage of the vague meaning of words, which proves excessive both when we extend it […] and when we compress it."[6]

Still, if idleness cannot be an inborn feature of the Romanians, nor diligence of the Germans for that matter, could not there be certain social, ideological or religious conditions that cause those attributes to become specific traits of certain nations? Even Costin agrees that "the people's habits grow out of the rules swaying them" and that "under liberal government people become enterprising, humane and righteous, while under tyranny the mores grow corrupt and many evil deeds are bred", even if, he adds, "to believe that they become hereditary and incurable is an error, nay a prejudice, of which no wise man should prove guilty."[7]

It is mainly religious tradition that is nowadays unanimously taken to have an influence on the attitude to labour. Everyone is by now familiar with the role that Protestant, particularly Calvinist, morals played in shaping a rigorous labour ethic that proved indispensable to the economic expansion of capitalism.[8] To what extent the Orthodox tradition was at all effective in this sense is, undoubtedly, an extremely important question. As we will see, the Transylvanian intellectuals of the early modern age tried to elaborate on the issue themselves, particularly relating to the much-debated issue of the rapport between working days and the numerous holidays prescribed by peasant religious tradition.

Secular ideologies and doctrines are also instrumental in the way work is evaluated. While the liberalism and pragmatism associated with the capitalist spirit encourage effort and drive, Marxist ideology, on the other hand, professes a more reserved attitude to labour, in maintaining that the latter, when practised in excess, is a dehumanising factor that severs the individual caught in its reifying mechanisms from his or her real essence. The communist doctrine considers labour a not too pleasant obligation; that is why it aims to increase productivity, so that the amount of time that one individual has to allot to it be reduced as much as possible. The ideal of Marxist ideology, as Francis Fukuyama, among others, has shown, is the four-hour working day, in order that the rest could be dedicated to the relaxation of the worker, able thus to practise sports and cultivate the arts.[9] Marxism even managed to put this principle into practice: indeed, in a communist or neo-communist regime most of the people never lend themselves to hard work for more than four hours a day, except that they employ the rest of the time in seeing to business less noble than that initially envisaged, such as relaxing with friends over a drink or two or watching television.

This example is also suggestive of the consequences of attitudes to labour that are triggered not only by a certain ideology, but also by the social-economic system associated with it, and especially by the arbitrary manner of distributing the end-results of production. Whether it practises an egalitarian type of redistribution or a strongly polarised one, if the system fails to encourage maximisation of labour by means of adequate material incentives and moral-religious recompense, the labour ethic will be seriously impaired.

The Romanian intellectuals of the early modern age were themselves alive to the issue. What meaning could labour on the nobles' estates have for the Transylvanian serf who had been accustomed, for hundreds of years, to his efforts remaining ineffectual as far as he was concerned, due both to economic exploitation and to the lack of a market where possible extra products could bring him profit? Was not the labour ethic definitely compromised by such a historical heritage, one able to stifle, in the peasant mentality, any drive towards personal thrift and saving, even after a change in the social, political and economic conditions?[10]

We will leave such general considerations aside and, in looking more closely at the inner mechanism of the Romanians' self-image, we will see that here labour is evaluated from a moral and even moralising perspective. Whether or not attributed to the Romanians, diligence is considered an important quality while idleness represents an equally major vice. The answers to the question of whether the Romanians are idle or diligent are numerous and complex: they range from the denial of the very validity of the question to the self-critical acknowledgement of the Romanians' specific idleness; from vehement arguments against the stance of foreigners in this respect to the search for causes and explanations, or to moralising urging.

"IDLE"

The motif of the Romanians' indolence comes to add yet another element to the series built on the logic of the negative side of the image, one that had the upper hand when it came to the realities of the present. As such, the motif is associated with other, related themes: lack of zeal for the national cause, often described by means of notions such as "laziness", "carelessness" and "apathy"; cultural backwardness and hostility to schooling, also due to inactivity, indifference and lack of energy; the peaceful and quiet nature the Romanians attribute to themselves, their calm, patience, and sometimes resignation and obedience—all signs of a slothful lifestyle that read mildness and lethargy as one of the specific facets of the nation.

From another point of view, idleness is a notion central to the discourse of social criticism that grew up in the wake of the Enlightenment. Alongside alcoholism, criminality and moral depravity, idleness is seen as one of the main consequences, and at the same time a cause, of the poverty and lack of civilisation that come with political and social oppression and, to a great extent, of the lack of culture, education and religious commitment. It is also to be invoked in explaining the dirtiness, insufficient nourishment, diseases, backward lifestyle and poverty of the population, in a complete and coherent picture that cannot afford to miss any of these pieces.

That this diagram of social criticism was forcefully imprinted into the social-political thinking and mentality of the Central European *Aufklärung* and its extensions into the first half of the nineteenth century, sheds clearer light on the substance of foreign criticism, too. Foreign observers almost always detect these elements in the Romanians' manners precisely and primarily because it is these very concepts with which the political thinking of the time operated, rather than because they were moved by any national hatred, as the accusations often suggest. They apply equivalent descriptions and value judgements to all populations with similar problems.[11] The best proof on this point is that the Romanian intellectuals too often come up with evaluations and images that are absolutely concordant with the foreign ones, informed by the same social criticism of enlightened extraction.

It cannot be claimed that the 1791 *Supplex* is a text critical of the Romanians, yet the Romanians' indolence is there the subject of a complex-free admittance. According to the act, should the élites of the Transylvanian Romanians continue to be disfavoured, they will be as unable as ever to bring the population onto the right path. Under such circumstances, "there is no hope for a love of culture from this nation and thus there is no promise of labour either; rather it is to be feared that ignorance, indolence and slothfulness, and all the vices arising therefrom, will swell in its womb, to the destruction of this our province."[12] Were we to see things from within the rhetoric of the document we can well imagine what the future might have brought, given that the demands of the *Supplex* were never fulfilled!

Obviously, the logic of the self-image had to have its way, to the effect that the 1814 petition of the people from Arad confirmed the above-quoted opinion relating to the Romanians' attitude to labour: besides being unlearned and given to theft and rebellion, "it also rarely happens that the Romanian sees devotedly to his work".[13] Of course, all those capital vices were exclusively due to the domination enforced by the Serbian ecclesiastical hierarchy.[14]

The journalistic work of the 1848 generation, as represented by Andrei Mureşanu, George Bariţ and Iosif Many, furthers the ideas of enlightened social criticism on both theoretical and pragmatic lines. Mureşanu in particular maintains the concept that lack of culture, and the other historically inherited drawbacks, have left a deep trace on the Romanian lifestyle, which translates as general inertia exhibited not only as to the overall progress of the nation, but even to the welfare of every individual. According to the Braşov-based poet and journalist:

> The more a people draws its might from the well of culture, the more it finds it in itself to see about the bettering of its state, and so the more it cherishes those matters whereof its welfare and material thriving are derived. In contrast, the more a people strays away from the light of good reason, the more it contents itself with little, disregards material satisfaction, and remains unfeeling to that natural urge to take care of the future and of that which nurtures the people itself as well as the men within it.[15]

Although its origins are indeed to found in the reason and "culture" so cherished by the enlightened minds of the Transylvanian School, this drive towards thrift and love of gain, the lack of which Mureşanu deplores in the Romanians, is actually something else: it is the mentality of the capitalist, of the enterprising bourgeoisie and of the individual's determined action and initiative. The Transylvanian intellectuals would like such liberal values, which encompass the dynamic, individualist ethic of the bourgeoisie's economic expansion, to spread among their fellow countrymen as well, so that the slowness and inefficiency of a traditional, rural, conservative and collectivist society be exploded in the process.

Mureşanu tries to render his readers sensitive to such ideals and, as usual, the foreign connection proves useful: "Let us throw a glance around and we will before long realise that this is the truth. Our neighbours make profitable use of every minute of their lives and save every penny, so that, in time, they can pride themselves on throwing the first seeds on their first lot, no matter how small." The Romanians, however, will not learn other, more lucrative professions, preferring to keep to their traditional crafts and to let things slide, in the interests of a principle of sheer neglect: "What use is there in worrying, God will take care of it all."[16]

George Bariț is of the same mind when he invokes the authority of a Saxon geographer whose stance he considers objective enough, even if not favourable to the Romanians. Bariț recommends that his readers lend their ears to his comments: "Wherever he may be, the Romanian is not too industrious; his needs are not too great and his habit is to make everything he uses with his own hands. Therefore the industry of this people is a mere swaddling infant."[17]

The Romanians' reluctance to take to industrial and commercial business, which Benigni notices in his work, is an important issue debated in the columns of the Brașov newspapers. "All our misery lies in the poor use we make of the goods of our country; we are not even good enough to clean our wool and we send it to foreign workshops to be spun and they send it back to us four times as expensive if not more. We won't grow our own silk and process it in the country, although in the warmest regions, along the Tîrnava or the Mureș rivers, they could do work as good as in northern Italy. Gentlemen, we don't even have factories! We like sugar, yet won't make it; and why not?" Transylvania's ground hides precious minerals "which our merchants are too lazy to look for and forge at home, so they bring them from others".[18] The Transylvanian Romanians' poverty, Bariț concludes, is not due to any lack of tools or to other unpropitious conditions, but primarily to the fact that they refuse to do anything about the resources of their country and will not work in order to put them to profitable use.

Underlying these considerations is the whole tradition of the eighteenth- and early nineteenth-century economic literature and policy of the Austrian Chamber (Hofkammer) and its effort to balance imports by the stimulation of autochthonous production. The Chamber was constantly trying to persuade the populations it governed that it was worthwhile breeding silkworms, cultivating potatoes, tobacco, sugar beet or primary materials for dyes.[19]

As mentioned above, the cliché of the Romanians' idleness was often circulated by the foreign observers of Romanian realities. The Romanian self-image often enters a dialogue with these foreign perceptions, by accepting their value judgements and possibly adding slight variations from within the body of stereotypes it has already embraced. Obviously, only certain images proposed by the foreigners are accepted, particularly those which explain the Romanians' indolence by referring it to unfavourable external circumstances.

Here too the type of argumentation is indebted to Enlightenment thought. As early as 1773, Michael von Heydendorff, an attendant of Joseph II during his travels through Transylvania, gave a significant answer to the emperor's question as to whether "there are good economic minds among the Romanians": "there are good minds given to economy among them, true, yet the majority are bad and idle. The nation in itself is naturally endowed with enough dexterity, yet it wants adequate training."[20]

Starting from such observations, the enlightened monarch himself would formulate a series of congruous remarks, to which any of his Romanian admirers of the first half of the next century could have subscribed: "I do not deny that in matters agricultural and economic the Wallachian is unskilled and his lands are but poorly cultivated. Yet what else can he do, when he is not sure of his property from one day to another and his master can summon him to work at will, every day, indeed every hour, as they often do. How could he, that being his state, see that his own land and labour thrive?"[21] In other words, the Romanian is idle, yet there are reasons why he is so, which makes him blameless.

In order to illustrate the same idea George Bariț also chooses the opinions of a foreigner, the Hungarian geographer József Dóczy, who writes, in Bariț's opinion, "without passion and like a friend" when he refers to the Romanians: "The Romanians are idle in all things, even though their minds are sound; and if they strive a little they can produce learned men and gifted artists."[22]

Equally significant is the translation of another foreign writer's opinions, those of Chr. Witt, physician in the Russian army, who views the realities of the principalities with an extremely critical eye. This time, obviously, Bariț is no longer emotionally on his side, yet he publishes his notes, which, as we will see, he does not refute completely. The Romanians, writes Witt, "are too little concerned with the cultivation of the land they inhabit [...] This people has fallen in the direst ineptitude and in the deepest moral corruption and degrading idleness, which makes it oblivious to the most urgent necessity of existence."[23]

Instead of discrediting such slander, Bariț chooses to look for plausible ways of explaining and justifying the type of behaviour Witt speaks about, thus implicitly admitting its existence. Who should be mindful of the cultivation of the land? asks Bariț. The land agents who are only after overnight fortunes, at the expense of the peasants and of the estates? Moreover, the attitudes Witt incriminates are due to the wars that had been ravaging the country, and are also to be observed in other peoples in similar distress: "It would have been good if someone had drawn a parallel on this point between the inhabitants of the Russian provinces and the Romanians, of whose land the neighbouring powers, the three and previously five of them, have made for years a ceaseless theatre of war, plague and oppression. Will it please your honours to search into the state of the commoners in other countries and see what it is that makes them better than the Romanians?"[24] Therefore, although the indolence is there, the Romanians are not to blame for it. Instead, the responsibility lies with the foreign powers; besides, not everyone else is less idle than the Romanians are.

Such a perspective also accounts for Bariț's discontent with such texts as that written by Witt. The issue at stake is not that they observe and describe the inactivity of the inhabitants, for they are right in maintaining that that is the case. What the Transylvanian intellectuals are really concerned with and fearful about is that people should not think that the Romanians alone are to be accused of idleness, that this flaw is a specific feature of theirs, one organically grown into their way of behaviour. Since there are others who, under similar conditions, behave in a similar way, it might well be conjectured that idleness is due to exterior circumstances; once these have been eliminated, the Romanians, too, will be able to straighten up.

Starting from the image of the Romanians' indolence, yet confident that it must and can be fought against, many Transylvanian intellectuals become primarily concerned with finding and giving the good pieces of advice that might extirpate that type of behaviour. While we may well doubt that their impelling appeals had any effect at all on the crowds they tried to move, such urging is, nevertheless, extremely telling of the mentality and self-image that was being fashioned by the élites.

Stoica de Hațeg, for instance, in a rector's circular letter of 1805 that was undoubtedly meant to make popular certain official instructions, advises the peasants to take to vegetable growing:

> Let every man hurry to work the land and feed their folk [...] Many of you have seen how the Germans, the French, the Italians, the Hungarians or the Serbs do their work; like them, mind your kitchen gardens, grow vines, but vegetables too [...] and all kinds of herbs for all kinds of broth. At night all should have a good sleep, for idling is misery [...] Thus, when we have all we need, we will be good hosts and brothers to all the enlightened and manly nations, but while laziness and lack reigns among the Romanians, others will rightly laugh and mock at us.[25]

The urging to work would strike more interesting notes once serfdom was abolished, after the revolution, thanks to the legislation passed by the Pozsony and Cluj Diets.[26] From that time on, it was said at the time, the Romanians would only have to work for their own benefit, therefore they had to abandon old habits and begin to work hard, all the more so as in their new position as landowners they would be confronted with competition specific to free production relationships. Whereas the serf's lot, irrespective of the servitude it presupposed, was inherited by the son from his father, one was now quite likely to lose one's property if a prodigal peasant was careless enough to have to sell his land or divide it among his numerous heirs. Property therefore had to be husbanded as well as one could; it had to be increased with new acquisitions, and the peasant was now bound to do better than ever before. "We expect the people to give proof of tenacious work", writes Bariț in 1848; "Such days as are not wanted for toil on the land should be used in work for pay on others' lands, for much is needed to support a house and a family; and then, children are many and wealth is shared out in as many parts, and if money in the cupboard is not enough then the sons or grandsons may come again to fear bondage to the lands of the wealthy. Let us teach them to work their land as well as they can, and milk it dry."[27]

However, this stirring to a life of labour, undertaken in the spring and summer of 1848, connoted a series of complex purposes, often ambiguous and slippery, given that from the very outburst of the revolution (i.e., long before serfdom was abolished as a result of the vote in the Cluj Diet at the beginning of June) the peasants expressed their revolutionary enthusiasm by a refusal to work and in mid-spring, at the height of the labour season, stopped performing the tasks [robote] they were supposed to carry out.[28]

Consequently, the gentry and the authorities, fearing that that year's agricultural production of the province was jeopardised, tried their best to persuade the peasants that they should go back to work; persuasion in this case meant either talking or, where possible, forcing them at gun-point, into doing their jobs. Similar efforts were made not only by the two Romanian bishoprics—traditional messengers of official demands—but also by the secular élite, now self-imposed as ideological leader of the nation. Both the moderates, like Bariţ or Cipariu, and the ultra-radicals who promoted a social programme attuned to peasant demands, like Bărnuţiu or Papiu Ilarian, were intent on urging the serfs to perform their tasks in all conscientiousness until the vote was passed by the qualified institutions to abolish their state. It is certain that the two groups were primarily concerned neither with the agricultural production of the province nor with the private interests of the noble owners, but with tactical and ideological points: they wanted to ensure that Romanian actions remained within the law since they feared that the anarchic tendencies of the peasants might discredit the political aims of the national movement.

An even more disturbing note was struck in the summer and winter issues of the popular paper edited by Iosif Many. The disturbance comes from the fact that, as the conflict between the Romanians and the Hungarians grew deeper and deeper, the Romanian peasants' refusal to work on the Hungarian nobles' estates acquired, as it did for the radical intellectuals as well, ethnic and political-national connotations. Yet Many, who was not greatly enthusiastic about the radicalisation of the national conflict (while being an adept of collaboration with the Hungarian revolution), went on advising the peasants to work on the estates of the well-to-do, even after serfdom had been abolished.

In support of his idea he brought both the arguments of enlightened social criticism and those underlying the enterprising mentality of the capitalist spirit, its sense of initiative and desire to prosper. No longer obliged to perform his toils, the peasant would gain more time, according to Many. This extra time should not be turned into leisure time, however, since it would, in all probability, be spent in pubs. On the contrary—and this is the last straw!—the ploughman should spend the extra time in working two or three times as much as he did before when he was a serf, for now he would be doing it for his own sake and would be earning money. It was, so to speak, the exact opposite of the ideal of the four-hour working day which Marx was about to elaborate at the time.

"Being now a free man, rid of bondage", writes Many, as if giving voice to the imaginary peasant he addresses, "what I have ever given in labour for others will from now on be my own. What time is left I will not idle away. I will gaily work for pay and thus my savings will rise higher and higher, so I can have enough if need arises. I will have the money to raise my children well, to send them to school so that they can learn what any man should learn in order to be a good citizen."[29]

What is more, Many initiates an almost direct and quite violent polemics with the Romanian radical intellectuals who urge the people to rebel and encourage them to cease working for their former owners and uphold their social demands. Many feels it is his duty to warn the peasants of the danger he believes can be sensed behind the turbulent discourse of these demagogues:

Take good care, for there are people in want who wrap their faces in lies and beat their breast that they are only after the public good, while solely hunting for their own, and declare they have mighty affidavit. Beware of them and search them well and judge for yourself before believing every word you hear [...] Will you listen to these false advisers and not work, and think that God has given you enough to cover your needs? But should you have enough only for this day and for the morrow, or perhaps for a whole year and the next too? Or is it that all you need is to feed your mouth and clothe your body, yours and your folk's? Will you spend your miserly life in shacks and huts for the rest of your days? [...] Brother! Hear my word and believe it is not enough to till your lot. For little will be gained of it. With the time you have and twice your might, work for pay on other good people's lands too, for you'll be better off yourself, as you have read here within. In one word, never yield to idleness, for idleness is the cushion of the devil.[30]

Many's apologetics with respect to labour and the enterprising spirit is not a context-based pose, meant to help the Hungarian authorities or Bishop Lemeny with their attempts at toning down the Romanians; that the Blaj-based intellectual professes the same ideas throughout his active career, particularly before the revolution, is proof of this. Significantly, Many, as well as other journalists, published translations from Benjamin Franklin's moralising writings, accompanied by their own comments and notes—thus offering a novel type of message to the Transylvanian public at the beginning of the modern age.[31]

Franklin's writings in their Transylvanian version mainly include advice for ensuring one's own wealth and welfare, with emphasis laid on the skill of earning and making profit. Their norms are actually the fundamental values of the bourgeois ethic and of the capitalist spirit: respect for money and gain, the cult of labour and of individual ambition, the enterprising spirit, thrift and husbandry. It was obvious, however, that the axiological universe of that paradigm, which the Transylvanian leaders promoted through their translations, rather jarred with the norms of a traditional society that sang to the tune of other mentalities and attitudes. Those markedly dynamic patterns of behaviour proposed by the American self-made man struck a blow at the slowness of a rural and conservative society that went by other rhythms of both time and action.

That time is money, and that wasting either is a crime; that rest and leisure, however short, are incompatible with the progress of the household or even with one's own inner peace, which can only be attained by ceaseless labour, are central ideas to Franklin's essays. They were certainly in accordance with the austere principles of the puritans or Quakers who had landed on American soil, but seemed much harder to swallow in a society where the labour and time wasted on the estates of the gentry, the low productivity of agricultural work and the general co-ordinates of a patriarchal existence were an invitation to dalliance and conservation rather than to promptness and dynamic progress. Likewise, the idea that labour, profit and temperance, matched with skill and especially with individual ambition, were the sure guarantees of success in life, was bound to have a hard time striking roots in a Transylvania that was not the land of all opportunities. "Help yourself and God will help you in return" is the lesson of bourgeois individualism, of confidence in one's own strength, which Franklin proposes to his readers. And this lesson itself came to displace an ethic of collective solidarity that any autochthonous mentality espouses as a guarantee of survival.

Despite their striking incongruity with the local values, then, it was these very recommendations that Franklin's Romanian translators selected for their own readers, persuaded that modernity and the capitalist spirit were indispensable for the economic advancement of the nation. The Transylvanian journalists explicitly targeted this message at the rural community: the "ploughmen" and the "land-toilers" are the constant recipients of the enlightened advice that idleness, time-wasting and lack of temperance are the causes of general poverty and misery; that labour, austerity and thrift are sure to rid them of their troubles.

The translators of Franklin's works show boundless confidence in the educational and exemplary value of the American writer's teachings. "The useful notes and wise rules that speak of his deep knowledge of life," writes Iosif Many in his annotations, "which did many people good in other countries, may serve us here as well. Brothers, should we alone be doomed to eternal poverty, when in other lands the life-experience of this or that man brings the good of the nations? Should we alone be deaf to the sound teachings of time and wisdom? No, my strong belief is that divine providence has saved happier days for our nation, too."[32] Elsewhere, Many states: "If ever there was a people in need of such teachings as are gathered here, that people is surely us, the Romanians."[33] It was an expression of the belief that, irrespective of the causes and circumstances that had generated it, indolence was a serious disease of the Romanian society, which could nevertheless be successfully fought against and finally eliminated.

"DILIGENT"

There were, nevertheless, opinions according to which the Romanians were indeed diligent, and their supposed idleness only a shameful piece of calumny that had to be denied. It sometimes happens that both clichés—of the Romanians' indolence and of the Romanians' thrift—are present in the same author, and even within the same document. In general, the answer to the question as to whether the Romanians are idle or diligent involved an ambiguity impossible to clarify.

Within their self-image, the idea that the Romanians are a "hardworking people" comes as a logical inference deriving from the motif of their being an "oppressed people". Their being exploited would make no sense if they were not hardworking, since the exploiters would not exercise their domination over a people that did not provide them with the best of profits. Conversely, of course, the nobility could easily maintain that it was precisely because of the peasants' laziness and inefficiency that so much was demanded from them. Interpretation here, as elsewhere, was necessarily relative.

In reality, neither of the two views was adequate, since, in the long run, everything boiled down to a question of productivity. Even the seemingly unfair and ill-conceived nature of agrarian relationships was merely an indication, in terms of social and labour relations, of this extremely reduced productivity, due, on the one hand, to the poor quality of the Transylvanian soil, and, on the other, to the primitive agricultural technology.[34]

This being the case, it was obvious that the Transylvanian noble had to demand a greater amount of statutory labour than his counterparts in Bărăgan or Alföld; to intensify exploitation in order to ensure, on the general scale of society, a reasonable level of production. Society's mental representations obviously favoured much more subjective interpretations of the same reality in dealing with the peasants' "laziness" or "industriousness", or with the "bad", "exploiting" nobles. Unfortunately, the biased perspective of the age (which was only natural for a view from within) would eventually make its way into the historiographical approach to the issue as well.

The theme of the Romanians' diligence, usually used to describe the peasants, consolidated throughout the period during which the political mentality of the successive generations of Transylvanian intellectuals was emerging from the Enlightenment and heading towards the Romantic age. The representatives of the Transylvanian School, many of whom were born into noble families and proudly acknowledged their origins, were able to look at certain social vices and flaws that were attributed to the peasants with a certain detachment, from a distance, as it were. Their criticism was delivered from the superior, fatherly, patronising position of the consciously rational senior. Their indisputable demophilia was, nevertheless, a different story from the democratic ideal professed by the 1848 generation. The Transylvanian *Aufklärers* could have subscribed at any moment to the Josephine formula: everything for the people, yet not too much by the agency of it.

In contrast, the 1848 generation claimed completely to identify with the peasants, and its members saw themselves as mere agents faithful to the latter's will. The peasants were seen as the embodiment of the national genius and specificity. Calling them lazy good-for-nothings would be synonymous with saying that the nation itself, in its most "authentic" essence, was guilty of indolence, which was quite different from a rational critique of certain social vices.

The idea of the Romanians' diligence is given a well-sustained, if only implicit, expression at textual level, by means of one of the basic themes of Transylvanian political petitioning: the argument that it is the Romanians who carry out Transylvania's public tasks and ensure the economic status of the province by means of taxes and services.[35] Just like Inochentie Micu's petitions or the memoirs of the bishops in the 1830s, the 1791 *Supplex* capitalises on this argument, which is somehow at variance with passages in the same document that speak of the Romanians' "idleness and sloth"—passages that have already been quoted above.

The *Supplex* only introduces the motif of Romanian diligence by an indirect reference. One example of explicitness in this point is the *Refutation* brought by an Enlightenment scholar with respect to the notes on the memoir published by Eder.[36] The document uses the very argument mentioned above in order to emphasise the Romanians' industry. Significantly, the author tackles the topic in polemical terms, that is, in the well-known combative style, demonstrating that the Romanians are not what foreigners claim them to be. Eder had called those who are like the Romanians (i.e., those situated outside the political-juridical system of the principality) "the idlers of the country"[37]. The reply reads as follows:

> The thoughtless insolence! The author calls "idlers of the country" those people who are of the same sort with the Romanians; hence, nor are the Romanians, to his mind, other than a pack of idlers. If the people who till the land and breed the cattle, the people who form the majority of the army and of the workforce of Transylvania, who provide for the soldier, for the judge and for the very author of those notes, if these people are the idlers [*trîntori* = also the Romanian for "drones"] of Transylvania, then I would like to know who are the busy bees of this country? Certainly not those who live by the diligence of the idling drones.[38]

Piqued at the harshness of the accusation, the reply goes as far as returning like for like; not only are the Romanians not idle, but the true idlers are precisely those who accuse them and live by their hard work.

In an effort to deny the Romanians' pessimistic self-perceptions, Dimitrie Țichindeal shows, in 1814, that among the Romanians too, throughout the provinces inhabited by them, are people with "a love of hard toil"[39]. In 1842, Simion Bărnuțiu renews the old argument of the Romanians as bearers of public tasks, and lays emphasis on the ingratitude such efforts receive in return: the Romanians "made the roads and guarded the bridges and had to pay the tolls too; they tilled the fields and the hills of the nobles and were left starving in the end".[40]

The *Appeal* to the Romanians of the Austrian Empire, launched in February-March 1849, which exalts the Romanians' long-proven diligence, is clearly at variance with Andrei Mureșanu's or George Bariț's discourse in favour of bourgeois industrial or commercial occupations, and thus prefigures agrarianism and the privileging of the rural economy. It involves an ideological purging of society (reduced thus to the peasantry), of the economy (equated with agriculture), and of daily behaviour (illustrated by the labour ethic). The three elements thus shape the ideal of a specifically Romanian national destiny: "Romanians! You have always worked hard for your daily bread and have earned your land by the sweat of your brow and hands, which is the noblest of work. May this be your concern from now on as well. It is the land that makes the country."[41]

Undoubtedly, underlying such slogans were also the conceptions of a Bărnuțiu or Bălcescu regarding a democratic republic made up of middle-class landowners[42], as a realisation of the regressive utopias centred on the golden age of the Roman colonies or of Mircea the Old's freeholders.[43]

A variant of the motif of the Romanians' diligence, one which perfectly illustrates the ambiguity of this theme within the Romanian self-image, is the stereotype of the hardworking Romanian woman. Damaschin Bojincă, for instance, draws up a grandiloquent list of Romanian qualities, of which industry seems to be one, yet only manifest in the female half of the nation: "Nowhere in other nations can be found women as hardworking as our Romanian peasant women [...] It is a matter of public knowledge, and all foreign writers admit that they are most tireless and skilled in weaving cloth [...], more so than any other women of other nations."[44] That the cliché is widespread is also proven by a text published in the *Mouthpiece of Enlightenment*. The editors draw attention to a passage published in the Saxon gazette *Transylvania*, which praises the industry of the men from Rășinari, while implying that the women of the area fall short of expectations in this respect ("The men are all hardworking and industrious and we would that the same could be said of the women"). The editors' note hastens to amend such a reversal of a well-established stereotype: "If that were proven true, it would be a rather rare exception from the rule in Transylvania, where the women are everywhere considered more industrious than the men."[45]

As can be seen here, the cliché of women's diligence, which may seem, on the face of it, a praiseworthy aspect (as in Bojincă), can be a double-edged weapon. If the women are so diligent, is that to say that the men are less industrious, or even that they are downright idle? The image of women as more hardworking than men casts a poorer light on the respective community, since, according to the extremely sexist conceptions of the age, the man was the head of the family and the representative element of society.[46]

There is yet another element that reinforced the potentially negative connotation of this stereotype. As Bojincă shows, it was largely embraced, probably even spread, by foreign observers. Indeed, they often drew attention to the diligence of Romanian women, which was taken as a sort of ethnographic curiosity, since their more or less superficial impressions were undoubtedly derived from the observation of the domestic and economic behaviour of peasant families. Foreigners often praised, and sometimes pitied, the daily life of the Romanian peasant woman, to whom both the picturesque garb and hard work came naturally. She was pictured as bustling around all day long, spinning and busy with all sorts of things, and when she rested, she continued to weave with one hand and knead dough with the other, sometimes breast-feeding her child at the same time.

The trouble was that such a picture fitted quite well with the way the Europeans perceived a series of extra-continental realities, as manifest, for instance, in the "savage" peoples, the Muslims or the Orientals.[47] The image of the men lounging in the shade while the women busied themselves around him with household jobs was central to the Europeans' perceptions of certain societies they considered backward, patriarchal, and prisoners of a slowness of which the men's indolence and inactivity were the best of symbols.

Nourished by the observance of somewhat similar situations, a more or less diminished variant of this mental representation influenced foreigners' perceptions of Romanian realities as well. It would eventually extend to reach the very self-image of the Romanians, with all its critical import.

However, the Transylvanian intellectuals often felt it their duty to deny foreign perceptions relative to Romanian idleness, and it was in fact out of such polemics and refutations that the most pregnant self-images of the Romanians' industriousness arose. Toma Costin engages in direct combat with a picture of the Romanians drawn by Martin Schwartner, according to which, besides their characteristic dissimulation and propensity towards theft or robbery, "the Romanians' laziness is truly off the scale; it can be seen even in the frequency of their holidays, as ordained by the Greek Church. Yet, even if the number of holidays were to be reduced, no one could convince the superstitious Romanians that work is allowed on these days."[48]

Costin argues against such affirmations by invoking, first, the well-known argument of the carrying out of public tasks. Furthermore, he asks, how can a nation be lazy which lives by such a laborious occupation as agriculture?

> The Transylvanian Romanians are faithfully carrying out public tasks, they (and I mean the serfs) spend most of the year in devoting themselves to tilling the land; they make brave soldiers, they support numerous families, they leave no patch of land untilled [...] No other worry is more trying to them than that they do not have enough land, for they would be willing to work even more, if only they had enough land. Therefore, at least to my mind, it is unjust to accuse of inertia a people that no one can find wanting in will to work, but only in the instruction that might show them how to cultivate a narrow stretch of land for a great profit.[49]

In other words, the Romanians would work more if the conditions existed for them to do so, which seems to make the later urgings of Bariţ and Many look futile, while the poor productivity, to which Costin admits, is simply the result of the Romanians' lack of education, a deficiency that, in enlightened thinking, is capable of explaining everything.

Nor are the Romanians' religious practices, Costin goes on, an argument by which their indolence can be proved. That "the Romanians' slothfulness feeds on their superstition in observing the holidays" is a statement "unworthy of belief. It is proven by everyday experience that the Romanians can hardly be persuaded not to work on Sundays, not to speak of the other, lesser holidays, particularly at the time of intensive work on the land, so that their priests are daily obliged to ask the help of the public authorities in constraining the peasants to observe the holidays."[50] In a similar way, Petru Maior (presumably the same person as Toma Costin) deplored in his sermons the fact that the peasants put their souls in danger by breaking the Third Commandment.[51]

At any rate, this was a complete reversal of some very widely spread perceptions. The nobles and the authorities at all levels complain repeatedly that the Romanians refuse to work on their many irregular holidays, which were even at odds with the Orthodox canons. Imperial edicts repeatedly try to reduce the number of holidays, in order to introduce into a society that proved quite reluctant to lend itself to the vivid rhythms of modernity, a more rational manner of administering time.[52] At the same time, however, Costin and Maior maintain that the Romanians work even on Sundays, obliging the authorities to interfere to put an end to their laborious zeal.

Certainly, as far as the facts go, the Romanians' folkloric and superstition-driven religion may well have made them more fearful of divine punishment on the day of Holy Sisoe or of other apocryphal saints than on the Sundays prescribed by the "official" religion. At any rate, all these paradoxical interpretations are yet further proof of the profound ambiguity inherent in the notions of "idleness" and "diligence", as caught in the intricate web of the Romanian self-image.

Far more interesting from a theoretical point of view are the arguments used by Eftimie Murgu, in his debate with Sava Tököly, in defence of the Romanians. In a demonstration typical of enlightened rationalism, Murgu shows the absolute logical irrelevance of such national stereotypes.

Being a general human feature due to random circumstances, idleness cannot be taken as a characteristic specific to the Romanians, irrespective of its prevalence among them:

Idleness, understood as a general corporal feature, might be conceived of as applying to all Romanians from a physical point of view, yet it could not be observed by experience in whole families, and even less in a whole nation. But the very observation of human nature gives plain proof to the contrary, as it clearly shows that idleness (in a moral sense) needs be considered from the viewpoint of certain wholly non-specific, therefore random, circumstances, which by no means should be taken as necessary and thus able to allow that certain general conclusions be drawn from the idleness of such and such an individual.

Murgu then triumphantly rounds off his demonstration: "That a Romanian might differ, in his being, from other mortals, is a position which only the Holy Father could sanction."[53]

Such a valuable theoretical elaboration, arguing for the universality of the human being and against the levelling of moral and behavioural features to national "specific" traits, was probably as far as the Romanians' reflection on the subject could go in terms of adequacy to reality. It was, nevertheless, at a considerable remove from the basic logic of the self-image, which claimed that the Romanians did differ, either for the better or for the worse, from other mortals, and sought to point out precisely what it was that told them apart from, not what brought them into the vicinity of, others. A definite answer, that is, a yes or a no, was needed to this new, obsessive question engendered by foreign calumny: Are the Romanians diligent or are they idle?

RESISTANCE TO DENATIONALISATION—OPEN TOWARDS ASSIMILATION OR RESISTANT TO IT?

The ability to resist denationalisation, to maintain their ethnic "purity" unaltered, was another essential element of the Transylvanian Romanians' self-image, one tightly linked to other themes relating to the Romanians' number, to their solidarity as a compact group, and to their age-old continuity in the geographical space of Romania as a whole and of Transylvania in particular. The special import and attention ascribed to the issue at the time—which I need not emphasise here—is to be accounted for in terms of at least two sets of circumstances. For one thing, denationalisation could be considered a real threat, fatal to the nation, given the political-national and cultural conditions in which the Romanians found themselves. Secondly, besides such concrete circumstances, it was only natural that the question should challenge a collective consciousness that was about to discover its modern national identity while obsessing over the search for, and definition of, its specificity. One of the major issues debated within the discourse on identity was: To what extent are the Romanians able to keep up their own way of being, both in the face of the threat posed by others and against the pressures of modernisation? The answer to that question is also able to provide an explanation for the mechanisms conducive to the rise of nationalism.

Romanian society experienced the pressure exerted by others and by the shock of modernisation with acute intensity; the impact was obviously bound to induce a state of crisis. Consequently here, as in the case of so many other themes, the Transylvanian intellectuals' opinions on the Romanians' ability to resist denationalisation varied to the utmost degree. Interpretation followed such Manichaean, contradictory lines as are specific to the torments of a restless self-consciousness.

In short, some of the significant interpretations generated by Romanian self-perception assumed that the Romanians were endowed with a remarkable capacity to oppose denationalisation, therefore any effort to assimilate them, however energetic, did not stand a chance. Other, equally relevant, positions insisted on the danger of assimilation, on the Romanians' malefic propensity towards trying to become "one of theirs".

The bivalent nature of the collective beliefs in this respect would eventually be captured in the highly expressive formula, "Don't forget you're a Romanian!" Despite its categorical and enthusiastic urging for the preservation of the national identity, the slogan also, and just as clearly, presupposes the possibility of denial. The ceaseless repetition of the appeal would have been futile in the absence of the threat that it attempts to avert. "Don't forget you're a Romanian" arises from the assumption that the possibility of forgetting is always there.

We should note from the very beginning that comments relating to Romanian denationalisation, to denial, to the abandonment of the national language and identity, are more frequent than those confessing (with unshaken self-assurance and as a matter of fact) a belief in the Romanians' ability to resist. Obviously, the question remains as to whether the pessimistic opinions do not actually function as mere signs of alarm, meant to stimulate and reinforce attitudes to the contrary, and whether, on the other hand, optimistic self-assurance is not a result of self-delusion and an attempt to dissimulate hidden worries.

THE CAPACITY FOR ETHNIC-RACIAL RESISTANCE

Following the first line of interpretation it can be claimed that no fear or doubt seems to shake trust in the Romanians' capacity for ethnic-racial resistance. The off-handedness manifest in the various relevant declarations stands in sharp contrast both to the real and serious threat posed by Hungarian and Serb pressure, and to other elements of the self-image, which exhibit a more tentative attitude to the Romanians' various qualities and features. Nevertheless, a great number of the most trustworthy Transylvanian leaders of opinion express the utmost degree of self-assurance and confidence in this respect, which demonstrates that this aspect had become forcefully established within the self-image. It was, undoubtedly, the expression of a deep conviction, grown out of the nationalism specific to the age. At the same time, however, as I stated above, it can also be considered as the outcome of a subconscious mechanism of symbolic self-defence in the face of a serious threat to the national existence and its projection in terms of identity.

The theme of resistance to denationalisation was not, however, a novelty. It was obviously indebted to certain perceptions, attitudes and behaviour proper to traditional peasant mentality with its reserve and mistrust with respect to foreigners and the hostility it exhibited at the very idea of coming into more intimate contact with outsiders.[54]

In spite of this heritage, however, which it incorporated, the Enlightenment remained unable to develop a well-articulated theory on this particular question, since it still lacked the doctrinal perspective on the nation that only Romanticism would produce. Petru Maior, for instance, tries to deny the quite popular theme of the denationalisation of the Romanian élites, yet goes no further than merely denying the phenomenon, without offering a persuasive argumentation: "There are quite few of them [the Romanian nobles opting for denationalisation] and they only comply to it out of great need; and they do not abjure both the nation and the

Eastern Church, to which every Romanian is devoted." Further on, however, Maior admits that "the cream of the Romanian nobles" have embraced Calvinism and now think of themselves as Hungarians.[55] Thirteen years later, Theodor Aaron takes up the theme in a commentary on his master, and proves extremely categorical too, yet still without any further explanation: "I believe it to be easier to unite water with fire than to turn the Romanians Slavic (Serb)."[56]

On the other hand, an intellectual like Eftimie Murgu, nourished with the new Romantic principles, offers an extremely elaborate theoretical argument in support of the idea that no nation, the Romanians included, can undergo a dissolution of its defining traits, which are hereditarily imprinted into the national specificity. Naturally, Murgu, just like the other scholars who would subsequently tackle the issue, develops his thesis along the co-ordinates of Herder's Romantic conception of the nation, which dominated the space of Central and Eastern Europe at the time.[57] Nationality is an organic, inborn given, conditioning one's development as a cultural being; it cannot be obliterated, forfeited or borrowed at will, since it is a metaphysical principle that transcends individual will.[58]

Murgu builds up his demonstration as a polemical response to Sava Tököly. The latter had claimed (as many Romanians did too, in fact) that in the event that "a Romanian fails to go up in the world, he then recants his nationality, feeling ashamed he was ever called a Romanian." According to Murgu:

> Such a supposition is completely groundless. In the first place, it is to be observed that a man can be silent about what his nation is, but cannot recant it. It cannot be denied that among the characteristics of nationalities the first and foremost is descent, as well as the national spirit specific to any nation. That characteristic is continuously transmitted by way of heredity. A sly deceiver may shut his eyes to all other particularities of his nationality, yet one of them will remain whether he wants it or not, since it does not depend on our observation, and therefore neither is it subject to our will, while still being recognisable and different from other nations. That particularity of every nation might be called the national character or the national specificity. This irrefutable inheritance that, as carrier of the national characteristics, alone defines nationality, is the implacable and protective divinity which is so adamant in resisting an integral transformation of the nation. Those who choose to be silent about their own nation may well display, by a change of language, a deceptive exterior aspect, yet can never adopt a true, authentic aspect of the nation they have newly adopted.[59]

As a consequence of this theory, Murgu goes on, cultivated Romanians do not repudiate their nationality, but most of them acknowledge it in full.[60]

George Bariţ writes at a time of fierce disputes surrounding Hungarian projects for denationalisation (the so-called fight for language of 1842)[61], yet he also feels persuaded that the Romanians cannot be assimilated. This is in fact one of the central themes of his political meditation, which he elaborates in quite carefully drawn demonstrations. As compared to Murgu, Bariţ founds his argumentation less on theoretical grounds than on a pragmatic analysis of the political-social and cultural-ideological realities capable of legitimating it.

In an article of 1842 he writes that the factors in favour of the maintenance of a national life for the Romanians from Transylvania are: a) their great number; b) the awakening of a self-consciousness and the acknowledgement of the mother tongue as an instrument of a national culture and literature; c) the church, considered as "the mightiest defence-wall of the Romanians' nationality"; and d) "the close national and religious communication" between the Transylvanian Romanians and the Romanians from the principalities, who would inspire the former with their model of national life.[62]

On the basis of these arguments, Bariţ repeatedly expresses his faith in the Romanians' capacity for ethnic-national resistance. He sometimes does so in relation to his fellow countrymen from the principalities (faced with the pan-Slav danger which threatened their political existence and extended its religious influence under the banner of Orthodoxy): "I believe that the Wallachians and the Moldavians, surrounded as they are today by Slavonic nations, are able to fight by themselves for their nationality and language, and also to keep up their forefathers' faith" since "they have now their constitution and national governments" which are "securely upheld by the common sense and public opinion that are growing in the spirit of the nation itself."[63] Elsewhere, too, he finds no reason why he should fear anything for the Transylvanians: "Any attempt to denationalise the Transylvanian Romanians is but a vain endeavour, a thing most repugnant to nature and a fight against an overbearing genetic majority, a blind uproar against a literature that can no longer decline and fall."[64]

One of the key ideas of Bariţ's discourse is that denationalisation is no longer possible "today", in the age of modernity. This is not only due to international public opinion and to the pre-eminence of the principle of nationalities within the system of ideas and practices proper to European foreign affairs. The decisive factors are the birth of the peoples' national consciousness as expressed in a modern culture, and the affirmation of their ethnic-cultural identity, which renders futile any attempt at assimilation.[65] "Could it be conceived that today, in the nineteenth century and with the political situation prevalent in Europe, a nation like that of the Romanians could fade away and then turn into something else if it well pleases some wise head or other?" asks the Braşov-based journalist in 1842.[66] If denationalisation could not affect the Romanians under medieval oppression, today it does not stand a chance.

On the other hand, Bariţ admits, it is also true that the Hungarian political élite has included among its national aims the assimilation of the nationalities.[67] But the attempt is both futile and impossible:

> This has been the way with the Romanians for centuries on end, and this will be the course of things for many centuries to come. Every struggle by those who would alter [= denationalise] the Romanians, this people of the highlands, will bend and come to pieces in front of their tenacious will. And in this the Romanian has no need for roving apostles, who would walk from village to village and come with all sorts of advice as to why he should not desert his religion, his nationality, his language and all the ancient customs.[68]

In a way that is absolutely paradoxical for the period in question, the ensuing conclusion is that there is no real danger of denationalisation. Moreover, the logical consequence is that the Romanians need neither worry nor do anything special in order to preserve their ethnic integrity: "A people, gentlemen, cannot be made into a bundle and thrown at once into the water; neither can it be made to contract consumption and die a slow death. The age of tyrannical measures is past now and never to return. For the which my belief in the Romanian's future is most strong, and I am certain that were he not to stir a finger for himself he would still endure well for a thousand years."[69] Certainly, should he agree to make some supplementary efforts all the same, the future of the nation would be the brighter.

As we will see below, Papiu Ilarian passes severe criticism on this conception, which Bariț and others had quite enthusiastically promoted in political articles in *Vormärz*. It is also true that Bariț himself seems, at a certain moment during the revolution, to contradict the ideas he had previously expounded. Before the second assembly in Blaj he presents (in a critical manner) the arguments employed by the Hungarians in their attempt to bring the Romanians round to an unconditional acceptance of the union with Hungary. But these arguments are identical to the opinions he had already professed and would still eventually maintain. All the same, the unflinching gazetteer betrays no confusion or acknowledgement of self-contradiction; on the contrary, he must have been quite persuaded of his own consistency, as far as he was concerned.

While presenting to the Romanians the advantages of an annexation to the new, liberal and reform-bent Hungary, writes the editor of the *Gazette*, the Hungarians are also trying to convince them not to fear a loss of nationality by that same union. "Nothing to fear here", says the Hungarian journalist quoted and criticised by Bariț, "for if they did not lose it when they were serfs, when their brains were lowly and unlearned, when they were cast down in poverty, now, when freedom warms their lives, when the light of culture guides them, when the properties they own put them in a position to use all advanced branches of industry, by no means will they lose it now." Although engaged in a polemics with his Hungarian adversary, Bariț's answer completely, if unknowingly (yet in a way truthful to his usual view), agrees with the opinions of his foil: "As to the extinction of the Romanian nationality, we will speak plainly and say that today we fear naught; for it is impossible, by the laws of nature, that the greater bowl be emptied into the lesser."[70]

Simion Bărnuțiu makes less frequent use of the theme of trust in the Romanians' capacity to resist denationalisation, which is, to a certain extent, due to his less numerous journalistic manifestations, as compared with Bariț. Nevertheless, another aspect is of more consequence here, one that will become quite apparent in Papiu Ilarian's case—namely, the paradox that the radical nationalists bring up the theme of assimilation much more frequently. They always have countless traitors and renegades to denounce, and thus justify their lack of trust in the nation's ability to resist. On the other hand, the moderates find no reason to fret about it; they remain calm and sure of their trust in the people, as sanctioned by Herder's theories and the positive clichés of the self-image.

In the "moderate", optimistic sense, Bărnuțiu declares at one point in the Blaj *Discourse*: "He who knows the Romanians' nature can see that they will not easily submit to the measures of Hungarianisation."[71]

However, in his well-known article "A shameful deal and an unfair rule", written in 1842[72], the perspective is more sensitive to nuance. Although belief in the Romanians' national sentiments receives passionate expression, the idea of the defence of their nationality appears rather in the form of an appeal to that end, the insinuation being that some things still remain to be taken care of in this respect. Indeed: "It would be a complete blunder to entertain the belief that the Romanians are void of sentiments for their honour, character and nationality." Yet, trust in their capacity to resist is expressed in the conditional, which makes room for a sinister piece of warning: "In the same way that the Hungarians, were they to renounce their language, would no longer be the mighty people they are now; so neither would the Romanians, in that same case, be a people any more, but only the scum of a people, whom everyone could employ to every villainy." The sinister prediction once admitted, trust may, and indeed must, be given the upper hand within the discourse of identity: "But this will never be the doing of the Romanians, for they are secure in their belief that, as the Hungarians have a right to their Hungarian tongue, so the Romanians have a right to their Romanian language."[73]

Timotei Cipariu, now in his hypostasis as a "moderate", a sceptic observer of national capabilities, seems to doubt the possibility that the Romanians' Hungarianisation could become a real fact, thus taking up the line of Bariţ's thought. He founds his conviction on an extremely pragmatic, if more rarely used, argument. The Romanians will not become subject to Hungarianisation because they see no benefit in such a transformation: "And what are the Romanians to expect from that change? No use whatsoever, and no hope. Or has the Romanian ever stooped so easily, and will he ever stoop?"[74] Surely, Cipariu's interpretation was making way for Papiu Ilarian's critical analysis: Were the Hungarians to offer advantages (the abolishment of serfdom, individual political rights, etc.) in exchange for the Romanians' learning of Hungarian—as both Széchenyi[75] and Wesselényi[76] suggest, in different variants—would the Romanians not find themselves heading towards denationalisation?

Trust in Romanian resistance to denationalisation was nevertheless grounded in particular on the general belief that the peasant majority of the nation had that particular tendency inscribed among its intimate and specific traits. The "people" invoked by the Romantics was undoubtedly the folkloric-ideological construct invented by Herder[77] and painted in idyllic shades by an Alecsandri or Coşbuc. Faithful to this perspective, the Transylvanian intellectuals refer repeatedly to the "archaic mentality" (actually a period piece flung in some corner of the archaeological museum of nationalist ideology), while legitimating their identity-related clichés on the basis of ethnographic observations.

The theme in question would derive its key arguments from that very sphere. "The Romanian finds no comfort in blending with foreign blood. He has preserved this domestic antipathy to this day", writes Cipariu. "It will be preserved from now on as well, and we find no reason why that antipathy should be disproved."[78] The process whereby ideology turns such ethnographic arguments into instruments to be used on all occasions (although, surely, they may sometimes have represented actual sociological realities) is significantly illustrated by Cipariu's calling them up in support of his defence of Transylvania's union with Hungary. Given that we are not disposed towards denationalisation, we may rest assured and accept this political solution and profit from the advantages it offers.

Bariţ, too, appeals to the traditional mentality. The Romanian peasant "cannot suffer the sight of his children putting on mixed habits"[79]—either in sartorial or, we might add, and even more so, in ethnic, terms. It is plain that such a people cannot be denationalised.

THE MIXED MARRIAGE AS A MEANS OF ALTERING ETHNIC PURITY

Another theme of wide circulation feeding on such ethnographic arguments and coming as a coda to the motif of Romanian resistance to denationalisation is the theme of the Romanians' ethnic purity as exhibited in discriminatory matrimonial behaviour, that is, hostility towards mixed marriages and to the idea of becoming related to foreigners.[80]

Here, as elsewhere, Petru Maior is the one who has a decisive say in establishing this feature in the national self-perception: "The Romanian people is to this day so weary of marrying women who are not Romanian that it very rarely happens for a Romanian to wed a wife of another tongue [...] That the Romanian has it in himself not to marry women of other tongues seems to me one of the reasons why [...] the Romanian tongue remains forever whole and unified."[81]

The obsession with ethnic purity and with racial "cleanliness", and the detestable connotations inherent in such terms and notions as relate to "crossbreeding"; the determined rejection of kinship or any intimate relationships with foreigners, which can only sully and mar the core of Romanian specificity—these are all essential elements of the discourse on identity. Not only marriage, but mere sexual intercourse with a foreign person is, in Maior's opinion, a sin that lays a heavy burden on the consciousness of the one who commits it. The Romanians, writes the rector of Gurghiu, "even when they confess their sins, by Christian law, to their confessor and spiritual father, if it so happens that they have committed the carnal sin with a woman of another nation, the burden being too heavy on their souls, they say that that woman was not Romanian."[82]

Damaschin Bojincă makes the same observation, which he reinforces with the idea of the endogamy specific to folk mentality: "Experience teaches us that it can rarely be said in truth of the Romanian that he be wedded to a woman of another nation, and neither does he choose a woman of such kinfolk as are of the same faith with him, nor even one of another village, and says he: Man ought to know the woman's kin and hearth."[83] The *Buda Lexicon* transposes the phenomenon onto a historical level by envisaging a wide span of time, thus hinting at the real ideological import of the motif of hostility to mixed marriages. After the Roman colonisation, the lexicon claims, many barbaric populations crossed the Dacian land, but "the overwhelming numbers of the Romanians, as well as their noble keenness not to mix in marriage with women of a foreign sort, prevented the Romanian tongue from too close a contact with the barbarian languages, whereby it would have surely been disfigured beyond recognition."[84]

Indeed, irrespective of the ethnographic reality whence it derived its legitimacy, the theme in question was the expression of an altogether differently oriented tendency, that is, the argumentation in favour of the indispensable theory of the purity of the Romanians' Latin origins. Knowing that the Romanians had inherited the full and complete stock of specific Roman features, their current matrimonial behaviour proved once again that the Romans did not marry Dacian women, thus preserving their ethnic purity unaltered, which they eventually passed on to their children and descendants. In subsequent decades, however, by a pirouetting metamorphosis typical of the cultural mechanisms by means of which images are transmitted, the idea would lose its initial function as an argument in an enlightened scholarly demonstration, and would activate to the full its nationalist connotations. As such, it would become an organic element of the Romantic conception of the peoples' capacity for national resistance.

At an early stage of the thesis, Petru Maior made a clear case for its intentions. Hostile foreign historians, envying the Romanians their illustrious origins, "say that the Romans who were sent by Trajan in Dacia took into wedlock Dacian women, out of which mixture grew a new breed of people, that is to say, not true Romans, but mongrels of Roman men and Dacian women".[85] Obviously, such an allegation (the very formula of the Romanians' ethno-genesis promoted today!) was taken to be an insult and a lie, since the Dacian men died in the war and so did most of their women and children, and the Roman veterans could not have stooped to marry barbarian spouses, while procreating in rather mysterious ways, on which Maior chooses not to insist.

Budai-Deleanu is thought to have taken, as a rule, a more moderate stance as to the theory of Latin purity; yet he too promotes it at a certain point, in his dissertation on the origins of the peoples of Transylvania. Some say we are the offspring of the Dacians, others "that we are a people born out of mixed marriages between the Dacians and the Romans", and yet others that "we are a cross of all the barbarian peoples who ever lived in Dacia, one after the other".[86] All these are, certainly, false opinions, the Transylvanian scholar goes on, deliberately forged to some political end by the Romanians' Hungarian and Saxon enemies.[87]

Elsewhere, however, Budai-Deleanu initiates an altogether different line of interpretation of mixed marriages and their effects on Romanian society: he admits, as an allowance to historical logic, "the fact that the Romans were pledged in matrimony to the Dacians"[88], even though he thus contradicts some of his previous affirmations.

It is also true that, with him, this new claim does not translate as derogation from the principle of the Romanians' exclusively Latin descent: it only entails a mere change in the way the theory will be argued. Language (rather than any occasional alliance) is, in Budai-Deleanu's opinion, the defining element of nationality. Or, since the Romanians speak an essentially Latin language, they can consider themselves the exclusive heirs of the Romans. The new conception nevertheless made room for a different attitude towards the motif of mixed marriages, as it could no longer embrace the old denial of their existence in a significant proportion.

Paul Iorgovici writes along the same lines. Contrary to a Maior or Bojincă[89], Iorgovici admits that "the Romanians used to live mixed with the Slovenes as they do now with the Serbs, from whom many a word have they borrowed [...]; no language and no nation can stay away from mixing", he adds.[90] Yet this has no bearing upon the core of the nation, which remains untouched by the Serbs, since nationality, the philologist from Banat believes, is defined by the historical origin, and especially by the primitive form, of the language.[91]

It was to be much later, in an age when Latinism was breathing its last, that Codru Drăguşanu (under the influence of less purist Wallachian traditions) was able to extend the frame of such rationalist considerations to the point where he could speak of the assimilation of the barbarian peoples within north-Danubian Roman frames.[92]

The idea that the phenomenon of mixed marriages had a tradition among the Romanians was too unpleasant a morsel to be swallowed easily by the collective imaginary of the time, and in fact it did not succeed in displacing the theory of the Romanians' ethnic purity. On the other hand, however, there were more and more observations of the current manifestation of the said process, which grew into a veritable stereotype. It does not follow, obviously, that relationships with foreigners began to be seen in a more favourable light; on the contrary, the cliché was meant to draw attention to the huge threat posed by mixed marriages to the need for national survival. According to the value hierarchy of the Romanian society at the beginning of the modern age, individual interests and sentiments had to bend to, and even coincide with, the common good.

The theme of the danger of mixed marriages becomes central to the explanation of such phenomena as denationalisation and assimilation. Its implications are, first, that it is the Romanians' fault, and not that of the foreigners, that there are fewer and fewer Romanians (in keeping with the self-critical dimension of the negative self-image), and, second, that the foreigners' methods of assimilation are indeed devious and subtle. As we have seen above[93], the representation of women as agents of the evil principle, appearing within society with the mission of tempting Romanian men and leading them astray, away from the right national path and into the space of perdition, is a strong image of the collective imaginary feeding on the misogynist tendencies of traditional mentality. The mixed marriage, incriminated by the discourse on identity, is almost always imagined as a relationship between a Romanian man and a foreign woman. And although women were in a position of complete inferiority within the moral economy of the family, the typical scenario invariably had the man betraying the public interest and even his national identity.[94]

An exception to this rule is to be found in Papiu Ilarian. While deploring the advancement of Hungarianisation among the Romanian élites in the decades prior to the revolution, Papiu shows that "the most honoured rectors and priests send their daughters to Cluj, Oşorhei, etc., where they can have commerce with Hungarian culture, whereof they come back with a good knowledge of the Hungarian language and garb, and it no longer agrees with them to be seeing Romanian lads, but they show an eagerness to converse with young Hungarian courtiers."[95]

On the other hand, Budai-Deleanu writes that the Hungarianisation of Romanian nobles who were seeking favours and benefits, "could not happen otherwise than by marriages" with Hungarian women, which ultimately led to assimilation.[96] Bojincă describes the methods employed by the Serbs in order to denationalise the Romanians (one such method being the schools), and shows that they are futile attempts, all except one: "Although the Serbs would leave no stone unturned in these matters, they hardly succeed in their doings, yet they sometimes happen to lay hands on some Romanian and betroth him, by ties of marriage, to the Serb nation."[97] Towards the middle of the century, Nicolae Tincu Velia uses similar terms: All Romanians understand the danger inherent in the Serbs' politics of denationalisation, "except those who are either turned Serb or fully entangled in family ties with the Serbs, or who live by their grace".[98] The conclusion to be drawn is clear: The only possibility of assimilation, the vulnerable spot of national resistance, was the pernicious marriage with foreign women.

Doubtless, the motif of the danger posed by mixed marriages finds its most spectacular expression in Moise Nicoară. As I pointed out in a previous chapter, his attitude cannot be separated from the psychological resentments of the child who lost his natural mother and then had to put up with a Serb stepmother. This scenario, often present in traditional mentality[99], was seen as a perfect illustration of the sly, insidious way in which foreigners managed to steal into Romanian souls and rule over them.

This being the case, it was only natural for Nicoară to make negative reference to Serb–Romanian mixed marriages: "If ever the son of a Romanian began to see the light they had to strip him naked, so that being among the Serbs he had to turn Serb, or else to wed a Serb's daughter unless he chose to starve to death."[100] Yet within his political-national representations, still indebted to an underlying type of "Illyrian" "nation-confession" solidarity, the most dangerous enemies are not the Orthodox Serbs (as they were for most people from Banat), but the Catholic Hungarians and Germans, the A-Romanians (as instruments of Viennese politics), and even the Greek Catholic Romanians. Such are the extensions of Nicoară's obsessions.

Ever since the times of Maria Theresa's policy of Catholic proselytism, "it has been by marriage with German and Hungarian women that the Romanian nation is fading away".[101] Imperial policy was intent on having the Romanians embrace Greek Catholicism solely in order to Germanise and Hungarianise them. How could this be? Well, simply because the Uniates, by abjuring their nationality and confession in order to advance to better positions, especially in the towns, always married foreign women: "Was ever seen a Uniate Romanian to wed a Romanian woman? And he who renounces not only the Romanians, but their church too, what does he do? He marries a Hungarian woman, another a German, and so on and so forth. Now tell me, what will his children be, when neither his woman nor anyone else knows he is a Romanian? [...] Will those babies be Romanian, when they always hear their parents speak ill of the Romanians and laugh at them together with other foreigners [...]?"[102]

Elsewhere Nicoară writes that, in order to reach its occult goals, the empire wants the bishopric of Transylvania to accept religious union, "if for nothing else, then only to get them round by and by, with promise of some office, to marrying, like all Uniates do, some Papist women; and then, slowly becoming one with the Hungarians and the Germans, to turn Papists themselves, while the Romanian name is sure to fail and fall".[103] Marriage with a foreign woman was therefore the most menacing strategy devised by the universal conspiracy with a view to destroying the Romanian national identity.

We should also note that, while mixed marriages acquired such absolutely negative dimensions within the discourse on identity, reality provided evidence of sometimes altogether different tendencies. Access to superior education, together with the erosion of the traditional mentality, entailed frequent deviations from the matrimonial rule banning interethnic alliances. The young intellectual nationalists—the first or second generation to have left the village world—could by no means be accused of a lack of national sentiments, and yet they were to break the old interdictions in all serenity. Budai-Deleanu married an Armenian, Maria de Mikolaewicze; George Bariţ a "Greek maid" from Braşov, Maria Velisar; Vasile Pop a Saxon lady, born Wagner; Vincenţiu Babeş a Viennese, Sofia Goldscheider; Petru Cermena a Serb woman, Maria Doctorovici; Pavel Vasici a Hungarian, Júlia Jancsó; Vasile Maniu a nephew of Kossuth, Olga de Lovich; and the list could go on.[104] The tolerant and cosmopolitan spirit specific to the heirs of the Enlightenment, as well as a typically Romantic sensibility, had already unleashed the free play of personal feelings in these people, even though their written opinions, still faithful to the canonical co-ordinates of the self-image, were sometimes at variance with their behaviour.

Some of them, for example Bariţ, Babeş or Vasici, may be said to owe the chance of meeting a foreign partner to certain of their own personal traits: their tolerance, modesty and openness to the values of others, as well as respect for the family, marriage and the role of women in society. Bariţ (who was to have nine children[105], just like Babeş[106]) or Vasici would devote a lifetime's journalistic work to observations on such topics[107], arguing for the improvement of inter-family relationships between parents and children, or husband and wife—issues that they treated on a par with that of national inequalities.

It would seem to follow from the above considerations that the materialisation of their matrimonial options may have been influenced by an anti-authoritarian type of attitude and behaviour (in the sense of such concepts as are theorised in Theodor Adorno[108]), one able to discourage, in their individual cases, the development of an ethnocentric type of personality.[109]

DENATIONALISATION: STIGMATISING THE ÉLITES AS PROMOTERS OF ASSIMILATION

Another line of interpretation bearing on the Romanians' capacity to resist denationalisation, one related to the image of mixed marriages, draws attention to the real danger of assimilation.

Central here is the widely spread motif of the Hungarianisation of the Romanian élites, and of the nobles in particular, as well as the theme of the renegades, or individual deserters from the national cause. In both cases, however, it is not the mass of the people that appears as subject to the process of assimilation. Given that in the Romantic conception the essence of the nation is represented by the peasant multitudes, and not by the cultured élites, the conclusion can be drawn that, all in all, the Romanians did rather well at resisting denationalisation. This is one of the core issues of Papiu's *History*: "Even though the learned embraced the Hungarian nation"—that is, the nobles, the priests, the élites as a whole—"or merely kept to themselves and had no word against Hungarianism, the forceful opposition came from the bulk of the Romanian people."[110]

On the other hand, it is still Papiu who foregrounds another, much more worrying, thesis. The Romanian nobles chose to trade their nationality in the Middle Ages for a series of political and material advantages[111]; the "mass of the people" remained untouched by assimilation, since they "took no part in the constitutional bounties, and, as a result, could not turn Hungarian either".[112] But in the present, at a time when the Hungarians were willing to offer the whole population individual political rights and an opportunity for social emancipation, were the Romanians not faced with the danger that, tempted by such advantages, the nation be affected by assimilation at its very core? Papiu's comment is the following:

> That the association of the inhabitants for common purposes notwithstanding their nationalities is able to lead to denationalisation was proved in all clarity by the aristocratic constitution of the Hungarian Country [in the Middle Ages] which had the Slav and Romanian nobles turn Hungarian. With the aid of wise politics, as was Széchenyi's, it might have happened that the other part of the people be Hungarianised as well by a settlement of common interests and of a common language rule.[113]

Papiu Ilarian thus comes to believe—and rightly so, we might add, although in sheer contrast with his national conceptions—that a "nation", in the political sense of the term (as well as the national identity associated with it), can build not only on ethnic-linguistic affinities, language and origins, but also on the identification of certain "common interests" of the inhabitants of the "country", and the stipulation of equal rights for all of them, as expressed in a uniform legislation.[114] The formula here is the French "voluntarist" model of the nation (versus Herder's "organicist" model); its materialisation was nevertheless strongly opposed by Romanian intellectuals from Transylvania.

Another young man of Papiu's generation, Ioan Puşcariu, gives an extremely explicit formulation of the same idea in a letter of March 1848:

> The Romanians have stood up to this day [= have resisted assimilation] only by keeping to their church and away from the rules. Now they have to abide by both Hungarian rules, which will presently lead to their denationalisation, in the same way that the Romans denationalised the whole world, first by conquering it, then by giving it citizen's rights, and in the end by having it speak their language. With us here, they have seen that no good comes of ill treatment, so now they wave the right of Hungarian citizenry, in which they surely imitate the French, who have mixed so many peoples by the power of one concept, that of *citoyen*. No, the Romanian can only fare worse from now on! So far they could hardly get them out of their caves in the Carpathians; now they mean to dazzle them with the splendours of Buda-Pest.[115]

It cannot be doubted that Papiu, Bărnuţiu or Puşcariu intend their scenarios as a warning against the danger of denationalisation for the use of their fellow countrymen, and feel they cannot be too vigilant about it. The paradoxical outcome of this attitude is that it is precisely the most radical nationalists who come to doubt the nation's capacity for resistance, in which the "moderates" believed without a second thought.

Even the denationalisation of the élites was seen as a phenomenon taking place on such a large scale that it seemed ultimately to bear on the whole nation. Papiu speaks of "the countless Romanians who embraced the Hungarian law", in referring to the early decades of the century[116]; in between 1830 and 1840 he observes again that "the Hungarians' attempts to Hungarianise the Romanians indeed had already made considerable progress", and "the Romanians, in their turn, no longer thought of themselves as respectable and civilised enough people unless they spoke the Hungarian language."[117] Romanian children were willingly sent to Hungarian schools, traditional customs were forgotten, the young readily Hungarianised their names, and Hungarian had begun to make its way into the internal administration of the Romanian churches, which was even more than the Hungarianisation acts had stipulated.[118]

In painting the catastrophic image of the Romanians' disposition towards assimilation, Papiu insists on this very deliberate embracing of Hungarian rules by the Romanians: the threat against the nationality of the latter came "not only from the Hungarians, but from the Romanians themselves, too, who were more and more eager to turn Hungarian, day by day".[119] The preference for the use of Hungarian in the Blaj bishopric "did so much for the Hungarians, more than they dared to hope by their own laws".[120] The Romanians from western areas, "far from opposing Hungarianism, gave it a warm welcome", and the worst of it was that the attitude was not confined to church élites, but seemed to spread among the body of the nation "from the bishop, through the clerics and the intellectuals, to certain villages where, in the Romanian churches, the Romanian pupils started to sing *keresztények sírjatok* ['Weep, thou Christians'—a Hungarian Catholic religious song]".[121] The very capacity for ethnic resistance on the part of the peasants is thus questioned and ultimately denied; the critical passion is poured forth in fits of anger and frenzied paradoxes: "Were Rákóczy himself to rise from the dead he would wonder at the way the times have changed, that the Romanians' bishop has now to ask permission from the Hungarians to translate the church books into Hungarian, whereas two hundred years ago the Hungarians had had the Romanians translate the liturgy into their national tongue."[122]

Enflamed by his own apocalyptic scenario, Papiu discharges his criticisms not only onto the renegades, but on those who still believe in the Romanians' capacities for national resistance, those who are not vigilant enough now, at the last hour before the tremendous threat becomes reality. He starts with Petru Maior himself, whom he cannot forgive for having said (in a phrase Papiu is careful to quote) that "the illustrious Hungarian nation has never done any injustice to the Romanians".[123] He continues with Bojincă and the other post-Enlightenment intellectuals from Banat, whom he accuses of being blind to the Hungarian threat because of their unilateral anti-Slav tendency. Again, Papiu quotes guilty paragraphs, such as those in which Bojincă shows that "the Romanians have wisely and diligently taken to learning the language of the country, Hungarian (whose sweetness (!) [the outraged exclamation mark is Papiu's] is rapture to foreign ears too)."[124]

The historian finally reaches the point he had envisaged from the very beginning, that is, a criticism of his contemporaries who, being neither traitors nor renegades, still play into the enemy's hands by "too generous a faith in the up-holding of the Romanian nationality, which they call 'genetic' [Papiu always uses the term with almost ironical undertones]".[125] In 1848, "the defenders of the union with Hungary [he probably refers, among others, to Cipariu] said that the genetic nationality, which has stayed unblemished for centuries, can never more be feared to perish"[126], as they thought that the Hungarians would never be able to extricate the national strain preserved in the Romanians' patriarchal traditions and ada-mantly kept up by the peasants.[127]

Their reasoning is faulty in the extreme, according to Papiu, thus reversing the argumentation developed by Bariț. If the Romanians were able to preserve their nationality in the Middle Ages by mere passive ethnic resistance (although the élites dropped it even then), today this is no longer possible. The current policy of deliberate denationalisation has at his disposal extremely efficient laws and insti-tutions (e.g. the school), faced with which the "genetic" nationality and passive resistance come to nothing. The means to end the fatal threat are to take direct national action, to fight against assimilation and especially to guarantee collective political rights (the "political nation", in the absence of which the "genetic" one is doomed to perish).[128]

Naturally, the revolution appeared as the inaugural moment of a new histori-cal age, the starting point of an overnight radical change of all negative realities. The nation would have a chance to rub away every speck of rust from its old body and come out again with a brand new face. The Romanians were gathering mo-mentum; instead of the old tendency to abjure their nationality and turn a deaf ear to the danger, a new attitude was setting in, one of conscious and active resis-tance. All were, obviously, signs of a reworking within the political imaginary of the revolutionary mythology.

It is also true that, although Papiu was the one who systematised the motif of the Romanians' denationalisation into a coherent theory, the theme is present, in different variants, throughout the cultural discourse of the time.

One of the more frequent variants is the theme of scorn for the mother tongue, which the Romanians obliterate while espousing foreign idioms. Since language is the prime and most visible element of identity, it follows that reticence in using it translates as hesitancy in assuming one's own ethnic-linguistic condition, felt as a burden by many. "Some are even ashamed to speak Romanian and among them-selves they would [rather] speak Greek or Hungarian or any other language that is not their own", writes Samuil Micu in 1796.[129] Budai-Deleanu shows that in the principalities "the nobles, although in no want of pure autochthonous words, de-spise them and would rather use foreign ones, which is to say Turkish and Greek"[130], but Transylvania is not exempt from such bad habits either:

Look at our noble throng
Bent on the Hungarian tongue
So today as for so long.[131]

Petru Maior deplores the fact that the foreigners' derision at the Romanians' national identity "leads no small number of Romanians, even those who have had an education, into cursing their own Romanian tongue, which they have no heart to learn better, but forsaking the language of their mothers they put on a show of their knowledge of some foreign tongues, like Turkish and Greek."[132] Andrei Mureşanu writes, in an ironical statement in 1844, that in the principalities, Romanian is the language of the state and of the church, "and, were it not for French, it may be the language of conversation as well, although so far it has been welcomed in few aristocratic houses, apart from among their servants".[133] Codru Drăguşanu applies the same judgement to the whole of Bucharest society, irrespective of their social condition: in "the Babylon of Romania", it is "not that the foreigners do not all speak the Romanian language, but in their own capital the Romanians speak the languages of all peoples. Among the upper class reigns the French language; the middle class has not yet forgotten its neo-Greek...; and then the commoners, as a function of where they were born, express their few ideas in Serb–Bulgarian, German–Hungarian, Russian, Italian–Spanish, Turkish and Otherish, and only rarely in Romanian."[134]

This long series of quotations, which might extend indefinitely, speaks for itself of the tenacity of the image, continuously circulated because ceaselessly nourished by unchanged realities. The need to use a more cultivated language than the mother tongue, the social prestige and culture it is able to confer, the access it grants to superior education and to a higher social or professional status, are temptations which the élites, with a taste for affirmation, found simply irresistible. At the same time, however, the use of a foreign language as a daily means of communication among one's fellow countrymen could be taken as a first step towards denationalisation. Consequently, the self-image severely reproves the new habit.[135]

The paradoxical consequences to which the disputes surrounding the question of whether the Romanians were or were not going through a process of denationalisation could lead are visible in the case of a press scandal which erupted in the summer of 1846.[136] It was provoked by the theatrical performances given in Blaj by a group of Hungarian itinerant actors.[137] Bărnuţiu, chased away from Blaj as a result of a personal conflict (in fact, one with both personal and political-national import) with Bishop Lemeny, wanted to take revenge on the clerics in Blaj and used this opportunity to blame the city of Blaj for embracing Hungarianism. He did so in a quite surprising manner, however, by writing anonymously for a Hungarian paper in Cluj, taking note both of the performance and of the ongoing Hungarianisation of Blaj while posing as an enthusiastic adept of Romanian denationalisation. Obviously, his intention was to shock by overcharge, and, indeed, his text is as shocking as can be. "The Romanians in Transylvania have never resisted Hungarianisation" is the beginning of Bărnuţiu's article! This, he says, has been plain to see during Lemeny's bishopric, when "the city of Blaj is becoming Hungarian and thereby more and more advanced on the way of progress".[138]

The moderates did have some idea about who was hiding beneath the cryptonym "B-r", as Bărnuţiu had signed his article in *Vasárnapi Újság*. Nor did they delay in replying. First, Bariţ shows that the accusations are unfair. Even if the people in Blaj go to a Hungarian theatre performance or even learn the language, no harm is done: "B-r wonders that our people in Blaj are ready to learn Hungarian. What is there to wonder about in someone learning the tongues of his country? Ask the Swiss: be they German, French, or Italian, aren't they learning one another's language?"[139]

Another reply to Bărnuțiu, by Cipariu, which was published in the *Gazette of Transylvania*, employs an even more critical tone. On reading the text in the Hungarian gazette, "many will be shaking their heads", frightened at the idea that even Blaj, the "hearth" of Romanianness, "is becoming Hungarian". What is written there in relation to the progress of the Hungarian language "is no fabrication", but the inhabitants of Blaj have no reason to blame themselves for it. Indeed, "there is no antipathy towards this language in Blaj; the Romanians, here as elsewhere in Transylvania, are ready to learn it with pleasure, not distaste, and not for some need either; they are aware of the importance this language has acquired of late, they sense the sympathy growing in the hearts of this noble Asian people for the Romanian nation."[140] The élites of this small isolated town are, it is claimed, thirsting for cultural manifestations, which they are able to enjoy so rarely, and "naturally, they cannot afford to deprive themselves of such small contentment for the mere prejudice that it is performed in Hungarian".[141]

The whole affair must have been deeply distressing for Cipariu: a lover of performances and social life, and at the same time persuaded he was a good Romanian, he sees the word spreading in the gazettes that, by satisfying that "small contentment" of his soul, he can be accused of being a renegade and traitor to the national interest. Hence he retaliates against Bărnuțiu by throwing at him the same old mortifying characterisation, which is considered to be the supreme insult and seems to be useful at all times. Although he knows quite well who "B-r" is, Cipariu feigns perfect innocence and tries thus to have Bărnuțiu hoist with his own petard: "The author of the article", the conclusion reads, "is no doubt an enthusiastic zealot of the Hungarianisation of the Romanians."[142] Obviously, for a nationalist like Bărnuțiu, there could be no insult more disparaging than that![143]

Another element is worth mentioning here, one that will throw light on the actual complexity of attitudes to denationalisation in contrast with the simplifying perspective of the radical nationalism of the time, and in particular with its historiographical extensions. Bariț and Cipariu, for example, maintained that the learning of the Hungarian language and its use as an instrument for communication with others (the "language of the country") or as a cultural vehicle, did not necessarily entail a process of denial and denationalisation. However, this position ran the risk of interfering with certain Hungarian ideological attitudes which others considered extremely dangerous. The foremost theoreticians of the unitary national state and of the Hungarian "political nation", Széchenyi or Wesselényi, held, as a rule, that their plans for promoting the Hungarian language and the measures for introducing it in the schools and churches of other nationalities, were not intended to displace the respective mother tongues either from the latter's memory or from the sphere of their private lives. The sole purpose, they claimed, was to achieve the exclusive use of Hungarian in the sphere of state life or in public relations of any sort.[144] Obviously, apart from any accusation of insincerity, the Romanian nationalists could have chosen to argue that such measures were bound to bring about the demise of the Romanian language, particularly as a language of culture, which could pave the way towards complete denationalisation.[145]

However, as we have seen, the complexity of the problem allowed, from a theoretical point of view, the free play of a wealth of interpretations and viewpoints. Room was made for all sorts of intermediary solutions, such as the *Projet de pacification*, or the Nationalities Act passed *in extremis* by the Hungarian revolution in the summer of 1849[146]—which were, to a certain extent, acceptable to the Romanian party as well. On the other hand, however, the historical reality offered much less room for a political realisation of refined solutions of the kind, while the ideological systems presiding over the social imaginary were even less permissive towards any tendency to legitimate compromises.

One frequent variant of the motif of the Romanians' assimilation is denationalisation seen as affecting individuals or small groups—renegades and traitors deserting the colours. As we have seen, the renegade as a figure within the self-image was almost always picked out from among the noble or intellectual élites, since the peasant, as incorruptible preserver of national specificity, was considered immune to such deviations.

The symbolic functioning of this variant of the theme of denationalisation is, again, open to diversity and nuance. Its primary role was, obviously, vehemently to condemn desertion, which it did on innumerable occasions; a more lenient attitude comes only from the enlightened intellectuals of the Transylvanian School, who are willing to find excuses and motivations where possible.

Yet, as usual, that critical role is far from covering the whole signifying potential of the theme. An equally urgent need was to draw attention to the sociological dimensions of a phenomenon often taken as widespread, and consequently to provide a warning as to its sombre consequences. The side effects of insistence and exaggeration in this respect were even beneficial to the inner balance of the self-image, as they gave a taste of consoling self-delusion: the large numbers, as well as the social and intellectual quality, of the renegades demonstrates, once again, how strong and worthy the Romanians might have been (and are, in fact) were it not for this deplorable tendency. They could have gone far, had all the individuals who strayed remained among their fellow countrymen! Self-delusion, and yet another excuse for the troubles of the present; also, a piece of warning and a call for the monolithic national solidarity of Romanian dreams.

As I have already mentioned, some of the late eighteenth-century intellectuals are less categorical in approaching the issue. In 1778 Samuil Micu writes, along the lines of an older stereotype, that in the past "there were more illustrious families among the Romanians". However, because of "the persecutions they endured and the hope of betterment", many Romanians passed from Orthodoxy to Calvinism and thus "renounce [their faith] and cry out loud that they are not Romanians". Still, Micu continues, "you are not to understand that I speak here of all Romanians, for there have been some, and still are, who, although they have changed faith or religion, have in no way denied their nationality, and, what's more, have vigorously employed their pens in the support and defence of their nation. Thus was Petru Dobra, director of public finances in Transylvania [...], and to this day there are others capable of such honourable conduct."[147]

Petru Maior largely shares Micu's opinions. He even dismisses the idea of the supposed denationalisation of the Romanian nobles as a calumny circulated by foreigners. He believes that "there are quite few of them and they only comply to it out of great need; and they do not abjure both the nation and the Eastern Church, to which every Romanian is devoted". Surely, what still grieves his heart is that in the seventeenth century,

> the cream of the Romanian nobles embraced the confession of the Helvetic law; and then the renegades, thinking that once religion changes so does nationality, reckoned in their weak minds that they were no longer Romanians but Hungarians. Such is their conviction that if someone calls them Romanians it angers them in the extreme, for to this day they are all taken as one, blood and religion, and even ceremonies. Still, for all that, could it be a crime to be called a Hungarian? Are there not a whole lot of Germans who pride themselves on being counted among the Hungarians?[148]

The message of the paragraph is clear: the "renegades" in question are, and must be, Romanians. Their being Calvinist and noble, or even their calling themselves "Hungarian", is of no consequence. Are there not others who do the same? The noble class [stare] in Transylvania is called, in conformity with the constitutional formulae, natio hungarica, but that affects neither the deep structures of the nationality nor the ethnic-linguistic identity of those people.

The question remained as to whether or not a different religious confession meant a sure way towards denationalisation. The enlightened intellectuals, whose philosophical-social outlook had evolved around the concept of religious tolerance, could not view a change of confession with too critical an eye (although they did not approve of it either, given the nationalist traditionalism they professed). The core of their argumentation was that a change of confession does not necessarily impinge upon the national, ethnic-cultural specificity. One could be a Romanian while being Catholic or Calvinist at the same time.[149] The question was raised in similar terms as far as social condition was concerned. Nobility, and the social-political privileges associated with it, were, it was argued, perfectly compatible with the quality of being Romanian and did not necessarily lead to denationalisation.

As can be expected, the Romantics, and Papiu in particular, would pass violent criticism on that conception. How could a Calvinist noble be a good Romanian too? According to the medieval constitutional system in Transylvania such double belonging to a privileged "nation" [= status] and to a "recognised" religion automatically excluded the person from the Romanians.

On the other hand, the 1791 Transylvanian Diet, which repealed the stipulations of the Supplex, as it (paradoxically enough) repudiated Maior's and Micu's writings, argued that the Romanians were not (de facto), or should not be (de jure), discriminated against from a political, social or religious point of view. If they belonged to a constitutional nation or religion, they enjoyed all the rights and privileges ensuing therefrom, while the ethnic-linguistic condition of the respective persons was a matter of individual concern which had no bearing on their social or confessional situation.

The interplay of social images and realities with respect to such a complex and delicate matter could undoubtedly make room for the most diverse interpretations. The enlightened intellectuals referred to certain families who had been en-nobled and religiously assimilated hundreds of years before, were now occupants of high positions in Transylvanian society and the administration, yet nevertheless preserved a sense of belonging to the Romanian community. They believed that the very existence of such families was a strong argument in favour of the idea that the social and religious conditioning in question should not, indeed does not, necessarily lead to denationalisation. The Romantics invoked examples to the contrary, of great Romanian families who had been assimilated and were thus proof positive that perdition awaited those who took that path.

Budai-Deleanu, in contrast to Micu and Maior, seems more inclined towards this latter interpretation. His attitude is also due to his always being more critical of the aristocracy, including the Romanian aristocracy. "In Transylvania", writes the author of the *Gypsiad*, "the noblemen (Romanian though they be) will not be called Romanians and hold the name in great disdain [...] with them, nobility transmutes both nationality and faith. As an example: If a Romanian becomes a nobleman, then he will be called Hungarian; likewise, if he becomes a Papist or a Calvinist, neither will he be called Romanian, but Hungarian; and this is how, in Transylvania, thousands of Romanians turned Hungarian!"[150] Although the very same phenomenon is at stake, where his colleagues tried to see things in a light favourable to the Romanians Budai-Deleanu only perceives the threat of national assimilation and nothing more.

Later Simion Bărnuțiu, although quoting Maior, sees things from a similar angle. He too tries, inspired by the Transylvanian School, to convince his fellow countrymen that a change of confession has nothing to do with one's nationality. He is nevertheless quite sceptical as to the echo that that conception could have among the Romanians:

> Were the Romanians to receive in their bosoms the Calvinist faith the Romanian nationality would be lost, for once Romanians move to another rite they will know nothing of the Ro-manian nation, as we have seen they did before the union with Rome and as is plain today with some of the most excellent families, especially in Hațeg, the county of Hunedoara, and even Făgăraș; for many cannot conceive how it could be that someone still belongs to the Romanians while, in terms of religion, he is part of the Reformed Church; they who are so weak of mind will not see that if there could be Romans in Italy while they were still of pa-gan faith, so much the more can someone stay Romanian and confess to it while being of the Calvinist faith; for the Calvinists are themselves Christian, and we should not mingle religious faiths and theologians' disputes with nationality.[151]

From a theoretical point of view (and a well-argued one, too), in Bărnuțiu's opinion, as in Maior's, there is no reason for the Calvinised nobles to be dena-tionalised. It is just that in practical terms, again in his opinion, things are quite bad, even if the virulence of his criticism is able to speak of a ray of hope lurking in some unacknowledged corner of his heart that such harsh reprimands might straighten the sinful.

An extremely severe line of criticism against the renegades and traitors to the national cause, in terms specific to the radical nationalism of the time, is opened by Damaschin Bojincă. From his point of view the existence of the phenomenon is fully recognised, while emphasis on it is even meant as a pedagogical means of reinforcing national solidarity and cohesion by exposing the despicable negative examples to public ridicule. The renegades' ingratitude towards the national community to which they should feel forever obliged is one of the educational themes in fact meant to stimulate their zeal and abnegation before the community, the subsuming of their individual interests to the higher common good of the Nation. According to Bojincă

> There are some who grow up and learn in institutions set up by zealous men for the good of the Romanian nation, then, at the public expense of the nation, they dress up in the cloak of science, within or outside the country, and then, like ungrateful cuckoos, they not only raise no finger on behalf of the culture of their people but stray away into foreign flocks and throw venomous arrows back at the breast which fed them and the loins of those who raised them. Yet many, having a mind to exculpate themselves for the coldness they show towards the national culture, say that they know the French language, and the Latin, and the Greek and others, and that is why they have no more need of Romanian books; but they forget that it is by the well-being and good name of their country that they eat their daily bread.[152]

Papiu also writes about the young renegades supported by the Ramonţai Foundation (he himself would have great trouble receiving a scholarship[153]), a foundation raised up "for the benefit of the nation, not of foreigners"[154], or about "the young men whom Bishop Aron raised with a mind that when their time came they be a help to the nation in return; but, with all the money spent on their education, they turned Hungarian".[155] The considerable debt every individual has to the nation must by all means be reimbursed, while failure to do so equals treason and assimilation into the foreign nation.[156]

Denationalisation being an abominable thing, the renegades were considered to be worse than foreigners, dangerous enemies who had turned against their initial condition which they now sought to defile by every means possible. "Since they follow the natural inclination of every proselyte", writes Moise Nicoară, "to show they are more devoted to their new faith and to their new nationality, they in truth become greater enemies of their own nation than the other nations themselves, so that they can conform to the irreconcilable spirit of their hosts."[157] The great noble families of Transylvania ("Iojika, Majlat, Lazar, Nalazi, Kendefi, Teleki and Bánfi", that is, almost all the houses of the Transylvanian high nobility) are, in Nicoară's opinion, of Romanian origin, but represent today "the most unyielding adversaries of this poor and numerous and so oppressed nation of ours".[158]

This represents a fairly odd paradox; the Romanians (in their renegade hypostasis) are their own oppressors—an idea also present in Papiu Ilarian: after the religious union, he writes, "the Romanian intellectuals who acquired some high office by this means embraced the Hungarian rule and then, like all recanters (renegades), proved even more dangerous to the Romanians than the Hungarians themselves."[159]

The danger posed by the renegades derived not only from their mere change of national identity but especially from their automatically joining the opposing camps, since they usually turned not simply into some indifferent foreigners but into true enemies of the Romanians. In 1848, Avram Iancu complains that "the Hungarianised Romanians" from Abrud "were working for the demoralisation of the people"[160], while Papiu shows that the army which General Bem led when he entered Transylvania was "alas, full of Romanians who were the bravest party of that army, in part forced, in part spurred on by the proclamation of that rebel bishop, Erdélyi, and of other Romanian renegades from Hungary, that they rise against their brothers".[161] Significantly, the Romanians in Bem's army were not simple soldiers, but "the bravest party of that army", since the most unyielding enemy was not the foreigner, but necessarily the Romanian renegade.

At times, the Romanian intellectuals seem to exhibit a true masochist pleasure in tracking down some fellow countryman who might be the cause of his brothers' misfortunes. Obviously, their findings only count as stereotypes of a self-consciousness going through a moment of crisis, regardless of whether of not some tattered diploma testifies to the "reality" of the respective image. For Şincai, one man who counts as a Romanian is Prince János Kemény ("the crestfallen Romanian"), under whose reign the *Approbatae* were drawn up which sanctioned (or introduced, in Şincai's opinion) juridical discrimination against the Romanians.[162] For Papiu it is the Hungarian revolutionary general János Czecz ("a Romanian, but of the renegades' stock").[163] For the Romanian deputies to the Pest Parliament it is Baron Miklós Jósika, who engaged in fierce disputes with the Romanian revolutionaries in 1848.[164]

The most famous renegades seem to be, in Papiu Ilarian's opinion, the Corvins themselves—an ambiguous symbol of the self-image, now all-glorious, the next moment the vilest of creatures.[165] The accusation is that, once in power, they failed to do anything good for their fellows, and even turned against them:

> Let us remember that Iancu the Romanian, whom the Hungarians call János Hunyadi, was the governor of the whole Hungarian Country and so powerful a man in his deeds that he alone made the Turkish Stanbul [= Constantinople] tremble with fear while Europe was trembling in front of the Turks; and his son, Matthias Corvinus, the greatest king of the Hungarians. And what good has come out of these Romanians for their nation? Have they helped the Romanian people rise to the dignity they deserved in their own country? Did Iancu help, in the years 1437 and 1438, the Romanians who lived then under the most unbearable and barbaric Hungarian oppression? Did he try then to stop the conjuration of the three nations against the Romanians?[166]

To sum up, we could say that the renegade would remain an extremely important element of the self-image, a reference point for the distinction between the good and the bad, or what counted as such for that image. Instead of being a bridge connecting the Romanians to others, he functions as a distance evaluator and passage marker along the malefic and contaminating frontier constantly pierced in either direction. Apart from these projections of the collective imaginary, the renegade functions as a sociological symbol speaking of the individual caught, as in a spider's web, in between the need for ethnic-national survival, the attractions offered by assimilation and acculturation, and the natural, yet difficult, ethnic and cultural blend.

THE SHAME OF BEING ROMANIAN

A frequent companion of the theme of denationalisation, meant as an explanation and by no means as an excuse, is the invocation of the shame felt by those Romanians who abjure their nation, coming with the realisation of their condition as renegades. Certainly, the frequency of the phrase is primarily explained by the need to censure that attitude in as vehement a tone as possible. Yet despite all the decidedly negative evaluation, the balance of the self-image would remain forever disturbed and impaired by such uncomfortable confession of the refusal of one's own identity. Even if limited to certain individuals, and sometimes to certain social-professional categories (the nobles, the intellectuals), the identity crisis inherent in the infamous formula was able to induce an extremely disturbing sense of collective embarrassment. It was a decisive step taken towards "self-hatred", a feature typical of the identity stigma at a "tribal" level.[167]

The phrase occurs in numerous significant texts of the age. Samuil Micu refers to the learned Romanians in Banat who "feel ashamed at being called Romanian and would they were called by any other name"[168], and to the situation of those in the principalities turned Phanariot, where "the Romanians had sunk so low that those who were boyars were ashamed to be called Romanians".[169] Budai-Deleanu speaks of the same Moldo-Wallachians who "Bow their heads in shame / At the sound of their name" and who have become strangers in their own country.[170]

Timotei Cipariu uses extremely violent images in painting the portrait of his fellow countrymen, while also trying to explain their attitude by the pressures and misfortunes they had to suffer:

> Some, so doing that they might relieve themselves of the burden that, like a mountain, weighed upon their shoulders, knelt before their tyrants, kissed the whip which had torn them, licked the spit from the dust and buried in it their shamed heads. A relief it was, sometimes, but on what opprobrious conditions, that they forget their blood and tongue! This sort of people did feel the shame at their doings that weighed on their consciences, but it was the situation that called for that sacrifice, when need was felt. And their sons, now born and raised in different cradles and among different ideas, took the name of Romanian as such an offence that they shrank before it could touch them.[171]

Condemnation is sometimes accompanied by moralising comments or by such advice and theory as might set the wrongdoers aright. The most widespread method is to invoke the Roman origins and "praised" nature of the Romanian nation. The motif is thus made to change direction; what is to be assumed is not shame, but pride in being Romanian, and those incapable of such sentiments should be driven away without scruple from the national community, as Stoica de Hațeg would put it: "And should there be Romanians who take shame in being called that, they should feel free to drop the name, while the name itself of the Romanian nation will remain worthy of praise in all great writings of the world."[172]

Some intellectuals, such as Bojincă, deny the very existence of such a phenomenon among the Romanians. It is nothing but a foreign calumny, they say, while the Romanians, far from feeling uneasy as to their own ethnic condition, take pride and joy in their identity and ethnonym, to which their Roman descent assuredly entitles them. Sava Tököly had stated (as had Micu, we might add) that the Romanian, having reached some position or other, "at once renounces his nation and shame takes hold of him for being said to bear the name of that poor Romanian nation".[173] Bojincă tries to demonstrate the fallaciousness of that position, maintaining that "the true Romanian will not renounce his people, nay, he will praise it and will be delighted to say, in all truth, that he is of the same blood with the glorious and enlightened Roman people."[174]

Nevertheless, other observers are of different opinions and try to probe, with remarkable psychological finesse, into the mechanisms of behaviour which illustrate the stigma of the shame of being Romanian. The priest Ioan Munteanu from Bihor wrote in 1846 to Bariț: "I find myself a stranger in my own country [...] I see myself surrounded by people of my own blood, but who have grown so corrupt that our national Romanian words make some laugh, others raise their fists in anger, and others feel such pity as one would confess when seeing among a crowd of pleasant faces some in which the traits are gone sour and hateful to the human sight!"[175] Besides derision and compassion, the condition of being Romanian provokes (among fellow countrymen too!) that feeling of revulsion and spite experienced by the stigma-bearer who rediscovers his own flaw by recognising it in his fellows. At the sound of Romanian words, Munteanu's interlocutors are reminded of their being Romanian themselves, which embarrasses and angers them since they would rather rid themselves of this shameful condition, a disgrace in their own eyes as it must be in the eyes of others.

Simion Bărnuțiu writes of those who "are uneasy and ashamed of being called Romanian"[176], and Nicolae Tincu Velia complains that in Vîrșeț "among almost nine thousand souls which have kept to the old Greek faith, you won't find ten who will confess they are Romanians, but all will say they are Serbs or Bulgarians", although, in his opinion, three-quarters of the town's population are of pure Romanian stock.[177]

The refusal by some to acknowledge their own identity because of the shame of being Romanian is a troublesome topic for Timotei Cipariu as well. He mentions several times the example of Dimitrie Cantemir who, he believes, although "one of the most arduous Romanian writers of literature [...] thought it more glorious to be of Tartar descent than to confess to what he was, a Romanian".[178]

The Romanians' cultural backwardness and lack of initiative in finding a way out of it puts him in an extremely bitter frame of mind. Although, evidently, it can be no cause for celebration, shame at being Romanian is no longer simply denied. Cipariu almost agrees with those who entertain that feeling, since their attitude seems well motivated by the sad realities of the Romanian condition.

It is no wonder, then, that the name of Roman is held in ridicule in this region today, and everyone who had known some advancement, frightened at the sight of our oppression, turned their faces away and ran like rabbits and buried themselves among the Serbs, the Hungarians, the Greeks, and even the Tartars, for fear someone might still call them Romanians. Only yesterday the Sturzas were up to their heads looking for ways to become kin with the Hungarian Thurzó family. Demetriu Cantemir [...] had rather show that his blood runs down from Chan the Tartar than keep to the Romanians.[179]

Cipariu reverses the givens of Stoica de Haţeg's argumentation and reconverts the pride at being of Roman descent into a state of disgrace; the Romanians' present degradation brings shame on their illustrious origins, since being born into a great family makes the descendants' decline even more opprobrious.[180] "It is high time we meditated upon these matters", the reverend from Blaj concludes, "for if we do not, beware, and know that our grandchildren will, for shame, make anything of themselves, even Turks."[181]

Ion Codru Drăguşanu confesses having himself committed the sin, and he does so in the easy and serene tone of his characteristic narrative style. At some point, the situation is such that he feels the pragmatic need to hide his identity. While in Moscow, he introduces himself as a "young Hungarian literate", the idea behind this false identity being that his chances of a job would thus considerably increase. It is true, the pilgrim admits, that such an attitude fell rather short of morality, "but here, *as on many other occasions* [emphases added], it was certainly welcome. Had I loosened the grip and confessed to being Romanian, because of the Russians' knowledge of part of the Romanians, everyone would have said, 'Can anything good come out of Nazareth?'"[182]

In any case, by labelling his attitude as a mere "white lie", Drăguşanu does not seem to trouble himself with any identity crisis presumably inherent in the sad necessity of camouflaging his own condition in this way.[183] On the contrary, he can even, ideally, imagine a severance from this identity, a detachment which he invokes with a pathos heralding Cioran's frenetic invectives, in a memorable phrase: "If I were to be born again, would it please Heaven I were born a Frenchman."[184] Why a Frenchman? Precisely because the Frenchman (of his time, at least) is, as the Romanian is not, full of pride at his unequalled condition and has no reason to feel ashamed about his state.

The meandering intricacy of such identity assuming and reassuming, in real or imaginary terms, undertaken at will or under the pressure of the most diverse internal or external constraints, is also expressively illustrated in a most humble act at the time of the revolution. Petru Pintye and Theodor Török, two insignificant office workers—of Romanian nationality, let us say—on the side of the Hungarian revolution, are caught by their fellow countrymen and probably forced to sign a declaration of faith, which they do in terms of disconcerting ingenuity: "I, the undersigned, confess that, being a Romanian, while happening among any society of other nations, will not hesitate to call myself a Romanian, so much the more as, on the occasion of the disarming of the Hungarians, being taken as a Hungarian, I would not confess to my being Romanian until finally giving this declaration."[185]

Was this, to the mind of its signatories, an act of assuming their own identity? Or, on the contrary, a repudiation? Who could tell? In all probability the two defendants, having lost all sense of orientation, could not tell in the long run who they really were, nor what was to be concealed and what to be taken as a matter of shame: their being Romanian? Their being Hungarian? Their having passed from the Romanians to the Hungarians or the other way round? An identity crisis was looming, feeding on their confusion.[186]

Yet while doubt could still persist in an individual consciousness caught in an ambiguous situation, at the level of the collective imaginary the revolution would, while at its peak (just as in 1989), attempt to eradicate the shame of being Romanian and relocate collective energies towards a new pride: "Can the Romanians still hang their heads in shame", writes Papiu Ilarian, "at the Romanian language, at our customs, clothes and old name? Are they still ready to deny their nation for some high offices or other private benefits, as they used to while under Hungarian persecution?"[187] The answer is a categorical "no". The mythology of the Blaj Assembly in May takes self-gratifying note of the renegades' re-conversion, of the return of the straying sons for whom the Romanian nation had until then been a matter of shame. With Vasile Nopcea leading, they vie with one another in unfurling their rediscovered identity. The pride they now feel at their fellow countrymen's spectacular triumph allows them to stand out from the bulk of foreigners with whom they had formerly tried to mingle, and the shame that had pushed them into hiding their true faces is now displaced and done away with. In Blaj, Papiu maintains that "among this procession one could see plenty of Romanians who used to pass for Hungarians, embarrassed at the name of Romanian, now shamed for having so sorrowfully strayed, and ready to grasp the hands of the true Romanians on their way to the great field of the gathering."[188]

The shame experienced at feeling ashamed of being Romanian is the new revolutionary formula meant to enrich the self-image as a miraculous antidote to the most disparaging connotation of the national identity. In fact, without ever being able to annihilate one another, shame and pride in being Romanian permanently generate and nourish each other in a dizzying swirl wherein the state of normality assumed without any inferiority or superiority complex appears as the tiniest ray of light, shimmering in the distance.

It is based on such co-ordinates that the whole scenario of resistance to denationalisation as a theme of the Romanian self-image unfolds. Being a Romanian at all costs and not being a Romanian at all are the two privileged landmarks delimiting the void between a great fear and a great hope. Being a Romanian (or anything else) and just that, without vanity and without lament, without headaches and without qualms of conscience, was a guilty sort of luxury which the collective imaginary of the nation refused to afford and which it has perhaps been unwilling to assume even to this day.

NOTES

1 For an analysis of the relationship between the labour ethic and cultural-religious traditions specific to various societies see 3:Fukuyama 1992, chp. 21, "The Thymotic Origins of Labour". Although I could not deny the existence of that relationship, on which the American author places strong emphasis, I would point out that the possibility always exists, as far as individuals and even nations are concerned, that the attitude to labour be modified, since it is conditioned not only by cultural heritage, but also by the current political or economic-social transformations. For a historical perspective, see 3:Le Goff 1978, pp. 19–144.

2 Tacitus, *Germania*, XIV–XV. Significantly, the issue of the Romanians' attitude to labour is widely capitalised upon in German images concerning them; see 3:Heitmann 1985, chps. VI, X.

3 Present, for instance, in Montesquieu, *L'Esprit des lois*, XIV, II, "*Combien les hommes sont différents dans les divers climats*".

4 1.9:Codru Drăgușanu 1980, pp. 166–167.

5 1.4:Murgu 1830; 1.9:Murgu 1969, p. 116.

6 1.4:Costin 1812a, p. 44; 1.9:Fugariu 1983, I, pp. 860–861.

7 *Ibidem*, pp. 43–44 and p. 860, respectively.

8 See 3:Weber 1934.

9 3:Fukuyama 1992, chps. VI, XXI.

10 Such a perspective capitalises on several "theories" concerning the Romanians' attitude to labour, famous in Romanian culture: Constantin Rădulescu-Motru, *Romanian Culture and Petty Politics* (1904) and Dumitru Drăghicescu, *On the Psychology of the Romanian People* (1907); see the editions Gheorghe Pienescu (2:Rădulescu-Motru 1984, pp. 52–54) and Elisabeta Simion (2:Drăghicescu 1995, pp. 386–389, 374–375), respectively. In fact, the two authors' approaches and arguments are, mostly, merely collections of national self-stereotypes, influenced by the methodology of the "psychology of peoples" (*Völkerpsychologie*) as practised by Lazarus, Steinthal and Wundt.

11 See, for social criticism of the Enlightenment and for the way it applies to Romanian realities, 3:Mitu M., Mitu S. 1996.

12 1.7:*Supplex 1791*, in 3:Prodan 1971, pp. 452, 464.

13 1.7:*Petition July 1814*, in 1.9:Păcăţian 1904, p. 140. For the relevant memoir see 3:Gyémánt 1986, p. 152.

14 *Ibidem*.

15 1.9:Mureşanu A. 1977, p. 84 (article "Property [wealth, estate]", in 1.2:*The Gazette*, VIII, 1845, no. 76–9).

16 *Ibidem*, pp. 84–85.

17 (Joseph) Benigni (von Mildenberg), "The Nature of the Transylvanian Peoples", in 1.2:*Journal for the Mind*, IV, 1841, no. 12, p. 93 (transl. from Benigni's manual, 1.5:Benigni 1837).

18 George Bariţ, "On the poverty we see overwhelming us in Transylvania", in 1.2:*The Gazette*, II, 1839, no. 18, pp. 71–72.

19 3:Moga 1936–1938; 3:Edroiu 1980; 3:Bodea 1982; 3:Andea S., Andea A. 1990.

20 1.9:Păcăţian 1904, p. 80.

21 *Apud* 3:Bernath 1972, chp. IX.

22 George Bariţ, "Knowledge of the soul", in 1.2:*Literary Paper*, I, 1838, no. 6, p. 47 (transl. from 1.4:Dóczy 1829–1830).

23 *Idem*, "On the Romanian disease", in 1.2:*Journal for the Mind*, VII, 1844, pp. 377–378.

24 *Ibidem*.

25 1.9:Stoica de Haţeg 1984, pp. 200–201.

26 See 3:Kovács 1973, pp. 15–31.

27 George Bariţ, in 1.2:*The Gazette*, XI, 1848, no. 45, p. 186.

28 3:Bocşan 1992, pp. 134–137.

29 Iosif Many, "A Word at its Time", in 1.2:*The Teacher*, I, 1848, no. 19–20.

30 *Ibidem*.

31 See 3:Mitu S. 1993a; *idem*, in The *"David Prodan" Notebooks*, I, 1994, no. 1. Also, 3:Zane 1980.

32 Iosif Many, "Golden rules", in 1.2:*The Teacher*, I, 1848, no. 4, p. 16.

33 *Idem*, "Poor Old Richard", in *ibidem*, no. 11, p. 43.

34 Even David Prodan, who, like any devoted Transylvanian militant historian (and Marxist too), is body and soul on the side of the peasants and, at the same time, a virulent critic of the exploiting nobility, admits that this is the case: "To conclude: the key to serfdom is to be found not in market production but in the poor technological resources of productivity of the soil, in comparison with the new demands of county economy" (3:Prodan 1989, p. 363).

35 See 3:Prodan 1971; 3:Teodor 1992; 3:Gyémánt 1986, pp. 455–482; 3:Maior L. 1992, pp. 5–21. The idea also surfaces in a popular verse circulated at the time of the revolution: "We gave them duties and we gave them rookies / We gave them grain and we gave them garb / Aren't we hardworking people!" The phrase "Aren't we hardworking people" recurs throughout the whole poem as a leitmotif allowing the Romanians to identify themselves in contrast to their Hungarian adversaries who are defined by the mirror phrase, "Aren't they a vicious people"; see 1.1:*Hardworking People* cca 1848.

36 The manuscript *Widerlegung der zu Klausenburg 1791 über die Vorstellung der Wallachischen Nation herausgekommen Noten* is published, in translation by Iosif Pervain, in 1.9:Budai-Deleanu 1970, pp. 37–114, the authorship established as such by the editor. Professor Pompiliu Teodor attributes it, however, to Samuil Micu, cf. 3:Teodor 1981–1982.

37 1.4:Eder 1791, "Praefatio editoris"; 1.9:Fugariu 1983, I, p. 154.

38 1.9:Budai-Deleanu 1970, p. 79.

39 1.9:Fugariu 1983, II, p. 276.

40 Simion Bărnuțiu, "A shameful deal and an unfair rule" (1842), *apud* 1.9:Bogdan-Duică 1924, p. 203.

41 1.9:Bodea 1967, p. 345.

42 See 3:Andrea A. 1973; 3:Zane 1977, *passim*.

43 Later, the model of a state of freeholders (*răzeși*) would be a particular concern of Eminescu; see 3:Ornea 1975, pp. 151–152, but esp. 3:Antohi 1994, pp. 104–135. For similar accents in Sadoveanu, 3:Manolescu 1993, pp. 209–247.

44 1.5:Bojincă 1832–1833, I, p. 210; 1.9:Bojincă 1978, pp. 123–124.

45 "Rășinari", in 1.2:*The Mouthpiece*, I, 1847, no. 32, p. 172. Also see 1.3:*Calendar Sibiu II*, pp. 67–69: "The wife wedded to a lazy husband".

46 Of extreme relevance to the misogyny of the age are the anecdotes published in the popular almanacs, which widely circulated the image of the garrulous, nagging, brainless, unfaithful etc. woman. See, for instance, 1.3:*Calendar Buda III* (Theodorovici), 1826, p. 33, "Some anecdotes"; 1.3:*Calendar Sibiu II*, 1856, pp. 60–61, "The man wedded to the bad wife."

47 See the same image as projected precisely onto the Transylvanian Romanians: "The Muslims, their wives and children", in 1.2:*Journal for the Mind*, III, 1840, no. 2, pp. 12–13; "The status of women in the East", in *ibidem*, VII, 1844, no. 25, pp. 197–200.

48 1.4:Costin 1812a, pp. 6–7; 1.9:Fugariu 1983, I, p. 857.

49 *Ibidem*, pp. 44–45 and p. 861, respectively.

50 *Ibidem*.

51 1.4:Maior P. 1809, pp. 42–43; 1.9:Fugariu 1983, I, pp. 799–800.

52 See 3:Răduțiu 1985; 3:Stefanescu 1995, chp. VI, "The agricultural calendar: Speeding up labour rhythms within the peasant household". Cf. 3:Le Goff 1978, pp. 66–79. For the issue of holidays in general see 3:Ghinoiu 1988; 3:Marian 1994.

53 1.4:Murgu 1830; 1.9:Murgu 1969, p. 116.

54 See 3:Mitu S. 1992.

55 1.4:Maior P. 1815, p. 7; 1.9:Fugariu 1983, II, pp. 233, 237.

56 1.4:Aaron Th. 1828, p. 78; 1.9:Fugariu 1983, II, p. 655.

57 See 3:Sundhausen 1973; 3:Wolf 1978; 3:Neumann 1986, pp. 177–206; 3:Karnoouh 1990.

58 3:Bocșan 1991; a relativising critique of Herder's ethnic-linguistic model of conceptualising the nation in 3:Karnoouh 1990, chp. III; also in 3:Marga 1994, pp. 10–17 (with a bibliography relating to eastern nationalism). Also see 3:Finkielkraut 1987, chp. I.

59 1.9:Murgu 1969, p. 198.

60 *Ibidem*, p. 300.

61 3:Arató 1960; 3:Arató 1983; 3:Gyémánt 1986, pp. 186–221.

62 George Bariț, "The Romanians and Hungarianism", in 1.2:*Journal for the Mind*, V, 1842, no. 9, pp. 68–69.

63 *Idem*, "The Romanians and Pan-Slavism", in *ibidem*, IV, 1841, no. 45, pp. 353–358; 1.9:Bariț 1962, p. 62.

64 *Idem*, "What is the will of the Transylvanian Romanians?", in *ibidem*, XI, 1848, no. 14–16; 1.9:Bariț 1962, p. 117.

65 This is, approximately, the argument launched today against Romanian nationalism in contemporary Transylvania: How can Hungary threaten Transylvania under the circumstances of today's international politics? And if that should happen, how could a Hungarian government manage a majority Romanian population?

66 George Bariț, "The Romanians and Hungarianism", in 1.2:*Journal for the Mind*, V, 1842, no. 9, pp. 68–69; 1.9:Bariț 1962, p. 65.

67 *Ibidem*, p. 69 and pp. 69–70, respectively.

68 *Idem*, "What is Pan-Wallachianism?", in 1.2:*Journal for the Mind*, VI, 1843, p. 43.
69 *Idem*, "What is the will of the Transylvanian Romanians?", in *ibidem*, XI, 1848, no. 14–16; 1.9:Bariț 1962, p. 116.
70 *Idem*, "Transylvania. Cluj, 9 May", in 1.2:*The Gazette*, XI, 1848, no. 36, p. 151; 1.9:Bariț 1962, pp. 119–120.
71 Simion Bărnuțiu, the Blaj *Discourse*, in 1.9:*Documents 1848 Transylvania* 1977–1988, IV, p. 19.
72 Published only eleven years later, Simion Bărnuțiu, "A shameful deal and an unfair rule", in 1.2:*Journal for the Mind*, XVI, 1853, no. 38, pp. 285–288; no. 39, pp. 295–298.
73 *Ibidem*,; 1.9:Bogdan-Duică 1924, p. 203.
74 Timotei Cipariu to George Bariț, a letter of February 1842, published in 1.6:*GBC* 1973–1993, IV, p. 169.
75 1.5:Széchenyi 1841; 1.5:Széchenyi 1842; 1.9:Széchenyi 1981, pp. 186–231. Cf. 3:Lupaș 1910; 3:Dragomir 1946; 3:Arató 1955; 3:Gyémánt 1986, pp. 194–195.
76 1.5:Wesselényi 1833; 1.5:Wesselényi 1843. Cf., besides the bibliography referred to in the preceding note, 3:Mikó 1943; 3:Trócsányi 1965; 3:Dărăban 1985.
77 See 3:Karnoouh 1990, chp. IV.
78 Timotei Cipariu, "The Union", in 1.2:*The Mouthpiece*, II, 1848, no. 67, p. 381.
79 George Bariț "What is Pan-Wallachianism?", in 1.2:*Journal for the Mind*, VI, 1843, pp. 42–43.
80 See 3:Mitu S. 1988b; 3:Mitu S. 1992, pp. 16–18. For the matrimonial interdiction for ethnic reasons, see 3:Trebici, Ghinoiu 1986, pp. 242–243.
81 1.4:Maior P. 1812, pp. 17–18; 1.9:Maior P. 1970, I, p. 106.
82 *Ibidem*.
83 1.5:Bojincă 1832–1833, I, p. 203; 1.9:Bojincă 1978, p. 122.
84 1.4:*Lesicon* 1825, p. 65; 1.9:Fugariu 1983, II, p. 612.
85 1.4:Maior P. 1812, p. 15; 1.9:Fugariu 1983, I, p. 872.
86 1.9:Budai-Deleanu 1991, I, p. 186.
87 Interestingly, contrary to Budai-Deleanu's claim, in the decades prior to the 1848 revolution the Hungarians, too, explicitly upheld the theory of the Romanians' Latin origins and even of the purity of their descent in the very terms employed by the Transylvanian School (see 3:Gyémánt 1986, p. 71; 3:Mitu M. 1995). Just like the Romanian scholars, the Hungarians were themselves ideologically motivated in promoting this thesis in an age when no one undertook scientific investigations for the sake of science itself (unfortunately, the habit was perpetuated for a long time in both nations): given that the main danger sensed by the Hungarian public consciousness was pan-Slavism, their aim was to stimulate such interpretations as could legitimate, from an ideological point of view, the Romanians' severance from the Slavs. As the Dacians were considered at the time (by Romanian scholars too) a people related to the Slavs, the Hungarians were keen on emphasising the Romanians' Latin origins alongside their turning to Western civilisation, religious union with Rome and the tendency to use the Latin alphabet—all elements capable of driving the Romanians closer to the Hungarians and away from the Slavs. Obviously, these were elements favoured by Romanian self-perception as well. Moreover, even though it was ideological motivation alone that led them to a, perhaps involuntary, selection of those specific traits as markers of Romanian identity, both the Romanians and the Hungarians would come earnestly to believe in the truth of the images they had tailored. As usual, the forging of national identity and of images of the other had too little to do with a rational analysis of reality.
88 1.9:Budai-Deleanu 1991, I, p. 206.
89 Stoica de Hațeg, too, wrote that there are "several villages of Russians [more exactly, people from Carașova] mixed with the Romanians", yet "it rarely happens that they become related by matrimony" (see Stoica de Hațeg 1984, p. 13).
90 1.9:Iorgovici 1979, pp. 111–113.
91 *Ibidem*.
92 1.9:Codru-Drăgușanu 1956, p. 229. I would also like to note here the methodological aims of my study: my concern is not with the pertinence or the degree of adequacy of these theories as related to the *historical reality* (particularly as I take this reality to be a nebulous element, still very poorly understood); I am only interested in them in terms of a relative validity, which can be checked either against a critical and rationalist model or in relation to an ideological elaboration.

93 See section II, 6, above, "The universal conspiracy against the Romanians".

94 Such ideological overemphasis on women's role in the process of denationalisation was also due to the symbolic position conferred at the time to the Woman–Mother, that is, that of a privileged transmitter and carrier of the national specificity by means of the "mother tongue"—the essential metaphysical principle of nationality in Herder's view. For the relationship between female sexual identity and nationalism in the modern age, see Alexandru Vári's excellent study, 3:Vári 1995 (with a bibliography).

95 1.5:Papiu Ilarian 1852(I), pp. 104–105. Could this passage be speaking of the memory of some sentimental failure of a former student in Cluj and clerk in "Oşorhei" feeling snubbed because some Romanian girl preferred a Hungarian colleague?... It might be a purely groundless speculation; yet, while we lack any other argument able to explain that exception, we might not be altogether off track here!

96 1.9:Budai-Deleanu 1991, I, p. 310.

97 1.9:Bojincă 1828, p. 19; 1.9:Fugariu 1983, II, p. 662.

98 Nicolae Tincu Velia to George Bariţ, a letter of April 1846, published in 1.6:Suciu I.D. 1945, p. 248. The preference for the Serbian variant is undoubtedly due to religious compatibility (although Bojincă had noted elsewhere that the Romanians refuse marriage with foreign women even "of such kinfolk as are of the same faith with him", 1.5:Bojincă 1832–1833, I, p. 203; 1.9:Bojincă 1978, p. 122).

99 *Exempli gratia*: the grandfather of the author of the present book, a native of Nicoară's natal area, married again, after the death of his Romanian wife (my grandmother), to a Hungarian woman.

100 1.9:Bodea 1943, p. 357.

101 *Ibidem*, p. 354.

102 *Ibidem*, pp. 365–366.

103 *Ibidem*, p. 286.

104 See 3:Mitu S. 1988b. Another interesting detail is that all sentimental affairs that post-revolutionary legends attribute to Avram Iancu, the national hero, revolve around foreign women, the most famous being Háni Farkas, the Hungarian lover who seems to have saved him from the disaster in Abrud. She would in fact get married in 1852 to one of the leaders of the 1848 Romanian resistance, Dimitrie Moldovan. Besides the study quoted above, see also 3:Hodoş 1923; 3:Lupaş 1932; 3:Dragomir 1965, pp. 286–287.

105 3:*Dictionary 1900*, p. 79, *sub voce* "Bariţiu, Ieronim G."; also see the diary fragments "Notes from my married life", published in 2:Boitoş 1942.

106 3:Cipăianu 1980, p. 19.

107 See part of these references in 3:*Ideology of Generation* 1968, pp. 262–265.

108 See 3:Adorno 1950.

109 Since my own biographical circumstances bear some resemblance to those discussed here (my wife is Hungarian), I wish to dispel any suspicion that I might be writing *pro domo mea*. I will add, therefore, from an academic methodological and authorial perspective, that the positive implications of mixed marriages are not of an exclusive and universal nature. It is preferable to approach them as social images and representations. Misogynists, nationalists, sado-masochists and any member of other similar categories may rest assured as to their freedom of matrimonial option. From a sociological point of view, it is by no means compulsory that a conjugal choice of the sort discussed above should change their convictions and type of behaviour.

110 1.5:Papiu Ilarian 1852(II), p. CXXV.

111 1.5:Papiu Ilarian 1852(I), p. 68.

112 1.5:Papiu Ilarian 1852(II), p. XIX.

113 *Ibidem*, pp. XLII–XLIII.

114 Such ideas were being advanced within the Hungarian ideology of the time by Count István Széchenyi, whom Papiu mentions too (see 1.5:Széchenyi 1841) or by the Transylvanian Baron Dénes Kemény, the leader of the liberal opposition in the Transylvanian Diet (see 1.5:Kemény D. 1861).

115 Ioan Puşcariu to George Bariţ, a letter of 26 March 1848, published in 1.9:Bodea 1967, pp. 316–317.

116 1.5:Papiu Ilarian 1852(II), pp. CIII sqq.
117 1.5:Papiu Ilarian 1852(I), pp. 104–105.
118 *Ibidem*, pp. 105–110.
119 *Ibidem*, p. 110.
120 *Ibidem*, pp. 108–109.
121 1.5:Papiu Ilarian 1852(II), pp. CXV–CXVIII.
122 1.5:Papiu Ilarian 1852(I), p. 108.
123 1.5:Papiu Ilarian 1852(II), pp. CIII sqq.
124 *Ibidem*.
125 *Ibidem*, pp. 72–73.
126 *Ibidem*, p. 164.
127 *Ibidem*, p. CXXV sqq.
128 *Ibidem*.
129 1.9:Fugariu 1983, I, p. 232 ("The reason for the fall of the Romanian nation", in *Short Information on the History of the Romanians*).
130 1.9:Budai-Deleanu 1970a, p. 49 (*Fundamenta grammatices linguae romaenicae*, 1821).
131 1.8:Budai-Deleanu 1974–1975, II, p. 39 (*The Gypsiad /A/*); p. 272 (*Three brave men*).
132 1.4:Maior P. 1812, pp. 329–330; 1.9:Fugariu 1983, I, pp. 919–920.
133 Andrei Mureșanu, "Notes on our poetry", in 1.2:*Journal for the Mind*, VII, 1844, no. 26, pp. 201–202; 1.9:Mureșanu A. 1977, p. 39.
134 1.9:Codru Drăgușanu 1956, p. 56.
135 It proved rather unsuccessful in this, if we come to think that in 1906, for instance, Nicolae Iorga was still fighting the French language, a favourite of the élites in Bucharest, and prompting student demonstrations which more often than not ended up in cavalry charges in the streets of the capital (see 3:Bulei 1990, pp. 352–362, "French mania and counter-reaction").
136 For details see 1.6:*GBC* 1973–1993, III, pp. 331–334; IV, pp. 265–167.
137 It was yet another theatrical performance in a foreign language (French plays on the stage of the National Theatre!) that provoked the 1906 incidents in Bucharest (see preceding notes). History keeps repeating itself, in "travesty" forms, as it most recently did with stage director Andrei Șerban's adventure at the National Theatre in Bucharest, where his directorship was contested on account of the same old obsession: National repertoire or universal repertoire?
138 B-r (Simion Bărnuțiu), *Magyar színészet Balásfalván* ("Hungarian theatre performance in Blaj"), in 1.2:*Újság*, 1846, no. 632, p. 391; 1.9:Bogdan-Duică 1924, pp. 220–221.
139 (George Bariț), "17 June st. v. 1846. Blaj", in 1.2:*The Gazette*, IX, 1846, no. 49, pp. 194–195; 1.9:Bogdan-Duică 1924, pp. 221–222.
140 a. (Timotei Cipariu), "20 June st. v. 1846. Hungarian theatre in Blaj", in 1.2:*The Gazette*, IX, no. 50, p. 197; 1.9:Bogdan-Duică 1924, pp. 222–223.
141 *Ibidem*.
142 *Ibidem*, p. 197, and p. 223, respectively.
143 However, Petru Maior, trying to explain the causes of the Romanian nobles' Hungarianisation, said in 1815: "Still, for all that, could it be a crime to be called a Hungarian?" (see 1.9:Fugariu 1983, II, p. 233).
144 1.5:Wesselényi 1843.
145 See 3:Gyémánt 1986, pp. 209–211.
146 See 3:Dragomir 1989, pp. 178–185, "The Romanian-Hungarian negotiations in the summer of 1849. Simonffy's intervention"; 3:Bocșan 1992, pp. 162–166; 3:Arató 1975; 3:Miskolczy 1981; 3:Kovács, Katus 1987, I, pp. 412–422.
147 1.9:Fugariu 1983, I, p. 10.
148 1.5:Maior P. 1834, pp. 32–34; 1.9:Fugariu 1983, II, p. 233.
149 See the same issue of the compatibility between "Romanianness" and any religious confession other than Orthodoxy (as captured in the formula "One cannot be a Romanian if one is a Catholic") in the intellectual debates of the inter-war period: 2:Ionescu 1937 (1990), pp. 194–214; cf. 3:Ornea 1995, pp. 91–94.
150 1.8:Budai-Deleanu 1974–1975, II (*The Gypsiad /A/*), pp. 104–105; 1.9:Maior P. 1976, II, p. 240.

151 Simion Bărnuțiu, "The Great Synod of the Bishopric of Făgăraș. *Prologus galeatus*" (1842), in 1.9:Bogdan-Duică 1924, p. 213.

152 1.4:Bojincă 1830, pp. 9–12; 1.9:Fugariu 1983, II, pp. 723–724.

153 See 3:Albu C. 1977, pp. 95–96.

154 1.5:Papiu Ilarian 1852(I), p. 200.

155 *Ibidem*, p. 216.

156 It was for similar reasons that the Ceaușescu regime would try in the 1980s to impose a tax to be paid by Romanian emigrants, which represented the equivalent of the sums previously invested by society in the education of the individuals in question.

157 1.7:*Memoir 1847*, in 1.9:Bodea 1943, p. 399.

158 *Ibidem*.

159 1.5:Papiu Ilarian 1852(I), p. 58.

160 Avram Iancu's report concerning the fighting of 1848–1849, drawn up in November 1849, re-edited in 1.9:Bodea 1982, II, p. 1037.

161 1.9:Papiu Ilarian 1943, p. 96.

162 1.9:Șincai 1967, p. 601; 1.9:Fugariu 1983, II, p. 51.

163 1.5:Papiu Ilarian 1852(II), p. 177.

164 "A national response to Baron Nic. Iojica by the Romanian deputies to the Hungarian Diet (...)", in 1.2:*Journal for the Mind*, XI, 1848, no. 32, pp. 2249–251; 1.9:Bodea 1982, II, p. 896.

165 The palimpsest of traces left by the inscriptions with which each generation chose to adorn Matthias Corvinus' statue in the central plaza of Cluj is the best proof on this point. Today, besides the inevitable inscription at the horse's feet, Matthias is spectacularly flanked by several tricolour flags, while the plaza is crossed by archaeological sections. Unfortunately, the space on the other side of the church behind the statue now only lends itself to a very peculiar type of digging, since the inter-war Romanian authorities decided to place underground public toilets here, for "obvious" reasons of public utility. For the toilets, see 2:Stanca 1987, p. 259.

166 1.5:Papiu Ilarian 1852(I), pp. 224–225.

167 See 3:Pițu 1991 and esp. 3:Antohi 1994, pp. 108–185. The formula with respect to the "shame of being Romanian" has been lately rediscovered and its use renewed at the level of public opinion by television producer Mihai Tatulici.

168 *Apud* 3:Prodan 1971, pp. 273–274.

169 Samuil Micu, *Short Information on the History of the Romanians* (1796), in 1.9:Fugariu 1983, I, pp. 236–238.

170 Ion Budai-Deleanu, *Three Brave Men*, in *ibidem*, II, p. 287.

171 1.1:Cipariu cca 1846.

172 1.9:Stoica de Hațeg 1984, p. 86.

173 1.4:Bojincă 1828, p. 88; 1.9:Fugariu 1983, II, p. 665.

174 *Ibidem*.

175 Ioan Munteanu to George Bariț, a letter of December 1846, published in 1.9:Bodea 1967, pp. 295–297.

176 Simion Bărnuțiu, "The Great Synod of the Bishopric of Făgăraș" (1842), in 1.9:Bogdan-Duică 1924, p. 214.

177 Nicolae Tincu Velia to George Bariț, a letter of April 1846, published in 1.6:Suciu I. D. 1945, p. 249.

178 Timotei Cipariu, "Which is the oldest Romanian book?", in 1.2:*The Mouthpiece*, II, 1848, no. 54, p. 304.

179 1.9:Cipariu 1972, p. 33.

180 *Ibidem*, pp. 33–34.

181 *Ibidem*, p. 34.

182 1.9:Codru Drăgușanu 1956, p. 220. See the *Gospel according to St. John*, I, 46.

183 The pilgrim actually camouflages his identity in the most literal terms, as he presents himself with an impressive "Hungarian" moustache, in conformity with the canon by which Hungarians were identified in the Romanian hetero-perception (see *loc. cit.*, previous note).

184 *Ibidem*, p. 254. In 1846, Dimitrie Brătianu wrote to Michelet using similar terms: *Maintenant, je sais qu'où finit la France, commence le néant* (*apud* 3:Antohi 1994, p. 257).

185 Declaration of faith given by Petru Pintye and Theodor Török, autumn of 1848, published in
    1.9:Dragomir 1944–1946, II, p. 420. Also there, a version in the Hungarian language of the
    same, declaring the two men's faith to the emperor.
186 Novelist Mór Jókai was to illustrate this play of double identity in one of his most renowned
    novels, *A szegény gazdagok* (The Poor Rich), published in 1860. The protagonist appears, during
    the day, as the Hungarian, Baron Lénárt Hátszegi, while at night he turns into Romanian
    bandit "Black Face". The metaphor was all the more telling as the acknowledged prototype for
    the character was one of the famous Romanian "renegades", Vasile Nopcea, a controversial
    character: supreme county administrator of Hunedoara, a conservative politician, but also vice-
    president of the Romanian delegation to Vienna during the revolution! Nopcea would be as-
    sailed by both Romanian and Hungarian parties as a representative of the high aristocracy,
    which the revolutionaries on both sides deeply abhorred. At the same time, Nopcea, just like the
    fictional Baron Hátszegi, "was a perfect example for this ethnic-cultural double condition of the
    nobles from Hațeg, who were partly devoted to their new Calvinist and Catholic faith, partly
    still loyal to their old traditions and customs, and thus accused of repudiation and denationali-
    sation from both sides while actually experiencing a bilingual and bicultural condition." See
    3:Mitu M. 1994, p. 118.
187 1.5:Papiu Ilarian 1852(I), pp. 227–228.
188 1.5:Papiu Ilarian 1852(II), p. 224.

IV. The Historical Dimension of the Positive Self-image

GENERALITIES

It is true that the negative dimension of their self-perception is central to the Transylvanian Romanians' social imaginary at the beginning of the modern age, as I have tried to show so far. On the other hand, however, it has to be pointed out, as a general rule, that national images are never univocal in their appreciative function; they never centre on one single evaluative obsession, be it positive or negative. Particularly when there is a tendency to subject them to tensions and distortions, under the pressure of difficult realities such as nationalism, the images exhibit an inextricable mixture of inferiority and superiority complexes, of positive and negative obsessions. Exaggerations in one direction trigger similar reactions in the other, as an attempt to provide the self-perception with some sort of balance, even though both the exaggerations in themselves, and the clash between their contradictory tendencies, are such as to cause profound crises in a tormented consciousness.

Another piece in the picture is the extreme degree of ambiguity inherent in the advancing of a positive self-image—a double-edged sword for the legitimating system of the national militant spirit. The Romanians may well present themselves in a favourable light, as, for instance, Petru Maior often does. They may well pride themselves on being on a par with the other nations in Transylvania; on having their own nobles, scholars and famous personalities; on enjoying citizens rights and an equal status with other nations. But if they do so, they undermine the very arguments that might have supported their battle for political-national rights, for the ending of the actual state of oppression and backwardness in which they find themselves. This is what Papiu Ilarian most explicitly censures when criticising his enlightened predecessors, particularly Maior, for having advanced statements in favour of the position presented above.

The paradoxical outcome of this situation is that favourable self-representation means, in certain circumstances, self-inflicted harm, since it deflates national activism. On the other hand, speaking ill of themselves and putting as much emphasis as possible on their degradation and decay may be the salutary thing for the Romanians to do, since such a discourse immediately gives an accusatory ring incriminating their oppressors, while stimulating collective efforts to seek a way out of the crisis.

We have seen that, when focused on the sombre realities of the present, the Transylvanian Romanians' self-image takes on overbearing negative tones, even going as far as to generate distortions, exaggerations and unjustified generalisations. Under such circumstances, given that a lucid and rational explanation of the causes of evil did not suffice for maintaining the fragile balance of a sensitised and vulnerable consciousness, the need was felt for some means of counteracting the negative self-perception and thus redressing the balance. Since the language of reason proved impotent in the face of burdensome realities, the solution seemed to lie in a number of substitution myths, which could replace unwanted evidence with illusory constructions, absorbed through the pores of emotion, affectivity, imagination and subjectivity.

In this case, since the present offered little satisfaction, the positive dimension of the self-image had to concentrate primarily on the past and on the future. Pride in a glorious and idealised past and hope in a luminous and auspicious future were the two main myths or collective sentiments by means of which the painful present could be exorcised and sloughed off.[1]

The main themes characteristic of these mythical compensatory spaces are of a strictly historical nature. The include the purity of the Romanians' Latin origins and their age-long continuity; the important role played by the Romanians as defenders of Christianity in the Middle Ages; belief in their preordained historical mission; their position as a sentinel guarding the Latin race, and Europe as a whole, at the mouth of the Danube, etc.

Closely connected with these themes, the positive image also circulated a number of motifs with greater bearing on the present. These motifs were themselves selected, however, from among the features and capacities with potential, which had been present throughout history and did not specifically relate to any particular circumstance. They included the numbers of Romanians and the fact they had spread widely; their resistance to denationalisation; their ethnic purity and originality; the values specific to an idealised rural universe (hospitality, goodness, lyricism); their belonging to the space of European civilisation; and the role of the principalities in coagulating and ensuring the prestige of the whole Romanian community.

These themes were not at all the outcome of a detached examination of the historical or present reality, in the sense of scientific observation or common logical deduction. Whether or not they had an intelligible or actual referent, these real or invented elements were turned into national myths and obsessions by means of emotional over-investment. They escaped the usual reference frame of relationships between reality and its reflection due to the function they were designed to fulfil—that of legitimating hopes and aspirations, of substituting unpleasant realities, of compensating an injured pride, of mending trust in the Romanians' own capacities, and of providing arguments in disputes with the competing national mythologies. Faced with an unsatisfactory reality and with foreign threats, the image turned into myth in order to build within the collective consciousness a second reality, a better reality and one more easy to bear.

No Different from Others: The Romanians' Growing Trust in Their Own Powers

The first step towards the building of a positive image was for the Romanians to gain trust in their own powers, to recover their lost dignity, to rid their minds of the idea that they were incapable of doing well. Bariţ observes that "before others started to belittle and defame us, not long ago we used to have all kinds of sayings to belittle and insult ourselves", and he shows that "this was so because we never thought nor trusted that something good could come out of us."[2]

That the Romanian nation was able to manage as well as others was an idea strongly influenced by the enlightened, optimistic belief in the capacity of every human personality to assert itself once unfavourable circumstances are done away with and the instinctive drive towards illumination unleashed. The Romanians, too, were inevitably endowed with that inborn propensity towards the good, which was a given for every human being on the face of the earth. This verity, so dear to enlightened rationalism, was able to place the Romanians on equal footing with other peoples, to provide them with belief in their chances for progress and success. Of course, for this latent possibility to become real, certain conditions had to be met, among which the foremost was, in the view of the Transylvanian *Aufklärers*, the illumination of the commoners by means of culture and religious morals.

A long-term, general and stimulating optimism as to the Romanians' ability to catch up with other nations therefore surfaces in a number of typical, enlightened texts that speak of the overall condition of the Romanians, written particularly during the first decades of the nineteenth century. In 1814, in one of the best-known annotations to his own fables, Dimitrie Ţichindeal builds such an image, one with an important echo both within its own time and on into posterity[3]: "The mind! Glorious nation of Dacians-Romanians in Banat, Wallachia, Moldavia, Transylvania, or the Hungarian Country, the mind! When you have seen the light of learning, when you have embraced good deeds, no other nation will be more excellent than you on the face of the earth."[4] As can be seen, the process of regaining belief in the Romanians' own powers comes, in the interests of eloquence, to take a radical leap to the other self-evaluating extreme, where it upholds the idea of a unique and glorious destiny reserved for the Romanian nation.

Apart from this rousing metaphor, Ţichindeal argues for his thesis in an extremely persuasive way by capitalising on the idea that evil cannot be associated with, nor embraced by, a particular people. Even though certain negative realities may seem to discount that theory, they are but appearances and the fruit of circumstance. The good, progress and enlightenment are infectious and will ultimately, and inevitably, displace barbarity and backwardness: "Looseness and depravation can never, in any people, be welcomed to stay, but only the divine light of reason and the civil observance of good deeds. I am assured that where barbarity and meanness reign, neither wise teachings nor good and just deeds can find their place. But these good deeds will be made room for in those hearts where gross and dull meanness does not prevail; and where it still does, it cannot continue until the end of time."[5]

The same optimistic philosophy concerning the perfectibility of the human condition in general, and of the condition of the Romanian nation in particular, is also manifest in Nicolae Horga Popovici, another provincial *Aufklärer* of the Arad area. Popovici shared with Țichindeal both the spiritual bent and his fate as an Orthodox vicar in some God-forsaken village lost among the still poorly reclaimed marshes of the Criș or Timiș lands.[6] He gives, in 1807, the outlines for a bright national self-image:

> For indeed, this nation of the Romanians has not received good learning in its bosom, but were she to open little by little, as our enlightened emperor hopes, she will, truly, stand by other great peoples and host the gifts of wisdom, and she will steer its progress towards the realm of happiness, which is the heart's truest desire, and she will take to such useful occupations as will make diligent craftsmen, busy merchants and faithful soldiers of her people; and be the man a high officer or a common ploughmen, he will see about his duty in all faith, knowing well what his business is [...] And thus we are to understand that there are good and trustworthy people among the Romanians too; except that they lack moral teaching, which should be a guide for any man from his early infancy.[7]

The lack of Christian morals and of an enlightened education is the one thing separating the Romanians from the happy condition of the civilised nations; otherwise, they are no different from such nations. Alternatively, the book of moral advice Popovici writes is precisely a means to mending this deficit.

Many other opinions are advanced promoting the idea of the Romanians' opportunities for progress, equal with those of any other country, as a means of regaining trust in their own powers. In 1819 Nicola Nicolau wrote that "nor can the Romanian people be said to be less endowed with natural gifts than the other peoples, which have for centuries been conversing with the enlightened teachings and sciences."[8] On the other hand, however, like many other Transylvanian intellectuals, the Brașov-based editor makes a strong case for the realisation of this possibility being dependent on the existence of a strong will and a determined cultural effort in this respect: "Yet for those important gifts [...] to bear good fruit and grow to thrive, much reading of books (precisely written to that end) is needed and desired."[9]

Zaharia Carcalechi also concentrates on these two ideas (belief in the national capacities and the need for a collective initiative to bring about their materialisation) in a much more eloquent, yet also more critical, demonstration: "We, today's Romanians [...], have our eyes covered in a mist that keeps the light of the Sun away from us! Can there not be gifted physicians among us who will know how to make our eyes clear, and that out of the will of the heart, and not for some profit or other [...]? Can there not be philosophers among us who will know how to teach us philosophy in the Romanian language? We can have it all, for we were born like other nations were, if only we had the will!"[10] The same combination of trust and remonstration is to be found in Stoica de Hațeg: "The heavens have bestowed on us, as on other nations, all that is needed for us to strive and be like others, not to lie tied to the earth, ground down as prisoners and covered in shame."[11]

Vasile Pop, too, expresses his confidence in the Romanians' ability to catch up with the other nations: "The Romanian spirit is no less diligent and searching than that of other nations, and were it to free itself from prejudice, and were the leaders of the nation to befriend such spirits to the slightest degree, we could employ our minds to many new and useful things."[12] "Late though it is", the scholar adds elsewhere, "our people has at least started to awaken and to see that we, too, are capable of good things."[13]

The noteworthy thing here, as in the case of the other statements, is the tentative, discursive placing of confidence as bearing on potentials and new beginnings, while complete achievement is projected onto a future horizon. Only the day to come can consecrate the true virtues and gifts of the nation and validate the optimistic confidence now entertained as to its normal and happy condition. Trust is gained, therefore, not only by picturing a bright future, but also by means of the heart-lifting observation that the first step has just been made on the right path. As Iosif Many puts it, "this is the dawning of the age of enlightenment for every nation. Let no one believe that the Romanians are only capable of herding sheep and other such occupations. My hope is that the future will refute this hardened opinion that others have formed of the Romanians."[14]

The formula was thus discovered which Romanian society would characteristically use in order to picture its own insertion in the historical time of the modern age, as a response to so many repeatedly resumed beginnings and an expression of the obsessive wish to recuperate its own belatedness: the time of awakening had come, everything would be fine starting tomorrow. The future would show that the Romanians, too, were as good as the other nations and would dissolve their shame at their own backwardness, together with all the other negative clichés which foreigners had used until then to defame them.[15]

Therefore, besides enlightened, optimistic confidence in the equal capacities of individuals and of the people, trust in the Romanians' own powers seemed to feed also on this particular representation of historical time, one that took the present as the zero point of a new era, or a critical moment able to turn historical tables and to offer the illusion that things would change dramatically, starting today. The nation was therefore expected to gather tremendous momentum. The Transylvanian intellectuals did not fail to recognise the huge speculative potential of the revolution, and began fashioning a self-image and a political discourse centred on national self-belief. Also, their duty was to keep the nation permanently in touch with that sentiment, since, in the absence of it, the nation was impossible to galvanise, given the overbearing fears and complexes that had petrified it before.

This is the path Simion Bărnuţiu, among others, takes in making his political discourse rely heavily on the mobilising potential of the representation of historical time. His *Provocation* is the first 1848 document intended to shock the collective mental frames of the Romanian élite into independent action and the inception of its own revolution, separate from the Hungarian one. Bărnuţiu "awakens" his fellow countrymen by means of the symbolic ring of history's alarm clock, set at the zero hour of a new age of enlightenment. "Today is the day of the resurrection of the nations who are dead. Hark, Romanians! So far you have been politically dead [...] Once again, brothers, today is the day of the rebirth of our rights. We want to overturn the tombstone, to untie the bonds that have kept our nation still for tens of hundreds of years, so that it can rise from the grave and live for ever."[16]

The Romanians' transfiguration, the entrance into the new era that will operate radical changes in their condition, thus revealing, in fact, their true nature and positive potential, is confidently celebrated in Bărnuţiu's discourse in Blaj: "Who will, from now on, have a heart to say that the Romanian does not wish for a happier state, that he remains unmoved at all summons, be they the sweet sound of liberty or the death sentence that is being prepared for him in the Hungarian assemblies? [...] It would be a thing most contrary to nature and a true impossibility" that "a whole people stand stock-still when the hour of its happiness is struck, and remain silent, like the deaf and the dumb, when its funeral bell tolls." In fact, "the Romanians' hearts have always beaten for liberty", which is also why they have risen on the present occasion.[17]

Bărnuţiu's attack is directed here precisely against that component of the self-image holding the Romanians to be helpless, idle, apathetic and incapable of working for the bettering of their fate. This state of lethargy will come to an end due, on the one hand, to external aggression, to the realisation of the deadly threat it poses, and, on the other, to the hope for a better future, inherent in the electrifying promise that the ideal of freedom can be achieved.

THE COMPENSATORY FUNCTION OF HISTORY

The instrumental function attributed to, and the evaluation of, historical time in the accounts relating to the Romanians' destiny highlights the idea that, in the case of the Transylvanian Romanians, national history played a crucial role in the regaining of trust in their own powers and, generally speaking, in the promotion of the positive dimension of the self-image. The past and the question of origins—important elements in any process of self-identification—were given extraordinary weight, given that the present, struggling to come to terms with incipient modernity, offered too poor a support for the building of a satisfactory and honourable identity.[18]

This being the case, for both the enlightened and, particularly, the Romantic spirit, the Romanians' chances of progress had to be justified by means of historical argumentation. The encouraging idea (of enlightened extraction) that the Romanians were good people, that they could succeed given that they were human beings, that is, that they had the propensity towards the good inborn in any human creature, was taken to be too abstract, too dryly rational to be able to communicate anything to an imaginary haunted by historical traumas and faced with unforgiving concrete realities, impervious to philosophical abstractions. The Romanians were able to succeed not because they were human beings, but because they were Romanians; the only valid and efficient arguments, able to inspire them with a belief in their chances for progress, were their noble Latin descent and glorious past.

In keeping with this line of thought, therefore, the first and adequate step to be taken on the way to progress was the collective realisation by the whole nation that it had descended from the Romans and that the history of the nation had once been a series of splendid events. Once this step had been taken, the Romanians, alive now to the sense of their destiny and true condition, would surely and naturally pursue the path opened up by their forefathers.

Knowledge of history was thus invested with the powers of a universal healer of all present and future ills. Evil was simply the outcome of the Romanians' ignoring their history, since it was only the ideal splendour of a mythical past that would give them an insight into their true condition, and not the troublesome present, which obscured and distorted it. Petru Maior was able to write his work, argues Bojincă, "because he saw that the dark degradation that had seized the Romanian nation was only due to the want of a history of the beginnings of the Dacians–Romans".[19] Elsewhere, in a comment on his own writings, he states:

> This history, as it was conceived to the praise of the nation, so shall it be an exemplum for the leading spirits of Wallachia and Moldavia. Let every one read this to the comfort of his soul, and see what his forefathers once were. But let him also search into what caused this beautiful country to drown in slowness, darkness and inactivity. Let the potent then chase away malignancy from the bosom of their country and, while reading the histories of their forefathers, let them never tire in seeing to it that it takes again the path of virtue, justice and bravery that its ancestors once trod.[20]

All evil is therefore "only due to the want of a history", a formula suggesting the double functioning of historical writing as both messianic and compensatory message. History, it is argued, is able to save and redeem the Romanians from the sins of today so that the morrow will find them clean and pure, while also bringing compensatory relief for the troubles of the present by projecting an existence in the illusory space of idealised myth-history.

It is to be noted that, prior to the inception of the modern age, that is, to the Transylvanian School, historiographical writing was not traversed by that identity-founding nationalistic thrill which would make such an impact on the contemporaries of the enlightened intellectuals and particularly of the Transylvanian Romantics, whose history books were brimful of such sentiments.[21] A certain neutral coldness and lack of any enflamed comments or affective involvement is to be observed in the accounts of certain episodes, such as that of Mihai the Brave, which would eventually come to be seen as key moments of national myth-history.

Mihai the Brave's case is more than appropriate here, since the "national signification" of the Wallachian prince's politics, as it would come to be perceived by Romanian self-consciousness, would only be "discovered", "highlighted" or, better put, "invented", with such theories as those launched by Florian Aaron or Bălcescu.[22] Until then, even Gheorghe Şincai, still indebted to traditional models of structuring historical narratives, had presented Mihai's odyssey in terms similar to those used to describe the political-military adventures of any other prince of the time.[23]

This is to say that, up until the beginning of the nineteenth century, history had not yet been completely turned into an instrument able to serve the tailoring of the national identity, as it would in the hands of the Romantics. Allusions bearing on contemporary issues were restricted to several themes of interest, such as the Romanians' Latin origins and whatever else could help in legitimating the political state of the Romanians from the Transylvanian principality. The histori-

cal approach was largely motivated by the mere, and only natural, intellectual curiosity that prompted an investigation of the past, while extra-scientific motives for
the practice of history were primarily of a moralising nature. The latter came in
the wake of a venerable tradition: history as a manual of life, that is, a sort of general panorama of worldly triumphs and vanities, of the mutability governing all
mundane political designs. Therefore, besides intellectual curiosity, the other instrument meant to legitimate this sort of historiographical sensibility was the
moralising dimension of a discourse venturing to encompass the general human
condition.

An altogether different note was struck with the historians of the modern age,
for whom history renounced such universalistic frames and wholly devoted itself
to the national interest. The idea of a disinterested investigation of the past or of
truth turned into a hollow cliché, since the primordial concerns, to which the new
historians openly confessed, lay elsewhere. The main purpose was to provide the
national community with a new identity, attuned to modernity, while the traditional means of self-identification were facing a crisis over the spectrum of various
renewals. To that end, the invention of a "new" tradition was called for, and the
mobilisation of a "new" past expected, able to offer symbolic support in the face of
the sudden, destabilising challenges of modernity.[24] Since the present was painful
and the future worrisome, history would be feverishly required to compensate for
all these troubles and uncertainties. Its "lessons" were no longer allowed to speak
of the inconstancy and worthlessness of human action as contrasted with the huge
theatre of universal history. On the contrary, such teachings were expected to
guide the vigorous march of the nation towards the luminous aim it was destined
to attain, and which, paradoxically, loomed from out of the mist of those long-
imagined origins.

In swerving from the general moralising, to the particular national, motivation
of history, the self-justifying texts of the Transylvanian historians at the beginning
of the modern age stressed its pedagogical function, indispensable to the progress
and especially to the self-awareness of the nation. The highlights were therefore
on the deliberate assuming of the function of generating collective identity, attributed to the discipline they practised. They wrote history in order to make the
Romanians into what they should be, that is, to make them "return" to their
"true" nature, which history was able to reveal—that history which was being
proposed, "discovered" or invented by the enlightened or Romantic scholars.
History (and the historians) would provide the Romanians with their identity, to
which the Romanians would have to conform (in the event that they had too
grievously strayed from it so far). It was the only way, the scholars maintained,
that the Romanians would be able to recapture their true essence, more or less
estranged or altered by the hardships of the times.

Dimitrie Iercovici's opinion is extremely telling of the ethnic pedagogy mentioned above. Although still impregnated with a moralising tendency it nevertheless exclusively centres on the strictly national relevance that the study of history
can have for the Romanians. He writes in 1794:

The teachings of history are a most precious thing and greatly useful to this world, for they, in informing men of all the events of times past, advise and show us how nations came, either by disobedience or by wicked pride, to fall out of memory and consideration and lose their name in this world. Second, they also teach us how the forgotten and fallen nations can rise again, by gentleness of conduct, cheerful obedience and the forgetting of the things which were the cause of their misfortune; how they can be born again and take back their name and, by making the lost glory their own again, welcome the light of a new age in their hearts.[25]

Although still heavily imbued with the idea of history as a lesson of the rise and fall of humankind[26], Iercovici's text also, and just as forcefully, foregrounds the new function of historiography: the generation of a new identity, a replica and transfigured copy of the "first" identity, the original one ("…how they can be born again", says Iercovici, significantly, in referring to the Romanians' general condition). The means to that end is, obviously, the mobilisation of the historical past. Or, for the lesson to be effective in revitalising national confidence, it is plain that the message of history can only be a encouraging and optimistic one, which the past will be carefully tailored to fit.

In fact, like any true enlightened intellectual of the Central European space, Iercovici is not yet ready to stake everything on the card of history, which is only called in to back up Christian teachings with a view to putting together a national pedagogy. Iercovici continues: "All these, without the learning of the Christian law and with the sole aid of historical teachings, can in no way be attained, for Christian morals are as tightly knit to the lessons of history as man's body with his soul and senses."[27]

One more reason why historical writing is unable, on its own, to ensure the progress of the nation, could be the Romanians' low cultural level, which prevents them from absorbing the revelations offered by historiography with respect to identity. However, the problem can be solved, Iercovici believes (and he proves quite insightful here, if we think of what was to come): the lesson of history should first and foremost indoctrinate the élites, on which its efficiency is to be tested in the first place. Then, we might add, the bulk of the nation, well framed by this ideological pattern, will also open up, according to its capacities for assimilation, to the national programme aimed at a positive redefinition of the self-image.

In all justice, will anyone say that the Romanian nation cannot, by the sole aid of the learning of history, straighten and rise from its dullness, for histories of the sort are not to be found written or published in the Romanian language? But a defence, like the one I give here, seems to me in want of sufficient grounds: for I am not speaking of those who husband their lives by the sweat of land labour and other such mechanical occupations, but of those who are by birth free and spared the hardships of a life of toil.[28]

Samuil Micu, in his *Short Information on the History of the Romanians* (1796, 1806) also insists on the primordial role that his history is meant to serve, that ism the animation of the people: "It is but a stain on the Romanians that they have no knowledge of the history of their people, for if we look around we see that all nations have put down on paper the deeds of their forefathers, and it is meet that all men who have their wits about them should know the history of their nation, which is the mentor of all things, be they religious or political, for it teaches not only by words, but also by examples."[29]

Micu does not tire of urging his fellow countrymen to write histories of the Romanians: "Either strive to that end yourself, or, should you feel unable, urge and help those who can, so that Romanian matters be shown in full and in particular and made known to the whole nation." The purpose is that "the good should pride themselves on their nation among others, while the wicked should bow their heads in shame and wipe their hearts of beastly sentiments and become Romanian men, which is to say thorough, for it is no trifle to have been born a Romanian."[30] Once again, history evinces its role as shaper of identity and tailor of the positive self-image: You cannot be a "Romanian man" ("men and Romans", writes Micu elsewhere[31]) unless you study history. Likewise, it is precisely the knowledge of history that will reveal the nobility of your condition, the "importance" of being a Romanian.

Initially launched by the enlightened intellectuals, the idea appears in practically identical terms in the writings of Transylvanian Romantic historians. Fifty years later, in 1847, August Treboniu Laurian wrote that the *Historical Journal for Dacia* was published in order that "the Romanian should understand he has to be a Romanian, to love his country, to love his nation, to learn how to respect himself and how to take care of his own future."[32] Again, the same old theme recurs: History alone is able to reveal a person's identity, to teach people how to be true Romanians (while so far they have been mere shadows, a degraded copy of primeval identity), and to inspire them with self-esteem and a positive evaluation of the national condition.

History as generator of national identity also performed a pragmatic role as a political weapon against those foreigners who denied the Romanians' status and rights. The unstable political situation the Romanians were in was closely related to their poor understanding of their own identity (due to a scant knowledge of history). It followed that the study of history, by causing them to assume their identity, would also be instrumental in chasing the enemy away from their frontiers.[33] Kogălniceanu, in his introductory lecture delivered at the Academia Mihăileană and also published in Transylvania in Bariț's papers, gives eloquent expression to this idea, taking his cue from the similar considerations advanced by Florian Aaron:

> We are in urgent need of a history of our country, be it only for the defence of our rights against the foreign nations. While we still lack a history, any foreign enemy will feel he has a right to come and say, as Mr. Aaron did: "The beginning of your people is unknown, the name you bear is not yours, nor the land you inhabit; your fate has been such that these things cannot change: forget your beginnings, throw away your name, or take the name I will give you, pack up your things and leave the land you live on, for it is not yours; all your strife is in vain, for you cannot be better than you are." And, in truth, all these things have been said to us by foreign people; our beginnings have been denied, our name altered, our land torn apart, our rights trampled over, only because we had not the consciousness of our nationality, only because we had no ground for understanding and defending our rights.[34]

George Bariț has an altogether different understanding of history, as we shall see below. When he refers to its strictly pragmatic dimension, he emphasises much more concrete and less spectacular aspects, since he is interested in its formative role in the area of civic and political culture: "Is it not a shame when we find ourselves in such want of historical notions that we cannot even understand properly a book or a gazette written with sharpness and good wit, or a parliamentary debate, so that we have been all too often in danger of losing our wits over all sorts of wicked snarls?"[35]

It is also true that in this article of 1845, dedicated to the importance and general ethno-pedagogical value of history writing, he also refers to its emotional impact on the collective psyche, as well as to the deciphering of the past as decisive for an understanding of the present and even of the future. "Is it not a natural inclination, which awakens in every sensible soul, to want to know where he comes from, what his kindred are, what his nation, what his country's troubles and misfortunes, what the life of his forefathers was, and other such matters? Is it not a disgrace when, ignorant of the past, we cannot understand the present nor see into the morrow?"[36]

Yet apart from this main tendency to stake everything on history as identity-giver and redeemer of the present, there are important voices expressing doubt that history, extraordinary though it may be, can work wonders in solving the problems of the present.[37]

Today's specialists[38] agree that the synthesis performed in 1848 between the theories of natural and of historical right, between liberal rationalism and organicist historicism, furnished the political ideology of the time with its doctrinal premises. Yet it is also true that some of the intellectuals of the age doubted (and maybe rightly so) that these two ways of thinking were truly compatible and wondered whether they should not opt for one of the two alternatives. My opinion is that in Transylvania, as in the rest of the Central and Eastern European space as a whole, the dominant doctrine throughout the first half of the nineteenth century was the organicist historicism of Herderian extraction, with occasional and only superficial additions of rationalist-contractualist ideas.

For the Transylvanian intellectuals of 1848, the liberal, national or democratic claims they made were primarily derived (in their essence, and not at a superficial declarative level) from the unshaken "certitudes" of the national history rather than from a real confidence in the power of reason, or of any abstract theory, to change a reality so rooted in its own past. No one was willing to accept the idea that the present was so hard to change and so unhappy because it was the outcome of a miserable past, while everyone was, at the same time, persuaded that there were indissoluble ties linking the present to the past. The solution, then, given the preference for the idea of those ties, was to "change" the past for the better by rewriting history; the present would thereby "improve", too, or at least trust would be built in the Romanians' abilities to change it.

Such rationale, elaborated at the level of the social imaginary of the time, provided political action with a much more profound motivation than an ideological attachment to the slogans of Western liberalism. Here (as almost everywhere else), the political ideology or "clear ideas" embodied in the doctrine were merely a superficial structure as compared with the political mythology and imaginary, with its social representations and collective beliefs, all deeply merged into the reflexive and emotional structures of society.

This being the case, the conclusion could be that such divergent opinions, voiced by Transylvanian intellectuals who doubted the "supremacy" of history although clearly at variance with mainstream sensibility, announced, however, the possibility of different thinking patterns other than the hegemonic tendency to conceive of the "national movement" and of the Romanians' condition in self-legitimating historicist terms.

Papiu Ilarian takes tentative steps in this direction when he criticises those "nationalist intellectuals among the Romanians" who, "neglectful of politics, spent their time in historical and literary inquiries. And even though their works awakened to some degree the Romanians' national spirit, and thus unwittingly triggered a natural opposition against Hungarianism, we still do not see that our historians and men of letters are in the least concerned with the political questions and relationships arising between the Romanians and the Hungarians."[39] Although he admits history is effective in defining identity, Papiu finds this is totally insufficient unless there is active involvement in the political problematic of the present. This is in fact in tune with the general thesis of his *History*, which maintains that self-consciousness, virtual identity, or the "genetic nationality", are worthless in the absence of determined will and effective action, of the nation's involvement in its most topical problems.

Andrei Mureşanu, too, is sceptical about the ability of history to solve by itself the problems of the present, unless there is energetic intervention on actual matters: "Brothers! We can no longer rely solely on ancient scripts without understanding how to read what is written therein and without giving proof that we deserve respect in total accordance with those scripts."[40]

The two examples mentioned above take a somewhat middle road in evaluating the role of history. There are other attitudes, however, which sharply deny historicism any relevance for the Romanians' topical interests.

Ion Budai-Deleanu, for instance, the Transylvanian thinker most powerfully influenced by the rationalism of the French Enlightenment, develops an extremely lucid and detached rationale behind his own historical and linguistic investigations: "The sole purpose of my entire research is to reach historical truth, or at least to come as close as possible to it, and I believe that every reader and every Romanian with brains about him is, and should be, indifferent to whether their nation descends from the Romans, from the Dacians or from any other people. Suffice it that the Romanians have formed on Dacian land a nation among the first ever, made of several millions of men."[41]

Budai-Deleanu's profession of faith is exemplary and, unfortunately, it has remained a model with little echo in the Romanian culture even to this day: the aim of any scientific research can only be the truth; no matter what history might reveal, for the better or for the worse, it cannot influence the way the Romanians' present problems will be solved and has nothing to do with their present condition, therefore today's interests should also be left aside when tackling the question of their illustrious origins; finally, if the Romanians need valid arguments for their cause they will only find them among the realities of the present, and had better leave history in the hands of the specialists.

It comes as no surprise, then, that, in keeping with his own deontology, Budai-Deleanu will be the only man of his time who acknowledges—*horribile dictu*—the existence of words of Dacian origin in the Romanian language (as only ill-meaning foreigners did in the age), even though he himself is in favour of a quasi-total extermination of such vestiges.[42]

Although keenly aware of the importance of history and a practitioner of historiography (or maybe precisely because of it), George Bariț, too, rejects history's relevance to the problems of the present in vehement yet beautifully drawn arguments. In 1848, and on other occasions too, he pleads for throwing history overboard, since it is only a source of prejudice, inequities and national adversities, and making use instead of the new grounds of reason and modernity. In his opinion (a mere *pium desiderium*, as will be proved later on), the Transylvanian Romanians will from now on

> leave behind all historical disputes surrounding the age of the peoples, on the historical naming of such and such a land, be it of the Transylvanian nobles, of the Saxons, or of the Szeklers, held either in friendship or adversity. All such matters will from now on only feed the historical inquiries, not politics, and even less the law. The Romanians will only know a country common to all, in which not only the age-old inhabitants but also those lawfully naturalised here after a ten years' stay will enjoy the rights of the oldest charters and all privileges.[43]

Besides the anti-historicist pathos, Bariț also upholds his plea with a pragmatic argument, which he invokes at the end of his dissertation: history may serve the Romanians, as is the case, for instance, with their exceptional endurance throughout the ages, but it can also easily turn against them, since it is, after all, merely a construction. Historical research may at any time bring to light some less convenient document or privilege. That is why the Romanians should base their efforts to build a future not on history, but on the modern ideas of freedom and equality of rights.

Bariț was not the only one who entertained such notions in 1848. The Romanian merchants from Brașov, the financial élites of the nation, communicated to Bishop Șaguna their concern about the way the Romanians' rights were to be defended: they demanded that history should by no means be invoked as an argument. "In treating this very important matter", they wrote, referring to the issue of the Romanians' admittance as a nationality, "by no means should the historical right be taken as a ground, no, not even for a single minute, but only the philosophical right".[44]

Bariț had in fact rejected the past as an argument before the revolution, in stating that history would be a useless and pernicious means of fuelling national resentments and hatred among peoples: "Why should we continue to look for comfort only in separation, divorce and mordant rejections, fearing even the weakest bonds? Why should we call up from the grave the shadows of our ancestors and thereby appal one another? Why should not we face the future with daring eyes?"[45]

The attempt to "call up" ancestors from their graves to come to the Romanians' side and support them in contemporary disputes[46] would nevertheless remain a frequent practice, welcomed by the Romanian social imaginary. While so trouble-stricken and seeming to endure such pain in the face of overwhelming hardships, who else could come to their rescue, by offering them the compensatory illusion of a happy resolution, than these fantasy ancestors, reaped from the golden pages of the national history?

LATIN ORIGINS

The motif of the Romanians' Latin origins is one extremely significant instance of the tendency of the self-image to look for positive elements in the past, while avoiding the present. In the wake of the Transylvanian School, the theme of Roman origins remained a fundamental element of the cultural discourse in Transylvania throughout the first half of the nineteenth century. Within the Transylvanian political-historical imaginary, it also functioned as the supreme argument legitimating the Romanian nation's accessibility to progress and thriving. Although reality was bleak and foreign criticism ever present, the Romanians showed complete confidence in their ability to find a way out simply because they were the descendants of the Romans. If the Romanians' ancestors were able to attain such a high degree of civilisation it was evident that the Romanians, too, had the same potential, as their descendants. This is what the Transylvanian intellectuals of the time advanced as a most serious and powerful argument.

The logic of such a deduction was reinforced by the theory of the *purity* of the Romanians' Latin origins. Understandably, the Transylvanians of the time needed that element within the scaffolding of a comforting self-image, which explains their tenacity in supporting it. "The Romanians are Romans" was a thesis readily embraced by August Treboniu Laurian, Simion Bărnuțiu and Alexandru Papiu Ilarian. According to this thesis, the Romanians were not only the inheritors of certain positive values and potentialities passed down to them, one way or another, through the ages, they were the very depository of the whole stock of creative capacities of their illustrious predecessors.

A related theme was that of the Romanians' resistance to denationalisation, of their ethnic purity, which, as we have seen, was backed up by ethnographic arguments bearing on the Romanians' matrimonial behaviour. The aim was the same: to demonstrate the purity of the Romanians' Latin descent and therefore their identification with the Romans.

Such a perspective was obviously able radically to modify, at the illusory level of the image, the givens of the Romanians' present condition as well. Instead of ranking lowest among the peoples of Europe, in point of degree of civilisation, freedom, political development and national self-assertion, they thus moved to the top of the list, since no other people around could claim as distinguished a descent as theirs, which was traced back to the conquerors of the world and the founders of modern civilisation in its European and Christian dimensions.[47]

Undoubtedly, the image was quite a slippery one, as can be seen in the epigonic motifs of Andrei Mureșanu's poetry and journalistic work.[48] Here, the Romanians' present degradation is pictured as all the sadder and the more unacceptable as they have fallen from such amazing heights, and, in fact, the huge contrast between the two hypostases is deliberately preserved for its shock effect, meant to arouse the stamina necessary for their awakening. Equally, the return from the abyss is also a promise of a growth as grandiose as the fall had been dramatic.

The theme of Roman origins is therefore meant to make a direct and concrete impact on the Romanians so that they can rise and bring to light their latent virtues, as Petru Maior himself had put it: "Seeing what noble blood is flowing through their veins, the Romanians shall try to follow their fathers in grace of soul and dignity of manners [...], as they have been endowed with excellent gifts from their mother nature, they shall be careful to become good citizens, of service to their country."[49]

Following the line of Maior's appeal, the Transylvanian intellectuals would never tire of underlining this ethno-pedagogical connotation of the motif of Roman origins, convinced that the promotion of that image would make a positive and consistent impact on the realities of the present.

In the *Antiquities of the Romans*[50], for instance, a work entirely devoted to an appraisal of the brilliant qualities of the Romanians' predecessors, Damaschin Bojincă shows that "the Romanian nation" had better find out more about the civilisation of "her Roman ancestors, if she wants to grow and benefit from the fruits of culture and the polish of refinement within and without, and if she desires, as she does, to make advancement and progress in the sciences, which are hard to gain without a full understanding of the writs, and particularly of the classics."[51]

Besides the ethno-pedagogical role of Roman civilisation as an exemplary model to be followed in an emotional-patriotic sense, Bojincă also invests the message with a more pragmatic import: Greek–Latin classicism is to be embraced for its scientific and cultural virtues as well. Serious schooling and a solid formation of both individual and nation presuppose a thorough study of the classic authors and ancient culture.

At the same time, another intellectual from Banat, Moise Bota, warns of the damaging consequences ensuing from the neglect of such training. The traitors, renegades and monsters of ingratitude who turn against their people are bred among those "who did not grow up with their folk" and "especially" among "those who were not nourished with the knowledge of those they sprang from, our Roman ancestors, those heroes and great men worthy of praise and eternal remembrance".[52] In other words, it is familiarity with Livy and Cicero alone that can arouse national sentiments and, more than that, can reveal the Romanians' true identity and sanction their pride in being Romanians. It was for this reason that the scholars of the time strove so hard to fathom all there was to know about ancient culture in every form of school and institution (which, after all, from the middle level onwards employed Latin as the language of study), and also to spread their findings among the masses of their less-educated fellow countrymen by means of a grandiose programme of translations from the classics, which filled the publications of the time from Bariţ's papers to the humblest village almanacs.[53]

This is also the argument that Bojincă uses in support of his efforts at popularisation. Elsewhere he insists on the possible effect that lack of knowledge, or, on the contrary, the "discovery", of the Romanians' Roman descent can have, in his opinion, on Romanian national pride, all the way down to folk perception. "Many stones bearing Roman inscriptions are being dug up in Transylvania, especially in the field called Prat, from Trajan, but our Romanians know nothing about it, and were they to know that the Stati, Lupi, Ulpi, Ghemeli and other names inscribed here were their grand ancestors they would doubtless raise their heads in a more manly manner."[54]

In fact, the idea that the Romanians are not "men" enough to make a point of their historical heritage, while others, less entitled to such boasting, do it without any scruple, was a cliché frequently used in the writings of the time.[55] We find it, for instance, in the *Romanian Library* of 1821: "Brothers! All nations, small and slow as they may be, are thirsting to read and know about the feats of their ancestors, even though much matter of pride they cannot have; so much the more it is meet that you read and know about the feats of the old Romans, your famed ancestors."[56]

Apart from this general evaluation of the role that the motif of Roman origins could have in stimulating national pride, it is also interesting to see the practical, concrete advantages that the intellectuals of the time believed it could bring as well.

It seems that the theme in question could be used in support of a range of causes and tendencies, irrespective of their orientation. Bărnuțiu, for instance, states, sententiously, that "Trajan's colonies are not sleeping, but they have awakened and become aware that they are called up to a higher culture, towards which they can only advance with the aid of their mother tongue."[57] In saying this, Bojincă has in mind a quite specific political aim: opposing the legislative projects of the Transylvanian Diet regarding the enhancement of the Hungarian language. Cipariu, too, writes that "the Romanians have in the history of their Roman ancestors examples of the most excellent virtues, be they domestic or public, political or military."[58] Yet he does so in articles written in April and May 1848, in which he pleads for the union of Transylvania with Hungary. Papiu Ilarian, on the other hand, employs the whole symbolism of the Romanians' Latinity in arguing for the Romanians' loyalty to the House of Habsburg. He thus operates a superposition of the "imperial" character of Rome onto the similar attributes of Vienna. "For centuries on end the Romanian has only known the mastery of an *imperator*. The Roman colonies had been established by *imperator*s. The Eastern rite was introduced by Byzantine emperors. For one hundred and fifty years now the Transylvanian Romanian has been spared the old tyrannies and calumny by the Austrian emperors, who are also called the emperors of the Romans; they were rid of serfdom solely by the grace of Emperor Joseph II, who proudly bore the name and is to this day the idol of the Romanians."[59]

The ironic thing is that the Uniate bishop of Oradea, Vasile Erdélyi, uses the theme of the Romanians' attachments to Rome in order to argue for the Romanians' involvement in the Hungarian revolution. Furthermore, the theme allows him to exalt the idea of a Hungarian state extending to the historical frontiers pledged to the crown of Saint Ștefan, a crown that itself bore, and in a double sense, too, the insignia of "Romanity": "In the tenth century AD the Hungarians and the Romanians chose as head of their nations Saint Ștefan, who then received two wreaths, one from Rome, the other from Constantinople, from the emperor of the Romans, so that both wreaths, the Romanian and the Hungarian, be joined together, just as the Hungarian and the Romanian have sworn brotherly devotion to one another."[60]

Even at the time of the revolution the popular paper *The Teacher of the People*, issued in Blaj and involved throughout the autumn of 1848 in a sustained propaganda campaign in favour of the recruitment initiated by the Hungarian authorities, began its work of political-nationalist education among the peasants with an article praising the virtues of the Romanians' Roman ancestors. "Today's Romanians" are told that "it is meet that we turn to them and know their life and customs, for it is the duty of the sons to pay attention to the ways of their parents, so that they receive good guidance and be able to follow them."[61]

A similar article makes the first page of the other popular weekly of the revolution, *The Friend of the People*, edited in Pest by Sigismund Pop. The virtues of the Romanians' Latin ancestors are invoked from the very beginning with the explicit aim of mobilising the Romanian masses to serve the Hungarian revolution.[62] This is yet another instance of the tendency of national images and stereotypes to serve as instruments of manipulation, in an infinite number of ways and on all occasions.

These miscellaneous examples might suggest that the invocation of the Romanians' Latin origins and of the ensuing virtues was felt at the time as an obligatory argument in legitimating any type of ideological discourse. Equally, one might understand that the theme of Roman origins could only be conceived in positive terms, while any possible view to the contrary was completely forbidden in the economy of the ideological prescriptions and of the political imaginary.

This was not quite the case. Undoubtedly, the glorification of Latinity was the dominant tendency of the age, while more reserved or even critical stances were fairly rare, featuring as isolated blasphemies uttered against the sacred collective certainties. Yet the latter tendency marks several moments of a necessary critical self-interrogation as to the fundamental verities of the self-image, of a lucid demythologising of such constructions. George Bariț, for instance, in translating the extremely accusatory remarks made by a foreign author about the Romanians, also mentions the opinion according to which "all their doings declare their having too long espoused idleness and disarray, although they pride themselves on their Roman origins".[63] Although elsewhere he chooses to retaliate in response to much more benign observations, this time Bariț prefers to remain silent, probably on account of the belief that such shaking of the reliquary of the national mythology might be of help from time to time.

Pavel Vasici is even more explicit. To an adversary from Banat who pleads for the introduction of the orthographic (and maybe even orthoepic) form *roman* [Roman] instead of *român* or *rumân* [Romanian]—forms which the Serbs used as well, to the damage of the Romanians' linguistic-national purity—Vasici gives an ironic response on behalf of good measure and common sense. "As to the name *roman*, do not take offence; were the Serbs to call us by the name of *roman*, *român* or *rumân* there is no harm to us [...]; let us be true to ourselves and acknowledge in our hearts that we are weak and frail, and let us try to illumine the Romanians, for should it be that they are Romans, the greater need they will have of illumination. What do you think, my good gentleman? Is the Romanian from Ghiroda kin to Cicero or Julius Caesar?"[64]

The critique of Latinism, coming also as a reaction to the Transylvanians' exaggerations, was obviously much more astute in the principalities. Kogălniceanu, for instance, in his 1843 lecture, rises against the "Romano-mania, or the mania of calling ourselves Romans, a passion that today has taken hold of Transylvania in particular and some of the writers in Wallachia". The champions of that tendency, "without bringing facts to uphold their words, believe that they will thus gain the world's respect and, when they proclaim they are Romans, they truly believe they are Romans and therefore the leading people in the whole world [...] Let us beware, gentlemen, of emulating this mania, which makes us subject to foreign ridicule [...]; otherwise, it might be that we well deserve Mr. Eliad's words, who says that it is only bankrupt nations that will not cease talking of their ancestors."[65]

In his *Memoirs* Timotei Cipariu also exercises the same unremitting lucidity, no longer satisfied with the illusory consoling myths of the self-image:

> It is no wonder, then, that the name of Roman is being put to slander in our land [...] The literate men of Europe begin to admit that our language has grown out of the Roman trunk, but when observing our state they shudder with disbelief and reckon our Roman descent goes no further than the talk we make of it. "It cannot be", they say or at least think to themselves, "that these be Roman people! Facts and deeds do betray those who are indeed Romans: the Italians, the Spaniards, the Gallic French; but these Romanians, where are the deeds that will make them worthy of the name? Doubtless, these were only the serfs of the Romans, from whom they stole the name and the language." What shall we reply to such men, fellow Romanians? It is high time we meditated upon these matters, for if we do not, beware, and know that our grandchildren will, for shame, make anything of themselves, even Turks.[66]

The national poet of the time (Andrei Mureşanu) himself, who actually makes prodigal use of Latinist imagery in his verse, is ready to take the opportunity of turning it upside down when he declares, with bitter irony:

> Enflamed your word is, Muse, of country when you speak,
> Of kin and fathers brave, of Rome and dear old days.
> In wonder I do tremble and ask, can you not see
> That our country's sold for money and cold grim darkness has our nation seized?[67]

Even his emblematic *Echo* leaves the Romanian collective imaginary the legacy of the same ambiguity inherent, he believes, in the Latinity associated with the Romanians' condition: "Now or never let us *give proof* [emphases added] to the world / That these veins are still warmed by Roman blood."[68] If the Romanians fail to give palpable and immediate proof, by their deeds, of their illustrious origin it will be denied to them, and rightly so.

Despite this array of doubts, anxieties, and even negative self-evaluations accompanying the motif in question, it can be argued as a conclusion that the existence of such critical rational considerations represented a sign of normality for the public spirit of the age. Even though Latinism was a hegemonic ideological principle, capable of ensuring cohesion and legitimating system of a society in search of certainties, the noteworthy deviations from the norm presented above show that pluralism of opinion and alternative options were not completely banished even in the case of this "primordial", if after all useless, issue of origins.

SAVIOURS OF CHRISTIAN EUROPE IN THE MIDDLE AGES

Another past-oriented positive theme of the self-image posits the Romanians as defenders of Christianity and of European civilisation in the Middle Ages. The main qualities presupposed by this role are, obviously, military proficiency and courage—important features of Romanian self-perception which we have seen underlined in other contexts as well. Petru Maior is again the one who lays down the bases of this stereotype: "Boundless would be the work of he who endeavours to write about all the deeds of the Romanians, which show forth the manly and brave nature of the Romanian nation."[69]

The competitive drive of the self-image, always taking foreign elements as a referent, is present here as well. In formulating and arguing for his idea, Maior starts from a statement by Anonymus, who says that in the age of Tuhutum the Romanians had been in a most precarious and downward state. Maior's response takes, obviously, the form of a denial, as he attempts to prove that the Romanians are not as cowardly or miserly as foreigners take them to be. In order to do that, he calls on the whole of medieval Romanian history as an argument in support of his demonstration. The great voivodes and military personalities Basarab I, Ştefan the Great, Vlad the Impaler and Iancu of Hunedoara are the pillars of this spectacular myth-history and the guarantors of a number of clichés. According to these examples, bravery, heroism and devotion are defining traits specific to this period of Romanian history. The elementary observation that the medieval age was everywhere a time of war and military bravery was obviously irrelevant for the upholders of that perspective.

The illustrious figures of the national history were also useful in demonstrating to foreigners, as well as to the Romanians themselves, that the Romanians were not only the numerous, silent and anonymous masses they were thought to be, but that they too had their renowned personalities, the embodiments of exceptional human qualities, whose universal value should be acknowledged and admired.

This is why the preference was for those personalities whose actions were of European import and who had gained foreign recognition for their deeds and qualities. This is true in the case of Iancu of Hunedoara, who was, at the time, the most frequently invoked personality, at least up until the reign of the figure of Mihai the Brave, forcefully launched by Florian Aaron's textbooks in Wallachia[70] and definitively established later, particularly due to Bălcescu's work. Iancu of

Hunedoara's Transylvanian origins and particularly his reputation as a champion of Christianity had a decisive say in establishing his popularity. Another impressive, if less frequently confessed, detail is that he attained a pre-eminent position in the Hungarian kingdom, which is to say within the very fortress of the traditional enemy. It was an occasion for soothing the Romanians' damaged pride and granting them unexpected satisfaction. The Romanian origins of Matthias Corvinus or Nicolaus Olahus were often invoked to the same effect.

In his study devoted to the Transylvanian voivode[71], Damaschin Bojincă is intent on evidencing these very aspects. He often emphasises the fact that "the much renowned hero Ioan Corvinus de Huniad, whom the whole world reveres, was born into the Romanian kin." Bojincă's purpose was to fashion the portrait of this personality as a European and tolerant character, a symbol of the peaceful cohabitation and mutual respect established among the nations of Hungary and Transylvania. It was a perfect occasion for forcing contemporary allusions: "The greatest and most famous hero of that age, Ioan, was of birth none other than a Romanian, a true patriot in body and soul, a lover of justice and truth and devoted in his generous heart to all sons of the country alike, be they of one nationality or another. He thus raised the country to the highest state of glory, and, with the courteous love of all his men, knew no foe mightier than he in the whole of Europe."[72]

Bojincă builds a similar image of Mihai the Brave, in whom he praises more than anything else his efforts to save Christianity and defend European civilisation. This hero "was the shield sworn to defend the whole of Christianity against barbaric tyranny, whom the whole of Europe beheld in wonder"; today's Romanians should know this so that they "see what their ancestors were once and their place in this world".[73]

This element of the self-image struggled for legitimacy in conditions of fierce competition, as I have already mentioned. In proudly sustaining the Romanian origins of Iancu of Hunedoara, Bojincă had to confront Hungarian historiography, itself obviously keen on attributing to the exceptionally competent governor of Hungary a convenient ethnic origin, in this case Hungarian.[74]

However, apart from the descent of particular personalities the very role and merit of defenders of Christianity is intensely disputed by the two competing national mythologies and self-images; it was an element on which the two self-perceptions placed extreme importance then, as well as later on. The Romanians vied with the Hungarians for pre-eminence not only in topical political or social matters, but even in the realm of symbols and national images, history and heroes, "specific" traits and position in Europe, all of which needed to be defended or gained in combat with the national enemy. What is more, many of these elements of the self-image were in fact "common goods", a universal patrimony, where others might well claim ascendancy (e.g., the role of defender of Christianity could have been challenged by any of the peoples to the south of the Danube, by Russia, Poland, Austria, Spain or anyone else). As such, they were, naturally, quite easy to prove as being the prerogatives of either the Romanians or the Hungarians, as consubstantial features of their heritage and historical destiny. The trouble started when the respective self-images, particularly those confronted with difficulties and abuses, attempted to claim *exclusive* ownership of those elements, while the clash of such more or less marked demands called forth nationalist pathos and large-scale conflicts, deeply rooted in the cultural and sensitive patterns of those nations.

This is the background against which the Romanians' dispute with the Hungarians over the role as defenders of Christianity was projected. The Romanian deputies to the Pest Parliament argued, in their polemical debate with Baron Miklós Jósika[75], for the need for a milder treatment of the Romanians by the Hungarians on account of the more conspicuous contribution of the former in performing that role, while the existence of competition in this respect was implicitly acknowledged:

> The Romanians raised their arms in faith and withstood the attack of the common enemies just like the Hungarians did, and more; in those battles which were of special benefit for the redemption of the country, the Romanians proved the more worthy of praise. And what have the Romanians received in return for their faith and civic devotion? Calumny (vile talk), scorn, misery, beastly abuse and serfdom. Transylvania stood up as a defence wall against Oriental barbarity, and this mighty wall was firstly the work of the Romanian people.[76]

George Bariț offers a noteworthy contribution on this topic. In his article *The Romanians and Hungarianism*[77] he approaches the Romanians' role and position in Europe and recognition of them at an international level. Starting from the appreciation that Europe has "a much poorer knowledge of us than they do of the Jews, who have their Moses", Bariț goes on to argue, probably on behalf of the idea that the Romanians, too, had their own prophets, that "in the days of old [...] it was the victory of Ioan Huniadi the Romanian, or of Ștefan of Moldavia [...] that the salvation of the Christians rested on" and that the Romanians were a "marginal European nation" meant to serve as "defence wall for the whole of Europe".

The Transylvanian journalist's concern is not simply that Europe does not acknowledge the Romanians' role as defenders of Christianity, but that today the Hungarians claim it for themselves (particularly as key figures of the resistance against Russian threats). What is important is not only that the Romanians be granted this merit but that it should not be transferred onto the Hungarians. Firstly, Bariț advances beautifully drawn arguments in favour of this latter part of his thesis. No other nation, and, therefore, we are led to understand, nor the Hungarians either, can assume this role any longer, since "both enlightened culture and wise politics are beginning to make of all Europe's states one big family, whose limbs can no longer act separately and move in ways which do not correspond to the interest of all the others".

On the other hand, *quod licet Iovi, non licet bovi*; what is forbidden to the Hungarians no longer applies to the Romanians. Due to their geographical position, to the national traits differentiating them from the Slavs and proving their kinship with the neo-Latin peoples, the Romanians are more than entitled to claim that role, as a nation who has been a "preserver [...] of the most precious channel of communication there is in Europe, which is the Danube".

The first sketches were thus drawn of an image which was to gain a great deal of ground, that is, the Romanians as sentinels of Latin Europe at the mouth of the Danube—an image meant, as Bariţ has it, to earn for them the attention and good will of the European community: "The Romanian nation has every right to the sympathy and aid of the nations of Europe, in as much as she is of a kind with most of them, as well as her being placed in that land which has inspired so much interest." This being the case, the time will come when "Europe will turn its eager and benevolent eyes onto the history of the Romanian nation [...], and will declare her right to the name of defence wall of Christianity."[78]

This is the core of Bariţ's argumentation: that the Romanians may also be called, as others unjustly are, "defenders of Christianity"; that they be acknowledged as such in the eyes of Europe as well as in their own eyes. The idea that they hold an important position in Europe and perform a necessary and well-determined function in the economy of the continent finds expression along the polemical lines of the self-image, as a point in their competition with the Hungarians. It is not they who are entitled to aspire to Europe's gratitude and sympathy, since the Romanians are the ones who bore the brunt of the battles with the Turks, who supplied the providential personalities who could ensure success in these battles, who are kindred with the peoples of Europe, not they, who are of Asian descent; it is the Romanians who can put up a natural barrier against the Slav threat looming large in the East.

Obviously, the Hungarians, too, could well claim that their history had had an anti-Ottoman dimension as well, that they were much closer to Western civilisation due to their geographical position and to the religion and feudal system they shared with the West, that they were that small nation at the borders of European civilisation, lost amidst the hostile ocean of pan-Slavism. But who could tell any more what the "true" facts were in the face of this dizzying swirl of national mythologies, when the truly significant ingredient able to fuel and justify such conflicting passions was the flickering reality of the images?

NOTES

1 For the mythologising of the past in Romanian culture, see 3:Pippidi 1993. If I were to push the interpretation here I would argue that the preference for the two temporal segments mentioned above may be said to parallel the so-called meta-narratives, or grand stories (grands récits), that Lyotard speaks about. The function of the latter would have been to legitimate knowledge up until the eve of post-modernism, either in the mythical (traditional) variant, bent on the past, or in the projective, modern one. The post-modern age would be characterised precisely by a lack of faith in such "ideological fairy-tales" with universalistic claims. See 3:Lyotard 1979 and 3:Călinescu M. 1987, chp. V.
2 George Bariţ, in 1.2:*Journal for the Mind*, II, 1839, p. 69.
3 See the overworked echo of Ţichindeal's modest work, due precisely to such enthusiastic projections regarding the Romanians' condition, from Ion Heliade-Rădulescu (1.5:Heliade 1838) to Eminescu's well-known mention in "Epigonii". In Banat and the area around Arad, the same image circulates, feeding on local patriotism (see the case of the Pedagogical College in Arad, a continuation of the famous Preparandia and the present promoter of that cult).
4 1.4:Ţichindeal 1814, pp. 274–275.

5 *Ibidem.*

6 Horga Popovici was a priest in Seleuş, in the valley of the Crişul Alb river, and Ţichindeal in Becicherec, Banat (see 3:*Dictionary 1900*, sub voce).

7 1.4:Horga Popovici 1807, "Foreword"; 1.9:Fugariu 1983, I, pp. 735–736.

8 1.4:Nicolau 1819, I ("Dedication"); 1.9:Fugariu 1983, II, p. 422.

9 *Ibidem.*

10 1.4:*The Adviser* 1826, p. 17; 1.9:Fugariu 1983, II, pp. 636–637.

11 1.9:Stoica de Haţeg 1984, p. 86.

12 Vasile Pop, preface to 1.4:Prale 1827; 1.6:*GBC* 1973–1993, V, p. 5.

13 Vasile Pop to George Bariţ, a letter of April 1838, published in 1.6:*GBC* 1973–1993, V, p. 23.

14 (Iosif Many), "Ş. St. Giorz, 15 March", in 1.2:*The Gazette*, VIII, 1845, no. 21, p. 81.

15 It is also true that this confidence in the healing virtues of the morrow is accompanied and undermined by an equally powerful doubt, which turns hope into anxiety and projects an uncertain and worrying future. Iosif Pop, for instance, a professor from Blaj involved in the conflict with Bishop Lemeny (significantly, he was to commit suicide in the long run), wrote in 1842: "A new age is about to begin for our nation: the light will either dwindle and perish and the darkness of despotism will blind poor Romanians for eternity, or it will guide us into better times" (1.1:Pop Iosif 1843). The same idea, in a formulation heralding Eminescu's discourse (and obviously influenced by folk paremiology) is present in one of Constantin Papfalvi's letters, written in 1846: "Are we from now on to advance on the way forward, or will we walk backwards like the crab?" (1.1:Papfalvi 1846).

16 1.9:Bărnuţiu 1990, p. 33. A similar formula, of much more modest eloquence, is present in a manuscript poem of the revolution period, probably an unintentional paraphrase of Mureşanu's *Echo*: "Rise, Romanian, come rise / For now your time has come" (1.1: *Poem Iancu* cca 1848).

17 Bărnuţiu's *Discourse* in Blaj, in 1.9:Documents 1848 Transylvania 1977–1988, IV. p. 1.

18 For a critique of this obsession with origins in Romanian culture, see 3:Magris 1986, chp. IX: "The origin, unreachable and always uncertain, is of little consequence, and Iorga himself cannot unravel the pristine stratum of his civilisation. As Curtius said, 'no origin of any people is known to history', for such origin does not exist in itself, but, by simply asking the question and starting investigations, historiography actually creates and documents it. Any genealogy goes as far back as the Big Bang; discussion around the Romanians' Latin origin or around the Dacian–Getic–Latin–Romanian continuity, so paramount in Romanian historiography and national ideology, is of no more consequence than the debate between Furtwangen and Donaueschingen on the sources of the Danube."

19 1.4:Bojincă 1828, p. 11; 1.9:Bojincă 1978, p. 10.

20 *Idem*, "The famous deeds and end of Mihai Viteazul (...)", in 1.2:*The Library*, III–IV, 1830, 1834; 1.9:Bojincă 1978, p. 82.

21 For the general historiographical atmosphere of those epochs, see 3:Teodor 1970; 3:Boia 1976; 3:Zub 1983.

22 See 1.5:Aaron F. 1835–1838; 1.9:Bălcescu 1986.

23 See 1.9:Şincai 1967.

24 For the "invention of tradition" and its problematic, see 3:Hobsbawm, Ranger 1983; 3:Karnoouh 1990.

25 1.4:Iercovici 1794, "To the reader"; 1.9:Fugariu 1983, I, p. 188.

26 Although, with him, this general human lesson itself seems especially destined for the Romanians, it "fits" in a particular way with their fate.

27 *Ibidem* (see previous notes).

28 *Ibidem.*

29 Samuil Micu, in 1.3:*Calendar Buda I*, 1806; 1.9:Fugariu 1983, I, p. 223.

30 *Ibidem*, pp. 223–224.

31 *Ibidem*, p. 224.

32 August Treboniu Laurian to Gheorghe Magheru, a letter of November 1847, published in 1.9:Bodea 1967, p. 312.

33 This close relationship between history and its quasi-military function has lately received renewed interest, leading to the powerful trend of "military historiography" supported by the

army's departments for research. Somehow, the militaries are persuaded they can defend their country (which remains their practically exclusive duty) by writing history...

34 Mihail Kogălniceanu, "Introductory lecture to the course of national history at the Academia Mihăileană", in 1.2:*Journal for the Mind*, VII, 1844, no. 11–13; 1.9:Bodea 1982, I, p. 215.

35 George Bariț, "History", in 1.2:*Journal for the Mind*, VIII, 1845, no. 49, pp. 389–391; 1.9:Bariț 1962, p. 88.

36 *Ibidem.*

37 A critical overview of "historicism" as general method of knowledge in 3:Popper 1979. Also see 3:Popper 1957.

38 3:*Ideology of generation* 1968, pp. 31–49; 3:Bocșan 1984; 3:Hitchins 1983, pp. 74–95, "Rumanian Intellectuals in Transylvania: The West and National Consciousness, 1830–1848"; 3:Bocșan 1992a.

39 1.5:Papiu Ilarian 1852(II), pp. CXVIII sqq.

40 Andrei Mureșanu, "A Word for education and the schools", in 1.2:*Journal for the Mind*, VII, 1844, no.50, pp. 391–393; 1.9:Mureșanu A. 1977, p. 67.

41 Ion Budai-Deleanu, *Romanian–German Lexicon* (1818), in 1.9:Fugariu 1983, II, p. 382.

42 See 3:Gheție 1966; 1.9:Budai-Deleanu 1970a, p. 11. However, the philologist from Lemberg could not entirely avoid the influence of the key ideas advanced by the Romanians' nascent national mythology, in the shaping of which he himself had a say by means of his notable contributions. Therefore, inconsistency is apparent in his work as well when, on other occasions, he exalts history's ability to redeem the Romanians of the troubles of the present.

43 George Bariț, "What is the will of the Transylvanian Romanians?", in 1.2:*Journal for the Mind*, XI, 1848, no. 14–16; 1.9:Bariț 1962, p. 115.

44 The representatives of the merchants from Brașov to Bishop Andrei Șaguna, a letter of 20 July 1848, published in 1.9:Dragomir 1944–1946, II, p. 170.

45 George Bariț, "Transylvania. Brașov (S. Wochenblatt)", in 1.2:*The Gazette*, X, 1847, no. 100, p. 397; 1.9:Bariț 1962, p. 100.

46 This would also be Eminescu's complaint: "At least leave the ancestors to rest in dusted chronicles", although he himself will not hesitate to call them up, in undoubtedly excellent verse, as an aid in the campaign aiming at the overturning of the liberal government, which, as a matter of fact, had just obtained the country's independence...

47 The idea is illustrated, for instance, in 1813, by Ioan Theodorovici Nica, in his poem *Song about the beginning and present condition of the Romanians*: "Hardly any other people / Of our Europe wide and large / Can of a great shining past / Speak with pride like us, Romanians." (See 1.8:Gherman 1977, pp. 59–61).

48 See the poems *A sigh* (1845) and *To my muse* (1847), in 1.8:Mureșanu A. 1988, pp. 29–32.

49 1.4:Maior P. 1812, "Foreword"; 1.9:Maior P. 1970, pp. 91–92.

50 The ambiguity of the ethnonym, used in almost all texts of the time, is also significant. *Romani*, when spelled with Latin letters, can be pronounced either *români* (Romanians) or *romani* (Romans), which is itself a validation of the deliberate confusion between the Romanians' ancestors and the Romanians themselves. *The Antiquities of the Romans* can therefore be read either as "The Antiquities of the Romans" or "of the Romanians".

51 1.5:Bojincă 1832–1833, I, pp. XII–XIII; 1.9:Fugariu 1983, II, p. 733.

52 1.4:Bota 1829, "Foreword"; 1.9:Fugariu 1983, II, p. 694.

53 See 3:Lascu N. 1974; 1.9:Marica 1969; 1.9:Răduică G., Răduică N. 1981. Also, texts which explain the Romanians' Latin origins and their Roman heritage can be encountered in the most popular specialised publications of the time: "The Old Romans' Customs of Raising their Children" and "Histories and Teachings of the Profane Writers, in particular of the old Romans, our illustrious ancestors", in 1.3:*Calendar Buda I*, 1811; "On some old customs of the Romanians, which were also performed by our renowned Roman ancestors...", in 1.3:*Calendar Sibiu I*, 1845, pp. 34–37; "On the old holidays of the Romans in use among today's Romanians", *ibidem*, 1847, pp. 36–38; "Traces of Roman Antiquities", in 1.3:*Calendar Brașov* (Bariț), 1853, pp. 27–43.

54 1.5:Bojincă 1832–1833, I, p. 87; 1.9:Fugariu 1983, II, p. 737. Note the subsequent debate in Romanian historiography around the existence of an awareness of Romanness at the level of traditional mentality, a debate with strong ideological undertones, responding, as can be seen, to the

exigencies of the self-image as well (3:Papacostea Ş. 1988; 3:Armbruster 1977, pp. 257–259; also in the latter, pp. 257–258 on the polemics involving Şerban Papacostea, Adolf Armbruster and Constantin Daicoviciu).

55 Romanian culture has perpetuated the cliché, visible today as well, in, for instance, the efforts made by some official institutions to promote in Romania and abroad a less "modest" image of the Romanians' spirituality, although the two centuries that separate the Transylvanian School from the present day have not seen a moment's rest in proclaiming, *urbi et orbi*, in a national effort, the Romanians' Latin origins and the extraordinary merits stemming from them.

56 1.2:*The Library*, I, 1821, pp. 82–83; 1.9:Fugariu 1983, II, p. 561.

57 Simion Bărnuţiu, "A shameful deal and an unfair rule", in 1.2:*Journal for the Mind*, XVI, 1853, no. 38–39; 1.9:Bogdan-Duică 1924, p. 203.

58 Timotei Cipariu, "The Union", in 1.2:*The Mouthpiece*, II, 1848, no. 67, p. 381.

59 1.9:Papiu Ilarian 1943, p. 63.

60 Bishop Vasile Erdélyi's circular letter of 13 December 1848, published in 1.9:Dragomir 1944–1946, II, p. 44.

61 "On the Old Romans", in 1.2:*The Teacher*, I, 1848, no. 2, p. 5.

62 See 1.2:*The Friend*, I, 1848, no. 1.

63 George Bariţ, "On the Romanian Disease", in 1.2:*Journal for the Mind*, VII, 1844, no. 48, p. 378.

64 Pavel Vasici, "Sir editor! (Literary Correspondence)", in 1.2:*Journal for the Mind*, II, 1839, no. 9–11. The article in question is "Entreaty to the Romanian Men of Letters" by Meletie Drăghici, in *ibidem*, no. 5, pp. 34–38.

65 Mihail Kogălniceanu, "Introductory lecture to the course of national history at the Academia Mihăileană", in 1.2:*Journal for the Mind*, VII, 1844, no. 11–13; 1.9:Bodea 1982, I, p. 219.

66 1.9:Cipariu 1972, pp. 33–34. This is exactly the image later circulated as an instance of Hermann von Keyserling's famous "national characters", which maintained that the Romanians were not truly "Latin" "in spirit" (despite the language), since their behaviour situated them in an altogether different pattern of civilisation: the Balkan, Oriental space (2:Keyserling 1929). See a pertinent critique (free from the nationalist-specificist conception of the nineteenth century or of such authors as Keyserling) of the way in which Romanian culture assumes and evaluates in the superlative its "Latinity", as if it were a merit in itself, in Claude Karnoouh. The French sociologist writes that, among the Eastern European countries willing to evidence their Western character, "the most amazing case is that of Romania, where the most exaggerated propaganda was enhanced as to the Latin origin of the language, as if the logical consequence of a common grammatical structure were the similarity between peoples who otherwise share little or nothing at all in point of cultural, religious or political experience" (3:Karnoouh 1990, chp. II). Also noticeable in such stance taking is a certain annoyance on the part of Western observers at the tedious reiteration of the Romanians' "Latinity". "Fine, you are Latin in your language and descent; so what?" In an inter-war Romanian variant, this attitude generated as exaggerated and irrelevant a tendency as the previous overemphasis on Latin origins: the Romanians' self-identification with a specific "Eastern spirit" (see 3:Petrescu 1991; 3:Antohi 1994, pp. 216–218, 268–271).

67 Andrei Mureşanu, *To my muse* (1847), in 1.8:Mureşanu A. 1963, p. 36.

68 *Idem, An Echo* (1848), in *ibidem*, p. 38.

69 1.4:Maior P. 1812, p. 112; 1.9:Maior P. 1970, p. 176.

70 1.5:Aaron F. 1835–1838; 1.5:Aaron F. 1839. See 3:Teodor 1968.

71 Damaschin Bojincă, "A Description of the Birth and Heroic Deeds of the Marvellous Hero Ioan Corvin de Huniad, Whose Name Has Travelled through the Whole of Europe", in 1.3:*Calendar Buda IV* (Neagoe), III, 1830, pp. 45–95.

72 *Ibidem*, pp. 47, 87–89; 1.9:Bojincă 1978, pp. 50, 57.

73 *Idem*, "The famous deeds and end of Mihai Viteazul, prince of the Romanian Country", in 1.2:*The Library*, IV, 1830, p. 30; 1.9:Bojincă 1978, p. 81.

74 See 1.4:Thewrewk 1825; József Kemény, in 1.2:*Társalkodó*, 1830, no. 17, pp. 133–135.

75 Jósika's article in 1.2:*Hírlap* 1848, no. 108; the reply of the eight Romanian deputies in 1.2:*Nemzet*, 1848, no. 66, pp. 1–2, reproduced in 1.2:*Journal for the Mind*, XI, 1848, no. 32, pp. 249–251, and partially in 1.2:*The Teacher*, I, 1848, no. 15, pp. 57–59.

76 "A National Reply given to Baron Nic. Jojica", in 1.2:*Journal for the Mind*, loc. cit.; 1.9:Murgu 1969, pp. 454–455.

77 George Bariţ, "The Romanians and Hungarianism", in 1.2:*Journal for the Mind*, V, 1842, no. 9–11, pp. 65–69, 73–77, 81–86.

78 *Ibidem*, p. 82.

V. The Positive Self-image:
Basics of National Identity

MORAL AND BEHAVIOURAL "QUALITIES": AN ETHNIC-PSYCHOLOGICAL PROFILE

I will try now to give a picture of a fairly narrow section of the ethnic-psychological profile that Transylvanian self-perceptions at the beginning of the modern age attributed to the Romanian nation. I will deal with a rather diffuse group of generally positive features, which, due to too little theoretical support, were not really able to coalesce into an autonomous, consistent theme. They are, to some extent, the counterpart of the moral "flaws" specific to the nation, which I have analysed in a previous chapter. Just as with those "flaws", there is no deep-running explanation or spirit of discrimination behind the process of ascribing to the Romanians "qualities" such as hospitality, mildness, good manners, serious-ness, or intelligence. Obviously, these are general attributes of the human being, present to an undoubtedly similar extent in the members of any human com-munity, at any point in time and space. Their canonisation within the self-image as defining features of the unique Romanian character, just like superficiality, inconsistency and dissent on the other hand, is simply the outcome of a rudimen-tary process of stereotype-formation, an attempt at describing reality by means of clichés and categories proper to the most elementary cognitive structures and mo-dalities of perception.

The portion of the ethnic-psychological profile to be sketched here does not include those much more consistent and frequent representations of the self-image which were stabilised into autonomous themes by a theoretical effort of systematisation and distinction, to be found elsewhere in the writings of the time. This is the case, among the qualities, of courage and devotion to national values; among the defects, of disunion and lack of solidarity; or, particularly, of attributes ranged in antithetical couplets: diligence/indolence, tolerance/xenophobia, mild nature/violent temperament, faithfulness, obedience and political moderation/a rebellious, trouble-raising spirit. Certainly, some of the traits approached here are closely connected with these more elaborate themes, from which they can only be severed for the sake of a clear analysis. Elements such as mildness, good hearted-ness, modesty, patience, resignation, gravity, or even hospitality, are especially concurrent with those partial clichés that make up the image of a tolerant, peace-ful people, subdued and faithful to the authorities.

It is also to be noted that these diffuse genetic "qualities" are primarily attributed to the Romanian peasant, as privileged depository of the Romanian specificity.[1] Romantic and Herderian thinking is thus taken as the basis for the image of an idealised rural universe, the hearth of Romanianness, at variance with the tenets of enlightened social criticism, according to which the misery, poverty and illiteracy of the village could only shape a totally inadequate moral and behavioural code and by no means the psychological profile of the nation.

The qualities in question are generally invoked as praiseworthy elements of a positive self-image. They thus oppose the self-denigrating incriminations from the negative "half" of the self-image, with which they are often in a more or less explicit polemics. A representation is thus built which is *on the whole*, and essentially, a eulogy. This is why the qualities are often indiscriminately subsumed to a general formula meant to emphasise the "special" virtues of the Romanian character.

Budai-Deleanu shows that the Romanian nation managed to overcome the trials of an inimical fate "solely due to her special virtues"[2], and Avram Iancu speaks of a people "which has been virtuous for centuries"[3]. Papiu Ilarian shows that, inscribed on the forehead of this people, one can read not only "all hardships of the past", but also "all those virtues that will redeem the present and the future"[4], since the Romanians are "endowed with splendid faculties, with sublime virtues"[5]. Bishop Şaguna commends to the emperor the "healthy nature of the Romanian peasants from Transylvania"[6]. Cipariu even offers an explanation of this absolutely positive way of being: thanks to their descent, the Romanians have the opportunity to imitate the "examples of the most excellent virtues, be they domestic or public, political or military".[7]

Two things are to be noted here. Firstly, the features which are said to be specific to the Romanians lose all neutrality or universal applicability and become perfect, particular qualities: they are no longer mere "characteristics" and "traits", but become "special qualities" or, most often, "virtues". Secondly, they are tightly linked to the past, the intimation being that they have belonged to the Romanians forever, so that the Romanians' present behaviour is simply the natural outcome of a venerable tradition that perpetuates the unchanging essence of an inherently positive national character.

More exact descriptions, able to outline such a positive picture of the psychological profile of the nation, are, however, rarer than enlightened critical analyses of the social realities and of their impact on the psychology, morals and behaviour of the Romanian people.

In 1805, in *Kurzgefasste Bemerkungen über Bukowina*, Budai-Deleanu draws such a psychological portrait of the Romanians, almost exclusively centred on positive features although sometimes more sensitive to nuances. His representation makes lavish use of a mechanism typical of the self-image, namely the "instrumentalisation of the qualities", which are attributed and invoked in order to legitimate various political, ideological or cultural options. The national "specificity" thus constructed can function as an argument in favour of a certain political idea or practical course of action, such as the promotion of Romanian clerks to the administration, or the rejection of governmental authoritarianism and arbitrariness. According to the magistrate from Lemberg:

The Moldavians are shrewder and wittier than the Russians. They, and all Romanians in general, are mainly characterised by a strong love of liberty and freedom, by a powerful attachment to their country, land, family and customs, which is why they very rarely emigrate. They cannot bear to be ordered about, especially by those of their own people; such authority must be aided by a fair amount of popularity. On the contrary, they will lend their ears to gentle and well-meaning talk. In general, they are more easily governable by wise guidance than by constraint. Once they have consented to a rule, they will remain faithful to it; and should the Romanian err and be punished for his transgressions, he will be content and say to himself, "'Tis law that struck me." On the contrary, should the punishment be groundless and arbitrarily inflicted by some master or civil servant, he will make a note of it, and will not fail, when he has the chance, to take revenge, on which he is no less keen than the Italians.

Budai-Deleanu also notes that the Romanians are to be praised for their hospitality.[8]

Several familiar stereotypes of the self-image are present here: the Romanian is intelligent (more intelligent than others) and fond of traditions and "liberty". This latter feature is also related to one of the basic issues of self-perception, namely the Romanian's attitude towards the authorities: violent and rebellious, as some would have it; peaceful and subdued in the opinion of others. As can be seen, Budai-Deleanu chooses the safe, middle way here.

Another significant description of the Romanian's (read the Romanian peasant's) psychological "specificity" belongs to Frenchman Hyppolite Desprez—a picture with which Papiu Ilarian agrees completely and which he translates in his *History*, since it fitted perfectly with the self-perception developed by the Romantic generation. Desprez sketches in firm brushstrokes the greatly influential image of a people that has preserved its original qualities despite an unfavourable fate. Its predisposition to irony, joined with grave melancholy, sobriety, authenticity and majestic simplicity, are those original psychological features that have allowed it to survive. This is a mental representation that was to make sustained and often successful efforts to explain the "miracle of the Romanians' endurance" in spite of all sorts of calamities, such as the migratory peoples, Phanariot domination or the Ceauşescu regime, thanks to a number of "abysmal" psychological elements such as its "humour", the boycott of History[9], or withdrawal into a grave inner space. Certainly, the image is ambiguous and risky, since it can easily slip into contrary themes, such as resignation, fatalism, inactivity or cowardice.

Despite this implicit ambiguity, in both Desprez and Papiu the perception develops along strictly positive co-ordinates and builds solely on praiseworthy attributes, which the French journalist warmly recommends, in the subtext, to his fellow countrymen on the banks of the Seine.

Instead of being crushed in despair because of animadvert oppression, they sharpened their ironic wit, which serves them to master all suffering. Their vivid and wise imagination leaves behind all present evils and travels to older times, where it chooses, to its own delight, to converse with most beautiful things. The Romanian peasant is thus the living proof of the precious alliance of enthusiasm with irony, and he has preserved this amiable and simple gravity intact, which used to be the mark of the ancient peoples and is today to be found only in the savages.[10]

Irony (rather than violent revenge, as Budai-Deleanu had maintained) as a means of compensating for suffering, an imaginative and "lyrical" disposition, an authenticity unmarred by modern civilisation and their transmission along a line of descent going back to an idealised antiquity, are several basic elements of the national self-image in its positive hypostasis.

Given the scarcity of well-developed descriptions of the Romanians' ethnic-psychological profile, we will have to search through a number of less prolific clichés, diffusely spread throughout the space of the social imaginary yet permanently recurrent in the political and cultural discourse of the time.

The Romanians' good heart is frequently invoked, captured in the expressive notion of "kindness", which was to know a long career in the social imaginary and philosophical speculation on the Romanians' moral traits. It seems, however, that this kindness often surfaces in somewhat paradoxical ways, since it is manifested towards those who least deserve such treatment. Ultimately, it would be preferable—such is the frequent suggestion—for the Romanians to give up such a kind attitude, which has not always done them good.

Damaschin Bojincă, for instance, writes that "the Romanians kindle so much kindness in their hearts" that they often choose to remain silent in the face of foreign calumny[11], which is not the best way to behave. "My people", he writes, "never does anyone any wrong"[12], while those whom it treats so kindly never fail to abuse it. The Romanians' kindness and mildness, for which they only receive unfair asperity in return, stir Papiu Ilarian's compassion: "For God's sake, have mercy on these good, obedient, mild and very poor people!"[13] The Romanians' mildness, as it is invoked here, goes hand in hand with their peacefulness ("the curse of bellicosity", writes Papiu, "has not befallen the Romanian"[14]), with a patient, malleable and obedient nature which the 1804 *Supplex* likens, in tune with certain popular perceptions, to the nature of an ox: foreigners have so many nasty things to say about the Romanians "because the Romanians are God's oxen, ready to follow whoever might call them".[15]

The Romanians' goodness is manifest in their forgiving nature (an article in the *Wiener Zeitung* in May 1848 stated that the Romanians "wanted to make the world see that they know not only how to endure, but how to forgive too"[16]) as well as in their gratefulness: the Romanians feel obliged to the House of Habsburg, Avram Iancu writes in June 1849, because "we are by nature inclined to gracious thankfulness".[17] The significant detail here is that such justificatory underlining of the Romanians' kindness was particularly vivid at the time of the revolution, when the generalised violence could have entitled some to different perceptions of the behaviour of the Romanians or of the other Transylvanian ethnic groups.[18]

The "instrumentalisation of the qualities" is also well illustrated by Damaschin Bojincă, who invokes the Romanians' generosity and merciful nature, as basic elements of their "kindness", in order to counteract Sava Tököly's contrary allegations. The Serbian author had stated that the Romanian language was spreading, especially in the villages, because the déclassé and "villains" of other nations preferred to take shelter with the Romanians, with whom they shared the same state of decay. Bojincă attributes the phenomenon to the Romanians' generosity, for which he gives psychological and religious reasons: "The poor of other nations seek the vicinity of the Romanians not because they are themselves in distress, but because the Romanian people, out of mercifulness, out of a natural tendency to help their neighbours and out of the urgings of their saintly religion, are ever ready to give alms and share all they have with the ruined and the destitute."[19]

The Romanians' kindness is also visible among themselves in the form of collective ethnic solidarity, especially at moments of crisis when such mutual support and mustering of common efforts are called for. The great fire that consumed Bucharest in 1847 was a perfect occasion for those who were otherwise extremely critical of the national specificity to eulogise the Romanians' charitable zeal and thus to deny their former judgements. Cipariu's *Mouthpiece of Enlightenment* stated that "the aid offered to the unfortunate in the Romanian Country is indeed a sign of such generosity and enthusiasm as have never been matched in the annals of humankind". It was also claimed that the Romanians had now given proof that "such nobility has found residence in their heart as can be seen in any people of the whole Europe".[20] Ioan Maiorescu shares similar views, which he expresses in an account sent to Bariț for publication: "Among the wounds afflicting us we can still taste the contentment of seeing how the character of the Romanian nation is being displayed in all its glory."[21] Seen in the context of his usual opinion of the realities of Bucharest, the fiery formulation of the Transylvanian scholar might be taken as a piece of irony, when in fact he means it in total earnest.

Along the co-ordinates of the self-image, calamity represents a propitious moment *par excellence* when the Romanians' essentially good heart manifests itself, even if it may have been concealed up until then by unfavourable circumstances.[22]

Closely connected with their goodness, Romanian "hospitality" was another quality that their self-perception (and other peoples' too, for that matter) obstinately attributed to itself as an essential constitutive feature. Among the Transylvanian intellectuals at the beginning of the modern age, too, it was taken as an undeniable factor, an indisputable given. Naturally, hospitality was primarily seen at work in the Romanians' relationships with foreigners and was taken as a sign of openness and respect towards them. Furthermore, foreigners themselves were the first to admit that this was the case, or so the story went, which was somewhat unusual, since foreigners, as was well known (as the self-image claimed), were usually either turned against the Romanians or ill-informed in their judgements.

Budai-Deleanu writes that "not even their fiercest enemies have denied the Romanians their hospitality. Even Captain Sulzer, who otherwise presents them in the worst of lights, has many good things to say about them, and from his own personal experience too."[23] The same idea appears in Eftimie Murgu: "The hospitality and magnanimity of the Romanians are acknowledged not only by their fellow countrymen, but by objective foreigners too."[24] Toma Costin reproaches Martin Schwartner precisely with remaining silent on the Romanians' hospitality[25], and Nicolae Horga Popovici writes that the Romanians are "happy to receive guests" and that they are "so friendly that few other nations can pride themselves on such fondness".[26]

Undoubtedly, foreigners did note the Romanians' hospitality in their texts, even though the Transylvanians were noticeably inclined to appreciate foreign testimonies only when favourable, and violently to reject them when adverse. Still, despite such over-invoked "proofs", the theme of the Romanians' hospitality, more than any other "quality" attributed to them (themselves mere general human traits), represents a perfect case for a better understanding of the mechanisms whereby a moral attribute or an element of civilisation, free of any ethnic or social conditioning, could be turned into a defining trait of the Romanians.

Nevertheless, hospitality, be it regarded from a Romanian or from a foreign perspective, is itself open to ambiguous connotations. It can easily be related to the image of "savages" who bring gifts to the civilised European traveller. As such, it is obviously connected to the backwardness and manner of behaviour of primitive populations, which, no matter whether they are taken to be inferior or not in point of cultural originality, are nevertheless something other than the model of modern civilisation to which the Romanians aspired.

On the other hand, cultural anthropology has long demonstrated that the *gift*—an essential social practice and institution among archaic populations—is by no means as devoid of ulterior motives as the uninformed and bewildered foreigners might think when faced with the signs of hospitality displayed by the "good savages". It has been shown that some compensation or other is always expected in return for a present. In fact, the gift is the equivalent of (and in fact the first step towards) relationships of exchange in more "evolved" societies: the disinterested offering of gifts is simply an appearance, since it always presupposes reciprocity, to the end of socially redistributing the means of subsistence.[27] From this point of view, the impressive amount of value placed on hospitality and generosity outside the sphere of folk culture, even at the level of the modern social imaginary, can be taken as the result of a survival to this day of the archaic mentalities associated with the institution of the *potlatch*.

Nevertheless, there is still another explanation for the surprising emphasis laid on such elements by both the Transylvanian intellectuals and foreign travellers, animated as they were by modern conceptions. We are dealing with a fundamental error of perspective, attributable to the Herderian cult of folk values.

In a modern understanding, and on the face of it, peasant mentality looks open and hospitable, particularly as manifest in the exterior forms displayed before foreigners taken as isolated individuals. In reality, however, the traditional community is particularly reluctant to establish contacts with outsiders, who are always perceived, given historical experience, as a potential threat. The lack of information on the foreign persons or communities with which the peasants have to deal at some point or another spontaneously generates mistrust, due to the fear of the unknown that the foreigner represents. On the other hand, the members of a peasant community are known to hold remarkably tightly together, in a collective reflex of defence.

The Romantics, who built their theories on Romanian rural virtues, whether foreigners or Romanians educated in the atmosphere of modern culture, looked at the traditional community from the outside and were consequently animated by totally different sensibilities and values. For the modern mentality, one grown on individualist bases *par excellence*, the collectivist values and the strong inter-human solidarity observed in the rural world wrongly appeared as "hospitality", as the expression of an opening to humanity as a whole, while they were actually turned almost exclusively on the community itself, which always feels threatened by the other in a hostile world.

Just like "hospitality", other clichés relating to the Romanians' "kindness" contributed to the shaping of a positive ethnic and psychological profile: modesty, good breeding, seriousness, "measure", genuineness.

The Romanians' modesty, another slippery term in the eulogising self-image, is unproblematic for Vasile Maniu ("the Romanians are good and modest"[28]). So it is for Codru Drăgușanu as well, who contrasts it with the well-known motif of the Hungarians' swagger—a typical case of building self-perception by antithesis with the negative image of the other: "The Hungarians of the steppe, who will wear their spurs even when bare-footed, are so full of rattle that they make a loathsome sight to look at, which the Romanians cannot be, no matter how poor."[29]

In an inconsistent way, yet typical for Drăgușanu's free spirit which will not abide by one single stereotype, the next move of his text is to incriminate the Romanians' boastfulness, again as compared with the Hungarians, only this time by way of similitude, not of contrast: "Hungary is also similar to Romania inasmuch as, even though a wealthy country, her inhabitants praise her to excess; as the saying goes, 'There's no axe like every Gypsy's axe.' The Romanians say that he who has a sip of the water of Dîmbovița will never leave the land; and the Hungarians say that there is no living outside Hungary; at any rate, not as good."[30] Codru Drăgușanu even attempts a sociological explanation of this feature, other than the determinist theories of the ethnic and psychological specificity: "That is so because these countries have been the gutter where all the nations of the world poured out their scum, which became the foam of our peoples and sucked their grease, as in the saying, 'Good country, bad deal.'"[31]

Drăgușanu's relativist imagologic perspective is also at work in his detached analysis of the "small" nations' tendency to praise themselves and exaggerate their own merits when confronted with the difficulties and crises of the process of modernisation and development. Such self-perspectives become even more risible when compared to a reality where these sort of problems have already been overcome, as is the case with the civilised north of Italy: "Look, brothers, and see that while the Romanians sing 'Dîmbovița, water sweet', and the Hungarians cry, 'Extra Hungariam non est vita', the Italians hold their tongues. The former feel the need to praise their countries, for every little thing declares the contrary, while here, Italy speaks for herself."[32]

At any rate, the theme of modesty remained a touchstone of the image of the ethnic-psychological profile of the nation, since its mere mention could turn into an argument capable of refuting it.

Good breeding, together with seriousness and a sense of measure, are themselves taken as defining traits of the Romanians, that is, primarily of the peasants, in keeping with the Romantic representation of a mild, peaceful and good-natured people. The sense of measure, the capacity to tell right from wrong, the golden, middle way are qualities allegedly forged by the hardships endured by the

Romanians throughout history, while other (particularly Western) peoples, dearer to the Fates, are less endowed with such qualities. From this point of view the elements in question are not only a sign of specificity, but also of the Romanians' superiority and, at the same time, one of the most enduring clichés of their spiritual and moral-philosophical self-definition.

Just like most of the features of the ethnic-psychological profile, the motifs of the Romanian's good-breeding and sense of measure appear among the Transylvanian intellectuals at the beginning of the modern age as pithy clichés or indisputable commonplaces, which seem to need neither supplementary explanations nor the elaboration of speculative theory to be met with later in Romanian culture.

The "survey" of certain, particularly ethnographic, realities is often the occasion for giving expression to the stereotype. Moise Nicoară, for instance, observes the Romanians along the Tîrnave rivers and remarks on "their manner of speech, their poised judgement married to a seemly conduct".[33] Codru Drăgușanu attributes that poise to their church rituals, which, in his opinion, display neither Catholic pomp nor Protestant simplicity and thus "choose the middle way between extremities and keep away from affectation".[34]

The Romanians' good breeding is recorded in Stoica de Hațeg as a sort of would-be traditional reluctance in the face of any form of abuse and triviality: "The Romanians of the old times had few swear words, such as those damning one's mother or dead kin, but nothing more. But when we had to deal with the Hungarian soldiers we could here names being called with respect to our law, the soul, the cross and the light."[35] As on numerous other occasions, ingenuity saves the rector-chronicler from the trap of ethnocentrism. The Romanians' imprecations of the "old times", that is, swear words "damning one's mother or dead kin", are looked upon with lenient eyes, while the truly obnoxious abuse seems to ensue from the mention of religious notions, which the Romanians have taken over from unruly foreigners. Certainly, such an interpretation involuntarily relativises the Romanians' indifference to licentious language.[36]

Ion Codru Drăgușanu (among other men of letters of the time) records, on the contrary, attitudes giving evidence of the frequency of that very bad habit.[37] In Transylvania, he writes, due to the judiciary tradition of punishing homicide by penalties differing according to the victim's social condition, "you can hear every fool shouting out whenever it pleases him, [...] 'I'll f...ing kill you and pay for your head at that!'"[38] Cipariu and Bărnuțiu, too, would develop a passion for collecting folk pornography, which can be found in their manuscript notes[39] and which the Romantic folklorists' prudery, as well as the clichés relative to the Romanian peasant's decency, could only overlook.

In contrast to such notes, which might have weakened confidence in the coherence of these themes, Papiu Ilarian canonises the Romanians' measure, good breeding, seriousness and gravity, to which he raises songs of praise at the hour of the revolution. Although, generally speaking, he makes no explicit mention, Papiu underlines these qualities in a markedly polemical fashion, seeking to deny those elements of the self-image or of others' perceptions which represent the Romanians as violent, troublesome, turbulent and rebellious, that is, deprived of a sense of measure, of the maturity and seriousness that could grant them access to the peaceful and balanced exercise of certain political rights. Papiu thus contributes, in a deliberate and programmatic manner, to the tailoring of those clichés. The elaboration is based on two basic operations: the recording of direct "observations" of Romanian behaviour in Blaj (actually, a selective reading of it through the lens of an idealised and mythologised gaze); and a subtextual denial of the validity of already existent stereotypes maintaining the contrary. The emotionally charged drive propelled by the revolution, its quality of a founding myth of national identity, bestowed on the themes under discussion the necessary eloquence and impact.

Papiu Ilarian, taking over his theme from the *Gazette of Transylvania*, wrote of Blaj that "the people who gathered together, during those three days, behaved with such calm and decorum that the Romanian nation will be honoured to have lived such moments for centuries on end."[40] As usual, the existence of such traits can be convincingly explained by invoking similar examples, as well as by the genetic transmission of the virtues of the Romanians' Latin forefathers: the peasants gathered for the assembly were seized by "a truly Roman gravity, as in a meeting where the people held counsel for the saving of the republic".[41]

The traits in question are seen as evidence of the Romanians' clear moral superiority over foreign peoples; while the "civilised people" of Berlin, Vienna, Pest or Cluj manifested their opposition to the reaction by hostile disturbance, by "chasing their ministers away [...], by mewing and howling and breaking windows"[42], the "fifty thousand unlearned Romanians considered all that to be mere folly, unworthy of a mature people and a serious cause" and thus refrained from any violent manifestation.[43] In short, seriousness, good manners and gravity are traits specific to the Romanians, which they had inherited on racial lines. "This admirable conduct of the Romanian people is an irrefutable proof that the oppression and tyranny they have suffered for centuries have not been able to wipe away the grave and serious character they inherited from their ancestors; that the Romanian, as his nature advised, has learned maturity in the school of ordeals."[44] Even the foreigners, as was the case with the Saxons for instance, "understood that the Romanian nation was not what they had said she was in their calumnies, but that she was an oppressed and yet dignified nation, a mature people".[45]

The seriousness thus attributed to the Romanians was also correlated with their "endurance", with the strength they exhibited in maintaining their specificity unaltered despite the meandering course of history, as an article published in 1853 in *The Romanian Telegraph* claimed: "Numberless years and centuries have passed over the Romanian people, numberless revolutions and political trials have shattered their existence; and yet they have remained what they were from the very beginning and what they can be seen to be today."[46]

Another trait of the Romanians' ethnic-psychological profile, in the variant imagined by the Transylvanian Romanians at the beginning of the modern age, was patience—another piece of the portrait of a peaceful and good-hearted people. This was particularly manifest in the Romanians' patient endurance of historical oppression. The absence of any violent response to such hardships, which their self-perception generally attributed to the Romanians, was taken as a prime moral and political virtue in harmony with the ideological heritage of Central

European enlightened legalism. As Bishop Şaguna put it in December 1848, it was precisely in trying to hold in check the excesses they were found guilty of by General Puchner that the Romanians had endured "the oppression and humiliation of our nation and of our religion, which we have borne for several centuries, in unrivalled patience".[47] *The Mouthpiece of Enlightenment* also spoke of this "quiet and long-suffering people"[48], and Şaguna showed again, in another speech, that the Romanian frontier regiments had always manifested "courage, faith and patience".[49]

Obviously, just like the other ethnic-psychological characteristics mentioned so far, the theme of patience is itself instrumentalised and functions as an argument in support of certain actions and tendencies or as a reply to unfavourable images constructed by foreigners. That the Romanians have patiently suffered all manner of wrongs for centuries on end is the perfect excuse for their present violence, which appears as the natural outcome of so prolonged a repression. In addition, since patience is one of their defining traits, accusations against their lack of restraint are obviously groundless. If they rose in 1848, it was only because of the unbearable treatment they had had to suffer, for otherwise it is well known that they are a patient people. "The Romanians who, starting this spring and until now, have so patiently suffered so much slander and pain", writes Papiu Ilarian, have finally taken action, at the call of the National Committee, as late as October 1848.[50]

The patience displayed until October (that is, until after the split between the Hungarian revolution and the "legitimate" authority in Vienna) is a theme with an clearly evident ideological import: the aim was to demonstrate that those who were the first to break the law and take violent action and thus start a "revolution" were the Hungarians, while the Romanians only acted after they had risen and therefore did nothing but fight for the restoration of the law.[51] Bărnuţiu argues along similar lines, at the very outbreak of events: the Romanian nation never meant to rise against the Hungarians "and this year, too, it acted like a pure maiden and with a patience unheard of in history, until it could no longer bear that terrorist faction and finally chose to use its right to defence and revenge".[52] Given the Romanians ethnic-psychological profile, they could only be "put out of countenance" or "lose their temper" because of external, that is, foreign, circumstances, and never as a result of an internal mood.

Depending on the diverse interpretations and interests the Romanians' patience could acquire the most varying connotations. Resignation, apathy and indifference to events was one such facet, which was itself prone to different evaluations. Papiu Ilarian defined the lack of interest and enthusiasm which, in his opinion, the Romanians from Hungary had manifested at the outbreak of the Hungarian revolution, as an absolutely positive "melancholy withdrawal of the people"[53], since it was simply, again in Papiu's opinion, the "instinctive premonition of the danger of Hungarianism".[54] Bariţ, on the other hand, in a 1844 article, disapproves of the Romanians' resignation and recommends the galvanisation of a "people that has too long lingered in apathy and fatal inertia, and has only rarely shown signs of life and feeling".[55] Even Papiu, in referring to the dark Middle Ages, deplores the resignation attributed to the Romanians, whom aristocratic oppression had presumably thrown into such sombre fatalism that all hope had died and whose every initiative, and thus any renewal whatsoever, was doomed to failure. The oppressed peasants "learned to obey all aristocratic tyrannies and to give up hope for a better future, as they were left worrying only about their daily bread. In the long run, all they could feel was that desperate resignation: 'That's the way it is'."[56] Like many other elements of the Romanians' ethnic-psychological profile, the sacramental formula of their ties with tradition also included a powerful negative potential.

Finally, another positive cliché relating to the Romanians' ethnic-psychological specificity, which punctuated the cultural discourse of the time, was the intelligence, or intellectual capacities, of the nation. Here, too, the polemical intention was brought to the fore. Foreigners, and the various sociological elements they exploited as well as the Romanians' own clichés—such as their cultural backwardness, their hostility to schooling, or the small number of intellectuals and of cultured élites—seemed to advance the image of a population deprived of intellectual aptitudes. Obviously, the Romanian scholars' efforts were aimed at showing that these factors were but random circumstances stifling a brewing mass of natural "exceptional" intelligence, which had only to wait for propitious external circumstances to express itself in perfect splendour.

It might be that the Romanians' enemies, who sought to benefit from the precariousness of the Romanians' cultural development, sometimes deliberately maintained this obliteration of the Romanians' intelligence. The Jesuits and the "co-habitant nations", writes Samuil Micu, "feared that the Romanians, who are otherwise extremely gifted", might escape from their grip were they to be allowed to exercise their intellectual capacities[57], all the more so as the Romanians were known to have "exceptional qualities and a sound mind".[58]

The free expression of the Romanians' uncommon spiritual resources was precluded, it was argued, not only by the foreigners' schemes but also by their own lack of trust in their national capacities. This could no longer be, since, as Vasile Pop wrote in 1827, "the Romanian spirit is no less diligent and searching than that of other nations".[59] In the case of the Transylvanian physician, the theme of the Romanians' intelligence was formulated in more moderate terms: intelligence was not seen as a personal asset of the Romanians; they were not more intelligent than others; it was just that the Romanians' level of intellectual possibilities was as high as that of other nations. Their intelligence was backed up in this case with typically enlightened arguments, capitalising upon the universality of human qualities. The Romanians, as a people, are intelligent, not due to some exceptional qualities but because every human being is endowed by his Creator with reason and intellectual capacity. All the Romanians had to do was exercise and explore these absolutely common resources.

Intelligence surfaces in different guises: wit, sharpness, a diplomatic spirit refined to the limits of shrewdness and cunning.[60] "The Romanian is smart", Sigismund Pop wrote in 1848[61], "naturally endowed with a sharp and keen mind".[62] In Wallachia, "the people are clever, and their countless troubles have taught them how to be tactful too", wrote Oprea Moroianu in 1853.[63]

However, it was also true that the Transylvanians were seriously circumspect about the idea of effortless wit, which they attributed, in accordance with a regional stereotype, to the Romanians from the principalities, often equating such superficiality with excess. They preferred the version of a grave, serious and "solid" "intelligence", refined by education and the cultivation of the mind, and detested the "shrewdness" proper to foreigners, to the urban spirit or even to the Wallachians. Papiu Ilarian, for instance, counts "astuteness" among the "moral plagues" which had corrupted the Transylvanian Romanians' spirit as a result of their damaging contact with the Saxons.[64]

Undoubtedly, the psychological, moral and behavioural traits analysed here (kindness, hospitality, modesty, good breeding, patience, seriousness, intelligence) are not the sole clichés defining the Transylvanian Romanians' self-perception of the time, in its positive variant. Nevertheless they outline a basic image of the ethnic-psychological profile, as the representation has come down to us, and can provide us with precious hints as to the mechanisms whereby several poignant contemporaneous collective obsessions have been formed today, as they were at the emergence point of modern nationalism.

The Number and Spreading of the Romanians

Another positive theme of the self-image that acquired a compensatory function with regard to contemporary uncertainties and troubles was that of the great number of Romanians. The picture of them as a strong and important people, be it by virtue of number only, was thus fashioned so as to fortify the strong belief in the destiny of the people and its potential for affirmation.[65]

Along the weft of its genesis and evolution this theme surfaces in two noteworthy manifestations. On the one hand, it springs from the continuation of the tradition of Romanian petitioning, most strongly visible in Inochentie Micu and the 1791 *Supplex*, for whom the multitude of the Romanians extant in Transylvania was of particular argumentative force in advocating political and national rights for this population in the respective province.[66] On the other hand, ever since the age of the Transylvanian School the numbers theme had been associated with awareness of the dimension of the Romanians' ethnic potential on the scale of the entire national space and beyond the frontiers of the historical provinces, too. The image was thus formed, at a particularly early date, of the numerousness of the Romanians, who stretched from the Nistru to the Tisza, let alone those who had crossed these boundaries and those who had become lost within foreign populations.

From the viewpoint of its relationship to the ideological background of the cultural age in which it became manifest, the theme under discussion should present a substantial affinity to the democratic sensibilities of Romanticism, for which the mob, or the "people", represented, by its numerical force, the favourite object of history and of social reality. However, even if nationalist, democratic and liberal Romanticism further enhanced and occasionally granted new meanings to the issue of the Romanians' number and their spread, the enlightened traditional basis that had ensured its initial starting point and its basic configuration is more obvious. Despite the ideological profile of the Enlightenment, which was more élitist and more detached from the many (see the difference between demophilia and democratism), the Transylvanian *Aufklärers* were no less proud then their Romantic successors of the numerousness of the Romanians, from which a series of positive aspects ensued. Evidently, the inconsistency manifested by the Romanian élites of Transylvanian society is able to explain why the enlightened intellectuals, often descendants of noble stock, nevertheless felt bound to stake their cards on the uncultured many, which was a matter of grievance to the enlightened intellectuals but which they were obliged to do for lack of any better option.

Generally, the entire incipient period of the modern age consecrated the absolutely positive connotation that defined the position of the many in the Romanian social imagery. It was not only that the precarious condition of the numerous individuals who formed the basis of society was by no means likely to engender a rejection of the masses; on the contrary, multitude was considered to be an element capable of compensating individual shortcomings and not of aggravating them, by multiplication and arithmetical progression. In the celebrated coinage of Negruzzi, the individuals that form the multitude are "stupid, but plenty",[67] therefore their number compensates for, rather than perpetuates, their personal handicaps. The coinage does not read "plenty, but stupid", as it could have done from a different perspective, for which number might appear futile for lack of quality. For the Transylvanian intellectuals, too, numerousness translated as rightfulness and force, constituting thus a value *per se*—one of the few undeniable things the Romanians had. What else would be left if they had to give up that argument as well?

As indicated in the title of this section, the theme can be divided into two main components: the Romanians' *geographical spreading* throughout the diverse historical provinces, and their *number*, or the *statistical* estimate of the nation's demographic expansion. The two scientific disciplines engaged in the configuration of this theme of the self-image are thus powerfully ideologised, acquiring an essential role in the articulation of the discourse on identity. Alongside history, philology and ethnography,[68] which are the traditional disciplines participating in the fashioning of national identity, geography and statistics are annexed to this effort as well, despite their more scientifically accurate propositions which ought to render them incapable of speculations and subjective approximations of a nationalist nature. It is, however, precisely their being put into the service of national ideas that explains the success experienced by these preoccupations in the epoch, in the attempt to subordinate science and, more generally, culture, to the necessities of political advocacy.

Thus geography and statistics (and, at a later date, demography) became two of the preferred *modi dicendi* of nationalism. The breathless mapping of the expansion and configuration of the national body, to which almost aesthetic forms and traits were attributed ("roundness", "achievement", "harmony", the fullness of a "rounded Romania" and the subsequent "Greater Romania"), and the passion for the idea of natural frontiers, rivers, mountains and seas that traced the spatial contour of national identity,[69] would fire each true nationalist's soul with mystical raptures.[70] In a similar manner, both statistical and demographic estimates, which engaged in passionate disputes with the falsified and tendentious positions advanced by others, added to this essential dimension of the process by which identity-related feelings were defined and assumed.

In the social imaginary of the Transylvanian Romanians at the beginning of the modern era, the issue of the Romanians' number and spread can be traced back, in its already strong formulation, to the writings of the scholars of the Transylvanian School. The two components of the issue were effectively associated and thus mutually fortified. The Romanians extended over all the historical provinces of "Trajan's Dacia", constituting everywhere the majority of the population; special emphasis was generally placed on the fact that they were more numerous in the space of these provinces than other ethnic groups. Additionally, examples of the extension of Romanianhood beyond the basic geographical area were also observed with satisfaction and minuteness. The reiterated recapitulation of the countless spaces inhabited by the Romanians was thus able to shape the spectacular and stimulating image of a numerous people that had made their presence felt in all European territories.

The sources of information used as a basis for this representation were, of course, the geography treatises and travel accounts of those foreign travellers who highlighted the expansion of the Romanian element. The Transylvanians' more personal notes were also useful, as was the case with their observations on the A-Romanians' massive settlement, during the second half of the eighteenth century, in the main cities of Austria, Hungary and Banat. One can remark, however, that all these pieces of information tended to be "aligned" and combined in such a fashion as to fit with the historical theories regarding the Dacian territory colonised by the Romans, which the Romanians continued to inhabit to the present day, within those very initial boundaries. Geography was therefore called upon in order to explain history, to which it became subordinate.

THE "SPREADING" OF THE ROMANIANS: THE NEED TO ENLARGE THE SPHERE OF NATIONAL IDENTITY

The spreading of the Romanians and the enumeration of the countries they inhabited always featured among the first issues tackled in the "manuals" designed to construct their national identity. Samuil Micu, for instance, in *Short Information on the History of the Romanians*, begins with a chapter that he calls *"The lands inhabited by the Romanians"*, in which he writes:

> In ancient Dacia, where the Emperor Trajan settled the Romans [= the Romanians] and which is bordered by the Tisza, the Prut, the Nistru and the Danube, there are more Romanians than any other ethnic groups. In Transylvania and Hungary up to the Tisza river, the Romanians supersede by their multitude all the other peoples that inhabit the land. In Wallachia and Moldavia, the Romanians are almost the unique dwellers of those lands. Besides these territories, there are Romanians who live in Basarabia, in Bugeac and Crimea, which are presently named the Little Tartar Country. Even under Slav rule, in the country called Nova Serbia [...] there are a lot of Romanians, and even south of the Danube, in Bulgaria. Furthermore, there are Romanians living in Macedonia, who also call themselves Valachs. [71]

Gheorghe Șincai also resorts to this image, underlining the idea of the spreading of the Romanians in an almost polemical manner. Evidently, foreigners are ready to deny even the undeniable data of geography when it comes to the Romanians: "The extent of this Dacian and Roman people [...] is more comprehensive than some assume", he writes in *Elementa linguae daco-romanae*. It encompasses "the whole of ancient Dacia", being delimited by "the Black Sea, the Nistru, the Carpathians, the Tisza and the Danube".[72] The natural frontiers theory, supported by ethnic and historical elements (delimiting the Dacia ruled by Trajan), was already completely formulated.[73] The perimeter was subsequently boosted to include areas such as those inhabited by the A-Romanians south of the Danube, then Pocutia, Podolia and Crimea[74]; mention was also made of the Romanian merchants' colonies in diverse European cities.[75] Even in a work such as *Advice on Agriculture,* Șincai renewed the issue of the Romanians' number and spread in order to sow the public consciousness of the age with pride in such impressive attributes, bestowed on the Romanians by divine grace. The Romanians "are so many and so extended by divine grace, that not one country but several contain them, for instance Wallachia and Moldavia, which the Romanians inhabit by nature, or Bucovina, and also countries that the Romanians inhabit alongside other nationalities, such as Transylvania, Banat, Maramureș and other countries under the rule of the crown of Hungary".[76]

Budai-Deleanu, in his turn, speaks of the "nation that inhabits the two principalities, of Wallachia and of Moldavia, and which in the lands of Transylvania, of Banat and of eastern Hungary is more numerous than any other",[77] while Petru Maior concentrates the idea, as he usually does, in a more suggestive image ("the limitless multitude of the Romanians who can be found from the Tisza to the Black Sea"[78]) thus pinpointing the essentials: the "limitless" number and the natural frontiers. The phrase "from the Tisza to the Black Sea" was to become common among the slogans relating to the theme under discussion.

Following in the footsteps of his enlightened forefathers and taking over, occasionally and textually, the formulas they had coined, Moise Nicoară refashions the image of the pan-Dacian territory that would be inhabited by the Romanians. As to its further "extent", he overlooks, nonetheless, the Roman heritage of the territories stretching south of the Danube, probably because of his heated debate with the A-Romanians of Vienna and Hungary—the Macedonians whom he counts in with the anti-Romanian occult conspiracy. Conversely, he often speaks of the Romanians in Russia and north of the Black Sea ("Nova Serbia") who had been brought from Banat and settled there starting in the eighteenth century and whose descendants he was to encounter in Bucharest, in 1810, as high-ranking officials in the army of the Tzar.[79] "The Romanians", Nicoară writes in an 1815 letter, "from the Tisza to the Black Sea, from the Danube to the Nistru, in Crimea on one side and in Crapacu on the other, at the limits of Poland, exiled and dispersed all over, represent a vast community, by their number and by the expansion of the space they inhabit, offering to the eyes of the foreign tourist the occasion to be amazed at the status of a nation so wretched and yet so numerous".[80]

The survey of the spaces inhabited by the Romanians would remain one of the favourite modalities of national education to which the Transylvanian intellectuals resorted. Their belief was that the mere invocation of this theme was likely to inspire their fellow countrymen with faith and courage, and to convince them that power lay in large numbers and that as long as action was taken there was room for hope of success. In the same spirit, *The Teacher of the People* and *The Friend of the People*, popular gazettes edited in 1848 in Blaj and Pest respectively, with the aim of educating the peasant masses by means of political propaganda, published several articles in which readers were informed in accessible language of the spread and number of the Romanian population.[81] Papiu Ilarian renewed in his *History* the motif of the natural ethnic frontiers conceded to the Romanians by divine grace—signs of a preordained mission to be accomplished: the Romanians, he writes, are surrounded by "what of Nature is most pleasant to the eye: the Carpathians and the Sea, confines traced by God's finger for a nation of giants".[82]

However, as we have already seen, outside this pan-Dacian perimeter which the Romanians had always inhabited and in the largest numbers, too, the issue of the spreading of the Romanians took particular note of the co-nationals who had chosen to be exiles among foreign peoples. Faced with the unrest then provoked by the precariousness of the national condition, the collective perception could not afford to disregard any member of the community, who, in fact, might serve to reinforce the fronts threatened by others.

Consequently, in its attempt at symbolical alleviation, the Transylvanian Romanians' self-image tended to swell in the extreme the sphere of the national body, by mixing in each and every element at hand. History-wise, diverse and uncertain ethnic groups were recuperated, such as the Cumanians, Petchenegs and Bissens, who were suddenly painted Romanian by Petru Maior's accomplished brush in a tendency to supplement certain historical deficiencies or gaps.[83] Geography-wise, particular emphasis was laid on the Roman stock extant south of the Danube—Morlacs, Kutso-Vlahs and Macedonians—now discovered with great satisfaction as an element able spectacularly to broaden the presence of the Romanians on the European continental stage.[84]

The generalised necessity for widening the sphere of national identity sprang from a desire on the part of the Romanians to reinforce their strength and from a feeling of insecurity realised in their becoming aware of their solitude among foreign and hostile nations. The discovery and, indeed, invention of nationals and co-nationals in exile played the role of displacing this solitude and this fear, which partly explains the aberrant search for Romanians among the Welsh or the Rheto-Romans of Switzerland[85] or, ultimately, the identification of the Romanians with the Romans. Papiu Ilarian claimed that a sense of security should entail from the Romanians' belonging to the neo-Roman community, as pan-Latinism was, *par excellence*, an ideological construct with the potential to set them free from the lingering feeling of insecurity and solitude: "Around you are yet millions of Romans, on the territories of Italy, our mother, as well as on the territories of France, our sister", who would assuredly second the Romanians on the way to emancipation.[86]

Of course, nor was the field of imaginary annexations free of competitive drives. In the same manner that the Romanians had incorporated others among themselves, the national perceptions of the Saxons or of the Serbs did the same with respect to the Romanians: the Romanians thus ended up with allogeneous origins, for example Slavic or German—a horrific absurdity in the eyes of the representatives of the Transylvanian School who were adepts of national Latin purity. Bojincă would reply to those "scribblers, or rather slaves", who, "having all the interest, work in the fanciful perspective of extending their nation by inclusion of the Romanians",[87] in the same polemical manner which Ioan Maiorescu would use in his confrontation with Schuller.[88]

A feature related to the motif of the spread of the Romanians was the *compact* nature of their population. They were not only the majority, but lived in a territorial continuum covering the areas they inhabited—an especially powerful argument supporting their national claims.

In the case of Eftimie Murgu, this feature stood in relation to the motif of the Romanians' collective solidarity as well as to that of their ethnic purity: "The Romanians have been numerous, and notwithstanding their exposure to sad circumstances their national bonds have been preserved; only a few of them are exiled, and their vast majority live in strict vicinity and do not suffer separation; this is the case in Banat, Transylvania, Wallachia, Moldavia and Macedonia."[89]

George Bariţ approaches the issue in an inherently polemical manner, by way of comparison to the situation of the Hungarians, in order to justify the Romanians' potential for national resistance and therefore prove the inefficiency and futility of any attempt at assimilating them. "Which of the two nations is more compact or more tried by heterogeneous nationalities? [...] Which of the two lives in greater segregation?" is the question posed by the Braşov-based journalist. The answer is that "only a few European countries are inhabited by nations as compact as the Romanians in the Romanian principalities", while in Transylvania, alongside the one million one hundred thousand Romanians, live another nine hundred thousand Hungarians, Saxons and "other national trifles".[90]

The problem that had been raised in a peaceful way by Bariţ, however, would be taken up, only this time under more dramatic circumstances, during the revolution. The compact character of the Romanians was advanced at that time as a decisive argument against the Hungarians at the climax of a life-and-death dispute: "Can you not see that both you and we", writes Prefect Buteanu to Major Csutak in April 1849, "are but two islands amidst millions of Slavs who are striving to engulf us? The Romanian element is much more compact, stretching from the Tisza to the Black Sea, more compact than yours, and cannot perish as a nation."[91]

In his turn, Avram Iancu addresses Lieutenant-Colonel Simonffy in June in similar terms: Why is it that the Hungarians do not want to win the sympathy of the Romanians, "a people that is compact by nature"[92], thereby securing a vital alliance between the two peoples? Again, Papiu Ilarian, in his *History*, focuses on the same attribute of national identity: contrary to the Slavs, who are divided by various particular traits within their own nation, "the Romanians form only a compact of eight million, they speak a unitary language, and in all their states a perfect homogeneity is manifest."[93] Therefore one should not fear the imminence of pan-Slavism.

Thus instrumentalised, the motif of the compact and homogeneous nature of the territorial disposition of the Romanians was used as a protective shield that was deployed depending on the direction from which diverse leaders of opinion believed that danger was looming.

THE NUMBER OF ROMANIANS: "WE ARE MANY", "WE ARE THE MOST NUMEROUS"

Apart from the manner of their spreading, the number of Romanians represents an issue of portentous consistency, both as an element of the self-image and as a political argument in support of national petitioning. In relative, adjectival evaluations, the Romanians are, variously, "many" or "the most numerous".

The first of the two variants suggests, in dithyrambic formulations, the idea of an incredible expansion, of the existence of vast numbers of Romanians, where number is undoubtedly considered a distinctive attribute of absolute particularity to the nation. Even if not always explicit, an exceptional virility appears, at least in the subtext, as a correlative element of the motif of the numerousness of the Romanians and as an ethnic specificity marker as well. Petru Maior mentions "the limitless number of the Romanians"[94] and "the overwhelming nation of the Romanians, spreading all over Transylvania"[95]; Şincai, too, thinks that "the Romanians are spreading east and west, in the largest of numbers, by divine grace";[96] the Buda *Lexicon* remarks on "the tremendous number of the Romanians"[97], while Budai-Deleanu[98] writes that "the Romanians dwelling in Dacia represent an important nation, made up of several millions." Significantly, in the case of the latter, the attribute *important* applied to the nation is equivalent to multitude, which means that number is also automatically quality. A foreigner, Dyonis Thalson, whose writings were also published in Romanian gazettes, coined an epoch-making formulation: In Dacia the Romanians are "myriad, like the stars in the heavens".[99] The simile, which would later be encountered during the revolution (for instance, in the case of Bărnuţiu's *Provocation*[100]) eloquently suggests the attributes of the multitude, of the millions of Romanians that rise and shine everywhere, like the stars of the firmament.

Obviously, if considered in terms of social segments, multitude is more pertinently applied to the peasants, to the "people", "which is most numerous", as Budai-Deleanu[101] writes, but also to "the numerous nobles of Transylvania" (as Papiu Ilarian[102] puts it), both categories enjoying the same superlative image with respect to numerical status.

The second variant of the theme of the number of Romanians, when not estimated in exact figures, emphasises their being a majority. In this case, not only are they "many", but "the most numerous", that is to say, numerically superior to the oppressive and competing Other. Of course, as the case presents itself the report could have had as its basis absolute statistical estimates and not a subjective adjectival description, since the issue of the Romanians' majority is manifest in the case of many foreign observers who were, so to say, detached by virtue of their very stance. This was the case with Emperor Joseph II, who appreciates that the Romanians are, beyond any doubt, "the most ancient and numerous population of Transylvania".[103] The association of majority with the idea of the antiquity and inherent priority of the Romanians represents an ideological correlation of great importance, which would later be encountered in a variety of Romanian intellectuals.

The 1791 *Supplex* promptly records with satisfaction the imperial opinion; the great sovereign, it states, "is fully convinced that the Romanians are much more numerous than the other nationalities of the province".[104] Samuil Micu supports the same idea: "The number of the Romanians of Transylvania is very large, so that it surpasses all the other nationalities considered in a cumulative manner."[105] Shortly after this statement, reported in the present tense, Micu speaks of the situation of the Romanians during the Middle Ages, suggesting a regressive deduction that will play an essential role in the polemics and argumentation of the national movement: the Romanians are at present the most numerous, as the population polls show, and, analogously, it can be concluded that as early as the Middle Ages, in the absence of such polls, the numerical rapport between the Romanians and the others was basically the same.

Of course, the issue of the Romanians' majority continued to have adherents even after the times of the Transylvanian School. It would be encountered, for instance, in the *Geography* edited by Nicola Nicolau ("The Romanians exceed by their number all the others considered en masse"[106]); and even in Papiu's *History*: "...the most numerous and most ancient nation of this country".[107] In the field of political discourse it remained a touchstone of the petitioning movement. It was invoked in all memoranda, from the demand of the people of Arad for a Romanian bishop[108] to the petitions in the wake of the revolution,[109] showing that "in all the lands inhabited by the Romanians, from the easternmost margins of the monarchy to the vicinity of the Tisza borderline, the Romanian nation corresponds to the greatest proportion, so that the lands here delimited are inhabited partly by Romanians and partly by other nationalities, of which the Romanians represent the majority, and only a small territory, where the Szeklers dwell, can be subtracted from this truth."[110]

It should be noted, nonetheless, that the invocation of multitude as generative of political rights was not the reflex of a democratic and individualist-egalitarian conception, as one might be tempted to think, not even at the height of the Romantic period. In the first place, because the number argument was more often than not preceded by the historical motivations of the Romanians' antiquity, priority, and "privileges", which entitled them to a better life. Secondly, because it became manifest particularly in the case of political memoranda and of moderate and legalist documents, number was not an argument of a philosophical or rationalist nature, as was the case with the abstract theories of the natural right laws. That the Romanians were many did not automatically entail political rights. The essential fact was that it was this multitude that paid taxes, volunteered soldiers and played an important role in the functioning of the empire; otherwise, without contributing much to the welfare of the society, whether a majority or not, the Romanians would not be entitled to perennial rights. Aligned to the historical organicist vision, the argumentation based on number was therefore used in a purely pragmatic and functional manner, in an attempt to tone down the Transylvanian liberalism of German orientation which emphasised the collective rather than the individual.

Besides such arguments with direct political import, the theme of the number of Romanians was used in "historical", in fact ideological, disputes or polemics meant to serve political and national ends. The problem of the continuity of the Romanians north of the Danube was, to this purpose, one of the most significant motifs.

As we have already seen in the case of Samuil Micu, the contemporary numbers of Romanians were taken as additional proof of the idea that they had been
just as numerous in the past, at the time of the Hungarian invasion, for instance.
It was, furthermore, a traditional argumentation in Romanian historiography, for
which the hypothetical premise stated above went without saying, thus making
room for the insinuation that such a large population could not have been engaged in migration.

Budai-Deleanu, in *De Originibus Populorum Transylvaniae*, suggestively invokes the numbers argument as a proof of Romanian continuity. Nowadays, he
writes, "there are at least five million Romanians in Wallachia, Moldavia, Transylvania and the parts of Hungary that once belonged to Dacia. National as well
as foreign sources show that they have ever been so numerous, if not more, on the
same sites, at the time of the coming of the Hungarians. If, then, this multitude
did not settle on these lands at the time of Trajan, I wonder under what rule they
could ever have been established here in Dacia?"[111] The basis of his argumentation lies as much in sources that could hardly have estimated the number of Romanians in Transylvania at the time of Gelu as it does in the logical assumption
that, given present characteristics, things must have been similar in the past.

Bariţ constructs his argumentation, in an 1842 article, along the very same
lines as Budai-Deleanu's theory (although, of course, he could not have had direct
knowledge of it). In a dispute with those who considered the Romanians as
"outsiders" in Transylvania, he states:

> I, for one, as I have previously stated on several occasions, affirm again that without further
> dispute to the purpose of finding the origin of this people, I see more than five million Ro-
> manians in the lands of ancient Dacia [...] Or, out of this total, more than one million two
> hundred thousand are inhabitants of Transylvania alone. Had they settled here only in the
> twelfth or the thirteenth centuries, tell me, what wretched and blindfolded politics could
> have been that which made those who claimed to be the masters of the land back then suffer
> such a population exceeding their number to settle among them?"[112]

Dyonis Thalson, whose interest lay in the continuity of the Romanians north
of the Danube, manipulated the issue of Romanian continuity south of the Danube to the same end. While on the northern bank of the river the Romanians
constituted a multitude, those on the southern bank were but few and insignificant.[113]

The thesis of multitude in favour of continuity is ambiguous and slippery, and
the adepts of the immigration theory could have easily turned it to their advantage. The Romanian intellectuals noticed the danger, and this perception would
significantly alter the thesis of the Romanians' number. The image of the Romanians as a numerous people reaching to all nooks and corners, an image which we
have seen was being fashioned within the Romanians' self-image as well as in the
perception of foreigners, could easily have led to the idea of the Romanians as
being endowed with spectacular virility, as a specific trait of the nation. Or, if the
Romanians were such a fast and successful breed, this could explain, on the co-
ordinates of the immigration theory, the reason for their contemporary multitude.
Initially, when they started out from south of the Danube, they were few, but it

was their vitality and their survival potential that caused a substantial demographic increase and therefore their numerical predominance.[114]

This foreign image explains why the Romanian intellectuals avoided stressing the idea of Romanian fecundity, even if it reinforced the issue of their multitude and that of a successful national perspective; even if it was easily sustainable, on the basis of ethnographic observations, whether foreign or national; and even if, generally speaking, it represented a multiple temptation favourable to the self-image. However, for fear that the continuity theory, an essential element of the national ideology, could thus be menaced, the fertility theory looked more like a perjury than anything else. Bariţ confronts the opinions of the Saxons, according to which "the Romanians are excessive breeders", which, the journalist continues, "they strongly believe and we strongly doubt".[115] Generally, Bariţ professes a demographic concept decidedly anti-Malthusian, lamenting rather the lack of density in the Romanian lands than the perspective of an exceptionally fecund population.[116]

However, irrespective of such speculations, which were founded on existing population statistics, all these tribulations evince the remarkable dimensions attained by the ideological manipulation of the motif of the Romanians' number.

Multitude can therefore be invoked to the most diverse ends. For George Bariţ, the Transylvanian Romanians' large number represents the foremost element that contributed to the maintaining of the Romanian national heartbeat in the province.[117] Similarly, Cipariu upholds by similar arguments the racial purity of the province: "The Romanian element is so numerous that there is no need for the reviving or revitalising of our blood by contact with foreign elements, as is the case with other nationalities."[118]

The same great number, which has been the Romanians' salvation in the past, represents the guarantee of their certain and luminous future, as Bariţ writes again in the spring of 1848: "And for those who are acquainted with the Romanians, they need only think of their multitude and they will see that nothing is to be feared for whatever may come after 1848."[119]

A somewhat paradoxical evaluation of the theme turned it into one of the reasons why the Romanians were oppressed. Foreigners feared them because they were numerous, thus discriminating against them and creating an inferior status for them. This is Samuil Micu's opinion: "Since there was a multitude of Romanians, who were impossible to drive away from their own country, the foreigners started calling them ingrate strangers in their own territories."[120] The *Memorandum* of 24 October 1849 applied the idea to Romanian–Serb relations on the Banat and Hungary: "It can easily be understood why the Serbian church officials were so intolerant of the Romanians, if we consider that the Serbs, who hold supremacy, are hardly a million, while the subordinate Romanians exceed three million inhabitants, and, consequently, this discrepancy of the peoples in question could only be appeased by spiritual oppression and by eliminating all the enlightened men of our nation."[121]

THE NUMBER OF ROMANIANS: THE WHIRLIGIG OF FIGURES

Of course, at a time when demographic statistics, polls, conscription and population programmes all enjoyed considerable progress,[122] it was only natural that the theme of the Romanians' number should not appear only as a set of adjectival approximations but as absolute evaluations and figures. However, the inebriating dance of subjective ideologisation was ready to concatenate even the apparently immobile world of figures. In the first place, the great national debates around the allegedly false and tendentious statistics represented one of the main factors of vilification. Secondly, the mystique of numbers, which were meant to express a palpable symbol of national solidarity, was prevalently manifest in the obsession with round figures, magical values (which were obtained, needless to say, by positive rounding) that were considered more eloquent than tedious statistical results.[123]

"Millions" is the preferred referent, and it was usually obtained by neglecting some odd hundreds or ten thousands, which were obviously less important. "You are millions, Romanians!" exclaims Papiu Ilarian[124], while the *Memorandum* of 26 September 1848 invokes the "millions of Romanians" who demand the unity of the national body under the aegis of the Austrian Crown.[125] The mere invocation of such a numerical scale was believed to be able to supplement courage, to legitimise Romanian claims and to trigger the granting of their rights.

The whirligig of figures starts from the 1791 *Supplex*, as related to the Romanians of the principality; "the supplicant nation", it states, "comprises almost a million inhabitants";[126] the Romanians represent "perhaps an exact million".[127]

Up to 1848, in conformity with the population polls and statistical enterprises,[128] the number of the Romanians soared to one million two hundred thousand, a figure that is often encountered among Romanian journalists as well.[129] Bărnuţiu, in the *Provocation*, meant, by slightly altering it, to stress that there was a discrepancy between this considerable figure and the totally inadequate political status of such a numerous population: "You, one million and three thousand individuals, do not count in the eyes of the world as a nation."[130]

The revolution no longer dabbled in such fragmented figures, which were rounded up without further explanations: "The Romanian nation counts one and a half million", writes Prodan Probul[131], while the Braşov merchants increase the figure to a higher amount; no matter whether nationality is "a great civil virtue" or simply "mere fanaticism", the latter write, it has to gain respect in the case of a population like that of Romanian Transylvania, "where the Romanians are, by their two million souls, more numerous and important than any other nation there abiding".[132] It should also be noted that these estimates refer only to the Romanians of Transylvania.

The number of Romanians took a further leap during the revolution, by the inclusion in the addition of diverse figures referring to the Romanian population of the various provinces of the Austrian Empire. The figure most often encountered was three million, which was obtained cumulatively from the number of Romanians in Transylvania and those of eastern Hungary. As they had formerly been estimated at one million[133], it is difficult to say by way of what mathematical artifice they could have soared so much in number, even allowing for the possibility of putting to account the Romanian population from the military borderline (approximately two hundred thousand). The need for a memorable figure, however, excluded these sorts of petty trifles and calculations.

Consequently, all official documentation of the nation, such as the petitions submitted to the emperor, exhibit the latter figure as a numerical marker of the main political claim, that is, the united national body of the Romanians of the monarchy. The Romanian nation is "the most numerous in the lands she inhabits, as she amounts to three and a half million",[134] according to the *Memorandum* of 25 February 1849, where the figure is amplified by more than half a million in order to be indicative of all the Romanians of the empire, including Bucovina and elsewhere. Subsequently, in the petition of 30 July 1849, among the enumeration of the losses that were inflicted on the Romanians ("the four hundred villages that were set on fire", and "the forty thousand casualties"), the "more than three million souls" constitute an eloquent reproach with respect to the fact that the nation was not included, as it had wished, in the new constitutional formula stipulated by imperial edict on 4 March 1849.[135]

Significantly for the unifying vision and for the necessity of always increasing the figures, the three million Romanians do not only appear in pro-Austria memoranda but also in arguments favourable to the Hungarians. Timotei Cipariu, for instance, in his series of articles in the *Mouthpiece of Enlightenment*, pleading for the union of Transylvania and Hungary, argues that only thus will the three million Romanians be added together, in Transylvania as well as in Western lands (Banat, *Partium* and Hungary).[136] From this point of view it is exactly this idea that the followers of the unification under the aegis of Austria were advocating, in a different political formula.

Irrespective of the form in which it could be arrived at, the figure became prominent in the social imaginary, acquiring an ideological identification function, as Vasile Maniu confesses in *The Sovereign People*: "Our brothers from Transylvania and Banat [...] amount to three million."[137]

Another figure, however, would make quite an impact at the same period on the social imaginary: the figure arrived at by adding up all Romanians at the level of the whole national territory. For a long while, or more specifically until the more accurate population polls undertaken in the principalities during the Organic Regulations, the round number circulated was that of five million. We encounter the same figure in Budai-Deleanu, in around 1815 ("The Romanians amount to approximately five million in Wallachia, Moldavia, Transylvania, and the parts of Hungary that were once Dacian"[138]), and in George Bariț, in 1842 ("Here we are, more than five million Romanians in the counties of ancient Dacia."[139])

Shortly after this there was an incredible leap to eight million, a figure at which the allegedly statistical estimate settled after 1848. Its "discovery" was facilitated by the progress experienced in the official polls on the one hand, and by the calculations of diverse foreign observers, authors of statistical and geographical estimates, travellers or international political journalists. This was the case with Kőváry and Wesselényi (who speak of seven or eight million[140]), with Desprez[141], and, of course, Vaillant[142], who plays a significant role in establishing a unitary image of the ethnic and geographical body of the Romanians, a denomination for this national ensemble (*La Roumanie*) and the round figure that circumscribes the dimensions of its power and importance as a European geo-political factor.

"Eight million souls", wrote Bariț in 1848.[143] The same "eight million Romanians of Trajan's Dacia" inspired Papiu Ilarian in 1852.[144] The *Mouthpiece of Enlightenment*, based on the *Erdélyország Statisztikája* written by László Kőváry, as well as the *Journal for the Mind*, both published in 1847, wished to be even more exact. Thus they claimed that, according to recent statistics, the figure to which the number of Romanians amounted was eight million two hundred and fifty thousand.[145] Cipariu worked during the revolution on translating an extremely eulogising article on the Romanians, published in the *Wiener Zeitung*, which advocated the unification of all Romanians (the principalities here included) under the aegis of Austria, transmitting the grandiose image of an "imposing, massive nation of six million inhabitants, under the sceptre of the Austrian Emperor". However satisfied he may have been with the opinions and appreciation expressed in the article, the editor from Blaj decided to correct the figures, in the sense of popular consecration, arriving at the idea that the new political regime could count on a prospective population of ten million inhabitants—the most ambitious figure encountered in the epoch.[146] This was basically Bălcescu's ideal as well, but the latter contented himself with the figure of "seven million Romanians".[147]

Leaving aside this kind of fluctuation, the formula "we are eight million Romanians" launched the figure that would be the most circulated around the 1848 revolution, by summing up various statistics and estimates of the time, from Dobrogea and Basarabia to Maramureș.[148] This calculation, in which a colossal national pride was invested, convincingly strengthened the belief that the Romanians represented a large and solid nation. It was thought that mere awareness of this element would boost hope and cause action, in the spirit of Avram Iancu's discourse in Blaj: "Look on this field, Romanians, we are as numerous as the pine-tree cones, we are numerous and we are strong, since God is with us."[149] Being numerous was equivalent to being strong; it was up to the Romanians, therefore, to break the chains of humiliation and be the makers of their own destiny.

A small-scale variant of the numbers theme is represented by the problem of figures during the revolution, an infinite source for the displaying of national pride, polemical drives and exaggerations. Estimates of the number of participants in the Blaj popular assemblies,[150] of the paramilitary Romanian troops, of the total losses suffered by the Romanians (the figure was forty thousand casualties), as well as of the number of Hungarian victims—all represented subjects of heated dispute, as if a plus or a minus of some thousand corpses could have altered the either just or hideous character of the civil war.

With respect to estimates of the losses, spectacular figures were used when it came to proving the Romanians' important contribution to the imperial cause, in what might well represent a case of historical mythologisation. The "hundreds of brave men" that are "as alert as sheep-dogs" in order to secure national values, in Andrei Mureșanu's[151] *Echo*, are a tell-tale symbol of the way in which the uprising of 1848 was perceived. "You have awoken in great numbers, as never seen before you"[152], writes Bărnuțiu in October, thus launching the myth of the one hundred thousand Romanians who enrolled overnight under the flag of Colonel Urban or of the Romanian legions. Besides such imprecise adjectives, some figures are given as accurate, for example, the one hundred and ninety-nine thousand soldiers of the legions[153]—a total arrived at as a result of a mechanical multiplication of the number of districts by a standard number of units, which could not be thoroughly checked during a totally unconventional war.

Mention should be made, at the end of this section, of some deviations from the fetishistic belief in the importance of number. Such deviations are nevertheless rare, even if this issue could easily have turned into a negative interpretation, intended to incriminate the image of a people that was constituted of anonymous masses, where great number outdid personality or the sense of an élite.

First of all, there are instances in which the thesis of the Romanians' large numbers is rejected. In the same manner, in which Bariţ discredited the stereotype of the Romanians' fecundity[154] on the grounds of his anti-Malthusian concept, Ion Codru Drăguşanu would be preoccupied with the lack of density of population in the principalities. Wallachia "resembles a newly founded colony and is scarcely peopled"[155], "its domains are more and more deserted by their residents".[156] He even wishes the French could come and "colonise our deserted lands",[157] while the idea of colonisation by the Germans was violently dismissed by Romanian journalism. In conformity with the pan-Latinist vision, the Romanians' neo-Roman racial affinities could only fortify the national body, which was, according to some, emaciated.

The number of Romanians, generally thought to be quite large, especially when it was important to provide encouragement, could also be considered small when used to serve other purposes and points of view. The Saxons or other neighbouring populations had nothing to fear from unification, wrote Bariţ, because "we are neither forty, nor eighty million"[158] (alluding to the peril of pan-Slavism). In other words, here the Romanians were no longer a people that could overwhelm by their multitude, as other images claimed. The same instrumentalisation can be found in Papiu Ilarian, for whom the Romanians of the Middle Ages were less numerous than the enemies they had had to confront.[159] It was solely in the event that number could be an argument for continuity that the Romanians' numerical importance could be modified, according to the ideological necessities.

An even more blatant deviation from the principle of the importance of multitude is recorded when the value, and not the dimension, represented by the Romanians, is contested. As soon as the Romanians are the beneficiary of a political, national and cultural education, Bariţ writes, "three million inhabitants will be just as good as six or nine", that is to say, the contemporary millions are not so important *per se*. According to the same logic, Cipariu affirms that the Romanians are "a numerous people, not in the political sense but in the sense of geographical extension".[160] Geographical extension, admirable as it may be, does not automatically entail a proportionate political development.

In the spirit of his rationalist scepticism and criticism, Cipariu several times denies, and with expressive vehemence, the importance of number. The Lilliputian Armenian community of Venice, he writes, has achieved in the field of culture more than the numerous Romanians have: "So much done alone by a small community, while our so many fellow countrymen reap not a thing!"[161] Elsewhere, lamenting on the rarity of literate people among the Romanians, the idea being that great number does not mean anything if quality is lacking, Cipariu exclaims: "The Saxons and the Hungarians, *respectu numeri* [as far as their number is concerned], are 1 to every 3 Romanians, but as to knowledge of reading, the Romanians do not even number 1 to 3 of them [...] *Numerus sumus* [We are but number], nothing else."[162]

This was, however, a mere reversal of the principle according to which great numbers generate rights and power and which represented one of those few compensatory certainties that nobody could take away from the Romanians.

LANGUAGE AND ALPHABET

Besides the functions it fulfilled as a means of communication and an essential pivot of social cohesion and support of cultural reflection and creation, language first and foremost represented the chief distinctive factor of national identity for the Transylvanian Romanians at the beginning of the modern age. In concordance with the Herderian ethnic-linguistic model of nationalism, language, just like nationality, was raised to the status of a metaphysical principle around which a cult of mystic adoration was built. The reflection on, and the "critical analysis" of, a transcendental phenomenon of this type, or "the philology" of the time, could not be, under such circumstances, other than an ideology *par excellence*.[163]

However, before ascending to the level of such a detached veneration of the beauty of the maternal language, the intellectuals of the time were confronted with endless difficulties determined by the use of Romanian as a language of culture and conversation for the élite, in other stylistic registers than that of popular expression and culture. These difficulties were due both to problems of a nature "external" to language (its discrimination as the language of administration and education, through various political and social conditionings), and to "internal" causes (the weak development of the cultural, scientific and socio-political language, but especially the absence of certain generally accepted stylistic and grammatical norms that structure a unitary "literary" language).[164] At the time, each intellectual wrote the way he thought fit, menacing the very possibility of efficient communication through the national idiom, the big problem being not disregard of the grammatical or orthographic rules but the absence of a normative system that could license conformity to, or transgression of, some canon. Each and every one of these intellectuals usually aimed at "correctness" and criticised the others for their "miscellaneous" and "maimed" language, but the notions remained absolutely subjective and relative.

The issue of the "poverty" of the language (at its highest level) raises other considerable questions. One solution would have been either to adopt the use of foreign idioms as languages of culture and conversation for the élite (which reopened the discussion regarding the risk of denationalisation) or to construct a new Romanian language through the transformation of the popular language into something else, with the help of the most various methods. This latter procedure was censured, this time from the perspective of the need for originality, for the specific genius and for linguistic purity.

Today, the best proof of the difficulties faced by the intellectuals of the time is their language itself, painstakingly fixed on the written page, with which they struggled, sometimes with lamentable results, in order to translate thoughts and feelings of an often remarkable depth. In many cases the texts written in Latin, German and Hungarian are much clearer and much more coherent than those written in the vernacular.[165]

This situation was fully acknowledged and often confessed by those who lived through it themselves, all the more so as they constantly had before them the example of the "more apt" idioms, which sanctioned a different fluency of speech. Obviously, at the level of the negative dimension of the self-image this was an extremely painful observation: as a corollary of their cultural backwardness the Romanians did not even have a "wealthier" language which could make possible a cultural creation to match that of others.

In 1825 Theodor Serb commiserated with Emanoil Gojdu, who was considered a nationalist "really inflamed towards the Romanians", for the fact that "he does not know Romanian all that well, as he is a great poet and writes so many beautiful things in Hungarian. He struggled with our language as well, but being influenced by much richer languages and not knowing the names of many ideas, he cannot figure them out."[166] Timotei Cipariu also invokes "the poverty we ceaselessly regret and feel, every time we cannot express our ideas smoothly and freely as we do in other European languages which are refined and elegant".[167] Papiu Ilarian, too, confesses in the preface to his *History*: "It is very difficult to write accurately and clearly in your own language all of a sudden and to ward off foreign expressions when you have learned all the sciences in foreign languages."[168]

That the Romanian language (due to some circumstances that undoubtedly exonerated it but could not ameliorate the situation) was less able, at that time, to express lofty ideas and sentiments, was a theme eloquently expressed by Andrei Mureșanu, through the metaphor of "the language for servants".[169] The poet denounces the practices of the élite, who believed that the Romanian language could be used only as an instrument of communication with servants and plebeians and by no means for the purposes of refined conversation, as capable of conferring distinction and social prestige, despite the cliché of the "sweetness" of the maternal tongue inherited from the Romanians' forefathers:

> They say language is sweet and that it sounds divine
> Among the other languages that it deserves to shine
> But I see in the salons, these are such shameful things
> To speak the servants' language is less the worth of kings![170]

Although in the principalities (Mureșanu resumes his idea in an article) it is the "sovereign" language of the state, Romanian "has been welcomed in few aristocratic houses, where only the servants speak it".[171]

Under such circumstances the Transylvanian School outlines the stereotype of the "lack of cultivation" of the Romanian language, one tightly linked, according to the optimistic enlightened philosophy, with the theme of the necessity and possibility of its "cultivation" henceforth. As we shall see below, the articulation of these motifs and strategies for action did not originate only in the mere recognition of some "objective" real difficulties, in the state of the language as such, but in a deeply ideological perspective. It is necessary that language be reformed and "improved" mainly because it is the first element of national identity, thus the creation of the respective identity should start from here.

In association with the motifs of cultural backwardness and of the lack of zeal for the national cause, the theme of the uncultivated language is expressed in a very plastic way by Samuil Micu: the Romanians, in his opinion "idle away when it comes to refining and polishing their language or when it is time to write and to learn, this being so bad a thing that it has bred stupidity and wickedness".[172]

Therefore, the cause of the Romanians' wretched situation was considered to reside in the decay of the language, an idea to be met with, a year later, in Radu Tempea as well. For him, the absence of a written grammar book—an aspect that clearly illustrates the neglect of the cultivation of the language—is the main reason behind all other misfortunes: "On the one hand, the Romanians lack this necessary skill and thus forget about our Romanian language (which springs from Rome), and on the other hand, they lack the proficiency and high sciences of books and thus have fallen in the obscurity of the mind and succumbed to witlessness and incognisance; and here we are! Today we are what we see before our eyes and what we feel we are!" "The inconstancy of leadership" had also contributed to the "spoiling" of the Romanian language "which stumbles even worse than before, having lost the great fluency of speech which our forerunners did not take the trouble to polish, so that ignorance and barbarity benumbed our nation and we fell prey to great sluggishness".[173]

Although in the first half of the nineteenth century the political and cultural progress of the nation slowly corroded the reason behind the lack of cultivation of the Romanian language, the theme is already present in Papiu Ilarian, who, besides his favourite themes, also deplores the fact that the young who "studied Hungarian and considered it the most cultivated and an absolutely necessary language, neglected Romanian, forgot it, kept it uncultivated".[174]

The natural corollary of the cliché of language neglect is its cultivation. For the enlightened intellectuals, this was an important prerequisite of their general pedagogic programme and at the same time a possibility that could unquestionably materialise, given their optimistic faith in the universality of the human being, in the equality of the chances of progress for all nations and all people.

In 1795 the same conviction is articulated in the *Notice of the Philosophical Society from Transylvania*: "All peoples have taken great pains in adorning their language style with distinctive and ordered words", hence, the Romanians, too, will welcome this tradition.[175] Budai-Deleanu faithfully sketches the trajectory of the leap from non-cultivation to the flourishing of the language; so far, Romanian has been "poor, rustic, uncultivated. The Wallachian writes the way he usually talks, without rules or prudent choice. In this language there is no vocabulary yet, no organised grammar, no orderly orthography." Still, "the Moldavian, and the Romanian language in general, has everything it takes to become in time a language equal, as far as culture goes, with Italian, if skilful people will polish it."[176] In translating one of Metastasio's plays, he embraces the same idea; he translates it "as a test, to show that Romanian can become as polished as Italian, through culture"[177]. The motivation for his action does not reside in the desire to offer a work of art to his co-nationals, but, more importantly, he wants to prove a point, namely to put to the test the cultural capacity of Romanian in comparison with the languages of other peoples.

Constantin Diaconovici-Loga, too, has faith in the potential of the Romanian language. Through derivation, he writes, "Romanian, which is now insipid and scarce, can become plentiful and cultivated."[178]

The political and cultural progress of the last two decades before the revolution offered even stronger reasons for this optimistic endeavour. In 1844 Andrei Mureşanu wrote that "Romanian has indicated even before that it welcomes a higher culture", and in the principalities "nowadays it is the language of the church, the language of the state and the dominant language"[179]. As usual, he stresses the fact that the value of the chances offered to the Romanians is strictly conditioned by their will and capacity to realise them: "So it is up to us to yield a culture to this language, which can warrant such a type of culture, and to preserve it with dignity so that in time it may function alongside the other cultivated European languages."[180]

Bariţ declares his confidence in the cultural potential of the language, still relying on the model of the national civility of the principalities—a key idea in his writings: "Romanian spoken on Romanian soil, irrespective of the complaints of some, has proved so far that it can be the language of government, of the church and schools, and, even more readily, of the crowd. What Romanian needs is an unencumbered growth, and as language of the artists it will reach a level that no other European language can reach in such a short time."[181]

THE IDEOLOGICAL RECONSTRUCTION OF THE LANGUAGE

As I have mentioned before, the problem of language cultivation is not merely a concrete problem, aiming at lexical enrichment, linguistic perfection and use in the cultural sphere. Firstly, language constitutes an ideological and identity problem. The construction of a modern national identity—the chief endeavour of the intellectual élite of the time—naturally presupposed the invention of a new language, adequate to this purpose. The new identity being presented as a rediscovery and restoration of the Romanians' original and essential Latinity—an eloquent cloth of nationality—it had to go back to its genuine form as well. Briefly, it was the fundamental justification of a radical Latinism, initiated by the Transylvanian School and solidly perpetuated in Transylvania in the first half of the following century.

However, the creation of a new—and artificial, one might say—language, in any case one totally different from the one then being spoken in all social areas, and one theoretically motivated, in an extremely convincing way, from the perspective of the ideology of the time, raised numerous sensitive problems. This typical tension between ideology and the social reality would generate a boundless diversity of variants and solutions as to the concrete ways of creating a new language. The fierce disputes and polemics on the topic would provide the main substance of the cultural effort of the time, from both a quantitative and qualitative point of view. Almost each cultivated Transylvanian intellectual would take it upon himself to devise, if not a grammar, then at least an orthographic system of his own, considered better, "purer" and truer than the ones competing with it. This huge collective effort would nevertheless come to be rightfully accused of sterility and vain wearying of the nation's creative capacities. But it could not be stopped, given the fact that what constantly set it in motion was that irrepressible tendency to look for a new identity, triggered by the shock of nationalism and modernisation, at a more general level.

This is not the place to retrace the history of the countless philological theories of the epoch.[182] I will simply mention here a few more important methods of fashioning a new language that would be "pure" and capable of expressing the Romanians' true national identity. One way to achieve it was by enriching the vocabulary with neologisms, obviously borrowed from the sphere of the neo-Romance languages if not from Latin directly. In contrast, another tendency proposed the purification and elimination of foreign lexical and grammatical elements and a return to an original form. Another method, which started from the premise that purification means lexical impoverishment, proposed the improvement of the language through its own resources, based on derivations from roots of Latin origin. Finally, another variant grounded the same lexical richness on internal resources, but by appealing to old words, even to unusable ones, from the traditional church language, or by bringing together the diverse dialectical forms extant in all the historical provinces. Similar discussions concerning the alphabet and orthography followed. Obviously, among all these attempts to reduce everything to the essentials there were many intermediary nuances, combinations and compromises, which went as far as accepting Slavic words or other solutions of a practical nature, farther away from the ideological content of the principles.

Beyond the more or less coherent practical way in which these ideas were applied, the deliberate effort at linguistic normalisation, meant as a builder of identity and of national self-stereotypes and acknowledged as such by its promoters, was extremely important from the point of view of the attitudes present at the level of the social imaginary.

Gheorghe Constantin Roja, the author of *The Skill of Reading Romanian* (1809), was one of those who formulated the desire to devise a new language as cleansed of foreign influences as possible. Even if such a language could not be understood by a large number of the population and would have to be learnt in school (as a foreign language, one might feel inclined to add), this was the only way:

> What can be more beautiful and easier for the Romanians than having their teachers instruct our sons in our pure dialect and, with its help, teach the sciences to them. These pupils will slowly come to impart their ideas in the immaculate Romanian language and then, in their turn, they will teach their sons in the same manner […] It does not really matter that not all of them will come to know this language, moreover, we will come to be as the other nations, because we will have an everyday language and a pure language that can only be learnt from books."[183]

Likewise, by means of such a language the Romanians would be able to understand others from other provinces, irrespective of dialectal differences.[184]

Roja was unquestionably influenced by the Greek model of language development, in both its popular (*dimotiki*) as well as savant (*katharevusa*) variant, but it should be added that other nations from the same area, too, while ushering in the signs of modernisation in too abrupt a manner, manifested similar tendencies to create a cultural, élitist language which could even be, ultimately, a foreign language!

Paul Iorgovici excellently highlights the practical difficulties and paradoxes brought about by this process of ideological language reconstruction. In his opinion, language can be purified and enriched through derivation from original Latin roots. Hence, "instead of using foreign words, we shall give birth to our own words, which to many might appear new, but in fact they are the words which we have, for various reasons, forgotten or which simply do not exist because of the poverty of our dictionary and grammar."[185]

In other words, language reconstruction could have surprises in store even for its own speakers, who would no longer recognise their own idiom.

The same problem is tackled by Gheorghe Şincai in 1783: "You who will read this book, you shall not judge me for the words that might seem new or foreign to you"; his purpose is "not to stray from the purely Romanian words (which is to say Latin of origin)". However, his readers' distrust is an error, because the language they speak is a degraded one.[186] The newly fashioned language represents but a mere return to the "true" language and its primordial purity.[187]

At first sight Budai-Deleanu seems to be a little more moderate in the way in which he sees the degree of innovation introduced by the newly cultivated language as compared to the quotidian idiom. In the dialogue he imagines between a "scholar" and a Romanian "schoolmaster" who specialises in philology, he writes: "The language of the Muses [...], as it is used for learning the sciences, can be found in all political peoples where such teachings are at home and is the same as the common language of the many[188]; it has only to be cleaned and purged of all the follies existent in the everyday language of the crowd, in one word, it is the language ordered and adjusted to grammatical rules", enriched with an adequate lexicon.[189]

Nevertheless, the perplexities of the two language-inventing alchemists were soon to appear. When faced with the above-mentioned idea, according to which the promotion of the newly cultivated language could be rather easily achieved, the teacher is seized with joy; nevertheless, he will implicitly be confronted with a contradiction: "So will we be able to learn the sciences in Romanian?" "Why not?" the teacher replies; the problem lies in that "of all who have written true Romanian so far, few can rise above the common language of the crowd, few are ready to go beyond the everyday language, and few have not already used plenty of foreign words without deliberateness or careful choice." A big question mark is raised here, which makes the teacher wonder: "So, have we spoken vile Romanian so far?"[190]

This was a new, violent nuance added to the negative self-image, able to trigger new identity crises: We do not even speak our own language properly; our condition is so precarious that its change must start from the deepest level, that of the words by means of which we structure our reality. Obviously the teacher tries to alleviate the torments of his pupil: it is impossible to have spoken bad Romanian so far, at the level of everyday language. But if people want to approach loftier subjects, this language reform is necessary.[191]

Unlike the three philologists quoted above, Radu Tempea avers sincere moderation as to the linguistic restructuring on Latin bases. He evokes the practical difficulties that such a transaction might imply, not seeking solutions to overcome them (as others do) but stressing the real disadvantages of an ideological language reconstruction, even if this ideal is not indifferent to him: "It is, and will be, difficult to bring language to its original genuineness, that is to Old Romanian (sprung from Rome), because if anyone should take up this endeavour, Romanian will turn out to be Latin or Italian; and he who will learn this unadulterated language, and who is not a Romanian, will not be able to understand either the church books or the everyday language now spoken; I suppose the unlearned Romanian might say this is maiming his mother tongue." A reversed paradox, this time: the new language, devised by the Latinists, is considered to be a degradation of the original language![192]

But, significantly, Tempea's grammar would not enjoy the same success as those of Iorgovici, Budai-Deleanu, Şincai or Maior, which gained historical visibility. Budai-Deleanu would even blame Tempea and Molnar-Piuariu for the prudence with which the two scholars promoted Latinism.[193]

According to its artisans, a fundamental process of ideological language reconstruction was its fashioning in conformity with all kinds of rules and linguistic norms, whether grammatical, lexical or orthographic. Iorgovici writes that "our language lacks ordering and enriching; this can only be done if we bring it to fixed rules"[194], and Şincai suggests the same in an even more expressive way, stating that "our language, like the people, should straighten and increase according to the norm left by His Majesty."[195]

The introduction of a new order and manner of language structuring, as well as the symbolic ordering of the social reality, represent a distinctively ideological type of action regarding both language and reality. The political myth of the reformatory authority of the good emperor is also at work here. The monarch's will to order straightens everything out, it "normalises" everything: the individual, society, even language, which needs to be ameliorated by rational criteria, just as other aspects of reality.

Following in the footsteps of the ideological model of enlightened despotism, the Transylvanian intellectuals constructed their own strategy for a "straightening of the nation", believing that grammar and the dictionary could order a (linguistic and social) world wandering in darkness, opprobrium and confusion.

The analogy, which turned out to be a true identification, between language and social reality transformed the process of language reconstruction into a primordial necessity. By straightening language, the state of the nation is automatically straightened, "because language and nation go at the same pace".[196] "From what we have said about Romanian so far", writes Paul Iorgovici, "we can understand many things about the state of the Romanian nation too."[197] The Romanian nation had decayed because language had been neglected, as had any sort of grammar and dictionary (which consequently engendered a cultural decline). This meant that the remaking of the initial language structure would transform it again into a new cultural vehicle, triggering the general progress of the nation.

This refuge in philology, like the attention granted to history, represents, in fact, a manner of ideological substitution of direct action in such fields as the economical or the political. Given that, in the respective spheres, one could not change much, the belief grew that bad things could be straightened out through the transformation of those purely ideological structures which seemed able to give in to direct action and be modified and "bettered" at will. If it was not possible to change the painful political or economic realities, the Romanians could, nevertheless, rewrite history and reform language; they could institute a completely new order in the illusory world of words, through grammars and dictionaries.

Under these circumstances, considering its vital importance for the destiny of the nation, the reconstruction of the language was declared not to be a matter that could be left to hazard, a prey to the people's diverse options, like a scientific problem or a matter of personal linguistic conduct. All the members of the national body had, necessarily, to comply with the ideological will that could restructure the new language. In the absence of the coercive means (the administrative power of the state or the cultural power of an institutionalised educational system) that might impose this will on the civil society, its introduction remained dependent on the symbolic pressure of "the national duty", of nationalism, as a hegemonic ideological system about to be constituted.[198]

"But let us leave aside what people say", the same Paul Iorgovici writes; "the more people, the more opinions; it is our duty to find the name we bear and the language we speak [...]. I know there will be many Romanians, who, either by ignorance or for other reasons, will stray through words from the root of our language. Everyone is free to think of everything the way they feel fit." But after this last enlightened concession made to tolerance for individual opinions, Iorgovici resumes the imperative of the ideological duty of national collectivism, leaving the task of its accomplishment, if the worst should come, to the future: "If these [the words derived from Latin roots] do not appeal to today's Romanians, I trust that they will appeal to our successors who will appreciate the assets of our nation and will strive to add new things to it, to the use of the nation."[199] Respect for language "purity" had become a question of national morality and the fulfilment of a destiny.

Even if such ideological commandments were pressing hard the linguistic, and especially orthographic, practice, one cannot say that lucid disavowals of such linguistic-ideological conformism were completely lacking, both at the level of everyday use and at the level of theoretical argumentation. They were favoured both by the absence, in civil society, of coercive means of ideological alignment, and by the existence of certain ideological pressures of a different nature which competed among themselves and weakened the main tendency, namely the nationalist Latinism. The Orthodox tradition, for instance, which linked the very specificity of its identity (and, as a prolongation, that of the nation) to the Slavic flavour of the language of church books or to the Cyrillic alphabet, introduced such a protean and diversionary factor into the main ideological stream, one which managed to erode the all-embracing character of the latter.[200]

Obviously, the Transylvanian intellectuals who averred their discontent at the philological fever of ideologisation could do this in the name of reason and common sense. Ioan Maiorescu, who always strove (although not always successfully) to be, as a philologist, an objective man of science and not a supporter of the partisan national ideology, deplores the manifestations of this ideologically motivated philological zeal: "When it comes to language, everyone would be a tailor. They smooth it and they comb it, until the skin is peeled off it; then they give it another skin to try on."[201]

In a letter to Papiu Ilarian, Simion Bărnuțiu is even more decidedly against the respective phenomenon; reading one of Carlo Cattaneo's reviews, which harshly criticises the sterile character of such Romanian philological disputes, the Transylvanian student from Pavia completely agrees with the Italian man of science: "The Romanians", Cattaneo says (in Bărnuțiu's translation), "instead of producing works of the mind, splendid and elegant, have only come up so far with grammatical issues [...]. Only three alphabets and fourteen different orthographic systems come between their few literati and the even fewer books they have."[202] Bărnuțiu declares himself a determined advocate of the abandoning of these futile disputes, which, in his opinion, divert the nation's cultural effort from the direction of original creation:

> The time has come to wake Romanians up not only in matters of orthography but in other, higher things of life as well, because, as you have already seen, foreigners already judge us, and rightfully so, because [...] over a span of seventy years the orthography issue was debated to saturation and the Romanians have argued enough so far saying that they could not produce any creative work, so now would be the right time to start doing that [...] I cannot explain why they have not done that so far, why they have not gone beyond orthography so far, why they are still mumbling their ABC, as Mr. Cattaneo rightfully claims.[203]

Today, an answer to Bărnuțiu's letter is not that hard to find: the importance of the respective matters came from the fact that they represented disputes over the national identity as it surfaced in the questions of language and the alphabet, while this long-debated identity constituted, in its turn, the main symbolic instrument of defence against the threat of the Other.

The Alphabet

Just as in the case of the language, the alphabet and orthography issue turned into a fierce battle over identity between the Latin and Cyrillic partisans. A third element of the dispute was the compromise solution represented by the transition alphabet, adopted, for instance, by George Bariț in his gazettes between 1840 and 1844.[204]

Almost all the important intellectuals of the time militated for the introduction of the Latin alphabet, even though many continued to publish or to write their correspondence in Cyrillic orthography, because of public preferences or simply out of habit. Nevertheless, if we consider both the remarkable persistence of Cyrillic writing and the vehemence with which the cultural leaders argued for the Latin script, we must admit that the endurance of the Cyrillic alphabet in Transylvania was not only due to traditional habits and routine but was also based on very solid ideological options.[205]

For the promoters of the Latin alphabet, its introduction represented, as naturally as possible, an identity problem, organically associated with the elaborate national ideology that was being fashioned at the time. A people with a Latin name, origin and language, it was argued, could only use the orthography corresponding to its specificity.

But even for the Orthodox Church hierarchy, which defended and cultivated the Cyrillic alphabet, the maintenance of the latter was still a question of identity, of defence of the national specificity. The Cyrillic script, which had illustrated the

Romanians' entire cultural being so far, was considered a distinctive mark of their Eastern faith defining their communitarian traits as compared to universalist and Catholic Latinism. A certain empirical logic seems to support this thesis. The introduction of the Latin alphabet represented newness as compared to the contemporary reality; it was equated with innovation and change—in a field of vital symbolic importance—so it could very easily be accused of triggering the loss of the Romanians' specificity and the alteration of their identity.

Consequently, the pleas of the "Latinisers" should be understood in relation to such a solidly grounded objection—including the point of view of their own system of argumentation—and not as a facile modernising response to an absurd and outdated conservatism of the *ancien régime* type. The advocates of the Latin alphabet had to beat their opponents with their own weapons (tradition being a natural basis of identity), which determined them to search for supplementary historical myths able to legitimate their position.

In the following we will look at these arguments, highlighting their special relevance from the point of view of national identity.

Samuil Micu, in his slow and burdened style, appealed to the most readily available historical motivation (the alphabet of the Romanians' ancestors), adding the pragmatic argument of the need for synchronisation and modernisation, given the fact that, at the time, the Latin alphabet was the orthographic vehicle of all civilised nations:

> Hence, the letters that the Romanians from Dacia have been using in their writing for some time are Slavic. And the old ones, the mother letters of the Romanians from Dacia, as those of the Romanians from Italy, are Latin. So, if we are willing to follow our forefathers and our great ancestors rather than foreigners; and rightfully admitting that they are quite useful both for education and for politics and that we shall be praised by other more cultivated peoples for our choice of adopting the old mother-tongue; given that all other skilful and learned peoples (not from the Romanian branch) use their mother-tongue, I thought it appropriate that we, Romanians, should use our fatherland's letters in this book.[206]

Budai-Deleanu produces a broader and more subtle argumentation. A key idea is that the Cyrillic alphabet represents a foreign force, altogether inappropriate to the internal structure of the language and to its specific genius. Between the alphabet and the language there has to be an intimate correspondence, the Transylvanian philologist believes, in perfect concordance with the linguistic theories of the time, since language is a living organism with specific properties (and not a mere linguistic sign, arbitrarily chosen and independent of the reality it designates, as the structuralists might say): "I will take it upon myself to demonstrate that the letters we call Slavic clash with the very being of our language, as the Turkish ones do too. Because, if we force the language, we might as well write with Turkish letters just as with the Slavic ones. But the question is: How will that affect the other language properties? Because each and every language has its own characteristics."[207]

But this difference between language and the alphabet generated a more serious problem than one might have imagined, a problem that was able to obdurate and alter the Romanians' very national identity. The Cyrillic alphabet hid the Latinate essence, both from the eyes of strangers and from the Romanians' own eyes; it estranged them from their real condition. A re-establishment of the original orthographic clothing alone could rebuild the transparency of identity: "Noticing that this type of text written with Slavic letters cannot be understood in other barbarian languages, we thought that we should write letters in the learned Latin mother-tongue and the sister of Italian."[208]

The "Latin—Wallachian" orthography was able to reveal the Romanians' Latin substance, concealed until then and forgotten under a barbarian, perverse and misrepresenting dress; identity, the ethnonym, Latin origins, the glory of the Romanians' condition—they would all appear in the right kind of light, clarity and splendour once the orthographic tailoring had been completed: "Romanian! Seeing how clearly, highly and joyfully this name shines after we have extricated it from its Cyrillic mesh and have dressed it in Romanian clothes, urge yourself to wear this name to your true praise."[209]

The obsessive drive to find a scapegoat to blame for all present troubles also surfaced in terms of the legacy of Cyril and Methodius. The script, it was argued, was to blame for the Romanians' backwardness and decay; Cyril and Methodius, as Vasile Gergely de Ciocotiş writes, were "the first and foremost cause of the wreck of our language" and, therefore, "it is mainly through them that the Romanians have been brought to a state of deep barbarity and covered in the dark mantle of ignorance".[210] The Cyrillic alphabet has led to this catastrophe because, in favouring Slavic loans, it transformed the language so that "bridled and alienated, our fading Roman language has declined and vanished, wandering and straying from the right path. Moreover, it has been burdened, precluded and completely severed from contact with other European languages, so that our language can no longer declare who we were."[211]

At this stage, the intellectual from Maramureş sounds another important note for the partisans of the Latin script, one that we have also seen in Samuil Micu: the need for synchronisation with the cultivated nations, and more than that, the need for the Romanians' harmonisation with Western European civilisation through the adoption of the alphabet that could introduce them into that community.

Besides the symbolic significance of the adoption of the alphabetic sign that would evince the Romanians' belonging to Western civilisation, the Transylvanian intellectuals insisted on underlining the practical importance of the respective orthographic alignment. For foreigners to be able to approach the Romanians and recognise their true origins and condition (since this would represent mutual welcoming steps towards the Romanians' integration into the European flux of the Enlightenment), it was necessary to adopt this indispensable communicational interface, a sign of identification and affinity. Budai-Deleanu states that he has used Latin letters in his lexicon primarily because "of the foreigners who might want to learn this language"[212], and Gheorghe Constantin Roja shows that "today, almost all the nations that write with Latin letters live in Europe"[213]. Timotei Cipariu, too, agrees that "almost all Europe writes with Latin letters"; even the Germans, the English or the Hungarians, who do not spring from the same Latin roots, still use this alphabet, "only the Romanian, who bears this name [...], of all the Romance peoples, writes with Cyrillic letters".[214]

The petition of 21 May 1848, addressed to the Hungarian government by the Romanians from the eastern parts of Hungary, takes this idea further, even stating that "Slavism" had deliberately compelled the Romanians to adopt the Cyrillic script in schools and churches, because "it wanted our nation separated from civilised Europe and lured through a moral sickening into the Slavic trap".[215]

Papiu Ilarian, already in Italy, sorrowfully deplores in a letter to Iacob Mureşanu the fact that the Cyrillic alphabet confers a totally different identity on the Romanians in the eyes of their Latin brothers: "Oh, Lord, the shame these Cyrillic letters bring to us! Please forgive me, because I do not want that anyone should consider me a pedant, but one needs to be abroad in order to properly see the way foreigners identify the strangeness of our Cyrillic letters and the barbarity of our blood." He insistently asks the editor of the *Gazette* to use Latin and not Cyrillic forms and letters in the publication, so that the Italians might see that the Romanians, too, are Latin![216]

However, since logical and pragmatic arguments are insufficient when it comes to an identity problem, the partisans of the Latin letters manifested the tendency to legitimate their position by invoking (or fashioning) certain arguments of a historical nature, that is, by inventing a Romanian tradition of the use of the Latin alphabet. Beyond the more general justification that it represented the alphabet of the Romanians' forefathers, the social imaginary tended to associate to these ideas a theory of the continuation of its use—a "logical" augmentation of the theory of the Romanians' continuity. Consequently, it was claimed that the Romanians had been using this alphabet all the time, along a historical line only interrupted by the conjectural replacement of the Latin with the Cyrillic script under Alexander the Kind as a consequence of the perverse advice of Metropolitan Bishop Theoctist. At that time all the old Romanian manuscripts written in the Latin script were allegedly burnt on the monarch's order, thus ensuring the definitive victory of the Cyrillic script and decisively preventing any Catholic attempts.

The enlightened Transylvanian intellectuals adopted this old scholarly tradition, enthusiastically launched in the Romanian culture by Dimitrie Cantemir[217], because it permitted an instrumentalisation that was extremely useful for the legitimising of certain ideological attitudes extremely important to them. On the one hand, it fortified the idea of the Romanians' Latinate essence, including the (of course illusory) trajectory of a continuity at the level of the written culture; on the other hand, it gave new historical justification to the religious union with Rome, due to the fact that the inflammatory/infamous gesture of Theoctist was regarded as an example of a typically "Greek" cunning blow at the ecumenical spirit of the Florence Council and at the religious unification then adopted.

The above-mentioned theory—an eloquent example of the fashioning of a historical-political justifying myth—was widely spread among the enlightened scholars[218], who, undoubtedly, sincerely believed in its truth; yet this aspect was but one of the natural results of any process of self-indoctrination and ideological intoxication.

Petru Maior suggestively resumes it, in building a whole justifying schema related to strictly contemporary ideological realities and priorities:

> Theoctist, knowing that the Romanian language is very similar to Italian, thought that if the Romanians kept using the same Latin letters that the Italians use, they would write books on the union, and when reading them, they would consider unification with the Romans and with

other Italians, their brothers, and so the Greek influence would decrease [...]. What Alexander and the Moldavians did was also accepted by the other Romanians, on this bank of the Danube, and all these Romanians with the same darkness of the mind and ignorance were covered.

The orthographic substitution led to the replacement of the Romanian language by the Slavic one in the church: "So, it is no wonder that this was followed by darkness, in which a lot of Romanians are still lying to this day."[219] Obviously, allusion to the current state of affairs was inevitable, given that the (negative, in this case) myth was but the symbolic original scenario of a reality reiterated in history, to the present day.

However, even in the stereotype-founding epoch of the Transylvanian School, there were lucid attitudes to be found as well, which attempted to see this tradition objectively and critically despite the fact that it might furnish precious arguments necessary to the process of fashioning the national identity. Although a firm advocate of Latin orthography, Budai-Deleanu—whose spirit was deeply marked by the sharp and cold rationalism of the French Enlightenment, more than other intellectuals of the time—attempted to back up his choice (in order better to validate it) on the solid grounds of objective truth and judgement and not on the moving sands of historicist mythology. His ambition was lucidly to debunk the historic-linguistic myth launched by Cantemir, even though his opinion (anyhow forgotten in a manuscript) could by no means compete with the seductive words of Petru Maior or persuade the generations to come, seized by the nationalist frenzy which was about to be born:

> Had the Romanians had a particular type of writing before adopting the Slavic script? And if so, what type of writing?...Obviously, we cannot decide that because there is no palpable proof to substantiate it. Thus in vain will strive those who claim that up until the reign of Alexander the Kind, the prince of Moldavia, the Romanians had taken over the script of their ancestors, namely the Latin, because for lack of the least bit of proof from that time, a letter or something, we cannot believe or totally reject this hypothesis and we cannot gullibly take their word for it either, at least not as truth-seeking men.[220]

Another savant philologist, Timotei Cipariu, adopts a similar position. Although he favours Catholicism as an ideological option, he manifests his scepticism at Cantemir's theory in the name of scientific rigour: "We do not know exactly from where the illustrious author took this historical-literary note."[221] Because he is engrossed in the problem of writing in the Latin script, also taking into consideration the point of view of its role as cultural-ideological interface between the Romanians and Catholicism, Cipariu attempts to resume the old discussion but this time with different arguments. Animated basically by the same tendency as Petru Maior, he replaces the ideologising scenario of the historical-ideological myth with a rational and critical argumentation: "One can believe that at the time there were books as well as church books, deeds and other authentic papers written in Latin, Polish, etc. However, one must admit that some princes and ladies were Catholic, and there were even some bishops who embraced the Latin rite with the respective monasteries and monks from Milcov, Argeş and Severin, so that books written in Latin, with Latin letters, could not be absent."[222]

The arguments for Latin orthography were so insistent and diversified because its promoters were aware of the fact that their attitude was open to a major accusation: the altering of the script is but a first step towards the alteration of the ancient faith, and, therefore to the loss of communal identity. For the traditional mentality and the way that the collective identity was defined at the time, the maintenance of religious specificity may then have been more important than mere belonging to an ethnic-linguistic community, expressed by distinctive traits at the level of high culture.

In trying to find a solution to this problem, the partisans of the Latin alphabet ceaselessly advised their public that the proposed innovation would not affect the Eastern religious tradition, held to by the latter with tenacity and conservatism. "If they adopt the Latin alphabet they should not be afraid that their law will be affected as well"[223], Petru Maior states. The Romanians' fear that in this way they might lose their faith had been induced, he argued, by "some of the Serbs and Greeks", who, "under the pretext of the law, scare them off from returning to their ancient script and urge them to preserve the Cyrillic script like the Serbs and the Russians, and so the Romanians are prisoners to the state of darkness and barbarity induced by the Serbs and the Russians".[224]

It is true that Maior himself half-admits that it was not only foreigners (invoked here as scare-mongers) who were the source of his co-nationals' attachment to the Cyrillic script. The Romanians' conservative prejudices (mentioned with a certain enlightened critical touch) also represented an equally, if not more, important cause. During the reign of Alexander the Kind, the Transylvanian scholar writes, "the Romanians foolishly thought that they would be vengefully cursed if anyone should find that they wrote with Latin letters. And this foolishness is still going on at present."[225]

The Romantic counterpart of Maior (as leader of the national opinion), Papiu Ilarian, also emphasised the internal reasons for the persistence of the Cyrillic script among the Romanians, with special critical virulence addressed to his co-nationals: "I will not have anyone explaining the letters situation to me. Why have the Romanians accepted them? And today, who is forcing them to keep them? It is not only the domination of the Serbs, because this domination implies more than the meanness of the Serbs, but also the Romanians' cowardliness, because in the same way that the Romanians do not always represent Romanianness, a couple of thousand Serbs do not mean that they are all Slavic."[226]

Just like Maior, who feared the public's reaction to the Latin alphabet, Budai-Deleanu also claims to be extremely obliging, even accepting the maintenance of the Cyrillic script in church books, in order to appease susceptibilities, even if we can infer that he was not over-pleased at having to make this concession. He did not intend to "renew the law in any way, because no one will touch the Cyrillic letters of the church books"; however, it was advisable that "a learned language" should adopt the new script, since "the Russians", the champions of Orthodoxy, "have long renounced their church language when it comes to political books and private letters, without harming in any way their faith".[227]

Budai-Deleanu's timorous pleading seems to imply that by keeping to traditional ways the Romanians would do nothing but prove themselves to be more Catholic than the pope—if such a formula could have had a place in the rigorous Eastern context of the respective discussion.

More sure of himself, Timotei Cipariu admits the existence of the same opposition towards the Latin alphabet, motivated both in terms of religion and identity, almost four decades after Maior and Budai-Deleanu. Yet without worrying about this, Cipariu, the first Transylvanian intellectual who dared to edit a gazette written in the Latin script and etymological orthography, resisted the Cyrillic script and the tradition that went with it, with inflexible detachment: "The smaller part of the Romanians are Uniate Catholics and they like better the Latin language and writing. The other, bigger part, the Greek-Slavic, fears that with the Latin letters the Catholic faith might insinuate into their being. The more learned undoubtedly understand that this conclusion and the fear that goes with it are unfounded. They know that almost all Europe writes with Latin letters."[228]

Of course, Cipariu was right when talking about the reservations of the Orthodox as to the adoption of the Latin alphabet, visible even in the principalities and not just in Transylvania. Almost all the intellectuals mentioned so far, who militated for the Latin alphabet, were Greek Catholics, and their Latin-historical and modernising-European motivation was strictly linked to their ideological and identity-related options of a confessional nature. It is true that the Orthodox could not generally bring theoretical arguments against the Latin alphabet, because in this way they would destroy the monolithic character of the ideological nationalist discourse. That is why their public statements are rarer, but when it came to practice, they watched closely and keenly over the maintenance of the Cyrillic alphabet in church and school books.

When necessary they found plenty of justifications, as Moise Nicoară did in his "political-religious" action between 1815 and 1819.[229] Initially militating, alongside Dimitrie Țichindeal, for the distancing of the Serbian ecclesiastical hierarchy, Nicoară was unquestionably supported by the Uniate bishopric from Oradea. Moreover, he received covert support from the Hungarian county authorities—maybe even from the imperial authorities—that had discreetly stimulated his action (if not implemented it from the very beginning, as the citizen from Arad himself would later claim)—in a concerted effort to weaken the Illyrian Orthodox bloc. The orthographic corollary of such an ideological tendency would have been the adoption of the Latin alphabet by the Orthodox Romanians from Arad and Banat, an idea welcomed with great warmth by Dimitrie Țichindeal. Eventually, Nicoară would react extremely violently when faced with this Latin and Catholic offensive, which he directly associated with ethnic assimilation by the Hungarians and the Germans, preferring to protect his identity in strict Orthodox contexts and coming back to conciliatory sentiments towards the Serbs. Undoubtedly, in this context, the graphic sign that was closest to the Romanian identity could only be the Orthodox Cyrillic one, even if the Latin nationalism learned by Nicoară directly from Maior[230] had initially convinced him to think otherwise: "I have never hesitated to tell the Romanians that I like more the Latin script than the Cyrillic or the Russian one, and my letters, which I have written with Latin characters to every Romanian I know, stand proof to this.[231] But there are far more things to take into consideration, and especially the great number of Romanians who do not know the Latin characters, and the ones who do know them cannot understand Romanian when reading them."[232]

The pragmatic argument in favour of the use of the Cyrillic script (i.e., the number of those who are not familiar with the Latin alphabet) is nevertheless immediately doubled by the ideological-national argument, one of a much more portentous import: "What will the priests say when they see that the schools employ those letters which none of them can understand. Undoubtedly they are afraid that, one of these days, they might be compelled to learn to read Hungarian."[233]

Under the circumstances, the graphical signs have an "ethnicising" function, they acquire a national connotation apart from their cultural denotation. Just as for their opponents the Cyrillic letters are not "Cyrillic", but "Serbian", "Greek" or "Russian", the Latin letters cease to be, depending on the way they are conceived, "Latin" or even "Romanian" and become "Hungarian" signs. Nicoară describes how

> I know a lot of people who loudly claim that they see no other way for the cultivation of the Romanian people other than accepting the "Latin" or the "Hungarian" letters. But, believe me, these men do not do this because of their discerning judgement or solid reason, but only to make themselves agreeable and show their obedience to those who outrank them. Such men cannot desire the well-being and the welfare of the country, but desire to lead the country into confusion, folly and even further ignorance.[234]

In Nicoară's paradoxical variant, cultural decay and blindness would not come from the abandonment of the Latin alphabet but from its acceptance, its adoption being a mere diversion implemented by the Romanians' opponents, meant to alter the Romanians' national specificity and identity. The crisis provoked by the reconstruction of the collective identity, under the shock of the nationalist ideology, brought to the surface the most surprising self-conscious attitudes and reactions.[235]

In 1853 Simion Bărnuțiu attempted to conciliate these contradictions concerning the graphical sign representing the national identity through their permutation into another, more profound and more important, sphere of the national realities. It cannot be denied, however, that his discourse also evinced a mode proper to a projected future and a present transition: "Our literati take it upon themselves to change the Cyrillic letters to Latin ones. It is not enough. A language mixed with foreign barbarian words is still an ugly language whether it is written with Latin letters or with Cyrillic ones. First and foremost, one would have to change the foreign words and feelings with national feelings, which we have lost through ignorance and bad cheating, and then to dress these ones with letters and deeds that are worthy of our forefathers' memory."[236]

Thus it was not enough to change the alphabet. Everything had to be reshuffled in order to rebuild the initial lost configuration of the Romanians' true national identity, transmitted from their forebears—the Romans. In order to find that identity it was mandatory that all elements be refashioned and rearranged in their right places, within a structure that could not coagulate in the absence of perfect semiotic harmony.

Bărnuțiu thus imagined a veritable semiotic triad, in which the national *sign* of collective will, solidarity and action had to correspond to the adequate *signified*—the Latin word—clothed in the Latin script of the corresponding *signifier*. Should the relation between these three be distorted, at any of its signifying levels, it would not be possible to reach the sign of Truth, the true sense of national identity.

CHURCH AND RELIGION

GENERALITIES: PRELIMINARIES AND CONTEXT

Generally speaking, church and religion were, for the Transylvanian Romanians at the beginning of the modern age, one of the most important elements by means of which they defined their national identity—an obligatory presence in any coherent representation of the self-image. Certainly, when a more individualised positing of this general dimension was called for and the need felt to define, in more concrete terms, which particular church or religion was most able to express their collective specificity, things became more complicated, given the Romanian plurality of confessions.[237] In Transylvania and the eastern parts of Hungary the Orthodox and Greek Catholic populations were fairly equal, both in number and in terms of their political and cultural "importance", that is, in terms of symbolic representation and legitimacy, as compared to the whole national body. (This latter aspect was, undoubtedly, much more open to debate and controversy than the former.)

Besides such confessional divergences, for the intellectuals of the time the most important type of collective solidarity and identity was, needless to say, the national one, based on Herderian ethnic and linguistic considerations. From this viewpoint, church and religion (just like any other area of spiritual life) were categorically subsumed to the idea of nationality: they thus lost any autonomy and became, just like history, tradition or culture, mere factors expected to express the national principle.

For a better understanding, such a perspective must be looked at in the context of two other far-reaching processes of utmost importance: a) the religious dominant of pre-modern collective sensibilities, and b) the "crisis of the church" in the modern age.

First of all, we need to remember that modern nationalism, a child of the élite, is not only an extension of the flimsy medieval, scholarly and "voivodal" national consciousness (or the sense of the existence of a "people", as Romanian historiography puts it), but also an inheritor of the ethnic and collective forms of solidarity manifest at the level of traditional peasant mentality.[238]

Certainly, the cultural identity of the peasant community also included the ethnic-linguistic factor (often in its regional-dialectal variations). However, here it functioned as a reality brought to the collective awareness in an empirical way, not as an ideological, let alone metaphysical, principle, as was the case with the national identity imagined by the Herderian Romantics. On the other hand, at an ideological level, the collective solidarity of the traditional village was structured to a decisive extent by the religious factor, that is, by its confessional option. In terms of the inner life of the individual, it was religious belief (which did not always perfectly coincide with the "official" confession) and the particular techniques by means of which the culture of the community ensured the salvation of souls, that played the most important part in defining an identity, not the ethnic-national destiny, which did not exist as an ideological principle.

As with modern nationalism, in terms of the cultural identity of the traditional communities, religion and nationality were tightly and inextricably linked together. The difference is that traditional mentality sanctions a reversed order of priorities. Church and religion are not expressions of the national principle, but the other way round; confession is the main element that defines us, while ethnicity is the particular way in which this essential condition attains particular realisations. Under such circumstances, as Keith Hitchins, among others, has shown, towards the middle of the eighteenth century the Orthodox Transylvanian peasant could still feel, identity-wise, closer to the Orthodox Serbs than the Greek Catholic Romanians (of a similar social condition).[239]

It was on such fertile ground that the "nations-confessions" of the eighteenth century were able to grow, such as the "Illyrian" type of solidarity.[240] Just like the modern forms of nationalism in their incipient stage, these are pre-Herderian ideological confections, circulated among the high-culture élites. An important role here was played by the state, which organised them by means of such privileged juridical bills as the *Declaratorium Illyricum* or Leopold's *Diploma of Religious Union*—acts that also functioned, for the respective solidarity, as founding stereotypes. Yet, contrary to Herderian nationalism, these ideological formations were not based on the metaphysical principle of the "people" (whose specificity found expression in its ethnic-linguistic marks), but on the much more mundane and empirical reality of the confessional-religious dominant, active at the level of those segments of the population that underwent a redefinition of identity.

Ultimately, besides many other aspects that I cannot dwell on here, the general crisis of the traditional identity, induced by the impact of modernity, would cause the new "national" élites to take refuge in the Herderian type of solidarity rather than to opt for other solutions more congenial to a *status quo* and a (real, not invented) tradition that were being contested in every possible way—solutions such as "regional patriotism" (*Landespatriotismus*), dynastic or juridical-constitutional patriotism or nation-confession.[241]

The second major element circumscribing the relationship between church and nationality is the general phenomenon of the "crisis of the church" in the modern age. I will not dwell extensively on it, since it has received consistent and comprehensive attention in a number of studies (among them Alain Besançon's splendid essay).[242] I will simply note that this particular crisis engendered a powerful secularisation of society and of individual consciousness, not so much by the progress of atheism as by the definitive confinement of church and religion to the tight recess of a Sunday exercise, conscientiously practised, yet completely divorced from the problems of daily life. Despite the apparent respect it and its attendants still enjoyed, the church was separated from the society, while the prominent role it previously played, minute by minute, in the inner life of the people, was taken over by a confused collection of pagan beliefs, nationalisms and other ideologies, by means of which these mundane principles and realities became the object of a daily veneration and of an idolatrous cult. The church itself, anxious to regain the attention of its scattered flock involved in the contingent matters of society, took to politics, social activism and national militancy. It thus willingly estranged itself from its unique and true mission. The circle of the crisis of the church was thus definitively rounded off, drawn by its own hands.

Obviously, from such a perspective the subsuming of church and religion to nationality and their being labelled as distinctive signs of the national identity by the Transylvanian intellectuals at the beginning of the modern age fit in perfectly with the wider context of a general evolution and are best explained as such.

REPRESENTATIONS OF THE RELATIONSHIP BETWEEN CHURCH AND NATIONALITY

Let us look now at the concrete way in which the social representations relating to the church and religion became part of the process of the Transylvanian Romanians' self-definition. We will thus survey the expressive themes that structured those images.

The church-nation relationship was frequently mentioned in texts of the time, which insisted on the motif of religion as a support of nationality. Petru Maior placed at the basis of this rapport the national relevance of the Romanian Church, the use of the vernacular in the Mass, as well as the case of religious literature. This particularity was also, in his opinion, a sign of the Romanians' superiority over all the other Christian peoples. "This blessing grants the Romanians superiority over all other Christian nations, be they Greek, Russians, Serbs or papists of any tongue [obviously, in the heat of his demonstration, Maior "forgets" about the Protestants], for none of these understand what is being read in the sacred liturgy and other church books [...]; while with the Romanians, the language that the common people speak is the same as that in which the holy books are written."[243]

The idea that church and faith had always been two of the most important means of individuality-conservation in terms of language and ethnicity, able to counteract denationalising pressures, becomes an element of political-historical analysis but also an omnipresent stereotype in the self-image. George Bariț, for instance, mentions, among the factors that allow the Romanians of Transylvania to keep a national life intact, the church, considered as "the most powerful defence-wall of the Romanians' nationality".[244] Gavril Munteanu, too, believes that "the Romanians owe their existence uniquely to religion, this strong protection against what the future has in store for them."[245] Papiu Ilarian writes that, in past ages, the Romanians' ancestors, faced with foreign oppression, "still found a shelter in their church, where they could soothe the wounds they had received from foreign barbarians", since faith, the church and language are "the most sacred and precious guardians of each people".[246]

As can be seen in these quotes, when it comes to their relationship with nationality, no significant distinction is maintained between the church (as an institution) and religion (as faith). This is, nevertheless, sometimes conducive to an undermining of the "church as defender of the nation" cliché. Papiu Ilarian himself, among others, severely criticises the "priesthood" and the church for their lack of national zeal. It is the institution of the church that has been managing the spiritual and cultural life of the Romanians for centuries, that has overseen the schooling and illumination of the people, and what has become of them? Obscurantism reigns among the people, while the church often serves as a means by which foreign interests and the threat of denationalisation penetrate their national space. Obviously, such a harsh critique, capable of shattering one of the basic stereotypes of the collective imaginary, would give rise to equally inflamed responses, such as that of the Greek Catholic bishopric of Oradea, which took deep offence at the attacks launched by the young people around Papiu.[247]

Certainly, it cannot be said that such critical stances managed to displace an idea that would continue to permeate Romanian culture, particularly since the distinction between the church and its superior hierarchy could at any moment easily brush away the contradiction.

On the other hand, there was another pervasive theme relative to the religion-nationality relationship that capitalised precisely on such matters of substance that told apart ethnicity from confession. As we have seen in the chapter devoted to the issue of resistance to denationalisation, the overlapping of religion and ethnicity was a phenomenon fiercely criticised both by the intellectuals of the Transylvanian School and by Bărnuțiu's Romantic generation.

Maior criticised "those renegades" who believed that "once religion is removed, nationality follows in its wake".[248] Bărnuțiu, too, took offence at the fact that "once the rite is taken away from the Romanian, he will know nothing of his nation either", yet disagreed in an extensive argumentation with those who

> cannot conceive how it could be that someone still belongs to the Romanians while, religion-wise, he is part of the Reformed Church; they who are so weak of mind will not see that if there could be Romans in Italy while they were still of pagan faith, so much the more can someone stay Romanian and confess to it while being of Calvinist faith; for the Calvinists are themselves Christian, and we should not mingle religious faiths and the theologians' disputes with nationality; nationality, or nation, or people, is one thing, and religion, or law, or faith, is quite another.[249]

In 1846 Bariț also concluded that "we have had enough experience to be able to tell nationality from religion".[250]

Why this frequent emphasis on the distinction between religion and nationality, elsewhere thought to be inseparable? Because, as the Transylvanian intellectuals claimed, there had often been, throughout history, Romanians who changed their confession and embraced Calvinism or Roman Catholicism. To insist on the equivalence between religion and nationality, on confession as a mark of national identity, on the fact that one could not be a Romanian unless one abided by the "Romanian law" (be it Orthodox or Greek Catholic), would automatically lead to the exclusion of those Romanians with a different confessional orientation from the national body. This was the exact opposite of the wishes of Maior or Micu, Bărnuțiu or Bariț. They fiercely criticised those Romanians who, by changing their faith, also abandoned their nationality, and tried to demonstrate that these were completely different things and that one could, and had to, keep one's ethnic-national identity even if opting for another confession.

Obviously, these intellectuals did not feel particularly easy about their co-nationals' religious conversion either, but the fact remains that, especially in this context, they criticised it only very little, if at all. Firstly, because it was simply the state of things and could not be ignored, and secondly, because the Enlightenment, in its Josephine variant, for instance, had deeply imprinted upon their consciousness the lesson of (particularly religious) tolerance. If an individual, making use of the free will of his conscience, wished to choose another confession, it was his political and natural right to do so. It was, nevertheless, contrary to the moral commandments, so the Transylvanian intellectuals believed, that he should, in the process, abandon his national community as well.

Certainly, such a distinction between religion and nationality was blatantly contrary to other systems of argumentation, which underlined the inseparability of the two. It could also be alleged, at least in theoretical terms, that the Romanians who also dropped their national identity on the way to a different faith were acting under the ideological pressure of the thesis maintaining that Romanianness necessarily equalled the two Oriental confessions that made up the "Romanian law".

The ambiguity of the answers given at the time to the question of whether one could still be a Romanian while being a Calvinist or a Roman Catholic; the risky tightrope that the Transylvanian intellectuals endeavoured to walk in their attempt to cover the distance between religion and nationality, can be demonstrated by means of two contradictory arguments. The first is to be found in Petru Maior's testament (a text of utmost importance for the inner life of its author), which announces the setting up of a scholarship fund at the Catholic college in Tîrgu Mureş, for the young men of his family, or otherwise "for any young Romanian man in the eminent county of Turda, preferably of noble family, be they Greek Catholic or Roman Catholic".[251] It follows that Maior can have seen no incompatibility between being a Roman Catholic and being a Romanian; furthermore (and, apparently, strangely enough for the author of the *Procanon*), Orthodox believers, although Romanian, were not able to benefit from this foundation—a decision that can be explained either in view of the difficulty of receiving Orthodox students in a Catholic college, or by a closer analysis of Petru Maior's choices regarding his national, confessional and social identity.

The second document that speaks of contrary orientations is a letter sent by the Roman Catholic inhabitants of Roşia Montană to Avram Iancu, in January 1849, in which they (in all probability as a response to the Romanian leaders' summons) reaffirm their loyalty to the imperial cause and at the same time express their desire for an amiable cohabitation with the Romanians. Significantly, at least a quarter of those who signed the letter bore clearly Romanian names ("Iosif Buzdugan", "Al. Cornea", "Ioan Dregan"), could probably speak Romanian, and may well have been considered as being of Romanian ethnicity. Yet, their Catholic orientation is reason enough for them to consider themselves, and to be considered, as members of another community, different from the Romanian one. As such, they related to the Romanians as strangers and, undoubtedly, would have to suffer, alongside the Hungarians, Germans or Czechs, the consequences of the Moîṭi's reprisals, which often ended, as they did in May 1849, in their setting part of the town on fire.[252] One cannot be a Romanian and a Catholic at the same time—such was the moral designed to rewrite the identity of these deviating, hateful people.[253]

In any event, all these vacillations as to the relationship between religion and nationality, which either underlined the distinction between the two or sought to consecrate their identification, advanced the ideal of the subsuming of confession to nation and the replacement of religion as ideological principle and identity-shaping dominant by the metaphysical principle of ethnicity. Nation-ethnicity became the new god of the modern age, which the Romantic intellectuals—the great priests of this new religion who fashioned its face and "acknowledged" its sacredness—wished to turn into the object of a daily mystical adoration by the crowds.

This pagan belief was to replace the old religion, whose emotional impact and force of persuasion it sought to undermine. As Papiu Ilarian admirably put it in his translation of, and comments on, Desprez, "the Romanian patriots choose to admire in this popular belief the naive cult of nationality and, driven by a zealous belief in this religion, they would be glad, I should think, to see the image of Trajan the Divine replace the saints of their church [...]; the Christian religion itself could not efface the Roman festivities and celebrations from the concerns of the Romanians. And all this declares the vigour and everlasting dominion of the Romanian nationality."[254] Church and religion, weaker than nationality, are definitively subordinated to the nation and have no other option than to identify completely with its destiny.

THE VENERABLE AGE AND PURITY OF ROMANIAN CHRISTIANITY AS FEATURES OF NATIONAL IDENTITY

That identification and profession of a common destiny were associated quite early on with a spectacular historical myth able to legitimate that destiny: the motif of the venerable age of Christianity in its Romanian variant. The age, continuity and pure Roman origins of the Romanian people had to find perfect equivalents in the similar attributes of the Romanians' religion. The Romanians, Petru Maior wrote in 1813, "are as singular in the age of their religion as they are most bright among the nations in their kin".[255]

The myth thus emerged of a people born Christian, who had received their belief directly from the apostles. In the same way that the Romans' blood had flowed unaltered in their veins, their Christian faith was the direct inheritor of the teachings preached by Christ's disciples themselves, a pure first-hand decantation of the original: "I am assured that the Romanians' ancestors", writes the same Maior in his church *History*—a natural counterpart of the other, national, *History*, "brought to Dacia Christ's faith in their bosoms just as they carried Roman blood in their veins, so that, among the Roman citizens whom Trajan sent to Dacia, some were Christians, some of whom, the older ones, may even have met the leaders of the apostles, Peter and Paul, and received the holy word from their mouths."[256]

The lack of any "official" data as to the moment of the Romanians' Christianisation or the missionaries who had performed their conversion (which the Germans, Slavs and Hungarians did possess) was turned into a positive argument in favour of the long presence of Christianity among the Romanians. They did not need missionaries to Christianise them, as the other peoples did, since they were born Christian and had always been Christian.[257] "That the Christian faith was received among the Romanians from the very beginning of the preaching of Christ's Gospel by the apostles in the old times, is proved without the shadow of a doubt by the fact that there is no writer who can be said to have recorded the beginning of the Romanians' turning to the Christian faith."[258]

Several years later Dimitrie Țichindeal would take over Maior's theory and give it even greater factuality by completely doing away with the few questions marks that the master had still preserved: "Some of our ancestors received the Christian faith from the mouths of the apostles Peter and Paul in Rome, and in the days of Emperor Trajan brought it here to Dacia: to Banat, to the Romanian Country and to Moldavia."[259] Țichindeal takes this as a basis in his argument for another very important idea, that is, the purity of the Romanians' Christianity: "A faith such as that received from the lips of the greatest apostles could only be of the purest stock and spared of any madness."[260]

In order that the preservation of this purity throughout the centuries should seem plausible, additional credibility came with the postulate of the Romanians' religious traditionalism, of their aversion to any sort of change, no matter how insignificant, in the "law". As can be expected, the empirical ethnographic observation could provide here a rich basis of argumentation.

Bariț values this conservative tendency: it is a natural thing that "the Romanian, now as ever, hates and banishes from his soul any innovation, small as it may be, in the least important religious customs."[261]

It is true that the positive evaluation of that inclination could easily clash with enlightened criticism, which was opposed to all prejudice and the rigidity of "obsolete customs". Nevertheless, in this respect the Transylvanian intellectuals preferred to sacrifice critical rationalism for the sake of historicist and national traditionalism. Faced with this taboo in religious tradition, Petru Maior, just like other enlightened intellectuals, tries to keep a balance between Voltairean ridicule and the nationalist discipline, in writing about "the ancestors' law and the churchly rule, to which many Romanians are still so devoted in their heart that in these matters they still fear their own shadow", that is, when it comes to changes in this respect.[262] Although Maior largely agrees with that conservative tendency, one can sense, in this passage, a certain touch of irony at the traditionalist stiffness of his co-nationals.

THE FOUR IDENTITY-RELATED FORMULAS OF ROMANIAN PLURI-CONFESSIONALISM

When a more exact circumscribing of the problems arising from the general issue of the Romanians' "church and religion" was envisaged, the immediate reality of an extreme confessional variety came into focus. At the level of the self-image, this state of things was translated as the motif of the Romanians' disunion, of their divided national will due to religious clashes.

Besides the fundamental scission between the two main confessions, the religious ideological spectrum was further complicated by the existence of various trends within the two: the "Latinist" tendency (otherwise defined, maybe excessively, as "ultramontane") of the Greek Catholics, as represented by bishops such as Atanasie Rednic, Ioan Bob and Ioan Lemeny; the Jansenist and Gallican orientation, with Uniates like Grigore Maior, Petru Maior or Simion Bărnuțiu; in the case of Orthodox believers from Hungary, the groups in the vicinity of the Serbian hierarchy who were in favour of the preservation of what they called the strictly Orthodox tradition, adherents to the Cyrillic alphabet and fierce adversaries of Greek Catholicism; other Orthodox tendencies, which favoured collaboration with the Uniate Church and the idea of adopting the Latin alphabet and the Gregorian calendar, as did Dimitrie Țichindeal in Banat, or the Transylvanian bishop Vasile Moga. The picture is even more complex than the sketch given here, as intermediary areas appeared even between these options.[263]

In a more simplified picture, three (or maybe four) main confessional formulas can be detected, each of them vying for supremacy in terms of identity: both for the conservation and promotion of their own identity and for claiming as great an amount of equivalence as possible between themselves and the national identity.

The first two formulas are represented by the legitimating ideological and identity-based systems of the two confessions, Uniate and Orthodox, which, despite the trends within and the projects of unification from without, were extremely keen on, and could by no means give up the idea of, the preservation of their own individuality, justified in dogmatic, historical and organisational terms.

The third formula, far from functioning as a compromise between the first two or as a link that might tone down confessional divergences, simply introduced yet another combatant in the dispute. This new confessional expression, which might be called the third way[264], was fairly ambiguous and, consequently, hard to define. Its adherents, usually of a Greek Catholic orientation (although sometimes Orthodox as well), primarily capitalised on the Eastern substance of the two Romanian confessions and thus searched for the common elements of identity to be found in the rite, the customs and, partially, in the canonical rights.[265] They wished for a national church that would be neither "Catholic" nor "Orthodox", but more than anything else "Romanian". What they implied here, however, by such terms as "Orthodox" and "Catholic", was primarily the other's formal dependence on the Serbian Metropolitan See of Sremski Karlovci or on the (Hungarian!) Roman Catholic Archbishopric of Esztergom, and not the dogmatic basis of the confession proper.

In reality, the promoters of this formula, usually men of the church, were absolutely adamant about preserving the dogmatic core of their faith, which, undoubtedly, was the most important religious ingredient and also the provider of the main element of identity for the respective confession. Moreover (as an unavoidable symbolic expression of this dogmatic core), they did not wish to undo their links with the supreme spiritual authority either: union with Rome for the Greek Catholics and communion with the patriarchy in Constantinople and the rest of the Orthodox world for the others.

This is why it can be said that each of the promoters of the third confessional way, whether Orthodox or Uniate, actually believed that such unity could be realised if the others renounced their formula, while they themselves were to keep the dogmatic core of their faith on which the new church would be founded and simply do away with the "extremist" exterior elements ("Latinist" or "Slavic") and with the subordination to a foreign hierarchical authority (at the medium, i.e., not supreme, level), be it Hungarian or Serb.

Obviously, in religious or dogmatic terms—which alone could be taken into account if it were, after all, religion and not the nationalist ideology that mattered—the hypocritical issue of "confessional unification" or of a national church could only be solved in practical terms by opting for one of the extant solutions at the level of historical reality: either the engulfing of one confession by the other or the unaltered preservation of the identity and integrity of each of them.[266] From this point of view, unlike the adherents of religious unification proper, the promoters of the "third confessional formula" (actually conceived as a way of advancing their own religious identity, either Uniate or Orthodox) gave proof not only of their confessionalism and attachment to their own religious faith, but also of a pragmatism and an insight which was ahead of their age.

There were also projects envisaging unification on strictly national bases, not on religious-dogmatic ones. These might be said to figure as a fourth tendency, although such a tendency was not as clearly delineated as the others, since, on the one hand, the actions (and sometimes even the persons) of its promoters could be identified with those of the adherents of the third way, and, on the other, it always relied on a number of isolated individuals, or a group of intellectuals, deprived of actual power over church structures and motivated by strictly political circumstances and intentions.

Such projects would be put forward as part of the ambience of Emperor Joseph's anti-papal policy, and particularly during the 1848 revolution when the formula of a national church was just another piece in the whole institutional picture projected by the leaders in the interests of the much-desired autonomous Romanian community. The belief was that the Romanian Metropolitan See, which enjoyed a certain type of autocephaly and comprised all the Romanian bishoprics of the monarchy, that is, both Orthodox and Uniate, was the institutional-organisational formula capable of solving this problem.[267]

Whom this metropolitan bishop (more of a superintendent than a divinely ordained high priest) was to mention in his prayers, or in what manner he would administrate the sacred communion, were, for the political leaders of 1848, mere useless theological conundrums which had nothing to do with the real problems of the nation.[268] Nevertheless, had such theological "trifles" (which were at the same time the basis of confessional identity) been abandoned, church and religion would have been completely bereaved of their true substance and become mere annexes to the nationalist ideology. They would have had to fulfil the propagandistic role[269] of leading their flock not so much to the salvation of their souls and towards the heavenly kingdom, as to the completion of the national destiny.[270]

We will survey in the following the way in which the identities of these confessional formulas manifested themselves, as well as their relationship with the overall image of the national identity, in looking at the expressive motifs and justifying themes that illustrate them.

THE GREEK CATHOLIC FORMULA

Naturally, Greek Catholicism built its identity schema primarily on arguments supporting the act of union with Rome and on the highlighting of certain

"Latinate" aspects. Inevitably, it was this element alone that could stress its particular character, its specific aspect, because its other feature, that is, the Eastern rite, could only underline its resemblance to the Orthodox faith and thus jeopardise its distinct identity.[271]

Following in the footsteps of a tradition of searching into the pragmatic reasons that might have motivated the authors of the union documents at the beginning of the eighteenth century, Bishop Inochentie Micu insists, in 1735, on the political, cultural and legal advantages that the religious union might have had for the Romanian population: "By uniting with the Catholic Church, the Romanian nation dismissed any impediment that might have prevented it from occupying public offices, and invented the Leopoldine diploma for any public high office."[272]

Such national advantages, which bore no connection to the spiritual content of the religious union, would generally be acknowledged, even by those who later on would contest Greek Catholicism for other reasons. Papiu Ilarian, for instance, who, unlike Micu, would deny the fact that union with Rome might have brought any political improvement, at least admits the existence of the incontestable cultural progress it might have triggered: "Through union with the Church of Rome, although the political and religious distance promised by the emperor's diplomas remained a mere stipulation, a new epoch is born for our intellectual culture."[273]

Adherence to Greek Catholicism was not simply identified by the respective faithful believers with accession to a better political and cultural status but was also considered a main factor of religious and confessional identity. Otherwise, especially once the differences in status between the Uniates and the Orthodox gradually disappeared (which, in some people's opinion, had never in practice existed), one might have said that religious union could no longer find any reason to exist.

In the circumstances, Greek Catholicism naturally built itself an auto-legitimising system based especially on arguments of an ideological nature; it also invented a justifying history, by, for instance, imagining a specific manner of symbolic correlation with the nation's interests.

Thus Greek Catholicism mainly insisted on presenting itself as a way of highlighting the Romanians' Western identity, as well as on the idea of their Latin heritage. It thus put forward the metaphor of the Romanians' attachment to Rome as a symbolic foundation for these two essential factors that defined the Romanians' collective identity. From this position, Eastern identity (which overlapped with Orthodoxy) was fought against in a polemics that mainly surfaced in attacks against the "Greeks".

In the eighteenth century and at the beginning of the nineteenth, the "Greeks" were a perfect target for attacks against Eastern identity, as they were most readily liable to contemporary negative allusions with respect to their cultural domination over the principalities and the Phanariots, but also the cultural-linguistic and economic competition between the Romanian and Greek communities of Braşov or Pest. Obviously, these "Greeks" are more of a conjectural metaphor, hostility towards them being in fact mitigated by opposition to their "Oriental" character, confused with the Orthodox confession, an opposition assumed in the name of Western identity, indicated by Rome and Catholicism. When the "Greeks", these necessary enemies, diminished as a concrete presence, the hostile image of the Eastern identity would shift its focus mainly onto the Serbs and the Russians, as symbols of Orthodoxy and of the opposing confessional identity.

In 1746 Gherontie Cotore perfectly illustrated this multiple ideological legitimisation of Greek Catholicism by means of his Latinist writings.[274] Firstly, he overlapped the religious union with the idea of Latin origins: "I know that we do not feel like separating from the Church of Rome, because we too are the offspring of Rome, and, during the reign of Trajan, our ancestors are said to have sprung from those parts of the country."[275]

He then dramatically stresses the motivations for differentiation from the "Greeks": they have been punished by divine wrath for the surrender of Constantinople to the Turks, as a consequence of their separation from the mother-church of Rome.[276] The Romanians, too, have been punished because of this schism, which is the cause of the present decay of their nation. The only chance of getting divine grace back is to return to the arms of the Roman Church, otherwise the Romanians will lose their souls and suffer great earthly sorrows:

> And the Greeks were punished because of this very fact, namely that they separated from the Church of Rome. [...] And our nation came to be dominated by the barbarians because of this very separation. [...] Remember this, oh once famous nation, so that, in falling prey to the artfulness of the Greeks [...], to the worldly kingdom, you might not lose, besides other punishments, the celestial world as well, which you will undoubtedly reach once you have united with the Head of the Church, which you have abandoned because of the ruse of the Greeks.[277]

Petru Maior, too, speculates on the antagonism between the East and the West, between the envious and corrupting "Greeks" and the "Italians" or the "Latins" who are our brothers and with whom we inevitably share the same religious and civilising identity. Maior detects the evil that had, by means of the foreigners' conniving, temporarily taken the Romanians away from the sphere of civilisation to which they would normally belong, at the moment of the legendary abandonment of the Latin alphabet in favour of the Cyrillic one—a graphical sign that overlaps with confessional identity. Obviously, "the cunning of the Greeks" was the cause of this deviation, while Metropolitan Bishop Theoctist simply acted as an instrument of these machinations. Maior writes that the bishop "thought that if the Romanians preserved the Latin letters for a longer period of time, given that the Italians too had the same letters, they would start writing books in favour of the already accomplished union, and, reading these books, the Romanians would agree to union with the Romans and the Italians, their brothers, and thus the deal with the Greeks would be abandoned. [...] Undoubtedly, the cause of the Romanians' misfortune is the domination of the Greeks, and after them, that of the Serbs over all Romanians and Italians."[278]

Just like Maior, Samuil Micu tries to fashion a new history of (let us say) the Romanians' "Greek Catholicism" in the years leading up to 1700, since the confession in question, identified, of course, in a rather confused way, had always represented the Romanians' true church. In the sixteenth century, Micu claims, during the Counter Reformation, "the Latin Catholics suffered many hardships, and so did the Romanians, and the princes of Transylvania thought it necessary to erase the Catholic faith for good and to instil the Calvinist faith into the Romanians"; obviously, "the Romanians are like stones when it comes to their Latin faith, ready to suffer all evil rather than abandon their mother-faith."[279]

In trying to delimit the sphere of their confessional identity, Micu places the Romanians alongside the Roman Catholics in their common fight against the advocates of reform, just as they had been allies before against the Greek Orthodox "schism". The affinity imagined by the Transylvanian scholar goes as far as delimiting the "Catholics abiding by the Latin law" from the Romanians, who would therefore be the "Catholics" abiding by the Greek law. And these denominations refer to the traditional Romanian Orthodox Transylvanian Church of the sixteenth century!

This paradoxical imprecision with respect to the notion of "Catholic" (based on the original etymological sense of the term) was common in the confessional vocabulary of the epoch, since the authors of the 1798 Orthodox project of church unification proposed that the new ecclesiastical structure should be called "the Eastern Church of Orthodox Greek rite, that is to say Catholic".[280] The problem was that the Greek Catholics who promoted it attributed to it a Latin connotation, meant to highlight the fact that the Romanian church, despite some brief accidents, had always been "Catholic", that is, united with the Church of Rome whose offspring it was.

The followers of the Transylvanian School also promoted the identity value of the Uniate Romanians' "Catholicism" towards the middle of the nineteenth century. In 1847 in the *Mouthpiece of Enlightenment*, Theodor Aaron, for instance (later churchman of the Lugoj Greek Catholic Bishopric), who resumed the philological-national polemics of Petru Maior), translated a text referring to the relationship between Roman Catholicism and Greek Catholicism, arguing for the essential identity of the two confessions. While differences in rites were to be respected, the essence of faith, that is, its dogmatic aspect, was common to both. In an epoch marked by confessional differences but also by unification projects based on national grounds, Aaron attempted to rediscover the semantics of the term "Catholic", vital to his confessional identity: "With the Romanians, the word 'Catholic' [...] came to designate a scornful word labelling the simple or the blind; in Hungary, the Romanians from Banat feel ridiculed when mocked at by the Serbs who call them 'Catholics'."[281] Aaron clearly condemns this mentality, showing that the characteristic denoting true religious identity must be assumed without any complex.

In the *Mouthpiece of Enlightenment* Timotei Cipariu, editor-in-chief of the gazette, also contributed to the fashioning of the Greek Catholic historical identity, stressing the resemblance to Western Catholicism, which might testify to a tradition of affinities and good mutual relations. The shift to Catholicism during the reign of Ioniță the Beautiful; marriages between the Romanian voivodes and Catholic ladies; the existence of certain bishops of the Latin rite in Argeș, Milcov or Severin represented just a few pointers, invoked in favour of the ideological legitimisation of confessional specificity and identity, as compared to the historical past and the nation's destiny.[282]

THE ORTHODOX FORMULA

The Orthodox believers were in a more favourable position than the Uniate Romanians with regard to the legitimisation of their identity schema. The appeal to tradition, on behalf of the Orthodox character of the Romanian church until the eighteenth century, represented a very solid argument, capable of identifying the Romanians' historical past with their Orthodox nature. Moreover, the prevalence of the same confession in the principalities was another legitimising evidence of the utmost relevance.

Under the circumstances, since they did not feel the need to fashion a more or less imagined past as the Uniates did, the Orthodox believers affirmed their identity particularly through an ideological confrontation with the Greek Catholics. The thing to be demonstrated was that the confessional option of the latter represented, in fact, a rupture with the Romanians' church body and tradition, and that atonement for the religious disputes could only be accomplished by their return to Orthodoxy. The fact that the Uniate Romanians abided by the same rite and Eastern "law" was one more justification able pave their way back to the mother-religion.

Thus the promoters of the Orthodox identity primarily dedicated their time to rejecting arguments in favour of religious union. Significantly, while the Uniate Romanians defensively upheld their position and mainly looked for reasons to support it, the Orthodox chose to assail the others, concentrating more on the debunking of the opponents' defence rather than on emphasising their own specificity. They did not have to defend themselves against anything, because, in their opinion, their position represented an organic, natural reality born with the nation, and not a choice deliberately assumed at a certain moment.

Moise Nicoară's arguments on these lines are comprehensive. Firstly, he rejects the thesis of the political and pragmatic advantages that such a religious union might have triggered, thus attempting to dismiss its original justification. In a dialogue with an imaginary interlocutor—an advocate of the union—the scholar from Arad rhetorically asks: "How much have the Romanians profited from this Union, and if they have, what are these advantages? [...] How many Uniate Romanians in high and even minor offices does he know in these counties? [...] Is there in all Hungary and Transylvania a single Uniate Romanian who is a landowner too or who honours or helps the Romanian nation in any way? No one can certify to this." In contrast, Nicoară believes, in a complete reversal of his opponents' argumentation, that there were Romanians in high office in Bihor before the religious union, but this is no longer the case.[283]

The danger of the religious union, he argues, firstly comes from what one might call (to use a consecrated phrase of the present) its anti-Romanian character. It is nothing but a diversionary tactic employed by foreigners in their attempts to denationalise the Romanians, since all Greek Catholics of a certain status actually mean to shift to Roman Catholicism so that they can eventually "Hungarianise" or "Germanise" themselves. Here, Nicoară very forecefully attacks the very Latin component of the Uniate confession—an element that brings its advocates closer to the Romanians' national enemies, which makes them all the easier to assimilate. Such an understanding permits an identification of Ortho-doxy with Romanianness and of Greek Catholicism with the foreigners, thus lay-ing the foundations for a future successful idea: that of Orthodox nationalism. According to Nicoară:

> The Uniate Romanians who study and thrive or simply learn trades, no sooner do they take off the ancient dress of the Romanian nation [...] than they abandon the Romanian church as well. They do not only abandon the Romanian Uniate Church but also totally relinquish its law, and since they are told from their early infancy that their law is the papist law, they do not want to know anything about the Romanian church and desert it and embrace the papist law. As a consequence they cannot be considered Romanian, and, thus, forsaking the law, they forsake their Romanian flesh and blood [...]; and has anyone ever seen a Uniate Romanian espousing a Romanian woman?[284]

Marriage to foreign women is thus the sure sign of denationalisation.

Nicoară also attempts to bring in theological arguments, bearing on the speci-ficity of the Catholic religion, in order to back up his anti-union philippics. "His [the Catholic's] law teaches him that he who does not obey the papist law will not deserve divine grace and will not be saved. Now you can understand all their do-ings by which they mean to turn all Romanians papists."[285]

Pursuing this Orthodox train of thought, strictly identified with the national interest, Nicoară comes to cultivate, from an ideological point of view, too, the idea of closeness to the co-religious people of other ethnic groups, such as the Serbs or the Russians.[286] The role of the Russians as protectors of Orthodoxy (due, if to nothing else, at least to their power) is invoked in support of the tradition of the ideological and confessional relations between Orthodox Transylvania and Russia throughout the eighteenth century[287]: "The Romanians who moved to Russia thrive so well that there are whole regiments of them in that country."[288] They occupy very high positions there, Nicoară states, which is in blatant opposi-tion to discrimination against them in the Austrian monarchy. Moreover, "when the Romanians were chased by law from Transylvania the Russians helped them, so that it once happened that an escaping Transylvanian bishop could make it to the Russian land and flee the claws of death."[289]

If the Greek Catholics were somehow able to rest assured because "Rome", Western identity, "the Italians", etc. supported them, the Orthodox, too, felt the need to invoke at times of spiritual crisis such confessional solidarity, relating to Eastern identity, to the Byzantine heritage, to Constantinople, Jerusalem or Mos-cow.[290]

Obviously, for other political or national reasons, this closeness too could be severely censured as sheer national betrayal, as Ion Ionescu of Brad does in 1849. He views things from the perspective of a Transylvanian settled in the principali-ties and educated there in the anti-Russian and liberal spirit of the enlightened scholars of Wallachia:

> The Russian propaganda in Banat and Transylvania is terrible for the Romanians. It en-trusts us with the name of brothers, having the same law and religion, and precisely because of this religion they manage somehow to mislead us into praising them. It is an awful thing to believe that the Russians [who had just occupied the principalities, defeating the advo-

cates of the revolution] are our brothers and friends. Because of this freedom the Hungarians meant to take our nationality away from us, and because of this religion the Russians attempted to enslave us. The wretched friars are the instruments of the Russians' ascendancy in Banat and Transylvania, and even Şaguna, the bishop of Sibiu, welcomed the Russians with open arms.[291]

Here, just as in the case of Moise Nicoară's incriminations against the Greek Catholics, the confusion triggered by the manipulation of confessional identities for the benefit of the national principle could lead to the most paradoxical and violent allegations.

The fusion of Orthodoxy and nationalism, the idea of founding a new church that was to be at the same time Orthodox and nationalistic, thus rejecting any possible project of confessional unification on more or less equal grounds, would materialise in the context of the action initiated by Şaguna, with a view to "restoring" an independent Orthodox Metropolitan Church.[292] The bishop and his supporters put forward their proposal by means of an extensive historical argumentation ("the Romanian Oriental Metropolitan Church of Alba Iulia" had supposedly existed "from the spreading of the Christian faith in this part of the country until the end of the seventeenth century"[293]). They also relied on the resourceful motivation of the particularistic-national character of the organisation and hierarchy of the Orthodox Church, opposed to Catholic universalism, which was incompatible, they believed, with such national structures. Only Orthodoxy (not Catholicism) could build such a national church because of certain specific and essential traits rooted in the very dogmatic core of the two confessions:

> The right of the Romanian church to have a [national] head is legitimised by its Constitution, based on the rite of the Oriental church, which requires that the church of a nation, from an administrative point of view, should be self-reliant and unconstrained by the church of any other nation.
>
> Besides this, the Oriental church is national because the Mass and the administrative issues are performed in the national language, and although the Oriental church has only one canonical right, still its administration is based on the needs, requests and habits of their own nations, because, finally, the priests, from the metropolitan bishop to the last deacon, have so far lived by the benevolence of the nations.
>
> The unity of the bishops, of the metropolitan bishops and of the patriarchs of different nations, having the same faith, conditioned by the Constitution of the Oriental church, does not depend on administrative matters but on purely dogmatic ones, which is to say on the sharing of the same dogmas, and on the observation of certain churchly habits, exclusively ceremonial, like the divine worship, which requires that, in the prayers for divine mercy, the holy bishop should mention the metropolitan bishop, who, in his turn, should mention the patriarch, even if this latter is a foreigner.
>
> According to its dogmas the Oriental church considers that its head is Jesus Christ. It thus urges us to believe in an unseen head, a belief that differs from the Roman Catholic Church, inasmuch as, from an administrative point of view, it appoints a head of the church elected by the very nation he represents, and even if some nations embrace the same faith the head can be different, collectively or individually. This is how, with the Greek and the Russians, for instance, the church is administrated by means of a synod, while with the Romanians it is administrated by a metropolitan bishop, etc. The Roman Catholic Church forms a perfect assemblage, both from a dogmatic point of view and from an administrative point of view, and its hierarchy has a system that disregards nationality. As a proof of what I have claimed so far you can take almost every page of the canonical law and of Oriental church dogma.[294]

On the solid basis of such argumentation, constructed by Şaguna in 1864 when he obtained the status of metropolitan see for his church, and in 1868 when the normative document legalising its functioning was adopted[295], Transylvanian Orthodoxy announced the future position of the Romanian national church. Its confessional tendency was to merge completely with the national identity. One could not be a true Romanian unless one was a true Orthodox believer, since the fate of the nation was one with the fate of its church. The evolution of the relationship between the ideology of autocephalic Orthodoxy and nationalism as an all-embracing social principle was to take one more step: the willing subordination of the national church (the offspring of a Byzantine-Russian tradition) to the one "Caesar" it itself acknowledged: the national state.

"THE THIRD WAY": UNITY OF CONFESSIONS

The pleas for a third confessional formula, one which would be neither Catholic nor Orthodox but specifically Romanian, and, in this sense, congruent with the Eastern tradition of the church rite practised by the Romanians, found solid bases in Greek Catholicism, which seemed to correspond, at least from a certain point of view, with all the criteria listed above. The only problematic point concerned the universalist nature of Catholicism in general (apart from the rite practised in a particular church), as symbolised by the special relationship it had with the papal see.

As far as this latter objection was concerned, there were, both within Catholicism and (on a larger scale) at the level of the papal policy regarding Eastern Catholicism, strong ideological elements able to legitimate the "specifist", local tendencies of the Uniate churches. After the 1596 Council of Brest the Catholic offensive of the Counter Reformation made decisively its own the idea of preserving the Eastern specificity of the new churches that had embraced the formula of religious union, precisely in order to draw them closer to Rome.[296] Petru Maior captured the essence of this policy in an extremely suggestive phrase, speaking of the need to tread softly on Orthodox sensibilities: "More flies will get stuck in honey than in vinegar."[297]

Secondly, at the end of the eighteenth century that tendency received an additional stimulus from another direction, that is, from Austrian state politics. The rationalist bent of Josephine policy, which sought to extend state control even over the church, thus subordinating it to its own interests, obviously came into conflict with Rome and opposed any ultramontane tendency. Gallicanism and Jansenism—which encouraged the particularism of the "national" Catholic churches and criticised papal policies—furnished the useful theoretical bases for the policy advanced under Emperor Joseph.[298]

It was on this fertile ground that Petru Maior's ideological efforts flourished, as, for instance, in his early work *Procanon*, in which he simply justifies, by means of Jansenist and Gallican arguments, the church politics of Joseph II, in a line of thought which he had undoubtedly embraced while in Vienna between 1779 and 1780.[299] In refuting the claims of the Western church to supremacy and papal infallibility[300], Maior cogently highlights the sources that had helped him articulate his opinions: "By the Lord's grace, the Germans have finally begun to see and discover all those schemes devised in Rome, and are now searching into the teachings of the Holy Fathers and into the old customs of the church and are putting them into practice, as can be seen from most of the decrees issued by the mighty Emperor Joseph II, which he has made known and obeyed everywhere."[301] Similar echoes, also due to a Viennese formation, can be found in Samuil Micu's work.[302]

At the same time, however, Maior's efforts laid the solid bases for a particularist, "specifist" line within the Greek Catholic Church of Transylvania, a line which wove its way until it identified with the nationalist idea of a Romanian Eastern Church, at least in project—which I have called the third confessional formula. Although derived from within Greek Catholicism and never intent on transgressing its limits, the new formula tried to re-tailor its identity on the basis of several elements taken as essential. They bore on Eastern specificity, on the idea of autonomy, on synodal bases (hence the attacks against papal supremacy and infallibility) and on the appeal for the preservation of the specifically Romanian tradition of this church.

The formula launched by Maior in *Procanon* and taken up again in his *History of the Church* in 1813, was to know a long career, illustrated towards the middle of the next century especially by Simion Bărnuțiu.[303] It obviously offered an extremely attractive solution for the materialisation of the political projects of completing a national church.

Like the other two confessional formulas, the tendency under discussion elaborated a tradition capable of legitimating it, and then tried to define itself against its adversaries: "The Romanians of Transylvania", writes Petru Maior, "became united with the Church of Rome in faith, not in law, for they have always kept the Greek law, even after the union, and to this day are loyal to it; and they do it even better and with more devotion than can be seen in the churches of the non-united Serbs."[304] These Romanians, united with the Roman Catholics in dogmatic terms, are, therefore, otherwise better "Orthodox" devotees than the Orthodox Serbs themselves![305]

The ceaseless oscillation between such paradoxical refusals of, and identifications with, one or the other of the two "competing" confessions with a view to evincing now the differences, now the common, "unifying" elements, and, ultimately, the superiority of the third formula, are the main technique it used for putting forth its identity-shaping potential.

The theme of the purity of the Romanians' variant of Christianity and the historical myth according to which they had preserved unaltered the faith they had received directly from the apostles, as they had done their Roman essence, were two convincing arguments used in support of the idea of Romanian superiority in religious terms. These arguments were also used to explain why the Romanians' faith was "better" both than that of the Latinist Catholics and that of the Orthodox Serbs, who had all deviated, one way or another, from the true, original Tradition. Țichindeal wrote that "a faith such as that received from the lips of the greatest apostles could only be of the purest stock and spared of any madness".[306]

Even if this theory did not give rise to a messianic pathos claiming to save the rest of humanity (as it did in the case of the Russians), it somehow tried to claim, as far as the Romanians were concerned, that they alone had preserved intact the spirit of the ecumenical synods from before the Great Schism. This was the doctrinal foundation lying beneath the claim that they were able to articulate a third confessional formula, a specifically Romanian one.[307]

Gheorghe Șincai, in the wake of Samuil Micu, was extremely eloquent in illustrating that concept, by stressing the specificity of the Romanians' confessional solution. The Romanians were even placed outside the religious disputes between the Orthodox and the Catholic believers, since they were the undisturbed repositories of the true faith: "In those times of unrest, the Romanians strove to keep the faith they had received from their beginnings and learned from the church, the holy synods of the world and the saintly fathers. The Greeks quarrelled with the Romans for their faith, but the Romanians know nothing of their discord, but, as I said, lived in faith and by the ancient teachings which their fathers and forefathers had received from the first Christian church."[308] The Romanians could be neither Orthodox nor Catholic, since they were Christians pure and simple, from the very beginning, from a time prior to the birth of such distinctions, and, therefore, they were better than either of the two parties.

The Romanians' Religious Disunity

One widespread theme, that relied on the evident reality of confessional pluralism, was that of the religious dissension that existed among the Romanians, of the divergences that turned brother against brother. The idea was merely a variant of a more ample motif within the self-image: that of discord and lack of "national" consensus[309] as a feature of Romanian specificity and of the psychological profile of the nation.

The image of the opposition between the two confessions was not only a representation of the actual existence of two different entities, but also the result of the symbolic legitimacy each of them sought for itself. From this perspective, they did not treat each other as two competing yet equal confessions, but each saw in the other a usurper, a deviation from the true faith as well as from the true church of the people.

From a historical perspective, the Greek Catholics saw themselves as the inheritors of the Romanian Church of Transylvania, which at the beginning of the eighteenth century, adopted in its entirety, together with its lawful shepherd, religious union with Rome. It thus kept intact the line of continuity for the Transylvanian diocese, particularly with regard to the preservation of the Eastern religious rite and tradition. That is why the Greek Catholic metropolitan see ("reestablished", in its own view, between 1853 and 1855 when the former bishopric had been raised to that rank) adopted the predicate "of Alba Iulia"[310], in memory of the "ancient" Metropolitan See of Bălgrad, whose successor it claimed to be. In view of such logic the Orthodox believers could be seen as having strayed from the body of the mother-church, as followers of those who did not obey the synodal decision of union with Rome, which is why their conversion and "return" to Greek Catholicism could only be a legitimate thing to hope for.

On the other hand, the Orthodox themselves fashioned their own story of continuity and legitimacy, based not only on ritual but also on dogmatic tradition, by insisting on the despotic and arbitrary nature of the religious union—a result of foreign intervention.

Nevertheless, despite these exclusionist self-legitimating systems underlying every stance taken, the intellectuals of the time, particularly those who diverged from the discourse of the church, tried to avoid the issue of the superior validity of either of the two confessions. They were driven to do so both by the idea of religious tolerance, which they had inherited from the Enlightenment, and by the stress laid on the overcoming of any confessional disputes and the highlighting of the necessity for national concord.

The response to the theme of the Romanians' religious disunity was therefore, as a rule, serious disapproval and bitterness, along the lines of the negative self-perception. One of the methods for exorcising evil and striking an inner balance within the image could be, as usual, an attack against foreigners. It was they who were to blame for the Romanians' internal disputes; it was they who had provoked the Romanians' religious dissension in order to divide and rule over them all the more easily.

Naturally, the idea was upheld by the promoters of radical nationalism especially. Petru Maior showed that guilt for the religious conflicts of the middle of the eighteenth century (especially for the slide into Orthodoxy) was to be thrown on "those who, to this day, have worked against the Romanians' being together, either united or not, and want them separated, as if they were two nations instead of one".[311] Papiu Ilarian thought that there was no objective difference of any consequence between Orthodoxy and Greek Catholicism, and claimed that "the hatred which the enemies' intrigues alone stirred among our Romanians, be they Uniate or not, was the cause of the Hungarian oppression".[312] True, Papiu did not overlook, as he never did, the portion of responsibility attributable to the Romanians, who, due to their guilty disputes, deliberately became the instruments of the foreigners' malefic actions: "The stupid fights for union or separation, fired by the foreigners, are more pernicious to the Romanians than the foreigners themselves", he wrote in 1852. Such fights started again, he goes on, because of "some Romanians who are guilty rather of baseness and servitude to the foreigners than of bigotry".[313]

Moise Nicoară illustrated a more special case relating to this theme. Since for him the Romanians' solidarity with the Orthodox Serbs was preferable to the unhealthy cohabitation with the Greek Catholic Romanians, Nicoară believed that the disunity provoked by foreigners was first and foremost a blow at the Romanian Serb Orthodox community, while attempts to bring together the Orthodox Romanians with their Uniate co-nationals were simply diversions perpetrated by the Romanians' enemies who sought to divide them!

> The emperor saw that, until recently, the Russians had long kept Moldavia and the Romanian Country under their rule and that in Serbia there were sill many Russians at Cerni's time. So, in all these parts, the Romanians and the Serbs were close to the Russians, which could not please His Majesty, particularly since the Serbs are of a kin with the Russians and speak the same language. This is why the noble gentlemen and the high officials of the crown began to feel sorry that the Romanians were close to the Serbs: they have now begun to wonder how they might separate the Romanians from the Serbs, if they cannot unite them [i.e. unite the Romanians with the Greek Catholics].[314]

Even the appointment of a Romanian, Vasile Moga, at the head of the Orthodox Diocese of Transylvania, instead of the Serb bishops who had previously held
the position, was, in the eyes of the former supporter of a Romanian bishop for
Arad, a perfidious manoeuvre meant to encourage the Transylvanian Orthodox to
make peace with the Greek Catholics and thus to pave the way to their destruction and denationalisation.[315]

Other intellectuals, of a more moderate nationalist orientation, contented
themselves with censuring such confessional disputes in a general way, not taking
them necessarily as an outcome of foreigners' actions. They simply chose to throw
light on the damaging nature of such conflicts, which the Romanians' own will
alone could overcome, and on the source of such conflicts in an obsolete tradition
of sectarian prejudice and fanaticism, which was incompatible with the liberty of
mind of modern man.

Budai-Deleanu, for instance, was critical of, yet did not vituperate against,
"those who, in our Transylvanian land, are called non-united", since "they would
rather speak the Serb language than welcome anything, precious as it might be,
from what the Uniates have discovered." He referred to the fact that, in their
works, Ioan Piuariu Molnar and Radu Tempea "shrank from guiding their language towards its true source, which is the Latin language, as they feared they
might turn papists!"[316] What he meant was that there was no room for confessional motivations and divergences in the sphere of grammar and philology.

Dimitrie Țichindeal, an Orthodox believer, also condemned religious dissent,
in an admirably poised and neutral tone, and claimed, in an otherwise optimistic
portrait of the pan-Romanian national community:

> Wherever they [the Romanians] might be, the primary source of disunion among them is
> that some are of the Uniate Greek law, while others follow the non-united Greek rule. The
> former call the latter non-Uniates, while the latter call the former Uniates. And the true
> brotherly and saintly name of Christian is kept by either for themselves. [...] Should the
> people in these lands refuse to throw away such vain beliefs and root out that old brawling
> for the law which is so hateful to the Lord, they will find the Turk and the slave within
> themselves![317]

Just like Țichindeal, Andrei Mureșanu believed that "the Romanians' grim
fate" sprang also from "the church upheavals, which have stifled all eagerness to
defend our nationality and made most of them bend to foreigners and serve their
purposes. The reason, then, why we are so behind, comes not so much from the
outside as from the inside."[318] Bariț, too, attacked, with mordant irony, these
anachronistic remains of some less enlightened times, which still kept a firm hold
on the Romanians' minds: "There is no persuading us, it seems, to take to the
practical sciences, for we have not yet even finished with confessional disputes
which still keep us lagging behind the other Europe, which, at the time of the Jan-
senists, under Joseph II, did away with such bothers once and for all!"[319]

The highly significant thing is, in fact, that after whole decades of attempts to
abandon religious strife, after so many appeals by both enlightened and Romantic
intellectuals for the completion of a monolithic national solidarity, after the moments of grace and unifying "unique will" of the revolution, the following decade

witnessed a peak of confessional dissent. Bishop Şaguna would go as far as forbidding clerics to subscribe to the *Gazette of Transylvania*, since he (absolutely unjustly) considered it a confessional mouthpiece of the Greek Catholics. The arch-Presbyterians from the Apuseni Mountains would even use their crosiers in order to bring straying sheep to the right path, the priests would refuse to solemnise mixed marriages unless the bride and groom accepted to become members of the flock they shepherded in so much strictness... and so on and so forth.[320] In 1855 Liviu Andrei Pop, the new rector of a poor region in the mountains, had some bitter remarks about this whole state of things: "I have lost hope that the Romanian could still make something of his future. Our priests here have sunk so low that they prefer to become friends with any foreign nation than to hold together among themselves, be they Uniates or not. They no longer even call one another Romanian, but the non-Uniates call the Uniates papists and the Uniates call the others Russians."[321]

Certainly, the time had not yet come for the poor intellectuals of the time, preoccupied and obsessed with the need to unify the strength and will of the national community, to understand that a resolute assertion of the various religious identities and pluralism, be it confessional, political or cultural, was but a sign of normality and of a healthy civil society; that these identities must be the outcome of a personal option, by an individual or by a group, and not of the pressure of a levelling ideological principle. As long as they did not engender violent crises and a medieval sort of fanaticism, and kept within the bounds of legality in a state aspiring to modernity, such confessional disputes evinced the survival of religious sensibilities as guarantors of social meaning and cohesion. Also, they pointed out the fact that nationalist ideology had not yet managed to impose itself as a comprehensive hegemonic ideological principle for the whole Romanian society of Transylvania. The new religion of the modern age had not yet been born in its fullness, although its apostles had already discovered the formulas of its universal success, forged in the catacombs—still isolated from the crowd—of the national culture.

NOTES

1 For the reasons behind this identification of the Romanians with the peasants, see (besides 3:Heitmann 1985, chp. I) 3:Pippidi 1993, p. 25.

2 1.9:Budai-Deleanu 1991, I, p. 312.

3 Avram Iancu to Lieutenant-Colonel Simonffy József, a letter of June 1849, published in 1.6:Maior L. 1972, pp. 86–89.

4 1.5:Papiu Ilarian 1852(II), pp. 229–230.

5 *Ibidem*, pp. 236–238.

6 1.7:*Speech February 1849*, in 1.9:Păcăţian 1904, p. 517.

7 Timotei Cipariu, "Union", in 1.2:*The Mouthpiece*, II, 1848, no. 67, p. 381.

8 1.9:Budai-Deleanu 1970a, pp. 37–39.

9 An idea present in Mircea Eliade, Lucian Blaga, Emil Cioran; cf. 3:Pippidi 1993, p. 29; 3:Antohi 1994, pp. 212–214, 272.

10 1.5:Papiu Ilarian 1852(II), pp. C–CII; Papiu's source is 1.5:Desprez 1850.

11 1.4:Bojincă 1828, pp. 14–15; 1.9:Fugariu 1983, II, p. 660.

12 *Ibidem*.

13 Al. Papiu Ilarian, "The addresses in M. Oșorhei", in 1.2:*Journal for the Mind*, XI, 1848, no. 13, pp. 99–101; reprinted in 1.2:*The Mouthpiece*, II, 1848, no. 66, pp. 375–376, and partially in 1.5:Papiu Ilarian 1852(II), pp. 105–106.

14 1.5:Papiu Ilarian 1852(II), pp. CX sq. About ninety years later an embittered Cioran would deplore what he called, in a Nietzschean reading, the absence of a conquering spirit in the Romanians, which should be able to muster national energies in order to serve an ideal superior to daily routine and materialism. Marshal Antonescu, on the other hand, would try to compensate for this deficiency by means of a campaign on the other side of the Nistru river.

15 1.7:*Supplex 1804*, in 3:Prodan 1970, pp. 82–89; 3:Prodan 1989, pp. 305–306.

16 "The Union of Transylvania with Hungary, a despotically proclaimed alliance", in 1.2:*Zeitung*, issue of 10 June 1848, article translated and re-edited in 1.9:Bodea 1983, I, p. 570.

17 Avram Iancu to Ioan Gozman, a letter of June 1849, published in 1.6:Maior L. 1972, pp. 92–93.

18 For the image of Romanian violence in 1848 as apparent in Hungarian sources, see 3:Mitu M. 1989–1993, pp. 565–567 for the press image; and 3:Mitu M. 1994, pp. 118–120 for Mór Jókai's prose. Faced with extremely severe foreign representations of the Romanians' conduct during the revolution, the urgent need was felt on the part of the latter to counteract them with images to the contrary.

19 1.4:Bojincă 1828, pp. 86–87; 1.9:Fugariu 1983, II, pp. 664–665.

20 "Bucharest", in 1.2:*The Mouthpiece*, I, 1847, no. 16, p. 74.

21 Ioan Maiorescu to George Bariț, a letter of March 1847, published in 1.6:*GBC* 1973–1993, I, p. 305.

22 A relevant analogy to such attitudes is to be found in the poem written by Adrian Păunescu on the occasion of the earthquake that devastated Bucharest 130 years later, on 4 March 1977. The formerly ill-mannered dubious individuals become, under the impact of the calamity, heroes fired by the noblest of sentiments (see 2:Păunescu 1977). Just as in the moments of grace of the 1989 revolution, the nation as a whole rediscovered its "true" virtues.

23 "Kurzgefasste Bemerkungen über Bukowina" (1805), in 1.9:Budai-Deleanu 1970a, pp. 37–39.

24 1.9:Murgu 1969, p. 298.

25 1.4:Costin 1812a, p. 46; 1.9:Fugariu 1983, I, p. 861.

26 1.4:Horga Popovici 1807; 1.9:Fugariu 1983, I, pp. 735–736.

27 See 3:Mauss 1973. Certainly, the economic function of the gift was accompanied by a magical signification, since it sanctioned the peaceful and trustworthy relationship between the parties involved.

28 [Vasile Maniu], "Hungary and Romania", in 1.2:*The People*, I, 1848, no. 19, pp. 75–76; 1.9:*The Year 1848*, III, pp. 484–487; 1.9:Bodea 1982, II, p. 899.

29 1.9:Ion Codru Drăgușanu 1956, p. 69.

30 *Ibidem*, p. 70.

31 *Ibidem*.

32 *Ibidem*, p. 72.

33 Moise Nicoară to Petru Maior, a letter of 5 to 8 December 1810, published in 1.9:Bodea 1943, p. 151.

34 1.9:Codru Drăgușanu 1956, p. 114.

35 "Stories of old" (1830), in 1.9:Stoica de Hațeg, 1984, p. 161.

36 A century later Mihai Ralea would give a totally different picture of the forms taken by Romanian trivial language: he maintains that swear words relating to religious realities are a characteristic of the people and an argument in favour of the Romanians' superficial religiosity: "The Romanian, as they say, holds nothing sacred; which means that he will break every spiritual value at the call of his logical instincts. Observe, for instance, our national swear words. Few other peoples are able to profane, in all voluptuousness, as it were, what should be held sacred, as some of our social strata do when they proffer words of abuse." ("National Atheism", in 2:Ralea, 1977, p. 598; 3:Ornea 1995, p. 104).

37 I would refer the reader to my manuscript study, "Licentiousness and triviality among the Transylvanian Romanians at the beginning of the modern age".

38 1.9:Codru Drăgușanu 1956, p. 106.

39 1.8:Pauleti 1980, pp. 418–419. I will give here, by way of a sample, a "folk rhyme" discovered by Simion Bărnuțiu and transcribed by Timotei Cipariu, published in *loc. cit.*: "Send me, mother, 'cross the valley, / Where men with big cock dally. / Nay, my dear, I will not, / For fear your soul might rot. / Send me, mother, drop your stitch, / For the cock will crack a breach."

40 1.5:Papiu Ilarian 1852(II), p. 256.

41 *Ibidem*, pp. 229–230.

42 *Ibidem*, pp. 213–214, 259–263.

43 *Ibidem*, pp. 259–263.

44 *Ibidem*.

45 *Ibidem*, p. 214.

46 "From the foot of the Surul hill", in 1.2:*The Telegraph*, I, 1853, no. 1, p. 2.

47 Bishop Șaguna's speech at the assembly of 28 December 1848 in Sibiu, published in 1.9:Păcățian 1904, p. 505.

48 1.2:*The Mouthpiece*, II, 1848, no. 68, p. 386.

49 1.7:*Speech February 1849*, in 1.9:Păcățian 1904, p. 517.

50 1.9:Papiu Ilarian 1943, p. 83.

51 See 3:Bocșan 1990; 3:Bocșan 1992.

52 Manifesto of the National Committee, dated 1 November 1848, published in 1.9:Bărnuțiu 1990, p. 67.

53 1.5:Papiu Ilarian 1852(II), pp. 53–55. For the various meanings of "melancholy" from a historical perspective, see 3:Starobinski 1966.

54 1.5:Papiu Ilarian 1852(II), *loc. cit.*

55 George Bariț, "Nationality", in 1.2:*Journal for the Mind*, VII, 1844, no. 51, p. 400; 1.9:Bariț 1962, p. 86.

56 1.5:Papiu Ilarian 1852(II), pp. 158–159.

57 Samuil Micu, *Historia Daco-Romanorum sive Valachorum* (1778), in 1.9:Fugariu 1983, I, p. 7.

58 *Ibidem*, p. 6.

59 Vasile Pop, "Foreword" to 1.4:Prale 1827; 1.6:*GBC* 1973–1993, V, p. 5.

60 The image of "Romanian intelligence" in the "French–Byzantine–Wallachian" variant of "wit", "sharpness", or of an "'esprit' in the French sense of the word", sometimes bordering on "slyness" and versatility, can be found both in foreign perceptions, i.e. German (3:Heitmann 1985, chp. IX; 2:Keyserling 1929) or Hungarian (3:Borsi-Kálmán 1994), and in Romanian images, such as the symbolic figure of Caragiale's "Mitică".

61 Sigismund Pop, in 1.2:*The Friend*, I, 1848, no. 2, coll. 27–28.

62 *Idem*, in *ibidem*, coll. 327.

63 Oprea Moroianu to Al. Papiu Ilarian and Iosif Hodoș, a letter of 11 October 1853, published in 1.6:Hodoș 1940, p. 17; 1.6:Pervain, Chindriș 1972, p. 230.

64 1.5:Papiu Ilarian 1852(I), pp. 121–122.

65 To this purpose, in *The Transfiguration of Romania*, Emil Cioran wished for a "Romania with the population of China and the destiny of France" (2: Cioran 1993a, p. 105).

66 See 1.7:*Memoir 1735*, in 1.9:Păcățian 1904, p. 60; 1.7:*Supplex 1791*, in 3:Prodan 1971, pp. 453, 465.

67 See the short story *Alexandru Lăpușneanu* (1840), in 1.5:Negruzzi 1857.

68 Evidently, the boundaries of the science in question not yet being traced at the time, its preoccupations were disseminated throughout the space covered by other cultural disciplines.

69 This type of perception is manifest in the social imaginary of many peoples: the Rhine borderline and the Hexagon in the case of the French people, the myth of the "three seas" bathing the frontier of Hungary in the Angevin period, the directions of Russian expansion according to the text of "the will of Peter the Great". Even the more recent European identity capitalises on geographical conditioning ("from the Atlantic to the Ural Mountains" or "from the Atlantic to the Danube Delta"), preferred over the much more logical extension of a spiritual, economic-financial or civilisational principle.

70 Of particular significance here could be the analysis of the febrile marks and lines that sketched frontiers and imaginary annexes, traced on the maps, atlases and manuals to be found in public libraries and old book shops, etc. The author of the present study himself possesses several such

atlases, on which he used to scribble expansion lines with the nationalist fervour of a young man. Unfortunately for the nationalists, the lack of application of "contemporary young men" to the study of geography frustrates their doctrine of one of its basic components.

71 1.9:Fugariu 1983, I p. 233.

72 1.4:Şincai 1805, pp. 4–5; 1.9:Fugariu 1983, I, p. 598.

73 It will be symbolically illustrated in Eminescu's *Doina* and defended politically by Ionel Brătianu in the peace treaties signed in the aftermath of the First World War.

74 In its turn, the extension of the frontiers of Romanianhood north of the Black Sea (of which Micu, Şincai or Moise Nicoară speak) will be consecrated by the military occupation of Transnistria under Marshal Antonescu, and by theoretical articles of Gheorghe Brătianu (see 2:Brătianu 1942).

75 1.9:Fugariu 1983, I, pp. 23, 598.

76 1.4:Şincai 1806, p. 150; 1.9:Fugariu 1983, I, p. 695.

77 1.9:Budai-Deleanu 1970a (1812), pp. 42–43.

78 1.4:Maior P. 1812, pp. 248–249.

79 1.9:Bodea 1943, p. 355.

80 Moise Nicoară to Bishop Samuil Vulcan, draft of a letter of 22 August 1815, published in *ibidem*, p. 167.

81 1.2:*The Friend*, I, 1848, coll. 327; "The Romanian", in 1.2:*The Teacher*, I, 1848, no. 1, pp. 3–4.

82 1.5:Papiu Ilarian 1852 (II), pp. 236, 238.

83 1.4:Maior P. 1812, pp. 142–178, 197–224; 1.9:Maior P. 1970, pp. 197–226, 241–263.

84 1.9:Şincai 1967, p. 49; 3:Capidan 1923; 3:Todoran 1983; Morangiés, "The Romanians of Anowallachia", in 1.2:*Journal for the Mind*, V, 1842, pp. 228–232, 233–237; Fr. Pouqueville, "Statistical table for the Romanians of Greece", in *ibidem*, IX, 1846, pp. 73–74; Leake, "The Romanians of Greece", in 1.2:*The Mouthpiece*, I, 1847, no. 49–50; Fallmerayer, "The Romanians of Greece", in *ibidem*, no. 51.

85 1.4:Bojincă 1828 (1.9:Bojincă 1978, p. 14); 1.4:Murgu 1830 (1.9:Murgu 1969, pp. 378–379, 382–384); "The Romanians of Switzerland, Moravia and Poland", in 1.2:*Journal for the Mind*, XXIV, 1861, pp. 287–288. For the same need to track down the co-nationals lost in bleak otherness among the Romanians of Wallachia and Moldavia respectively, see 3:Mitu M., Mitu S. 1996.

86 1.5:Papiu Ilarian 1852 (II), pp. 236–238.

87 1.9:Bojincă 1978, p. 8.

88 Ioan Maiorescu, "Refutation of the opinion of Mr. I. K. Schuller on the German origin of the Romanian language", in 1.2:*Journal for the Mind*, X, 1847, no. 15–22 (as an answer to an article from 1.2:*Archiv*, I, 1843, no. 1, pp. 67–108).

89 1.9:Murgu 1969, p. 246.

90 George Bariț, "Romanians and Hungarians", in 1.2:*Journal for the Mind*, V, 1842, no. 9–11; 1.9:Bariț 1962, p. 70.

91 Prefect Ioan Buteanu to Major Kálmán Csutak, a letter of April 1849, published in 1.9:Bodea 1982, II, p. 1081.

92 Avram Iancu to Lieutenant-Colonel József Simonffy, a letter of June 1849, published in 1.6:Maior L. 1972, pp. 86–89.

93 1.5:Papiu Ilarian 1852 (II), p. CXIII.

94 1.4:Maior P. 1812, pp. 248–249; 1.9:Fugariu 1983, I, p. 899.

95 1.4:Maior 1813, p. 71; 1.9:Fugariu 1983, II, p. 169.

96 1.4:Şincai 1806, p. 150; 1.9:Fugariu 1983, I, p. 695.

97 1.4:*Lexicon* 1825, p. 65; 1.9:Fugariu 1983, II, p. 612.

98 Ion Budai-Deleanu, *Romanian-German Lexicon* (1818), in 1.9:Fugariu 1983, II, p. 382.

99 Dyonis Thalson, "The Romans", in 1.2:*The Mouthpiece*, I, 1847, no. 47, p. 264.

100 1.9:Bărnuțiu 1990, p. 34.

101 1.9:Budai-Deleanu 1991, I, p. 314.

102 1.5:Papiu Ilarian 1852(II), p. CXXXVI.

103 *Apud* 3:Bernath 1972, chp. IX.

104 1.7:*Supplex 1791*, in 3:Prodan 1971, pp. 450, 462.

105 Samuil Micu, *Historia Daco-Romanorum sive Valachorum* (1778), in 1.9:Fugariu 1983, I, p. 8.
106 1.4:Nicolau 1814–1815, p. 49; 1.9:Fugariu 1983, II, p. 207.
107 1.5:Papiu Ilarian 1852(II), pp. 135–136.
108 1.7:*Petition July 1814*, in 1.9:Păcăţian 1904, p. 147.
109 See, for instance, 1.7:*Petition February 1849*; 1.7:*Memorandum March 1849*; 1.7:*Address November 1849*.
110 1.7:*Memorandum March 1849*, in 1.9:Păcăţian 1904, p. 539.
111 1.9:Budai-Deleanu 1991, I, p. 188.
112 George Bariţ, "What is the matter with the Romanians?", in 1.2:*Journal for the Mind*, V, 1842, no. 35, pp. 273–275; 1.9:Bariţ 1962, p. 75.
113 Dyonis Thalson, "The Romans", in 1.2:*The Mouthpiece*, I, 1847, no. 47, p. 264.
114 An extreme variant of this Hungarian hetero-image of the Romanians, in the spirit of the positivist and scientific nationalism of the twentieth century, would be the "goat-milk" theory, according to which the Romanians' fecundity is due to the consumption of such products as noticed in the case of the A-Romanian shepherds.
115 George Bariţ, "Response to the German papers of Braşov and Sibiu", in 1.2:*The Gazette*, X, 1847, no. 96, pp. 381–382; 1.9:Bariţ 1962, p. 98.
116 See 3:*Ideology of generation* 1968, pp. 265–266. Obviously, the speculations of the epoch regarding the Romanians' fecundity were a far cry from any clear understanding of the real demographic tendencies. For any traditional regime of population previous to the nineteenth-century demographic revolution, a high birth rate, going up to the biological limit of procreation, is more than frequent. It is nonetheless compensated by the almost identical level of infant mortality, which translates as a very slow natural increase (see 3:Chaunu 1971, pp. 95–170; 3:Lebrun 1985). Despite all these considerations, and, furthermore, despite the precautions of the Transylvanian intellectuals at the beginning of the modern era, Romanian culture would see the symbolic shaping of Transylvania as an "ethnic reservoir", a symbol of national vitality.
117 George Bariţ, "Romanians and Hungarians", in 1.2:*Journal for the Mind*, V, 1842, no. 9–11; 1.9:Bariţ 1962, p. 68.
118 Timotei Cipariu, "The Union", in 1.2:*The Mouthpiece*, II, 1848, no. 67, p. 381.
119 George Bariţ, "What is the will of the Transylvanian Romanians?", in 1.2:*Journal for the Mind*, XI, 1848, no. 14–16; 1.9:Bariţ 1962, p. 116.
120 Samuil Micu, "Short Information on the History of the Romanians" (1796), in 1.9:Fugariu 1983, I, pp. 231–232.
121 1.7:*Petition October 1849*, in 1.9:Păcăţian 1904, p. 625.
122 See 1.9:Răduţiu, Gyémánt 1995.
123 A good contemporary analogy is that of the "two million" Hungarians whom the Democratic Union of the Hungarians of Romania (UDMR) estimate live in Romania—a figure preferred to the quite different results of official surveys.
124 1.5:Papiu Ilarian 1852 (II), pp. 236–238.
125 1.7:*Memorandum September 1848*, in 1.9:Bodea 1982, II, p. 911.
126 1.7:*Supplex 1791*, in 3:Prodan 1971, pp. 454, 466.
127 *Ibidem*, p. 479.
128 See 1.9:Răduţiu, Gyémánt 1995, pp. 696–697 (annex no. 7, "The Population of Transylvania as divided into ethnic groups, 1690–1847").
129 George Bariţ, "What is the will of the Transylvanian Romanians?", in 1.2:*Journal for the Mind*, XI, 1848, no. 14–16; 1.9:Bariţ 1962, p. 116.
130 1.9:Bărnuţiu 1990, p. 33.
131 The appeal, addressed by Sub-Prefect Simion Prodan Probul to the Hungarian citizens of Aiud on 19 October 1848, published in 1.9:Bodea 1982, II, p. 990.
132 The Braşov merchants to Andrei Şaguna, a letter of 20 July 1848, published in 1.9:Dragomir 1944–1946, II, p. 169.
133 1.9:Răduţiu, Gyémánt 1995, pp. 698–699. Andrei Mureşanu speaks of 1,800,000 Romanians in Transylvania and Hungary, and adds that, according to one member of the Hungarian Diet, these were merely one hundred thousand. "The hard lie of statistics", Mureşanu notes (see An-

drei Mureșanu, "The reason why we are so belated", in 1.2:*Journal for the Mind*, VI, 1843, no. 42, pp. 329–31; 1.9:Mureșanu A. 1977, p. 38.

134 1.7:*Petition February 1849*, in 1.9:Păcățian 1904, p. 519.

135 1.7:*Response July 1849*, in *ibidem*, p. 609.

136 Timotei Cipariu, "The Union", in *The Mouthpiece*, II, 1848, no. 65, p. 367.

137 Vasile Maniu, "Hungary and Romania", in 1.2:*The People*, I, 1848, no. 19, pp. 75–76; 1.9:Bodea 1982, II, p. 899.

138 1.9:Budai-Deleanu 1991, I, p. 188.

139 George Bariț, "What is the matter with the Romanians?", in 1.2:*Journal for the Mind*, V, 1842, no. 35, pp. 273–275; 1.9:Bariț 1962, p. 75.

140 László Kőváry, "Excerpt from *The Statistics of Transylvania*", in 1.2:*The Mouthpiece*, I, 1847, no. 41, p. 226; 1.5:Wesselényi 1843; 1.5:Kőváry 1847.

141 1.5:Desprez 1850.

142 1.5:Vaillant 1844.

143 George Bariț, "What is the will of the Transylvanian Romanians?", in 1.2:*Journal for the Mind*, XI, 1848, no. 14–16; 1.9:Bariț 1962, p. 116.

144 1.5:Papiu Ilarian 1852 (II), pp. CII-CIII.

145 László Kőváry, in 1.2:*The Mouthpiece*, I, 1847, no. 41; 1.5:László Kőváry 1847; "The Number of the Romanians", in 1.2:*Journal for the Mind*, X, 1847, pp. 255–256.

146 "Austria and the Danubian Principalities (according to the Viennese Gazette)", in 1.2:*The Mouthpiece*, II, 1848, no. 70, pp. 393–395 (translated from 1.2:*Zeitung*, 1848, no. 116); 1.9:Bodea 1982, I, pp. 428–429, 433.

147 See 1.9:Bălcescu 1974, pp. 171–178.

148 See, for instance, the article "The Number of the Romanians", in 1.2:*Journal for the Mind*, X, 1847, no. 31, pp. 255–256. For the same figure, encountered during the revolution, see 3:Berindei 1974, p. 39.

149 These words are attributed to Iancu by Alecu Russo, a participant in the second national assembly in Blaj (1.9:Russo 1908, p. 80).

150 In May, *The National Mouthpiece* candidly wrote, "We hardly know how to estimate the participation in the assembly." Some, it claimed, spoke of 15,000; others of 95,000. In full modesty, the paper chose an intermediary figure: "We would say forty or fifty thousand." (1.2:*The Mouthpiece*, II, 1848, no. 1, pp. 1–4).

151 1.8:Mureșanu A. 1963, p. 38.

152 1.9:Bărnuțiu 1990, p. 62.

153 3:Bariț 1994, pp. 340–341.

154 This is only theoretically speaking; in reality, he was to be the father of nine children (see 2:Boitoș 1942).

155 1.9:Drăgușanu 1956, p. 93.

156 *Ibidem*, p. 102.

157 *Ibidem*, p. 231.

158 George Bariț, "A deadly article", in 1.2:*The Gazette*, XII, 1849, no. 25, p. 97; 1.9:Bariț 1962, p. 136.

159 1.5:Papiu Ilarian 1852(I), pp. 22–26.

160 Timotei Cipariu, "Principles of Language and Writing", in 1.2:*The Mouthpiece*, II, 1848, no. 59, p. 332.

161 *Idem*, "Letters of Italy" (1852), in 1.9:Cipariu 1972, p. 140.

162 Timotei Cipariu to George Bariț, a letter of March 1848, published in 1.6:*GBC* 1973–1993, IV, p. 299.

163 Firstly, see the excellent study by Sorin Antohi, "The Words and the World. The Making of the Socio-Political Language in Romanian Culture", in 3:Antohi 1994, pp. 136–174. For the political implications of the language problem, see 3:Gyémánt 1986, pp. 183–221.

164 Obviously, there is a strong interconnection between the two plans—a truism and a sophism that the partisans and the opponents of the use of the Romanian language as cultural idiom always exploited in their argumentation: Is Romanian uncultivated because discriminated against, or is it discriminated against because it is uncultivated?

165 Note here the famous example of Avram Iancu, who was said to write better in Hungarian, which he practised in the Piarist college in Cluj, than in Romanian. The cumbersome style of his letters, full of Hungarian expressions, is relevant in this sense. Cf. the opinion of Professor Liviu Maior, the editor of Iancu's correspondence, communicated during his courses on the 1848 revolution.

166 Theodor Serb to Moise Nicoară, a letter of 6 January 1825, published in 1.9:Bodea 1943, p 384. Gojdu was to hold this position all his life, given that even his testament, through which he willed his famous foundation to the young Romanians, is written in Hungarian (see 1.1:Gojdu 1869; 2:Gojdu 1888; 3:Cordoş, Jude 1989–1993).

167 Timotei Cipariu, "Principles of Language and Writing", in 1.2:*The Mouthpiece*, I, 1847, no. 6, p. 26.

168 1.5:Papiu Ilarian 1852(II), pp. X–XI.

169 See the same formula in 3:Antohi 1994, pp. 136–174.

170 Andrei Mureşanu, *To my Muse* (1847), in 1.8:Mureşanu A. 1963, p 36.

171 *Idem*, "A Few Reflections upon our Poetry", in 1.2:*Journal for the Mind*, VII, 1844, no. 26, p. 201; 1.9:Mureşanu A., 1977, p. 39.

172 Samuil Micu, *Short Information on the History of the Romanians* (1796), in 1.9:Fugariu 1983, I, pp. 232–233.

173 1.4:Tempea 1797: "Foreword"; 1.9:Fugariu 1983, I, p. 315.

174 1.5:Papiu Ilarian 1825(II), pp. CXVIII sqq.

175 1.9:Fugariu 1983, I, p. 199.

176 Ion Budai-Deleanu, *Kurzgefasste Bemerkungen über Bukowina* (1805), in 1.9:Budai-Deleanu 1970a, p. 39.

177 1.9:Fugariu 1983, II, p. 150.

178 1.4:Diaconovici-Loga 1822, pp. 142–143; 1.9:Diaconovici-Loga 1973, p. 133.

179 Andrei Mureşanu, "A Few Reflections upon our Poetry", in 1.2:*Journal for the Mind*, VII, 1844, no. 26, p. 201; 1.9:Mureşanu A. 1977, p. 39.

180 *Idem*, "The Romanian and his Poetry", in 1.2:*The Telegraph*, I, 1853, no. 41–43; 1.9:Mureşanu A. 1977, p. 134.

181 George Bariţ, "The Moldavian-Romanian Land (Its Future and Positioning)", in 1.2:*Journal for the Mind*, III, 1840, no. 25, pp. 193–200; 1.9:Bariţ 1962, p. 58.

182 See 3:Marino 1964; 3:Seche 1966; 3:Gheţie 1966; 3:Macrea 1969.

183 1.4:Roja 1809, p. 14; 1.9:Fugariu 1983, I, p. 819.

184 *Ibidem*.

185 1.4:Iorgovici 1799, p. 30; 1.9:Iorgovici 1979, p. 145.

186 1.4: Şincai 1783, p. II; 1.9:Fugariu 1983, I, p. 34.

187 This nostalgia for an original purity and correctness, altered by the hardships of the times, is an enduring heritage in Romanian culture; the new orthographic regulations of the Academy are an excellent proof to the point.

188 In more pedantic terminology, one might say that the "common language" can only be-come (back) to a state of "in-itself"-ness if sieved through the filter of ideological reconstruction; here, the distance separating the language "in itself" from the "common language" is in fact equivalent to the Kantian gap between "the thing in itself" and the "phenomenon", even if, in this case, bridging proves to be theoretically possible.

189 Ion Budai-Deleanu, *The Romanian Manual for Romanian Grammatical Rules* (1815–1820), in 1.9:Budai-Deleanu 1970a, pp. 132–133.

190 *Ibidem*.

191 *Ibem*.

192 1.4:Tempea 1797, "Foreword"; 1.9:Fugariu 1983, I, p. 317.

193 1.9:Budai-Deleanu 1970a, pp. 117–118.

194 1.4:Iorgovici 1799, pp. 72–73; 1.9:Iorgovici 1979, pp. 229–231 (also p. 231, note 76, see the editors' considerations).

195 1.4:Şincai 1783, p. II; 1.9:Fugariu 1970, I, p. 75; 1.4:Iorgovici 1799, pp. 81, 10–11; 1.9:Iorgovici 1979, pp. 247, 105–107.

196 1.4:Iorgovici 1799, pp. 81, 10–11; 1.9:Iorgovici 1979, pp. 247, 105–107.

197 *Ibidem*, p. 81 and p. 247, respectively.

198 For the relation between language, "intelligentsia", civil society and the ideological pressures, see 3:Antohi 1994, pp. 145–146, 163–164.

199 1.4:Iorgovici 1799, pp. 77–79; 1.9:Iorgovici 1979, pp. 239–243. How strikingly the coercion of an ideological principle can be refracted at the level of idiomatic practice has been proved by the linguistic conformism to the famous "wooden language", both in the communist years and afterwards (see 3:Thom 1987).

200 This happened in a manner analogous to the way in which the nationalist principle, resuscitated during Ceaușescu's regime, supplanted the ideological hegemonic Marxist system precisely against its promoters' will, because it offered an alternative to the latter. See this thesis in 3:Verdery 1991.

201 Ioan Maiorescu, in 1.2:*Literary Paper*, I, 1838, no. 16, p. 122.

202 Simion Bărnuțiu to Al. Papiu Ilarian, a letter of December 1852, published in 1.6:Pervain, Chindriș 1972, II, p. 40.

203 *Ibidem*, pp. 48–49 (a letter of January 1853).

204 *The Journal for the Mind* adopted the transition alphabet in 1840, and *The Gazette* in 1844. From 1852 onwards they would be partially printed in Latin letters but the definitive passage to this alphabet would occur only in 1862 (see 3:Marica 1977, II, p. 19). For the whole problematic of the age of the transition alphabet, see the wonderful book by Ștefan Cazimir, 3:Cazimir 1986.

205 In popular almanacs or in the Orthodox Church printings, the Cyrillic alphabet would survive until the beginning of the twentieth century.

206 1.4:Micu 1801, pp. III–IV; 1.9:Fugariu 1983, I, pp. 529–530.

207 Ion Budai-Deleanu, *Basics of Romanian Grammar* (1815–1820), in 1.9:Budai-Deleanu 1970a, p. 111; 1.9:Fugariu 1983, II, pp. 139–140. Obviously, Budai-Deleanu was wrong: any language can be written in any other alphabet. The irony was that the Turks themselves adopted the Latin alphabet after the Kemalist Revolution, for the sake of modernisation, ignoring in a salutary way their own identity-related orthographic obsessions. Because they have similar phonemes (e.g. "ș"), the Turks even adopted characters from the Romanian alphabet (see 3:Graur 1974, p. 146).

208 1.9:Fugariu 1983, II, pp. 144–145.

209 1.4:Crișan-Körösi 1805; 1.9:Fugariu 1983, I, p. 594. A sample of the original orthography reveals to us how "clearly" this "Romanian" language sounded in that dress: *Romane! Vediand quőt de chiár, inalt si sulléget extralucesce acest Nome, dòpa ce l'am desbracat d'in flócce le lui Cyrill...*

210 1.4:Gergely de Ciocotiș 1819, "Foreword"; 1.9:Fugariu 1983, II, p. 500.

211 *Ibidem*.

212 Ion Budai-Deleanu, *Basics of Romanian Grammar*, in 1.9:Fugariu 1983, II, pp. 144–145.

213 1.4:Roja 1809, pp. 16–18; 1.9:Fugariu 1983, I, p. 820.

214 Timotei Cipariu, "Principles of Language and Writing", in 1.2:*The Mouthpiece*, II, 1848, no. 57, p. 320.

215 1.7:*Petition May 1848*, in 1.9:Păcățian 1904, p. 345; 1.9:Bodea 1982, I, p. 510. The noteworthy fact is that the Hungarian ideology of the time also professed this idea, underlining the Romanians' Latin essence and their affinity with the Western space of civilisation in order to stimulate and legitimate the Romanians' separation from the Orthodox Slavic bloc (with Russia as the shadow governor), in trying to attenuate the obsession of the "surrounding" (see 3:Gyémánt 1986, p. 71). The memoir deliberately welcomes this idea in order to attract the sympathy of the Hungarian decision factors.

216 Al. Papiu Ilarian to Iacob Mureșanu, a letter of December 1852, published in 1.6:Pervain, Chindriș 1972, I, p. 173.

217 1.9:Dimitrie Cantemir 1981, chp. V, "On the Moldavian Letters".

218 See also 1.4:Micu, Șincai 1780, pp. II–IV; 1.9:Fugariu 1983, I, p. 22.

219 1.4:Maior P. 1812, pp. 327–330.

220 Ion Budai-Deleanu, *Basics of Romanian Grammar* (1815–1820), in 1.9:Budai-Deleanu 1970a, pp. 111–112.

221 Timotei Cipariu, "Which is the Oldest Romanian Book?", in 1.2:*The Mouthpiece*, II, 1848, no. 54, p. 304.

222 *Ibidem*.

223 1.4:Maior P. 1812, p. 334; 1.9:Maior P. 1970, II, p. 74.

224 *Ibidem*.

225 *Ibidem*, pp. 335–336 and p. 75, respectively.

226 1.5:Papiu Ilarian 1852(II), pp. CX sqq.

227 1.9:Budai-Deleanu 1970a, pp. 122–123.

228 Timotei Cipariu, "Principles of Language and Writing", in 1.2:*The Mouthpiece*, II, 1848, no. 57, p. 320.

229 For this movement, see 1.9:Bodea 1943; 3:Bocșan 1982; 3:Bocșan, Lumperdean, Pop 1996, pp. 122–125 (with bibliography).

230 See the correspondence between Maior and Nicoară in 1.9:Bodea 1943, pp. 145–153.

231 Nicoară does exactly the opposite, thus proving in an exemplary manner that ideology can topple all realities. While the Latinists, such as Cipariu or Laurian, use, out of habit, Cyrillic script in their private correspondence, the traditionalist Nicoară writes for private use in Latin characters! It is true that his Romanian autographs in the Latin script are primarily from his young days, since, later, he would use the Cyrillic script. But this evolution closely follows his ideological options, in all their paradoxes (see the autographs of the respective persons in B.A.R., Bucharest: Rom. ms. 3455, Nicoară's notes and correspondence; Rom. ms. 996, Laurian's correspondence with Bariț; Rom. ms. 994, Cipariu's correspondence with Bariț).

232 1.7:*Last Appeal August 1819*, in 1.9:Bodea 1943, p. 344.

233 *Ibidem*.

234 *Ibidem*.

235 However, to this day, in various parts of Eastern Europe, the ideological dispute with respect to the two alphabets is still sensed, if not, sometimes, resumed in all fierceness. In the former Yugoslavia, for instance, after a period of more or less marked tendencies towards the Latin alphabet, the Serbs strongly adopted the Cyrillic system as a consequence of the conflict with Catholic and "Latin" Slovenia and Croatia. For example, in the 1980s Belgrade Television subtitled foreign films in the Latin alphabet, which is no longer the case today. In the same period, Basarabia, for instance, registered a reversed evolution, meant to underline its new identity and the distancing from Moscow. On the other hand, to this day Romanian Orthodox church writings use stylised Latin characters in headlines, vignettes, etc., whose form reminds one of the old Cyrillic alphabet, as a reminiscence of the traditional Cyrillic script.

236 Simion Bărnuțiu to Al. Papiu Ilarian, a letter of February 1853, published in 1.6:Pervain, Chindriș 1972, II, p. 58.

237 For a general discussion of ecclesiastical history and the history of the religious life, as well as for their relationship to various ethnic and national aspects, see 3:Bocșan, Lumperdean, Pop 1996; 3:Crăciun, Ghitta 1995.

238 Romanian historiography makes a grievous mistake when it dissociates only poorly, if at all, between these two aspects bearing on any discussion of the medieval nation. Having discovered the concept of "medieval nation", one able to prolong backwards the obsessions of modern nationalism, Romanian historians tend to cram under this all-encompassing umbrella every element of ethnic-national specificity, be it part of high culture, state politics, or "instinctive" popular sentiments. Medieval nationalism, manifest in the system of classification of the medieval universities or in the political, cultural and religious tendencies of the "national" fragmentation of the universal body of the Christian Republic, is completely different from the cultural identity of the traditional rural community. This archaic collective solidarity is not a medieval reality but a feature of any pre-modern folkloric culture, be it of the eighteenth century, of the Middle Ages or of Antiquity, and, generally speaking, of any "primitive" population based on an oral culture. Any attempt to approach it from a methodological perspective other than that of ethnology and cultural anthropology is indeed meaningless.

239 3:Hitchins 1983, pp. 7–28; 3:Hotea 1988–1991, p. 174.

240 See 3:Turczynski 1976.

241 See 3:Hobsbawm, Ranger 1983; 3:Antohi 1994, p. 277.

242 3:Besançon 1978; also see 3:Finkielkraut 1987, and the classic study of Julien Benda, 3:Benda 1928.

243 1.4:Maior P. 1812, p. 333; 1.9:Maior P. 1970, II, p. 73.

244 George Bariț, "The Romanians and Hungarianism", in 1.2:*Journal for the Mind*, V, 1842, no. 9, pp. 68–69.

245 Gavril Munteanu to George Bariț, a letter of July 1846, published in 1.6:*GBC* 1973–1993, VI, p. 211.

246 Al. Papiu Ilarian (on behalf of the Romanian students in Vienna) to the Synod of the Greek Catholic bishopric, a letter of September 1850, published in 1.6:Pervain, Chindriș 1972, I, p. 210.

247 Papiu's correspondence with Alexandru Roman (a close friend of Bishop Erdélyi) and Iacob Mureșanu is extremely telling in this respect (see 1.6:Pervain, Chindriș 1972, II, pp. 233, 304 sqq.).

248 1.5:Maior P. 1834, p. 32; 1.9:Fugariu 1983, II, p. 233.

249 Simion Bărnuțiu, "The Great Synod of the Făgăraș bishopric. *Prologus galeatus*", in 1.2:*Journal for the Mind*, VI, 1843, no. 4–5; 1.9:Bogdan-Duică 1924, pp. 213–214.

250 George Bariț, "Reflections occasioned by M. A. Gérando's description of the Romanians", in 1.2:*Journal for the Mind*, IX, 1846, no. 6; 1.9:Bariț 1962, p. 91.

251 1.6:Maior P. 1968, p. 134.

252 See 3:Dragomir 1965, pp. 153–154.

253 See the same thesis of the incompatibility between "Romanianness" and Catholicism in the intellectual debates of the inter-war period, as vehemently defended by Nae Ionescu: 2:Ionescu 1937 (1990), pp. 194–214; 3:Ornea 1995, pp. 91–94.

254 1.5:Papiu Ilarian 1852(II), pp. C-CII.

255 1.4:Maior P. 1813: "Foreword"; 1.9:Fugariu 1983, II, p. 165.

256 1.4:Maior P. 1813, p. 4; 1.4:Maior P. 1976, II, pp. 100–101. The 1791 *Supplex* had already formulated the idea but in a much more moderate manner: with Trajan's followers, "especially in the fourth century", spread in Dacia "the Christian faith, according to the rite of the Eastern Church" (1.7:*Supplex 1791*, in 3:Prodan 1971, pp. 443, 455).

257 For the same idea in Șaguna's case, see 3:Hitchins 1977, pp. 249–251. Vasile Pârvan, and particularly some of his disciples, would not be content with this priority either, which meant that they pushed the obsession with oldness even further by means of the theory of the quasi-Christian monotheism or henotheism of the Getes (see 2:Pârvan 1982, pp. 91–95). Certainly, insofar as they were Indo-Europeans, the Dacians' faith could only be based on the tripartite pantheon of these populations (3:Dumézil 1981–1986), but this is already a question of the science of mythology, not of the mythologising of science.

258 1.4:Maior P. 1813, p. 4; 1.9:Maior P. 1976, II, p. 100.

259 1.4:Țichindeal 1814, p. 482, "Moral of the fable of the sparrow and the other birds"; 1.9:Fugariu 1983, II, p. 277.

260 *Ibidem*. With the fable-writer from Banat the thesis of Romanian purity serves, in the subtext, also as an argument legitimating Romanian separation from the Serb hierarchy; Romanian tendencies cannot be condemned as a dangerous invention since they simply cannot err in church matters.

261 George Bariț, "What is pan-Wallachianism?", in 1.2:*Journal for the Mind*, VI, 1843, p. 42.

262 1.4:Maior P. 1813, p. 92; 1.9:Maior P. 1976, II, p. 133.

263 See the case of Moise Nicoară, an Orthodox believer who initially moved away from the Serbs and came closer to Țichindeal and the Uniate bishop of Oradea, then turned to the Serbs again yet did not wholly accept the supremacy of the hierarchy in Sremski Karlovci, but also became a fierce enemy of Catholicism and even of Greek Catholicism. According to his nationalism, he was, as far as confession was concerned, exclusively "on the Romanians' side", yet in practice he denied, ideologically speaking, all actual confessions which his co-nationals effectively embraced (see 1.9:Bodea 1943; 3:Bocșan, Lumperdean, Pop 1996, pp. 122–125).

264 An identity-based formula which was to make quite an impact on the Romanian social imaginary.

265 At the time, the Greek Catholics were, from a "logical" point of view, placed in a more advantageous position than the Orthodox adherents in promoting the formula of a national "new church". If you wish to change anything—the former appeared to tell the other party—so that, by means of this innovation, we can have a new formula for a national church, all you have to do is follow our example and adopt the religious union, which preserves the Eastern substance of the rite yet diverges from Slav-oriented Orthodoxy and thus represents, *par excellence*, a "third

way" which will be uniquely ours, a national, Romanian solution. Surely, the Orthodox party retaliated, particularly as the status of their church ameliorated, either by insisting on the "Catholic" dominance of the union or by devising their own theory of the national-confessional specificity and inviting the Uniates to come (back) to the ancestors' church, so that its national character could be reinforced. In arguing for the Romanian Orthodox metropolitan see, the leaders of Banat would also make use of a solid argument: Since there is no visible head of the Orthodox Church, as there is for the Catholic Church (the invisible head of the Church being Jesus Christ), we are all the more able to raise national, particularist churches with autonomous leadership, which will only be directly "subordinated" to, and otherwise in continuous communication with, the divinity (see 1.7:*Petition October 1849*, in 1.9:Păcăţian 1904, pp. 624–25).

266 The forced "reunification" of the Uniate and Orthodox Churches in 1948, but also the underground survival and the post–1989 revival of Greek Catholicism, have been a convincing illustration to the point. As to the ecumenical ideal, unless it is a mere utopia, it seems that it can only be achieved in a distant future; cf. Pope John Paul II (3:Giovanni Paolo II 1994, chp. XXII).

267 See 3:Bocşan, Lumperdean, Pop 1996, pp. 61–182.

268 Nor was a person willing to fulfil that function easy to find. Various intellectuals, some of whom were of a very "lay" cast of mind (Samuil Micu, Petru Maior, Moise Nicoară, Gheorghe Lazăr, Simion Bărnuţiu) would in turn be considered by their coteries as candidates for such high ecclesiastical positions (see 3:Păcurariu 1981; 3:Bîrlea 1987; 3:Păcurariu 1992; 3:Bocşan, Lumperdean, Pop 1996) even if it was obvious that they could never have received the approval of the political authorities (as the legal procedures required) and not even the vote of their own church synods. When, in 1850, the suggestion was made to Andrei Şaguna that he, together with his whole church, embrace Greek Catholicism so that the confessional unity of all the Romanians could be achieved and he become their national metropolitan bishop, he indignantly refused such a "betrayal" of his faith (see 3:Bîrlea 1987, pp. 239–243). For the relationship between nationalism and confession in Şaguna's case, in which the second element clearly had the upper hand, see 3:Hitchins 1977, pp. 174–175, 215–216, 250, 284 ("It is true that Şaguna judged the idea of nationality with a detachment that was utterly foreign to men like Bărnuţiu and Raţiu. He could not share their faith in it as the key to human development, for that was the role he assigned to the Christian religion." "In an age of nationalism he was not a nationalist.")

269 "Priests, hold up the cross! for Christian is the army / Freedom the word and its grand holy purpose." See Andrei Mureşanu's *Echo*, in 1.8:Mureşanu A. 1988, p. 34.

270 For the messianic Romantics, under the influence of Lamennais's Christian socialism—the true "theology of salvation" at the beginning of the modern age (see 3:Breazu 1973)—there could be no contradiction between the two objectives, as long as the will of the "people" equalled God's will. The completion of the national destiny presupposed the fulfilment of the divine designs, while collective redemption was only possible within, and by the agency of, the mystical body of the Nation.

271 This explains why, in the most difficult moments, when its identity is threatened, Greek Catholicism stresses even more its relation with Rome and its "Catholic" dimension, in order to avoid the disintegration of its specificity and its dissolution into Orthodoxy. This is what happened, for instance, in the communist and post-communism periods.

272 1.7:*Memoir 1735*, in 1.9:Păcăţian 1904, p. 60.

273 1.5:Papiu Ilarian 1852(I), pp. 195–196. It is, in fact, a conclusion as to the "advantages" that this act of union could bring the Romanians, which the Romanians' national historiography and culture would perpetuate almost unchanged, as in so many other cases, from Papiu and the other Romantics to this day.

274 Gherontie Cotore, *On the Schism of the Greeks; idem, On Those Petty Articles Which Have Caused so Much Grudge*, 1746 (fragments in 1.9:Comşa 1944, pp. 94–98).

275 *Ibidem*, p. 96.

276 This is probably a myth deliberately devised by the Counter Reformation in order to attract the Orthodox to the union, but also to exonerate the West and Catholicism of the "fault" of "having abandoned" their Christian Orthodox brothers in the hands of the barbarians. It is the same old and embarrassing story, an illustration on the theme of the "*miserabilism*" of the small peoples,

"abandoned" by the West, as the Eastern peoples were, in Yalta, thrown "into the claws of barbarism".

277 1.9:Comșa 1944, pp. 96–98.
278 1.9:Maior P. 1812, pp. 328–329; 1.9:Maior P. 1970, pp. 68–69.
279 Samuil Micu, *Short Information on the Romanians' History* (1796), in 1.9:Fugariu 1983, I, p. 231.
280 3:Bocșan, Lumperdean, Pop 1996, pp. 80–83, 112–116 (with bibliography for the 1798 moment).
281 Theodor Aaron, in 1.2:*The Mouthpiece*, I, 1847, no. 52, p. 291.
282 Timotei Cipariu, "Which Is the Oldest Romanian Book?", in *ibidem*, II, 1848, no. 54, p. 304. For the establishing of a Greek Catholic identity with the Romanians from Bihor, see 3:Barbu 1992.
283 1.9:Bodea 1943, p. 364.
284 *Ibidem.*
285 *Ibidem.*
286 If I may draw a scarcely palatable parallel, I would state that, years ago, a similar motivation pushed the nationalist politician Corneliu Vadim Tudor to take a stand in favour of the Bosnian Serbs.
287 See 3:Dragomir 1914; 3:Dragomir 1917. For the relations with the Serbs, see 3:Anuichi 1980.
288 1.9:Bodea 1943, p. 355.
289 *Ibidem.* In his later days Nicoară would even send memoirs to the Russian diplomats, in which he presented the "political-religious" actions he had taken while younger and solicited Moscow's help for the Romanian Orthodox people of Banat (see 1.7:*Memoir 1847 Russia*, in *ibidem*, pp. 404 sqq). The problem of the "Russian help" sought by the Transylvanian Romanians, also motivated by religious affinities, would be brought to the fore again, in dramatic terms, in 1848–1849. For the way in which the Transylvanian Saxons asked for Russian help in 1848, which they painfully regretted afterwards, see 3:Cosma 1995.
290 See 3:Hitchins 1983, pp. 7–28, "Religion and Rumanian National Consciousness in Eighteenth Century Transylvania".
291 Ion Ionescu of Brad to A.G. Golescu, a letter of 26 February 1849, published in 1.9:Bodea 1982, II, pp. 1010–1011.
292 See 3:Bocșan, Lumperdean, Pop 1996, pp. 145–148; 3:Hitchins 1977, pp. 87–89; also here, pp. 248–249, on the first sketches of the theory of Orthodoxy as an essential element of Romanianness in the writings of Andrei Șaguna.
293 1.7:*Memorandum 1850 Șaguna*, in 1.9:Păcățian 1904, p. 664. Also see 1.5:Șaguna 1849; 1.5:Șaguna 1850; 1.5:Șaguna 1860, vol. II, *passim*.
294 1.7:*Petition October 1849*, in 1.9: Păcățian 1904, p. 624–625.
295 3:Hitchins 1977, pp. 242–247.
296 Cf. 3:Halecki 1962; 3:Teodor 1995.
297 1.4:Maior P. 1813, p. 48; 1.9:Maior P. 1976, II, p. 119.
298 3:Teodor 1984, pp. 91–94.
299 3:Protase 1973, pp. 38–68.
300 1.9:Maior P. 1894, Title II, chp. 4, "Foolish is the Pope's vanity"; 1.9:Maior P. 1976, I, 23 sqq.
301 *Ibidem*, p. 17.
302 See, for instance, 1.4:Micu 1781, p. I; 1.9:Fugariu 1983, I, pp. 30–31. Cf. 3:Teodor 1984, pp. 90–91.
303 Simion Bărnuțiu, *The Great Synod of the Făgăraș bishopric* (1843) and *The Metropolitan See of Alba Iulia. A Word at its Time on the Liberty and Unification of the Romanian Church* (1854), see 3:Teodor 1983, pp. 102–104.
304 1.4:Maior P. 1813, p. 88; 1.9:Fugariu 1983, II, p. 174.
305 In the same sense, Orthodox parishioner Țichindeal wrote, "the Uniate keeps the fast better than we do" (see 1.4:Țichindeal 1814, p. 479; 1.9:Fugariu 1983, II, p. 276), and thus sanctioned the same paradox: the Uniates are more "Orthodox" than the Orthodox believers themselves and can keep the "Eastern specificity" even better than the non-Uniates, who are contaminated by religious "impurities" of Serb extraction.
306 *Ibidem*, p. 482 and p. 277, respectively.

307 For the nationalist ideology, this formula would be all the more commendable as it was not "contaminated" by any foreign influence and managed to remain specific and original. It would have been unacceptable, for instance, for the Romanians to have been Christianised by the agency of others, by foreign missionaries, or by means of contacts with other peoples. If they could not go as far as to claim that they had invented Christianity (as the adherents of the theory of Gete monotheism would, later on, in a disguised way), they could at least declare that they were the ones who had best preserved it, in its authentic form.

308 1.9:Fugariu 1983, II, p. 78.

309 The analysis of this cliché of self-perception as it appears in the speeches of president Iliescu, for instance, could be the object of a much more interesting study. For a tentative attempt, see 3:Pasti 1995, pp. 153–159, "The illusions of the 'national consensus'".

310 3:Bocșan, Lumperdean, Pop 1996, pp. 161–165.

311 1.4:Maior P. 1813, p. 113; 1.9:Fugariu 1983, II, p. 179.

312 1.5:Papiu Ilarian 1852(I), pp. 60–63.

313 *Ibidem*.

314 1.9:Bodea 1943, p. 356.

315 *Ibidem*, p. 358.

316 1.9:Fugariu 1983, II, p. 144.

317 1.4:Țichindeal 1814, p. 479, "Moral of the fable of the sparrow and the other birds"; 1.9:Fugariu 1983, II, p. 276.

318 A.N. [Andrei Mureșanu], "The reason why we are so belated", in 1.2:*Journal for the Mind*, VI, 1843, no. 42, pp. 329–331.

319 George Bariț, "Souvenirs of my travels", in 1.2:*The Gazette*, XV, 1852, no. 88; 1.9:Bariț 1962, p. 154.

320 Cf. 1.9:Pușcariu 1889, pp. 120–160; 1.6:*GBC* 1973–1993, III, pp. 107–108.

321 Liviu Andrei Pop to Al. Papiu Ilarian and Iosif Hodoș, a letter of February 1855, published in 1.6:Pervain, Chindriș 1972, II, p. 255.

VI. Conclusions

Most of the conclusions to be drawn from the discussion of the topics on which we have focused have been given as a coda to each chapter or section. What, then, could be offered as a final conclusion at the end of this study? One truism to be borne in mind is that the process whereby a self-image of the Transylvanian Romanians was being configured at the beginning of the modern era had to come to terms with a number of extremely complex and difficult questions. The answers to the big questions of any collective interrogation on identity—"Who are we?" and "Why are we the way we are?", and not otherwise—were far from offering simple, soothing solutions.

Firstly, the sombre reality nourishing the self-image was such as to suggest a predominantly negative perception. In political and national terms, the Romanians complained about their not being acknowledged as a politically viable entity within the constitutional mechanism of Transylvania and Hungary, and about the absence of any institution that might have allowed their national community the right to representation in, and access to, the realm of power. Despite the efforts of Emperor Joseph's regime to better their juridical and formal status, the Romanians continued to be seen as tolerated, along the lines of a tradition of political practices and perspectives established in Transylvania.

True, at the level of the self-image, such problems could be somehow isolated, accounted for and explained away by blaming them on foreign domination and oppression: evil was thus exorcised by relegating its origins to a sphere extraneous to the Romanians. There were also the Danubian principalities, which offered the consoling proof that certain national associations and institutions could exist, and in the form a sovereign state, too.

Reality was even direr in the social sphere, at the level of everyday existence, when it came to the Romanian population's material living conditions and its degree of culture and civilisation. Here things were even worse than with respect to the question of political emancipation and existence, since the disaster came in palpable, concrete forms. Its causes could no longer be as easily dissociated and placed somewhere out there, since they were too evidently anchored in the very core of Romanian existence.

What is more, the Romanian intellectuals themselves admitted that the resolution of the political-national problems and of the issues bearing on society and on civilisation could not go one without the other. However, in this case, were they not coming dangerously close to the point of view upheld by those who justified the lack of political rights for the Romanian nation by the general backwardness of the population?

It was this very serious backwardness that struck the eye and gained the observers' attention, whatever the motivation or justification. The population's misery and poverty, the precarious conditions of existence and illiteracy, as well as the evils they entailed in social and moral terms, or in terms of civilisation (dirtiness, decay, indolence, drunkenness, violence, superstitions), considered, this time, to affect both the principalities and Transylvania, were, as we have seen, descriptive elements of the self-image which could be neither ignored nor satisfactorily justified in Romanian society's attempt to define itself.

Those who were alive to such questions found themselves faced with a dilemma: the emphasis on the issue of responsibility for the present state of things, the excessive preoccupation with finding older or newer causes for it, or with explanatory exterior circumstances—was not all this in fact an attempt to flee reality, a refusal to take responsibility and assume a self-evident condition?

This is the first problem in relation to the fashioning of a self-image for the Romanian society: reality was too tough to be faithfully incorporated in an image. On the one hand, such an image was bound to damage the already sensitised self-esteem of a community that had only recently become self-aware. On the other, even if due respect were paid to the values of truth and objectivity, the following question arose: Was not such a negative image likely to discourage society's efforts towards emancipation, to blunt the enthusiasm needed for its awakening and self-trust?

The insolubility of this aporia also explains its tenacious persistence in Romanian culture: the flight from reality, in other words the illusion and the lie, cannot function as a basis for steady and efficient construction. But can a damaged and sensitised consciousness bear any sort of truth?

Another problem made an even more remarkable impact on the building of the Romanian self-image. Difficult as the reality might have been, it became even more so when described and analysed through the lens of foreign observers.

There are several factors at work here. For one thing, since the Romanian intellectuals were few in number[1] and enjoyed only limited material possibilities of expression[2], it was natural that foreigners who approached Romanian issues in widely circulated writings should be more numerous. Also, foreigners were more often than not the *first* to tackle a particular problem, which explains why Romanian writings, even the substantial contributions to the point, were most often replies, answers or arguments for or against an opinion that had already been expressed by a foreigner.

In most cases, Romanian writing at the time did not make a direct and first-hand approach to the issue of the Romanians' specificity and lifestyle, but only appeared in the form of replies to a foreign reference, which was either refuted for its mistakes, exaggerations and distortions, or accepted as the truth, while a more sensitive motivation was sought for certain negative traits of the image.[3]

There is not only an objective reason for this situation, that is, the higher numbers of foreigners, but also a subjective one, relating to the Romanians' unwillingness to insist on an extremely disheartening reality. Since they could neither fake nor overtax it, they were, paradoxically, left to prefer having others speak about them, so that they could then work on this basis in searching for nuances and justifications.

The worst of it was that this state of affairs was solely due to certain exterior circumstances; otherwise, it must have been extremely unpleasant to hear foreigners advance such opinions and descriptions.

Firstly, national pride was all the more damaged when the negative images were presented by foreigners before the whole of Europe. Secondly, and naturally, the foreigners' observations and judgements were sometimes less pertinent, either due to superficial consideration or to lack of better knowledge, which was easy to understand, or out of ill will or antipathy. Here lay the biggest problem. The negative images sketched by foreigners, whether exaggerated or accurate, biased or faithful, could easily turn into crushing arguments, with practical effects, in the hands of the Romanians' political and national adversaries, whereby they could justify their oppression and domination.

Under such difficult circumstances a polemical attitude and the questioning of such images became, for the Romanian intellectuals, an acute necessity, not so much for the sake of a disinterested pursuit of the truth in a theoretical dispute, but as a weapon in political-national confrontations. The Transylvanian Romanians' self-image would be shaped accordingly: the prime concern was not the need for self-knowledge or an inner drive towards a better understanding of their own specificity, but the necessity of replying to the attacks and denigration of others. The Romanian intellectuals were primarily careful to demolish foreign images, and only in the second place keen on constructing an image of their own. They had to prove first that they were not what foreigners said they were; self-questioning would only be approached afterwards.

These are the roots of an essential feature of the Transylvanian Romanians' self-perception in the modern age: its intrinsic *nationalism*. The self-image is polemical, offensive, strongly oriented towards the outside, against all those who wrong and jeopardise the Romanian nation; it never starts from the Romanians' own reality but only refers to the adverse perceptions of others.

Both elements presented here are the premises for a distorting self-image, or, more exactly, for an erroneous understanding and interpretation of reality. A double pressure drives the image further and further away from reality: first, the reality is too sombre and discouraging to be unreservedly accepted, and second, the image would sooner relate to other illusions and images than respond to *real* topical problems.

This tension between image and reality threatened to place self-understanding and judgement on the moving sands of some illusory territories, to base them on lies and fakes, and thus to induce a grievous collective self-identification crisis. The features singled out, usually mere flaws and qualities of any human being, were emotionally overcharged as a function of a self-image that violently jarred with both its true ego and with the surrounding world.

Those flaws and qualities thus became obsessive inferiority and superiority complexes, which primitive fears or vanities related to an imaginary world of illusory *alter egos*, of omnipresent enemies hatching a universal conspiracy. Fear of this universal threat engendered the jealous privileging of those traits that were specific to the Romanians, that singled them out and that they alone possessed— "they alone" according to the criteria of this sick consciousness that simply missed the banal truth that the real features that *bracket together* human communities are much more numerous and more important than those which differentiate them. Hospitality, humour, tolerance or a poetic gift, or, on the contrary, idleness, superficiality or incoherence were proclaimed as Romanian national defining traits, as if they could be other than mere universal attributes describing the morals, behaviour or creative capacity of any human being at any moment in time and at any point in space.

The testimonies and texts analysed in this book suggest, I believe, the fact that, nevertheless, the Transylvanian intellectuals who laid the foundations for a modern self-image often managed to avoid these traps and to give evidence of balance, reason and lucidity in the face of such a burdensome "imagological" situation. Taken as a lesson of history, their travail is worthy of notice and even of a touch of warm sympathy and deference.

Obviously, this heritage is still manifest in Romanian spirituality. Whether or not it will be able to tame its own harmful potential in other ages, which may not be so difficult but are certainly deprived of enlightened élites devoted to the ideal of reason and tolerance, the credo of a Bariţ or Cipariu, is a question over which the honest researcher will have to puzzle even more when approaching the space of contemporary reality.

Notes

1 A study on the Romanian intellectuals of Transylvania in the first half of the nineteenth century, especially from the point of view of their formation, in 3:Gyémánt 1986, pp. 336–362; a briefer account in 3:Hitchins 1983, pp. 74–95, "Rumanian Intellectuals in Transylvania: The West and National Consciousness, 1830–1848", where it is shown that there were approximately 10,000 literate people and only several hundreds of graduates in a population of almost two million people.
2 The sociological analysis of the cultural institutions and of the Romanian intellectual readership of the time, in 3:Marica 1977, pp. 11–111, "Contributions to the issue of the subscribers to the Romanian periodicals up until the First World War"; as well as in 3:*Ideology generation* 1968, pp. 10–31, 160–236.
3 See 3:Mitu S. 1994, pp. 106–108.

VII. Bibliography

1. PERIOD SOURCES

1.1. UNPUBLISHED MANUSCRIPTS AND DOCUMENTS

Alpini 1845. A letter of 21 July 1845, Constantin Alpini, rector of Mediaș to Vasile Moldvai, copy transcribed in the annexes to the manuscript study of Coriolan Suciu, "Other fragments of the Lemeni process" (in Romanian) (1.1:Suciu 1938), ms. in the Cluj Institute for History (Ioan Chindriș).

Aurora 1838–1840. Manuscript journal of the pupils in Blaj, 1838–1840; period copies of excerpts from it in B.A.R., Bucharest, Rom. ms. 460–461.

Cipariu cca. 1846. Timotei Cipariu, "A literary note" (in Romanian), ms. in the State Archives in Cluj, the Blaj Stock, the "Timotei Cipariu" Collection, no. 2749.

Cipariu cca. 1849. Timotei Cipariu ["Up, let's stand up for our rights and country!" (in Romanian)], untitled poem printed as leaflet, in the State Archives in Cluj, the Blaj Stock, the "Timotei Cipariu" Collection, no. 2801.

Cipariu 1850. Timotei Cipariu, *From the North of Dacia, 10/22 Febr.* (in Romanian) [1850, account of travel through Bucovina], B.A.R. Bucharest, Rom. ms. 994, f. 207r–208v.

Cipariu 1853. A letter of 27 December 1853, Timotei Cipariu to Iacob Mureșanu, unpublished ms. transcribed by Dr. Ioan Chindriș, at the Cluj Institute for History.

Complaint 1842. The complaint submitted to the Blaj bishopric by the Greek Catholic community in Budiul de Cîmpie (in Romanian), dated 1 June 1842, ms. in the State Archives in Blaj, the Greek Catholic Metropolitan See Stock, no. 593/1842.

Crainic 1845. A letter of 22 May 1845, Simion Crainic to the rectors' assembly in the Blaj diocese, ms. in the State Archives in Cluj, the Blaj Stock, the "Ioan Lemeni" Collection, no. 3703 (under no. 3702 a copy, different handwriting).

Crișan 1842. A letter of 15 June 1842, George Crișan, superintendent of the Pogăceaua district to Bishop Ioan Lemeny, ms. in the State Archives in Cluj, the Greek Catholic Metropolitan See Stock, no. 699/1842.

Dragomir 1845. A letter of 21 March 1845, Ioan Dragomir to Ștefan Moldvai, ms. in the State Archives in Cluj, the Blaj Stock, the "Ioan Lemeni" Collection, no. 3764.

Gojdu 1869. Period copy of Emanuil Gojdu's will (drawn up on 4 November 1869), ms. in the National Museum of Transylvanian History, cat. no. M1928–1929.

Hardworking People cca 1848. ["Aren't we hardworking people" (in Romanian)], anonymous verse transcribed at the epoch, ms. in the Central University Library in Cluj, the Stock of Mikó Rhédei's correspondence, box 77, no. 9, f. 1r+v.

Many 1838a. Iosif Many, "Prayer" (in Romanian), poem published in the manuscript journal *Aurora* (Blaj) in 1838, copied at the epoch by Nicolae Pauleti, B.A.R., Bucharest, Rom. ms. 460–461, f. 34v.

Moldvai 1843. A letter of 28 July 1843, Vasile Moldvai, priest in Uifălău to Grigore Moldvai, ms. in the State Archives in Cluj, the Blaj Stock, the "Ioan Lemeni" Collection.

Papfalvi 1846. A letter of 4 May 1846, Constantin Papfalvi to Vasile Moldovan, copy transcribed in the annexes to the manuscript study of Coriolan Suciu, "Other fragments of the Lemeni process" (in Romanian) (1.1:Suciu 1938), ms. in the Cluj Institute for History (Ioan Chindriş).

A Poem. Iancu cca. 1848. "A Poem. Iancu" (in Romanian), anonymous poem transcribed at the epoch, ms. in the Central University Library in Cluj, the Stock of Mikó Rhédei's correspondence, box 77, no. 9, f. 1v–2r.

Pop 1843. The declaration of Ioan Pop, priest in Budiul de Cîmpie, made in Blaj on 22 September 1843, concerning the Lemeni process; ms. in B.A.R., Cluj, Archive Stock, no. 3632.

Pop Iosif 1843. A letter datable after 14 June 1843, Iosif Pop, teacher in Blaj, to Nicolae Maniu, the Greek Catholic rector of Sibiu (copy transcribed by historian Nicolae Albu), ms. in the Cluj Institute for History (Ioan Chindriş).

Raţiu 1845. A letter of 1 July 1845, Vasile Raţiu to Timotei Cipariu, copy transcribed in the annexes to the manuscript study of Coriolan Suciu, "Other fragments of the Lemeni process" (in Romanian) (1.1:Suciu 1938), ms. in the Cluj Institute for History (Ioan Chindriş).

Suciu 1938. Coriolan Suciu, "Other fragments of the Lemeni process" (in Romanian), the continuation of the study 3:Suciu 1938a, remained in manuscript due to the intervention of the Metropolitan See in Blaj; autograph ms. in the Cluj Institute for History (Ioan Chindriş).

1.2. PAPERS AND PERIODICALS*

Archiv. Archiv des Vereins für Siebenbürgische Landeskunde (Sibiu), 1843–1848.

Blätter. Blätter für Geist, Gemüt und Vaterlandskunde (Braşov), 1842–1848.

The Friend. The Friend of the People (in Romanian) (Pest), 1848.

The Gazette. The Transylvanian Gazette (in Romanian) [Starting 3 January 1849: *The Transylvania Gazette*; from 1 December 1849: *The Gazette of Transylvania*] (Braşov), 1838–1855.

Híradó. Erdély Híradó [The Transylvanian Herald] (Cluj), 1840–1848.

Hírlap. Pesti Hírlap [The Pest Gazette], 1848.

Journal. Historical Journal for Dacia (in Romanian) (Bucharest), 1845–1848.

The Library. The Romanian Library (in Romanian) (Buda), 1821, 1829–1830, 1834.

Literary Paper. Literary Paper (in Romanian) (Braşov), 1838.

The Mouthpiece. The Mouthpiece of Enlightenment (in Romanian) [Starting May 1848: *The National Mouthpiece*] (Blaj), 1847–1848.

Nemzet. Nemzet [The Nation] (Pest), 1848.

Journal for the Mind. Journal for the Mind, Heart and Literature (in Romanian) (Braşov), 1838–1861.

The People. The Sovereign People (in Romanian) (Bucharest), 1848.

Satellit. Satellit des Siebenb. Wochenblattes (Braşov), 1840–1848.

Századunk. Századunk [Our Century] (Bratislava), 1840.

Társalkodó. Nemzeti Társalkodó [National Dialogues] (Cluj), 1830.

The Teacher. The Teacher of the People (in Romanian) (Blaj), 1848.

The Telegraph. The Romanian Telegraph (in Romanian) (Sibiu), 1853.

Újság. Vasárnapi Újság [The Sunday Paper] (Cluj), 1846–1848.

Wiener Allgemeine. Wiener Allgemeine Literaturzeitung (Vienna), 1813.

Zeitung. Wiener Zeitung (Vienna), 1848.

1.3. CALENDARS

Calendar Braşov (Bariţ). *Calendar for the Romanian people...* (in Romanian) (ed. George Bariţ. Braşov: Römer & Kramner, 1852–1853).

Calendar Buda I. Calendar for A.D. [...] *Made to show the position and climate of the Hungarian Land and of the principalities of Transylvania, Wallachia and Moldavia* (in Romanian) (ed. Samuil Micu, Gheorghe Şincai, Petru Maior. Buda: the University Press, 1806–1821).

---

* The years of publication of the periodicals (papers and calendars) listed here do not refer to the whole periods in which they were issued, but only to the intervals of interest for the present study.

Calendar Buda II (Carcalechi). *Calendar for A.D.* [...] *Made to show the position and climate of the Hungarian Land, of the Great Principality of Transylvania, of Wallachia and Moldavia* (in Romanian) (ed. Zaharia Carcalechi. Buda: the University Press, 1817–1818, 1825).

Calendar Buda III (Theodorovici). *Calendar for A.D.* [...] *Made to show the position and climate of the Hungarian Land, of the Great Principality of Transylvania, of Wallachia and Moldavia* (in Romanian) (ed. Ion Theodorovici. Buda: the University Press, 1824–1853).

Calendar Buda IV (Neagoe). *Calendar for A.D.* [...](in Romanian) (ed. Ştefan P. Neagoe. Buda: the University Press, 1828–1832; starting 1829: *Romanian Calendar*).

Calendar Sibiu I. Calendar... (in Romanian) (Sibiu: Barth Press, Clozius Press, 1792–1849).

Calendar Sibiu II. Calendar... (in Romanian) (Sibiu: the Diocese Press, 1852–1856).

1.4. OLD BOOKS (1780–1830)

Aaron Th. 1828. Theodor Aaron, *Short Appendix to Petru Maior's History* (in Romanian). Buda: the University Press, 1828.

Advice 1816. *Advice for preventing and curing the illnesses spreading throughout the country and those binding spells and some sporadic diseases, that is to say, of the kind that comes here and there, striking horned cattle, sheep and pigs* (in Romanian). Buda: the University Press, 1816.

The Adviser 1826. *The Adviser of the Young in Which There Is Counsel on How to Have True and Useful Commerce with Books* (in Romanian). Buda: the University Press, 1826 [although the front cover mentions Gheorghe Lazăr as author of the work, the real author must be Zaharia Carcalachi, who signs the dedication to the book and who probably opted for that substitution for promotional reasons, with a view to impressing the readers].

Barruel 1803. L'Abbé Augustin de Barruel, *Mémoires pour servir à l'histoire du Jacobinisme*. Hamburg: P. Fauche, 1803.

Bojincă 1827. Damaschin Bojincă, *Animadversio in Dissertationem Hallensem sub titulo: Erweis dass die Walachen nicht römischer Abkunft sind*. Pest: Landerer Publishers, 1827.

Bojincă 1828. Damaschin Bojincă, *A Sickened Response to the Foul Words Uttered in Halle in the Year 1823* [...](in Romanian). Buda: the University Press, 1828.

Bojincă 1830. Damaschin Bojincă, *The Manual of Good Conduct to Be Consulted by Parents and Put to Good Use by the Romanian Youth* (in Romanian). Buda: the University Press, 1830.

Bota 1829. Moise Bota, *Poems Spurring the Romanian Youth to Studying Hard, as a Gift of Gratefulness for the Bright New Year MDCCCXXIX* (in Romanian). Buda: the University Press, 1829.

Carcalechi 1826. Zaharia Carcalechi, *The Adviser of the Young* (in Romanian). Buda: the University Press, 1826.

Costin 1812a. [Toma Costin?], *Discussio descriptionis Valachorum Transylvanorum editae patrioticis paginis (Vaterländische Blätter) Nris 83, 84, 85 Viennae 1811. Auctore I.G.*. Pest: Trattner Press, 1812.

Costin 1812b. [Toma Costin?], *Észrevételek Tekéntetes Schwartner Márton úr Magyarország statistikájában az oláhokról tett jegyzésekre* [Observations regarding the considerations made by the honourable Martin Schwartner in reference to the Romanians in his statistics of Hungary]. Pest, 1812.

Crişan-Körösi 1805. [Ştefan Crişan-Körösi], *Ortographia latino-valachica*. Cluj: The Press of the Lutheran College, 1805.

Decree 1786. [Imperial Decree for the Settlement of the Laws of Marriage in Transylvania] Sibiu: 1786.

Diaconovici-Loga 1821. Constantin Diaconovici-Loga, *Appeal for the Publication of Romanian books* (in Romanian). Buda: the University Press, 1821.

Diaconovici-Loga 1822. Constantin Diaconovici-Loga, *Romanian Grammar* (in Romanian). Buda: the University Press, 1822.

Dóczy 1829–1830. József Dóczy, *Európa tekintete természeti, műveleti és kormányi állapotjában* [Inquiry into the natural and cultural state and of the governing forms in Europe], IX. Vienna, 1829–1830.

Eder 1791. *Supplex Libellus Valachorum Transsilvaniae iura tribus receptis Nationibus communia postliminio sibi adseri postulantium. Cum notis historico-criticis I.C.E.* [Joseph Karl Eder] *civis transilvani* [The Appeal of the Romanian Transylvanians who demand to be given back the rights common to all three acknowledged nations. With historical-critical notes by I.C.E., a citizen of Transylvania]. Cluj: Martin Hochmeister Press, 1791.

Engel 1794. Johann Christian Engel, *Commentatio de expeditionibus Traiani ad Danubium et origine Valachorum*. Vienna, 1794.

Gergely de Ciocotiş 1819. Vasile Gergely de Ciocotiş (trans. from G.I. Wenzel), *The Man of the World or Several Rules of Civility, Elegance, Good Conduct and True Graciousness for the Use of the Romanian Youth* (in Romanian). Vienna: Dim. Davidovici Press, 1819.

Horga Popovici 1807. Nicolae Horga Popovici, *A Mirror Shewn to the Wise Man, including Stories of Old and Useful Teachings, on How Welcome It Is to Know Yourself and Be Kind to Your Neighbour as Signs of Wisdom* (in Romanian). Buda: the University Press, 1807.

Iercovici 1794. *History of Alexander the Great from Macedonia* […](in Romanian), trans. and preface by Dimitrie Iercovici. Sibiu: Petru Barth Press, 1794.

Iorgovici 1799. Paul Iorgovici, *Observations on the Romanian Language* (in Romanian). Buda: the University Press, 1799.

Lexicon 1825. Romanian–Latin–Hungarian–German Lexicon (in Romanian). Buda: the University Press, 1825.

Maior P. 1809. Petru Maior, *"Didahii", which is to say teachings for raising the young after the dead infants are buried* (in Romanian). Buda: the University Press, 1809.

Maior P. 1812. Petru Maior, *History of the Beginning of the Romanians in Dacia* (in Romanian). Buda: the University Press, 1812.

Maior P. 1813. Petru Maior, *History of the Romanians' Church* (in Romanian). Buda: the University Press, 1813.

Maior P. 1814a. Petru Maior, *Animadversiones in Recensionem Historiae de origine Valachorum in Dacia*. Buda: the University Press, 1814.

Maior P. 1814b. Petru Maior, *Response to the Slander Against the Person of Petru Maior, the Author of the History Treating of the Beginning of the Romanians in Dacia* (in Romanian). Buda: the University Press, 1814.

Maior P. 1815. Petru Maior, *Reflexiones in Responsum Domini recensentis Viennensis ad Animadversiones in Recensionem Historiae de origine Valachorum in Dacia*. Pest: Trattner Press, 1815.

Maior P. 1816. Petru Maior, *Contemplatio Recensionis in valachicam anticriticam Literarii Ephemeridibus Viennensibus, nro 7, Februar, 1816, divulgatae*. Buda: the University Press, 1816.

Micu 1781. Samuil Micu, *Dissertatio canonica de matrimonio juxta disciplinam graecae orientalis ecclesiae*. Vienna: Kurzböck Press, 1781.

Micu 1801. Samuil Micu, *Book of Prayers for Devout Christians* (in Romanian). Sibiu: Martin Hochmeister Press, 1801.

Micu, Şincai 1780. Samuil Micu and Gheorghe Şincai, *Elementa linguae daco–romanae sive valachicae*. Vienna: Kurzböck Press, 1780.

Murgu 1830. Eftimie Murgu, *Widerlegung der Abhandlung welche unter dem Titel vorkömnt* […] *durch S.T. in Ofen 1827 und Beweis dass die Wallachen der Römer unbezweifelte Nachkömmlinge sind*. Buda: the University Press, 1830.

Nicolau 1814–1815. Nicola Nicolau (ed.), *Geography or the Mapping of the Earth* (in Romanian) I–II. Buda: the University Press, 1814-1815.

Nicolau 1819. Pierre Blanchard, *The New Plutarch or the Short Version of the Lives of the Most Famous Men and Women of Every Nation, from the Earliest Times to This Day* (in Romanian), I–II, ed. Nicola Nicolau. Buda: the University Press, 1819.

Prale 1827. *The Psalter of the Prophet King David* (in Romanian), trans. Ioan Prale. Braşov: Sobeli Press, 1827.

Roja 1809. Gheorghe Constantin Roja, *The Art of Spelling the Romanian Language with Latin Letters*, (in Romanian). Buda: the University Press, 1809.

Schwartner 1089. Martin Schwartner, *Statistik des Königreichs Ungarn*, I. Buda, 1809.

Sulzer 1781–1782. Franz Joseph Sulzer, *Geschichte des transalpinischen Daciens, das ist Walachei, Moldau und Bessarabiens, im Zusammenhange mit der Geschichte des übrigen Daciens*, I–III. Vienna, 1781–1782.

Şincai 1783. Gheorghe Şincai, *The Great Catechism* (in Romanian). Blaj: The Seminary Press, 1783.

Şincai 1805. Gheorghe Şincai, *Elementa linguae daco-romanae sive valachicae* (second edition). Buda: the University Press, 1805.

Şincai 1806. Gheorghe Şincai, *Advice for the Good Use of Field Economy to Benefit the Romanian Schools from the Hungarian Land and its Unified Parts* (in Romanian). Buda: the University Press, 1806.

Teaching 1820. *Theological Teaching on the Ways and Duties of a Good Christian* (in Romanian). Sibiu: Barth Press, 1820.

Tempea 1797. Radu Tempea, *Romanian Grammar* (in Romanian). Sibiu: Petru Barth Press, 1797.

Thewrewk 1825. József Thewrewk [Török], *Három értekezés Hunyadi Székely János, magyarországi Kormányzó [...] törvényes ágyból lett születésének bebizonyítására* [Three dissertations which give true account of the birth of Ioan Huniade the Szekler, governor of Hungary [...], of lawfully wedded husband and wife]. Bratislava, 1825.

Tököly 1823. [Sava Tököly], *Erweis dass die Wallachen nicht Römischer Abkunft sind [...]*. Halle, 1823.

Tököly 1827. S.T. [Sava Tököly], *Demonstration that the Wallachians or else called Romanians are not of Roman descent [...]* (in Romanian). Buda: the University Press, 1827.

Ţichindeal 1814. Dimitrie Ţichindeal, *Philosophical and Political Teachings Whose Moral Wisdom Is Shown in Fables and Examples* (in Romanian). Buda: the University Press, 1814.

1.5. BOOKS (1831–1861)

Aaron F. 1835–1838. Florian Aaron, *Brief Account of the History of the Wallachian Principality* (in Romanian), I–III. Bucharest: I. Eliad's Press, 1835, 1837, 1838.

Aaron F. 1839. Florian Aaron, *Manual of the History of the Romanian Principality* (in Romanian). Bucharest: Sf. Sava Press, 1839.

Barac 1836. *Arabian Nights* (in Romanian), I, trans. Ioan Barac. Braşov, 1836.

Bălcescu/Russo 1850. Nicolae Bălcescu, *Song To Romania* (in Romanian). Paris: De Soye, 1850.

Benigni 1837. Joseph Benigni von Mildenberg, *Handbuch der Statistik und Geographie des Grossfürstenthums Siebenbürgens*, I–III. Sibiu, 1837.

Bojincă 1832–1833. Damaschin Bojincă, *The Ancient Times of the Romans* (in Romanian), I–II. Buda: the University Press, 1832–1833.

Desprez 1850. Hippolyte Desprez, *Les peuples d'Autriche et de la Turquie. Histoire contemporaine des magyars, des roumains et des polonais*, I–II. Paris, 1850.

Heliade 1838. Ion Heliade-Rădulescu, preface to Dimitrie Ţichindeal, *Philosophical and Political Teachings Whose Moral Wisdom Is Shown in Fables and Examples* (in Romanian), ed. Ion Heliade-Rădulescu. Bucharest: Heliade Press, 1838.

Kemény D. 1861. Dénes Kemény, *Honegység* [Unity of the Country], ed. Gábor Kemény. Cluj, 1861.

Kőváry 1847. László Kőváry, *Erdélyország Statisztikája* [Statistics of Transylvania], I. Cluj, 1847.

Laurian 1849. August Treboniu Laurian, *Die Romänen der Österreichischen Monarchie*, I–III. Vienna, 1849.

Maior P. 1834. Petru Maior, *History of the Beginning of the Romanians in Dacia* (in Romanian), eds. Iordache Mălinescu and Damaschin Bojincă. Buda: the University Press, 1834.

Negruzzi 1857. Constantin Negruzzi, *The Indiscretions of Young Age* (in Romanian). Iaşi: Bermann Press, 1857.

Papiu Ilarian 1852(I). Alexandru Papiu Ilarian, *History of the Romanians from Higher Dacia* (in Romanian), vol. I, 2nd edition. Vienna: C. Gerold & Son Press, 1852.

Papiu Ilarian 1852(II). Alexandru Papiu Ilarian, *History of the Romanians from Higher Dacia* (in Romanian), vol. II. Vienna: C. Gerold & Son Press, 1852.

Széchenyi 1841. István Széchenyi, *A Kelet népe* [The People of the East]. Pest, 1841.

Széchenyi 1842. István Széchenyi, *A Magyar Akadémia körül* [On the Hungarian Academy]. Pest, 1841.

Şaguna 1849. Andrei Şaguna, *Reminder of the Historical Right to Autonomy of the Romanians' National Church of Eastern Faith in These Provinces of the Austrian Monarchy and Coda* (in Romanian). Sibiu, 1849.

Şaguna 1850. Andrei Şaguna, *Coda to the Reminder of the Historical Right to Autonomy of the Romanians' National Church of Eastern Faith in These Provinces of the Austrian Monarchy* (in Romanian). Sibiu, 1850.

Şaguna 1860. Andrei Şaguna, *History of the Universal Eastern Orthodox Church* (in Romanian), I–II. Sibiu, 1860.

Vaillant 1844. J.A. Vaillant, *La Romanie ou l'histoire, langue, littérature, orographie, statistique des Romans*, I–III. Paris, 1844.

Wesselényi 1833. Miklós Wesselényi, *Balítéletekről* [On Prejudice]. [Apocryphal place of publication: Bucharest] [Leipzig], 1833.

Wesselényi 1833. Miklós Wesselényi, *Szózat a magyar és szláv nemzetiség ügyében* [Discourse on the question of the Hungarian and Slav nations]. Leipzig, 1843.

1.6. Published Correspondence: Volumes and Sets

GBC 1973–1993. *George Bariţ and His Contemporaries* (in Romanian), I–IX, co-ord. Ştefan Pascu and Iosif Pervain, ed. Ştefan Pascu, Iosif Pervain, Ioan Chindriş, Titus Moraru, Gelu Neamţu, Grigore Ploeşteanu, Mircea Popa, Dumitru Suciu, Ioan Buzaşi, George Cipăianu, Ioan Gabor, Gheorghe Asanache, Alexandru Matei. Bucharest: Minerva, 1973, 1975, 1976, 1978, 1981, 1983, 1985, 1987, 1993.

Hodoş 1940. Enea Hodoş, *Letters* (in Romanian). Sibiu: Veştemean Press, f.a. [preface dated 1940].

Hodoş 1944. Enea Hodoş, *From the Correspondence of Simeon Bărnuţiu and His Contemporaries* (in Romanian). Sibiu: O.L. Veştemean Press, 1944.

Maior L. 1972. Liviu Maior, *Avram Iancu. Letters* (in Romanian). Cluj: Dacia, 1972.

Maior P. 1968. Petru Maior, *Letters and New Documents* (in Romanian), ed. Nicolae Albu. Bucharest: Publishing House for Literature, 1968.

Pervain, Chindriş 1972. Iosif Pervain and Ioand Chindriş (eds.), *The Correspondence of Alexandru Papiu Ilarian* (in Romanian), I–II. Cluj: Dacia, 1972.

Suciu I.D. 1945. I.D. Suciu, *Nicolae Tincu Velia (1816–1867). His Life and Work* (in Romanian). Bucharest: Bucharest Institute for National History, 1845 (documentary annexes: "The Correspondence of Nicolae Ticu Velia" [in Romanian]).

1.7. Political Memoirs and Petitions

Address April 1849. *The Address of the Romanian Delegation in Vienna to General Jellačić* (in Romanian), of 28 April 1849, published in 1.9:Păcăţian 1904, pp. 546–548.

Address November 1849. *Homage Address of 15 November 1849 by the Romanians from the Arad diocese* (in Romanian), submitted to Emperor Franz Joseph, published in 1.9:Păcăţian 1904, pp. 631–633.

Appeal April 1850. *Appeal by the Romanian Leaders of the County of Somcuta in Favour of the Former Deputy Sigismund Pop* (in Romanian), published in 1.9:Dragomir 1944–1946, I, pp. 192–195.

Last Appeal August 1819. *Last Appeal of 15 August 1819, drawn up by Moise Nicoară and destined to the Emperor Francisc I* (in Romanian), published in 1.9:Bodea 1943, pp. 298 sqq.

Memoir 1735. *Memoir addressed to the emperor on 8 March 1735 by Bishop Ioan Inochentie Micu-Klein* (in Romanian), published in 1.9:Păcăţian 1904, p. 60.

Memoir 1846 Răşinari. *Memoir addressed to the emperor in 1846 by the Romanian community in Răşinari* (in Romanian), published in 1.9:Păcăţian 1904, pp. 165–169.

Memoir 1847. *Memoir addressed to the Sublime Porte by Moise Nicoară in 1847* (in Romanian), published in 1.9:Bodea 1943, pp. 393 sqq.

Memoir 1847 Russia. *Memoir addressed by Moise Nicoară in 1847 to the Russian ambassador in Turkey* (in Romanian), published in 1.9:Bodea 1943, pp. 404 sqq.

Memoir August 1848. *Memoir made by Solicitor Miclăuș concerning the state of the Romanians from the Imperial Land* (in Romanian), published in 1.9:Dragomir 1944–1946, II, pp. 178 sqq.

Memoir September 1848. *Memoir addressed to the Austrian Parliament by the Romanians from Transylvania* (in Romanian), drawn up in Blaj on 26 September 1848, published in 1.9:Bodea 1982, II, pp. 910–913 (translation from the German original, published on pp. 913 sqq.).

Memorandum March 1849. *The Memorandum of 5 March 1849, addressed to the Austrian government by the Romanian delegation in Vienna* (in Romanian), published in 1.9:Păcățian 1904, pp. 535–541.

Memorandum January 1850. *The Memorandum of 10 January 1849, submitted to the Austrian government by the Romanian delegation in Vienna* (in Romanian), published in 1.9:Păcățian 1904, pp. 649–657.

Memorandum 1850 Șaguna. *The Memorandum addressed to the Austrian government by Bishop Andrei Șaguna at the beginning of the year 1850* (in Romanian), published in 1.9:Păcățian 1904, pp. 658–667.

Petition July 1814. *Petition of the Romanians from the Arad diocese* (in Romanian), submitted to the emperor in July 1814, published in 1.9:Păcățian 1904, pp. 140–148.

Petition May 1848. *Petition of the Romanian people from Hungary and Banat* (in Romanian), addressed to the Hungarian government on 21 May 1848, published in 1.9:Păcățian 1904, pp. 344–347; 1.9:Bodea 1982, I, pp. 509–511.

Petition June 1848. *Petition of 18 June 1848 by the Romanian delegation in Vienna* (in Romanian), published in 1.9:Păcățian 1904, pp. 369–370.

Petition February 1849. *Petition of 25 February 1849 by the Romanian delegation in Vienna* (in Romanian), published in 1.9:Păcățian 1904, pp. 519–522.

Petition July 1849. *Petition of 18 July 1849 by the Romanian delegation in Vienna* (in Romanian), published in 1.9:Păcățian 1904, pp. 599–605.

Petition October 1849. *Petition addressed on 24 October 1849 to the Austrian ministry by the delegates from Banat concerning the hierarchical schism of the Serb Church* (in Romanian), published in 1.9:Păcățian 1904, pp. 623–627.

Petition December 1849. *Petition of December 1849 by the people of Lugoj to the emperor* (in Romanian), published in 1.9:Păcățian 1904, pp. 636–637.

Petition January 1850. *Petition of January 1850 by Bishop Erdélyi to the emperor* (in Romanian), published in 1.9:Păcățian 1904, pp. 641–648.

Response July 1849. *Response of 29 July 1849 by the Romanian delegation in Vienna to the previous reaction of Minister Bach* (in Romanian), published in 1.9:Păcățian 1904, pp. 607–611.

Bishop Șaguna before Emperor Franz Joseph (in Romanian), published in 1.9:Păcățian 1904, pp. 516–519.

Supplex 1791. The memoir *Supplex Libellus Valachorum* (in Romanian) of 28 March 1791, addressed to Emperor Leopold II, published in 3:Prodan 1971, pp. 443–466.

Supplex 1804. *Memoir addressed to the emperor by the representatives of the Romanians in 1804* (in Romanian), published in 3:Prodan 1970, pp. 82–89.

1.8. POETRY: VOLUMES AND SETS

Budai-Deleanu 1974–1975. Ion Budai-Deleanu, *Works* (in Romanian), I–II, ed. Florea Fugariu. Bucharest: Minerva, 1974, 1975. Vol. I: *The Gypsiad (B)* (in Romanian); vol. II: *The Gypsiad (A)* (in Romanian); *Three Brave Men* (in Romanian).

Cipariu 1976. Timotei Cipariu, *Poems* (in Romanian), ed. Nicolae Albu. Cluj: Dacia, 1976.

Gherman 1977. Mihai Gherman (ed.), *The Transylvanian School (Poems, Prose, Translations)* (in Romanian). Cluj: Dacia, 1977.

Mureșanu A. 1963. Andrei Mureșanu, *Poems and Articles* (in Romanian), ed. D. Păcurariu. Bucharest: Publishing House for Literature, 1963.

Mureșanu A. 1988. Andrei Mureșanu, *Poems. Articles* (in Romanian), ed. Ion Buzași. Bucharest: Minerva, 1988.

Pauleti 1980. Nicolae Pauleti, *Writings. Original Poems. Folklore. Translations from Ovid* (in Romanian), ed. Ioan Chindriș. Bucharest: Minerva, 1980.

1.9. ANTHOLOGIES, DOCUMENT COLLECTIONS, WORKING TOOLS, CRITICAL EDITIONS, SUBSEQUENT RE-EDITS

Bariț 1962. George Bariț, *Social–Political Writings* (in Romanian), ed. Victor Cherestesiu, Camil Mureșan, George Em. Marica. Bucharest: Publishing House for Politics, 1962.

Bălcescu 1974. Nicolae Bălcescu, *Works* (in Romanian), I, ed. G. Zane and Elena G. Zane. Bucharest: Publishing House of the Academy, 1974.

Bălcescu 1986. Nicolae Bălcescu, *The Romanians Under the Rule of Mihai Voyvod the Brave* (in Romanian), ed. Daniela Poenaru. Bucharest: Publishing House of the Academy, 1986. [Vol. III in the *Opere* series].

Bărnuțiu 1990. Simion Bărnuțiu, *The Blaj Discourse and Writings from 1848* (in Romanian), ed. Ioan Chindriș. Cluj: The World Union of Free Romanians, 1990.

Bocșan Leu 1988. *Memoir-writing at the time of the 1848 Revolution in Transylvania* (in Romanian), ed. Nicolae Bocșan and Valeriu Leu. Cluj: Dacia, 1988.

Bodea 1937. [Moise Nicoară], *Fragments of Biography* (in Romanian), published by Cornelia Bodea, in *Hotarul*, IV, 1937, no. 5.

Bodea 1943. Cornelia C. Bodea, *Moise Nicoară (1784–1861) and the role he played in the struggle for the national–religious emancipation of the Romanians from Banat and Crișana* (in Romanian), part I. Arad: Diocese Press, 1943 (documentary annexes).

Bodea 1967. Cornelia Bodea, *The Romanians' Fight for National Unity. 1834–1849* (in Romanian). Bucharest: Publishing House of the Academy, 1967 (documentary annexes).

Bodea 1982. Cornelia Bodea, *The Year 1848 and the Romanians. A History in Dates and Documents* (in Romanian), I–II. Bucharest: Scientific and Encyclopaedic Publishing House, 1982.

Bogdan-Duică 1924. Gheorghe Bogdan-Duică, *The Life and Ideas of Simion Bărnuțiu* (in Romanian). Bucharest: Cultura Națională, 1924.

Bojincă 1978. Damaschin Bojincă, *Writings. From the Ideal of Enlightenment to the National Ideal* (in Romanian), ed. Nicolae Bocșan. Timișoara: Facla, 1978.

Brătescu 1988. *Health Care. The First Medical Studies in the Romanian Language (1581–1820)* (in Romanian), ed. G. Brătescu. Bucharest: Medical Publishing House, 1988.

BRV 1903-1944. Ioan Bianu, Nerva Hodoș, Dan Simionescu, *Old Romanian Bibliography (1508–1830)* (in Romanian). Bucharest, 1903, 1910, 1912–1936, 1944.

Budai-Deleanu 1970. Ioan Budai-Deleanu, *New Writings* (in Romanian), ed. Iosif Pervain. Cluj: Dacia, 1970.

Budai-Deleanu 1970a. Ion Budai-Deleanu, *Linguistic Writings* (in Romanian), ed. Mirela Teodorescu and Ion Gheție. Bucharest: Scientific Publishing House, 1970.

Budai-Deleanu 1991. Ion Budai-Deleanu, *De originibus populorum Transylvaniae.* [On the Origin of the Peoples of Transylvania], ed. Ladislau Gyémánt, I–II. Bucharest: Encyclopaedic Publishing House, 1991.

Cantemir 1981. Dimitrie Cantemir, *Description of Moldavia* (in Romanian), ed. Leonida Maniu. Bucharest: Minerva, 1981.

Cipariu 1972. Timotei Cipariu, *Diary* (in Romanian), ed. Maria Protase. Cluj: Dacia, 1972.

Codru Drăgușanu 1956. Ion Codru Drăgușanu, *The Transylvanian Pilgrim* (in Romanian), ed. Romul Munteanu. Bucharest: ESPLA, 1956.

Codru Drăgușanu 1980. Ion Codru Drăgușanu, *The Transylvanian Pilgrim* (in Romanian), ed. Corneliu Albu. Bucharest: Sport-Turism, 1980.

Comșa 1944. Nicolae Comșa, *The Romanian Manuscripts from the Central Library in Blaj* (in Romanian). Blaj: Lumina Press, Miron Roșu, 1944.

Diaconovici-Loga. Constantin Diaconovici-Loga, *Romanian Grammar* (in Romanian), ed. O. Șerban and E. Dorcescu. Timișoara: Facla, 1973.

Documents 1848 Transylvania 1977–1988. *Documents concerning the 1848 revolution in the Romanian Countries. C. Transylvania* (in Romanian), I–IV, ed. Ştefan Pascu and Victor Chereşteşiu. Bucharest: Publishing House of the Academy, 1977, 1979, 1982, 1988. (The first volume published as *The 1848-1849 Revolution in Transylvania* [in Romanian]).

Dragomir 1944–1946. Silviu Dragomir, *Studies and Documents concerning the revolution of the Romanians from Transylvania in 1848–1849* (in Romanian), vol. I-III. Sibiu: Cartea Românească Press in Cluj, 1944–1946.

Fugariu 1970. Florea Fugariu (ed.), *The Transylvanian School* (in Romanian), I–III. Bucharest: Albatros, 1970.

Fugariu 1983. Florea Fugariu (ed.), *The Transylvanian School* (in Romanian), I–II. Bucharest: Minerva, 1983.

Iorgovici 1979. Paul Iorgovici, *Observations concerning the Romanian language* (in Romanian), ed. Doina Bogdan-Dascălu and Crisu Dascălu. Timişoara: Facla, 1979.

Maior P. 1894. Petru Maior, *Procanon* (in Romanian), ed. C. Erbiceanu. Bucharest: The Press for Church Books, 1894.

Maior P. 1970. Petru Maior, *History of the Beginning of the Romanians in Dacia* (in Romanian), I–II, ed. Florea Fugariu. Bucharest: Albatros, 1970.

Maior P. 1976. Petru Maior, *Writings* (in Romanian), I–II, ed. Florea Fugariu. Bucharest: Minerva, 1976.

Marica 1969. George Em. Marica, *Journal for the Mind, Heart and Literature. Analytic bibliography, with a monograph* (in Romanian). Bucharest: Publishing House for Literature, 1969.

Mureşanu A. 1977. Andrei Mureşanu, *Reflections* (in Romanian), ed. Livia Grămadă. Cluj: Dacia, 1977.

Mureşanu A. 1988. Andrei Mureşanu, *Poems. Articles* (in Romanian), ed. Ion Buzaşi. Bucharest: Minerva, 1988.

Murgu 1969. Eftimie Murgu, *Writings* (in Romanian), ed. I.D. Suciu. Bucharest: Publishing House for Literature, 1969.

Papiu Ilarian 1943. Al. Papiu Ilarian, *History of the Romanians from Higher Dacia. Sketch of the Third volume* (in Romanian), ed. Ştefan Pascu. Sibiu: Dacia Traiana, 1943.

Papiu Ilarian 1981. Al Papiu Ilarian, *Anthology* (in Romanian), ed. Corneliu Albu. Bucharest: Scientific and Encyclopaedic Publishing House, 1981.

Păcăţian 1904. Teodor V. Păcăţian, *The Golden Book or the Political–National Confrontations of the Romanians under the Hungarian Crown* (in Romanian), second edition, I. Sibiu: Iosif Marschall Press, 1904.

Pervain 1970. Iosif Pervain, *Ion Budai-Deleanu. New Writings* (in Romanian). Cluj: Dacia, 1970.

Pervain 1971. Iosif Pervain, *Studies in Romanian Literature* (in Romanian). Cluj: Dacia, 1971 (the documentary annexes).

Puşcariu 1889. Ilarion Puşcariu, *Documents of Language and History* (in Romanian), I. Sibiu: Archdiocese Press, 1889.

Răduică G., Răduică N. 1981. Georgeta Răduică and Nicolin Răduică, *Romanian Calendars and Almanacs. 1731–1918. Bibliographic Dictionary* (in Romanian). Bucharest: Scientific and Encyclopaedic Publishing House, 1981.

Răduţiu, Gyémánt 1995. Aurel Răduţiu and Ladislau Gyémánt, *The Repertoire of Statistic Sources concerning Transylvania. 1690–1947* (in Romanian), f.l., Encyclopaedic Universe, f.a. [1995].

Russo 1908. Alecu Russo, *Writings* (in Romanian), ed. Petre V. Hanes. Bucharest: Romanian Academy, 1908.

Stoica de Haţeg 1981. Nicolae Stoica de Haţeg, *The Chronicle of Banat* (in Romanian), ed. Damaschin Mioc. Timişoara: Facla, 1981.

Stoica de Haţeg 1984. Nicolae Stoica de Haţeg, *Writings. The Chronicle of Mehadia and the Herculane Baths. Stories of Old for Romanian School Children. A Miscellany* (in Romanian), ed. Damaschin Mioc and Costin Feneşan. Timişoara: Facla, 1984.

Széchenyi 1981. István Széchenyi, *Közjóra való törekedések. Szemelvények* [Exertions towards the Public Benefit. A Selection], ed. Samu Benkő. Bucharest: Kriterion, 1981.

Şincai 1967. Gheorghe Şincai, *Works. I. The Chronicle of the Romanians* (in Romanian), vol. I, ed. Florea Fugariu. Bucharest: Publishing House for Literature, 1967.

Teodor 1972. Pompiliu Teodor, *Avram Iancu in the Memoirs* (in Romanian). Cluj: Dacia, 1972.
The Year 1848. The Year 1848 in the Romanian Principalities (in Romanian), I–IV. Bucharest: Göbl Press, 1902–1910.

2. SOURCES REFERRING TO OTHER PERIODS (LATE NINETEENTH TO TWENTIETH CENTURY)

Blaga 1994. Lucian Blaga, *The Trilogy of Culture. II. The Mioritic Space* (in Romanian). Bucharest: Humanitas, 1994.
Blandiana 1991. Ana Blandiana, *100 Poems* (in Romanian), f.l. Tinerama, 1991.
Boitoș 1942. Olimpiu Boitoș, "George Barițiu's Diary" (*Notes from my married years*) (in Romanian), in *Literary Studies* (in Romanian) (Sibiu), I, 1942.
Brătianu 1942. Gheorghe I. Brătianu, "Ethnic Space, Vital Space, Space of Safety" (in Romanian), in *The Annals of the Academy of Moral and Political Sciences* (in Romanian), II, 1942.
Cioran 1992. Emil Cioran, *La tentation d'exister. Paris: Gallimard, 1956.*
Cioran 1993a. Emil Cioran, *The Transfiguration of Romania* (in Romanian). Bucharest: Humanitas, 1993.
Cioran 1993b. Emil Cioran, *Conversations with Cioran* (in Romanian). Bucharest: Humanitas, 1993.
Drăghicescu 1995. D. Drăghicescu, *On the Psychology of the Romanian People. Introductory* (in Romanian), ed. Elisabeta Simion. Bucharest: Albatros, 1995.
Gojdu 1888. *The Annals of Gojdu's Foundation* (in Romanian), vol. I (1870–1883). Budapest: Sam. Márkus Press, 1888.
Harris 1964. Tomás Harris, *Goya, Engravings and Lithographs.* Oxford, 1964
Ionescu 1937(1990). Nae Ionescu, *The Compass. 1926–1933* (in Romanian), ed. Mircea Eliade. Bucharest: Cultura Națională, f.a. [1937]. (Reprint: ed. Dan Zamfirescu. Bucharest: Roza Vînturilor Publishing House, 1990.)
Jurma 1994. Gheorghe Jurma, *Discovery of Banat* (in Romanian). Reșița: Timpul, 1994.
Keyserling 1929. Hermann Keyserling, *Das Spektrum Europas.* Heidelberg: Niels Kampmann, 1929.
Maior L. 1993. Liviu Maior, *Alexandru Vaida-Voivode between Belvedere and Versailles (notes, memories, letters)* (in Romanian). [Cluj] Sincron, 1993.
Pascu I.G. 1995. Ioan Gyuri Pascu (lyrics and music), "Africa (such a burning dream)" (in Romanian), in *The Jazzoline Engine* (in Romanian), sound recording, Europa Records [1995].
Păunescu 1977. Adrian Păunescu, "Rising by life from the dead" (in Romanian), in *Flacara*, XXVI, 1977, no. 10, 10 March, pp. 12–13.
Păunescu 1993–1994. Adrian Păunescu, *The Grey Trilogy. I. The Romaniad* (in Romanian). Bucharest: Păunescu Publishing House, 1993–1994.
Pârvan 1982. Vasile Pârvan, *Getica. A proto-history of Dacia* (in Romanian), ed. Radu Florescu. Bucharest: Meridiane, 1982.
Phoenix. Nicolae Covaci (music), Șerban Foarță, Andrei Ujică (lyrics), "The Small Gypsiad" (in Romanian), in *Flute Bud* (in Romanian), L.P., Electrecord, f.a.
Ralea 1977. Mihail Ralea, *Writings* (in Romanian), II, ed. N. Tertulian. Bucharest: Minerva, 1977.
Rădulescu-Motru 1984. Constantin Rădulescu-Motru, *Energetic Personalism and Other Writings* (in Romanian), ed. Gh. Al. Cazan and Gheorghe Pienescu. Bucharest: Eminescu, 1984.
Stanca 1987. Horia Stanca, *Fragmentarium. Cluj* (in Romanian). Cluj: Dacia, 1987.

3. SECONDARY SOURCES (SPECIALISED BIBLIOGRAPHY)

Adorno 1950. Theodor W. Adorno et alii, *The Authoritarian Personality.* New York: Harper and Row, 1950.
Adriaenssen 1991. Cristine Adriaenssen, *Auguste de Gérando, Ein Französichen Zeuge des Ungarischen Reformären (1819–1849).* Frankfurt am Main, Bonn, New York, Paris, 1991.

Albu C. 1977. Corneliu Albu, *Alesandru Papiu Ilarian. His Life and Activity* (in Romanian). Bucharest: Scientific and Encyclopaedic Publishing House, 1977.

Alexandrescu 1983. Sorin Alexandrescu, "'Junimea': Discours politique et discours culturel", in *Libra. Études roumaines offertes à Willem Noomen*. Groningen, 1983, pp. 47–79.

Allport 1954. Gordon W. Allport, *The Nature of Prejudice*. New York: Doubleday and Company Inc., 1954.

Andea A. 1973. Avram Andea, "Simion Bărnuțiu's Conceptions on the Questions of Freedom and Property" (in Romanian), in *Studia Universitatis "Babeș-Bolyai", Historia*, XVIII, 1973, fasc. 1, pp. 33–50.

Andea S., Andea A, 1990. Susana Andea and Avram Andea, "The Continental Blockade and Some Aspects of Austrian Economic Policy in Transylvania (1806–1813)" (in Romanian), in Nicolae Bocșan, Nicolae Edroiu, Aurel Răduțiu (eds.), *Culture and Society in the Modern Age* (in Romanian). Cluj: Dacia, 1990, pp. 64–75.

Anderson 1991. Benedict Anderson, *Imagined Communities. Reflections on the Origins and Spread of Nationalism*. Revised Edition. London: Verso, 1991 [first edition, 1983].

Anghelescu 1971. Mircea Anghelescu, *Romanian Pre-Romanticism (up to 1840)* (in Romanian). Bucharest: Minerva, 1971.

Anghelescu 1975. Mircea Anghelescu, *Romanian Literature and the Orient (the Seventeeth through the Nineteenth Century)* (in Romanian). Bucharest: Minerva, 1975.

Antohi 1991. Sorin Antohi, *Utopia. Studies in the Social Imaginary* (in Romanian). Bucharest: Scientific Publishing House, 1991.

Antohi 1994. Sorin Antohi, *Civitas imaginalis. History and Utopia in Romanian Culture* (in Romanian). Bucharest: Litera, 1994.

Anuichi 1980. Silviu Anuichi, *Romanian–Serb Church Relationships in the Seventeeth and Eighteenth Centuries* (in Romanian). Bucharest, 1980.

Arató 1955. Endre Arató, "A magyar nemesség és az osztrák udvar nemzetiségi politikája a szabadságharc előtt" [The national politics of the Hungarian nobles and of the Viennese Court before the revolution], in *Századok* [Centuries], LXXXIX, 1955, no. 2, pp. 191–210.

Arató 1960. Endre Arató, *A nemzetiségi kérdés története Magyarországon 1790–1848* [The history of the national issue in Hungary. 1790–1848], I–II. Budapest, 1960.

Arató 1975. Endre Arató, "Az 1849. évi júliusi nemzetiségi törvény és helye Európában" [The Law of Nationalities of July 1849 and its place in Europe], in *Kortárs* [The Contemporary], 1975.

Arató 1983. Endre Arató, *A magyarországi nemzetiségek nemzeti ideológiája* [The national ideology of the nationalities in Hungary]. Budapest, 1983.

Armbruster 1977. Adolf Armbruster, *La romanité des Roumains. Histoire d'une idée*. Bucharest: Publishing House of the Academy, 1977.

Baczko 1984. Bronislaw Baczko, *Les imaginaires sociaux. Mémoires et espoirs collectifs*. Paris: Payot, 1984.

Barbu 1992. Violeta Barbu, "The Uniate Roman Romanian Church in search of an identity: The question of the rite and the Jesuit missionaries' activity" (in Romanian), in *Historical Journal* (in Romanian), 1992, no. 5–6, pp. 529–547.

Bariț 1994. George Bariț, *Choice Periods from the History of Transylvania. Two Hundred Years Ago* (in Romanian), vol. II, ed. Ștefan Pascu and Florin Salvan. Brașov: Inspectorate for Culture, 1994.

Bîrlea 1987. Octavian Bîrlea, *The Metropolitan See of the Unitarian Romanian Church, proclaimed in 1855 in Blaj* (in Romanian). Munich, 1987.

Benda 1928. Julien Benda, *La trahison des clercs*. Paris: Grasset, 1928.

Berindei 1974. Dan Berindei, "The Internal Programme of the Romanian Revolution of 1848-1849" (in Romanian), in Nichita Adăniloaie and Dan Berindei (co-ord.), *The 1848 Revolution in the Romanian Principalities* (in Romanian). Bucharest: The Publishing House of the Academy, 1974.

Bernath 1972. Mathias Bernath, *Habsburg und die Anfänge der rumänischen Nationsbildung*. Leiden: Brill, 1972.

Besançon 1977. Alain Besançon, *Les origines intellectuelles du léninisme*. Paris: Calmann–Lévy, 1977.

Besançon 1978. Alain Besançon, *La confusion des langues. La crise idéologique de l'Église*. Paris: Calmann–Lévy, 1978.

Bochmann 1977. Klaus Bochmann, "Der Zivilisationbegriff in der Rumänischen Literatur der Aufklärung der Romantik bis 1848", in *Synthesis,* IV, 1977.

Bocșan 1973. Nicolae Bocșan, "The Polemics of Damaschin Bojincă and Eftimie Murgu with Sava Tököly" (in Romanian), in *Banatica,* II, 1973, pp. 363–382.

Bocșan 1982. Nicolae Bocșan, "Early Liberalism with the National Movement in Banat" (in Romanian), in Nicolae Edroiu, Aurel Răduțiu, Pompiliu Teodor (eds.), *State. Society. Nation. Historical Interpretations* (in Romanian). Cluj: Dacia, 1982.

Bocșan 1984. Nicolae Bocșan, "Social and Democratic Options in the Shaping of Modern National Solidarity. 1821-1848" (in Romanian), in Ștefan Ștefanescu (co-ord.), *The Romanian Nation. Birth. Affirmation. Contemporary Horizon* (in Romanian). Bucharest: Scientific and Encyclopaedic Publishing House, 1984, pp. 338–377.

Bocșan 1986. Nicolae Bocșan, *Contributions to the History of the Romanian Enlightenment* (in Romanian). Timișoara: Facla, 1986.

Bocșan 1990. Nicolae Bocșan, "Revolution and the Revolutionary with the Transylvanian Romanians in 1848 (March–August)" (in Romanian), in *Studia Universitatis "Babeș-Bolyai", Historia,* XXXV, 1990, fasc. 1, pp. 26–53.

Bocșan 1991. Nicolae Bocșan, "The Evolution of the Idea of the Nation with the Romanians from Transylvania and Banat. 1840–1860" (in Romanian), in *Revue de Transylvanie,* I, 1991, pp. 38–63.

Bocșan 1992. Nicolae Bocșan, "The 1848 Revolution" (in Romanian), in vol. *The Memorandum. 1892–1894. Romanian Ideology and Political Action* (in Romanian). Bucharest: Progresul Românesc, 1992 (second edition, 1994), pp. 128–169.

Bocșan 1992a. Nicolae Bocșan, "From the 1848 Revolution to Dualism" (in Romanian), in vol. *The Memorandum. 1892–1894. Romanian Ideology and Political Action* (in Romanian). Bucharest: Progresul Românesc, 1992, pp. 107–127.

Bocșan 1994. Nicolae Bocșan, "The Revolution in March–August 1848. The Use of the Term", in *Colloquia,* I, 1994, no. 1, pp. 157–171.

Bocșan 1995. Nicolae Bocșan, "Contributions to the History of Revolutionary Mentality. The Notion of Revolution with the Transylvanian Romanians (Sept. 1848–Aug. 1849)" (in Romanian), in Nicolae Bocșan, Nicolae Edroiu, Liviu Maior, Aurel Răduțiu, Pompiliu Teodor (eds.), *David Prodan. The Authority of the Model* (in Romanian). Cluj: Publishing House of the Romanian Cultural Foundation, 1995, pp. 175–189.

Bocșan, Duma, Bona 1994. Nicolae Bocșan, Mihai Duma, Petru Bona, *France and Banat. 1789–1815* (in Romanian). Reșița: The History Museum, 1994.

Bocșan, Lumperdean, Pop 1996. Nicolae Bocșan, Ioan Lumperdean, Ioan-Aurel Pop, *Ethnie et confession en Transylvanie (du XIIIᵉ au XIXᵉ siècles).* Cluj: Publishing House of the Romanian Cultural Foundation, 1996.

Bodea 1960. Cornelia C. Bodea, "The 1848 revolution in Transylvania and Hungary as seen by John Paget" (in Romanian), in *Studies and Materials of Modern History* (in Romanian), 1960, 2, pp. 187–221.

Bodea 1982. Cornelia Bodea, "Préoccupations économiques et culturelles dans les textes transylvains des années 1786–1830", in Romul Munteanu (co-ord.), *La culture roumaine à l'époque des Lumières,* I. Bucharest: Univers, 1982, pp. 227–261.

Boia 1976. Lucian Boia, *The Evolution of Romanian Historiography* (in Romanian). Bucharest, 1976.

Boia 1991. Lucian Boia, "Vers une histoire de l'imaginaire", in *The Annals of the Bucharest University. History* (in Romanian), XL, 1991, pp. 3–22.

Boia 1995a. *Romanian Historical Myths* (in Romanian), (dir.) Lucian Boia. Bucharest: University Publishing House, 1995.

Boia 1995b. *The Myths of Romanian Communism* (in Romanian), (dir.) Lucian Boia. Bucharest: University Publishing House, 1995.

Bolovan I. 1994. Ioan Bolovan, "Considerations regarding the cholera epidemic in 1848 in Transylvania" (in Romanian), in Sorin Mitu and Florin Gogîltan (eds.), *Studies in the History of Transylvania* (in Romanian). Cluj: The Association of Historians from Transylvania and Banat, 1994, pp. 164–167.

Borsi-Kálmán 1994. Béla Borsi-Kálmán, "Les Roumains aux yeaux des Hongrois. Stéréotypes et lieux communs 'hongrois' sur les 'Roumains': Bêtises, Généralités, Sémi-Vérités par rapports à la conscience et la stratégie nationale", in G. Bădărău, L. Boicu, L. Nastasă (co-ord.), *History as a Reading of the World* (in Romanian). Iași: The Academic Foundation "A.D. Xenopol", 1994, pp. 455–459.

Bourdieu 1971. Pierre Bourdieu, "Le marché des biens symboliques", in *L'année sociologique*, XXII, 1971, pp. 49–126.

Breazu 1973. Ion Breazu, "Lamennais with the Transylvanian Romanians in 1848" (in Romanian), in *idem, Studies of Romanian and Comparative Literature* (in Romanian), II, ed. Mircea Curticeanu. Cluj: Dacia, 1973, pp. 118–141.

Bulei 1990. Ion Bulei, *At the Time When the Century Was Dawning...* (in Romanian). Bucharest: Eminescu, 1990.

Capidan 1923. Theodor Capidan, "Petru Maior and the A-Romanians" (in Romanian), in *Literary Junimea* (in Romanian), XII, 1923, no. 4-5.

Carmilly-Weinberger 1994. Moshe Carmilly-Weinberger, *History of the Jews from Transylvania (1623–1944)* (in Romanian). Bucharest: Encyclopaedic Publishing House, 1994.

Cazimir 1986. Ștefan Cazimir, *Alphabet of Transition* (in Romanian). Bucharest: Cartea Românească, 1986.

Călinescu M. 1987. Matei Călinescu, *Five Faces of Modernity: Modernism. Avant-Garde. Decadence. Kitsch. Postmodernism*. Duke University Press, 1987.

Chaunu 1971. Pierre Chaunu, *La civilisation de l'Europe des Lumières*. Paris: Arthaud, 1971.

Chelcea 1991. Septimiu Chelcea, "The Romanians' Self-Image" (in Romanian), in *Journal of Psychology* (in Romanian), XXXVII, 1991, no. 1–2, pp. 25–30.

Chelcea 1994a. Septimiu Chelcea, "The Students' Ethnic Attitudes During the Transition Period" (in Romanian), in *Magazine of Social Research* (in Romanian), I, 1994, no. 3, pp. 67–75.

Chelcea 1994b. Septimiu Chelcea, "The Ethnic Attitudes and their Valorisation" (in Romanian), in *Romanian Sociology* (in Romanian), 1994, no. 2–3.

Chelcea 1994c. Septimiu Chelcea, "The Romanians' Ethnic Attitudes" (in Romanian), in *Romanian Sociology* (in Romanian), 1994, no. 2–3.

Chindriș 1983. Ioan Chindriș, *Alexandru Papiu Ilarian's Revolutionary Ideology* (in Romanian). Bucharest: Political Publishing House, 1983.

Cipăianu 1980. George Cipăianu, *Vincentiu Babeș (1821–1907)* (in Romanian). Timișoara: Facla, 1980.

Condeescu 1946. N.N. Condeescu, *Ion Codru Drăgușanu and France* (in Romanian). Sighișoara: Neagu Press, 1946.

Cordoș, Jude 1989–1993. Nicolae Cordos and Maria Magdalena Jude, "Documentary Contributions concerning Emanuil Gojdu and his Foundation" (in Romanian), in *Acta Musei Napocensis*, 26–30, II/History, 1989–1993, pp. 573–590.

Cornea 1972. Paul Cornea, *The Origins of Romanian Romanticism. Public Spirit, Movement of Ideas and Literature Between 1780 and 1840* (in Romanian). Bucharest: Minerva, 1972.

Cosma 1995. Ela Cosma, "The Image of the Russians in Saxon Media in 1849" (in Romanian), lecture delivered at the symposium *The Image of the Other in Transylvania* (in Romanian), Cluj, 5–6 May 1995.

Crăciun, Ghitta 1995. Maria Crăciun and Ovidiu Ghitta (eds.), *Ethnicity and Religion in Central and Eastern Europe*. Cluj: Cluj University Press, 1995.

Cudalbu-Slusanski 1937–1938. O. Cudalbu-Slusanski, "Contributions à la biographie de J.A. Vaillant (1805–1886)", in *Mélanges de l'École Roumaine en France*, XIV, 1937–1938.

Dărăban 1985. Valentin Dărăban, "Miklós Wesselényi between democracy and nationalism" (in Romanian), in *Acta Musei Porolissensis*, IX, 1985, pp. 723–729.

Delumeau 1978. Jean Delumeau, *La peur en Occident (XIVᵉ–XVIIIᵉ siècles). Une cité assiégée*. Paris: Fayard, 1978.

Dictionary 1900. The Dictionary of Romanian Literature from the Origins to 1900 (in Romanian). Bucharest: Publishing House of the Academy, 1979.

From Hist. Trans. (II) 1963. *From the History of Transylvania* (in Romanian), II, second edition. Bucharest: Publishing House of the Academy, 1963.

Djuvara 1989. Neagu Djuvara, *Le pays roumains entre Orient et Occident: les Principautés danubiennes au début du XIXᵉ siècle*. Paris: Publications Orientalistes de France, 1989.

Dragomir 1914. Silviu Dragomir, *Church Relationships of the Romanians from Transylvania with Russia in the Eighteenth Century* (in Romanian). Sibiu, 1914.

Dragomir 1917. Silviu Dragomir, "The Relationships of the Romanian Church with Russia in the Seventeeth Century" (in Romanian), in *The Annals of the Romanian Academy. The Records of the History Department* (in Romanian), s. II, 1917, pp. 34–42.

Dragomir 1946. Silviu Dragomir, *Studies and Documents concerning the Revolution of the Transylvanian Romanians in 1848–49* (in Romanian), vol. V, "The History of the Revolution" (in Romanian). Cluj, 1946.

Dragomir 1965. Silviu Dragomir, *Avram Iancu* (in Romanian). Bucharest: Scientific Publishing House, 1965.

Dragomir 1989. Silviu Dragomir, *Studies regarding the History of the Romanian Revolution of 1848* (in Romanian), ed. Pompiliu Teodor. Cluj: Dacia, 1989.

Duby 1988. Georges Duby, *Mâle Moyen Age. De l'amour et autres essais*. Paris: Flammarion, 1988.

Dumézil 1981–1986. Georges Dumézil, *Mythe et épopée*, I–III. Paris: Gallimard, 1981–1986.

Durandin 1989. Catherine Durnadin, *Révolution à la française ou à la russe. Polonais, Roumains et Russes au XIXᵉ siècle*. Paris: P.U.F., 1989.

Duțu 1982. Alexandru Duțu, *Comparative Literature and the History of Mentalities* (in Romanian). Bucharest: Univers, 1982.

Dyserinck 1981. Hugo Dyserinck, "Komparatistische Imagologie", in *idem, Komparatistik. Eine Einführung*. Bonn: Bouvier, 1981, pp. 125–133.

Edroiu 1980. Nicolae Edroiu, "Economic Literature of the 1780-1820 Period and Romanian Society", in Pompiliu Teodor (ed.), *Enlightenment and Romanian Society*. Cluj: Dacia, 1980, pp. 40–54.

Febvre 1930. Lucien Febvre, "Civilisation. Évolution d'un mot et d'un groupe d'idées", in vol. *Civilisation. Le mot et l'idée*. Paris, 1930, pp. 1–55.

Finkielkraut 1987. Alain Finkielkraut, *La défaite de la pensée*. Paris: Gallimard, 1987.

Fukuyama 1992. Francis Fukuyama, *The End of History and the Last Man*. New York: Free Press, Macmillan, 1992.

Furet 1978. François Furet, *Penser la Révolution française*. Paris: Gallimard, 1978.

Georgescu 1971. Vlad Georgescu, *Political Ideas and the Enlightenment in the Romanian Principalities (1750–1831)*. Boulder: East European Quarterly, 1971.

Gellner 1983. Ernst Gellner, *Nations and Nationalism*. Oxford: Blackwell, 1983.

Gheție 1966. Ion Gheție, *The Linguistic Work of Ion Budai-Deleanu* (in Romanian). Bucharest: Publishing House of the Academy, 1966.

Ghinoiu 1988. Ion Ghinoiu, *The Ages of Time* (in Romanian). Bucharest: Meridiane, 1988.

Ghitta 1994. Ovidiu Ghitta, "Draft for a historiography of the Religious union in north–western Transylvania" (in Romanian), in Sorin Mitu and Florin Gogîltan (co-ord.), *Studies in the History of Transylvania* (in Romanian). Cluj: Association of Historians from Transylvania and Banat, 1994, pp. 88–96.

Girardet 1986. Raoul Girardet, *Mythes et mythologies politiques*. Paris: Seuil, 1986.

Giurescu C.C. 1977. Constantin C. Giurescu, *Controversial Issues in Romanian Historiography* (in Romanian). Bucharest: Albatros, 1977.

Godechot 1963. Jacques Godechot, *Les révolutions (1770–1799)*. Paris: P.U.F., 1963.

Goffman 1963. Erving Goffman, *Stigma. Notes on the Management of Spoiled Identity*. Englewood Cliffs, N.J.: Prentice-Hall, Inc., 1963.

Graur 1974. Al. Graur, *Brief Treaty of Orthography* (in Romanian). Bucharest: Scientific Publishing House, 1974.

Gyémánt 1986. Ladislau Gyémánt, *The Transylvanian Romanians' National Movement between 1790 and 1848* (in Romanian). Bucharest: Scientific Publishing House, 1986.

Habermas 1973. Jürgen Habermas, *Erkenntnis und Interesse*. Frankfurt am Main: Suhrkamp, 1973.

Halecki 1962. O. Halecki, "Das Problem der Kircheunion in der osteuropäischen Geschichte", in *Österreichische Osthefte*, IV, 1962, no. 1, pp. 1–5.

Heitmann 1985. Klaus Heitmann, *Das Rumänenbild im deutschen Sprachraum. 1775–1918. Eine imagologische Studie*. Köln: Böhlau, 1985.

Hitchins 1969. Keith Hitchins, *The Rumanian National Movement in Transylvania, 1780–1849*. Cambridge, Massachusetts: Harvard University Press, 1969.

Hitchins 1977. Keith Hitchins, *Orthodoxy and Nationality. Andrei Șaguna and the Romanians of Transylvania, 1846–1873*. Cambridge, Massachusetts: Harvard University Press, 1977.

Hitchins 1983. Keith Hitchins, *Studies on Romanian National Consciousness*. Pelham N.Y., Montreal, Paris, Lugoj, Roma: Nagard, 1983.

Hobsbawm 1990. Eric J. Hobsbawm, *Nations and Nationalism since 1780: programme, myth, reality*. Cambridge: Cambridge University Press, 1990.

Hobsbawm, Ranger 1983. Eric J. Hobsbawm and Terence Ranger (eds.), *The Invention of Tradition*. Cambridge: Cambridge University Press, 1983.

Hodoș 1923. Enea Hodoș, "Avram Iancu's Young Years" (in Romanian), in *The Year-Book of the Institute for National History* (in Romanian) (Cluj), II, 1923, pp. 381–383.

Hotea 1988–1991. Meda Diana Hotea, "Manifestations of Peasant Collective Mentality in the Middle of the Eighteenth Century in Transylvania" (in Romanian), in *Sargetia*, XXI–XXIV, 1988–1991, pp. 173–177.

Ibrăileanu 1970. Garabet Ibrăileanu, *The Critical Spirit in Romanian Culture* (in Romanian), ed. Constantin Ciopraga. Iași: Junimea, 1970.

Ideology of generation 1968. *The Ideology of the 1848 Romanian Generation in Transylvania* (in Romanian), by George Em. Marica, Iosif Hajós, Călina Mare, Constantin Rusu. Bucharest: Political Publishing House, 1968.

Iercoșan 1983. Sara Iercoșan, *Junimism in Transylvania* (in Romanian). Cluj: Dacia, 1983.

Giovanni Paolo II 1994. Giovanni Paolo II, *Varcare la soglia della speranza*. Milano: Mondadori, 1994.

Iorga 1981. Nicolae Iorga, *History of the Romanians in Travel Accounts* (in Romanian), ed. Adrian Anghelescu. Bucharest: Eminescu, 1981.

Isar 1991. N. Isar, *French Journalists and the Romanian Cause (1834–1859)* (in Romanian). Bucharest: Publishing House of the Academy, 1991.

Iscru 1975. G.D. Iscru, *Contributions Regarding the Village Educational System in Wallachia Until the Middle of the Nineteenth Century* (in Romanian). Bucharest: Didactic and Pedagogical Publishing House, 1975.

Isopescu 1930. Claudiu Isopescu, *Il viaggiatore transilvano Ion Codru Drăgușanu e l'Italia*. Rome, 1930.

History Pedagogy (II) 1966. *From the History of Romanian Pedagogy. An Anthology* (in Romanian), II. Bucharest: Didactic and Pedagogical Publishing House, 1966.

Istrate 1982. Ion Istrate, *Romanian Literary Baroque* (in Romanian). Bucharest: Minerva, 1982.

Karnoouh 1990. Claude Karnoouh, *L'invention du peuple. Chroniques de Roumanie. Essai*. Paris: Arcantère, 1990.

Kovács 1973. Iosif Kovács, *The Abolishment of Feudal Bonds in Transylvania* (in Romanian). Cluj: Dacia, 1973.

Kovács, Katus 1987. Endre Kovács (editor-in-chief), László Katus (editor), *Magyarország története. 1848–1890* [History of Hungary. 1848–1890], I. Budapest: Akadémiai Kiadó, 1987 (vol. 6/1 from Pach Zsigmond Pál (co-ord.), *Magyarország története tíz kötetben* [History of Hungary in Ten Volumes]).

Lascu N. 1957. Nicolae Lascu, *Ovid in Romania* (in Romanian). Bucharest, 1957.

Lascu N. 1974. Nicolae Lascu, *The Ancient Classics in Romania* (in Romanian). Cluj: Dacia, 1974.

Lascu V. 1981. Viorica Lascu, "A.T. Laurian's Encounter with Italy" (in Romanian), in *Apulum*, XIX, 1982, pp. 287–292.

Lebrun 1985. François Lebrun, *La vie conjugale sous l'Ancien Régime*. Paris: Armand Colin, 1985.

Le Goff 1978. Jacques Le Goff, *Pour un autre Moyen Age. Temps, travail et culture en Occident*. Paris: Gallimard, 1978.

Le Rider 1990. Jacques Le Rider, *Modernité viennoise et crises de l'identité*. Paris: P.U.F., 1990.

Lessing 1930. Theodor Lessing, *Der jüdische Selbsthass*. Berlin: Jüdischer Verlag, 1930.

Lovinescu 1972. E. Lovinescu, *History of Modern Romanian Civilisation* (in Romanian), ed. Z. Ornea. Bucharest: Scientific Publishing House, 1972.

Lupaș 1910. Ioan Lupaș, *Count István Széchenyi and the Politics of Hungarisation* (in Romanian). Sibiu, 1910.

Lupaș 1932. Ioan Lupaș, "A Female Friend of Avram Iancu" (in Romanian), in *The Literary and Artistic Truth* (in Romanian), 1932, no. 123.

Lyotard 1979. Jean-François Lyotard, *La condition postmoderne. Rapport sur le savoir*. Paris: Minuit, 1979.

Macrea 1994. D. Macrea, "The Transylvanian School and the Questions of Romanic Linguistics" (in Romanian), in *Linguistic Research* (in Romanian), XIV, 1969, no. 1, pp. 7–13.

Magris 1986. Claudio Magris, *Danubio*. Milano: Garzanti, 1986.

Maior L. 1967. Liviu Maior, "Aspects of the Organisation of Romanian Administration in the Years 1848–1849 in Transylvania" (in Romanian), in *Acta Musei Napocensis*, IV, 1967, pp. 563–570.

Maior L. 1968. Liviu Maior, "One Instance of French–Romanian Relationships: H. Desprez" (in Romanian), in *Studia Universitatis "Babeș-Bolyai", Historia*, XIII, 1968, fasc. 2, pp. 103–115.

Maior L. 1972. Liviu Maior, "The Administrative Organisation of the Apuseni Mountains as 'Romanian country' by Avram Iancu" (in Romanian), in *Studia Universitatis "Babeș-Bolyai", Historia*, XVII, 1972, fasc. 2, pp. 39–45.

Maior L. 1992. Liviu Maior, *The Memorandum. The Political–Historical Philosophy of Romanian Petitioning* (in Romanian). Cluj: Publishing House of the Romanian Cultural Foundation, 1992.

Manolache, Dumitrașcu, Pîrnuță 1968. A. Manolache, Gh. Dumitrașcu, Gh. Pîrnuță, *The Pedagogical Thinking of the 1848 Generation* (in Romanian). Bucharest: Didactic and Pedagogical Publishing House, 1968.

Manolescu 1993. Nicolae Manolescu, *Sadoveanu or the Utopia of the Book* (in Romanian). Bucharest: Minerva, 1993.

Marcu 1935. Alexandru Marcu, *Simion Bărnuțiu, Al. Papiu Ilarian and Iosif Hodoș. Their Studying in Italy* (in Romanian). Bucharest, 1935.

Marga 1985. Andrei Marga, *Action and Reason with Jürgen Habermas* (in Romanian). Cluj: Dacia, 1985.

Marga 1992. Andrei Marga, *The Pragmatic Reconstruction of Philosophy* (in Romanian), I. Cluj: "Babeș-Bolyai" University, 1992.

Marga 1994. Andrei Marga, *Explorations in Actuality* (in Romanian). Cluj: Apostrof Library, 1994.

Marga 1995. Andrei Marga, *The Philosophy of European Unification* (in Romanian). Cluj: Apostrof Library, 1995.

Marian 1994. Simeon Florea Marian, *The Romanians' Revels* (in Romanian), I–III. Bucharest: Publishing House of the Romanian Cultural Foundation, 1994.

Marica 1976. George Em. Marica, "Conscience civique et conscience littéraire en Transylvanie à l'époque de 1848", in *Cahiers roumains d'études littéraires*, 1976, no. 2, pp. 21–37.

Marica 1977. George Em. Marica, *Studies on the History and Sociology of Romanian Transylvanian Culture in the Nineteenth Century* (in Romanian), I. Cluj: Dacia, 1977.

Marino 1964. Adrian Marino, "The Romanian Enlightened Minds and the Question of 'Language Cultivation'" (in Romanian), in *The Romanian Language* (in Romanian), XIII, 1964, no. 5, pp. 467–480; no. 6, pp. 571–586.

Marino 1992. Adrian Marino, *The Biography of the Idea of Literature, Vol. II: The Age of Lights, the Nineteenth Century* (in Romanian). Cluj: Dacia, 1992.

Marino 1995. Adrian Marino, *Pro Europe. Integration of Romania. Ideological and Cultural Aspects* (in Romanian). Iași: Polirom, 1995.

Mauss 1973. Marcel Mauss, "Essai sur le don. Forme et raison de l'echange dans les sociétés archaïques", in *idem, Sociologie et anthropologie*. Paris: P.U.F., 1973.

Mauzi 1969. Robert Mauzi, *L'idée du bonheur dans la littérature et la pensée française au XVIII siècle*. Paris: Armand Colin, 1969.

Mazilu 1976. Dan Horia Mazilu, *The Baroque in Seventeeth–Century Romanian Literature* (in Romanian). Bucharest: Minerva, 1976.

Mazilu 1984. Dan Horia Mazilu, *Romanian Literature in the Age of the Renaissance* (in Romanian). Bucharest: Minerva, 1984.

Mazilu 1986-1987. Dan Horia Mazilu, *Oratorical Prose in Old Romanian Literature* (in Romanian), I–II. Bucharest: Minerva, 1986-1987.

Mîrza 1987. Iacob Mîrza, *School and Nation (The Blaj Schools in the Age of National Rebirth)* (in Romanian). Cluj: Dacia, 1987.

Mikó 1943. Imre Mikó, *Széchenyi és Wesselényi nemzetiségi politikája* [Széchenyi's and Wesselényi's National Policy]. Cluj, 1943.

Miskolczy 1981. Ambrus Miskolczy, "Roumanian Hungarian Attempts at reconciliation in the spring of 1949 in Transylvania. Ioan Dragos's Mission", in *Annales Universitatis Scientiarum Budapestinensis de Rolando Eötvös Nominatae. Sectio Historica*, XXI, 1981, pp. 61–81.

Mitu M. 1989–1993. Melinda Mitu, "The Romanian Revolution of 1848–1849 in Transylvania as Mirrored in the Newspaper *Márczius Tizenötödike*" (in Romanian) (I), in *Acta Musei Napocensis,* 26–30, II/History, 1989–1993, pp. 555–571.

Mitu M. 1992. Melinda Mitu, "Iosif Many's Journalistic Work in Hungarian" (in Romanian), in *Studia Universitatis "Babeş-Bolyai". Historia*, XXXVII, 1–2, 1992, pp. 75–80.

Mitu M. 1994. Melinda Ildikó Mitu, "The Romanians' Origin, Continuity and Ethnonym in László Kőváry's View" (in Romanian), in Sorin Mitu and Florin Gogîltan (eds.), *Studies in Transylvanian History. Regional Specificity and European Openness* (in Romanian). Cluj: Association of Historians from Transylvania and Banat, 1994, pp. 116–121.

Mitu M., Mitu S. 1996. Melinda Mitu and Sorin Mitu, "Ein ungarischer Reisender aus Siebenbürgen in der Walachei in der Zeit des Vormärz", in Sorin Mitu and Florin Gogîltan (eds.), *Interethnische- und Zivilisationsbeziehungen im siebenbürgischen Raum. Historische Studien*. Cluj: Verein der Historiker aus Siebenbürgen und dem Banat, 1996, pp. 209–231.

Mitu S. 1987–1988. Sorin Mitu, "Italy in 1850 in the Public Consciousness of Transylvanian Romanian Society" (in Romanian), in *Acta Musei Napocensis*, 26–30, II/History, 1987–1988, pp. 1127–1139.

Mitu S. 1988a. Sorin Mitu, "Interférences roumano-italiennes en 1850: Sensibilités révolutionnaires et réactions idéologiques" (I–II), in *Studia Universitatis "Babeş-Bolyai". Historia*, XXXIII, 1988, fasc. 1, pp. 84–98; fasc. 2, pp. 78–95.

Mitu S. 1988b. Sorin Mitu, "Love and the National Sentiment" (in Romanian), in *Echinox*, XX, 1988, pp. 65–92.

Mitu S. 1991. Sorin Mitu, "The Irish Model and the Transylvanian Romanians (1838–1848)" (in Romanian), in *Studia Universitatis "Babeş-Bolyai". Historia*, XXXVI, 1991, 1–2, pp. 65–92.

Mitu S. 1992. Sorin Mitu, "The Image of the Frenchman in Peasant Traditional Mentality" (in Romanian), in *Studia Universitatis "Babeş-Bolyai". Historia*, XXXVII, 1992, 1–2, pp. 3–22.

Mitu S. 1993a. Sorin Mitu, "Benjamin Franklin in the Romanian Culture of Transylvania at the Beginning of the Modern Age", in *Transylvanian Review*, II, 1993, no. 1, pp. 49–57.

Mitu S. 1993b. Sorin Mitu, "Methodological Aspects of the Research in Comparative Imagology" (in Romanian), in *Studia Universitatis "Babeş-Bolyai". Historia*, XXXVIII, 1993, 1–2, pp. 89–121.

Mitu S. 1994. Sorin Mitu, "Aspects of the Transylvanian Romanians' Self-Image. 1800–1850. The Negative Dimension" (in Romanian), in Sorin Mitu and Florin Gogîltan (eds.), *Studies in Transylvanian History. Regional Specificity and European Openness* (in Romanian). Cluj: Association of Historians from Transylvania and Banat, 1994, pp. 106–115.

Moga 1936–1938. Ioan Moga, "Austrian Economic Policy and Transylvanian trade in the Eighteenth Century" (in Romanian), in *The Year-Book of the Institute for National History* (in Romanian) (Cluj), VII, 1936–1938, pp. 86–165.

Monglond 1930. André Monglond, *Le préromantisme français*, I–II. Grenoble, 1930.

Moscovici 1990. Serge Moscovici (ed.), *Psychologie sociale*. Paris: P.U.F., 1990.

Mungiu 1995. Alina Mungiu, *The Romanians after '89. The History of a Misunderstanding* (in Romanian). Bucharest: Humanitas, 1995.

Mureşanu C. 1982. Camil Mureşanu, "The Echo of the Civil War in U.S.A. in the Transylvanian Romanian Media" (in Romanian), in Nicolae Edroiu, Aurel Răduţiu, Pompiliu Teodor (eds.), *State. Society. Nation. Historical Interpretations* (in Romanian). Cluj: Dacia, 1982, pp. 353–359.

Mureșanu C. 1991. Camil Mureșanu, "Nation, Nationalism, Nationalities, Minorities" (in Romanian), in *Tribuna,* XXXV, 1991, no. 37–38, 40–42.

Muscă 1980. Vasile Muscă, "Social Coordinates and Moral Values in the Transylvanian Enlightenment. Deistic Order—Social Happiness—Reason", in Pompiliu Teodor (ed.), *Enlightenment and Romanian Society.* Cluj: Dacia, 1980, pp. 207–220.

Neamțu 1988. Gelu Neamțu, "On How People Acted in the Spring of the 1848 Revolution in Transylvania" (in Romanian), in *The Year-Book of the 'A.D. Xenopol' Institute for History and Archeology* (in Romanian), XXV, 1988, pp. 311–318.

Netea 1966. Vasile Netea, *George Barițiu. His Life and Activity* (in Romanian). Bucharest: Scientific Publishing Press, 1966.

Neumann 1986. Victor Neumann, *Spiritual Junctions* (in Romanian). Bucharest: Eminescu, 1986.

Nicoară S. 1993. Simona Nicoară, "The Image of America in Romanian Culture of the Early Modern Epoch", in *Transylvanian Review,* II, 1993, no. 1, pp. 58–65.

Nicoară T. 1990. Toader Nicoară, "Mental Climate and Political Climate in the Romanian Principalities in the Second Half of the Seventeeth Century and the First Decades of the Eighteenth" (in Romanian), in Nicolae Bocșan, Nicolae Edroiu, Aurel Răduțiu (eds.), *Culture and Society in the Modern Age* (in Romanian). Cluj: Dacia, 1990, pp. 15–32.

Ornea 1975. Z. Ornea, *Junimea and Junimism* (in Romanian). Bucharest: Eminescu, 1975.

Ornea 1995. Z. Ornea, *The '30s. The Romanian Extreme Right* (in Romanian). Bucharest: Publishing House of the Romanian Cultural Foundation, 1995.

Papacostea S. 1988. Șerban Papacostea, "The Romanians' Awareness of Romanianness in the Middle Ages" (in Romanian), in *idem, The Rise of the State in the Romanian Middle Ages. Critical Studies* (in Romanian). Cluj: Dacia, 1988, pp. 222–230.

Papadima 1975. Ovidiu Papadima, *Hypostases of Romanian Enlightenment* (in Romanian). Bucharest: Minerva, 1975.

Pasti 1995. Vladimir Pasti, *Romania in Transition. The Fall into the Future* (in Romanian). Bucharest: Nemira, 1995.

Pavel 1994. Dan Pavel, "'Awake, Romanian!' An Inquiry into the Ideology of Nationalism" (in Romanian), in *Polis,* 2/1994, pp. 153–170.

Păcurariu 1981. Mircea Păcurariu, *History of the Romanian Orthodox Church* (in Romanian), II. Bucharest, 1981.

Păcurariu 1992. Mircea Păcurariu, *History of the Romanian Church in Transylvania, Banat, Crișana and Maramures* (in Romanian). Cluj, 1992.

Petrescu 1991. Dan Petescu, "'Tentatio Orientis Interbellica'", in Al. Zub (ed.), *Culture and Society. Studies on the Romanian Past* (in Romanian). Bucharest: Scientific Publishing House, 1991.

Pippidi 1980. Andrei Pippidi, "Naissance, renaissance et mort du 'Bon Sauvage': à propos des Morlaques et des Valaques", in *idem, Hommes et idées du Sud–Est européen à l'aube de l'âge moderne.* Paris, Bucharest: CNRS, Publishing House of the Academy, 1980.

Pippidi 1993. Andrei Pippidi, "Myths of the Past. The Crossroads of the Present" (in Romanian), in *Xenopoliana,* I, 1993, 1–4, pp. 22–31.

Pițu 1991. Luca Pițu, *The Romanian Sense of Self-Hatred* (in Romanian). Iași: European Institute, 1991.

Popa L. 1994. Liliana Popa, "German–Romanian Partnership in the Sibiu Press Affair" (in Romanian), in *The "David Prodan" Notebooks* (in Romanian), I, 1994, pp. 103–110.

Popper 1957. Karl Raimund Popper, *The Open Society and its Enemies.* London: Routledge and Kegan Paul, 1957.

Popper 1979. Karl Raimund Popper, *The Poverty of Historicism.* London: Routledge and Kegan Paul, 1979 (first edition, 1957).

Prodan 1967–1968. D. Prodan, *Serfdom in Sixteenth-Century Transylvania* (in Romanian). Bucharest: Publishing House of the Academy, 1967–1968.

Prodan 1970. D. Prodan, *Another Romanian Supplex Libellus. 1804* (in Romanian). Cluj: Dacia, 1970.

Prodan 1971. D. Prodan, *Supplex Libellus Valachorum or the political Struggle of the Romanians in Transylvania during the 18th Century.* Bucharest: Publishing House of the Academy, 1971.

Prodan 1979. D. Prodan, *Horea's Mutiny* (in Romanian), I–II. Bucharest: Scientific and Encyclopaedic Publishing House, 1979.

Prodan 1989. D. Prodan, *The Question of Serfdom in Transylvania. 1700–1848* (in Romanian). Bucharest: Scientific and Encyclopaedic Publishing House, 1989.

Protase 1973. Maria Protase, *Petru Maior: A Founder of Consciousnesses* (in Romanian). Bucharest: Minerva, 1973.

Protopopescu 1966. Lucia Protopopescu, *Contributions to the History of Education in Transylvania. 1744–1805* (in Romanian). Bucharest: Didactic and Pedagogical Publishing House, 1966.

Radosav 1985. Doru Radosav, "The Image of Africa in the Romanian Culture of the First Half of the Nineteenth Century. Geographical Horizon—Mental Horizon" (in Romanian), in Nicolae Edroiu, Aurel Răduțiu, Pompiliu Teodor (eds.), *Medieval and Modern Romanian Civilisation. Historical Studies* (in Romanian). Cluj: Dacia, 1985, pp. 249–259.

Răduțiu 1985. Aurel Răduțiu, "Labour and fete days in Transylvania (seventeenth–eighteenth centuries)" (in Romanian), in Nicolae Edroiu, Aurel Răduțiu, Pompiliu Teodor (eds.), *Medieval and Modern Romanian Civilisation. Historical Studies* (in Romanian). Cluj: Dacia, 1985, pp. 215–230.

Reszler 1981. André Reszler, *Mythes politiques modernes*. Paris: P.U.F., 1981.

Ricoeur 1986. Paul Ricoeur, *Du texte à l'action. Essais d'herméneutique*, II. Paris: Seuil, 1986.

Said 1978. Edward W. Said, *Orientalism*. New York: Pantheon, 1978.

Seche 1966. Mircea Seche, *Draft for a History of Romanian Lexicography* (in Romanian), I. Bucharest: Scientific Publishing House, 1966.

Shafir 1983. Michael Shafir, "Political Culture, Intellectual Dissent and Intellectual Consent. The Case of Romania", in *Orbis*, 27, 1983, pp. 393–420.

Simpson, Yinger 1985. George Eaton Simpson and John Milton Yinger, *Racial and Cultural Minorities*. New York, London, 1985.

Smith 1986. Anthony D. Smith, *The Ethnic Origins of Nations*. Oxford: Blackwell, 1986

Sőtér, Pándi 1965. István Sőtér (co-ord.), *A magyar irodalom története* [History of Hungarian Literature], vol. III: Pál Pándi (editor), *A magyar irodalom története 1772–től 1849–ig* [History of Hungarian Literature from 1772 to 1849]. Budapest: Akadémiai Kiadó, 1965.

Spengler 1923. Oswald Spengler, *Der Untergang des Abendlandes. Umrisse einer Morphologie der Weltgeschichte*. Munich: Oskar Beck, 1923.

Starobinski 1966. Jean Starobinski, "Ironie et mélancolie", in *Critique* (Paris), 1966, 227–228, pp. 291–308, 438–457.

Suciu 1938a. Coriolan Suciu, "Fragments from the Case: The Teachers from Blaj vs. Bishop Lemeni (1843–1846)" (in Romanian), excerpt from *Christian Culture* (in Romanian). Blaj, 1938.

Suciu 1938b. Coriolan Suciu, "Preamble to the Lemeni case. II. The so-called attempts on Bărnuțiu's life" (in Romanian), in *Christian Culture* (in Romanian), XVIII, 1938, no. 12, pp. 730–746.

Sundhausen 1973. Holm Sundhausen, *Die Einfluss der Herderschen Ideen auf die Nationsbildung bei den Völkern der Habsburger Monarchie*. Munich, 1973.

Szaluta 1987. Jacques Szaluta, *La psychohistoire*. Paris: P.U.F., 1987.

Ştefanescu 1995. Barbu Ştefanescu, *Agricultural technology and labour rhythm in the peasant household of Crişana in the eighteenth century and the first decades of the nineteenth century* (in Romanian), doctoral thesis. Cluj: "Babeş-Bolyai" University, 1995.

Tacciu 1973. Elena Tacciu, *Romantic Mythology* (in Romanian). Bucharest: Cartea Românească, 1973.

Tacciu 1982–1987. Elena Tacciu, *Romanian Romanticism. A Study of Archetypes* (in Romanian), I–III. Bucharest: Minerva, 1982–1987.

Talmon 1968. J.L. Talmon, *Romantisme et Révolte*. Paris: Flammarion, 1968.

Teodor 1968. Pompiliu Teodor, "Aaron Florian's Contribution to the Development of National Historiography" (in Romanian), in *Acta Musei Napocensis*, V, 1968, pp. 577–586.

Teodor 1970. Pompiliu Teodor, *The Evolution of Romanian Historical Thought* (in Romanian). Cluj: Dacia, 1970.

Teodor 1981–1982. Pompiliu Teodor, "A Controversial Polemical Writing in the Age of the Supplex" (in Romanian), in *Studies and Conferences* (in Romanian) (Satu Mare), V–VI, 1981–1982, pp. 203–209.

Teodor 1984. Pompiliu Teodor, *European Communications in the Enlightenment* (in Romanian). Cluj: Dacia, 1984.

Teodor 1992. Pompiliu Teodor, "The National Movement in the Eighteenth Century" (in Romanian), in *The Memorandum. 1892–1894. Romanian Ideology and Political Action* (in Romanian). Bucharest: Progresul Românesc, 1992 (second edition, 1994), pp. 92–106.

Teodor 1995. Pompiliu Teodor, "The Romanians from Transylvania between the Tradition of the Eastern Church, the Counter Reformation and the Catholic Reformation", in Maria Crăciun and Ovidiu Ghitta (eds.), *Ethnicity and Religion in Central and Eastern Europe*. Cluj: Cluj University Press, 1995, pp. 175–186.

Thom 1987. Françoise Thom, *La langue de bois*. Paris: Julliard, 1987.

Tocqueville 1981. Alexis de Tocqueville, *De la démocratie en Amérique*. Paris: Garnier–Flammarion, 1981.

Todoran 1983. Romulus Todoran, "Samuil Micu and the A-Romanians" (in Romanian), in *Linguistic Research* (in Romanian) (Cluj), XXVIII, 1983, no. 2, pp. 97–100.

Tonnelat 1930. E. Tonnelat, "Kultur. Histoire du mot, évolution du sens", in *Civilisation. Le mot et l'idée*. Paris, 1930, pp. 61–73.

Topliceanu, Ucrain 1989. Iulian Topliceanu and Constantin Ucrain, *Avram Iancu's Army* (in Romanian). Cluj: Dacia, 1989.

Tóth 1944. Zoltán I. Tóth, "Cotore Gerontius és az erdélyi román nemzeti öntudat ébredése" [Gherontie Cotore and the awakening of Romanian national consciousness in Transylvania], in *Hitel*, 1944, pp. 84–95.

Tóth 1946. Zoltán I. Tóth, *Az erdélyi román nacionalizmus első százada 1697–1792* [The first century of Romanian nationalism in Transylvania]. Budapest, 1946.

Tóth 1959. Zoltán I. Tóth, *Az erdélyi és magyarországi román nemzeti mozgalom (1790–1848)* [The national movement of the Romanians from Transylvania and Hungary (1790–1848)]. Budapest, 1959.

Totu, Florea, Abrudan 1984. Maria Totu (co-ord.), Petre Florea, Paul Abrudan, *Men of Duty. 1848–1849. Short Dictionary* (in Romanian). Bucharest: Military Publishing House, 1984.

Trebici, Ghinoiu 1986. Vladimir Trebici and Ion Ghinoiu, *Demography and Ethnography* (in Romanian). Bucharest: Scientific and Encyclopaedic Publishing House, 1986.

Trócsányi 1976. Zsolt Trócsányi, *Miklós Wesselényi*. Budapest, 1965.

Turczynski 1976. Emanuel Turczynski, *Konfession und Nation. Zur Frühgeschichte der serbischen und rumänischen Nationsbildung*. Düsseldorf: Schwann, 1976.

Turliuc 1994. Cătălin Turliuc, "Nationalism and Ethnicity. Historiographic and Methodological Considerations" (in Romanian), in G. Bădărău, L. Boicu, L. Nastasă (eds.), *History as a Reading of the World* (in Romanian). Iași: "A.D. Xenopol" Academic Foundation, 1994, pp. 425–439.

Țîrcovnicu 1964. V. Țîrcovnicu, "Damaschin Bojincă, Enlightened Pedagogue" (in Romanian), in *Pedagogical Review* (in Romanian), XIII, 1964, no. 2, pp. 53–64.

Țîrcovnicu 1970. V. Țîrcovnicu, *Contributions to the History of Romanian Education in Banat (1780–1918)* (in Romanian). Bucharest: Didactic and Pedagogical Publishing House, 1970.

Țîrcovnicu 1978. V. Țîrcovnicu, *History of Education in Banat until 1800* (in Romanian). Bucharest: Didactic and Pedagogical Publishing House, 1978.

Urechia 1892–1901. Vasile A. Urechia, *History of the Schools between 1800 and 1864* (in Romanian), I–IV. Bucharest, 1892–1901.

Van Tieghem 1924–1948. Paul Van Tieghem, *Le préromantisme. Études d'histoire littéraire européenne*, I–V. Paris, 1924-1948.

Vári 1993. Alexandru Vári, "The image of the United States of America as reflected in the *Gazette of Transylvania* (1838–1848)" (in Romanian), in Nicolae Bocșan, Nicolae Edroiu, Vasile Vesa, *European Junctions. History and Society in the Modern Age* (in Romanian). Cluj: Dacia, 1993, pp. 106–115.

Vári 1995. Alexandru Vári, "Alice through the Looking Glass or Preliminaries to an Imagology of Women in Transylvanian Urban Milieux at the End of the Nineteenth Century" (in Romanian), in Sorin Mitu and Florin Gogîltan (eds.), *Private Life, Collective Mentalities and Social Imaginary in Transylvania* (in Romanian). Cluj: Association of Historians from Transylvania and Banat, 1995–1996, pp. 284–292.

Verdery 1988. Katherine Verdery, "Moments in the Rise of Discourse on National Identity. I: The Seventeenth through the Nineteenth Century", in I. Agrigoroaiei, Gh. Buzatu, V. Cristian (eds.), *The Romanians in World History* (in Romanian), vol. III/1, Iași: "Al. I. Cuza" University, 1988, pp. 25–60.

Verdery 1991. Katherine Verdery, *National Ideology under Socialism: Identity and Cultural Politics in Ceausescu's Romania*. Berkeley: University of California Press, 1991.

Veress 1982. Endre Veress, *A budai Egyetemi Nyomda kiadványainak dokumentumai* [Documents concerning the publications of the Buda University Press], ed. Sámuel Domokos. Budapest, 1982.

Volovici 1991. Leon Volovici, *Nationalist Ideology and Antisemitism: The Case of Romanian Intellectuals in 1930's*. Oxford: Pergamon Press, 1991.

Weber 1934. Max Weber, *Die protestantische Ethik und der Geist des Kapitalismus*. Tübingen: J.C.B. Mohr, 1934.

Wolf 1978. Iosif Wolf, "Herder's Legacy to the Ideology of the 1848 Romanian Generation" (in Romanian), in *Marisia*, VIII, 1978, pp. 146–156.

Zane 1977. G. Zane, *N. Bălcescu. The Work. The Man. The Age* (in Romanian), second edition. Bucharest: Eminescu, 1977.

Zane 1980. G. Zane, "On the Rules of Proper Conduct in Economic Life" (in Romanian), in *idem*, *Studies* (in Romanian), ed. Elena G. Zane. Bucharest: Eminescu, 1980, pp. 344–357.

Zeletin 1991. Ştefan Zeletin, *The Romanian Bourgeoisie. Its Origin and Historical Role* (in Romanian). Bucharest: Humanitas, 1991.

Zieglauer 1881. Ferdinand von Zieglauer, *Die politische Reformbewegung in Siebenbürgen in der Zeit Joseph's II. und Leopold's II*. Vienna, 1881.

Zub 1981. Al. Zub, *Writing and Making History (Romanian Historiography after 1848)* (in Romanian). Iași: Junimea, 1981.

Zub 1983. Al. Zub, *Triumphant Was the Idea (Notes on Romanian Historicism)* (in Romanian). Iași: Junimea, 1983.

Index

Caesar, Julius, 194
Călinescu, Matei, 198
Cantacuzino, Constantin, 119
Cantemir, Dimitrie, 19, 167, 239–40, 271
Capidan, Theodor, 267
Caragiale, Ion Luca, 266
Caraşova (Krassóvár), 172
Carcalechi, Zaharia, 73, 95–6, 121, 126, 180
Carmilly-Weinberger, Moshe, 123
Carpathian Mountains, 68, 73, 156, 217–8
Cattaneo, Carlo, 47, 236
Caucasus, 62
Cazimir, Ştefan, 271
Ceauşescu regime, 121, 124, 175, 205, 271
Central Europe, 33, 51, 147, 185
Central and Eastern Europe, 187
Cermena, Petre, 110, 129, 155
Chaunu, Pierre, 268
Chelcea, Septimiu, 13, 51
China, 266
Chindriş, Ioan, 54–6, 120, 123–4, 129, 266, 271–3, 276
Chişineu Criş (Kisjenő), 33
Christian socialism, 106, 274
Cicero, 191, 194
Cioculescu, Şerban, 55
Cioran, Emil, 57–8, 63–4, 67, 76, 118, 122, 127, 168, 264–6
Cipăianu, George, 173
Cipariu, Timotei, 9, 16, 23, 25, 43–6, 50–2, 54–6, 58, 63, 66, 68–9, 71–2, 75, 79, 83, 86, 97, 104, 106–7, 110, 115, 118–24, 127–9, 138, 150, 158, 160, 166–8, 172, 174–5, 192, 194, 201, 204, 207, 210, 223, 226–9, 238, 240, 242, 255, 264, 266, 268–72, 275, 280
civilisation, 7, 75, 78, 83, 91, 100, 106, 108, 190, 201, 208, 254, 277–8; as citizenship, 106; autochthonous, 115; culture and, 72; European, 74, 79, 104, 178, 195–6, 198; foreign, 98; French, 98, 103; lack of, 133; low level of, 81; model of, 74; modern, 44, 68, 94, 102–3, 206; opposed to culture, 99, 105; Roman, 191; urban, 107; Western, 108, 172, 198, 238, 271
Cluj (Kolozsvár; Klausenburg), 12–3, 36, 40, 54, 83, 93, 120, 122, 137, 153, 159, 173, 175, 211, 270
Codru Drăguşanu, Ion, 40–1, 55, 60, 63–6, 70–1, 74, 79, 83, 92–3, 100, 102–3, 105,

115, 119–23, 125–7, 129, 131, 153, 159, 168–9, 172, 174–5, 209–10, 227, 265, 269
Comlăuş (Komlós), 19
Comşa, Nicolae, 118, 123, 274–5
Condeescu, N.N., 127
confessional (religious) identity, 241, 244–5, 248, 251–61, 264
conservatism, 97–8, 126, 134, 139, 237, 241, 250; social, 93, 108
Constantinople, 41, 59, 165, 193, 251, 254, 257
Cordoş, Nicolae, 270
Cornea, Alexandru, 248
Cornea, Paul, 129
Coruţ, Pavel, 53
Corvinus (family), 165
Coşbuc, George, 111, 150
Cosimelli, Antonio, 44
Cosma, Ela, 275
Costache, Veniamin, 53–4
Costin, Toma, 24, 50–1, 131–2, 143–4, 170–71, 207, 265
Cotore, Gherontie, 59–60, 80, 118–9, 254, 274
Cotruş, Aron, 111
Crainic, Simion, 110, 129
Crăciun, Maria, 272
Crimea, 216–7
Crişan, George, 35, 54
Crişan-Körösi, Ştefan, 271
Crişul Alb (Kőrös) (river), 180, 199
Croatia, 272
Csutak, Kálmán, 219, 267
Cudalbu-Sluşanski, O., 55
Curtius, Ernst Robert, 199
Cyril, 238
Czecz, János, 165

Dacia, 41, 43, 68, 115, 152, 216–7, 220, 222, 225–6, 237, 249–50, 273
Daicoviciu, Constantin, 201
Danube, 23, 178, 196–9, 216–8, 221–2, 240, 266
Danubian principalities: see Romanian principalities
Dărăban, Valentin, 172
De Originibus Populorum Transylvaniae (Budai-Deleanu), 222
Debrecen (Debreţin), 110

161, 177–8, 183–4, 188, 190, 193, 195–6, 198, 224, 237, 239, 244, 251, 253–6, 258–62
Lemberg (Lvov), 200, 204
Lemeny, Ioan, 35, 53–4, 114, 116, 119, 129–30, 139, 159, 199, 250
Leopold I (of Habsburg), 23, 93, 245
Lessing, Theodor, 118
Leu, Valeriu, 52, 124
liberalism, 128, 132, 134, 173, 187, 257; Codru Drăguşanu and the spirit of, 93; in Hungary, 149; moderate, 97–8; radical, 97; Transylvanian, 221; Western, 187
Library of the Romanian Academy, 12
Livy, 191
Lovich, Olga de, 155
Lovinescu, Eugen, 126
Lugoj (Lugos; Lugosch), 28, 255
Lumperdean, Ion, 272–6
Lupaş, Ioan, 172–3
Lyotard, Jean–François, 126, 198

Macedonia, 216, 219
Macrea, Dimitrie, 270
Magheru, Gheorghe, 199
Magris, Claudio, 122, 199
Maior, Grigore, 251
Maior, Liviu, 52, 55, 125, 170, 264–5, 267, 270
Maior, Petru, 9, 15–7, 20–5, 37–8, 46–7, 49–51, 53, 56, 62, 73, 77, 128, 144, 146–7, 151–2, 157–8, 162–3, 171–2, 174, 177, 183, 191, 195, 200–1, 217, 220, 234, 239–42, 246–51, 254–5, 259–60, 262, 265, 267, 271–6
Maiorescu, Ioan, 16, 50, 52, 63, 70, 82–3, 88, 99–100, 103, 106, 119, 121, 123–4, 126–27, 207, 219, 235, 265, 267, 271
Maiorescu, Titu, 97, 100, 103
Maniu, Nicolae, 35, 54
Maniu, Vasile, 155, 209, 225, 265, 269
Manolache, A., 127
Manolescu, Nicolae, 171
Manuilovici, Archimandrite, 36
Many, Iosif, 40, 42, 54–5, 79, 83, 88, 97, 101, 104–6, 111, 115, 122, 127, 129, 134, 138–40, 144, 170, 181, 199
Maramureş (Máramaros), 52, 217, 226, 238
Marcu, Alexandru, 129
Marga, Andrei, 12–3, 127, 171
Maria Theresa (of Habsburg), 154

Marian, Simion Florea, 171
Marica, George Em., 12, 56, 200, 271, 280
Marino, Adrian, 121, 126–7, 270
Marx, Karl, 138
Marxism, 5, 129, 132, 271
Matthias Corvinus (Matei Corvin; Mátyás király), 165, 175, 196
Mauss, Marcel, 265
Mauzi, Robert, 128
Mazilu, Dan Horia, 118–9
Mediaş (Medgyes; Mediasch), 54, 119
Mehadia (Mehádia), 45
Metastasio, Pietro, 231
Methodius, 238
Metternich-Winneburg, Klemens Lothar, Prince Wenzel von, 31, 41, 87, 120
Michelet, Jules, 175
Mickiewicz, Adam, 105–6
Micu, Inochentie, 28, 53, 141, 214, 253
Micu, Samuil, 8, 16, 37, 43, 53, 60, 68, 70–1, 92, 94, 119–20, 158, 161–3, 166–7, 171, 175, 185–6, 199, 213, 216, 220–3, 230, 237–8, 247, 254–5, 260–1, 266–8, 270–1, 274–5
Mihai the Brave (of Wallachia), 26, 114, 183, 195–6
Mihuţ, Ioan, 50
Mikó, Imre, 172
Mikolaewicze, Maria de, 155
Milcov (bishopric), 240, 255
military historiography, 125, 199
Mircea the Old (of Wallachia), 26, 142
Mîrza, Iacob, 127
Miskolczy, Ambrus, 174
Mitu, Melinda, 54–5, 170, 172, 176, 265, 267
Mitu, Sorin, 51, 55, 121–3, 126–7, 129, 170–3, 267, 280
moderates, 75, 114, 138, 149–50, 156, 159
Moga, Ioan, 170
Moga, Vasile, 251, 263
Moldavia, 53, 64, 179, 183, 216–7, 219, 222, 225, 240, 250, 262, 267
Moldovan, Dimitrie, 119, 124, 128, 173
Moldovan, Ştefan, 35, 54
Moldvai, Ştefan, 128–9
Monglond, André, 129
Montesquieu, Charles de Secondat, Baron de La Brède et de, 77, 126, 169
Moroianu, Oprea, 213, 266
Moscovici, Serge, 53